Know Thy Enemy

Social, Economic and Political Studies of the Middle East and Asia

FOUNDING EDITOR: C.A.O. VAN NIEUWENHUIJZE

VOLUME 126

The titles published in this series are listed at *brill.com/seps*

Know Thy Enemy

Evolving Attitudes towards "Others" in Modern Shiʿi Thought and Practice

By

Meir Litvak

BRILL

LEIDEN | BOSTON

Cover illustration: The Shrine of Fatima Masumeh with gold dome and blue minarets in city of Qom, Iran. Photo by Inna Giliarova.

Library of Congress Cataloging-in-Publication Data

Names: Litvak, Meir, author.
Title: Know thy enemy : evolving attitudes towards "others" in modern Shiʿi thought and practice / by Meir Litvak.
Description: Leiden ; Boston : Brill, 2021. | Series: Social, economic and political studies of the Middle East and Asia, 1385-3376 ; vol. 126 | Includes index.
Identifiers: LCCN 2020052245 (print) | LCCN 2020052246 (ebook) | ISBN 9789004439207 (hardback) | ISBN 9789004444683 (ebook)
Subjects: LCSH: Shīʿah—Relations. | Shīʿah—Relations—Judaism. | Shīʿah—Relations—Sunnites.
Classification: LCC BP194.15 .L58 2021 (print) | LCC BP194.15 (ebook) | DDC 297.2/8—dc23
LC record available at https://lccn.loc.gov/2020052245
LC ebook record available at https://lccn.loc.gov/2020052246

Typeface for the Latin, Greek, and Cyrillic scripts: "Brill". See and download: brill.com/brill-typeface.

ISSN 1385-3376
ISBN 978-90-04-43920-7 (hardback)
ISBN 978-90-04-44468-3 (e-book)

Dedicated to my mother

Contents

Acknowledgements XI
A Note on Transliteration XII

Introduction 1
1 Othering and Islam: a Historical Note 7
2 The Modern Other as Enemy 19
3 Structure of the Book 30

1 **From Westoxication to the Decline of the West** 34
1 The Western Threat 38
2 The "Great Satan" 40
3 Khamenei and the Cultural Onslaught 42
4 The Cultural Onslaught: Past and Present 43
5 The Inevitable Fall of the West 47
6 The Decline of the West: a Comparative Perspective 49
7 Western Moral and Social Decadence 51
8 Humanism and the Decline of the West 55
9 The West's Decline as a Divine Punishment 59
10 The Islamic Revolution and the Fall of the West 61
11 Responses to the Clash of Civilizations 62
12 Shīʿī Views on the "End of History" 65
13 Conclusion 71

2 **The Jews as Enemies of Shīʿīsm** 73
1 Anti-Judaism in Traditional Shīʿīsm 75
2 From Anti-Judaism to Modern Anti-Semitism 77
3 The Islamic Republic: Anti-Zionism and Anti-Semitism 79
4 The Jews as the Enemy 84
5 Jewish Conspiracies and the Early Shīʿa 87
6 The Jews, the Mahdī, and Their Final Fate 104
7 Conclusion 109

3 **Extending a Hand to "Our Sunnī Brethren"** 112
1 Historical Foundations of the Sunnī-Shīʿī Rift 112
2 Attempts at Rapprochement in the Nineteenth and Twentieth Centuries 116

3 Minimizing the Sectarian Rift 121
4 Reaching Out to Sunnīs 123
5 Nullifying the ʿUmarkoshān Celebrations 128
6 Redefining the Nine Rabīʿ Celebrations 132
7 The Nine Rabīʿ Celebrations: Popular vs. Official Islam 136
8 Reinterpreting Rabīʿ Ninth: Ideology and Tactics 140
9 Clerical Power Struggle or Sectarian Rapprochement 145
10 Conclusion 148

4 **Anti-Wahhābī and Jihādī-Salafī Polemics: from Apologetics to Denunciation** 151
1 Wahhābism and the Shīʿa: the Historical Background 152
2 Exacerbation of the Sunnī-Shīʿī Rift: the Islamic Republic vs. the Jihādī-Salafī Challenge 154
3 Shīʿī Deconstruction of Wahhābī Doctrines 156
4 Wahhābī Obscurantism vs. Shīʿī Rationalism 162
5 Wahhābism and the Other Enemies of Islam 167
5.1 *Wahhābism's Jewish Origins* 168
5.2 *Wahhābism as Protégé of British Imperialism* 172
6 The Wahhābīs and Jihadi Salafists 174
7 The Takfīrī Trend: the Child of Wahhābism 177
7.1 *The Takfīrīs and Islamic Unity* 179
8 ISIS as Harbingers of the Mahdī 181
9 The Jihādī-Salafists, the Jews, and the West 184
10 The Takfīrīs as Non-Muslims 187
11 Conclusion 190

5 **Liberty and Its Boundaries vis-à-vis Dissent and Apostasy** 194
1 Critique of Liberal Negative Liberty 197
2 Spiritual Liberty as True Liberty 203
3 Islam as the Guarantor of Liberty 205
4 Positive Liberty and Its Application 207
5 Limits on Freedom under Islam 210
6 Freedom, Apostasy, and Treason 217
7 The Reformist and Liberal Approach 222
8 Conclusion 230

6 **The Deviationist and Misguided Bahāʾī Sect** 234
1 A Deviationist Sect – Not a Religion 239
2 Critiquing Bahāʾī Doctrines 242
3 Bahāʾīsm as a Political Enemy 250
4 Liberal Voices 261
5 Conclusion 264

7 **Feminism: The "Gift" of the West to Islam** 267
1 Feminism and the West 271
2 The Feminist Challenge to Islamic Law 276
3 The Feminist Threat to Morality 281
4 Countering Islamic Feminism 285
5 Conclusion 290

Conclusion 292

List of Sources 303
Index 371

Acknowledgements

The research and publication of this book were made possible thanks to the generous support of the Israeli Science Foundation founded by the Israel Academy of Sciences and Humanities.

Special thanks are due to several good friends and colleagues. Esther Webman had been a close friend and colleague for years. She not only read early drafts of some chapters and made valuable comments, but exchanging ideas with her with was always very stimulating. Tragically, she passed away prematurely before the book came out, but my gratitude to her will always remain. My close friend Iddo Landau has read drafts of a few chapters and in addition to his valuable comments he offered important corrections that spared me from falling into risky pitfalls. My friends Bruce Maddy Weitzman and Joshua Teitelbaum were extremely helpful in exchanging views and ideas and in helping me to better articulate some of my ideas. David Yeroushalmi and Miriam Nissimov were most helpful in overcoming the challenges posed by various Persian-language neologisms.

The staff members of Widener Library at Harvard University and of Souraski library at Tel Aviv University have been very helpful in providing me with valuable sources. The Alliance Center for Iranian Studies has always been the most hospitable venue for conducting this research. Special thanks are due to Nikki Littman and Belina Nueberger for language editing my non-native English. Thanks are also due to Brill's editorial staff for their editorial expertise and guidance. Needless to say, all shortcomings and faults in the book are mine alone. Finally, I wish to thank my wife Nava and my children Omri and Adi for their continued support and patience during the years of working on this book.

A Note on Transliteration

As the book relies heavily on Persian-language and Arabic sources, I have used the transliteration system as recommended by IJMES for the sake of maximum consistency at the cost of sacrificing the Persian pronunciation of various terms. In few cases of well-known persons e.g. Khomeini, Khamenei, Mojtahed-Shabestari as well as in the case of few geographic places the common English form has been used.

The following letters have been used for the Arabic and Persian letters

ʾ	Arabic and Persian hamza
ʿ	Arabic ʿayn
ح	Ḥ
ذ (Persian)	Z̲
ص	Ṣ
ض (Arabic)	Ḍ
ض (Persian)	Ż
ط	Ṭ
ظ	Ẓ

Long vowels:

آ	Ā
ا	ā
و	ū
ي	ī

Introduction

"Any person, whose path is not the path of Islam is our enemy," declared Ayatollah Rūḥollah Khomeini (d. 1989) leader of the 1979 Revolution prior to the March 1979 referendum, which approved the formation of the Islamic Republic of Iran.[1] Pursuing the same line of thought, Ayatollah ʿAlī Khamenei, Khomeini's successor as Supreme Leader, asserted that the Islamic Republic had faced enemy conspiracies from the onset, because it had established a unique, morally superior system of government. He has, therefore, repeatedly called for vigilance against the "enemy" who threatens Islam and the Iranian nation.[2] These statements were, and still are, part of a broader religious and cultural phenomenon of "othering," or drawing a clear distinction between the collective self and the "other", which is essential for articulating the Shīʿī and any other religious worldview. The construction of the "self" for any group has, throughout history, arisen from differences between groups, and responses to them range from complete rejection to wholesale acceptance. The disliked "other" may be a foreigner who triggers xenophobic reactions, or a member of an alternative group within the same society, which engenders alterophobia. In fact, some scholars argue, that dislike of "others" has been a persistent condition of society throughout history."[3]

The politicization of Shīʿīsm in the modern period, which culminated in the establishment of the Islamic Republic, sharpened the "self-other" distinction into a more dichotomous "friend-enemy" juxtaposition. The evolving re-articulations of the "others" in modern Iranian Shīʿī thought and practice, particularly since the 1979 Revolution – be they Westerners, jihādī-Salafī Sunnīs, Jews, feminists, or Bahāʾīs – and the formulation of boundaries between Shīʿīs and these "others" are the subject of the present study. The examination of such attitudes and practices will shed light not only on the formation of modern Shīʿī identity, but also on modern Islamism at large.

---

1 Rūḥollah Khomeini, *Ṣaḥīfa-i nūr: majmūʿa-i rāhnimūdhā-i imām-i Khomeini* (Tehrān: Vizārat-i Irshād-i Islāmī, 1995), vol. 7 p. 457, vol. 21 p. 212.

2 Muḥammad Ḥusayn Reżāʾī (ed.), *Dushman shināsī dar kalām-i imām-i Khamenei* (Muʾasasa-i farhangī valāʾ-i muntaẓar (aj), 1392/2013), 37; "Dushman shināsī," farsi.khamenei.ir/keyword-print?id=1022; "Bayānāt-i maqām-i muʿaẓẓam-i rahbarī beh munāsabat-i rūz-i mubāraza bā istikbār-i jahānī," 9 Abān 1375/October 30, 1996, http://www.leader.ir/fa/speech/1346.

3 Hakan T. Karateke, H. Erdem Çıpa and Helga Anetshofer (eds.), *Disliking Others: Loathing, Hostility, and Distrust in Premodern Ottoman Lands* (Boston: Academic Studies Press, 2018), xi–xii.

 | DOI:10.1163/9789004444683_002

The concept of othering highlights how societies create a sense of identity, belonging, and social status by constructing social categories as binary opposites and by stigmatizing differences, real or imagined, between the in-group (us) and the out-group (them or the "other").[4] Social identities are *not* natural, but are constructed, negotiated, and contested as historical processes. They are relational as groups typically define themselves in relation to "others." Identity has little meaning without the "other", as by defining itself a group automatically defines "others," and vice versa, the portrayal of the "other" is crucial to the way a group sees itself. Thus, the ancient Greeks and Chinese viewed the world as divided between them and barbarians, the Jews created the Jews-gentile antithesis, and the Muslims divided historically the world between believers and infidels.

Within this larger context, religious identities are defined not only by the sets of beliefs and practices that coreligionists share, but also through the religious community's differentiating itself from other communities. They are dynamic and constantly in evolution. This is particularly true in modern times as people are more exposed to new stimuli and challenges and apparently feel a greater need to reassert their identity or sets of collective identities that may provide important "anchors" in a world that is constantly in flux. Identities are thus context dependent and discursively constructed in ever-new ways.[5]

According to Okolie, identity is rarely claimed or assigned for its own sake. Definitions of the self and of the "other" are tied to rewards and punishment, both material and symbolic, which is why identities are contested. The distinction between self and "other" and the representation of each group are often embedded in power relations, as both dominant and weak groups formulate dichotomies between the self and the "other". The very process reflects these power differentials.[6] Accordingly, social institutions like the law, the media, education, and religion hold the balance of power through their representation of what is accepted as "normal" and what is considered other and "different." In sociological terms, the underlying aim is to construct and represent the "other"

4 Sune Qvotrup Jensen "Othering, identity formation and agency," *Qualitative studies* 2:2 (2011): 63–78; Jean-François Staszak, "Other/Otherness," in *International Encyclopedia of Human Geography*, eds., R. Kitchin and N. Thrift (Oxford: Elsevier, 2008), vol. 8, p. 43–47.

5 Anna Triandafyllidou and Ruth Wodak, "Conceptual and methodological questions in the study of collective identities: An introduction," *Journal of Language and Politics* 2, no. 2 (2003): 206.

6 Andrew C. Okolie, "Introduction to the Special Issue-Identity: Now You Don't See It; Now You Do." *Identity: An International Journal of Theory and Research* 3:1 (2003): 2.

as pathological and morally inferior, and thus make the subordinate individual or group aware of their inferior status.[7]

In the Shīʿī case, however, the "other"s, e.g. the West, Wahhābī and jihādī-Salafī Islam and possibly also Zionism, are conceived as formidable foes who threaten the Shīʿa, the Islamic Republic, and Islam in general, even though they are considered morally and intellectually inferior. This process both reflects and enhances the Shīʿī self-perception as a "saved community" (*al-firqa al-nājiyya*) – that is, God's chosen community, the righteous few who are besieged by powerful and hostile "others," but which will be saved by God at the end of time. It emanates from the historical reality of past Shīʿī weakness and suffering, augmented by the bitter Iranian experience of two centuries of foreign intervention and exploitation. In the Islamic Republic, it serves the regime's political needs in that it presents Iran as successfully confronting formidable enemies. Besides reflecting Shīʿī conviction of the rightness of its cause, it also conveys a growing confidence in the future. At the same time, in the domestic Iranian arena, othering serves to preserve the dominant power structure, since it is the ruling establishment that determines who the "other" is (feminists, Bahāʾīs, or religious liberals), and how they should be treated or suppressed, especially when they are perceived as challenging the dominant power structure.

Anthropologists Gerd Baumann and Andre Gingrich have proposed three fundamental "grammars" or structures of identity and alterity (otherness, i.e. the characteristics of the "other"), in which figures of alterity can be portrayed in sociocultural contexts, and connected with social agencies. First is a dichotomous "orientalizing" structure of the self and the "other" by negative mirror imaging: "What is good in us is lacking in them," but it also adds a subordinating reversal: "What is lacking in us is (still) present in them, it thus entails a possibility of desire for the 'other' and even sometimes a potential for self-critical relativism."[8] Though the concept originally drew on Edward Said's critique in *Orientalism*, in the context of the present study it is best applied to the Shīʿī discourse on the West, the Jews, the Bahāʾīs, as well as the Wahhābī and jihādī-Salafī camps in Islam.

7 Gayatri Spivak cited in Jensen "Othering, identity formation and agency;" Monika Fludernik, "Identity/alterity," in *The Cambridge Companion to Narrative*, ed. David Herman (Cambridge: Cambridge University Press, 2007), 260, 266; Staszak, "Other/Otherness," p. 44.

8 Gerd Baumann and Andre Gingrich, (eds.), *Grammars of Identity/Alterity: A Structural Approach* (Oxford/New York: Berghahn, 2004), x.

The second structure of "segmentation" operates via context-dependent and hence differentiated levels of selfing and othering among parties conceived as formally equal. Although it allows for the fusion and fission of identity/alterity in a highly context-sensitive manner, it is nearly always subject to disputes about primacy. It allows, for instance, for a shift from enemy to friend, and thereby enables the formation of alliances and the neutralization of conflicts. This structure is particularly helpful in analyzing the shifting official attitude towards mainstream Sunnī Islam in view of the rising threat of jihādī-Salafī groups in the Muslim world and the anticipation of a joint Shīʿī-Sunnī front against the West and Zionism. The third structure is that of "encompassment." It works "by a hierarchized sub-inclusion of 'others' who are thought, from a higher level of abstraction, to be really 'part of us'" and can therefore be appropriated easily. It thus includes some, but never all, "others," and tends to minimize the otherness of those it includes.[9] This structure, too, helps clarify the Shīʿī-Iranian presentation of mainstream Sunnī Islam as being part of the Islamic nation, while adhering to an incorrect interpretation of "pure Muḥammadan Islam" as not equal to the Shīʿa.

In several important studies, Russi Jaspal applied the Identity Process Theory (IPT), which provides an integrative theory of identity threat and coping.[10] IPT outlines (i) the necessary components of a positive identity; (ii) the psychosocial contexts in which a person's identity is susceptible to threat; and (iii) the strategies that are most likely to be implemented by an individual or a group coping with threats. In the context of the present study, the strategy employed refers to the self-perception of Shīʿī identity as the epitome of true Islam, which was threatened by intolerant Sunnī trends in the past, as it is nowadays by Western culture, Bahāʾīsm, and feminism.

According to Jaspal, the individual or group needs to perceive appropriate levels of self-continuity; uniqueness of the self and differentiation from relevant "others" (or distinctiveness); competence and control over one's life and future (or self-efficacy); feelings of worth and value (or self-esteem); significance and purpose of one's life (or meaning); a feeling of belonging to social groups and networks (or belonging); and compatibility and coherence between elements of their identities (or psychological coherence). IPT holds that if the individual or social group cannot achieve appropriate levels of these

9 Baumann and Gingrich, *Grammars of Identity/Alterity*, x, xi.

10 Rusi Jaspal and Marco Cinnirella, "Coping with potentially incompatible identities: accounts of religious, ethnic and sexual identities from British Pakistani men who identify as Muslim and gay," *British Journal of Social Psychology* 49, no. 4 (2010): 849–70; Rusi Jaspal and Marco Cinnirella, "The construction of ethnic identity: Insights from identity process theory," *Ethnicities* 12:5 (2012): 503–530.

principles, identity is threatened. Perceived changes, or symbolic threats, in the surrounding social environment may disrupt the unifying psychological thread between past, present, and future. A key tenet of IPT is that the individual or social group will attempt to alleviate identity threats by engaging in various coping strategies, such as denial, re-conceptualization of the threatening situation, or group mobilization against the threatening stimulus.[11]

These insights are particularly helpful in the present study, as the "West," Bahāʾīs, and Feminism are perceived as posing a symbolic threat to Shīʿīsm, while Sunnī jihādī-Salafīsm, as well as the Jews and Zionism, are presented as posing a more physical threat. The process of othering such external threats highlights their false ideological or theological basis, as well as their negative attributes and nefarious activities. By presenting the Shīʿa as the complete opposite of these negative traits and as the unbroken saga of a continuous struggle for true faith and justice, this process enhances a sense of Shīʿī distinctiveness, self-esteem, and self-efficacy, in addition to bolstering its internal unity and coherence. Put together, the concept of "othering," and particularly of IPT, are very useful in analyzing the formation and articulation of Shīʿī attitudes towards various "others." In particular they help understand the Shīʿī efforts to enhance Shīʿī in-group efficacy, as well as internal solidarity and cohesion; the feelings of belonging in the broader Muslim world, and the maintenance of the Iranian regime's official ideology. These are achieved by highlighting the threat posed by various "others," and the moral and intellectual superiority of the Shīʿī in-group.

The Enemy is a special case of the "other", according to Harle. The enemy represents evil (the Devil), while the self represents the Good (or God). The relationship between the enemy and the self adds hostility and violence to identity-creating relationships. While the "other" simply defines our identity by excluding him/her, the enemy determines the very nature of the conflict. It specifies who the enemy is and describes the latter's basic nature; furthermore, it explains why this is so.[12]

Howard Stein argues that group self-definition and cohesiveness are achieved by highlighting the contrast with and opposition to an historical enemy who is perceived, through psychological projection, as embodying characteristics

11 For a comprehensive discussion and analysis of IPT, see Glynis M. Breakwell, *Coping with Threatened Identities* (London: Methuen, 1986); Rusi Jaspal and Glynis M. Breakwell (eds.), *Identity Process Theory: Identity, Social Action and Social Change* (Cambridge: Cambridge University Press, 2014).

12 Vilho Harle, "Otherness, identity, and politics: Towards a framework of analysis," *The European Legacy* 1, no. 2 (1996): 410; Vilho Harle, "On the Concepts of the 'Other' and the 'Enemy'," *History of European Ideas* 19, nos. 1–3 (1994): 28.

that are disavowed in one's own group. In times of conflict, the split between self and "other" often generates a contrast between good and evil, which oversimplifies and often demonizes the "other". Participants in conflicts tend to subscribe to "mirror images" of their own group and the enemy "other". When one "others" another group, one points out its perceived weaknesses in order to make one's own group seem superior. The need to have enemies and even to create them is ever-present in the human psyche, and "rituals [to overpower its evil] will continue to be enacted in order to maintain a psychological distance from the enemy."

Yet, according to Stein, whenever similarities cannot be acknowledged, hostility increases. As a result, "the adversaries are locked in a permanent dance." They are in fact a cultural pair, since self-definition is impossible without reference to the "other". The cultivation and availability of such an indispensable enemy is a recurrent feature of a group's own internal self-regulation. In the process of othering, the group consciously exaggerates differences and rescinds affiliative feelings. Thus, he adds, "We" must not allow ourselves to feel that we have much, if anything, in common with our enemy – even though the unconscious commonality underlies the very choice of enemy – for this would deprive "us" of the use of this enemy as a repository for disavowed impulses, feelings, and aspects of the self.[13]

The paradox of psychological closeness and distance lies in that a group feels driven to act against the perceived "enemy" to create a chasm of separation, precisely when it feels overrun, contaminated, indeed "possessed" by an enemy who can no longer be kept at a safe distance through group rituals. Thus the group feels compelled to purge itself of attributes it can no longer completely disassociate from, nor repress.[14] As will be shown below, this maxim is particularly pertinent to the Shīʿī perception of the West.

In a study on the reflection of the Arab-Israeli conflict in Israeli school textbooks, social psychologist Daniel Bar-Tal has shown that societies involved in intractable conflicts develop suitable psychological tools that enable them to cope successfully with conflict situations. Beliefs that support these tools include a deep-rooted certainty regarding the justice of one's cause, delegitimization of the adversary, positive self-perception, and feelings of victimhood. Put together, these beliefs constitute an ethos that supports a continuation of the conflict, as they are reflected in language, stereotypes, images, myths, and

13 Howard F. Stein, "The Indispensable Enemy and American-Soviet Relations," *Ethos* 17, no. 4 (December 1989): 480–481.

14 Stein, "The Indispensable Enemy and American-Soviet Relations," 494.

collective memory.[15] Participants in conflicts tend to subscribe to ethnocentric "mirror images" of their own and their enemy's country – in which ones' own country is believed to be moral, whereas one's enemy's is believed to be diabolical. Likewise, one's own actions are attributed to altruistic motives, but identical actions taken by an enemy are perceived as self-serving. Cognitive consistency is thus maintained through the application of double standards when judging the morality of each group's actions. Ethnocentric beliefs may be maintained by simply ignoring contradictory evidence and by decreasing the salience of information that is inconsistent with a moral self-image and a diabolical enemy-image.[16] As will be shown below, these observations apply to the Shīʿī encounter with perceived rivals/enemies as well.

1 Othering and Islam: a Historical Note

The praxes of othering discussed above are not and have never been exclusive to the Shīʿa, but are found in every religion. In pagan religions, however, the multiplicity of gods represents a multiplicity of truths that can coexist. The shift from one religion to another does not entail the dichotomous rejection of one truth and acceptance of another, but rather an addition and endorsement of one more god or gods as well as multiple truths. Conversely, monotheistic religions tend to see themselves as the sole custodians of truth. Therefore, they view other religions not simply as mistaken, but at best as sinful and at worst as enemies of the one true God and message. Consequently, the attitude towards other religions among monotheists is usually more exclusive and often hostile.[17]

---

15 Daniel Bar-Tal, "Societal Beliefs in Times of Intractable Conflict: The Israeli Case," *International Journal of Conflict Management*, 9 (1998): 22–50; Idem, "From Intractable Conflict Through Conflict Resolution to Reconciliation: Psychological Analysis," *Political Psychology* 21, no. 2 (June 2000): 351–365.

16 G.N. Sande, George R. Goethals and Lisa Ferarri, Leila T. Worth, "Value Guided Attributions: Maintaining the Moral Self Image and the Diabolical Enemy-Image," *Journal of Social Issues*, 45 (1989): 91–93.

17 For examples of Jewish Othering during the biblical period, see Laurence J. Silberstein, "Others within and others without: Rethinking Jewish identity and culture," in *The other in Jewish Thought and History: Constructions of Jewish Culture and Identity*, eds., Laurence J. Silberstein and Robert L. Cohn (New York: NYU Press, 1994), 1–34. The literature of the 'Othering' of Jews by Christians is vast, for a few examples, see Yaacov Deutsch, *Judaism in Christian eyes: ethnographic descriptions of Jews and Judaism in early modern Europe* (Oxford: Oxford University Press, 2012); Marvin Perry, *Jewish-Christian*

A comprehensive analysis of the phenomenon of othering in relation to Islam as a religion and culture is beyond the scope of this study. Still, a few short references will help put the Shīʿī case in a proper historical context. The evolution of Islam from a small religious community in Mecca into a religious-political one following the Prophet's migration to Medina in 622 was marked by the Constitution of Medina (*ʿahd al-umma*), which described the Muslims as "*umma dūn al-nās*," that is, a community distinct from the rest of humankind. The early Muslim community defined itself against three "others": pagans, Jews, and Christians. The Qur'ān and early Muslim tradition viewed Islam as superseding the two previous monotheistic religions, which had supposedly falsified and corrupted God's true message to humanity. Islam by contrast, was the correct and, therefore, final expression and implementation of divine revelation. Islam set itself against Christianity in various Qur'ānic verses that reject the incarnation and the trinity, and against Judaism by rejecting numerous Jewish laws and practices. But, as Bernard Lewis observed, more important than the rejection of Judaism and Christianity was the rejection of paganism in the early Islamic period. Inevitably, the struggle against paganism brought Islam closer to Judaism and Christianity, seen if not as allies, then as kindred faiths opposed to a common adversary.[18]

Still, the othering of Christians and Jews was not identical. The Prophet's contacts with Christians were less important and far less contentious than those with the Jews. His relations with the Christian tribes and settled communities were in general regulated by agreements according to which the Christians were permitted to practice their religion and run their own affairs, on condition that they pay a fixed tribute, provide supplies to the Muslims during war and refrain from usury. Thanks to these more peaceful relations with the Prophet, references to the Christians in Qur'ān are more favorable than those to Jews.[19]

Conversely, as a result of the Prophet's clashes with the three Jewish tribes in Medina, the portrayal of the Jews in the principal religious texts, the Qur'ān and [Sunnī] ḥadīth, is fairly negative in view of their alleged sins against previous prophets and particularly against Muḥammad. Thus, the Qur'ān contains more hostile references to the Jews than to Christians. A much-quoted passage

---

encounters over the centuries: Symbiosis, prejudice, holocaust, dialogue (New York: Peter Lang Publishing Incorporated, 1994).

18 Bernard Lewis, *The Jews of Islam* (Princeton: Princeton University Press, 1984), 12.

19 Kenneth Cragg, *Muhammad and the Christian: a question of response* (Darton, Longman & Todd, Limited, 1984); Jacques Waardenburg, "The Early Period, 610–650," in *Muslim Perceptions of Other Religions: A Historical Survey*, ed., Jacques Waardenburg (Oxford: Oxford University Press, 1999), 8–9.

from the Qur'ān reflects the Prophet's differential attitude towards the two groups: "You will find that the people most hostile towards the believers are the Jews and the polytheists. And you will find that the nearest in affection towards the believers are those who say, 'We are Christians'." (Qur'ān 5:82).[20] As a punishment for their deviation from the earlier true Mosaic revelation of monotheism, and for their refusal to acknowledge Muḥammad's prophecy, the Jews incurred the wrath of God and are condemned to dispersal and humiliation among the nations. The Christians are only described as 'misguided'."[21] The Qur'ān charges both religions of rigid and excessive practices of worship.[22] The cumbersome nature of Jewish law and of the Jews for being excessive in matters of the law drew criticism in later periods as well.

Modern polemicists see the overly spiritual orientation of the Christian teachings at the expense of laws regulating conduct as reflecting a lack of orientation in worldly affairs and an inadequate guidance of society. This, they say, is why Christianity allows worldly ideologies to fill in the gap. By way of contrast, Islam offers the perfect middle between these two religions as it provides an all-embracing program for the solution of spiritual, as well as social and economic problems and needs.[23] In the theological sphere various writers charge the Jews of excess in denying the prophecy of Jesus altogether, while accusing the Christians of laxity by elevating him to the status of deity. Again, Islam takes the (correct) middle path.[24]

---

20 Tr. Ṭalāl Itānī, https://www.clearquran.com/001.html.

21 Lewis, *The Jews of Islam*, 11, Norman A. Stillman, "Anti-Judaism and Antisemitism in the Arab and Islamic Worlds Prior to 1948," in *Antisemitism: A History*, eds., Albert S. Lindemann and Richard Levy (Oxford: Oxford University Press, 2010): 212–221.

22 Meir J. Kister, "On 'Concessions' and Conduct: A Study in *Ḥadīth*," *Studies on the First Century of Islamic Society*, ed., G.H.A. Juynboll (Carbondale: Southern Illinois University Press, 1982), 91.

23 For criticism of the excessive Jewish laws, see Kamila Adang, "Medieval Muslim Polemics against the Jewish Scriptures," in *Muslim Perceptions of Other Religions*, ed., Jacques Waardenburg, 143, 145, 147; For criticism of Christianity, see Isabel Stümpel-Hatami, "Christianity as Described by Persian Muslims," Ibid., 231.

24 Mājida Aḥmad Sulaymān Yāqūt, *Fatḥ al-bārī fī sharḥ Ṣaḥīḥ al-Bukhārī: dirāsa fī al-manhaj wa-al-maṣādir* (Alexandria: Dār al-Maʿrifa al-Jāmiʿīyya, 2014), vol. 15, 200; Būdan Daḥmān, *Wasaṭiyyat al-Islām bayn al-Yahūdiyya wal-naṣrāniyya: dirāsa muqārina* (MA Thesis), https://vb.tafsir.net/tafsir52961/#.W88eknszYkI; "Ayatollah Vaḥīd Khorāsānī: Qur'ān, bashar rā as ifrāṭ wa-tafrīṭ dar mowred-i ʿĪsā najāt mīdahad," 24 Farvardīn 1390/April 13, 2011, https://www.isna.ir/news/9001-09767/آیت-الله-وحید-خراسانی-قرآن-بشر-را-از-افراط-و-تفریط-در-مورد.

Yet, in the course of the tenth and fifteenth centuries the image of the Jews in literary Arabīc texts varied from negative to neutral to positive.[25] Medieval Muslim theologians were engaged in polemics against the various religions they encountered following the expansion of the Muslim state. Fundamentally, these polemics reflect the basic Muslim view of other religions as deviations from the one primordial religion, which culminated in Islam.

Within this context, Muslim theologians, whether Sunnī or Shīʿī, invested much greater effort in anti-Christian polemics than in polemics against Judaism. The affinity between Judaism and Islam as the two strictly monotheistic religions based on law, left little space for specific theological disagreement between the two religions, except for the Jewish rejection of Muḥammad as a prophet, which Muslim authors connected with the Jews' earlier rejection of Jesus. In contrast, Muslim authors could neither accept nor understand the dogmas of Christianity. The smaller size of the Jewish community and the intensified Muslim clash with the Crusaders after the twelfth century were additional factors in this differential approach. At the same time, the pervasive idea viewed the Christian community as simply having been led astray, as opposed to the Jewish community, which was in active rebellion against God. Yet, Stillman notes, there was not much comparable in Islam in quantity – and only rarely in sheer vitriol – to the Christian polemics against Jews.[26]

The recognition of Judaism and Christianity as containing a genuine, even if distorted, divine revelation served as the basis for subsequent Islamic tolerance towards them. Such tolerance did not mean equality, but was an act of benevolence by the superior religion and acceptance of subordination by the tolerated religions. Overall and with few exceptions, in the premodern era, Muslim societies were far more tolerant towards religious minorities than Christian Europe.[27] The crisis of the Muslim world following its painful encounter with Western imperialism eroded Muslim tolerance and produced ideological animosity towards both the Christian and the Jewish minorities, which were now identified as the main beneficiaries of a growing Western influence and of various reform efforts carried out by Muslim rulers.[28]

---

25 William M. Brinner, "The Image of the Jew as 'Other' in Medieval Arabic Texts," *Israel Oriental Studies* XIV (1994): 228–229.

26 Camila Adang, "Medieval Muslim Polemics against the Jewish Scriptures," 144; Hava Lazarus-Yafeh, "Some neglected aspects of medieval Muslim polemics against Christianity," *Harvard Theological Review* 89, no. 1 (1996): 63; Abbas Barzegar, "The Persistence of Heresy: Paul of Tarsus, Ibn Saba', and Historical Narrative in Sunni Identity Formation," *Numen* 58 (2011): 222; Stillman, "Anti-Judaism and Antisemitism," 217.

27 Lewis, *The Jews of Islam*, 14–20.

28 On the changing attitudes towards Christians, see Bruce Masters, "The 1850 Events in Aleppo: an aftershock of Syria's incorporation into the capitalist World System," *International Journal of Middle East Studies* 22:1 (1990): 3–20; Leila Fawaz, *An occasion*

If Judaism and Christianity were indeed major "others" to pre-modern Islam, it makes sense that the mutual othering between Islam or Muslims and the West in the modern era was to become the focus of scholarly attention. Focusing on the knowledge-power nexus depicted by Michel Foucault, Edward Said argued in his highly influential *Orientalism* that Western culture had structured scholarly cultural and popular discourse around a stereotyped image of the "Orient" or Islam as the ultimate feared and abhorred "other." Moreover, the West, or the self, was portrayed as a positive mirror image of everything that was wrong with the Orient and Islam. Said's *Orientalism*, however, reified the West as a highly monolithic and almost unchanging entity in its racist othering of the East. Similarly, Arshin Adib-Moghaddam charges that "our whole cultural constellation is susceptible to accentuating the inevitability of conflict between supposedly homogenous constructs, especially between 'Islam' and the 'West.' and that violence between 'us' and 'them' is a 'natural' fact of history, or that our differences demand subjugating the 'other'."[29]

Other scholars adopt a more nuanced and multifaceted approach. David Blanks and Michael Frassetto maintain that while the East has always held a certain fascination for Westerners, the European view of the "other", like its view of the self, has revolved around an ever-changing set of historical circumstances ever since classical times. The encounter with the Muslim "other" was elemental to the shaping of the Western worldview. This was especially true during the centuries that began with the Crusades and ended with the dismemberment of the Ottoman Empire. The West's need to construct an image of the Muslim "other" was a twofold process that came to dominate the pre-modern discourse on Islam. On the one hand, it created an image of the Saracen, Moor, or Turk that was wholly alien and wholly evil, with the Muslim becoming, as it were, a photographic negative of the ideal Christian self-image. By debasing the image of their rivals, Western Christians were enhancing their own self-image and trying to build self-confidence in the face of a more powerful and more culturally sophisticated enemy. At the same time, and unlike Said, they point to a more complex picture. Thus alongside hostility there was also cooperation, conscious cultural borrowing, and even scholarly appreciation

---

for war: civil conflict in Lebanon and Damascus in 1860 (Berkeley: University of California Press, 1995); Eugene L. Rogan, "Sectarianism and Social Conflict in Damascus: The 1860 Events Reconsidered," *Arabica* 51, no. 4 (October 2004): 493–511. For the rise of anti-Semitism in the Arab world, see: Sylvia G. Haim, "Arab Anti-Semitic Literature," *Jewish Social Studies* 17, no. 4 (1955): 307–12; Bernard Lewis, *Semites and Anti-Semites* (London, 1997); Robert Wistrich, *Muslim Anti-Semitism: A Clear and Present Danger* (New York: American Jewish Committee, 2002).

29 Arshin Adib-Moghaddam, *A Meta-History of the Clash of Civilizations: Us and Them Beyond Orientalism* (London: Hurst, 2011), 4.

of Islamic culture. The methods these scholars used and the conclusions they drew would find their way into popular literature.[30]

Similarly, Noel Malcolm points to a "long-running, continuous traditions of direct hostility to both Islam and the Ottoman Empire" in Europe. Yet, ever since the 17th century a new paradigm emerged alongside the older one, expressing "a growing appreciation" of various aspects of Ottoman rule as well as positive statements about Muḥammad and Islam, "which are indeed remarkable." Yet, he cautioned that many of the contributors to this paradigm "were engaged in some kind of shame-praising activity vis-à-vis their own society."[31] American scholar William Brinner, for one, maintains that since Jews were the only other left within most of Christendom, the concept of "other" in Christian religious and literary texts was focused primarily on them rather than on Muslims.[32]

With the winding down of the Cold War, American political scientist Samuel Huntington published his grim forecast of an imminent "clash of civilizations." Accordingly, at the global level of world politics the primary clash was expected to break out between the West "and the rest," while at the local level it was to be between Muslim groups and adjacent groups from other civilizations. Huntington furthermore asserted that the underlying problem for the West was not Islamic fundamentalism but Islam itself. His analysis, which aroused a heated debate among Western and Middle Eastern scholars and intellectuals, could be seen as one more manifestation of othering, even though Huntington insisted that he had sought to preempt such a clash, not to promote it.[33]

Similarly, the emergence of the West as "other" in Muslim eyes was a product of a long process of cultural construction and was hence never monolithic. It started as indifference and lack of interest in what had been perceived as a morally inferior and militarily weaker culture. Yet, in view of repeated Muslim military defeats by Europeans and growing Western economic and political intrusion into Muslim lands since the eighteenth century, it evolved into a growing interest in, and even admiration for, the sources of Western success and

30 David R. Blanks and Michael Frassetto, "Introduction" in *Western Views of Islam in Medieval and Early Modern Europe: Perception of Other*, eds., Blanks and Frassetto (New York: St. Martin, 1999), 1–8. See also William Montgomery Watt, *Muslim-Christian Encounters: Perceptions and Misperceptions* (London: Routledge, 2013).

31 Noel Malcolm, *Useful Enemies: Islam and The Ottoman Empire in Western Political Thought, 1450–1750* (Oxford: Oxford University Press, 2019), 410–412.

32 Brinner, "The Image of the Jew as 'Other' in Medieval Arabic Texts," 228.

33 Samuel P. Huntington, "The clash of civilizations?" *Foreign affairs* (1993): 22–49; and his book *The clash of Civilizations and the Remaking of World Order* (New York: Simon & Shuster, 1996).

power.[34] At the same time, from the mid-nineteenth century onward, Western cultural influence was increasingly perceived as a challenge and threat to the Islamic worldview, culture, and identity. For quite a few Muslim or Islamic thinkers the West had been transformed into the menacing "other".[35]

Turning to intra-Muslim othering, the contrast between the collective we and the "other" has been a major feature in the evolution of Shīʿīsm as a minority group in Islam. The root of what would become in the course of years the core of Shīʿī identity and religion was the dispute over the personality, qualifications, and authority of the rightful successor of the Prophet Muḥammad, who died in 632 CE. The majority of the Muslim community followed Abū Bakr (d. 634), ʿUmar b. al-Khaṭṭāb (d. 644) and ʿUthmān b. ʿAffān (d. 656), as the Prophet's legitimate caliphs (successors). By contrast, the minority, which subsequently termed itself as *Shīʿat ʿAlī* (ʿAlī's faction) regarded ʿAlī b. Abī Ṭālib, the Prophet's cousin and son-in-law as the only rightful heir, since he was a member of the Prophet's family (*ahl al-bayt*) and therefore possessed some of the Prophet's charisma; in addition, the Prophet had nominated him as such.[36] The subsequent Shīʿī sense of injustice was augmented by Caliph ʿAlī's failure to stave off the challenge posed by Muʿāwiya, the governor of Damascus and a member of the Umayyad family, and culminated with ʿAlī's assassination in 661 and Muʿāwiya's complete victory.

As Najam Haider observed, it would be wrong to speak then of a distinct Shīʿī community in any modern sense of the term.[37] However, what would

---

34 Bernard Lewis, *The Muslim Discovery of Europe* (New York: Norton & Co, 1982); Geert Jan van Gelder and Ed de Moor (eds.), *The Middle East and Europe: Encounters and Exchanges* (Amsterdam: Rodopi, 1992); Jacques Waardenburg, "The Modern Period: 1500–1950," in *Muslim Perceptions of Other Religions*, 75–80; Mansoor Moaddel, *Islamic Modernism, Nationalism and Fundamentalism: Episode and Discourse* (Chicago: University of Chicago Press, 2005), 52–101.

35 Bassam Tibi, *Islam Between Politics and Culture* (New York: Palgrave, 2001), 188–230; Nathan C. Funk and Abdul Aziz Said, "Islam and the West: Narratives of conflict and conflict transformation." *International Journal of Peace Studies* (2004): 11–13; Ana Belén Soage, "Islamism and Modernity: The Political Thought of Sayyid Qutb," *Totalitarian Movements and Political Religions* 10, no. 2 (2009): 189–203.

36 The literature dealing with the issue of succession is vast. For a thorough historical analysis, see Wilfred Madelung, *The Succession to Muhammad: a Study of the Early Caliphate* (Cambridge: Cambridge University Press, 1997); For an analysis focusing on the centrality of charisma, see Hamid Dabashi, *Authority in Islam: from the rise of Muhammad to the establishment of the Umayyads* (New Brunswick: Transaction Publishers, 1989).

37 Najam Haider, "The Myth of the Shīʿī Perspective: Identity and Memory in Early Islam," in *Routledge Handbook on Early Islam*, ed. Herbert Berg (London: Routledge, 2018), 210.

become the constitutive myth of the Shīʿa,[38] was the traumatic slaughter on 10 Muḥarram 61/October 10, 680 of ʿAlī's son, Ḥusayn, along with 70 of his supporters in the battle against the Ummayad army in Karbalāʾ, Iraq. This tragedy led to the evolution, in Michael Fischer's words, of the Karbalāʾ paradigm, which still dominates the Shīʿī worldview, and its attitude towards the majority in the Islamic community, including the condition of humanity as a whole. It symbolized the distortion of Islamic history and the epitome of everything that was wrong with the world with the victory of evil over justice.[39]

While support for ʿAlī was motivated by a mix of political, personal and social factors, it evolved in the course of subsequent decades into a fully-fledged sectarian cleavage encompassing religious, social, and political principles. The dominant majority, which emerged as Sunnī Islam, became in many ways the major "other" against which Shīʿīsm viewed and defined itself in the course of history. As a result, Shīʿī doctrines and practices evolved primarily, but not exclusively, through a dialectic interaction with this majority, involving both opposition and rejection, coupled with a conscious, yet unwitting, borrowing from and accommodation with the Sunnī majority.[40] Still, in the arenas of law and theology, community memory was kept alive through the practice of historical narration, playing a key role in the shaping and preserving of a distinct Shīʿī identity vis-à-vis the Sunnī majority. In addition, while Shīʿīs often needed to protect themselves from the overbearing power of and occasional repression by a Sunnī majority, they always sought to win over Sunnīs through proselytization. Overall, Shīʿīs perceived themselves as the elite (*khāṣṣa*) among Muslims, while the Sunnīs were perceived as plebs (*ʿāmma*).[41] In addition, throughout history Jews, and since the mid-nineteenth century Bahāʾīs as well, served as "others" against whom Shīʿīs defined themselves. After the

38 In its anthropological meaning, myth is a narration of past events, which a group of people tells itself about itself. It may have a factual historical basis, but as the original factual source undergoes a process of elaboration and reinterpretation over time, it acquires epic dimensions. Myths usually have several functions. They reveal the meaning and order of the world; they shape the group's sense of self by placing it within an historical chain of events; they sanction specific models of behavior; and explain why evil and chaos exist.

39 Michael Fischer, *Iran: From Religious Dispute to Revolution* (Cambridge, Mass.: Harvard University Press, 1980), 7–8, 10–11.

40 With regard to the early Shīʿī legal debate on the status of martyrs, which was conducted in constant awareness of Sunnī views, see for example Robert Gleave, "The Status of the Battlefield Martyr in Classical Shiʿi Law," in *Concepts of Martyrdom in Modern Islam: Political and Social Perspectives of Sacrifice and Death*, eds. Meir Hatina and Meir Litvak (London: I.B. Tauris, 2016), 52–75.

41 Kamran Scot Aghaie, "The Origins of the Sunnīte-Shi'ite Divide and the Emergence of the Taziyeh Tradition." *TDR/The Drama Review* 49, no. 4 (2005): 45; Barzegar, "The Persistence of Heresy," 208–209.

1960s, however, the West became the ultimate "other" in the Shīʿī discourse, as numerous Iranian writers expounded on the threat it posed to Iranian cultural and national identity.

The conflict with the Shīʿa played a key role in the formulation of a distinct Sunnī identity as well. As the dominant majority, the Sunnīs were initially less anxious to articulate a full-fledged comprehensive doctrine, and Sunnīsm evolved more as a rejection of Shīʿī claims. Occasionally, from the ninth century onwards, the othering of the Shīʿīs was manifested in discriminatory measures and sectarian frictions. The ʿAbbāsid caliph al-Mutawakkil (r. 847–861), for instance, instituted the cursing of ʿAlī from the pulpits and destroyed the tombs of his descendants in Iraq. According to Laoust, the breach between the two communities during this period became more profound and more violent than that which separated Islam from Christianity and Judaism.[42] With the intensification of the conflict between the Shīʿī Būyīd amīrs and the ʿAbbāsid caliphs and possibly also in response to the concurrent intellectual flourishing of the Shīʿa, the ʿAbbāsid caliph al-Qādir promulgated the "Qādiriyya Treatise" (*al-risāla al-Qādiriyya*) in 409/1018, which fully defined and articulated the principles of the Sunnī doctrines against Shīʿīsm.[43] Sunnī polemicists employed a set of pejorative terms against Shīʿīs, such as "rejectionists" (*al-rāfiḍa, rawāfiḍ*), or "those who curse and reject" (*ahl al-sabb wal-rafḍ*), which alluded to Shīʿī rejection of the first three caliphs, and therefore referred to them as to a "fifth column" within the umma, insincere and with ulterior motives.[44] Even worse were the terms "the accursed sect" (*al-tāʾifa al-malʿūna*) and "the demonic community" (*al-umma al-shaytāniyya*).[45] Presumably one of the most humiliating Sunnī practices was to "Judaize" Shīʿīsm, as manifested in the maxim "the *rāfiḍa* (i.e. Shīʿīs) are the Jews of our umma." The equation implies not only resemblance in characteristics and attributes, but also in intention and action.[46]

---

42 Barzegar, "The Persistence of Heresy," p. 209; Hugh Kennedy, "al-Mutawakkil ʿAlā Allāh," EI2 – https://referenceworks.brillonline.com/entries/encyclopaedia-of-islam-2/al-mutawakkil-ala-llah-SIM_5658?s.num=1&s.f.s2_parent=s.f.book.encyclopaedia-of-islam-2&s.q=Mutawakkil; Henri Laoust, "La pensée et l'action politiques d'al-Mawardi." *Revue des études islamiques* 36 (1968): 44.

43 Udjang Tholib, *The Reign of the caliph al-Qadir billāh (381/991–422/1031)* (PhD Dissertation, McGill University, 2002), 250–267.

44 For the evolution of this term, see Etan Kohlberg, "The Term *Rāfiḍa* in Imāmī Shīʿī Usage," *Journal of the American Oriental Society* 99, no. 4 (October–December 1977): 677–679; Barzegar, "The Persistence of Heresy," 222.

45 http://www.buraydahcity.com/vb/showthread.php?t=32867.

46 Steven Wasserstrom, "Shīʿīte and Jew between History and Myth," in *Between Muslim and Jew: The Problem of Symbiosis under Early Islam* (Princeton: Princeton University Press, 2014), 93–135; Barzegar, "The Persistence of Heresy," 223.

The Ottomans, who regarded themselves as the champions of Sunnī Islam and were engaged in a prolonged conflict with the Iranian Ṣafavīd dynasty, treated their Shīʿī subjects as suspected "others." Until the mid-nineteenth century, they banned the public commemorations of the ʿĀshūrāʾ, and sought to curb Shīʿī missionary efforts in Iraq. At other times, the Ottomans subordinated religious considerations to administrative efficiency and employed Shīʿī families as tax farmers.[47] Alongside continued sectarian tensions and othering by both groups, various attempts at ecumenical reconciliation between Sunnīs and Shīʿīs took place throughout the twentieth century, but with limited success.[48]

An essential feature of othering in Islam, Christianity and Judaism was religious polemics, which played an important role in their doctrinal, social and organizational consolidation of identity. They served scholars from each religion to prove the veracity of their own religion, to articulate and refine the doctrines of their group and to refute opposing dogmas and historical claims of their rivals. In Islamic history polemics served to delineate Sunnī and Shīʿī group membership as early as the 2/8 century. For Shīʿīs, they were an essential means to convince the ordinary believers to remain loyal to the group when they faced difficulties and persecutions, and to convince Sunnīs to endorse Shīʿīsm.

Therefore, Shīʿī polemics always maintained a dual intertwined approach. The first was defensive seeking to validate various Shīʿī claims, from Ali's precedence in the Prophet's succession to the continued presence of the Hidden Imām. In the modern period it meant inter alia defending Shīʿī Islam from the perceived threat of western ideas and from charges of polytheism (*shirk*) raised by Wahhābīs. The second approach was offensive, seeking to refute the actions and doctrines of their rivals, be they Sunnīs in the past or Bahāʾīs and feminists in the modern period.[49]

---

47 For Ottoman discriminatory policy in Iraq, see Meir Litvak, *Shiʿi Scholars of nineteenth-century Iraq: the ʿUlamaʾ of Najaf and Karbalaʾ* (Cambridge: Cambridge University Press, 2002), 115–164. For the more pragmatic employment of Shīʿī tax farmers in Lebanon, see Stephen Winter, *The Shiʿites of Lebanon under Ottoman Rule, 1516–1788* (Cambridge: Cambridge University Press, 2010).

48 For such efforts, see Rainer Brunner, *Islamic Ecumenism in the 20th Century: The Azhar and Shīʿism between Rapprochement and Restraint* (Leiden-Boston: Brill, 2004); Elisheva Machlis, *Shiʿi Sectarianism in the Middle East: Modernisation and the Quest for Islamic Universalism* (London: I.B. Tauris, 2014), 47–48, 52–53, 82–113.

49 See both approaches in the writings of ʿAlāma ibn Muṭahhar al-Ḥillī (d. 726/1325), in Tarik Al-Jamil, "Ibn Taymiyya And Ibn Al-Mutahhar Al-Hilli: Shi'i Polemics And The Struggle For Religious Authority In Medieval Islam," in *Ibn Taymiyya and His Times*, eds., Yossef Rapoport and Shahab Ahmed (Karachi: Oxford University Press, 2010), 235–240.

Religious polemics required knowledge, often very thorough, of the texts and doctrines of the rival. This was fairly easy in inter-Muslim disputes as Shīʿī teachers and students often attended Sunnī learning circles, and occasionally borrowed heavily from Sunnīs in matters of law with necessary adaptations to suit their own doctrinal beliefs.[50] Selective appropriation of Sunnī material as part of polemics and apologetics was essential, as it was clear that the more powerful or self-confident Sunnīs would reject the validity of the Shīʿī sources. In addition, proving the Shīʿī case through a subversive reading of their rivals' religious texts was viewed as a more effective psychological weapon affecting both friend and foe.[51]

Once they enjoyed state patronage under the Ṣafavīds, the Shīʿī clerics could employ a more assertive polemical approach with the aim of converting Sunnīs to Shīʿīsm.[52] At the same time, the Shīʿī scholars "did not perceive the Jews as a serious intellectual challenge," which necessitated similar efforts, and there is little evidence that they engaged in composing original polemical works against Jews. As late as the 19th century, the Shīʿī writers did not read Jewish and Christian scriptures in their languages, and were familiar only with the Pentateuch rather than the entire Biblical corpus. Instead, they used works written by converts to Islam or translations by Christians.[53]

The presence of Christian missionaries, however, aroused already from the 17th century onward the sensitivities of Muslim scholars, Sunnīs and Shīʿīs, and gave rise to rich and sophisticated polemical literature. During the early 19th century, the Shīʿī writers developed an entire polemical genre of *radd-i padrī* (refutation of the padre) to refute the argumentations of the British missionary Henry Martyn (d. 1812) and of other missionaries. The threat posed by the missionaries is evident in extensive use of new sources. In his disputes against Jews, Aqā Muḥammad ʿAlī Bihbihānī Kirmānshāhī (d. 1801), for example used

50 Al-Jamil, "Ibn Taymiyya And Ibn Al-Mutahhar Al-Hilli," 230–231, 240; Devin J. Stewart, *Islamic Legal Orthodoxy: Twelver Shiʿite Responses to the Sunnī Legal System* (Salt Lake City: University of Utah Press, 1998), 73–111.

51 See for example, the extensive use of Sunnī authorities by Shaykh Jaʿfar Kāshif al-Ghitāʾ (d. 1812), in his correspondence with the Wahhābī Amīr ʿAbd al-ʿAzīz b. Saʿūd in 1810 as he defended the Shīʿa from charges of polytheism in Meir Litvak, "Encounters between Shīʿī and Sunnī ʿUlamaʾ in Ottoman Iraq," *Division and Ecumenism in Islam: The Sunna and Shiʿa in History*, eds., Ofra Bengio and Meir Litvak (New York: Palgrave-McMillan, 2011), 74–77 and chapter 4 below.

52 Rula Jurdi Abisaab, *Converting Persia: Religion and Power in the Safavid Empire* (London: I.B. Tauris, 2004), 16, 40.

53 Reza Pourjavady and Sabine Schmidtke, "Muslim Polemics against Judaism and Christianity in 18th Century Iran. The Literary Sources of Āqā Muḥammad ʿAlī Bihbahānī's (1144/1732–1216/1801) Rādd-i shubahāt al-kuffār," *Studia Iranica* 35, no. 1 (2006): 71, 87.

old polemics from earlier centuries. But in his anti-missionary work, he relied on many more sources closer to his time. Other clerics, most notably Mulla Aḥmad Narāqī of Kāshān (d. 1829) cooperated with Jews in translating and understanding parts of the Bible in composing his polemical tracts against missionaries. In other words, the Christian missionary threat engendered a Shīʿī-Jewish exchange concerning the Hebrew Bible.[54]

Though much of the *radd-i padri* was reworking of old themes used for centuries, Abbas Amanat discerns two new approaches: one, use of *uṣūl al-fiqh* (principles of jurisprudence) technique to question Jesus' prophecy and the second an emphasis mostly among the Ṣūfī writers on the evolutionary (*takvīnī*) nature of prophethood as a proof of Islam's validity.[55] The anti-missionary polemics written in Persian to refute Christian doctrines did not aim to convince Christians but to bolster Iranians' belief in Shīʿī Islam.

Similarly, the anti-Western polemics during the 20th century disputed western ideas from liberalism to Marxism as well as aspects of western lifestyle as a means to defend Shīʿī-Islamic beliefs. The threat and challenge posed by Western ideas required greater familiarity with Western thought and societies. In this case, citing western critics on the ills of their societies was a powerful rhetorical strategy as it projected greater authenticity. Here too a generational difference is evident. The older generation of clerics used only Persian and Arab sources. Some of the younger ones have had direct access to western sources through translations, while others either could read western works in their original languages or have even studied in western universities in order to better grapple with the Western challenge.

Polemics always required extensive use of rationalist argumentation since reliance on one's own sacred texts would never convince a rival who rejects such texts altogether. Here, the Shīʿī endorsement of the rationalist Muʿtazilī theology and the continued development of the methodology of ijtihād proved very effective. At the same time, the Shīʿī polemicists certainly gave priority to their own sources whenever there was a contradiction between the Qur'ān or Shīʿī ḥadīth and other scriptures.

---

54 Schmidtke and Pourjavady, "Muslim Polemics against Judaism and Christianity in 18th Century Iran," 76, 84; Daniel Tsadik, "Nineteenth Century Shīʿī Anti-Christian Polemics and the Jewish Aramaic Nevuat Ha-yeled [The Prophecy of the Child]," *Iranian Studies*, 37, No. 1 (Mar., 2004): 5, 13.

55 Abbas Amanat, "Mujtahids and missionaries: Shiʿi responses to Christian polemics in the early Qajar period," in *Religion and Society in Qajar Iran*, ed., Robert Gleave (London: Routledge, 2004), 256.

Among the most common techniques of Shīʿī polemicists across the years was to trace and highlight discrepancies, contradictions, corruption and distortions in the rivals' sacred texts or highlighting conflicts and internal criticisms within their ranks that undermine their message or appeal. Another common means was subversive reading of the rival's text in order to prove the truth of Shīʿīsm, for instance in predicting the prophecy of Muḥammad and the emergence of the twelve Imāms. Occasionally, such readings involved outright distortions or fabrications as was the case with various charges against Bahāʾīs as agents of the US and Israel. Very often polemicists juxtaposed the utopian Islamic ideal against the grim reality in the rival's side, or offered generalizations on the rivals by ignoring diversity within the rival's ranks or by highlighting the most extreme elements of the others. Likewise, polemics occasionally resorted to a-historical arguments by ignoring changes and developments that affect them.

2 The Modern Other as Enemy

As part of the global phenomenon of soaring religious fundamentalism, the rise of radical Islam or Islamism since the 1970s has made the issue of religious othering more pertinent and more violent. Islamism maintains an exclusivist claim to the truth and has used the rhetoric of othering to justify itself. Determining who falls within the category of true believers and who remains outside has proven to be a key concern for advocates of Islamism.[56] The concept of the world as a battlefield where the forces of good and evil are fighting against each other, of a perennial universal battle going on everywhere and at all times, is common to most prophetic religions, but it is especially characteristic of the fundamentalist groups within them. Fundamentalists view history as a cosmic struggle between good and evil, using stark binary dichotomies to describe the opposing camps. Although rhetoric stresses that the main battle is spiritual, it is not less real. It is being fought in the realms of personal spiritual and moral development, as well as in the sphere of ideas, worldviews, and ideologies. If the world is a battlefield, and if personal or collective salvation or damnation is at stake, then the opponent or the "other" becomes ipso facto an enemy. Islamic fundamentalism offers a radical reinterpretation of traditional Islamic concepts. Its discourse on the subject of battle serves to warn believers

56 Naser Ghobadzādeh & Shahram Akbarzādeh, "Sectarianism and the prevalence of 'Othering' in Islamic thought," *Third World Quarterly* 36, no. 4 (2015): 691.

against those identified as enemies, and mobilize them for the struggle against perceived enemies who need to be vanquished.[57]

Often, radicals view lapsed or deviating members of their own religion as more dangerous, at least in the short run, than members of other religions. The reason is their supposed deviousness, which threatens the community from within and prevents it from attaining its spiritual or political goals. These generalizations apply to Sunnī radicals as well. If the West and the Jews serve as their ultimate external "other", the Shīʿīs and Ṣūfīs fulfil the same role, albeit within Islam. Thus the great Ḥanbalī scholar Taqī al-Dīn Aḥmad ibn Taymiyya (d. 1328), who is revered by present-day Salafists, and Muḥammad b. ʿAbd al-Wahhāb (d. 1792), founder of the Wahhābī sect, described the Shīʿīs as "the greatest harm" (*ashaddu al-ḍarar*) to religion, more so than the Jews and the Christians. Following their cue, modern Islamist polemicists denounce the Shīʿīs as "enemies of God." This approach, which produced a voluminous polemical literature between the sects of Islam centuries ago, has acquired a new momentum in the past four decades.[58] It culminated in the calls of Abū Muṣʿab al-Zarqāwī (d. 2006), the first leader of al-Qāʿida in Iraq, who claimed that "the danger of the *rāfiḍa* is greater and their damage more lethal to the umma than the Americans." He therefore called for the "total annihilation" of "the apostate agents headed by the *rāfiḍa*." By 2011, al-Qāʿida affiliates had killed more Shīʿīs (the internal enemy) than Americans (the external enemy) in Iraq.[59]

The process of othering in Shīʿīsm underwent radicalization to the binary enemy-friend dichotomy with the politicization of the Shīʿa since the 1963 mass protests in Iran. However, following the 1979 Revolution it became a crucial pillar in the Islamic Republic's official ideology and strategy of survival.

---

57 David Zeidan, "The Islamic fundamentalist view of life as a perennial battle." *Middle East Review of International Affairs* 5, no. 4 (2001): 27; Mark Juergensmeyer, *The New Cold War? Religious Nationalism Confronts the Secular State* (Berkeley: University of California Press, 1993), 156–160.

58 Muḥammad b. ʿAbd al-Wahhāb, *Risāla fī al-radd ʿalā al-rāfiḍa* (Sanʿā: Dār al-athār, 2006); see the *fatwā* by the Saudi shaykh ʿAbd al-Raḥman al-Barrāk that said that the Shīʿī "threat to the Muslims is greater than that of the Jews or Christians," http://www.alkhayma.com/politics/albrak19122006.htm; *Maʿlūmāt muhimma ʿan al-rāfiḍa aʿdāʾ Allah*, 11, http://www.dd-sunnah.net/forum/showthread.php?t=13767; *"Mukhtaṣar taʾrīkh al-rāfiḍa saraṭān al-umma,"* http://www.masr4host.org/~amhzn/vb/showthread.php?t=4496, see also Meir Litvak, "More harmful than the Jews: anti-Shīʿī polemics in modern radical Sunnī discourse," in *Le Shīʿisme imamite quarante ans après: Hommage à Etan Kohlberg*, eds. Muhammad Ali Amīr-Moezzi, Meir M. Bar-Asher and Simon Hopkins, (Paris: Brepols Publishers, 2008), 285–306.

59 Cited in Nibras Kazimi, "Zarqawi's Anti-Shiʿa Legacy: Original or Borrowed?" *Current Trends in Islamist Ideology* 4 (November 2006): 67; Ghobadzādeh & Akbarzādeh, "Sectarianism and the prevalence of 'Othering' in Islamic thought," 693.

The division of the people into "our own people" (*khōdihā*) and "others" (*gheyr-i khōdihā*), that is the enemies of the revolution, the so-called liberals, the secular and Westernized intellectuals, became a recurrent motif in the dominant religious and political discourse.[60]

Every revolutionary regime needs internal and external enemies in order to preserve the ideological fervor among the population and its monopoly of power.[61] In the Shīʿī-Iranian case, the consolidation of the revolutionary regime required the articulation of new positions on a variety of ideological issues, among them attitudes towards old and new adversaries. Following Langmuir's observations regarding medieval anti-Semitism,[62] it is conceivable that the fear of waning ideological commitment among the Iranian population in the course of time required greater demonization of the various enemies and of the threat they pose to Islam. As an ideological and essentially right-wing regime in the sense that it believes in shaping human consciousness by spiritual rather than by material means, the Iranian government built a powerful apparatus of indoctrination through a wide plethora of printed, electronic, and visual media designed to mold the proper Shīʿī-Islamic person, and inure him/her to various inimical ideologies. Moreover, Adib-Moghaddam's charge applies well to Iran as he speaks of "a system of control, constituted by many discourses, permeated by entrenched ideologies, and many disciplines" all of which "ensure a permanent reactivation of 'us' versus 'them' mentality."[63]

The violent struggle for power led by Khomeini and his clerical supporters against the other members of the revolutionary coalition, which brought down the Shāh, exacerbated the perception of rival "others" as enemies. The 1981 Iraqi invasion of Iran, with the tacit support of most Arab states, and the subsequent eight-year-long war with its heavy human toll, as well as the confrontation with

---

60 Navid Kermani, "The Fear of the Guardians: 24 Army Officers Write a Letter to President Khātamī," in *The Twelver Shia in Modern Times: Religion, Culture & Political History*, eds., R. Brunner & W. Ende (Leiden: Brill 2001), 358–359.

61 An example of the fever against internal enemies is the Stalinist regime in the Soviet Union, particularly after 1929, see Robert Conquest, *The Great Terror: Stalin's purge of the thirties* (New York: Random House, 2018). An example of building an external enemy is Nazi anti-Jewish ideology, see Saul Friedländer, *Nazi Germany and the Jews, 1933–1945* (New York: Harper Collins, 1997), 73–111.

62 Gavin Langmuir, *Toward a Definition of Antisemitism* (Berkeley: University of California Press, 1990), 9–10, 100–134.

63 Adib-Moghaddam, *A Meta-History of the Clash of Civilizations*, XIV. Shabnam J. Holliday, *Defining Iran: Politics of Resistance* (Surrey: Ashgate, 2011), 4, 82, analyzes the construction of Iranian national identity under the Islamic Republic "in relation to both an internal 'other' and an external 'other,'" but this important discussion is beyond the scope of the present study.

the US following 1979–1981 hostage taking, deepened the siege mentality of the ruling clerical establishment in Iran and its self-perception as being surrounded by enemies. This view of the world, clearly manifested in Khamenei's words "there is no creature without enemy," produced a massive indoctrination and socialization process designed to create the aura of a revolution besieged by enemies who seek to destroy it. Accordingly, the existence of an enemy is not a transient reality but a permanent one. Moreover, the enemy is present with a clearly defined action plan in all fields – from culture through the economy and politics.[64] This ideological and political vantage point gave birth to a vibrant debate in modern Iranian Shīʿīsm on the need to "know thy enemy" (*dushman shināsī*), the threat he poses to [Shīʿī] Islam, and the ways to confront and defeat him.[65]

Regional changes at the beginning of the twenty-first century appeared to favor the Shīʿīs. The success of the Lebanese Ḥizballah in driving Israel out of Lebanon in 2000 enhanced its prestige even among the Sunnī masses as it stood in sharp contrast to the lethargy and failures of the veteran Sunnī-dominated Arab governments. The partial defeat of the anti-Shīʿī Ṭālibān regime in Afghanistan by the Americans in 2001 and, more importantly, the downfall of the Baʿth regime in Iraq following the 2003 U.S. invasion enhanced Iran's regional position. The shift of power in Iraq from the Sunnī minority to the Shīʿī majority affected the regional balance of power between the two sects, and was instrumental in the rise of Iran as a regional power. These changes exacerbated the sectarian Sunnī-Shīʿī rift in the region, particularly following the rise of Sunnī jihādī-Salafī movements, which espoused a vehement anti-Shīʿī ideology. Concurrently, they emboldened the Shīʿīs' self-confidence and generated significant changes in Shīʿī views of the self and required the reformulation of central doctrinal positions towards their various rival "others."

Whereas in the premodern period Sunnīs constituted the main antagonistic "other", the modern Shīʿī discourse identified two types of enemies. The external enemies, according to Khomeini and Khamenei, were "world arrogance," that is the U.S., and the "network of global Zionism." These enemies appear in different forms. At times they take a harsh and hostile face of wolves while at others they take the deceitful face of foxes. However as Khamenei included

64 "Mu'alafahā-i shenākht-i dushman chīst?," 7 Mehr 1392/September 29, 2013, http://www.ghatreh.com/news/nn15863623.

65 The publication of a book dedicated to Khamenei's views and statements on this topic, *Dushman Shināsī dar Kalām-i Imām-i Khamenei* as well as the availability of this search category in his official website, which presents all his speeches and statements on *dushman shināsī*, are two pertinent examples of its importance in addition to many hundreds of publications in all media.

"Zionist capitalists" among the key decision makers of world arrogance, alongside owners of companies and cartels that held the world by the throat, it seems that the term Zionist enemy in fact referred to Jews in general.[66] Lower-level writers were more forthright and, basing themselves on the Qurʾān, saw the Jews as a special category of enemies distinct from other disbelievers.[67]

The internal enemies were those who opposed the Islamic government, among them the hypocrites (*munāfiqīn*) and those who want to mislead the people against the revolution. Therefore, Khamenei at times described the internal enemy as more dangerous than the external one, although the two were always linked together. He thus described any internal criticism and casting doubt at the regime as assisting the external enemy. At other times, the external enemy allegedly used Iranian intellectuals in order to disseminate Western ideas and sow disbelief. Indeed, according to Khamenei, global arrogance, the external enemy, was widely active throughout Iran in the universities, high schools, the press, and the media. Vigilance against the enemy ought therefore not to be relaxed, not even for one moment, as the search for the enemy everywhere was a divine duty.[68] Considering these dangers, the role of the leadership in recognizing the enemy and his local followers, i.e. West-leaning intellectuals, was one of the most important factors in the survival and victory of the Islamic Revolution.[69]

The calls for vigilance, while serving the regime's goal to preserve a siege mentality that would justify political repression, reflected deep suspicions

---

66 *Dushman shināsī dar kalām Imām-i Khamenei*, p. 58; "Dushman shināsī az dīdār-i maqām-i muʿaẓẓam-i rahbarī (1)," 25 Mehr 1388/October 17, 2009, https://rasekhoon.net/article/show/145713/(1); "Dushman shināsī dar kalām Imām va-rahbarī (powerkī)," *Kayhān* 30 Shahrīvar 1393/September 21, 2014; "Bayānāt dar dīdār-i zāʾirān va-mujāvirān-i ḥaram-i muṭṭahar-i rażavī," 1 Farvardīn 1389/March 21, 2010, http://www.ghadeer.org/BsnText/13260.

67 "Mowżūʿ-i pazhūhesh (2) dushman shināsī," *Maʿārif-i Islāmī* 68 (1386/ 2007), https://Ḥawza.net/fa/Magazine/View/5387/5606/54392; Javād Bakhtiyārī, "Dushman shināsī dar Qurʾān bā taʾkīd bar dushmanī-i Yahūd," Muʾasasa-i amūzeshī-i pazhūheshī-i imām Khomeini, http://www.hawzah.net/fa/Seminar/View/78647/.

68 *Dushman Shināsī dar Kalām-i Imām-i Khamenei*, 79, 90, 99; "Murūrī bar kitāb-i dushman shināsī az manẓar-i rahbarī," 12 Abān 1395/November 2, 2016, http://teeh.ir/fa/news-details/2329/مروری-بر-کتاب-«دشمن شناسی-از-منظر-رهبری»; "Dushman-i bīrūnī va-durūnī-i inqilāb-i Islāmī," 1/6/1394/August 23, 2015, https://www.farsnews.com/news/13940529000720/; "Dushman shināsī az manẓar-i maqām-i muʿaẓẓam-i rahbarī," *Maʿārif* 64 (Esfand 1387/February 2009), https://hawzah.net/fa/Magazine/View/5211/6900/83079; "Dushman shināsī dar kalām Imām va-rahbarī."

69 *Dushman shināsī dar kalām Imām-i Khamenei*, 40 "Dushman shināsī az manẓar-i maqām-i muʿaẓẓam-i rahbarī."

and possibly also resentment against those social groups that produced or sustained intellectuals. Significantly, a *Kayhān* article equated their effect on society to that of microbes and viruses. The implication, though not stated explicitly, was clear: Just as the body needs to overcome and eliminate these threatening microbes, so should Muslim society deal with its enemies in the same manner.[70]

In many of his speeches Khamenei has enumerated the reasons behind the enemy's hostility to Islam and particularly to the Islamic Republic. Recognizing and fearing its inherent advantages, the enemies of Islam are aware that any country adhering to Islam can attain the peak of civilization. They fear the Islamic awakening, which challenges their own domination. They know that Iran is the flag carrier of this awakening and that its calls for the unity and empowerment of Islam raise the hopes of the Muslim nations and all oppressed peoples. The "enemies" oppose the very essence of the Islamic Revolution, as well as the principles it advocates. The revolution stands against oppression, as well as against the domination, exploitation, and humiliation of the world's nations by the superpowers and it struggles against the imposition of Western culture on the Muslim nations. At the same time, the revolution champions ideals that its enemies reject, such as the defense of any nation or person that endorses the path of Islam or the affirmation of Iranian independence, national identity, and Islamic values. In addition, they fear the power and scientific progress that Islam boosts.[71] While some of these charges of Western fear of political Islam are valid, they also serve as an obvious example of psychological projection, where one side attributes to the "other" the harmful or problematic aspects of the self. In Khamenei's case the fear of a Western "cultural offensive" (*tahājum-i farhangī*) against Islam constitutes the mirror image to the fear and animosity he attributes to the West.

Following Khamenei's cue, Brigadier General Yadollah Javānī, a leading theoretician of the Revolutionary Guards, discussed the question why the Iranian nation and the Islamic Republic had enemies. He argued that the unique essence of Iranian identity comprised "Islam, revolution and historical depth."

---

70 "Dushman shināsī dar kalām Imām va-rahbarī (powerkī);" "Dushman shināsī żarūratī barāye jāmi'a," *Kayhān*, 18 Khordād 1394/June 8, 2015; "Murūrī bar kitāb-i dushman shināsī az manẓar-i rahbarī;" "Dushman-i bīrūnī va-durūnī-i inqilāb-i Islāmī"; "Dushman shināsī az manẓar-i maqām-i mu'aẓẓam-i rahbarī;" "Dushman shināsī dar kalām-i Imām va-rahbarī."

71 *Dushman shināsī dar kalām-i Imām-i Khamenei*, 35, 40; Muḥammad Javād Salmānpūr, "Dushman shināsī va-dushman setīzī az dīdār-i Imām (rh)," *Miṣbāḥ* 7:30 (Tīr 1378/ July 1999), 65; "Dushman shināsī az manẓar-i maqām-i mu'aẓẓam-i rahbarī;" Āyat Muẓaffarī, *Rāhbordhā-i dushman shināsī* (Qom: Zamzama-i Hidāyat, 1392/2013), 45–61.

Based on these characteristics, "Iranians seek to build Islamic civilization, defend the oppressed and the poor, and stand against the oppressors." But, he went on, these characteristics are diametrically opposed to our "avaricious enemy and its tendency to bully and plunder" weaker nations. Javānī's inevitable conclusion was that "for the Iranian nation ... the existence of the enemy is definite, permanent, and inevitable."[72]

Considering the reasons behind their hostility, the enemies continue to seek to undermine and weaken Iran's Islamic identity and system, which are based on the doctrine of "governance of the jurist" (*Vilāyat-i Faqīh*) and the leadership of the clergy in society and separate them from the people. For decades they strove to undercut the people's belief in pure Islam, to deny the eternal validity of Islamic law, to separate Islam from politics and disseminate instead a false submissive version of Islam. They sought to denigrate Islamic culture and obliterate Iran's authentic values, rooted in Islam, in order to destroy the national and religious vitality of the Muslims, and of the Iranian nation in particular. The reason was their understanding that a nation that did not adhere to its culture would lose its independent thinking and fall under foreign domination and rule.[73]

With the threat of the enemy looming so large, the official discourse depicted awareness of the enemy's goals as a national and religious duty (*taklīf sharʿī*), a question of "acknowledging the unity of God and worship" (*towḥīd and ʿibādāt*), and as an essential prerequisite for the attainment of felicity (*saʿādat*) for mankind.[74] The threat emanating from their enemies was a major theme in the Qur'ān and the Traditions (*aḥādīth*) – a third of all Qur'ānic passages according to some writers. The Qur'ān spoke of three types of enemies:

---

72 Yadollah Javānī, "Cherā dushman dārīm," *Ṣubḥ-i Ṣādiq*, July 7, 2017.

73 *Dushman shināsī dar kalām Imām-i Khamenei*, 54, 59, 89, 91; Salmānpūr, "Dushman shināsī va-dushman setīzī az dīdār-i Imām (rh)," 66; Fāṭima Omīdī, *Āyīn-i Pāsdārī pīrāmūn vaḥdat, basīj, dushman shināsī* (Tehrān: Nashr-i Shahīd, 1392/2013), 107–122; "Dushman shināsī az manẓar-i maqām-i muʿaẓẓam-i rahbarī;" "Dushman shināsī az dīdār-i maqām-i muʿaẓẓam-i rahbarī (2)," 25 Mehr 1388/October 17, 2009, http://rasekhoon.net/article/show/145714/; Muẓaffarī, *Rāhbordhā-i dushman shināsī*, 61–102.

74 *Dushman shināsī dar kalām Imām-i Khamenei*, 90; Muẓaffar Hājiyān Ḥusayn Abādī, "Dushman shināsī żarūrat-i millī," 29 Mehr 1396/21 October 2017, http://eskimia.ir/دشمن-شناسی،-ضرورتی-ملی/; "Dushman Shināsī dar Kalām Imām va-rahbarī (powerkī);" "Mu'alafahā-i shenākht-i dushman chīst?"; Mahdī Ṭā'ib et al., *Tabār-i inḥirāf: pazhūheshī dar dushman'shināsī-i ta'rīkhī* (Qom: Mu'asasa-i farhangī-i valā'-i muntaẓar, 1390/2011), 4; Muḥammad Taqī Zāhidī, "Ta'rīkhcheh-i tharvat andūzī-i zarsālārān-i Yahūd," 22 Azar 1392/December 13, 2013, https://www.mashreghnews.ir/news/270442-تاریخچه-ثروت-اندوزی-زرسالاران-یهود/; "Mowżūʿ pazhūhesh (2) dushman shināsī."

the polytheists, the hypocrites, and the Jews (One should note that few writers put the Jews at the head of the five categories of enemies). The correct understanding of these groups is essential for the proper assessment of the enemies confronting today's Islamic Republic, since the failure to do so would inevitably lead to the path of extinction.[75]

Typical of Islamist writers, the early Islamic period, and in the Shīʿī case the tragic history of the imāms ʿAlī and Ḥusayn, not only serves as a major source of historical reference and a source of inspiration, but also as a painful lesson regarding the particular importance of in-depth knowledge of the enemy. The IRGC organ *Pāsdār-i Islām*, for one, cited Imām ʿAlī, who had warned against minimizing the danger of the enemy even when the latter seemed weak and, more importantly, against believing the enemy when he spoke softly. Ḥujjat al-Islam Muḥammad Taqī Zāhidī cited the sixth Shīʿī Imām, Jaʿfar al-Ṣādiq (d. 765), as saying that the essence of religion was love of God and enmity towards His enemies. Thus the official Tebyān website equated hypocrites like Ṭalḥa and Zubayr, who had betrayed Imām ʿAlī, with those who took part in the revolution against the Shāh, but later on turned against the Islamic Republic. As both men were killed in the battle against ʿAlī in 656, it is possible that the article pointed to the desired end of present-day enemies.[76] As the enemies had a well-conceived plan against the Revolution, Khamenei stressed the necessity of confronting them with a counteraction plan that centered on adherence to and strengthening of the Islamic faith. As the major pillar of resistance against the enemy, religion gave one strength and resilience.[77]

The conceptualization of politics in the form of friend-enemy formulation is not unique to Islamism but is also found in Carl Schmitt's political theory. Schmitt, the leading legal theoretician of Nazi Germany, argues that "the specific political distinction … is that between friend and enemy" and that a state

75 A group of authors, *Darsnāmah-i taʾrīkh-i taḥlīlī-i dushman shināsī* (Qom: Muʾasasa-i Iṭṭilāʿ rasānī va-muṭālaʿāt-i farhangī-i Lawḥ va-Qalam, 1383/2004), vol. 1, 13–14; "Dushman shināsī va-rāhkārhā-i muqābala bā ān az manẓar-i Qurʾān chīst?" http://www.islamquest.net/fa/archive/question/fa35070; Ḥusayn Abādī, "Dushman shināsī żarūrat-i millī"; Khātamī, "Dushman shināsī az dīdgāh Imām ʿAlī (ʿalayhi al-salām);" "Dushman shināsī," http://www.masjed.ir/fa/article/2816/دشمن-شناسی.

76 Aḥmad Khātamī, "Dushman shināsī az dīdgāh-i Imām ʿAlī," *Pāsdār-i Islām* 209 (1378/1999), https://hawzah.net/fa/Magazine/View/89/3409/15864; Zāhidī, "Taʾrīkhcheh-i tharvat andūzī-i zarsālārān-i Yahūd;" Farukhandeh Zorgān, "Dushman shināsī az manẓar-i Imām ʿAlī `ʿalayhi al-salām," *Kayhan*, 15 Mordad 1385/August 6, 2006; "Teknīkhā-i dushman shināsī az manẓar-i Imām ʿAlī," 27 Abān 1388/18 November 2009, https://article.tebyan.net/107858/.

77 *Dushman shināsī dar kalām Imām-i Khamenei*, p. 107–108; "Muʾalafahā-i shenākht-i dushman chīst?"; "Dushman shināsī va-rāhkārhā-i muqābala bā ān az manẓar-i Qurʾān chīst."

can only be legitimate if its legal boundaries embody a clear friend-enemy distinction. In order to achieve this aim, Schmitt implies, a sovereign dictator must unite the community by appealing to a clear friend-enemy distinction, as well as through the suppression, elimination, or expulsion of internal enemies who do not endorse that distinction. In so doing, the sovereign dictator expresses the community's understanding of what is normal or exceptional and of who belongs, thus creating a homogeneous medium, which Schmitt considers to be a precondition of the legitimate applicability of law. Contrary to Schmitt, the friend-enemy dichotomy in the Shīʿī worldview is founded on moral Islamic principles and criteria, which relate to the perceived threat to the community's spiritual and moral integrity. Schmitt on the other hand maintains that the drawing of a friend-enemy distinction is never a mere reaction to a threat or to a predetermined form of existence that is already a given. Rather, it actively constitutes the political identity or existence of the people, and determines who belongs to the people.[78]

Overall, the post-revolutionary Shīʿī-Iranian discourse towards "others" reflects a dualist self-perception also found among other Islamist movements. One side is that of a besieged religion, surrounded and threatened by external and internal enemies in the past and in the present. The other side is of a powerful revolution that has and will continue to overcome its enemies and is hence destined to triumph in the future.[79] According to the official narrative, the 1979 Revolution awakened the Iranian nation from its slumber and slackness; it revolutionized Islamic ideologies and transformed all global equations of power. In other words, the revolution has dealt a serious blow to all "devouring forces" in the world. The conclusion is that Iran is stronger than its enemies and should never fear them.[80] For forty years the enemies have clung to their hostility one writer asserted, and have taken every opportunity to harm the "great nation of Iran." But recognizing and learning the enemy will eventually lead him to despair and defeat, as has been the case since the revolution.[81]

78 On Schmitt's friend-enemy concept, see idem. *The Concept of the Political. Expanded Edition* (1932), trans. by G. Schwab (Chicago: University of Chicago Press, 2007), 19, 26, 46–48; Lars Vinx, "Carl Schmitt", *The Stanford Encyclopedia of Philosophy* (Spring 2016 Edition), https://plato.stanford.edu/archives/spr2016/entries/schmitt/; Gabriella Slomp, *Carl Schmitt and the Politics of Hostility, Violence and Terror* (New York: Palgrave-McMillan, 2009), chapters 1–3.

79 See similar feelings among Sunnī movements in Emmanuel Sivan, *Radical Islam: Medieval Theology and Modern Politics* (New Haven: Yale University Press, 1990).

80 *Dushman Shināsī dar Kalām Imām-i Khamenei*, 47, 80, 104–105, 109; "Bayānāt az dīdār-i jamʿī az rūḥāniyān," 11 Mordād 1368/August 2, 1989, http://farsi.khamenei.ir/speech-content?id=2151.

81 Ḥusayn Abādī, "Dushman shināsī żarūrat-i millī."

When considering the othering discourse in Iran, one ought to remember that the Iranian religious, intellectual and clerical arenas are far from monolithic. They can each be divided into three major camps or discourses: religious conservative (*Uṣūl garā*, often translated as "principlist"), reformist (*Iṣlāḥgarā*) and liberal.[82]

The conservative camp refers to an array of forces that had previously identified themselves as conservative, fundamentalist, neo-fundamentalist, or traditionalist. They are the largest and politically dominant clerical faction supported by Supreme Leader Khamenei and are organizationally associated with the *Jāmiʿa-i rūḥāniyat mubāriz* (society of militant clergy). They espouse an absolutist and legalistic Islam, premised on the notion of "duty," as well as on a strict and, if needed, forceful and violent enforcement of religion onto all facets of the social and political spheres and moral codes in the public sphere. They believe that Iran must remain true to its revolutionary goals of 1979, and fear that compromising on revolutionary principles would threaten the pillars of the Islamic Republic. Many of them are ardent supporters of the principle of the absolute authority of the ruling jurist (*vilāyat-i muṭlaq*), which may even position him above Islamic law. Therefore, they do not tolerate dissent and make few concessions to the popular will and contemporary realities, particularly on issues pertaining to gender equality. They regard enmity toward the United States and Western culture as a fundamental pillar of the revolution and central to the very identity of the Islamic Republic. Hence, they oppose economic opening to the world, which might open up Iran to foreign cultural influences. Instead, they promote economic self-sufficiency titled "resistance economy." While they cherish the sanctity of private property, they support the dominant role of the state in the economy.[83]

A more militant hardline faction emerged in the late 1990s in response to the electoral victories of the reformists in the 1997 presidential elections. These radical or neoconservatives, many of them laymen, argued that the revolution had lost its way with the election of Akbar Hāshimī Rafsanjānī (d. 2017) to the presidency in 1989 and therefore advocated a return to the ideological purity

---

82 For a comprehensive analysis of the Iranian intellectual-political map, see Mehran Kamrava, *Iran's Intellectual Revolution* (Cambridge: Cambridge University Press, 2008).

83 Kamrava, *Iran's Intellectual Revolution*, 79–119; Maziar Behrooz, "Factionalism in Iran under Khomeini," *Middle Eastern Studies* 27, no. 4 (Oct., 1991): 597–614; Said A. Arjomand, *After Khomeini: Iran under his Successors* (Oxford: Oxford University Press, 2009), 65–68; Ziba Mir-Hosseini, "The Conservative–Reformist Conflict Over Women's Rights in Iran," *International Journal of Politics, Culture and Society* 16, no. 1 (Fall 2002): 37–38; Roxanne D. Marcotte, "Religion and Freedom: Typology of an Iranian Discussion," *Australian Religion Studies Review* 18, no. 1 (2005): 49–67.

of the early days of the revolution. The most prominent politician associated with this group was former president Maḥmūd Ahmadinezhad (2005–2013) and his clerical mentor Ayatollah Muḥammad Taqī Miṣbāḥ Yazdī, the leading hardliner within the clerical establishment.[84]

The reformist camp advocated a more flexible interpretation of religion to accommodate social changes, while at the same time attempting to preserve Islam's spiritual nature. It sought to reconcile Islam with democracy, human rights, and improvement in gender equality as a way to adapt religion to the needs of a changing society and to keep it relevant in the eyes of a broader and younger public. In domestic policies, the reformists wanted the regime to pay more attention to issues such as unemployment, poverty and corruption, instead of adhering to the rigid revolutionary ideology of the early 1980s. On foreign policy, they sought the normalization of Iran's relations with the outside world, including the West. Organizationally the reformists were closer to the minority group the *Majmaʿ-i Ruḥāniyūn Mubāriz* (Association of Militant Clergy, MRM) in the clerical establishment. They achieved temporary prominence with the unexpected victory of Seyyed Muḥammad Khātamī in the 1997 presidential elections and the 2000 Majlis elections. However, with the return to more overt political repression in April 2001, the ideological debate in Iran became largely one-sided as the reformist spokesmen were gradually and systematically silenced. The reformists somewhat recovered following Ḥasan Rouhani's election to the presidency in 2013. Rouhani, however, was ideologically less committed to reform than Khātamī.[85]

The conservative and reformist groups supported the *Vilāyat-Faqīh* doctrine and system, though they differed over its correct scope. Both supported the stability and long-term survival of the Islamic Republic, but disagreed over the best means to preserve it. Contrary to these two groups, the small group of liberal clerics and religious intellectuals questioned, if not challenged, the doctrinal validity of the dominant system in Iran. Rather, they gave priority to democratic principles in their interpretation of religion. They rejected any

84 Ali Ansari, *Iran under Ahmadinejad: The politics of confrontation* (Abingdon: Routledge, 2017), 16; Anoushiravan Ehteshami and Mahjoob Zweiri, *Iran and the Rise of its Neoconservatives: The Politics of Tehran's Silent Revolution* (London: I.B. Tauris, 2007). On Miṣbāḥ Yazdī, see Farhang Rajaee, *Islamism and Modernism: The Changing Discourse in Iran* (Austin: University of Texas Press, 2007), 172–179; Sussan Siavoshi, "Ayatollah Mesbah Yazdi: Politics, Knowledge, and the Good Life," *The Muslim World*, vol. 100 (January 2010): 124–144.

85 Meir Litvak, "Iran," in *Middle East Contemporary Survey 2000*, Bruce Maddy-Weitzman, ed., (Tel Aviv: Moshe Dayan Center for Middle Eastern and African Studies, 2002), 206–245, Marcotte, "Religion and Freedom," 64.

coercion in the application of religious law as opposed to the very essence of religion. The most notable members of this group were the clerics Muḥsin Kadīvar, Ḥasan Yūsufī Eshkivarī and Muḥammad Mojtahed-Shabestari and the philosopher Abdul Karim Soroush. Significantly, Kadīvar and Eshkivarī had been imprisoned for their views and all four thinkers are in exile. Still they posed an important intellectual challenge to the dominant discourse in Iran.[86]

3 Structure of the Book

Considering the evolution and momentous changes in the nature of othering in modern Shīʿī thought and practice, the present study aims to address this issue thematically, devoting each chapter to the discourse on a specific "other" moving from the external to the internal enemies.

Chapter 1 discusses the evolving ideological attitudes towards the West, which Khamenei defined as the greatest enemy of Islam in the modern period. The chapter analyzes the shift from the fear of the West's cultural offensive to the articulation of a dogma predicting the imminent decline of Western civilization. It examines, inter alia, how the Shīʿī writers contend with modern Western thought on global development, such as Samuel Huntington's *Clash of Civilization* and Francis Fukuyama's *End of History* theories in order to articulate an idyllic Shīʿī end of history. Overall, this discourse is examined in light of broader sociocultural developments, particularly concern over the growing

86 On Kadīvar see, Yasuyuki Matsunaga, "Mohsen Kadivar, an Advocate of Postrevivalist Islam in Iran," *British Journal of Middle Eastern Studies* 34, no. 3 (2007): 317–329; Farzin Vahdat, "Post-revolutionary discourses of Muḥammad Mojtahed Shabestari and Mohsen Kadivar: Reconciling the terms of mediated subjectivity," *Critique: Critical Middle Eastern Studies*, 16 (Spring 2000): 31–54. On Eshkivarī, see Ziba Mir-Hosseini and Richard Tapper. *Islam and democracy in Iran: Eshkevari and the quest for reform* (London: I.B. Tauris, 2006). On Mojtahed-Shabestari, see Farzin Vahdat, "Post-revolutionary Islamic modernity in Iran: the intersubjective hermeneutics of Mohamad Mojtahed Shabestari." *Modern Muslim Intellectuals and the Qur'an* (2004): 193–224; On Soroush, see Valla Vakili, "Debating Religion and Politics in Iran: The Political Thought of Abdolkarim Soroush," Council on Foreign Relations, January 1996 – http://www.drsoroush.com/PDF/E-CMO-19960100-Debating_Religion_and_Politics_in_Iran-Valla_Vakili.pdf. See also, Mahmoud Sadri, "Sacral Defense of Secularism: The Political Theologies of Soroush, Shabestari, and Kadivar," *International Journal of Politics, Culture and Society* 15, no. 2 (Winter 2001): 257–270; Tauseef Ahmad Parray, "Iranian Intellectuals on 'Islam and Democracy' Compatibility: Views of Abdulkarim Soroush and Hasan Yousuf Eshkevari." *Journal of Middle Eastern and Islamic Studies (in Asia)* 7, no. 3 (2013): 43–64.

appeal of Western culture among Iranian youth together with the confidence, typical of many religious groups that the future belongs to them.

Chapter 2 analyzes the shift from traditional attitudes and polemics against the Jews to a modern, politicized anti-Semitic discourse. In particular, it discusses the emergence of a new discourse, which presents the Jews as enemies of Shīʿīsm from its inception to the present. Accordingly, Jewish manipulations are responsible for the distortion of Islam following the Prophet's death, and have caused many of the tragedies that have befallen the Shīʿīs throughout their history. In addition, the Jews and Zionists are presented as standing behind all the hostile "other"s analyzed in the book.

Chapter 3 examines the Shīʿī attempts to defuse the sectarian rift with the Sunnī majority in two ways: The first is through the emphasis on the common Islamic cause against the West and Zionism; the second is through the banning of popular Shīʿī practices, such as cursing the first three Caliphs, that alienated Sunnīs, and the ensuing internal debate over this policy. The chapter also examines the gap between the official discourse and popular practices that were slow to change despite indoctrination from above.

Conversely, Chapter 4 investigates the Shīʿī discourse against Wahhābism and jihādī-Salafī trends, the two fiercest ideological enemies of Shīʿīsm in the Sunnī camp. It traces the evolution from a defensive discourse vis-à-vis Wahhābism, characterized by apologetics designed to prove that Shīʿīs were legitimate Muslims, to a broad denunciation of Wahhābism and jihādī-Salafī ideologies as crude, duplicitous, and intellectually inferior distortions of Islam. It also highlights the Shīʿī attempt to forge a common cause with mainstream Sunnī Islam against them by accusing them of being close to the West and to Zionism, and by branding the jihādī-Salafists as non-Muslims.

Chapter 5 shifts the discussion to the internal "others" as it discusses the Shīʿī debate on the meaning and scope of the concept of liberty within the Islamic system. It analyzes the dominant perception of liberty as voluntary submission to God and liberation from one's whims and desires, and the way this discussion addresses and opposes Western liberal notions of "negative" and "positive" liberty. The chapter then examines the implications of this debate on the accepted scope and boundaries of liberty allowed within an Islamist system and its application to so-called apostates who challenge these boundaries.

Chapter 6, addresses the polemics and actions against the Bahāʾī minority in Iran. It traces the presentation of Bahāʾīsm as an illegitimate deviationist sect that lacks any sound religious principles, and the rhetorical devices used to deconstruct Bahāʾī doctrines and modes of action. It also shows how the linkage that is made between the Bahāʾīs and external hostile "others," such as Western political and cultural imperialism, fuses religious and nationalist motifs, which depict the clergy as the champions of Iranian nationalism. While this discourse serves to exclude and oppress the Bahāʾīs, it also reflects Muslim fear of them as agents of modernity.

Chapter 7 analyzes the hostile representation of feminism as a Western-inspired threat to the three pillars of Islam: the centrality and stature of the Sharīʿa; the family, which is regarded as the bastion of proper religious life; and the monopoly of male clerics over the interpretation of religion. Special attention is given to the critique of Islamic feminism, which was portrayed as a sophisticated yet devious challenge to a clerical-led system. The book's conclusion points to the common and different motifs and features in the polemics against the different "others," as well as their reflection on modern Shīʿī self-perceptions.

Any study on public discourse raises the questions whether the material collected is sufficiently representative and did not overlook important positions and trends, considering the wealth of printed and electronic publications in Iran. This abundance enables those who are interested to focus on key sources and expand from them by ever widening circles through references, approvals or disputes. The writings of the leaders are an obvious starting point as they set the contours for the various debates. All of Khomeini's writings have been published in print and electronically. His sermons and statements have come out in official compilations.[87] Supreme Leader Khamenei's personal websites contain all his speeches as well as his rulings and books. Similarly, numerous clerics from all ranks have their personal websites, which contain their articles, sermons and interviews as well as many of their books. There are also smaller compilations containing the Leader's statements on specific topics.

Official Q&A websites such as Porseman and Rasekhoon as well as government research centers such as Mouood Cultural Institute and Ḥażrat-i Valī-i ʿAṣr Institute provide the authoritative clerical and governmental position on a broad array of political and theological questions. Numerous scholarly journals focusing on historical, theological, doctrinal, legal and philosophical issues provide the views and analysis of academics affiliated with Iranian universities and scholarly bodies.

Since the Shīʿī clerical establishment has never been monolithic, different opinions and views have always aroused lively debates and disputes, which refer the readers to an ever-expanding pool of sources. Thus, the writings of

87 Most important is *Ṣaḥīfa-i nūr: majmūʿa-i rāhnimūdhā-i imām-i Khomeini* (Tehrān: Vizārat-i Irshād-i Islāmī, 1995).

reformist or dissident clerics provide an important source, not only of their own ideas, but also for their more conservative rivals whose views they dispute.

The present study does not presume to have covered every single statement said or written on the topics discussed. Still, I am convinced that the picture presented here is comprehensive and reflects faithfully the breadth of the Shīʿī discourse, considering the tendency of Shīʿī writers to address each other's writings and recirculate crucial themes and arguments through numerous venues, thereby minimizing the possibility of missing them. Overall, while offering insights to Shīʿī perceptions of "others," the present study also sheds new light on Shīʿī self-perceptions and thus contributes to a better understanding of modern Shīʿism.

CHAPTER 1

From Westoxication to the Decline of the West

One of the principle elements of the evolving Islamic ideology that preceded the 1979 Iranian Revolution was the dichotomy, in Hamid Dabashi's words, between "an injured self and a hostile Other. The injured self, as it was collectively created, is the most compelling force in the contemporary Iranian psyche; the hostile Other is the visceral denial of 'The West.'" "More than anything else," Dabashi added, "it is this collective discontent against an imaginative construction called 'The West' that deeply animated the revolutionary movement."[1]

The encounter with the "West" in strategic, economic, and cultural spheres played a crucial role in modern Iranian history and generated processes of change in all fields of life. Therefore, this often painful encounter with the West and the changing attitudes toward it can also shed light on the changing self-perception of the Iranian elites, particularly since the 1979 Revolution. Animosity toward the West, primarily the United States, has dominated Iran's intellectual and ideological discourse since the early 1960s. The anti-West discourse emerged as the outcome of a growing sense of threat to Iranian culture and national identity from the overbearing Western cultural and economic domination, disillusionment with Western and universal philosophies of liberation, and resentment of Western support for Muḥammad Reża Shāh's oppressive regime (1941–1979), which flew in the face of their lofty ideas of freedom and progress. It rearticulated the dilemma of Iranian intellectuals in terms of an essential choice between cultural authenticity – "a return to the self" – and subservience to the West.[2]

The idea of the West in the Islamist Iranian perspective shows considerable continuity from the idea of "cultural alienation" raised by history professor Fakhr al-Dīn Shādmān's in the 1950s until the current official discourse of the Islamic Republic. The "West" is not used as a geographic term, since it includes countries like Japan, Israel, and, occasionally, Russia, Rather, it has been used historically as an economic and political notion to represent the world's

1 Hamid Dabashi, *Theology of Discontent: The Ideological Foundations of the Islamic Revolution in Iran* (New York: New York University Press, 1993), 5.

2 Mehrzad Boroujerdi, "The Ambivalent Modernity of Iranian Intellectuals," in *Intellectual Trends in Twentieth-Century Iran: a critical survey*, ed. Negin Nabavi (Gainesville: University of Florida Press, 2003), 11–23; Ali Mirsepassi, *Intellectual Discourse and the Politics of Modernization Negotiating Modernity in Iran* (Cambridge: Cambridge University Press, 2004), 76–79.

 | DOI:10.1163/9789004444683_003

wealthier and more technologically advanced nations and, most importantly, as a cultural and ideological concept, associated for most of these Iranian thinkers with modernity.[3] In a book published by Iran's Islamic Revolution Guards Corps, Muḥammad Bāqir Ẕū al-Qadr traces the cosmic essence that separates the "East" and "West" back to the writings of the great mystic Shihāb al-Dīn Yaḥyā Suhrawardī (d. 1191). Accordingly, the "East" represents the source and principle of light, life, and purity and the place where the angels are found; the "West," on the other hand, is "the symbol of darkness ... the valley of decline and fall and the site of evil and malice."[4]

In modern discourse, the West is identified with a series of attributes, most importantly, humanism, namely, "the human condition that sees humanity as independent and free of anything above and beyond it," as well as materialism, rationalism, positivism, empiricism, imperialism, scientism, secularism, individualism, pragmatism, and utilitarianism. None of these elements stand alone but are all part of a comprehensive whole.[5] According to this perception, which reflects a deep sense of affront and humiliation caused by perceived Western arrogance, the essence of the West is disregard and denigration of everything outside it. Iran's Supreme Leader Khamenei emphasized the West's rejection of the ideas and traditions of all previous cultures and civilizations as inferior and backward. Pushing the dichotomy back in time, Reża Dāvarī (b. 1933), who was described as "the philosophical spokesman of the regime,"[6] argued that a major result of this spirit and essence was a loathing of the East, which dates back to ancient Greek animosity toward Iranians.[7]

---

3 Jalāl Āl-i Aḥmad, *Gharbzedegī* (Tehrān, multiple editions), 22–23; Ehsan Bakhshandeh, *Occidentalism in Iran: Representations of the West in the Iranian Media* (London: I.B. Tauris, 2015), 9–11.

4 Muḥammad Bāqir Ẕū al-Qadr, *Qiṣṣa-i ghurbat-i gharbī: goftārī dar mabānī-i farhang va-tamaddun-i gharb* (Tehrān: Dāneshgāh-i farmāndehī va-setād-i dowra-i ʿālī-i jang, 1381/2002), 10–11.

5 Reża Dāvarī Ardakānī, *Dar bārah-i gharb* (Tehrān: Intishārāt-i Hermes, 1393/2014), 31, 111–112; Maḥmūd Zamānī, "Gharb az aghāz tā pāyān," http://rasekhoon.net/article/show/764209; Muḥammad Ḥusayn Jamshīdī, "Tahājum-i farhangī (3): Mabānī-i niẓām-i farhangī-i gharb," *Muṭālaʿāt-i rāhbordī-i Basīj*, 7–8 (1374/1995), 21–48; Muḥammad Ḥusayn Jamshīdī, "Tahājum-i farhangī (4)," *Muṭālaʿāt-i rāhbordī-i basīj* 9–10 (1996), 56–79; Ẕū al-Qadr, *Qiṣṣa-i ghurbat-i gharbī*, 81–117; Farhad Khosrokhavar, "Neo-Conservative Intellectuals in Iran," *Middle East Critique* 10, no. 19 (2001): 5–30.

6 For Dāvarī's intellectual stature and role in the Islamic Republic, see Mehran Kamrava, *Iran's Intellectual Revolution* (Cambridge: Cambridge University Press, 2008), 66–67; Farhang Rajaee, *Islamism and Modernism*, 186.

7 Bashgāh-i khabar-negārān-i javān, "Tamaddun-i gharb dar sar'āshībī-i suqūṭ," 27 Dey 1391/ January 16, 2013, https://www.yjc.ir/fa/news/4234980/تمدن-غرب-درسراشیبی-سقوط; Maqām-i muʿaẓẓam-i rahbarī, "Zavāl va-ufūl-i tamaddun-i gharb dar kalām-i rahbarī,"

Anti-West ideology is not unique to Iran but was a local manifestation of the broader phenomenon of Occidentalism. Occidentalism stems from the problematic binary of the Occident and a wide range of "Eastern" cultures – be they nineteenth-century Russia, pre-World War II Japan, or the Muslim world. The Occidentalist view of the West, particularly the United States, is of a cold, mechanical civilization lacking spirit or soul. The West is guided by the calculated utilitarianism and rationalism of applying means to aims, in other words, the accounting of money, interests, and scientific evidence, but the aims are seen as misplaced and morally wrong. The West is essentially a bourgeois society, addicted to comforts, animal-like lust, self-interest, and security. It is, by definition, a society of cowards, who prize life over death. By contrast, the Occidentalists see their own culture as guided by faith, spirituality, and morality as well as healthy collectivism, which puts the common good of the community above the selfish interests of the individual.[8] In addition, Occidentalists often view the Jews as the evil force behind the West or epitomizing the West.[9] Hence, Islamist movements, both Sunnī and Shīʿī, speak of a Western (or Crusader) Jewish alliance and offensive against Islam.

As part of this debate, Shīʿī polemicists resort to the sharp, almost essentialist Islam-West dichotomy, often associated with the much-maligned Orientalist discourse.[10] An indication of the importance of Occidentalism is the development of a special subject of Occidentology (*gharbshināsī*) within

May 1, 2013, http://mkhb.r98.ir/post/114; Dāvarī Ardakānī, *Dar bārah-i gharb*, 31, 120; ʿAlī Aṣghar Kowthari, "Zavāl-i tamaddun-i gharb," May 2, 2013, http://kosari113.mihanblog .com/post/543.

8 Ian Buruma and Avishai Margalit, *Occidentalism: The West in the Eyes of Its Enemies* (New York: Penguin, 2005); James G. Carrier, ed., *Occidentalism: Images of the West* (Oxford: Clarendon Press, 1995); Bakhshandeh, *Occidentalism in Iran*, 11–15.

9 For example, Shahriyār Zarshinās, a conservative intellectual close to the Islamic Revolution Guard Corps (IRGC), attributed the growth and idea of capitalism to Jewish spirit and thinking, cited in "Gozāreshī az kitāb-i mabānī-i naẓarī-i gharb-i modern," 5 Abān 1388/October 27, 2009, https://hawzah.net/fa/Article/View/82468/; Seyyed Muḥammad Bāqir Roknī, *Akhlāq-i Yahūdī va-tamaddun-i gharb* (Tehrān: Nashr, 2010) and favorable reviews of this book, http://www.tebyan.net/newindex .aspx?pid=934&articleID=743460, http://teeh.ir/fa/news-details/1945, and http://teeh .ir/fa/news-details/1945/. See also, "Qawm-i Yahūd va-taskhīr-i jahān," November 2, 2016, http://www.rasanews.ir/print/458897, which highlights the "role of the Jewish people and Torah theories" in the "formation of the 500-year history of Western civilization."

10 For such an analysis, see Sadik Jalal al-Azm, "Orientalism, Occidentalism, and Islamism: Keynote Address to 'Orientalism and Fundamentalism in Islamic and Judaic Critique: A Conference Honoring Sadik Al-Azm,'" *Comparative Studies of South Asia, Africa and the Middle East* 30, no. 1 (2010): 6–13.

the indoctrination program of the Basīj militia that serves as a central instrument of governmental control in the Islamic Republic.[11]

Meherzad Boroujerdi analyzed the Iranian turn against the West as a form of nativism, namely, an intellectual doctrine "that calls for the resurgence, reinstatement or continuance of native or indigenous cultural customs, beliefs, and values" – the doctrine, in the Iranian case, that affirms one's Perso-Islamic heritage.[12] As Ali Mirsepassi has shown, this nativist movement has its roots in the strong Western tradition of the Counter-enlightenment, from Joseph de Maistre (d. 1821) and Johann Gottfried Herder (d. 1803) through to Friedrich Nietzsche (d. 1900), Martin Heidegger (d. 1976), and Carl Schmitt (d. 1985).[13] These figures continue to serve as sources of authority for the post-revolutionary discourse as well.

Mehdi Parvizi Amineh and Shmuel N. Eisenstadt set the Iranian case in the broader context of modern fundamentalist movements that promulgate a totalistic ideological denial of the premises of the Enlightenment, especially the emphasis on the autonomy and sovereignty of reason and the individual. They often ground their rejection of the Enlightenment in the universalistic principles of their respective religions as newly interpreted by them. These movements build on the earlier "nativistic" movements but reinterpret them in radical, political, modern, communal, and national ways.[14]

Animosity to US policy and Western culture became an official policy of the Islamic Republic, manifested in the labeling of the United States as the "Great Satan" and the number one enemy of the Muslim world as well as in the slogan "Death to America" chanted in public rallies. This animosity has remained a prominent feature in the ideology and discourse of the Islamic Republic to the present day. Yet, the growing self-confidence of the Iranian elites in recent

---

11 The program includes topics such as "the critique of modernity, crisis of modernity (ethical, identity, environmental, economic and philosophical)" and "the Islamic Revolution and the West," Saeid Golkar, *Captive Society: The Basij Militia and Social Control in Iran* (Washington DC: Woodrow Wilson Center Press, 2015), 64–65. See also the publication of a scholarly journal called *Gharb shināsī bonyādī,* dedicated to the philosophical study of the West, by the Institute for Humanities and Cultural Studies in Tehrān. For the journal website, see http://occidentstudy.ihcs.ac.ir/.

12 Mehrzad Boroujerdi, *Iranian Intellectuals and the West: The Tormented Triumph of Nativism* (Syracuse: Syracuse University Press, 1996), 14.

13 Ali Mirsepassi, "Religious Intellectuals and Western Critiques of Secular Modernity," *Comparative Studies of South Asia, Africa and the Middle East* 26, no. 3 (2006): 416–433.

14 Mahdī Parvizi Amineh and Shmuel N. Eisenstadt, "The Iranian Revolution: The Multiple Contexts of the Iranian Revolution," *Perspectives on Global Development and Technology* 6, no. 1 (2007): 129–157.

years, as Iran has overcome a series of internal crises and external challenges, produced two other approaches to the West.

The first, which was espoused by the former president, Muḥammad Khātamī (1997–2005), found some positive elements in Western culture, e.g., the fusion between religiosity and democracy among the eighteenth-century Puritans in America. This approach saw no harm in a certain degree of opening to the West, as it no longer feared that Western culture would undermine Iran's Islamic identity and advocated a "dialogue of civilizations."[15]

The second approach, advocated by the dominant conservative camp headed by Khamenei, which is the subject of this chapter, contains two seemingly contradictory arguments. The first emphasizes the continuous threat posed by the West to the Islamic Republic not only by economic pressures but, more disturbingly, by waging a "cultural onslaught" (*tahājum-i farhangī*) against Islam and the Islamic government. The second argument emphasizes the short-term Western threat but views the West as a decadent civilization that is destined to collapse. It also expresses great confidence in the Muslim world and Iran as the rising force in the global arena.[16] The purpose of this chapter is to analyze the major characteristics of this dual discourse on the Western cultural offensive and the inevitable decline of the West.

1 The Western Threat

The turn of Iranian intellectuals against the West is usually traced to the early 1950s, particularly following the US-organized coup against Prime Minister Muḥammad Mosaddeq in August 1953. Earlier generations of thinkers had viewed the West as a source of inspiration and model for emulation which could help salvage Iran from its weakness and backwardness. Henceforth, intellectuals began to see the West as the source of Iran's problems and Westernization as a threat.

Shādmān was among the first to describe Iranian society as suffering from cultural alienation. He warned against the pseudo-modernists, the *fokolī*, who believed that mere imitation of Europeans would guarantee progress and lead

15 For detailed analyses of Khātamī's ideas, see David Menashri, *Post-Revolutionary Politics in Iran: Religion, Society, and Power* (Portland: F. Cass, 2001), 205–220; Farid Mirbagheri, "Narrowing the Gap or Camouflaging the Divide: An Analysis of Muḥammad Khatami's 'Dialogue of Civilizations'", *British Journal of Middle Eastern Studies* 34, no. 3 (December 2007): 305–316.

16 "Furūpāshī-i Amrīkā nazdīk ast," 22 Dey 1392/January 12, 2014, http://www.farsnews.com/newstext.php?nn=13921022001517#sthash.TGqv9nLj.dpu.

to a modern civilization. Depicting Western civilization as a foe, he warned that its victory in Iran would "be our last defeat, for there will be no more Iranian nation left to endure [another] loss from another enemy."[17] Jalāl Āl-i Aḥmad (d. 1969) drew on this alienation in his influential book *Gharbzedegī* (Westoxication), in which he decried the submission to and superficial imitation of Western ways. He claimed that both led to the loss of Iran's authentic identity and its political and economic subjugation to the United States. In the face of this onslaught he described Islam as the major force that could help Iran to preserve its identity and independence.[18] ʿAlī Sharīʿatī (d. 1977), moving from Āl-i Aḥmad's diagnosis to a revolutionary response, presented the struggle of the world's downtrodden (*mustażʿafān*), led by Shīʿī Islam against the West with US imperialism at its helm, as the modern phase in the millennia-long struggle between monotheism and polytheism.[19]

Among the Shīʿī clergy, Khomeini, the founder of the Islamic Republic, incorporated many of the elements of the anti-Western, anti-enlightenment discourse as a central component in his religious and political doctrine. According to his discourse, the West could be summed up as one concept, designating cultural intrusion, political repression, and enslavement alongside economic exploitation, imperialism, neocolonialism, and American arrogance. In 1963, when he emerged as a national figure opposing the Shāh's policies, Khomeini declared that "the world must know that all difficulties that Iran and the Muslim people have are the work of Westerners and the Americans." Adding nationalist grievances to his religious argument, Khomeini accused the US-led West of enslaving Iran and exploiting its resources by using the Pahlavī monarchs as their local proxies.[20]

His disciple and associate, Ayatollah Murtażā Muṭṭaharī (d. 1979), who would emerge as the leading intellectual cleric, viewed the West in essentialist terms. He acknowledged the West's scientific and technological achievements – even its promotion of justice – and saw no harm in borrowing and adopting these aspects of Western culture. But, like all other Islamic thinkers, he derided the separation between belief and knowledge and, even worse, the West's materialism and war against religion, and rejected Western political and cultural imperialism. He therefore regarded the attraction of various Iranian intellectuals

17 Cited in Ali Gheissari, *Iranian Intellectuals in the 20th Century* (Austin: University of Texas Press, 1998), 86.

18 Dabashi, *Theology of Discontent*, 80–82.

19 Ibid., 129–132.

20 Mehran Kamrava, "Khomeini and the West," in *A Critical Introduction to Khomeini*, ed. Arshin Adib-Moghaddam (Cambridge: Cambridge University Press, 2014), 149–169; Rūḥollah Khomeini, *al-Ḥukūma al-Islāmiyya* (Beirut: Dār al-Ṭalīʿa, 1979), 7.

toward the West as a disease. As, in his opinion, Islam was fundamentally and inherently opposed to oppression and imperialism, confrontation with the West, at least on the cultural and ideological level, was inevitable.[21]

2 The "Great Satan"

Following the 1979 Revolution, animosity towards the West, represented primarily by the United States, became a major pillar of the Islamic Republic's official ideology. The choice to label it the "Great Satan" referred to the multiple threats posed by America's Western culture. Just like the Qur'ānic Satan, *al-Waswas* (the Whisperer), who whispers in the soul of believers to lure them away from God and religion, so does Western culture appeal to the basest human traits such as greed and sexual promiscuity, hence its great appeal among misguided Muslims. Just as the Qur'ānic Satan seeks to distance believers from God, so, according to Khomeini, do the modern satanic forces, which comprise of the West and the Jews, conspire against the Muslims in order to "extirpate Islam" and sow doubt and confusion in the hearts of Muslims. By working together with local Westernized intellectuals to plant the false idea that Islam, like Christianity, was concerned with only rituals and faith, these forces sought to undermine, in particular, Islam's most important feature: the comprehensive system of law that governs society and state. Their reason for targeting Islam was the realization that "Islam and its ordinances" was the "main obstacle in the path of their materialistic ambitions." In addition, the West resists the righteous cause of Islam to expand to the "four corners of the globe."[22]

As Abbas Amanat showed, the emphasis on the polluting effects of Satanic temptations associated with Western culture, such as music, paintings, movies, and unveiled women, on the believer's body and soul resonated well with the

---

21 Dabashi, *Theology of Discontent*, 174; Murtażā Muṭṭaharī, *Yāddāshthsar'āshībīā-i ustād-i Muṭṭaharī* (Tehrān: Intishārāt-i Ṣadrā, 1377/1998), vol. 2, 251; Seyyed 'Abbās Rażavī, "Shahīd-i Muṭṭaharī va-ru'ya-i digār tamaddun-i gharb," *Ḥawza* 105–106 (1380/2000): 342–383; 'Alī Aṣghar Ṭālib-nezhād, Seyyed Muḥammad 'Alī Taqavī, and Mohammd Javād Ranjkesh, "Vakāvī-i dīdār-i ayatollah Muṭṭaharī dar mowred-i tamaddun-i modern-i gharb va-chegūnegī ta'ammol bā ān," *Pazhūheshī naẓariyyahā-i ijtimā'ī mutafakkirān-i musalmān* 8, no. 2 (1397/2018): 115–116, 122–123.

22 Khumaynī, *al-Ḥukūma al-Islāmiyya*, 7; Rūḥollah Khomeini, *Islam and Revolution: Writings and Declarations of Imam Khomeini*, trans. Hamid Algar (Berkeley: Mizan Press, 1981), 27, 47, 109, 127; Dabashi, *Theology of Discontent*, 426.

centrality of ritual purity in Shīʿī doctrines and popular beliefs.[23] The depiction of the United States as the Great Satan was intended among other things to ensure a complete conflict between Iran and the West from not just an historical but also an eschatological point of view.[24]

Khomeini warned his followers in the late 1980s that although it had been "cut off" from Iran's resources thanks to the Revolution, the United States never ceased plotting against Iran; just as the believer had to constantly fight worldly temptations, standing up to the cultural onslaught of the West and the Soviet Union is extremely difficult and "may even result in hunger and martyrdom."[25] Khomeini kept up his animosity toward the West until his death. His political will and testament (*vaṣiyatnāmah*) contains at least twenty-one charges against the dangers of the "oppressive, pagan West" to Islam. He described the United States as "the foremost enemy of Islam ... a terrorist state by nature that has set fire to everything everywhere." Echoing Āl-i Aḥmad and Franz Fanon (d. 1961), Khomeini expressed his wrath at the harm caused to Iran by the Westernized intellectuals who "have become estranged with their own cultures and they have come to regard the peoples of the super-powers as being of races and cultures superior to their own."

However, in this document written six years before his death, a certain change is already apparent in Khomeini's attitude. He no longer described Iran as a hapless victim of Western conspiracies but as a state that, thanks to Islam, was able to stand on its own, and he noted with satisfaction that since the Revolution, the United States has been "dumbfounded and disgraced in its dealings with the dauntless Iranian nation."[26]

The 1990 collapse of Communism, seen as an essentially Western ideology by both Shīʿīs and Sunnīs, hardened the belief of Iranian conservatives that the United States and its allies would be next. The underlying tone of many editorials in conservative media outlets at that time was the inevitability of the fall of the United States and, with it, Western civilization and the subsequent resurgence of Islamic civilization and its golden era.[27]

---

23 Abbas Amanat, *Apocalyptic Islam and Iranian Shiʿism* (London: I.B. Tauris, 2009), 199–200, 205.

24 William O. Beeman, "Images of the Great Satan: Representations of the United States in the Iranian Revolution," in *Religion and Politics in Iran: Shiʿism from Quietism to Revolution*, ed., Nikki Keddie (New Haven: Yale University Press, 1983), 191–217.

25 Rūḥollah Khomeini, *Ṣaḥīfa-i nūr: majmūʿa-i rāhnimūdhā-i imām-i Khomeini* (Tehrān: Vizārat-i Irshād-i Islāmī, 1995), vol. 21, 27.

26 *The Political Will of Imam Khomeini*, http://www.alseraj.net/maktaba/kotob/english/Miscellaneousbooks/LastwillofImamKhomeini/occasion/ertehal/english/will/.

27 Muḥammad A. Tabaar, "The Beloved Great Satan: The Portrayal of the U.S. in the Iranian Media Since 9/11," *Crossroads* 6, no. 1(2006): 23.

3 Khamenei and the Cultural Onslaught

Animosity toward the West has remained a major tenet of Iran's cultural and ideological discourse under Khamenei. His speeches and statements are replete with warnings about the "plots" and threats against Iran by the "enemy," first and foremost, the West led by the United States. Iranian school textbooks, which serve to convey the official worldview to the next generation, describe the West as "an oppressive, criminal force that has attempted to conquer the Muslim world, exploit its natural wealth, oppress its people, and crush its spirit."[28] Following this line, Ẕū al-Qadr maintained that the West seeks to eliminate all other cultures and civilizations and absorb them into its own "digestive" system. The West seeks to overpower the entire world, particularly the Islamic East and the Islamic awakening, and, even more specifically, to eliminate the Islamic Republic of Iran. Western enmity to the Islamic Republic is fundamental and unbreakable, he concluded.[29]

Khamenei's greatest concern, however, has not been a military invasion of Iran. Rather, he and the conservatives within the Iranian establishment have warned against the Western-led cultural onslaught designed to spread "Western vice" and cultural influence that will undermine Islamic morality and the foundations of Iranian society and change the cultural and Islamic identity of Iranian society in order to bring about the demise of the Islamic system in Iran. Of particular concern in this regard was the waning religious and revolutionary fervor among the masses, especially, the young.[30] According to Rajaee, Khamenei may have been inspired to adopt the theme of the Western cultural onslaught by a public letter written by thirty-five conservative professors in June 1991 in which they coined the term. The letter claimed that the undermining of tradition, the family, and social mores caused by the spread of notions

---

28 Mehran Golnar, "Socialization of Schoolchildren in the Islamic Republic of Iran," *Iranian Studies* 22, No. 1 (1989): 43.

29 Ẕū al-Qadr, *Qiṣṣa-i ghurbat-i gharbī*, 3, 10–11, 15.

30 Khamenei's pronouncements on the subject were collected and published by the Ministry of Culture and Islamic Guidance in 1996 under the title, *Culture and the Cultural Invasion* (*Farhang va-tahājum-i farhangī*). A subsequent and shorter collection of such statements is available at http://toorenamaree.blogfa.com/post/8. Compilations of his subsequent statements on this issue were published on various semi-official websites, e.g. *Bayānāt-i Imām-i Khamenei dar bārah-i tahājum-i farhangī*, http://toorenamaree.blogfa.com/post/8; *Manshūr-i sokhnān-i maqām-i muʿaẓẓam-i rahbarī dar mowred-i tahājum-i farhangī*, May 25, 2012, http://bidaricyberi.blogfa.com/post-54.aspx.

such as "one-world culture," "the global village," and "the new world order," constituted a Western cultural invasion of Iran.[31]

4 The Cultural Onslaught: Past and Present

Khamenei linked the present-day cultural onslaught to the beginning of British imperialist encroachment on Iran in the early nineteenth century. With the old imperialist method no longer effective, the colonial powers have, he claimed, found new ways to dominate other countries, namely, by superimposing their culture, a new method he called "postmodern colonialism."[32] "We are subject to the cultural assault," which, he stated, is part of "a hundred-year history of assault against Islam" and is based on the premise that Western culture is superior and "should become the dominant culture, accepted by everyone." Culture is the means, but he sees the aim of the assault as Western domination and control of the entire world. On some occasions he was more specific and charged that the final aim of the cultural onslaught is to bring the world under the control of international Zionism.[33]

Khamenei distinguished between a necessary "cultural exchange" – a peaceful borrowing of the fruits of knowledge and science from others from a position of strength – and the evil "cultural onslaught." As examples of the former, he gave the peaceful adoption of Islamic culture by the peoples of South-East Asia several centuries ago and the spread of the Persian language, which

31 *Kayhān*, June 27, 1991 cited in Rajaee, *Islamism and Modernism*, 167. The term itself dates to at least the mid-1970s when the Pahlavī establishment raised the specter of the "onslaught of cultures" (*hujūm-i farhanghā*) from the outside in an attempt to reach out and coopt moderate intellectuals. See Negin Nabavi, "The Discourse of 'Authentic Culture' in Iran in the 1960s and 1970s," in *Intellectual Trends in Twentieth-Century Iran*, 96. For the Islamic Republic, the Pahlavī system was the prime example of such an onslaught.

32 "Bayānāt dar dīdār-i mas'ūlān-i niẓām," July 21, 2013, http://farsi.khamenei.ir/speech-content?id=23175; Khamenei's speech to residents of Qom, January 8, 2005, cited in Karim Sadjadpour, *Reading Khamenei: The World View of Iran's Most Powerful Leader* (Carnegie Endowment for International Peace, 2008), 18.

33 "Farhang va-tahājum-i farhangī dar āyīnah-i rahbar-i inqilāb," March 29, 2012, http://www.farsnews.com/newstext.php?nn=13910120000657; "Didār-i a'żā'-i shūrā-i 'āli-i inqilāb-i farhangī bā rahbar-i inqilāb," June 13, 2011, http://farsi.khamenei.ir/news-content?id=12693; "Al-Imām al-Khamenei: Amrīkā wal-ṣahāyīna yu'ādūna Irān li-anna al-Islām huna akthar burūzan," April 25, 2017, https://www.tasnimnews.com/ar/news/2017/04/25/1389363/الإمام-الخامنئی-امریکا-والصهاينة-يعادون-ايران-لأن-الإسلام-هنا-أكثر-بروزاً. Khamenei also ordered the Basīj to be fully involved in this new war by forming new units to enforce Islamic norms in society (Golkar, *Captive Society*, 77).

became the language of high culture and government in India. By contrast, the British eliminated every native language that rivaled theirs as part of their subjugating process. The modern Western cultural onslaught, he added elsewhere, is nothing but war by other means, waged by the West in order to uproot Iran's national culture and forcibly impose new beliefs through missionaries and Westernized intellectuals in order to dominate Iran politically. On various occasions, he has equated the Western cultural onslaught with "a cultural act of plunder, a cultural massacre." With Iran's arid condition on his mind, he likened the need to defend Iran from the cultural onslaught to the need of a person who possesses a source of pure water to protect it from a nearby source of poisonous water.[34]

Iranian school textbooks reiterate the message that "the enemies of this people" have launched "a soft war" and a cultural offensive in an attempt to assault Iranian culture and "create havoc."[35] Others have elaborated on the evils of the cultural onslaught, which consists of the intentional and systematic imposition of the assaulting culture, destruction or total obliteration of the targeted culture, and its capitulation to the aggressive assaulting party. They contend that the cultural onslaught targets the younger generations, thereby leading to the spread of corruption, anti-Islamic ideas, and loss of identity.[36] Some of these writers have likened it to the "gradual death of the nation" and described it as the greatest problem of the Muslim world.[37] The cultural onslaught discourse has been exacerbated by the growing fear and resentment of the increasingly popular notion of globalization, which Iranians, like Islamists elsewhere, have associated with Americanization.[38]

---

34 "Bayānāt dar dīdār-i javānān-I astān-i Khorāsān-i shimālī," October 14, 2012, http://farsi.khamenei.ir/speech-content?id=21252; "Khaṭar al-ghazw al-thaqāfī," https://library.tebyan.net/fa/Viewer/Text/141579/0; "Pīsh raft yā pas raft? Naqd-i algū-i gharbī az manẓar-i rahbar-i muʿaẓẓam-i inqilāb-i Islāmī," April 14, 2015, http://www.farsnews.com/newstext.php?nn=13930802000542; Menashri, *Post-Revolutionary Politics*, 188.

35 The textbook *Defense Readiness* cited in Eldad J. Pardo, *Imperial Dreams: The Paradox of Iranian Education* (The Institute for Monitoring Peace and Tolerance in School Education [IMPACT-SE], May 2015), 11–12.

36 Ismāʿīl Valīzādeh, "Tahājum-i farhangī va-rāhhā-i muqābala bā ān," *Maʿārif* 69 (1388/2009), https://hawzah.net/fa/Magazine/View/5211/7149/87155; Ḥamīd Javādānī Shāhdīn, "Darāmadī bar shenākht-i abʿād-i tahājum-i farhangī va-naḥwa-i muqābala bā ān," *Rūsh shināsī-i ʿulūm-i insānī* 35 (1382/2003): 85–104.

37 "Tahājum-i farhangī, marg-i tadrījī-i yek millat," http://sbmu.ac.ir/?siteid=426&pageid=22839; *Hamshahrī*, September 29, 2004; *Javān*, March 10, 2005; *Qods*, June 9, 2005.

38 For the Arab Islamist perception of globalization, see Esther Webman, "Arab Perceptions of Globalization," in *Middle Eastern Societies and the West: Accommodation or Clash of Civilization*, ed. Meir Litvak (Tel Aviv: Dayan Center, 2006), 177–198. The number of

Dr. Muḥammad Ḥusayn Jamshīdī of Modarres University presented the cultural onslaught facing Iran as the latest manifestation in a long historical chain going back to Pharaoh's misrepresentation of the Prophet Mūsā as a sorcerer. He suggested that all wars throughout history have been cultural wars that originated in cultural clashes. However, the contemporary offensive differs, in his opinion, from all previous cases in both its scope and content. As it has encompassed every aspect of individual and social life, it aims at the total negation and emasculation of Islamic culture and civilization in order to facilitate Western cultural, political, and economic domination. Moreover, it is far more perilous than military or political attacks, as those who are subjected to the latter are fully aware of them and can call upon the people to rise up in protest. The cultural onslaught, on the other hand, is covert "like termites inside a tree that gradually suck away at its insides." The overall result of this offensive is the dissemination of hopelessness and the disbelief that one's culture is capable of progress. It thus leads to submission and subjugation to foreign cultures alongside self-destruction and collapse in all areas of society.[39]

Khamenei insists that Iran has been the most important target of the Western cultural onslaught because it is "more Islamic" than other countries and because it has confronted the dominant Western system and proved to be on the side of truth.[40] School textbooks explained the targeting of Iran as a result of the success of the 1979 Revolution, which "shook the very foundations of the oppressors' power" and "by making other Muslims aware of the power of Islam, endangered the West's interests in many parts of the world, especially in the Islamic countries." Thus, they claim, "from the beginning, [Iran] became the target of the enmity and conspiracies of the superpowers."[41] Others have attributed the West's targeting of Iran to its unique Shīʿī identity, which, they claim, provides answers to all aspects of life at all times and

---

books and articles published in Iran on globalization and its cultural impact exceeds the hundreds.

39 Muḥammad Ḥusayn Jamshīdī, "Tahājum-i farhangī: Tahājum-i farhangī chīst?," *Muṭālaʿāt-i rāhbordī-i basīj* 3–4 (1373/1994): 75–112. See a similar description of the threat in Murtażā Ashrāfī, "Tahājum-i farhangī (nātū-i farhangī)," 24 Abān 1393/November 15, 2014, http://pajoohe.ir/تهاجم-فرهنگی-ناتوی-فرهنگی_a-44577.aspx.

40 "Niẓām-i jumhūrī-i Islāmī, muhimtarīn-i hadaf-i tahājum-i farhangī-i istikbār ast," *Akhbār-i Shīʿīyān* 68 (1390/ 2011): 1–3; "Bayānāt dar dīdār-i aʾima-i masājid-i astān-i Tehrān," 21 Mordād 1395/August 11, 2016, http://farsi.khamenei.ir/speech-content?id=34109; "Naẓariyat-i bīdārī-i Islāmī va-pāyān-i makātib-i umanīstī," 31 Mordād 1395/August 21, 2016, http://farsi.khamenei.ir/print-content?id=25076 (last accessed July 19, 2015).

41 *Grade 8 History textbook*, 93 and *Grade 11 History textbook*, 155 cited in Saeed Paivandi, *Discrimination and Intolerance in Iran's Textbooks* (Washington, D.C.: Freedom House, 2008), 51.

constitutes the most serious rival to Western ideology due to its reliance on divine foundations.[42] They believe that the best way to confront the Western cultural onslaught is to raise popular awareness of the Western threat to Iran's culture and identity, expand religious activities and adhere to the teachings of Islam as expounded by the Islamic Republic.[43]

The specter of the cultural onslaught has, in some ways, continued the older theme of *gharbzedegi* but with a few important differences. The pre-Revolution anti-Western criticism represented an opposition trend operating within a state that appeared captivated, if not dominated, by Western culture. It was defensive in nature, responding to a widespread sense of the threat of the loss of identity to a powerful, domineering Western culture. It was critical of Iranian society but sought its internal spiritual regeneration and the return to its true self. The cultural onslaught discourse, on the other hand, emerged a decade after the Revolution and the establishment of Islamic rule which should, theoretically, have molded a new Islamic person. After all, it was Khomeini who claimed in 1982 during the war with Iraq that "the people of Iran were the best people throughout history," since their enthusiasm for battle and embrace of martyrdom had no precedent in Islamic history, even during the time of the Prophet and Imām ʿAlī.[44] Following such claims, it was difficult to accuse or criticize Iranian society of being Westoxicated. Still, such a society had to be shielded and protected from Western culture, just as pious believers must always guard themselves from temptation and sin.

In other words, instead of looking inward at the Iranians themselves, advocates of the new discourse have been facing a supposedly easier task of shielding their society from foreign contamination. Yet, in their repeated invocation of the ever-present cultural onslaught, Iran's leaders have not only expressed the fear prevalent among all religious preachers of the continuous threat of temptation and moral corruption over the soul of the believers. Rather, they have also implicitly acknowledged the continued allure of Western ideas for ordinary laypeople and intellectuals years after the Revolution, thereby

42 "Ahdāf-i keshvarhā-i gharbī az tahājum-i farhangī," 16 Dey 1391/January 11, 2013 http://www.siasi.porsemani.ir/node/1738.

43 Valīzādeh, "Tahājum-i farhangī va-rāhhā-i muqābala bā ān"; Shāhdīn, "Darāmadī bar shenākht-i abʿād-i tahājum-i farhangī;" "Leader Urges Vigilance Against U.S. Infiltration," *Kayhān*, September 16, 2015, http://kayhan.ir/en/news/18450/leader-urges-vigilance-against-us-infiltration.

44 Khomeini, *Ṣaḥīfa-i nūr*, 16: 96–100.

conceding a certain failure of their efforts or perhaps even fear over the weakness of their ideology.[45]

Equally important, the constant hammering of the cultural onslaught theme serves the regime politically. Every revolutionary regime needs enemies, both internal and external, in order to preserve the fading ideological fervor among the population years after the Revolution and to justify repressive measures against dissidents. In the Iranian case, the cultural onslaught served to suppress secularists and reformists who challenged the regime's ideology by depicting them as facilitators of the Western cultural onslaught. In many of his speeches, Khamenei has played on the deep-seated and widespread resentment toward foreign meddling in Iranian affairs by insisting that the external enemy uses the cultural onslaught in order to spur and stimulate the internal enemy, meaning reformist or liberal elements who oppose government policies. He has thus branded them not just political rivals of the regime but semi-traitors to the nation.[46]

5 The Inevitable Fall of the West

The 1990s marked a shift in the Shīʿī discourse on the West. It still depicted the United States as Satan waging a cultural onslaught on Iran's Islamic culture. But, the tone became increasingly triumphant, portraying the West as a decadent civilization doomed to decline with Islam gradually and inevitably returning to its rightful leading role in history. This new discourse is profoundly nationalist, reflecting great pride in the Iranian nation and the success of the Revolution in restoring Iran's true independence from the West – an independence which had been lost since the nineteenth century – and paving the way for the restoration of Iran's glory.

The extensive discussion on the imminent decline of the West has been influenced by several factors. First and foremost, the Islamic Republic's success

---

45 For the great interest in Western philosophy and intellectual thought, see Mehrzad Boroujerdi, "Iranian Islam and the Faustian Bargain of Western Modernity," *Journal of Peace Research* 34, no. 1 (February 1997): 1–5. See also the poll conducted in Iran in September 2002 which showed popular support for a rapprochement with the United States in Patrick Clawson, "The Paradox of Anti-Americanism in Iran," *Middle Eastern Review of International Affairs* 8, no. 1 (March 2004): 16–24. The embarrassed authorities sentenced those responsible for conducting the poll to jail for eight and nine years respectively for "publishing nonscientific research."

46 *Manshūr-i sokhnān-i maqām-i muʿaẓẓam-i rahbarī dar mowred-i tahājum-i farhangī*; "Dushman shināsī az manẓar-i maqām-i muʿaẓẓam-i rahbarī," *Maʿārif* 64 (1387/2009), https://hawzah.net/fa/Magazine/View/5211/6900/83079.

in overcoming a series of external and domestic challenges enhanced the self-confidence of the Iranian elite to stand up to the West. The regional changes following the US invasion of Iraq, the US stumble in the Iraqi quagmire, and global developments such as China's economic surge and Europe's demographic problems enhanced Iran's belief in the inevitable decline of the West and Iran's rise to regional leadership. In addition, Iran's leaders probably believed that highlighting the West's structural ills and imminent fall would be an effective way to counter the attraction of various aspects of the Western lifestyle and ideas among significant segments of Iranian society. It was equally important to refute the ideas of a new "fourth generation" of Iranian intellectuals, who had developed a more balanced and even appreciative view of the West than their pre-Revolution predecessors.[47] Finally, Ahmadinezhad's election as president in 2005 marked the rise of the new generation, graduates of the Iran-Iraq War, to political prominence with the determination to rekindle the now faded spirit of the Revolution. Members of this generation had not been traumatized by American intervention in Iranian domestic affairs, which culminated in the toppling of Prime Minister Muḥammad Mosaddeq in August 1953. Instead, they had grown up with the belief that Western machinations had robbed Iran of victory over Iraq.[48]

Yet, while predicting the imminent decline and fall of the West, Shīʿī spokespeople kept warning of the growing threat of the Western cultural onslaught. This paradox is not unique to Iran. In April 1929, Stalin justified the use of harsh repressive measures in implementing the Five-year Plan by the argument, which contradicted classical Marxist theory that the more the Soviet Union advanced toward socialism, the more class warfare would intensify as the opponents of socialism would strengthen their struggle against it.[49] Similarly, Iran's leaders claim that the West's cultural soft war escalates precisely when its weaknesses and internal failings become more visible. Dāvarī, for example, has explained that the present-day Western cultural onslaught is particularly aggressive because it reflects not the power of the West but its weakness. Iranians should not, however, belittle the threat of this onslaught or believe that it can be repulsed by ordinary means. The West is weaker than it was in the nineteenth century but not in comparison to the peoples it wishes to dominate.[50] Put differently, even if the decline of the West is inevitable in

---

47 On the division into waves, see Rajaee, *Islamism and Modernism*, 197–235.

48 Ray Takeyh, "A Profile in Defiance," *The National Interest*, March 17, 2006.

49 Robert Gellately, *Stalin's Curse: Battling for Communism in War and Cold War* (Oxford: Oxford University Press, 2013), 24–25.

50 Reża Dāvarī Ardakānī, "Daʿvat-i dīnī va-tahājum-i farhangī," *Mashriq* 2–3 (1995):17.

the long run, it is still currently capable of corrupting Iran's soul and thus poses a threat. In a way, the cultural onslaught could be described as the swan song of the decaying Western civilization.

It can be argued that these two supposedly contradictory visions complement each other and are typical of the perception of history shared by most modern religious or politically radical movements. Modern Islamic fundamentalist or revivalist movements emerged in response to a sense of deep malaise in their societies, which was caused by Western-like modernity. However, as Uriah Furman noted, true believers are certain that the outcome of the struggle has been predetermined: reality will change and the correct cosmological and universal order will be restored, meaning that the civilization of Islam will triumph, the West will decline, non-Muslims will return to their "natural" status, and the word of God will prevail on earth.[51]

6 The Decline of the West: a Comparative Perspective

The idea of the decline of the West is neither new nor unique to Iran. It was first raised by romanticist writers in late eighteenth-century Europe in reaction to the atrocities committed during the French Revolution, which they associated with the Enlightenment. According to the conservative Iranian revolutionary worldview, the nihilism and decadence of contemporary Europe are the direct result of the triumph of liberalism.[52] The publication of Oswald Spengler's *The Decline of the West* (*Der Untergang des Abendlandes*) in 1918 (and the second volume in 1922) was an important landmark in the discourse of "decline" due to its attempt to devise a comprehensive philosophical cyclical scheme on the rise and decline of cultures. Spengler viewed cultures as living organisms with a life cycle of birth-development-fulfillment-decay-death or, in his words, "spring, summer, autumn, and winter." The high watermark of a society or civilization is its phase of fulfillment, the so-called "culture" phase. After each culture has reached its prime, it inevitably degenerates into what Spengler calls "civilization." The "civilization" phase witnesses drastic social upheavals, mass movements of peoples, ongoing wars, and constant crises. These cycles are part of the structure of the world, and nothing can be done to change or arrest them. Spengler asserted that the West was in its "winter"

51 Uriah Furman, "The Future of Islam, the Future of the West in Fundamentalist Islamic Theology," *HaMizrah Hahadash* 51(2012):132. (Hebrew).

52 Arthur Herman, *The Idea of Decline in Western History* (New York: Simon and Schuster, 1997), 39–40.

phase, manifested inter alia in the exhaustion of mental organization, materialism, the decline of religion, the cult of science and utilitarianism, democracy, and plutocracy. As much as it was an attempt at analysis (and a highly problematic one), Spengler's ideas reflected the mood of his age.[53]

The other Western prophet of decline, Arnold Toynbee (d. 1975), sought a sounder historical and philosophical basis for his magnum opus *A Study of History* (1934–1961), which claimed to portray the rise and decline of twenty-six civilizations throughout history. Toynbee maintained that civilizations come into being by overcoming obstacles, such as geographic or climatic challenges. They exist because they are able to provide the correct response to a challenge. Once established, they grow in proportion to their ability to control their environment; but then, the process of decadence sets in as they offer the same responses to ever changing challenges. Civilizations are constantly beset with new threats from outside, though more often, it is a threat from inside – a revolt by the "internal proletariat" – which breaks up a society. As in Spengler's schema, the dominant minority loses its nerve or, alternatively, becomes decadent, frivolous, and ostentatious.[54]

The idea of the rise and decline of societies and civilizations existed in Islamic political thought thanks, primarily, to the concepts developed by the early Muslim scholar Ibn Khaldūn (d. 1406).[55] Perceptions of decline appeared in Ottoman political writings of the seventeenth century, though research today sees them as reflecting cultural trends or reactions to internal sociopolitical changes more than valid historical analyses.[56] Likewise, Iranian intellectuals from the mid-nineteenth century were preoccupied with the decline of modern Iran particularly in view of its glorious past. Conversely, modern Islamist writers from Muḥammad Rashīd Riḍḍā (d. 1935) to Yūsuf Qaradāwī (b. 1926), while often lamenting the status of Islam, enthusiastically endorsed the notion of the "decline of the West."[57]

The contemporary Iranian discourse on the future decline of the West differs significantly from the formula devised by Ibn Khaldūn. It does not follow

53 For an analysis of Spengler's work, see Klaus P. Fischer, *History and Prophecy: Oswald Spengler and the Decline of the West* (New York: P. Lang, 1989); Herman, *Idea of Decline*, 221–255.

54 Arnold J. Toynbee, *A Study of History*. In 12 Vols (Oxford: Oxford University Press, 1961); Herman, *Idea of Decline*, 256–294.

55 ʿAziz al-ʿAzmah, *Ibn Khaldun* (London: Routledge, 1990); Yves Lacoste, *Ibn Khaldun: The Birth of History and the Past of the Third World* (London: Verso, 1984).

56 Bernard Lewis, "Ottoman Observers of Ottoman Decline," *Islamic Studies* 1 (1962): 71–87.

57 See Uriya Shavit (ed.), *The Decline of the West: The Rise of Islam? Studies in Civilizational Discourse* (Tel Aviv: Hakibbutz Hameuchad, 2010). (Hebrew).

Ibn Khaldūn's cyclical approach but is based on the monotheistic linear view of history from creation to redemption, with its own optimistic perception of the "end of history." Moreover, according to Ibn Khaldūn, an important element in the decadence and decline of urban societies in the Middle East was the loss of the warlike, desert qualities and the adoption of a "soft" urban mentality. Conversely, the Iranian discourse emphasizes the West's inherent aggressive and militaristic characteristics in addition to its spiritual and moral decadence. Ibn Khaldūn's model was deterministic, but though it purported to be universal, it was heavily influenced by the Middle-Eastern and North-African specific context of the contrast between the desert and the sown, a situation that does not apply to the modern Islam-West dichotomy. Similarly, while Iranian writers often refer to Spengler and Toynbee when discussing the West and endorse Spengler's criticism of liberal democracy, they do not share the latter's conceptualization of culture having the life cycle of a living organism. This is because of their linear historical belief that while the revived Islamic civilization may face constant external and internal threats, it is largely immune from this type of decline due to the inherently superior qualities of Islam.

As was the case with pre-Revolution writings, the new discourse on Western decline is part of a broader and more universal Occidentalist discourse which draws inspiration from the counter-enlightenment trend in Europe including its views on the future of the West. Western writings on decline serve as a reference and also buttress the Islamist argument, since they are regarded as an admission of Western guilt and failure. This new discourse also perhaps reflects subtle or subconscious esteem toward the West or Western sources.[58] While it shares various ideas with the Sunnī Islamist criticism of the West and belief in the ultimate victory of Islam, the Iranian discourse fuses it with unique Shīʿī ideas about the eventual outcome of the historical process.

7 Western Moral and Social Decadence

Supreme Leader Khamenei took the lead in highlighting the structural social and cultural crisis of Western civilization and advocating its imminent decline, particularly as the 2003 American invasion of Iraq was proving a failure.[59] In

58 In addition to Spengler, Toynbee, and Heidegger, see Seyyed Muḥammad ʿAlī Mudarrisī (Ṭabāṭabāʾī), *Tamaddun-i mādī gerāyāne mā gharbīhā: dīdār-i jamʿī az dāneshmandān-i gharbī dar naqd-i tamaddun-i gharb* (Qom: Intishārāt Shafaq, 1382/2003), which analyzes Western critics of the West.

59 As of May 2020, Khamenei's official website has published passages from 32 speeches and sermons, which contain his critical analysis of the ills of Western civilization, "Boḥrān-i

various statements he predicted that the present Iranian generation would witness the fall of Western civilization due to its internal contradictions, absence of logic, brutal conduct, and lack of consideration for human principles. Speaking to students of the Ayatollah Mujtahidī Seminary, Khamenei promised them that: "You young people will see that day that, because of the absence of spirituality, this civilized Western world will be stricken by perdition and destruction; from the peak of capability and power it shows today, it will fall to the depths of misery and powerlessness."[60]

Khamenei did not ignore the West's technological and scientific achievements. Rather, he reversed the Shīʿī trope of the pure inner self (*bāṭin*) and the impure exterior (*ẓāhir*) to claim that these were mere external features (*ẓawāhir*) in contrast to the West's *bāṭin*, which is materialistic and contaminated by lust, sin, and immorality. At best, these technological achievements were the means, he asserted, that enabled the West to impose its tyranny on the rest of the world. Moreover, he maintained that science and technology could not offer solutions to society's moral and social problems. In a series of rhetorical questions, he asked whether humanity was content after two to three centuries of materialistic Western domination. Has Western culture been able to heal the old ills of humanity? Have poverty, famine, oppression, and discrimination disappeared? And have society's sacred values been secured? His own response was obvious: Western society during the period of imperialism and exploitation had pursued the wrong path and was unable to offer any remedy for humanity's suffering. The root cause of humanity's internal decay and imminent fall was the ideological and philosophical essence of Western civilization, that is, secularism, humanism, and the reliance on rationalism, science, and positivism. All of these had led to the rejection of spirituality, the exclusion of morality and religion from the public sphere, the centrality of capitalism and imperialism, and the exploitation of other nations.[61] Following

---

gharb," http://farsi.khamenei.ir/keyword-print?id=2236. As early as February 2012, an admiring blogger had highlighted Khamenei's repeated predictions of the imminent fall of the West as one of fourteen examples of his farsighted vision of historical processes, "Nigāhī beh taḥaqquq-i ʿajīb 14 pīsh-bīnī-i buzurg-i Imām-i Khamenei," February 4, 2012, http://iran313.blogfa.com/post-114.aspx.

60 Khamenei "Sibk zendegī," October 15, 2012, http://farsi.khamenei.ir/speech-content?id=21293; "Bayānāt dar dīdār-i ṭulāb va-asātīd-i madrasa-i ʿilmī-i ayatollah mujtahidī," 21 Khordād 1383/ June 10, 2004, http://farsi.khamenei.ir/speech-content?id=1138.

61 "Pīsh-bīnī-i suqūṭ-i gharb tavassoṭ-i maqām-i muʿaẓẓam-i rahbarī.," 15 Ābān 1390/ November 6, 2011, http://siasi.porsemani.ir/node/1806; "Rahbar-i muʿaẓẓam-i inqilāb: Khaṭṭ-i kullī-i niẓām-i Islāmī chīst?," April 28, 2013, http://www.hoviatema.ir/export/print/445?module=news; "Gharb az ban-bast idīʾūlūzhīk khārij mīshavad?," 5 Dey 1391/ December 25, 2012, https://www.bultannews.com/fa/news/116796/. For Khamenei's

Khamenei, this theme was disseminated in a variety of media from Friday sermons and scholarly articles to newspapers articles.

Echoing German philosopher Martin Heidegger's critique on modernity, various Shīʿī writers have denounced the centrality of technology and industrial production in the West, which regards humans as no different from machines and as small cogs in a huge industrial apparatus. Dāvarī, for example, described technology as a dominant mode of thinking in the West, becoming a major force of oppression instead of liberation.[62] The moral crisis resulting from the domination of machines has become a "malignant cancer" in Western societies, producing aggressive states and brutal wars, added an anonymous blogger. A third writer concluded that the "spirit of machinism," which ignores the spiritual dimension of humans, has produced a major identity crisis in the West, which will inevitably lead to decline and destruction.[63]

Khamenei pointed out the glaring contradiction between the West's self-perception of standing on the moral high ground and its criminal and bullish conduct toward other peoples, which would, he asserted, bring about its fall.[64] The paradise promised by the Renaissance had turned into hell. The end result of the Western experiment has been Fascism, Nazism, or Communism, or, alternatively, the absolute rule of liberalism manifested in "America and its

favorable views toward science and scientific research, see Sadjadpour, *Reading Khamenei*, 22–24.

62 ʿAlī Javādī, "Umanīsm: inḥiṭāṭ-i maʿnavī va-fasād-i akhlāqī-i gharb," *Resālat*, March 5, 2009; Dāvarī cited in Zamānī, "Gharb az aghāz tā pāyān;" Khūshyār Būrūmand and Seyyed Ḥasan Ḥusaynī, "Barresī-i rūyikard-i Heidegger dar muvājaha bā teknūlūzhī," *Gharb shināsī bonyādī* 5, no. 1 (1393/2014): 8–11; Ẕū al-Qadr, *Qiṣṣa-i ghurbat-i gharbī*, 126; Aṣghar Ṭāhirzādeh, *ʿIlal-i tazalzul-i tamaddun-i gharb* (Iṣfahān: Lub al-Mīzān, 1388/2009), 163–164.

63 Maḥmūd Ḥakīmī, "Gharb bīmār ast (8): Gharb va-mashīnīzm" *Darshā-i maktab-i Islām* 10, no. 11 (Abān 1348/October 1969), 779; ʿAlī Akbar Rashād, "Tajdīd-i ḥayāt-i dīnī va-maʿnavīgarā'i dar gharb-i muʿāṣir," July 15, 2014, http://rashad.ir/2017/09/13/تجدید-حیات-دینی-و-معنویت-گرایی-در-غرب/. Ironically, and without equating the Iranian writers with the Nazis, there is an interesting similarity with Nazi Germany's scathing criticism of the dominant role of technology in Western culture alongside its massive investments in modern scientific and technological development. For the German phenomenon, see Jeffrey Herf, *Reactionary Modernism: Technology, Culture, and Politics in Weimar and the Third Reich* (Cambridge: Cambridge University Press, 1986). For Iranian investments in science, see Abdol S. Soofi and Sepehr Ghazinoory, eds., *Science and Innovations in Iran: Development, Progress, and Challenges* (New York: Palgrave Macmillan, 2013).

64 "Tamaddun-i gharb dar maʿraż-i suqūṭ va-sar nīgūnī ast," April 17, 2013, http://www.iribnews.ir/fa/news/28332.

darling Israel." All the crimes of the past 150 years are, he claimed, the outcome of the ideas of the Enlightenment.[65]

An *I'timād-I millī* editorial published during the 2006 Israeli-Lebanese war saw it as one more link in a long chain of Western crimes that foretold and hastened its doom. It referred back to the flames of war which had erupted in Europe and claimed millions of innocent lives, causing, it maintained, many Western intellectuals and philosophers to reconsider their way of thinking about Western civilization. The realization that, in spite of expressions of modernity such as enjoying cinema and theatre, building railways, and colonizing thousands under the pretext of modernization, a civilized Western person could also "kill hundreds of thousands of innocent human beings, simply by pressing a button or pulling on a lever, was a horrifying nightmare." Numerous western thinkers such as Voltaire (d. 1778), Montesquieu (d. 1755), Rousseau (d. 1778), Gobineau (d. 1882) and Nietzsche, had spoken of the excellence of Europeans, but the outcome was ruinous. Conversely, Spengler was among the first intellectuals to despair of the conduct of the West. Now, close to a century later, we must, the editorial asserted, once again use Spengler's term, the decline of the West. "A storm of Muslim wrath is brewing, which will inflict a major defeat on America and Israel," it concluded.[66]

Historian Ḥasan Vā'izī drew lessons from the collapse of the Soviet Union to predict the future fall of the United States. His 2003 book, which received the blessings of Khamenei's office and reportedly sold over 80,000 copies, explained that the idea that governed the Soviet Union and the United States, that is, materialism without spirituality, contrasted with human nature and was thus bound to fail. This one-dimensional view of humans, which typifies the United States, was, he claimed, condemned to annihilation. The search for spirituality had initially driven many Americans to Hindu mysticism, Buddhism, and similar cults, but they came to realize that these were in fact charlatanism and many started turning to Islam. In order to preempt this development, the US elites equated Islam with terrorism and resorted to invading and conquering other countries. Vā'izī concluded that while the United

65 Maqām-i mu'aẓẓam-i rahbarī, "Zavāl va-ufūl-i tamaddun-i gharb dar kalām-i rahbarī;" "Pīsh-raft yā pas-raft? Naqd-i algū-i gharbī az manẓar-i rahbar-i mu'aẓẓam-i inqilāb-i Islāmī," April 4, 2015, http://www.farsnews.com/newstext.php?nn=13930802000542.

66 "Israel's Crime: Decline of the West," *I'timād-i Millī*, August 6, 2006, NTIS, US Dept. of Commerce. See similar charges in "Nābūdī-i Shī'a beṣūrat-i narm az dīdār-i fransīs Fūkūyāmā," *Islam Times*, 18 Esfand 1395/March 8, 2017, https://www.islamtimes.org/fa/article/616178.

States might have occasional short-term victories, it would ultimately face destruction or decline.[67]

8 Humanism and the Decline of the West

The West's greatest fault, according to this discourse, was the adoption of humanism (*insān-madārī* and *insān-gerā'ī*) as the central pillar of its civilization and of modernity. As one writer explained, the roots of humanism go back to ancient Greece, when the gods were seen to compete with human beings. It took a new form during the Renaissance, and by leaning on human sensualities and carnal desires, it was transformed into a philosophy that considers the human material dimension to be the yardstick and value of every affair. According to this interpretation, humanism puts humans at the center of the world and seeks to please them instead of God. It regards humans as self-regulating creatures, who become the main pivot of being and the sole source of knowledge, intellect, and moral values rather than God and whose thoughts, and actions have priority over all else. Humanism, therefore, confines everything to "human criteria" and turns away from the spiritual sphere under the pretext of gaining control of nature. It has created a world in which everything is planned and arranged by people for their own sake and has become a self-adulating, egotistical, and egocentric idea. Humanism did not only reject divine religions but in fact invented a new religion.[68]

Member of the Assembly of Experts Ḥujjat al-Islām Aḥmad Beheshtī conceded that humanism might have had some positive aspects, as it awakened

67 Vā'izī to *Ya Lesaratol-Ḥusayn*, March 5, 2003, cited in https://www.balatarin.com/permlink/2010/1/10/1909036. See also his "Shikl gīrī-i ṭarḥ-i furūpāshī-i shūrāvī hazīnehā-i khārijī va-dākhilī," 7 Esfand 1386/February 26, 2008, http://www.rasekhoon.net/article/show-2934.aspx. For similar comparisons of the past Soviet collapse to the inevitable Western collapse, see Muḥammad Ṣādiq Kūshkī, "Ravand-i furūpāshī-i tamaddun-i gharb az pīrūzī-i inqilāb-i Islāmī aghāz shodeh ast," 17 Azar 1390/December 8, 2011, https://www.mehrnews.com/news/1485518 and Tabaar, "The Beloved Great Satan," 23. For other views celebrating large-scale conversion to Islam in the West, see Ayatollah 'Alī Akbar Rashād, "Mowj-i Islām-gerā'ī dar jahān gharb," http://rashad.ir/category/آثار/غرب‌شناسی/.

68 'Alī Khāliqī Afkand, "insān madārī (umanīsm)," *Imām-i Khomeini va-goftemān-i gharb* (Tehrān: Anjuman-i ma'ārif-i Islāmī, 1379/2000), http://www.ghadeer.org/Book/15/2336; Muhammad Taqi Misbah Yazdi, *Freedom: The Unstated Facts and Points*, trans. Mansoor Limba (Tehrān: Ahl al-Bayt World Assembly, 2005), 38–39; Zamānī, "Gharb, az aghāz tā pāyān"; Ẕū al-Qadr, *Qiṣṣa-i ghurbat-i gharbī*, 93–96; Hādī Vakīlī, "Naqd-i mabānī-i umanīstī-i ḥuqūq-i bashar-i gharbī," *Kitāb-i naqd* 36 (1384/2005): 129–154; "Pīsh-bīnī-i suqūṭ-i gharb tavassoṭ-i maqām-i mu'aẓẓam-i rahbarī."; "Gozāreshī az kitāb-i mabānī-i naẓarī-i gharb-i modern."

people's awareness to despotism, human misery, and arrogance; had it succeeded, the world would be filled with ideal people. But, in reality, humanism failed to advance its supposedly lofty goals. Even worse, the greatest murderers in history, Stalin and Hitler, were supported in the name of humanism. Similarly, Beheshtī pointed to the crimes committed by the Americans in Vietnam, Iraq, and Afghanistan, the French in Algeria, and the Zionist oppression of the Palestinians – all sustained by humanism – and concluded that humanism had never protected the oppressed.[69]

Similarly, Dāvarī depicted humanism as the "pivotal axis of Western history," the rise of humans who consider themselves the beginning, end, and center of the universe. And this, he believes, is where the "West's fundamental flaw lies," and from whence its inevitable collapse will derive. For Dāvarī, the West and modernity are synonymous. While modernity may manifest itself in various fields such as capitalism or political liberalism, it eventually takes shape as imperialism. At the same time, Dāvarī pointed to the practical equivalency between modernity and humanism, which he defines as "a condition in which man considers himself worthy of conquest over all other beings, and he assumes that with his willpower and his rationality, he can bestow order on everything."[70] Dāvarī rejects the association of humanism and subjectivity (namely, the autonomy of the self) with such virtues as self-respect, freedom, responsible individuality, mutual respect and responsibility, and social accountability. Instead, modernity, which might be one of humanity's greatest achievements, is also the age of "oppression, rape, and pillage," "despotic rule," "slavery to machines," "revolt ... subversion ... heedlessness ... egoism ... hubris," and "a period of decline for divine thought and human alienation." In today's West, Dāvarī maintains, "the air is depressing, doors are shut, heads are confused, hands are hidden, breaths are cloudy, hearts are heavy and tired, trees are skeleton-like, the earth is barren, the sky is dusty and confining."[71] No system based on flawed premises can sustain itself indefinitely, and the West is

69 Aḥmad Beheshtī, "Islām va-umanīsm," *Ufq-i ḥawza* 28, 9 Tīr 1382/June 3, 2003, https://hawzah.net/fa/Magazine/View/6435/8078/106170/.

70 Reża Dāvarī Ardakānī, *Tamaddun va-tafakkur-i gharbī* (Tehrān: Sāqī, 1380/2001), 11; Dāvarī, "Is Philosophy Global or Regional?," http://rezadavari.ir/index.php?option=com_content&view=article&id=324:is-philosophy-global-or-regional&catid=32:archive&Itemid=76; See also Rajaee, *Islamism and Modernism*, 187.

71 "Murūri bar athār va-andīshehā-i Reża Dāvarī Ardakānī," 22 Khordād 1394/June 12, 2015, http://www.irna.ir/fa/News/81643158/; Kamrava, *Iran's Intellectual Revolution*, 66; Rajaeei, *Islamism and Modernism*, 187; Vāʿizī, "Shikl gīrī-i ṭarḥ-i furūpāshī-i shūrāvī hazīnehā-i khārijī va-dākhilī."

no exception. Therefore, "the era of the West, and the eclipse in the history of sacred thought and the alienation of man, will come to an end," he concluded.[72]

Dāvarī goes beyond the political arena to the philosophical sphere in locating the crisis of the West. The "Promethean passion," Dāvarī states, is the guiding principle of the West; just as the mythical Prometheus sought to bring the secret of fire from heaven to earth, the "Promethean passion" of the West is the yearning for a utopia, and the existence of a utopian vision is inherent and essential for the West. The Western utopia is modernity, in other words, an ideal society that will replace the system of knowledge or philosophy, previously based on God's ordinances, for one based on human reason, intellect, and science, that is, the ideals of the Enlightenment. This yearning is found, he asserts, in the writings of every major Western writer such as Hobbes (d. 1679), Hegel (d. 1831), or Rousseau. However, Dāvarī adds, this Western approach is not an expression of reason and intellect; instead, it is a symptom of poverty of the mind and a lack of knowledge and understanding of the divine revelation and arrogance.[73] Modernity is the utopia of the West, but it suffers today from a deep crisis manifested in the emergence of post-modernism, which denies all the grand narratives of history. Thus, in Dāvarī's opinion, the two processes – the disappearance of all utopias and the emergence of post-modernism – signify the decline and imminent fall of the West.

According to Dāvarī and others, a crucial point standing at the core and essence of the West is the close and inseparable link between philosophy and power. While they acknowledge the past achievements of Western philosophy, even though they rejected its premises, they all insist that present-day Western philosophy suffers from a major crisis. Accordingly, Western civilization suffers from intellectual sterility, exhaustion, and the loss of internal vitality, a political Parkinson's disease, social AIDS, and a malignant civilizational cancer, all of which stem from the weakness of belief.[74] Rationalism, which rel-

---

72 Cited in Kamrava, *Iran's Intellectual Revolution*, 66.

73 Reża Dāvarī Ardakānī, "Autopia va-ta'rīkh-i jahān-i jadīd," n.d. http://rezadavari.ir/index.php?option=com_content&view=article&id=450:2015-06-14-11-21-38&catid=43:2015-06-13-12-02-50&Itemid=79; Zamānī, "Gharb, az aghāz tā pāyān."

74 Maqṣūd Ranjīr, "Falsafa va-siyāsat-i gharb dar andīsheh-i Dāvarī," *Pegāh-i ḥawza* 317, no. 24 (1390/2011): 8–16, http://www.hawzah.net/fa/Magazine/View/3814/7847/101231/فلسفه-و-سیاست-غرب-در-اندیشه-داوری; Seyyed Ḥusayn 'Alavī, "Gharb-i modern az nowzāyī tā nāzā'iyī," *Risālat*, 17 Esfand 1391/March 7, 2013; Muḥammad 'Abdollahī, "Bīst dalīl barāye furūpāshī-i Amrīkā," 23 Mehr 1390/October 15, 2011, https://www.farsnews.com/news/13900723000034/20; 'Alī Reża Ṣadrā, "Āsīb-i shināsī-i jahānī-shodan va-jahānīsāzī bā model jahānīgerā'ī-i mahdaviyat," *Qabasāt*, 33 (1383/2004): 155–176, http://ensani.ir/fa/article/7278/.

egated religion to the margins, produced a negative and destructive effect that contains nothing except for despair and indifference and results, inevitably, in nihilism.[75]

Seyyed Ḥusayn ʿAlavī of Muṣṭafā University, among others, explains the causal connection between Western humanism and the West's intellectual and philosophical stagnation and moral degradation, which in itself marks or justifies the end of Western civilization. During the early phase of the modern age, from the time of Descartes (d. 1650) and Kant (d. 1804), Western philosophers believed, he states, that reason, separated from revelation, could discover and explain everything. Yet, only 150 years after Kant, the West experienced a deterioration which has produced an opposite mood typified by emptiness, despair, and arrogance and personified by Nietzsche, who challenged religious morality and developed the idea of the "Superman" and the morality of masters and slaves. Western philosophy has ever since suffered from stagnation, according to ʿAllawi, without even one philosopher worthy of that title. Instead, there are thinkers, such as Karl Popper (d. 1994), Hanna Arendt (d. 1975), Jurgen Habermas (b. 1929), and Anthony Giddens (b. 1938), who formulate theories that justify the rule of the elites over the people. In ʿAllawi's eyes, the few Western thinkers who voiced semi-metaphysical ideas were desperate yet arrogant post-modernists who believed they could thus revive the moribund Western civilization. This, he concludes, is the end of a civilization that sought to replace God with arrogant people.[76]

Among the worst consequences of humanism, according to the dominant Shīʿī view, was a deep moral crisis and the spread of corruption throughout all spheres of life. Since humanism revolves around people and there is nothing above them, people have no sense of responsibility toward anything; they only look after their own interests and seek to take advantage of everything regardless of the price.[77] Not surprisingly, Iranian writers find a direct correlation

---

75 Mujtabā Ḥaddādī, "Ufūl-i gharb-i modern va-talāsh barāye takhrīb-i Islām," *Risālat*, 17 Esfand 1389/March 8, 2011; Ẓū al-Qadr, *Qiṣṣa-i ghurbat-i gharbī*, 126; "Pīsh-bīnī-i suqūṭ-i gharb tavassoṭ-i maqām-i muʿaẓẓam-i rahbarī."

76 ʿAlavī, "Gharb-i modern az nowzāyī tā nāzāʾiyī." See also Masʿūd Rażavī, who uses Nietzsche's ideas both as a critique and a symptom of Western decadence, *Pāyān-i taʾrīkh: Suqūṭ-i gharb va-aghāz-i ʿaṣr-i sevom* (Tehrān: Shafīqī, 1381/2002) and Mūsā Najafī, who cites both Nietzsche's and Heidegger's criticism of the decadence of Western culture in his *Naẓariyat-i tamaddun-i jadīd-i Islāmī: Falsafa-i takāmul-i tamaddun-i Islāmī va-jawhar-i ufūl-i yābande-i tamaddun-i gharb* (Iṣfahān: Armā, 1392/2013), 113. For other writers who emphasized the prevalence of post-modernism as the symbol of Western decline, see "Goftār-i pīshīn: cherā bāyad gharb rā shenākht," July 11, 2006, http://www.tebyan.net/index.aspx?pid=24112.

77 Javādī "Umanīsm: inḥiṭāṭ-i maʿnavī va-fasād-i akhlāqī-i gharb."

between the decline of religion and the many socioeconomic ills in Western societies, seeing it as a reflection of Western moral corruption and decadence.[78] They, like the Soviets of the 1950s and 1960s, cite Western statistics showing the rising rates of crime, divorce, drug abuse, and prostitution in order to prove their point.[79]

One salient feature of the perceived Western decadence is sexual promiscuity, and in Khamenei's words, the "unforgivable sin" against women of defining them as mere objects of pleasure. Khamenei also lashed out at the "normalization of sin" which has become a distinct feature of Western culture, particularly "the great sin of homosexuality becoming a virtue." He predicted that the irreparable damage to family values would lead to the West's collapse.[80] Khamenei's personal representative in the Revolutionary Guards, Ḥujjat al-Islām ʿAlī Saʿīdī, followed suit by explaining that the entry of one hundred active homosexuals to the US Congress following the 2012 elections was a clear sign of the West's decay. Brigadier General Muḥammad Reża Naqdī, then commander of the Basīj militia, predicted that the "European race, just like the dinosaurs, is in the process of extinction," due to "the prevalence of homosexuality and living with animals."[81]

9 The West's Decline as a Divine Punishment

The 2008 financial crisis that engulfed the United States and Europe elicited worldwide criticism of capitalism and its excesses. For the Shīʿī spokespeople,

---

78 "Rafsanjani Delivers Tehran Friday Prayer Sermons," *Radio Tehran*, January 10, 2003; "Ayatollah Javādī Āmolī: Amrīkāʾīhā ʿaql nadārand," 21 October 2012, http://www.asriran.com/fa/print/237623; Mahdī Nāṣirī, *Islām va-Tajaddud* (Tehrān: Ṣubḥ, 1380/2001), 219–220; "Nābūdī-i Shīʿa beṣūrat narm az dīdār-i fransīs Fūkūyāmā"; Fuʾād Ayzadī, "Amrīkā va-abr qudratīʾāsh," May 18, 2013, http://farsi.khamenei.ir/others-note?id=21786; ʿAbdollahī, "Bīst dalīl barāye furūpāshī-i Amrīkā."

79 "Pīsh-bīnī suqūṭ gharb," *Siyāsat-i rūz*, November 8, 2005; ʿAbdollahī, "Bīst dalīl barāye furūpāshī-i Amrīkā"; "Amrīkā va-asāsān ʿgharbʾ rū beh-sūye furūpāshī pīsh mīravad," May 10, 2011, http://u313yasin.blogfa.com/post-100.aspx. See also "Naqdī: idīʾūlūzhīhā-i gharb beh ban bast rasīdeh ast," 18 Ordībehesht 1394/May 8, 2015, http://www.isna.ir/fa/news/94021810069.

80 "Imam Khamenei Blasts West's View of Women," *Sayyid ʿAlī*, August 12, 2015, http://sayyidali.com/getting-to-know/imam-khamenei-blasts-wests-view-of-women.html; "Khamenei sibk zindigī."

81 "Rāhyābī 100 hamjins bāz beh kongreh-i Amrīkā suqūṭ-i siyāsī-i gharb ast," June 14, 2013, http://www.tasnimnews.com/fa/news/1394/06/28/69893; "Sirdār-i Naqdī: nezhād-i urupaʾi dar hāl-i inqirāż ast," 3 Bahman 1394/January 23, 2016, https://www.tasnimnews.com/fa/news/1396/11/03/1636397.

the crisis served as further vindication of the deep malaise of Western societies but, more importantly, as an indicator and precursor of the coming fall of the West and liberal democracy. Khamenei, for instance, explained that the United States was "in a full-blown crisis" because its "corrupt foundation has been exposed to the American people" and predicted that the Occupy Wall Street Movement that emerged in 2011 would "bring down the capitalist system and the West."[82] Similarly, Ḥujjat al-Islām Seyyed Muḥammad Mahdī Mīr-Bāqirī, head of the Farhangistān-i 'Ulūm-i Islāmī in Qom, attributed the financial crisis to the ideological crisis of Western civilization that was based on humanism, liberalism, and nationalism.[83] The daily *Kayhān* recalled American arrogance and smugness following the collapse of the former Soviet Union and their belief in themselves as "the world's absolute power." The Americans, the writers emphasized, presented liberal democracy as the savior of the world in place of wrecked socialism, but the modern socioeconomic reality proves otherwise: the "whole world has accepted that liberal capitalism has been defeated. America's financial crunch is the beginning of the end."[84]

According to Ḥujjat al-Islām Muḥammad Taqī Rahbar of the Tablīghāt-i Islāmī Organization, the insoluble crisis from which the United States was suffering having plundered the entire world for decades, was a fulfillment of the Qur'ānic passage: "So, when they had forgotten the warning they had received, We opened the gates to everything for them. Then, as they reveled in what they had been given, We struck them suddenly and they were dumbfounded" (Sūrat al-An'ām, 44–45). Rahbar expressed his hope, based on this passage, that the oppressed peoples of the world would rise up against the evil US rulers and celebrate their defeat and death.[85] Likewise, Ayatollah Aḥmad Jannatī (b. 1927) head of the Council of Guardians, described the financial crisis as a

---

82 "Iranian President in Gilan, Blames Neo-Colonialism for Financial Crisis Speech by Iranian President Maḥmūd Ahmadinezhad to the People of Rasht in Gilan Province," *Islamic Republic of Iran News Network Television (IRINN)*, October 16, 2008, OSC [CIA Open Source Center]; Khamenei's office published a collection of his statements on the subject titled: *The End of the West: An Essay on the Statements of the Exalted Leader of the Revolution Regarding the Capitalist System* (*Pāyān-i Gharb: Justārī dar bayānāt-i rahbar-i mu'aẓẓam-i inqilāb* (*madda ẓilluhu al-'ālī*) *pīrāmūn niẓām-i sarmāyeh-dārī*) (Tehrān: Kitāb-i Farda, 1390/2011); "Khamenei Claims Occupy Wall Street Protests Will Topple US Capitalism," *The Guardian*, October 12, 2011, http://www.theguardian.com/world/2011/oct/12/iran-us-protests-topple-capitalism.

83 Muḥammad Mahdī Mīr-Bāqirī, "Boḥrān-i idī'ūlūzhīk-i tamaddun-i gharb 'āmil 'Ījād bohran-i Iqtiṣādī shode ast," April 19, 2014, http://www.hamandishi.ir/news/216675/.

84 *Kayhān*, October 15, 2008; *Kayhān*, May 27, 2014.

85 "Ra'īs sāzimān-i basīj-i masājid-i sepāh: tamaddun mottakī bar sarmāyeh-dārī-i gharb rū beh ufūl ast," June 8, 2013, http://www.farsnews.com/newstext.php?nn=13920218001340; Muḥammad Taqī Rahbar, "Tamaddun-i gharb dar sar'āshībī-i suqūṭ," pt. 1 *Pāsdār-i Islām* 324 (1387/ 2008): 1–3 and pt. 2, *Pāsdār-i Islām* 326 (1387/ 2009): 12–15.

"punishment from God," adding that the "unhappier they are, the happier we become."[86] Ahmadinezhad described the crisis as signifying the "end of capitalism," explaining that the reason for the West's defeat "is that they have forgotten God and piety." Visiting Damascus in early May 2009 he declared that Iran was leading a "new order" that would replace the now obsolete "old order" led by the United States and the West.[87] Following the controversial presidential elections of June 2009, Ahmadinezhad boasted that "as soon as the new government is formed, it will enter the global sphere with a power that is ten times greater than that of the West and overthrow the West from its hegemonic position."[88]

10 The Islamic Revolution and the Fall of the West

The 1979 Revolution has been seen by many as the decisive event that precipitated the fall of the West, as it undermined the very existence and value system of the West and the capitalist world. According to a *Fars News Agency* article, the Revolution generated a global religious awakening that would bring about the collapse of the globalization of western culture. Going further, Ḥusayn Rūḥānī of Iṣfahān University claimed that the Islamic Revolution had not only shaken the foundations of modernity but was offering a comprehensive alternative with which to run the world. Since the victory of the Revolution, he asserted, the West was sinking deeper and deeper into the morass and mire of its own creation, and the United States as the leader of the West had encountered numerous defeats.[89]

Muḥammad Taqī Rahbar claimed that one of the major blessings of the Islamic Revolution was that it shattered the myth of Western superiority and "tore the deceptive fiber of this civilization."[90] In a similar vein, a writer in

86 "Tehran Begins to Feel the Pain of Finance Crisis," *Washington Times*, November 5, 2008. See "Mideast Mirror, Section C (Turkey & Iran)" *Kayhān*, October 15, 2008 for similar predictions. See also Ahmadinejad's statement that a "new era is starting" after the "definite defeat of capitalism," *Christian Science Monitor*, November 9, 2009.

87 Cited in Memri, Inquiry & Analysis Series Report No. 517, May 29, 2009, http://www.memri.org/report/en/print3334.htm; *Islamic Republic of Iran News Network Television (IRINN)*, October 16, 2008, NewsEdge Document Number: 200810161477.1_f7b708afa060bb55.

88 Roger Cohen, "Iran's Tragic Joke," *New York Times*, July 21, 2009.

89 Rajaee, *Islamism and Modernism*, 168; "Jahānī shodan inqilāb-i Islāmī va-pāyān-i ta'rīkh," 22 Farvardīn 1394/April 11 2015, https://www.farsnews.com/news/13940119001061; Ḥusayn Rūḥānī, "Dāneshgāh farāmūshī inḥiṭāṭ-i gharb," *Kayhān*, 4 Shahrīvar 1393/August 26, 2014.

90 Rahbar, "Tamaddun-i gharb" pt. 3, *Pasdar Islām* 327–328 (2009). See also Majīd Mūsā Mukhtārī, "Ufūl-i gharb va-ilzāmāt barpāyī tamaddun-i Islāmī," *Javān*, June 13, 2009; Mūsā Najafī, "Falsafa-i takāmul-i bīdārī-i Islāmī va-jawhar-i ufūl-i yābande-i tamaddun-i gharb,"

the *Tasnim* news agency asserted that the Islamic Revolution had destroyed American strategy in the Middle East and awakened pro-Islamic, anti-Western, and anti-Zionist protest and revolutionary movements throughout the region. While prompting the United States to spend huge amounts of money engaging in military interventions to prevent the outbreak of other revolutions, the Islamic Revolution altered the regional and global balance of power against the West and in favor of Islam.[91]

In his introduction to *What is Philosophy?*, which was published shortly after the victory of the Islamic Revolution, Dāvarī described the revolution as a reaction to Westoxication, portending the end of Western domination and the beginning of a new era in which religion would dampen the "holocaust of Westoxication." Similarly, Ẕū al-Qadr sees the Revolution as an uprising against the liberal capitalist hegemony of the West and the regimes associated with it. Yet, despite his earlier assessment of the Revolution's achievements, Dāvarī later yearned for or anticipated the outbreak of another global revolution, "which will undermine the West and, when expanded, overthrow it. With this revolution humanity can renew the forgotten covenant of the past and a new era will be established."[92]

11 Responses to the Clash of Civilizations

While participants in the decline discourse found it useful to cite Western writers who shared their critical view of the West, they also grappled with ideological advocates of the West. Of these, two writers elicited many passionate reactions and therefore merit special attention here: Samuel Huntington (d. 2008) with his pessimistic "Clash of Civilizations"[93] and Francis Fukuyama's triumphalist "The End of History?"

Justārhā-i siyāsī-i mu'āṣir 2, no. 2 (2011): 84–85; Kūshkī, "Ravand-i furūpāshī-i gharb az pīrūzī-i inqilāb-i Islāmī aghāz shodeh ast"; Ayzadī, "Amrīkā va-abr qudratī'āsh."

91 "Naqsh-i inqilāb-i Islāmī dar ufūl-i Amrīkā va-gharb," 16 Bahman 1392/February 5, 2014, http://www.ghatreh.com/news/nn17859353. See also "Naẓarī-i bīdārī-i Islāmī va-pāyān-i makātib-i umanīstī."

92 Reża Dāvarī Ardakānī, *Falsafa Chist?* (Tehrān: Anjuman-i Islāmī-i Ḥikmat va-Falsafa-i Iran, 1980), 57, 60, cited in Farzin Vahdat, "Post-Revolutionary Islamic Discourses on Modernity in Iran: Expansion and Contraction of Human Subjectivity," *International Journal of Middle East Studies* 35, no. 4 (2003): 608; Ẕū al-Qadr, *Qiṣṣa-i ghurbat-i gharbī*, 3.

93 Samuel Huntington, "The Clash of Civilizations?," *Foreign Affairs* 72, no. 3 (1993): 22–49. Huntington expanded his thesis to a book, *The Clash of Civilizations and the Remaking of World Order* (New York: Simon and Shuster, 1996). The number of references to Huntington in the Iranian print and electronic media is too vast to be enumerated here.

Huntington's main argument was that in the post-Cold War era, cultural communities, the largest of which are civilizations, were replacing Cold War blocs and the fault lines between civilizations were becoming the central lines of conflict in global politics. He rejected the notion that there could be a "universal civilization" as a Western idea that was at odds with the particularism of most other societies. According to Huntington, as modernization bolsters the power and self-confidence of non-Western – particularly Asian – societies, it strengthens their commitment to their indigenous culture and thereby leads to rejection of the West. In raising the threat of a clash of civilizations, Huntington argued that at the macro or global level of world politics the primary clash would be between the West "and the rest," while at the micro level it would be between Islam and others.[94]

Huntington's ideas aroused mixed reactions among Shīʿī writers.[95] Reformists, who tacitly supported President Khātamī's dialogue of civilizations, criticized Huntington's major argument as an expression of Islamophobia and Orientalism. For them, his approach stemmed from a belief in the superiority of Western civilization and represented Islam in the superficial and denigrating way that was typical of Western Orientalism.[96] The mainstream, however, endorsed Huntingdon's diagnosis of a cultural and ideological clash between Islam and the West – a staple, in many ways, of modern Islamist thought – but rejected his solutions. They accepted his observations that the relative, or even absolute, decline of the West was the outcome of the deep structural crisis of Western society. Western civilization, they agreed, is moving toward nihilism and emptiness, as rationalism, which marginalized religion, produced a negative and destructive effect that can offer nothing except indifference, despair, and hopelessness. In what can be described as a mirror image of the situation in Iran (though not necessarily wrong), they attributed the "clash" theory to the West's need to find an enemy against which it would unite and which would provide it with a sense of purpose as a way out of its internal crisis; it was an excuse for the continued activities of the Western war machine, which was looking to justify its domination over other civilizations. Muḥammad Jaʿfar Afsā pointed to Huntington's double standard in this context: while treating Western policies as legitimate "security measures," Huntington categorizes

94 Huntington, *The Clash of Civilizations and the Remaking of World Order*, 94, 101, 217.

95 Due to lack of space only those reactions pertaining to the relations between Islam and the West will be discussed here.

96 See, for example, ʿAbbās ʿĪsā-zādeh and Seyyed Ḥusayn Sharaf al-Dīn, "Naẓariyat-i barkhōrd-i tamaddunhā chahārchūb-i mafhūm-i dark-i Islām harāsī," *Gharb shināsī bonyādī* 8, no. 2 (1395/2016): 47–52.

similar policies by Islamic countries as belonging to the realm of the "clash of civilizations."[97] These writers accepted Huntington's view of Islam as the major rival of the West, confident that following the inevitable decline of the West, the flag of Islam would rise in all corners of the world.[98]

While others from the mainstream have accepted the notion of the clash, they have described it as one between opposing models of globalization rather than civilizations. Dr. ʿAlī Reża Ṣadrā of ʿAlāma Ṭabātabāʾī University spoke of the evolving clash between three types of globalization: economic globalization, the false American globalization, namely the imposition of American culture on the world, and finally the Islamic-Shīʿī (*Mahdavī*) globalization, the all-inclusive spiritual and economic model which is the true solution for humanity's problems.[99]

Ḥujjat al-Islām Dr. Aḥmad Rahdār of Bāqir al-ʿUlūm University criticized Huntington's analysis of the causes of the conflicts and tensions between civilizations. Agreeing that the Western model is not universal, he attributes this to the capricious and materialistic nature of American culture, which could not serve as a spiritual model for other peoples. Likewise, the reason for the agitation in the Muslim world is not Islam, as Huntington claims, but poverty, oppression, and alienation from tyrannical rulers. Hence, the reason for the future decline of the West is not the clash of civilizations but rather the secularism and absence of spirituality that lead Westerners astray and destroyed any purpose in life. According to Rahdār, it is other civilizations, particularly Islam, that provide the answers to humanity's existential problems thanks to their spiritual dimension.[100]

---

97 Ḥaddādī, "Ufūl-i gharb-i modern va-talāsh barāye takhrīb-i Islām;" Daʾūd Mahdavī Zādehgān, "Rīsheh-yābī-i naẓariyat-i barkhōrd-i tamaddunhā," *Ḥukūmat-i Islāmī* 11(1378/1999): 193–194; Kowthari, "Zavāl tamaddun-i gharb"; Muḥammad Jaʿfar Afsā, "Naẓariyat-i barkhōrd-i tamaddunhā," *Farhang-i kowthar* 41 (1379/2000): 18–21.

98 Ḥusayn Rūḥānī, "Furūpāshī-i Amrīkā vāqiʿiyatī-i maḥtūm," *Kayhān*, May 27, 2014; Ḥaddādī, "Ufūl-i gharb-i modern." For a less passionate approach, see Muḥammad ʿAlī Tavānā, "Islām va-naẓariyat-i pāyān-i taʾrīkh," *Taʾrīkh dar āyīnah-i pazhūhesh* 8, no. 3 (2011): 71–86.

99 Ṣadrā, "Āsīb-i shināsī jahānī-shodan va-jahānīsāzī bā model jahānī-gerāʾī mahdaviyat;" Afsā, "Naẓariyat-i barkhōrd-i tamaddunhā," 18–20.

100 Aḥmad Rahdār, "Barresī-i panj-i naẓariyya dar bāb-i pāyān-i modernīte," *Maʿrifat* 68 (May 16, 2010): 43–59, http://www.hawzah.net/fa/article/articleview/89074.

12 Shīʿī Views on the "End of History"

If Huntington elicited a range of responses, few Western writers have aroused so much anger among Shīʿī and Sunnī Islamists as Fukuyama did with his controversial "End of History" theory. Fukuyama drew on the philosophy of Hegel, who saw history as a linear procession of epochs moving toward a specific condition – the realization of human freedom as a result of a dialectic conflict between ideas. He therefore saw the fall of Communism in the late 1980s as marking the end of the historical ideological struggles of the twentieth century and the triumph of liberal democracy and economic liberalism. Looking for future challenges to this triumph, Fukuyama examined the potential rise of destructive forms of nationalism and fundamentalist religion but found them unlikely to prevail. Thus, he argued, the triumph of liberalism was likely to be permanent and history in the sense of a clash of ideas had come to an end.[101]

A host of Iranian writers attacked Fukuyama's theory as arrogant and condescending, with some of them emphasizing his alleged animosity toward Islam and support of Zionism.[102] They criticized his theory for being based on universalist "historical materialism" (ironic considering his reliance on Hegel) and a belief in the laws of nature and liberal democracy. In other words, they rejected the Western meta-historical concepts, which view historical developments as based solely on earthly processes, since such views lead to atheism. Rather, in their meta-history God plays a decisive role – if not now then at least on the Day of Judgment. They argued that Shīʿī Islam, unlike the one-dimensional materialistic Western notion of humanity, is more comprehensive, as it takes into consideration people's spiritual and material attributes and regards the moral and spiritual aspect of human civilization as essential.[103] ʿAlī Muḥammadpūr dismissed the ostensible contrast of Fukuyama's naive and optimistic approach with Huntington's bleak forecast for the future. Fukuyama

---

101 Francis Fukuyama, "The End of History?," *The National Interest* 16 (1989): 3–18. He expanded his ideas into a book, *The End of History and the Last Man* (New York: Avon Books, 1992).

102 "Nābūdī-i Shīʿa beṣūrat-i narm az dīdār-i fransīs Fūkūyāmā," *Islam Times*, 18 Esfand 1395/ March 8, 2017, https://www.islamtimes.org/fa/article/616178/; Bahār Raḥmat, "Naẓar-i Fūkūyāmā jāponī al-aṣl va-tabaʿ-i Amrīkā dar mowred-i vilāyat-i faqīh," April 19, 2011, http://baharrahmat.mihanblog.com/post/40; Ḥasan Ijrāʾī, "Fūkūyāmā va-mahdaviyat: az afsāneh tā vāqiʿiyat," *Sāʿat-i ṣifr* 16, December 9, 2002, http://www.parsine.com/fa/news/58818.

103 Tavānā, "Islām va-naẓariyat-i pāyān-i taʾrīkh"; Ḥasan Ḥażratī and Nafīse Falāḥpūr, "Muqāyasa-i andīsheh-i mahdaviyat-i Shīʿa ithnā-ʿasharī va-naẓariyat-i pāyān-i taʾrīkh-i Fūkūyāmā," *Taʾrīkh-i Islām* 83(1388/ 2009): 161–186; Ijrāʾī, "Fūkūyāmā va-mahdaviyat: az afsāneh tā vāqiʿiyat"; Rahdār, "Barresī-i panj-i naẓariyya."

believes that after the predicted clash of civilizations and the disappearance of rival civilizations, Western liberal democracy will dominate the world. In contrast to Western historical teleology, as they understood it, the Iranian critics presented the Shīʿī concept of progress, namely, advancement toward spiritual perfection through a constant struggle between truth and falsehood. They contrasted two visions of the course of history. Fukuyama, following Hegelian dialectic logic, sees all humanity as basically the same and believes that the dialectic process of historical development will culminate in the consolidation of Western liberal democracy. Shīʿīsm, on the other hand, recognizes the differences between various cultures and regions but believes that humanity will advance toward convergence and unity through spiritual progress under the banner of Islam.[104]

Rejecting Fukuyama's premise that the fall of Communism meant victory for liberal democracy, various Iranians writers insisted that it reflected the failure of the entire project of Western Enlightenment. Liberal democracy, with its focus on earthly and material matters, cannot, they claimed, offer any future vision for humanity nor can it realize the true aspirations of humanity; the world will therefore remain a prisoner to oppression and injustice. In implicit endorsement of Huntington's views, they maintained that with the fall of Communism, Western capitalism faced a much more formidable enemy: Islam, with its values and its morality. Muḥammad ʿAlī Tavānā of Shīrāz University criticized Fukuyama for failing to appreciate the dynamism and vitality of Islamic culture as a rising force in both the post-Communist world and the West. Muḥammadpūr, likewise, highlighted the ideological and cultural decline of the West, Israel's defeat, and the great victories of the Muslim countries, which will thus invalidate Fukuyama's theory.[105]

In 2001, shortly after 9/11, a *Kayhān* editorial titled "The End of History is the Beginning of Our Path" dismissed Fukuyama's premature triumphalism. It offered its own version of history and concluded:

104 ʿAlī Muḥammad-pūr, "Fūkūyāmā ham iʿtirāf mīkonad," *Amān* 5 (1386/ 2007): 18–22, http://www.hawzah.net/fa/magazine/magart/6024/6029/63103; Ḥażratī and Falāḥpūr, "Muqāyasa-i andīsheh-i mahdaviyat-i Shīʿa"; Tavānā, "Islām va-naẓariyat-i pāyān-i ta'rīkh"; Aḥmad ʿAlī Niyāzī, "Pāyān-i ta'rīkh dar andīsheh-i Fūkūyāmā va-naẓariyat-i mahdaviyat," *Sangar-i sāybarī*, November 22, 2010, http://cyberbunker.blogfa.com/post/1270.

105 Tavānā, "Islām va-naẓariyat-i pāyān-i ta'rīkh"; Muḥammad-pūr, "Fūkūyāmā ham iʿtirāf mīkonad"; Shahriyār Najafpūr, "Muṭālaʿa-i taṭbīqī-i naẓariyat-i pāyān-i ta'rīkh-i Fūkūyāmā," https://rasekhoon.net/article/show/120494/; Rūḥānī "Furūpāshī-i Amrīkā vāqiʿiyatī-i maḥtūm,"; ʿAlī Reża Samīʿī Iṣfahānī and Yaʿqūb Karīmī Menjarmuʿe, "Pāyān ta'rīkh yā bohran-i idī'ūlūzhī," *Dānesh siyāsī va-beyn milalī* 1 (1391/2012): 23–24.

> Today is the end of history for the failed liberal democracy. The train of progress has come up against the fortress of capitalism. Amid the ruined remains of democracy we will be able to lead mankind toward salvation and security with the light of guidance which Imām Ḥusayn, peace be upon him, has placed in our hands for shedding light on bewildered humanity at the end of history.[106]

Fukuyama's critics argued that the true end of history will come in two phases. First, the consolidation of the "universal governance of the jurist" (*vilāyat-i faqīh jahānī*), in other words, the Iranian system of government that will spread throughout the world as the government of the downtrodden (*mustaż'afān*). This phase will pave the way for the second phase, "the governance of the Mahdī" (*ḥukūmat-i mahdaviyat*), in other words, the Shī'ī messianic vision of the coming of the Twelve Imām as the Mahdī. This end of history, unlike Fukuyama's, is not determined by earthly historical processes but by God's will. It is impossible to predict when it will take place, and the various Shī'ī writers are very careful not to arouse irresponsible messianic expectations; it is, however, inevitable and will, they claim, come to pass.[107]

On comparing the two notions of the end of history, the polemical practice of earlier Islamist modernists has been used, namely, contrasting the more negative aspects of the Western capitalist world with an idyllic future vision of Islam.[108] The Mahdaviyat concept is, according to Iranian scholars, truly universal, and in contrast to Fukuyama's ethnocentric view, will bring together East and West in harmony. Moreover, in the Western liberal "end of history" humanity will not attain true happiness, since liberalism has not solved the conflict between social equality and liberty. Humanity will thus remain hungry for justice, awaiting the coming of the Imām Mahdī who will save it from oppression and elevate it to the realm of sanctity and perfection.[109] In offering

---

106 *Kayhān*, October 20, 2001 cited in Tabaar, "The Beloved Great Satan," 65.

107 Tavānā, "Islām va-naẓariyat-i pāyān-i ta'rīkh"; "G̱harb va-ākhar al-zamān," pt. 2, http://www.mahdaviat.porsemani.ir/content/۲غرب-و-اخرالزمان; Ismā'īl Shafī'ī Sarvestānī, "Gharb va-ākhar al-zamān," (2002), http://www.iec-md.org/farhangi/gharb_aakheroz zamaan_shafiei-sarvestaani.html; Murtażā Shīrūdī, "Inqilāb-i Islāmī va-chisti niẓām-i āyandeh-i jahānī," *Ḥuṣūn* 11 (2007): 42–65, http://www.ensani.ir/fa/content/122667/default.aspx; 'Abd al-Quyūm Sajjādī, "Jahānī-shodan va-mahdaviyat: dō negāh beh āyandeh," *Qabasāt* 33 (1383/2004): 129–142.

108 For this practice, see Houchang Chehabi, *Iranian Politics and Religious Modernism: The Liberation Movement of Iran under the Shah and Khomeini* (London: I.B. Tauris, 1990), 75.

109 Niyāzī, "Pāyān-i ta'rīkh dar andīsheh-i Fūkūyāmā"; Najafpūr, "Mutala'a-i taṭbīqī-i naẓariyat-i pāyān-i ta'rīkh"; Muḥammad Akhavān, "Mahdaviyat va-jang-i tamaddunhā," *Intiẓār Mow'ūd* 16 (1385/2006): 4–5; Qanbar 'Alī Ṣamadī, "Doktrīn-i mahdaviyat

the global Mahdaviyat vision, these writers appear to affirm Bassam Tibi's observation that only Western and Islamic civilizations have universal claims.[110]

The idea that the universal governance of the jurist will precede and precipitate the coming of the Mahdī contradicts traditional Shīʿī eschatology. According to earlier Shīʿī literature, the Mahdī's return was to be preceded by a period of natural catastrophes and human strife or, more specifically, a sequence of five events or signs involving struggles and battles. The Mahdī himself would arise as the "Lord of the Age" or the "Lord of the Sword" to lead his "army of wrath" in its reconquest of the world. The main idea of the anticipated rise of the Mahdī was the redemption of his Shīʿī followers from the oppression that has dominated the world since the Prophet's death and the punishment of their tormentors. This literature was formulated in periods of political distress as a way to offer Shīʿī believers hopes for a better future and a means to adhere to their faith despite the hardships.[111]

By contrast, the process presented by the Iranian writers mentioned above reflects the different political and psychological reality of a self-confident and optimistic Iranian outlook. The historical Mahdī was supposed to redeem his followers from their Sunnī oppressors. But, as with the change that has taken place in the Āshūrā commemorations since the 1970s, the West, particularly the United States, has replaced the Sunnīs as the evil oppressor.[112] Nonetheless, according to the new interpretation, by the time the Mahdī comes, the power of the West will be long gone.[113] Instead of the vengeful traditional eschatology, the new approach is more conciliatory, describing the Mahdavi "end of history" as bringing East and West together but under Shīʿī, not Western, hegemony.

---

va-naẓariyat-i pāyān-i ta'rīkh: vīzhegīhā va-tafāvothā," 19 Mordād 1390/August 10, 2011, http://www.intizar.ir/vdcgrq934ak93.pra.html. Last accessed June 11, 2012; "Jahānī-shodan inqilāb-i Islāmī va-pāyān-i ta'rīkh."

110 Bassam Tibi, *The Challenge of Fundamentalism: Political Islam and the New World Disorder* (Berkeley: University of California Press, 1999), 5.

111 Jassim M. Hussein, *The Occultation of the Twelfth Imam* (London: Muhammadi Trust, 1982), 26–27; David Cook, "Messianism in the Shiʿite Crescent," *Current Trends in Islamist Ideology* 11 (2011): 91–103. (For additional discussions on the rise of the Mahdī, see Chapter 2.)

112 Kamran Scot Aghaie, *The Martyrs of Karbala: Shīʿī Symbols and Rituals in Modern Iran* (Seattle: University of Washington Press, 2004), 80–81. Radical populist groups within the Iranian system continue to disseminate the more apocalyptic view of the coming of the Mahdī, see Amanat, *Apocalyptic Islam and Iranian Shiʿism*; Cook, "Messianism in the Shiite Crescent;" Mariella Ourghi, *Schiitischer Messianismus und Mahdī-Glaube in der Neuzeit* (Würzburg: Ergon, 2008).

113 See, for example, Najafī, *Naẓariyat-i tamaddun-i jadīd-i Islāmī*, 239.

It seems that in the effort to lessen the appeal of Western liberalism, the Shīʿī writers tried to present a benign image of Shīʿī eschatology of global peace and harmony. This image differed sharply from the more vengeful eschatological version that had evolved in the past as part of the conflict with the Sunnī majority and emerged at present in the context of the struggle against the violent jihādī-Salafists.

In addition to expressing this new self-confidence, another possible explanation for this new messianic interpretation is the need to preserve the belief in the Mahdī, which is so central to Shīʿīsm, in a situation where Iran is ruled by the purportedly perfect system of *vilāyat-i faqīh*. Put differently, if the regime can claim that Iran is on its way toward realizing utopia on earth, the surrounding region and the world will still be in need of salvation. This new understanding might also have been an attempt to preempt potential pondering by Shīʿīs or criticism by Sunnī Salafists over the belated coming of the Mahdī, at a time when a powerful Shīʿī religious government is in power and he thus no longer needs to remain in hiding from his potential enemies.

The upheaval that has shaken the Arab world since 2011 initially aroused hopes in Iran for the emergence of a new Islamic Middle East under its leadership. The anticipated regional change was viewed as reinforcement of the inevitable decline of the West. Ahmadinezhad, with his usual flair, described the fall of the Tunisian and Egyptian presidents, Zein al-ʿAbidin Ben ʿAlī and Husni Mubarak, as part of "a global revolution, managed by the imām of the age" and predicted the formation of a world government, ruled by the Twelfth Imām, i.e., the Mahdī. Khamenei, on the other hand, was more down to earth and depicted the change as a clear indication of a regional Islamic awakening and the strategic weakening of the United States. In a speech to the Assembly of Experts in September 2014, for example, he spoke of the inevitable fall of Western power and called upon the Iranians to prepare themselves for the new world order in which Iran would play an important role due to its great capabilities and thanks to Islam and Iranian culture.[114]

Yet, Khamenei was apparently apprehensive that the frequent talks about the imminent fall of the West might end up in grave disappointment should this fall be delayed. Therefore, his office published a statement clarifying that

---

114 "Bayānāt dar dīdār-i jamʿī az madāḥān," May 1, 2013, http://farsi.khamenei.ir/speech-content?id=22443; "Taʾammolī bar Bayānāt-i rahbar-i inqilāb dar dīdār-i khobregān-i rahbarī," pt. 2, *Bultan News*, March 14, 2014, http://www.bultannews.com/fa/news/195528. See also Khamenei's speech "Bayānāt dar dīdār-i shirkat konandegān dar 'kongreh-i jahānī-i jarayānhā-i ifrāṭī va-takfīrī az dīdgāh-i ʿulamāʾ-i Islām," November 25, 2014, http://farsi.khamenei.ir/speech-content?id=28278; ʿAli Parchami, "The 'Arab Spring': The View from Tehran," *Contemporary Politics* 18, no. 1 (2012): 35–52.

he had never set a precise time or date for the inevitable decline and fall of Western civilization but rather anticipates it due to his observations of the internal weaknesses of Western society and the awakening of Islam and the unity of the Muslim people.[115]

The signing of the July 2015 nuclear agreement between Iran and the six world powers (the Joint Comprehensive Plan of Action) intensified the debate between those who saw it as a first step in improving Iran's relations with the world community, and those who regarded it as a threat to the foundations of the Islamic system. Khamenei, who had approved the agreement, was adamant about preventing any deeper economic or cultural integration with the world powers, and particularly any rapprochement with the United States, fearing its implications on the Iran's political, social, and cultural situation.[116] Similar to his past warnings, he came out with a series of declarations, which called upon the Iranians to be on the alert: "The main purpose of the enemies is for Iranians to give up on their revolutionary mentality.... Economic and security breaches are definitely dangerous and have dire consequences but political and cultural intrusion by the enemy is a more serious danger that everyone should be vigilant about."[117] In other words, although the West is destined to decline, it is still capable of threatening the revolution and the country. The specter of the ongoing Western threat thus served as an excuse for the regime to subsequently embark on the largest wave of arrests of dissidents since the large-scale 2009 protests against the fraudulent presidential elections.[118]

On October 14, 2018 Khamenei released a draft of the "Islamic-Iranian Blueprint for Progress," a document including "the ideal horizon of the country for the five decades to come." Under the projected "new Islamic civilization" Iran will, by 2065, enjoy "the leadership of a just, courageous, and capable *Faqīh* [jurist]," and based on "Islam-based policies, rules, and structures," it will be "an international pioneer in producing Islamic human sciences and elevated culture." It will be the leader of a new Islamic civilization, among the top

115 "Pīsh-bīnī-i suqūṭ-i gharb tavassoṭ-i maqām-i muʿaẓẓam-i rahbarī."

116 Alex Vatanka, "Pulling the Strings – How Khamenei Will Prevent Reform in Iran," *Foreign Affairs*, November 25, 2015, https://www.foreignaffairs.com/articles/iran/2015-11-25/pulling-strings.

117 "Leader Urges Vigilance Against U.S. Infiltration," *Kayhān*, September 16, 2015, http://kayhan.ir/en/news/18450/leader-urges-vigilance-against-us-infiltration. Khamenei's official website produced twenty-seven speeches between March and November 2015 (1394 in the Iranian solar calendar), in which he warned of the threat of "the enemy's influence" on Iran, "Nufūẓ-i dushman," http://farsi.khamenei.ir/newspart-index?tid=6592.

118 "Largest Wave of Arrests by Iran's Revolutionary Guards Since 2009," *Center for Human Rights in Iran*, November 19, 2015, http://www.iranhumanrights.org/2015/11/irgc-intelligence-arrests/.

five countries of the world in producing ideas, science, and technology and one of the top ten largest economies. The blueprint envisages a semi-utopian Islamic-Iranian civilization free of Western cultural or ideological influence or threat and emphasizes the harmony between "reason and ḥadīth; science and religion." However, its insistence on the need to prevent the "formation of threats to the Islamic Republic of Iran" and develop the Basīj implies that despite the proclaimed confidence in its inevitable fall, the Western challenge would not disappear.[119]

13 Conclusion

The Shīʿī discourse on the decline of the West should be viewed within the broader debate about Iran's ideological and political path. The West is still a principal "other" for the regime, as it represents the very opposite of its Islamic cultural and ideological essence yet has an ongoing if not increasing allure among segments of the population.

The contradiction between the continuous warnings against the cultural onslaught that threatens the foundations of Iran's Islamic society and the confidence regarding its inevitable and even imminent demise can, at least partially, be explained by the identity process theory. The response to the supposed threat of the West to the identity of the group is an elaboration on the historical depth and uniqueness of the in-group, the East, coupled with calls to mobilize the in-group against this threat.[120] The Western threat cannot be dismissed as a simple pretext for the continual repression of political dissidents. Rather, it reflects a common feature of many modern fundamentalist

---

119 "Farākhwān-i rahbar-i inqilāb barāye takmīl va-irtiqāyi algūyī pāyeh-i Islāmī Irānī pīshraft," 22 Mehr 1397/October 14, 2018, http://farsi.khamenei.ir/news-content?id=40693. Khamenei first raised the concept of "Islamic Iranian progress" on December 1, 2010. On May 24, 2011 he appointed the board of the Center of Islamic Iranian progress, which began publishing a scholarly journal carrying that name in 2012, see "Intiṣāb-i raʾīs va-aʿżāʾ shūrā-i ʿālī-i markaz algūyī Islāmī-Irānī pīshraft," 3 Khordād 1390/May 24, 2014, http://www.icana.ir/Fa/News/165265. Quite a few of the earlier articles that explained it underscored the contrast between progress based on Islamic principles and ideals and progress based on the materialist Western model, e.g., Zaynab Sanchūlī, "Tabyīn-i mahiyat-i algūyī Islāmī Irānī pīshraft," *Alguyi pīshraft Islāmī Irānī* 2, no. 3 (1392/2013): 79–104 and Shuʿayb Bahmand, Masʿūd Jaʿfarī-nezhād, and ʿAlī Reża Golshānī, "Żarūrathā-i tadvīn-i algūyi Islāmī Irānī pīshraft az manẓar-i rahbar-i muʿaẓẓam-i inqilāb-i Islāmī," *Pazhūheshhā-i Inqilāb-i Islāmī* 19 (1395/2017): 107–129.

120 Rusi Jaspal and Marco Cinnirella, "The Construction of Ethnic Identity: Insights from Identity Process Theory," *Ethnicities* 12, no. 5 (2012): 503–530.

movements, combining fear for their cultural identity and cohesion and deep pessimism over the weak nature of humans, which makes them susceptible to the temptations of Western culture and modernity, in the short term with absolute confidence in their victory and success in the long term. The theme of the inevitable decline of the West has been integrated into the traditional Shīʿī messianic belief as a precursor phase for the coming of the Mahdī, who will establish a universal rule of justice instead of the oppressive and corrupt Western system. However, unlike the traditional approach and the apocalyptic view of radical Sunnī jihādī-Salafī organizations, the Iranian vision speaks of a gradual, non-violent "end of history" following the universal rule of the jurist.

There is, however, a paradox: while discussion on the inevitable fall of the West continues, Iranian society itself is undergoing great changes. Some of these, such as a rising marriage age, higher divorce rates, and lower birth rates, have made Iranian society look like Western societies, according to the sober acknowledgement of one Iranian official. Equally significant are the more positive public attitudes toward Western culture; even President Ḥasan Rouhani found it necessary to complete his PhD studies at a British university. One cause of this attitudinal change is disappointment in the state's Islamist ideology.

In view of this growing similarity to the West, it is difficult to gauge just how many Iranian still believe in the inevitable fall of the West. While quite a few advocates of the decline theme genuinely believe in what they say, their discourse may also be viewed as an attempt by the Islamist Republic to boost morale regarding their inevitable long-term victory in light of their failure to instill values among a growing number of subjects.

CHAPTER 2

The Jews as Enemies of Shīʿism

The "Jewish people are the greatest enemy of Islam" and Jews are "the most corrupt" and "seditious group among all human beings" are but two of the many harsh statements against the Jews and Judaism raised in the post-1979 Shīʿī discourse.[1] The prevalence of anti-Jewish statements and the extensive preoccupation with the Jews in modern Shīʿī discourse reflects the role of anti-Semitism alongside anti-Zionism as an important building block in the Islamic Republic's official ideology. Moreover, the alleged Jewish enmity to Shīʿī Islam places them as a central and powerful enemy in the pantheon of the "others" who stand in contrast to the modern Shīʿī-Islamic "self." The current discourse thus emphasizes the importance of studying the Jews as part of the theme of knowing the enemy.

The current anti-Jewish discourse constitutes both continuity and a departure from past Shīʿī attitudes toward Jews, but it is decidedly more one-dimensional and hostile than before. It also borrows from modern European anti-Semitism and is suffused with historical anachronisms when it refers to seventh-century Jews as Zionists or capitalists. Its spokesmen are mainly middle-ranking clerics and writers as well as various organs of religious propagation and writers of semi-official blogs, who actually work for the government and disseminate the official position. The ongoing coverage of such writings by governmental news agencies associated with hardliners in the clerical establishment may point to the factional affiliation of the producers of this discourse.

Although this discourse has been influenced by the Sunnī Islamist one, it retains distinct Shīʿī features, which seem to have attained greater scope and power in recent years. More importantly, they are articulated as part of a more

1 "Qawm-i Yahūd rā behtar beshenāsīm," 26 Khordād 1392/June 16, 2013, http://article.tebyan.net/248084; "Ayatollah Mesbah Yazdi speech on the Jews," January 20, 2010, http://www.terrorism-info.org.il/en/article/18156; Mahdī Taʿeb, ed., *Tabār-i inḥirāf: pazhūheshī dar dushman shināsī-i taʾrīkhī* Vol. 1 (Qom: Muʾasasa-i farhangī valāʾ-i muntaẓar, 1390/2011), 8; Seyyed ʿAlī Ḥusaynī Qūrtānī, "Yahūd rā behtar beshenāsīm," 7 Khordād 1391/May 27, 2012, http://rasekhoon.net/article/print/213036/; "Yahūdiyān, sarsakhtarīn-i dushmanān," 23 Khordād 1393/June 13, 2014, http://mouood.org/component/k2/item/20369; "Buzurgtarīn-i dushman-i idīʾūlūzhīk-i Islām, Amrīkā ast, yā Inglīs, yā vahhābiyān va-salafiyān," http://www.islamquest.net/fa/archive/question/fa29589. The number of books and articles dedicated to the discussion of Jewish enmity toward Islam and Shīʿism in particular is too vast to be enumerated here.

 | DOI:10.1163/9789004444683_004

comprehensive vision of Islamic history. This phenomenon is best explained by two insights. The first, formulated by Esther Webman, is the evolution of the Jew into a metaphor for evil. In other words, the "Jew" is constructed as a functional metaphor, an all-purpose villain, to explain the changing circumstances and catastrophes that have befallen Arab societies.[2] The second is David Nirenberg's definition of "Judaism" and "anti-Judaism." "Judaism" is not only the religion of a specific people with specific beliefs but also a category, a set of ideas and attributes with which non-Jews can make sense of and criticize their world. Hence, "anti-Judaism" is not simply an attitude toward Jews and their religion but "a powerful theoretical framework for making sense of the world." Accordingly, "anti-Judaism puts old ideas about Judaism to new kinds of work in thinking about the world; to show this work engaged the past and transformed it; and to ask how that work reshaped the possibilities for thought in the future." Anti-Judaism thus invoked the threat of Judaism to make critical sense of its cosmos.[3] Nirenberg's observation is particularly helpful in explaining the Shīʿī Iranian case, with the Jews serving as the explanation and source of many of the misfortunes that have befallen the Shīʿīs in history and associated with the perceived modern threats to the correct Shiʿi Islamic way of life. A case in point is Ayatollah Jaʿfar Subḥānī's argument that the slogan "fewer children better life," originally used to promote birth control, is Jewish, and his subsequent identification of the Westernized lifestyle as Jewish and therefore a threat to Islam.[4]

In analyzing the psychological motives underlying the manifestation of anti-Semitism and anti-Zionism in Iran, Rusi Jaspal described them as strategies for coping with identity threat and helping to restore feelings of belonging within the Muslim world and beyond. Accordingly, the accentuation of intergroup (Muslim-Jewish) distinctiveness is conducive to the accentuation of intra-group (Muslim) belonging.[5] In other words, anti-Semitism is also part of Shīʿī-Iranian efforts to soften the Sunnī-Shīʿī cleavage by blaming the Jews, rather than mainstream Sunnīs, for Islam's perceived deviation from its correct historical and moral path. Since anti-Semitism in the Islamic Republic has

2 Esther Webman, "The 'Jew' as a Metaphor for Evil in Arab Public Discourse," *The Journal of the Middle East and Africa* 6, no. 3–4 (2015): 275–292.

3 David Nirenberg, *Anti-Judaism: The Western Tradition* (New York: W.W. Norton, 2013), 3, 5, 169, 464.

4 "Ayatollah Subḥānī: farzand-i kamtar zindigī behtar, shiʿārī Yahūdī va-bar khīlāf-i Islām ast," 15 Shahrīvar 1389/September 6, 2010, http://www.irna.ir/fa/NewsPrint.aspx?ID=2000621401.

5 Rusi Jaspal, "Anti-Semitism and Anti-Zionism in Iran: The Role of Identity Processes," *Israel Affairs* 19, no. 2 (2013): 267–284. Jaspal further developed these ideas in his book *Antisemitism and Anti-Zionism: Representation, Cognition, and Everyday Talk* (London: Routledge, 2014).

been the subject of quite a few studies, the focus of this chapter now turns to analyzing those aspects that pertain to the portrayal of the Jews as enemies of Shīʿīsm as part of the broader phenomenon of consolidating the boundaries between Shīʿīs and "others."

1 Anti-Judaism in Traditional Shīʿīsm

Pre-modern Shīʿīsm espoused a dual approach toward the Jews. Like Sunnī Islam, it blamed the Jews for rejecting the teaching of the Prophet Muḥammad, for distorting and falsifying the true scriptures given to them by Moses, and for a host of immoral activities. Unlike Sunnī Islam – and most likely due to the adoption of pre-Islamic Zoroastrian concepts of ritual purity – Shīʿī doctrine traditionally regarded the Jews as ritually "unclean."[6]

In the sphere of reglious polemics, Muslim writings against Judaism, both Sunnī and Shīʿī, took second place to those against Christianity; the Jews did not posed the same challenge due to their smaller number and the absence of a strong external church backing them. The two most predominant themes were locating internal contradictions in the Jewish scriptures in order to prove their forgery or falsification by the Jews or proving the prevalence of abrogation (*naskh*) in the Jewish scriptures in order to show that the Bible had been abrogated by the Qurʾān.[7] Muslim polemics against Christianity declined significantly in the post-classical age of Islam, following the conversion of the vast majority of Christians to Islam. They were revived in the nineteenth century in an effort to refute Christian missionaries who came to the Muslim world.

At the same time, early Shīʿī traditions often equated Shīʿīs with the biblical "Children of Israel" or, more moderately, saw the Jews as a prototype of Shīʿīsm, similar to Christianity which viewed itself as the "true Israel" (*verus Israel*).[8] Joel Kramer went further and stated that a "striking socio-religious

---

6 For the transfer of such themes from Zoroastrianism to Shīʿīsm, see Sorour Soroudi, "The Concept of Jewish Impurity and its Reflection in Persian and Judeo-Persian Traditions," *Irano Judaica*, III (1993): 1–29. For Jewish impurity in Shīʿī law, see Daniel Tsadik, *Between Foreigners and Shiʿis: Nineteenth-Century Iran and Its Jewish Minority* (Stanford: Stanford University Press, 2007), 17–21.

7 Camilla Adang, *Muslim Writers on Judaism and the Hebrew Bible: From Ibn Rabban to Ibn Hazm* (New York: Brill, 1996); Moshe Perlman, "The Medieval Polemics Between Islam and Judaism," in *Religion in a Religious Age*, ed. S.D. Goitein (Cambridge, MA: Association for Jewish Studies, 1974), 103–38.

8 For an analysis of this dualism, see Meir Barasher, "Les fils d'Israël, prototypes de la Chi'a: Notes sur quelques traditions exégétiques du chi'isme duodécimain," *Perspectives (Revue de l'Université Hébraïque de Jérusalem)* 9 (2002): 125–137; Steven Wasserstrom, *Between Muslim*

phenomenon during [the Būyīd] period [945–1055] was a rapprochement between Jews and Shīʿīs."[9]

Following the unification of Iran by the Ṣafavīd dynasty in 1501 and the transformation of Shīʿīsm into the religion of state, attitudes toward Jews worsened significantly. In earlier periods economic competition between Shīʿīs and Jews in the areas of present-day Iraq might have bred such antagonism. But this could not have been the case in Ṣafavīd Iran, as the Jews were a small and poor community that played an insignificant role in Iran's economy and society.

One possible reason for Shīʿī intolerance, which was also occasionally directed against heterodox Islamic sects in Iran, was the Shīʿīs' sense of insecurity, prompted by their own fate as a persecuted minority in the more distant past. The self-confident majority Sunnīs, on the other hand, could afford to be more generous toward minorities, although this tolerance diminished as of the late nineteenth century with the growing sense of the Western threat to Islam. Another reason for this intolerance may have been Sunnī polemics against Shīʿīsm, which pointed to parallels between the Shīʿī and Jewish doctrines and culminated in the maxim "the *rāfiḍa* [Shīʿīs] are the Jews of our umma [community]."[10] The charge of Shīʿī similarity or even identity with the Jews and Judaism has become much more prevalent and virulent among modern-day Wahhābīs and Salafists.[11] One way of refuting such accusations has been to take a stronger anti-Jewish position.

In addition to imposing social and economic restrictions on the Jews and disseminating anti-Jewish statements in both juridical treatises and religious polemics against Judaism, Shīʿī Iran was the only Muslim country to conduct mass enforced conversions of Jews.[12] These anti-Jewish tendencies continued well into the nineteenth century under the Qājār dynasty. While all

---

and Jew: The Problem of Symbiosis under Early Islam (Princeton: Princeton University Press, 2014), 93–135.

9 Joel L. Kramer, *Humanism in the Renaissance of Islam: The Cultural Revival During the Buyid Age* (Leiden: Brill, 1992), 79.

10 For an analysis of these parallels and of the cultural implications of this maxim, see Wasserstrom, *Between Muslim and Jew*, 93–135.

11 For an analysis of these charges, see Isaac Hasson, *Contemporary Polemics Between Neo-Wahhabis and Post-Khomeinist Shiʿites* (Washington DC: Hudson Institute, 2009).

12 Vera Moreen, "The Problems of Conversion Among Iranian Jews in the Seventeenth and Eighteenth Centuries," *Iranian Studies* 19, no. 3–4 (1986): 215–228; Roger M. Savory, "Relations Between the Safavid State and Its Non-Muslim Minorities," *Islam and Christian-Muslim Relations* 14, no. 4 (2003): 435–458; Rula Jurdi Abisaab, *Converting Persia: Religion and Power in the Safavid Empire* (London: I.B. Tauris, 2011), 63, 103–104, 127; Mehrdad Amanat, *Jewish Identities in Iran: Resistance and Conversion to Islam and the Bahāʾī Faith* (London: I.B. Tauris, 2011), 37–60.

non-Muslim minorities faced discrimination, the Jews fared worse than the Christians because they were less important economically.[13]

A new element appearing in the late nineteenth century was the influence of European racism and the myths of Aryan racial superiority on various Westernized Iranians. Such ideas retained a certain degree of influence during the reign of Reżā Shāh (1925–1941), and were also manifested in the prevalence of anti-Jewish attitudes in popular culture.[14]

2 From Anti-Judaism to Modern Anti-Semitism

In the post-World War II period, Muslim writers, both clerics and laypeople, have focused on the West, which is associated with Christianity, but they deal mostly with its secular aspects. Judaism and Jews became popular targets of Islamic polemics or attacks, not because they may attract Muslims but because they are associated with Western-dominated modernity and the dichotomy between the West and Islam. In addition, the establishment of Jewish sovereignty challenges the proper world order in which, according to the Islamic view, Jews should be inferior to Muslims. Hence, the anti-Jewish discourse combines both traditional and modern themes, but the latter can be seen as more forceful today, because they reflect the sense of Muslim frustration and anger at the modern world and serve the Iranian regime's need to produce enemies.

The reign of Muḥammad Reżā Shāh, however, was the "golden era" of Iranian Jewry, which reached unprecedented achievements both intellectually and materially. It was also a period of extensive Iranian-Israeli economic, military, and strategic cooperation. Nonetheless, various clerics and pro-Islamist intellectuals continued to propagate strong anti-Zionist and anti-Jewish views.[15] The growing rift in the early 1960s between Muḥammad Reżā Shāh and the

13 For the situation of the Jews in the Qājār period, see Tsadik, *Between Foreigners and Shi'is*; David Yeroushalmi, *The Jews of Iran in the Nineteenth Century: Aspects of History, Community, and Culture* (Leiden: Brill, 2009); Daniel Tsadki, "Judeo-Persian Communities of Iran, v. Qajar Period (1786–1925)," *Encyclopedia Iranica*, http://www.iranicaonline.org/articles/judeo-persian-communities-v-qajar-period.

14 Amnon Netzer, "Antisemitism in Iran, 1925–1950," *Peamim* 29 (1987): 6–8 (Hebrew). For popular attitudes, see Orly Rahimiyan, "'The Jew Has a Lot of Money, Too': Representations of Jews in Twentieth-Century Iranian Culture," in *Constructing Nationalism in Iran: From the Qajars to the Islamic Republic*, ed. Meir Litvak (Abingdon: Routledge, 2017), 173–189.

15 David Menashri, "The Jews of Iran: Between the Shah and Khomeini," in *Anti-Semitism in Times of Crisis*, ed. Sander Gilman and Steven Katz (New York: New York University Press, 1991), 353–371; Mahdi Ahouie, "Iranian Anti-Zionism and the Holocaust: A Long Discourse Dismissed," *Radical History Review* 105 (2009): 58–78.

Islamic opposition exacerbated Islamist Iranian animosity toward Israel due to the latter's alliance with the Shāh. A more important shift took place in Iranian intellectual discourse, which increasingly depicted the West as the source of Iran's problems. This change impacted attitudes toward Zionism and Judaism, which were now perceived by the Shāh's opponents as offshoots of Western imperialism established in order to oppress the Muslims.[16]

These developments reflected a shift in Iran from traditional anti-Judaism to modern anti-Semitism. Anti-Judaism refers to disdain for Jews and hostile attitudes toward Judaism and aims primarily at undermining Judaism's religious validity. The shift to anti-Semitism is evident in the growing demonization of the Jews as an active threat to Islam and Iran and the reliance on conspiracy theories, themes, and terminology borrowed from European anti-Semitism. The heavy political component of the new discourse, shown by linking the Jews to other modern political enemies of the Shīʿa, similarly marks this transition.[17]

It was Khomeini, who made anti-Semitism a central component of Iran's Islamic ideology. Already on the first page of his major ideological treatise, *Vilāyat-i Faqīh: Ḥukūmat-i Islāmī* (The governance of the jurist: Islamic government), Khomeini charged that Islam was "from the very beginning ... afflicted by the Jews, for it was they who established anti-Islamic propaganda and engaged in various stratagems" against the Muslims. Following their ancestors, he went on, the Jews and Christians conspired against Islam in the modern period as well, seeking to undermine its most important feature of being a comprehensive and total system of law that governs society and state. For that purpose, the Jews joined hands with other groups – "more satanic than them" – in order to facilitate the imperialist penetration of the Muslim countries. Their main goal was the "extirpation of Islam" and the sowing of doubt and confusion in the hearts of Muslims, since "Islam and its ordinances were the main obstacle in the path of their materialistic ambitions." In addition, the West, with both its Jewish and Christian elements, resists the just cause of Islam and its expansion to the "four corners of the globe." According to Khomeini, the Jews, "may God curse them ... are opposed to the very foundations of Islam and wish to establish Jewish domination throughout the world." Like other Islamic thinkers, Khomeini sometimes describes the Jews as treacherous agents of the

16 Ibid., 60–63.

17 For the difference between anti-Judaism and anti-Semitism, see Gavin Langmuir, *Toward a Definition of Antisemitism* (Berkeley: University of California Press, 1990), particularly 57–99; Susannah Heschel, "Historiography of Antisemitism Versus Anti-Judaism: A Response to Robert Morgan," *Journal for the Study of the New Testament* 33, no. 3 (2011): 257–279.

West and, at other times, as the real power that stands behind the West's offensive against Islam.[18] Linking Judaism and Zionism, Khomeini maintained that the most overt manifestation of the Jewish-Christian conspiracy against Islam was the establishment of Israel by Western imperialism in order to oppress the Muslims. Both Khomeini and Khamenei, stated that the occupation of Palestine by the Jews is part of a satanic design by the British and the Americans to "sow the seeds of disunity among Muslims."[19]

3 The Islamic Republic: Anti-Zionism and Anti-Semitism

Ever since assuming power in 1979, the new Iranian leaders sought to render their anti-Jewish animosity more presentable. Spokesmen for the Islamic regime claimed to distinguish between Zionists, whom they vehemently opposed, and Jews, who should be treated with tolerance.[20] Under the Islamic regime Iranian Jews enjoy tolerance though not full equality. This attitude presumably seeks to demonstrate that under the benevolent rule of Islam Jews can live peacefully as a protected subordinated minority and that there is therefore no justification for the aspiration of Jewish sovereignty, i.e., Zionism. The Iranian Constitution allocated one seat in parliament to a representative of the Jewish community, who always backs the regime's anti-Zionist line. Moreover, reflecting a shift from traditional religious anti-Judaism to modern ideology is the nullification of the issue of Jewish impurity, so important in the past, as stated by Khamenei.[21] Similarly, Iranian discourse distinguishes between the

---

18 Rūḥollah Khumaynī, *Al-Ḥukūma al-Islāmiyya* (Beirut: Dār al-Ṭalīʿa, 1979), 7; Rūḥollah Khomeini, *Islam and Revolution: Writings and Declarations of Imam Khomeini*, trans. and annot. Hamid Algar (Berkeley: Mizan Press, 1981), 27, 47.

19 Hamid Dabashi, *Theology of Discontent: The Ideological Foundations of the Islamic Revolution in Iran* (New York: New York University Press, 1993), 426; "Leader: Muslims can no more remain indifferent towards suppressions of Palestinians (24.4.2001)," http://www.khamenei.de/imam_gb/news/news2001/april2001.htm.

20 Rūḥollah Khumaynī, *al-Qaḍiyya al-filasṭīniyya* fī *kalām al-imām al-Khumaynī* (Beirut: Dār al-wasīla, 1996), 47–51; ʿAlī Akbar Vīlāyatī, *Irān wa-*falasṭīn *(1867–1937), judhūr al-ʿalāqa wa-taqallubāt al-siyāsa* (Beirut: Dār al-Ḥaqq, 1997), 14; ʿAlī Khamenei, *Felestīn az manẓar-i ḥażrat-i Ayat Allah al-ʿuzmā Khāmenehi* (Tehrān: Inqilāb-i Islāmī, 1391/2012), 44, 392.

21 "9320–3: Physical contact with non-Muslims," http://www.khamenei.de/imam_gb/fatwas/12quesions.htm. While a few conservative clerics, most notably Ayatollah Muḥammad Taqī Bahjat, still regard non-Muslims as internally and spiritually unclean, other leading clerics such as Grand Ayatollahs Javād Tabrīzī, Vaḥīd Khorāsānī, and ʿAlī Sistānī adopted the new approach, see Markaz-i millī-i pāsokhgūyi-i beh suʾālāt-i dīnī, "Nejes-i būdan ahl-i kitāb," 30 Mordād 1389/August 21, 2010, http://www.pasokhgoo

local Jewish community, which "behaves well" and knows its place as a subordinated minority, and the Jews as a collective or concept.[22]

Thus, the post-1979 Shīʿī discourse conflates the Jews with other modern perceived threats and challenges to (Shīʿī) Islam and Iran, namely, the West in its various manifestations that range from the Freemasons to capitalism and popular culture, Wahhābism, and radical Sunnī jihādī-Salafīsm.[23] While Shīʿī Islamists, like their Sunnī counterparts, reject Western cultural influence as an anathema to authentic Islamic culture, they have not shied away from borrowing anti-Jewish ideas from that same West in the service of their cause.[24]

Yet, as far as ideology and religious discourse about the Jews as a historical or cultural collective are concerned, there is hardly any distinction between Judaism and Zionism. Anti-Jewish expressions and motifs appear in the writings and statements of clerics, in scholarly books and articles published by the Qom learning complex, in pseudo-scholarly TV programs, and in tens if not hundreds of semi-official websites and blogs focusing on Judaism.[25] Israel has

---

.ir/node/17135; "Kuffār aʿam az ahl-i kitāb va-ghayr-i ān ṭibq-i fatāwā-i Ayat Allah Bahjat nejes hastand," 3 Esfand 1389/February 22, 2011, http://www.porseshkadeh.com/Question/25560.

22 There are some exceptions to this approach. Ayatollah Rūḥollah Qarahī, for example, accused Iranian Jews of serving Israel and Zionism, "Yahūd shināsī az nigāhī-i ustād-i Qarahī," 23 Azar 1390/December 14, 2011, http://boyekhoshebandegi.blogfa.com/post/31.

23 Salmān Qāsimī, *Yahūdiyān banī Isrā'īl va-farāmāsōnarī* (Iṣfahān: Kiyārād, 1391); Hārūn Yaḥyā, "Dāstān-i ḥaqīqī-i Qābāla," *Mowʿūd*, 62 (1385/ 2006): 34–39; "Asrār-i farāmāsōnhā: Yahūdiyān-i farāmāsōn chegūneh jahān rā idāra mīkonand?," 18 Khordād 1396/June 8, 2017, http://www.historywonders.ir/2017/06/08/; "Farāmāsōnarī farzand-i khwānde nā-mashrūʿ-i Yahūd," http://masoner.persianblog.ir/post/7/; "Nemādhā-i muhim Yahūdī va-māsōnī," 23 Tīr 1392/July 14, 2013, https://www.porseman.com/article/134966/نمادهای-مهم-یهودی-و-ماسونی; "Irtibāṭ-i farāmāsōnarī bā ṣahyūnīsm va-shayṭān-parastī," 16 Esfand 1393/March 7, 2015, http://www.adyannet.com/fa/news/14930. The Masonic conspiracy was invented by right-wing groups in Europe as early as the eighteenth century and has been a popular theme in both anti-Semitic and anti-Enlightenment literature ever since. "Freemasonry," *Holocaust Encyclopedia*, https://www.ushmm.org/wlc/en/article.php?ModuleId=10007186. The first lodge of the Freemasons in Iran was established in 1858 by the reformist Mīrzā Malkam Khān. It later became synonymous in the minds of the clergy with negative Western influence. Hamid Algar, "An Introduction to the History of Freemasonry in Iran," *Middle Eastern Studies* 6, no. 3 (1970): 276–296.

24 Henri Ford's *The International Jew* was translated into Persian, published by the official Islamic Culture and Relations Organization, and displayed at the Iranian pavilion at the 2005 international book fair, "The Booksellers of Tehran," *The Wall Street Journal*, October 28, 2005. See also the publication of David Duke's, *Bartarī ṭalabī Yahūd* (Tehrān: Amīr Kabir, 1393/2014).

25 The term semi-official refers to websites and organizations that are not officially part of the government, but are financed by it and reflect its views.

often been referred to as "the Jewish entity," a "bunch of Jews,"[26] with the Jews in the diaspora being referred to as Zionists.[27]

Various writers, such as Ayatollah Rūḥollah Qarahī, director of the Mahdī seminary in Qom, rejected any distinction between Judaism and Zionism, asserting that they are "made of the same cloth."[28] Like their Sunnī counterparts, the semi-official *Tebyān* website described Zionism as the manifestation of Jewish corruption.[29] Others have explained that the Jews dominate the world through the "Zionist lobby."[30]

Since Islamists have often failed to draw sharp distinctions between the past and the present,[31] they apply the label Zionist anachronistically to the past. Grand Ayatollah Ḥusayn Nūrī-Hamadānī (b. 1925), for example, referred to the Jews of Medina at the time of the Prophet as "the center of Zionists."[32] Ḥujjat al-Islam Muḥammad Ibrāhīm-niyā of the Anṣār al-Mahdī organization accused Zionist Jews of playing a key role in the traumatic event that gave birth to the Shīʿa, namely, the usurpation of the caliphate from ʿAlī, the Prophet's

---

26 *Siyāsat-i rūz*, April 8, 2003 (FBIS-DR); *Intikhāb* (*Entekhab*), April 20, 2003; *Iran*, May 15, 2003.

27 *Kayhān*, June 13, 2002; *Jumhūrī-i Islāmī*, May 20, 2003.

28 "Yahūdīhā va-ṣahyūnīsthā az yek qimāsh hastand," n.d., http://mahdaviun.blogfa.com/post-36.aspx; "Yahūd shināsī az nigāhī-i ustād-i Qarahī;" "ʿIlal va-ʿavāmil-i dushmanī-i Yahūd bar Islam," 24 Bahman 1391/February 12, 2013, http://www.mouood.org/component/k2/item/7960-علل-و-عوامل-دشمنی-یهود-با-اسلام.html. Ḥasan Raḥīm-pūr Azghadī, a prolific anti-Jewish writer, calls his blog "Ṣahyūnī setīzī" (Anti-Zionism), but his URL address is under the Iranian category of anti-Semitism, see http://antisemitism.blogfa.com/post-1.aspx; Aḥmad Karīmyān, *Yahūd va-ṣahyūnīsm: taḥlīl-i ʿanāṣir-i qawmī, taʾrīkhī va-dīnī-i yek fājiʿa* (Qom: Bustān, 1389/2010).

29 "Vaʿdah-i ilāhī nisbat beh nābūdī-i Yahūdiyān," 2 Azar 1391/November 22, 2012, http://www.tebyan.net/newindex.aspx/index.aspx?pid=934&articleid=751771. See also Ḥujjat al-Islām Abū-l-Fatḥ Daʿvatī in "Dirāsa ḥawla ẓuhūr wa-burūz wa-ʿaqībat qawm al-Yahūd min manẓar al-Qurʾān al-karīm," September 22, 2009, http://iqna.ir/ar/news/1828520, and "Ānūsī chīst va-cherā bāyad muslimīn ānūsīhā rā beshenāsad," 31 Mehr 1389/October 23, 2010, http://www.andishehha.com/view/6048.

30 "Yahūdiyān-i makhfī," 23 Shahrīvar 1390/September 14, 2011, http://www.mouood.org/component/k2/item/2022-یهودیان-مخفی.html.

31 Jacob Lassner, *The Middle East Remembered: Forged Identities, Competing Narratives, Contested Spaces* (Ann Arbor: University of Michigan Press, 2000), 28. See also Emmanuel Sivan, *Islamic Fundamentalism and Anti-Semitism* (Jerusalem, 1985) (Hebrew), who explained that modern fundamentalists seek to "settle historical accounts" with the enemies of Islam in earlier times.

32 *Iran*, May 15, 2003; IRNA, January 17, 1998; "Ayatollah Nouri-Hamedani: 'Fight the Jews and Vanquish Them So As To Hasten the Coming of the Hidden Imam,'" MEMRI, Special Dispatch Series no. 897, April 22, 2005, https://www.memri.org/reports/ayatollah-nouri-hamedani-%E2%80%98fight-jews-and-vanquish-them-so-hasten-coming-hidden-imam%E2%80%99.

cousin and son-in-law, following the Prophet's death.[33] The two most blatant expressions of the confluence between anti-Zionism and anti-Semitism in Iran are the dissemination of the notorious anti-Semitic tract, *The Protocols of the Elders of Zion*, and Holocaust denial.[34] In recent years, the *Protocols* have been widely cited by numerous clerics and other writers as an authentic historical document exposing Jewish machinations. In the words of Basīj writer Keyvān Majīdī, if the Jews claim that the *Protocols* are a forgery, then "how can it be that all the plans and pledges given in these protocols have taken place without pre-planning."[35]

Iran's Holocaust denial is a manifestation of anti-Semitism disguised as anti-Zionism. Using the pretext of the Zionist fabrication of the Holocaust, Iran distorts and denies Jewish history by presenting their worst tragedy as a scam, even though it has nothing to do with Zionism per se. This denial appeals to the anti-Semitic tendency to charge the Jews with unscrupulous plotting in order to achieve illegitimate and immoral goals, mainly financial extortion.[36]

---

33 "Naqsh-i Yahūdiyān-i *ṣahyūnīst* dar ghasb-i khilāfat-i amīr al-mu'minīn ṣalvāt-i Allah ʿalayhi wa-salam," http://intiqam.blogfa.com/post-23.aspx; Ḥujjat al-Islām Muḥammad Reżā Ṭabāṭabā'ī, "Naqsh-i jarayān-i Masīḥī-Yahūdī dar tarbiyat-i Yazīd," 15 Abān 1393/November 6, 2014, http://www.farsnews.com/printable.php?nn=13930812000133; "Yūḥānā muʿallīm-i Yazīd beshenāsīd," 19 Abān 1392/November 10, 2013, http://www.mouood.org/component/k2/item/15236-یوحنا-معلم-یزید-را-بشناسید.html. See also the website http://www.yahood.net, which focuses on Judaism and Jews and speaks about Zionist extremism throughout history.

34 Orly R. Rahimiyan, "The Protocols of the Elders of Zion in Iranian Political and Cultural Discourse," *The Global Impact of the Protocols of the Elders of Zion: A Century-Old Myth*, ed. Esther Webman (London: Routledge, 2012), 196–219; "The Protocols of the Elders of Zion, An Iranian Perspective," MEMRI, Special Dispatch Series no. 98, June 7, 2000, https://www.memri.org/reports/protocols-elders-zion-iranian-perspective; "Iranian TV Series Based on the Protocols of the Elders of Zion and the Jewish Control of Hollywood," MEMRI, Special Dispatch Series no. 705, May 1, 2004, https://www.memri.org/reports/iranian-tv-series-based-protocols-elders-zion-and-jewish-control-hollywood, and "Antisemitism and Holocaust Denial in the Iranian Media," MEMRI, Special Dispatch Series no. 855, January 28, 2005, https://www.memri.org/reports/antisemitism-and-holocaust-denial-iranian-media.

35 Keyvān Majīdī, "Vāqiʿiyat-i Yahūd setīzī: protokolhā-i zuʿamā'-i ṣahyūn," 18 Dey 1389/January 8, 2011, http://basij-ganjnameh.persianblog.ir/post/84/ (Last accessed March 10, 2013).

36 For analysis of Holocaust denial in Iran, see Meir Litvak, "The Islamic Republic of Iran and the Holocaust: Anti-Semitism and Anti-Zionism," *The Journal of Israeli History* 25, no. 1 (2006): 267–284; Meir Litvak, "Iranian Anti-Semitism and the Holocaust," in *Antisemitism Before and Since the Holocaust: Altered Contexts and Recent Perspectives*, ed. Anthony McElligott and Jeffrey Herf (New York: Palgrave-McMillan, 2017), 205–229;

Finally, practicing certain intellectual gymnastics, differentiations are made by some between Judaism "as a divine message," which is part of the holy scriptures, and "the people called Jews," whose history is replete with "hostility, slander, schemes, and conspiracies."[37] Quite a few writers have rejected, however, the charges of anti-Semitism, describing this allegation as a malicious ploy in the psychological warfare used by the Zionists to justify their illegitimate presence in Palestine. Others have described it as a fiction created by Jewish historians in order to portray the Jews as innocent victims and hide their own malicious schemes.[38] One writer, for example, denied the existence of anti-Semitism, explaining that it is "Jewishness" itself that is the problem. Being Jewish is essentially both embracing a sense of superiority over other people and imbibing deep fears and paranoia from them. Judaism is, he claimed, neither a race nor a religion but a "mental disease." The only cure for this disease is for the Jews to reject and deny Judaism, he concluded.[39]

Most writers, when speaking of the Jewish-Muslim and, particularly, the Jewish-Shīʿī conflict, have referred to the Jews as a "people" (*qawm*) and

---

Matthias Küntzel, *Unholy Hatreds: Holocaust Denial and Antisemitism in Iran*, Vidal Sasson International Center for the Study of Antisemitism, no. 8, 2007; Ahouie, "Iranian Anti-Zionism and the Holocaust;" Soli Shahvar, "The Islamic Regime in Iran and Its Attitude toward the Jews: The Religious and Political Dimensions," *Immigrants & Minorities* 27, no. 1 (2009): 94–98.

37 Muḥsin Muḥammadī, "Muvājaha-i Islām bā ṣahyūnīsm, tamadduni ast neh siyāsī," 15 Azar 1395/December 5. 2016, https://www.farsnews.com/news/13950915000103; Mahdī Khazʿalī, "Poshtbordeh ānūsīhā," 15 Mordād 1389/6 August 6, 2010, http://k4t8u2.blogspot.com/2010/10/blog-post_7023.html; "Hizbullah Deputy Secretary-General Sheik Naim Qassem on the Difference Between Jews and Zionists," MEMRI, Clip no. 1298, October 17, 2006, https://www.memri.org/tv/hizbullah-deputy-secretary-general-sheik-naim-qassem-difference-between-jews-and-zionists/transcript; Mujtabā Ranjī, "Ishtirākāt-i ʿaqīdatī Vahhābiyat va-Yahūdiyat," 20 Esfand 1393/March 11, 2015, http://www.jahannews.com/sound/411939.

38 Ibrāhīm Rajablū, "Jang-i ravānī-i ṣahyūnīsm, mafāhīm va-mażamīn," *Ḥawza* 189, 28 Mordād 1385/August 19, 2006; "Tuhmat-i Yahūdsetīzī be mathābat-i yek silāḥ-i siyāsī manfaʿat ṭalabāneh," 27 Farvradīn 1389/April 16, 2010, http://www.farsnews.net/newstext.php?nn=8901141028; Muʾasasa-i muṭālaʿāt-i va-taḥqīqāt-i beyne almilalī, *Az afsāneh-i Yahūdīsetīzī tā vāqiʿiyat-i Islām setīzī* (Qom, 1394/2015); ʿAlī Reżā Sulṭān-Shāhī, *Yahūd setīzī (anti Semitism) vāqiʿiyat yā dastavīz-i siyāsī* (PhD diss., Dāneshgāh-i āzād Islāmī, 1381/2002); "Naqsh-i ṣahyūnīsm dar Yahūd setīzī," 7 Mordād 1387/July 28, 2008, http://www.aftabir.com/articles/view/politics/world/c1c1217232350_zionism_p1.php; "Aligārshī-i Yahūdī va-usṭūra-i inkīzīsion," 25 Tīr 1395/July 15, 2015, http://www.mouood.org/component/k2/item/36945.

39 "Ḥimāyat bī qayd va-sharṭ az Yahūdiyān tahdīdī ʿalayh-i javāmiʿ-i basharī," 23 Farvardīn 1389/April 12, 2010, http://www.farsnews.net/newstext.php?nn=8901211582. It was disseminated in other blogs and websites dedicated to fighting Zionism, e.g., http://zionistregime.blogfa.com/post-43.aspx and http://4palestine.blogfa.com/post-65.aspx.

explained that Jewish identity is based on genealogical continuity and not religious belief since affiliation to Judaism is only by blood.[40] The use of the term "*qawm*" probably stems from this emphasis on a continued Jewish identity and the actions of those Jews who converted to Islam but allegedly harmed Islam from within as part of the Jewish scheme.[41] In other words, Jewishness was and is an immutable attribute regardless of conversion to other religions. This designation differs from the dominant Arab terminology that refuses to recognize Jewish peoplehood and insists that Jews only share a religious belief. While such discourse contains racist undertones, it is different from racist Western anti-Semitism since it focuses on the religious and cultural conflict and the idiom of speech is religious rather than racial.

4 The Jews as the Enemy

The central theme of the anti-Semitic discourse in Iran constitutes an almost classic case of psychological projection by depicting the Jews as historical enemies who are motivated by hatred against Islam and the Muslims, in particular, Shīʿīsm.[42] If the West is currently the greatest threat to Islam, then the Jews, portrayed as Islam's greatest enemy from its inception, now merge with the West in the modern age. Such a formulation presents Shīʿīsm as not only a major target or victim of Jewish animosity but also its complete and morally superior opposite.

Starting from a pure theological vantage point, a state-controlled Q&A website on Islam cites five categories of enemies enumerated in the Qur'ān with the Jews as a category of their own, distinct from ordinary infidels, pagans, and hypocrites and second only to Satan, thus indicating their central position. Other writers maintained that the Qur'ān places the Jews as the number one enemy, ahead of the pagans and Christians.[43] The Jews thus wage a war

---

40 Zāhidī, "Ta'rīkhcheh-i tharvat andūzī-i zarsālārān-i Yahūd." See also Mu'asasa-i farhangī va-iṭṭilāʿ-i rasānī-i Tebyān, *Yahūda dīnī ke dar rāh-i shaytān qadam bar mīdārad* (Qom: 1395/2016), 1–2.

41 See the sources cited in note 1 above.

42 Psychological projection denotes a shift of the border between the self and the world in favor of the self, attributing to the "other" those repulsive or harmful aspects of the self.

43 "Dushman shināsī va-rāhkārhā-i muqābala bar an az manẓar-i Qur'ān chīst?," http://www.islamquest.net/fa/archive/question/fa35070; a group of authors, *Darsnāmah-i ta'rīkh-i taḥlīlī-i dushman shināsī*, vol. 1 (Qom: Mu'asasa-i iṭṭilāʿ rasānī va-muṭālaʿāt-i farhangī-i lawḥ va-qalam, 1383/2004), 14.

on Islam on a broad front, ranging from brutal murders through economic investments to cultural raids. According to this narrative, they play a key role in disseminating Islamophobia (*Islam setīzī*) all over the world; as one writer explained, wherever there is injustice and oppression against Muslims, there are Jews standing behind it. Elsewhere it has been charged that all prominent Muslim intellectuals who were critical of religion, most notably Aḥmad Kasravī (assassinated in 1946 by Islamist terrorists) and Salman Rushdie, were influenced by the Jews or had been members of "Zionist freemason" organizations.[44] The arch conservatives Miṣbāḥ Yazdī and Ḥujjat al-Islam Mahdī Ṭā'ib, head of the Iranian Ammār think tank that advises Khamenei, accused the Jews of seeking to rule the world and destroy Islam.[45]

The reasons for the Jews' enmity toward Islam are, apparently, ingrained in their negative traits, which are enumerated in the Qur'ān and have been revealed by their conduct throughout history. Key among these are disobedience and defiance of God and brutality "even toward their own women and children,"[46] as "there is no difference between them and animals."[47] The Jews harbor aggression and rancor against all others and are hostile toward reason. They are depicted as cunning, manipulative, and lacking any conscience; they are, in addition, morally corrupt and thus threaten the morality of the family, the bastion of Muslim society. In discussing Jewish conspiracies against Iranian youth, one of the Shīʿī writers charged that "Yiddish music" influenced heavily the "rootless jazz music" in America and consequently "the Jewish Michael

---

44 Ghulām Reżā Kāẓimyan-Pūr, "Taṭābuk va-hamhangī-i Vahhābiyat va-Yahūdiyat dar te'ōrī va-ʿamal," 20 Abān 1393/November 11, 2011, http://www.tajlil.com/fa/pages/?cid=41328; "Naqsh-i Yahūdiyān dar tarvīj-i Islām setīzī," http://qods.persianblog.ir/post/153; "ʿIlal va-ʿavāmil-i dushmanī-i Yahūd bar Islām."

45 Intelligence and Terrorism Information Center, January 25, 2010, http://www.terrorism-info.org.il/malam_multimedia/English/eng_n/html/iran_e048.htm; "Head of Iranian Think-Tank Advising Khamenei: The Jews Want Nuclear Bomb to Kill Muslims and Achieve World Domination," MEMRI, Clip No. 4042, February 1, 2013, https://www.memri.org/tv/head-iranian-think-tank-advising-khamenei-jews-want-nuclear-bomb-kill-muslims-and-achieve-world/transcript; "Khamenei Associate Mahdī Taeb: 'The Jews … Are The Only Ones Who Need Weapons Of Mass Destruction In Order To Rule The World – Because There Are 1.4 Billion Muslims And None Of Them Agree To Jewish Supremacy,'" MEMRI, Special Dispatch no. 6759, January 27, 2017, https://www.memri.org/reports/khamenei-associate-Mahdī-taeb-jews-are-only-ones-who-need-weapons-mass-destruction-order.

46 Qūrtānī, "Yahūd rā behtar beshenāsīm."

47 "ʿIlal va-ʿavāmil-i dushmanī-i Yahūd bar Islām."

Jackson overcame church music."[48] Some have gone further to describe the Jews as "enemies of religion" and of humanity as a whole, having made efforts throughout history to confront, destroy, and eliminate the truth in order to preserve their identity.[49] Jews are, in addition, notorious for their greed and dubious financial and economic practices, ranging from money lending, hoarding of gold, to playing a major role in the American slave trade. All of these traits, which are associated with Western capitalism, stand in complete contrast to the ideals and essence of Islam and thus accentuate the stereotypization of the "other."[50] It should be noted that while describing the Jews as the greatest enemy during the formative Islamic period, the official website *islamquest.net* conceded that in recent centuries the imperialism of Christian countries committed no fewer crimes against Islam and the Muslims.[51]

A prominent theme among Shīʿī writers is alleged Jewish racism, which is rooted in the Jewish belief in being the chosen people and their insistence that God's message was aimed solely at the Jews. This racism is seen to be manifested in Jewish contempt toward all others, voluntary seclusion from others, and belief that Jewish identity is based on blood. Some have even claimed that the Jews never hesitate to commit crimes against others due to this belief in

---

48 "Dunyā bāzīcheh dast-i Yahūd," http://montazer-mousa.blogfa.com/post/14; "ʿIlal va-ʿavāmil-i dushmanī-i Yahūd bar Islām;" "Goftegū-i ʿAlī Khalīl Ismāʿīl bā dustān-i javān dar masjid Imām-i Sajjād ʿalayhi al-salām," http://atm.parsiblog.com/Posts/119/; ʿAlī Akbar Rāʾifī-pūr, "Vāqiʿiyat-i Yahūd setīzī 1," 24 Bahman 1387/February 12, 2009, http://antisemitism.blogfa.com/post-1.aspx; "Towtīʾah-i Yahūd barāye javānān-i Irānī," http://javanetaki.blogfa.com/category/5/توطئه-یهود-برای-جوانان-ایرانی; *Kayhān*, June 30, 2016.

49 Ṭabāṭabāʾī, "Naqsh-i jarayān-i Masīḥī-Yahūdī dar tarbiyat-i Yazīd"; "ʿIllat-i dushmanī-i Yahūdī bā Islām: nezhād parastī," 30 Bahman 1395/February 18, 2017, http://mastoor.ir/content/view/7996/1; "Falsafa-i ikhtilāf-i Yahūdiyān bā Shīʿīyān," 13 Dey 1393/January 3, 2015, http://www.welayatnet.com/fa/news/51395; "ʿIlal va-ʿavāmil-i dushmanī-i Yahūd bar Islām;" Ismāʿīl Shafīʿī Sarvestānī, "Naqsh-i Yahūd dar vāqiʿa-i Karbalāʾ," 13 Mehr 1395/October 4, 2016, https://www.ourpresident.ir/analysis/report/2-مهم-نقش-یهود-در-واقعه-کربلا; "Rivāyat-i Ḥujjat al-Islām Ṭāʾib az naqsh-i Yahūd dar dastgāh-i khilāfat-i Muʿāwiya," 22 Dey 1391/January 11, 2013, http://www.farsnews.com/newstext.php?nn=13911021000692; a group of authors, *Darsnāmah-i taʾrīkh-i taḥlīlī-i dushman shināsī*, 20.

50 Keyvān Majīdī, "Vāqiʿiyat-i Yahūd setīzī (2)," 18 Dey 1389/January 8, 2008, http://basij-ganjnameh.persianblog.ir/post/84/; Zāhidī, "Taʾrīkhcheh tharvat andūzī-i zarsālārān-i Yahūd"; Aḥmad Karīmyān, "ʿAvāmīl-i nifrat az Yahūd (7)," http://rasekhoon.net/article/show/750799/; "Yahūdiyān rāz-i sarmāyeh dārī modern," http://www.bashgah.net/fa/content/print_version/23593.

51 "Buzurgtarīn-i dushman-i idīʾūlūzhīk-i Islām, Amrīkā ast, yā Inglīs, yā vahhābiyān va-salafiyān."

their racial superiority.[52] ʿAlī Akbar Rāʾifī-Pūr concluded that any group holding such views or behaving in this way would incur similar hatred as the Jews.[53]

The unanimous view in the Shīʿī discourse is that Islam, particularly Shīʿīsm, rejects and fights these supposed Jewish attributes, worldview, and conduct, and this is why it became the main target of Jewish enmity from its very inception.[54] Qarahī, who earlier described the Jews as a mix between demons (*jins*) and humans, went further and established a clear-cut contrast between the doctrine of *vilāyat-i faqīh*, the ideological foundations of the Islamic Republic, and *vilāyat-i shaytān* (the rule of Satan), which he associated with the Jews: "If it is not the rule of God, then naturally it is the rule of the Jews and Christians," he charged, and "who are the Jews? They are the tools of Satan (*abzār-i shaytān*)."[55]

5 Jewish Conspiracies and the Early Shīʿa

The Islamic sources – the Qurʾān, ḥadīth, and the early biographies of the Prophet – narrate the early Islamic past as marked by conflicts that would influence much of its future. In fact, the prophetic material contained in the Qurʾān and the life story of Muḥammad become mutually intelligible through the creation of a narrative of confrontation between prophecy and its "Jewish" enemies. The source of this Jewish enmity and its greatest sin is the opposition to the Prophet: the rejection of his message and the efforts to foil his mission.[56]

---

52 Reżā Muṣṭafavī, *Al-Tiyām: farjam shināsī-i jarayānhā-i taʾrīkh* (Tehrān, 1395/2016), 118–119; "Yahūdiyān, sarsakhtarīn-i dushmanān;" Ṭabāṭabāʾī, "Naqsh-i jarayān-i Yahūdī-Masīḥī dar tarbiyat-i Yazīd;" al-Arqam al-Zuʿbī, "Ḥaqāyiqī dar bārah-i Yahūdiyat," *Maʿrifat* 74 (1382/2004): 57–65; Muḥammad Mahdī Ḥamīdī, "Yahūd az manẓar-i taʾrīkh," 30 Farvardīn 1396/April 19, 2017, http://www.bonyadmahdi.com/sysnews/cid/373; "Jarayān shināsī-i taʾrīkhī-i nufūẕ bā tamarkuz bar Yahūd," 14 Bahman 1395/February 2, 2017, http://www.mehrnews.com/news/3895081. Needless to say, the charges about Jewish insistence of the purity of blood are unfounded as people could and did join Judaism through conversion.

53 Rāʾifī-Pūr, "Vāqiʿiyat-i Yahūd setīzī 1." For other justifications of anti-Judaism, see Najāḥ al-Ṭāʾī, *Faḍāʾiḥ Yahūd mutalabbisūn bil-Islām* (Beirut: Dār al-hudā li-iḥyāʾ al-turāth, 1422/2001), 7; "Nigāhī beh Kītāb az afsāneh-i Yahūd setīzī tā vāqiʿiyat-i Islām setīzī," 19 Ordībehesht 1394/May 9, 2015, http://www.rasanews.ir/print/259737.

54 Muḥammadī, "Muvājaha-i Islām bā ṣahyūnīsm tamadunī ast neh siyāsī."

55 "Sokhanrānī-i ustād-i Qarahī dar ayām-i ʿĀshūrāʾ," 21 Azar 1390/December 12, 2011, http://www.shabestan.ir/detail/News/90013.

56 ʿAlī Akbar Mahdīpūr, *Taʾrīkh-i Islām bā rūyikard-i dushman shināsī* (Qom: Naghmat, 1390/2012), 31–35; Ṭāʾib, *Tabār-i inḥirāf*, 19; "ʿAmaliyāt-i Yahūd barāye muqābala bā piyāmbar (S) (radpāy-i Yahūd dar ḥavādith-i ṣadr-i Islām)," https://hawzah.net/fa/Article/

All Muslim writers, Shīʿīs and Sunnīs alike, view the life time of the Prophet Muḥammad and the ensuing generations as the formative period of Islamic history or, in Douglas Pratt's words, the "originating paradigms" which shaped Islam and have determined Islamic history ever since.[57] This period is the key to understanding history through to the present day, and many writers see a direct link between past and present enemies and their actions against Islam. For both Sunnīs and Shīʿīs, the clashes between the Prophet and his adversaries, particularly the Jewish tribes of Medina, serve as the explanatory model for Muslim-Jewish relations for all times, because the enmity of the Jews in the Qurʾān is not tied *explicitly* to events in the life of the prophet Muḥammad or his community. In Nirenberg's words, it is not historical but constant, serving as the screen against which humanity's progress toward prophetic truth is projected.[58]

As the Prophet struggled to spread his message and consolidate his community, he encountered opposition from three different parties[59] or "enemies" in modern Shīʿī parlance: the Jews, the Christians, and the "hypocrites" (*munāfiqūn*).[60] The Shīʿī discourse debates which was the worst enemy, with the overwhelming majority agreeing that the Jews had been the greatest and "most implacable" enemies, because of their well-ordered organization and advanced culture. As proof, they have pointed to the greater number of passages (one-sixth of all passages) in the Qurʾān devoted to criticizing or warning about Jews compared with other groups, and the harsher words used against them by the Prophet. Most significant in their eyes are Jewish conspiracies and treasonous acts against the Prophet, culminating in the effort to murder his

---

View/97206. The story can be traced to Muḥammad Bāqir Majlisī, *Biḥār al-anwār*, (Beirut: Dār iḥyāʾ al-turāth al-ʿArabī, 1983) vol. 15, 51, 53, 117, and 127.

57 Douglas Pratt, "Muslim–Jewish Relations: Some Islamic Paradigms," *Islam and Christian–Muslim Relations* 21, no. 1(2010): 12.

58 Nirenberg, *Anti-Judaism*, 149–150.

59 The relationship between Muḥammad and the Jews has been the subject of numerous studies. Among the most important are: Michael Lecker, *Jews and Arabs in Pre-and Early Islamic Arabia*, vol. 639 (Aldershot: Ashgate, 1998); Michael Lecker, *Muslims, Jews and Pagans: Studies in Early Islamic Medina* (Leiden: Brill, 1995); Uri Rubin, "The 'Constitution of Medina' Some Notes," *Studia Islamica* 62 (1985): 5–23; Arent Jan Wensinck, *Muhammad and the Jews of Medina*, vol. 3. (Berlin: K. Schwarz, 1975).

60 Sunnīs apply this term to people who pretended to be Muslims during the Prophet's lifetime but who secretly retained their pagan beliefs and sought to undermine the Muslim community. Shīʿīs applied it to those Muslims who had pretended to be loyal to the Prophet but in fact betrayed his wish to appoint ʿAlī as his successor. Today, the term is used in Iran to denote dissidents who claim to be good Muslims but disagree with the regime's policies.

ancestors in order to prevent his birth and the attempt to poison him which hastened his death, as well as the wars he waged against them.[61]

Of particular importance in the context of the present chapter is the supposed major Jewish role in a series of events which resulted, according to the Shīʿī view, in the corruption and divergence of Islam from its correct path to the detriment and misfortune of the Shīʿa. This narrative emerged in response, at least in part, to Sunnī claims against the Shīʿa. According to Steven Wasserstrom, a common approach among Sunnī writers was the personification of doctrines, particularly those developed by dissident sects, by ascribing them to purported founding figures. This occasionally resulted in sects being related to wholly spurious, concocted originators: "it would be difficult to find a Muslim heresy that was not at one time or another traced back to a Jewish originator."[62] Such attribution seemed to have served several purposes. It absolved the "true" Muslims from responsibility for internal conflicts that harmed Islam. Likewise, it downgraded dissident sects by associating them with a despised outsider or, in Nirenberg's words, had the effect of "Judaizing" rivals. It also served to vilify the Jews as enemies of Islam.

The Shīʿīs had already suffered this fate of "becoming Jewish" in the classical age of Islam, since, according to their Sunnī critics, the exaltation of ʿAlī by the early Shīʿī movements was an imitation of the Israelites' worship of the golden calf. These critics even went so far as to give Shīʿī Islam a specifically Jewish paternity, claiming that it was the Jew ʿAbd Allah ibn Sabaʾ who convinced the Muslim community to elevate ʿAlī above all others and who drove the Islamic community into dissension and disarray by inciting the rebellion against Islam's third caliph, ʿUthmān b. Affān. The Shīʿīs, of course, deny the charge and claim that Ibn Sabaʾ was an imaginary figure.[63] Countering these accusations

---

61 For a few examples, see "Dar mowred-i nufūẕ-i Yahūd dar Islām towżīḥ bedīn," http://www.porseshkadeh.com/mob-question/25952; Qūrtānī, "Yahūd rā behtar beshenāsīm;" "Qawm-i Yahūd rā behtar beshenāsīm;" "Yahūd dushman-i aṣlī-i Imām-i Zamān (ʿajala Allah taʿālā farajahu)," 27 Abān 1391/November 17, 2017, http://www.shia-news.com/fa/news/46588; "Yahūdiyān, sarsakhtarīn-i dushmanān." According to Sunnī and Shīʿī traditions, Muḥammad's Jewish wife, Ṣafiyya, tried to murder him by poisoning his food, but he understood her scheme and refrained from eating it.

62 Wasserstrom, *Between Muslim and Jew*, 157. For this tendency among modern Salafists, see Hasson, "Contemporary Polemics Between Neo-Wahhābīs and Post-Khomeinist Shiʿites," 19.

63 Ibid., 158; ʿAbbas Barzegar, "The Persistence of Heresy: Paul of Tarsus, Ibn Sabaʾ, and Historical Narrative in Sunnī Identity Formation," *Numen* 58 (2011): 210, 212–216; *A Shiʿite Encyclopedia* (Ahlul-Bayt Digital Islamic Library Project, 2017, electronic edition), 938. Few Shīʿī writers have accused ʿAbdallah ibn Sabaʾ of sowing discord among the Muslims against the Shīʿa in "Yahūdiyān-i makhfī."

by Judaizing the Sunnīs would have been too provocative for the Shīʿī minority, therefore, the Shīʿīs, particularly in recent times, responded by presenting themselves as much greater victims of Jewish enmity and machinations than the Sunnīs. Such claims, while not absolving the Sunnīs from any wrongdoing, softened Shīʿī criticism against them by portraying ordinary Sunnīs as unwitting dupes of both the Jews and of a few truly evil and unscrupulous Muslims. This approach enabled Ḥujjat al-Islam Hāmid Kāshānī, a prolific contributor to the official propagation media, to separate a small group of Sunnīs (around ten to fifteen percent) who had allegedly fallen under the Jewish spell from the majority of innocent Sunnīs, whom he addressed as "brothers."[64] Thus, by turning against the common enemy, the Jews, a common bond with a broad strata of Sunnīs remained possible.

At the same time, such claims serve to portray Shīʿīsm not only as a victim of Jewish manipulation but also as the Jews' absolute and morally superior opposite; if the Jews, who represent evil, are first and foremost the enemies of Shīʿīsm, then Shīʿīsm must be the epitome of virtue. Moreover, Shīʿīsm, as the correct and pure Islam, has never been affected by the Jews.[65] Sunnī Islam, on the other hand, has been influenced by the Jews, and therefore the dichotomy between Sunnīsm and Judaism is not as deep. Indeed, some have even explained that "infected Islam" (*Islam-i vīrūsī*), namely, mainstream Sunnī Islam, never posed a problem to the Jews. The Jews wanted to dominate the world and did not care about a religion that was not opposed to their goals when it relinquished the political sphere and accepted the legitimacy of all Muslim rulers. The real challenge to Jews, they claimed, was posed by true revolutionary Islam as advocated by Khomeini, which denies the legitimacy of corrupt rulers.[66] This lack of a clear contradiction between Sunnī Islam and the Jews had a major impact on their relationships. Ḥujjat al-Islam Muḥsin Muḥammadī of the Institute of Applied History in Qom thus maintained that throughout history the Sunnīs turned against the Shīʿa but not against the Jews, while

---

64 "Barresī-i nifāq va-khaṭarnaktar az nifāq," 4 Abān 1394/October 26, 2015, http://iusnews.ir/fa/news-details/183224/.

65 See, for example, a sermon by Ayatollah Qarahī in which he explained that the secret of guarding oneself from Jewish influence is adherence to the Shīʿī imams, "Vīlāyat; kelīd-i uṣūl-i dīn/ramz-i maṣūniyat-i iʿtiqādāt az nufūẕ-i Yahūd chīst?," 26 Mehr 1394/October 18, 2015, http://www.mehrnews.com/news/2942890/.

66 "Cheh kesī Yahūdī ast? M'uasses-i Shīʿa yā muḥaddith-i sunnī?!," http://bedat.blogfa.com; "Janghā-i khulafāʾ va-manfaʿat-i Yahūd az ān," http://jscenter.ir/judaism-and-islam/jewish-intrigue/5507.

Israel never had a problem with Sunnī Islam, only with Shīʿīsm.[67] The sharp contrast between Judaism and Shīʿīsm is manifested in Nūrī-Hamadānī's explanation that Jewish enmity together with Muslim lack of awareness of social obligations (*takālif*), were two important reasons for the failure to implement the *vilāyat-i faqīh* and Islamic government during the Great Occultation of the Twelfth Imām (941). In other words, Jewish enmity was a major factor in preventing Shīʿīsm from attaining self-fulfillment prior to the 1979 Revolution. Mahdī Ṭāʾib brought this dichotomy into the present, by portraying the Islamic Republic as the main bulwark against global Jewish domination.[68]

Many of the charges of Jewish manipulations appear in early Shīʿī sources, and relate mostly to the clashes between the Prophet and the Jewish tribes of Medina. The modern discourse under the Islamic Republic, however, represents an increase in quantity and scope, greater elaboration of the plots, and a stronger link between these past conspiracies and present-day threats to Islam.

An early common Muslim contention against the Jews was the falsification of the true message that God had conveyed to them through Moses and the forging of false scriptures instead of those given by God. The present narrative goes further by speaking of Jewish strategy and plots to weaken and undermine Islam by falsifying it and diverting it from its correct doctrinal, moral, and historical path. According to this narrative, the Jews have sought throughout history to corrupt the beliefs of other peoples by penetrating them from within and implanting their own beliefs and ideas.[69] For example, the Jews sought to destroy Islam immediately after the death of the Prophet, employing measures such as the dissemination of the "Torah and Jewish ideas" among Muslims. By spreading these "poisonous ideas," they succeeded in contaminating the pure beliefs of Islam, thereby facilitating the corruption of this "divine religion" and bringing it to the same state as Judaism and Christianity. The Jews were, in addition, very active in fomenting sedition among Muslims. So extensive was Jewish role and involvement in Islamic affairs, Ḥujjat al-Islam Muḥammad

---

67 Muḥammadī, "Muvājaha-i Islām bā ṣahyūnīsm tamaddunī ast neh siyāsī;" "Ahl-i Sunnat va-Yahūd," http://fa.tarikh.org/index.php/نکات-ناب/معاونت-علمی/item/1751-اهل-سنت-و-یهود.

68 "Dushmanī-i Yahūd va-bī tavajjuhī-i musalmānān beh takālif-i ijtimāʿī. Baʿith-i ʿadam-i tashkīl-i ḥukūmat-i Islāmī dar dowra-i ghaybat ast," 3 Abān 1394/October 25, 2015, http://vasael.ir/fa/print/1239; "Ṭāʾib: Mashāʾī Abū Bakr-i zamān va-nufūẕī-i Yahūd ast," 14 Tīr 1395/July 4, 2016, http://www.entekhab.ir/fa/news/30644.

69 See, for example, in "Yahūdiyān-i makhfī," the assertion that many Jews "dressed as Christians," assumed leadership of the Church, and spread corruption in its ranks.

ʿAlī Manṣūrī Damghānī of the Mouood Institute explained, that it would require more than 200 seminary meetings to cover it.[70] Ḥujjat al-Islam Muḥsin Muḥammadī, among others, compared the excessive influence of the Jews following the Prophet's death with the present-day threat of Western cultural influence on Iran.[71]

One particular charge is that the Jews sought to undermine the idea of the *Imāmat*, the leadership of the Islamic community designated for ʿAlī and his descendants. In the words of Ḥujjat al-Islam ʿAbd al-Qādir Saʿādatī, a researcher on Jews in Tabrīz, the Jews had been major facilitators of this deviation from the principle of *Imāmat*, which become the source of many divisions among Muslims ever since.[72] In a similar vein, the authors of *Mahār-i inḥirāf*, a book dedicated to describing the Jewish role in numerous religious deviations in Islamic history, explained that understanding the true causes for the deviation of Islam in this early period is crucial for exposing present-day Jewish and Zionist conspiracies against Islam.[73] The perpetrators of these acts had been "Jews in Muslim garb," that is, converts to Islam who remained Jewish in their soul and mind and sought to distort and corrupt Islam from within. The most famous or notorious of these converts was Kaʿb al-Aḥbār (d. 652–653), whose close relations with the second caliph, ʿUmar b. al-Khaṭṭāb, are discussed below.[74] These converts attempted to falsify if not replace whole passages from the Qurʾān, disseminated false exegeses and interpretations of the Qurʾān, fabricated numerous ḥadīth designed to harm ʿAlī's cause, and falsified Islamic history.[75] A *Fars News Agency* article, applying modern-day terminology to the

70 "Vāqiʿiyat taḥrīf-shodeh dar taʾrīkh-i Islām: goft va-gūyī ikhtiṣāṣī bā ʿalāmah moḥaqqiq sayyid Jaʿfar Murtażā ʿĀmilī," *Mowʿūd* 76 (1386/ 2007): 14–19, http://www.hawzah.net/fa/Magazine/View/4227/5729/570578C; "Naqsh-i Yahūd dar taḥrīf-i ḥādithat-i Ghadīr Khumm," 22 Dey 1388/January 12, 2010, http://www.askdin.com/showthread.php?t=2437; "Naqsh-i Yahūd (ṣahyūnīsm) dar vāqiʿa-i Karbalāʾ," http://21122012.blogfa.com/post-38.aspx.

71 "Jarayān shināsī taʾrīkhī-i nufūẕ bā tamarkuz bar Yahūd."

72 Muʾasasa-i taʾrīkh-i taṭbīqī, "Barresī-i ikhlālgarī va-nufūẕ-i farhangī-i Yahūd pas as riḥlat-i piyāmbar-i Islām (a) dar goftegū bā Ḥujjat al-Islām Saʿādatī," 31 Mordād 1395/ August 21, 2016, shorturl.at/inuwL; "Ayatollah Qarahī: Abā Sufyān va-Muʿāwiya musalmān nā-būdand/Barresī-i ʿIlal-i ʿĀshūrāʾ va-taʾrīkh-i Karbalāʾ," 29 Mehr 1394/October 21, 2015, http://www.mehrnews.com/news/2946109.

73 Ḥusayn Ilāhī, ʿAlī Yazdānī, and Ḥasan Kāẓimzādeh, *Mahār-i inḥirāf: Bāzgavī-i ḥavādith pas az riḥlat-i piyāmbar akram* (s) (Qom: muʾasasa-i taʾrīkh-i taṭbīqī, 1393/2014), 3.

74 M. Schimitz, "Kaʿb al-Aḥbār," *Encyclopaedia of Islam* (*EI2*) (Leiden: Brill, 1978) 4: 316–17. For a Shīʿī view, see *A Shiʿite Encyclopedia*, 938–947.

75 "Yahūdiyānī keh iddiʿāʾ-i musalmānī mīkonand," 23 Khordād 1393/June 13, 2014, https://www.mouood.org/component/k2/item/20370; Ilāhī, Yazdānī and Kāẓimzādeh, *Mahār-i inḥirāf*,

past, charged these converts with implementing a "policy of influence," which is associated in the modern discourse with the abhorred Western cultural influence as well as espionage and subversion in order to strike at the Muslim community in Medina.[76]

The suspicious attitude toward these converts is not unique to Shīʿīsm and is also prevalent in Sunnī Islam under the category of Isrāʾīliyyāt – Judeo-Christian traditions that allegedly entered Islamic exegesis and distorted it.[77] Yet, several points regarding the converts seem to be unique here and deserve elaboration. First is the major role and impact attributed to the Jews regarding key events that were detrimental to the Shīʿa. Accordingly, these converts did not act as individuals but were motivated by their Jewish identity or nature and operated as part of the broader Jewish scheme against Islam. Their actions and those of any other Jews therefore reflect upon all Jews at all times. Second is the association of these early converts with modern Jewish converts to Islam in Iran and, even more importantly, to Bahāʾīsm, as proof of the ongoing Jewish effort to harm Islam from within. Third is the equation of the alleged impact of the early converts on Sunnī Islam with the similarly alleged Jewish penetration of Christianity and its falsification by the Jews, in particular, the Jewish-born Christian apostle Paul. Paul is renowned in Christian tradition for separating the new Christian faith from Judaism by rejecting Jewish law and insisting on Christ's Lordship, crucifixion, and second coming. The Qurʾān, on the other hand, regards Jesus as a human prophet and denies the historical veracity of his crucifixion and resurrection. Muslim writers have therefore viewed Paul's ideas as intentionally leading the Christian community astray by falsifying

---

117–118, 123–126; "Siyāsathā-i sāzimān-i nifāq barāye nābūdī-i Islām pas az piyāmbar (s)," pt. 2, http://www.fa.tarikh.org/index.php/پیامبر-اعظم/تاریخ-انبیا-و-معصومین-ع/item/1302-سیاست های-سازمان-نفاق-برای-نابودی-اسلام-پس-از-پیامبر-ص-بخش-سوم?tmpl=component&print=1; Ayatollah Muḥammad Amīnī Golestānī, "Intiqām-i Yahūdiyān az Imām ʿAlī (A)," http://ahdema.ir/انتقام-یهودیان-از-امام-علی-ع; al-Ṭāʾī, *Faḍāʾiḥ-i Yahūd mutalabbisūn bil-Islām*; "Āsīb shināsī-i taʾrīkh-i Islām va-naqsh-i Yahūd dar ān," http://analytichistory.blogfa.com/post-3.aspx.

76 "Naqsh-i Yahūd dar vaqāyiʿ-i taʾrīkh-i Islām," 7 Bahman 1386/January 27, 2008, http://www.farsnews.com/printable.php?nn=8609240312.

77 For a Shīʿī view of Isrāʾīliyyāt, see Georges Vajda, "Isrāʾīliyyāt," *Encyclopaedia of Islam, Second Edition* http://dx.doi.org/10.1163/1573-3912_ei2glos_SIM_gi_01840; Y. Tzvi Langermann, "Medical Israiliyyat? Ancient Islamic Medical Traditions Transcribed into the Hebrew Alphabet," *Aleph: Historical Studies in Science and Judaism* 6, no. 1 (2006): 373–398; *A Shiʿite Encyclopedia*, 829; "Ayatollah Jaʿfar Subḥānī: mushkil-i Isrāʾīliyyāt dar ḥadīth, bekhāṭir-i bidʿathā-i ṣadr-i Islam ast," 27 Tīr 1390/January 17, 2012, http://www.hawzah.net/fa/News/View/88892.

the true story of Jesus and his mission and laying the foundations for false Christian theology, doctrines, and practices in contravention of God's original intention.[78] Many Shīʿī writers have not only denied Paul's role in separating Christianity from Judaism but attributed his activities to the broader Jewish propensity to oppose God's will and subvert other religions. Paul played a key role in the Jewish scheme to infiltrate Christianity from within in order to divert it from its true path. They therefore view Paul as a model for the Jewish converts to Islam who similarly distorted true Islam and have even suggested that because of these converts, Sunnī Islam suffered the same deformation that took place in Christianity. In other words, the errors of Sunnī Islam are products of the Jews.[79]

A major issue in this context that Shīʿī historiography and polemics have grappled with is the need to explain the turn of most of the Prophet's Companions (*ṣaḥāba*) against ʿAlī, the Prophet's cousin, son-in-law, and rightful heir according to Shīʿī belief immediately after the Prophet's death. A major point in the contemporary Shīʿī narrative is the attribution of a key role in these developments to the Jewish converts and through them to the Jews as a whole. The event that might serve here as a starting point took place in the portico (*saqīfa*) of the Banū Sāʿidah in Medina, a few hours after the Prophet's sudden death on 11 Rabīʿ awwal, 632, when the nascent Muslim community was in confusion. While ʿAlī was preparing the Prophet's body for burial, ʿUmar b. al-Khaṭṭāb, one of the Prophet's closest companions, took advantage of the divisions among the Medinese elite and swore allegiance to Abū Bakr, another close companion of the Prophet, thereby installing him as the first caliph or the heir of the Prophet.[80]

---

78 Barzegar, "The Persistence of Heresy," 218; Mahdīpūr, *Taʾrīkh-i Islām bā rūyikard-i dushman shināsī*, 10, 24–25, 49.

79 Ṭāʾib et al., *Tabār-i inḥirāf*, 191–92; "Yahūdiyān-i makhfī"; Ilāhī, Yazdānī, and Kāẓimzādeh, *Mahār-i inḥirāf*, 163; "Yahūdī makhfī yā ānūsī," 12 Dey 1391/January 1, 2013, http://afshin1939.persianblog.ir/post/633; "Yahūdīzādehgān musalmān nemā (bakhsh-i pāyānī)," http://khoroosh.parsiblog.com/category/یهود/. See also the favorable reviews in Yūsuf Rashād, *Naqsh-i āfarīnī-i Yahūdiyān-i makhfī dar Masīḥiyat*, trans. ʿAbbās Kosnakī (Tehrān: *Mowʿūd*, 1390/2011), http://www.hawzah.net/fa/News/View/94273 and http://teeh.ir/fa/news-details/2733/.

80 For a detailed analysis of the event, see Wilfred Madelung, *The Succession to Muhammad: A Study of the Early Caliphate* (Cambridge: Cambridge University Press, 1997), 30ff; Seyyed Ḥusayn Muhammad Jafri, *The Origins and Early Development of Shia Islam* (London: Longman, 1979), 23–43; Hamid Dabashi, *Authority in Islam: From the Rise of Muhammad to the Establishment of the Umayyads* (New Brunswick: Transaction Publishers, 1989), 75–120; G. Lecomte, "al-Saḳīfa," *EI2* http://dx.doi.org/10.1163/1573-3912_ei2glos_SIM_gi_04068. The number of Sunnī and Shīʿī sources in Arabic and Persian is too vast to be referenced here.

The Saqīfa meeting is the starting point for a series of historical developments that led to the emergence of the Shīʿa as an idea or faction and, subsequently, a separate school within Islam. The crux of the Shīʿī sense of injury was the moral and doctrinal sin committed by the usurpation of the caliphate from ʿAlī, which launched the path of Islam's deviation. Shīʿī distress was augmented by the fact that seventy-two days earlier, on 18 Ẕū al-Ḥijjah, the Prophet, who was returning to Medina after completing his last pilgrimage to Mecca, stopped at the Ghadīr Khumm oasis where he declared: "to whomsoever I am mawlā, ʿAlī is also their Mawlā." Both Sunnīs and Shīʿīs accept the veracity of the event but differ over its meaning. The Shīʿīs interpret the word *mawlā* as "master" and thus regard Muḥammad's statement as a clear-cut designation of ʿAlī as his heir and maintain that the community at large had also viewed it as such. The Sunnīs, on the other hand, construe the word *mawlā* as "friend" and thus deny that Muḥammad's statement had any political meaning or intention.[81]

For centuries, Shīʿī writings and polemics blamed several Companions, led by ʿUmar and Abū Bakr, for the usurpation of the Prophet's succession from ʿAlī and for his later tribulations.[82] While not exonerating these Companions, the modern discourse highlights the Jewish role in these events. According to Ibrāhīm-niyā and Manṣūrī Damghānī, the glaring contradiction between Ghadīr Khumm and the Saqīfa meeting could only be the result of conspiracy and sedition. It took the Americans and the British thirty years to carry out the sedition of 1388 (the mass protest demonstrations against the regime following the rigged 2009 presidential elections), yet a major sedition took place only seventy-two days after the Ghadīr event. Who else but the "Zionist Jews" could have connived such a conspiracy, the Shīʿa writers maintain. It is only logical that the Jews had been the mastermind behind the Saqīfa plot considering their continuous clashes with the Prophet and the numerous warnings against them in the Qurʾān. Likewise, they accuse Jewish converts of suppressing

---

81 L. Veccia Vaglieri, "Ghadīr Khumm," *Encyclopaedia of Islam*. New Edition, vol. 2, 993–94; Madelung, *The Succession to Muhammad*, 253.

82 For Shīʿī criticism of the Companions as hypocrites and even apostates, see Etan Kohlberg, "Some Imami Shīʿī Views on the Sahabah" *Jerusalem Studies in Arabic and Islam* 5 (1984): 143–175. Muḥammad Riḏā al-Muẓaffar, *Saqīfa* (Beirut: Mu'assasat al-aʿlamī lil-maṭbūʿāt, 1973) and Jaʿfar Naqdī, *al-Anwār al-ʿalawiyya wa-al-asrār al-murtaḍawiyya fī aḥwāl Amīr al-Muʾminīn wa-faḍāʾilihi wa-manāqibihi wa-ghazawātihi* (Najaf: al-Maṭbaʿa al-Ḥaydarīyya, 1962), who represent the more traditional approach, do not mention a Jewish role in the Saqīfa meeting.

ḥadīths that highlighted ʿAlī's designation and forging hundreds of contrary ḥadīths that denied his rights.[83]

Jewish actions are explained in three complementary motifs: Jewish enmity toward the Prophet's household and ʿAlī in particular; allegations of close friendship and collaboration between the Jews and those Companions who had played the most harmful role in the conspiracies against ʿAlī and Fāṭima (d. 632), the Prophet's daughter and ʿAlī's wife; and the attribution of Jewish ancestry to many of these Companions.

The Jews allegedly hated ʿAlī for several reasons. First, due to their evil nature, the Jews had always opposed true men of God. Therefore, they fought against ʿAlī just as they had persecuted Jesus and Muḥammad. Various Shīʿī sources attribute Jewish animosity toward ʿAlī to his actions in the battle against the Jewish tribe of Banu Qurayẓa, in which he killed many of them, and to his central role in the conquest of the Jewish oasis of al-Khaybar.[84] Concurrently, ʿAlī was among the very few who had, from early on, distrusted the Jewish converts to Islam, primarily Kaʿb al-Aḥbār, whom he viewed as a liar and hypocrite. Moreover, former Khamenei's representative in Iṣfahān Muḥammad Dashtī stated, ʿAlī had "fought the hypocrites, the polytheists, and the Jews" all his life. Kaʿb, "the international Jew," who knew that "Jewish influence would be eliminated forever" once ʿAlī assumed the reign of leadership, focused his efforts against ʿAlī. He therefore played a key role in driving many of the early Muslims away from ʿAlī and was the person who advised ʿUmar not to appoint ʿAlī as his successor.[85]

---

83 "Saqīfat banī Isrāʾīl," http://intiqam.blogfa.com/post-23.aspx; "Gozāresh-i Fars az neshest-i ʿnaqsh-i Yahūd dar vāqiʿa-i khūnīn-i Karbalāʾ (2)," 27 Abān 1391/November 17, 2012, http://www.farsnews.com/newstext.php?nn=13910826000113; Muḥammad Mahdī Ḥamīdī, *Dushmanān-i mahdaviyat cherā? Va-chegūneh?* (Iṣfahān: Markaz-i taḥqīqāt-i rayānah-i qāʾimiyya Iṣfahān, 1387/2008), 96–98; "Jarayān shināsī taʾrīkhī-i nufūẕ bā tamarkuz bar Yahūd."

84 "Naqsh-i Yahūd dar shahādat-i Imāmān," http://www.ahbab14.blogfa.com/post/26; "ʿUmar wal-Yahūd: dirāsa nafsiyya fī khalfiyat ʿUmar al-dīnīyya," pt. 2, https://groups.yahoo.com/neo/groups/al-sadeq/conversations/messages/60377; "al-Radd al-ṣārim ʿalā aʿdāʾ al-Imām al-qāʾim," May 4, 2016, https://www.facebook.com/123825401328114/photos/a.227440030966650.1073741828.123825401328114/229390314104955/?type=3; Muḥammad Dashtī, *Rahāvard-i mubārazat-i ḥażrat-i zahrāʾ ʿalayhā al-salām* (Iṣfahān: Markaz taḥqīqāt-i rayāneh-i qāʾimiyya-i Iṣfahān, n.d.) Electronic edition, 19; "Yahūdīzādehgān musalmān nemā."

85 *A Shiʿite Encyclopedia*, 940; "Barresī ikhlālgarī va-nufūẕ-i farhangī-i Yahūd;" "ʿUmar wal-Yahūd;" Dashtī, *Rahāvard-i mubārazat-i ḥażrat-i Zahrāʾ*, 18, 29; al-Ṭāʾī, *Faḍāʾiḥ-i Yahūd mutalabbisūn bil-Islām*, 99; "Kaʿb al-Aḥbār, shakhṣi ke dar musalmānān nufūẕ kard va-talāsh kard taʿlīmāt-i Yahūd rā vārid-i Islām konad," http://tvshia.com/fa/content/50285.

Jewish enmity toward the Prophet's household reached a new low with their active role in the assassination of ʿAlī, the poisoning of Fāṭima, and the death of the other ten imāms. The allegation that Ibn Muljam, the Khārijī zealot who murdered ʿAlī in 661, was the son of a Jewish mother and thus a Jew can be traced to Muḥammad Bāqir Majlisī's seventeenth-century ḥadīth compendium, *Biḥār al-anwār*, if not earlier. The story carried on through the twentieth century, as Shaykh ʿAbbās Qommī (d. 1941) even cited a ḥadīth in which the Prophet had warned ʿAlī that his assassin would be Jewish. The official state media of the Islamic Republic, for its part, have disseminated the charge several times.[86] Pre-modern Shīʿī tradition attributed the death of nine Shīʿī imāms to poisoning by the tyrant Umayyad and ʿAbbāsid caliphs.[87] Various, though not all, modern writers have maintained that Jews were those who poisoned these imāms either on behalf of the Sunnī rulers or of their own volition. Ibrāhīm-niyā adds Fāṭima to this toll. Her death only six months after the Prophet's demise could not, he claimed, have been natural. Since the Jews had poisoned all other imāms, they must have poisoned her as well, he concluded.[88]

Contrary to ʿAlī's valiant stance against the Jews, the modern Shīʿī narrative portrays Abū Bakr and ʿUmar as their close friends. Charges of close friendship

86 Majlisī, *Biḥār al-anwār* vol. 42, 262–263; ʿAbbās Qommī, *Muntahī al-amāl fī tawārīkh al-nabī wal-āl ʿalayhim al-salām* vol. 1 (Tehrān: Bāqir al-ʿUlūm, 1384/2005), 258; Naqdī, *Al-Anwār al-ʿalawiyya wal-asrār al-murtaḍawiyya*, 376; "Āyā ibn Muljam Yahūdī būd?," 28 Tīr 1393/July 19, 2014, https://www.farsnews.com/printnews/13930427000047. The same post appeared in the following semi-official websites: http://meysammotiee.ir/post/1377; http://www.mashreghnews.ir/news/328533; http://www.jahannews.com/analysis/370980; Dashtī, *Rahāvard-i mubārazat-i ḥażrat-i Zahrā'*, 121; "Cherā ibn Muljam qātil Imām ʿAlī (ʿa) shod," 25 Tīr 1394/July 16, 2015, http://snn.ir/fa/news/425891; "Begīrad farzand-i zan-i Yahūdī rā," http://masaf.ir/View/Contents/29817/; "Yahūd setīzī rā ṣahyūnīsthā rāh endākhteand," October 17, 2018 cited in "At Antisemitic Conference In Tehran, Iranian Presidency Official Denies Holocaust: 'In Fact, We Do Show Antisemitic Behavior, And If We Are Not Doing Something Against The Jews, We Feel Bad – It Is Part Of Our Culture,'" MEMRI, Special Dispatch no. 7758, November 12, 2018, https://www.memri.org/reports/antisemitic-conference-tehran-iranian-presidency-official-denies-holocaust-fact-we-do-show.

87 See for example, ʿAbbās Qommī, *Muntahī al-amāl* vol. 1, 342, vol. 2, 62, 172, 310; Moojan Momen, *An Introduction to Shīʿī Islam* (New Haven: Yale University Press, 1985), 28, 37, 39, 40, 42, 43, 44.

88 "Naqsh-i Yahūd dar vaqāyiʿ-i ta'rīkh-i Islām;" "Yahūdī zādehgan musalmān nemā;" "Naqsh-i Yahūd dar shahādat-i Imāmān;" "Naqsh-i Yahūd dar shahādat-i ahl-i bayt," http://dar-al-quran.ir/اخبار/مناسبت-ها-1508/نقش-یهود-در-شهادت-اهل-بیت-ع; Ḥamīdī, *Dushmanān-i mahdaviyat cherā va-chegūneh*, 125, 128, 147; Muḥammad Ibrāhīm-niyā, "Naqsh-i Yahūd dar shahādat-i ḥażrat-i Zahrā' salām Allah ʿalayhā," http://intiqam.blogfa.com/post-24.aspx; "Inqilābīm, sarbaz rahbarīm," July 26, 2016, http://www.pictaram.org/post/BIYE7yuDAdR; "Aghāz-i intiẓār-i ta'rīkh," http://karbarayezohor.blogfa.com/post/39.

between Jews and ʿAlī's opponents appeared in early Shīʿī writings including ḥadīths attributed to the Eleventh Imām, Ḥasan al-ʿAskarī (d. 260/874).[89] However, they appear to have increased in scope, level of detail, and richness of plot in the more modern narrative. Thus, according to this motif, Abū Bakr's father had been a teacher for the Jews, and his daughter, ʿAisha (d. 678), was treated by a Jewish woman with a Jewish talisman when she was ill. Moreover, both men allegedly accepted Islam only after hearing from their Jewish friends that the Prophet was destined to rule the Arabs and that their conversion was part of a Jewish scheme. In fact, it is asserted that the Jews promoted Abū Bakr at the very beginning of the Prophet's mission as part of their plan to dominate the young Muslim community.[90]

The modern Shīʿī writers have claimed that following the Saqīfa meeting, "the Jewish organization" (*sāzemān-i Yahūd*) and the "descendants of Jews" (*Yahūdīzādehgān*) played an active role in instigating ʿUmar and Abū Bakr's assault on Fāṭima's house that resulted in her injury and the miscarriage of her unborn son, Muhsin.[91] Abū Bakr's expropriation of the Fadak oasis, which the Prophet had taken from the Jews of Khaybar and given to Fāṭima, has been seen in both traditional and modern Shīʿī discourse as a leading example of his injustice toward the Prophet's family. The modern narrative now explains it as a manifestation of Abū Bakr's friendship with the Jews, who wanted to avenge their loss.[92] As a result of these developments, the Jews, according to Ḥujjat al-Islam Saʿādatī, exerted immense influence and power "in the political, social, ideological, and cultural spheres" of the nation of Islam.[93]

The Jewish connection is even stronger in the case of ʿUmar, a subject of Shīʿī animosity for centuries, with references to his familiarity with the Jewish

---

89 Shaykh Ṣadūq, *Kamāl al-Dīn wa-tamām al-niʿma* (Qom: Mu'assasat al-nashr al-Islāmī, 1363/1984), 463; Majlisī, *Biḥār al-anwār* vol. 52, 6.

90 "Naqsh-i Yahūd dar vaqāyiʿ-i ta'rīkh-i Islām"; "Poshtībānī-i Yahūd az saqīfa gerāyān," https://forum.hammihan.com/thread101903.html (last accessed June 24, 2017); "Inḥirāf ʿAbd al-Raḥman Dimashqiyya (w) ʿAlī al-Rubayʿī ʿan al-Islām," August 5, 2012, https://www.facebook.com/alsadreeon/posts/401495023231756; Ilāhī, Yazdānī, and Kāẓimzādeh, *Mahār-i inḥirāf*, 5.

91 Dashtī, *Rahāvard-i mubārazat-i ḥażrat-i Zahrā'*, 42; Ibrāhīm-niyā, "Naqsh-i Yahūd dar shahādat-i ḥażrat-i Zahrā' Salam Allah ʿalayhā;" "Dawr al-Yahūd fī al-mu'āmara/Mu'āmarat al-Muslimīn ʿalā al-nabī Muḥammad," September 15, 2013, http://marwan1433.blogspot.co.il/2013/09/11.htm; "Naqsh-i Yahūd dar vaqāyiʿ-i ta'rīkh-i Islām;" "Naqsh-i Yahūd dar shahādat-i ḥażrat-i Fāṭima (s)," http://fa.alkawthartv.com/news/119907; Ḥamīdī, *Dushmanān-i mahdaviyat cherā va-chegūneh?*, 100–101.

92 Dashtī, *Rahāvard-i mubārazat-i ḥażrat-i Zahrā'*, 57–58; "Naqsh-i Yahūd dar shahādat-i Imāmān;" "Yahūdi zādehgān musalmān nemā (bakhsh-i pāyānī)."

93 "Barresī-i ikhlālgarī va-nufūẓ-i farhangī-i Yahūd." See a similar claim in Ilāhī, Yazdānī, and Kāẓimzādeh, *Mahār-i inḥirāf*, 58.

scriptures appearing in Sunnī sources as well.[94] The current narrative goes further in portraying ʿUmar as a close friend of the Jews and a person who had been heavily influenced by them before he became a Muslim and, most importantly, afterwards, when he served as their "fifth column" or agent in Medina. He reportedly retained his strong "tendency toward Judaism" even after becoming a Muslim despite the Prophet's strong warnings against this practice."[95] It is claimed that once he became caliph, ʿUmar enlisted the Jewish converts to stave off the crisis of legitimacy they were facing in light of ʿAlī's great social, moral, and scholarly stature. ʿUmar appointed Kaʿb al-Aḥbār, who had played a key role in driving many of the Companions away from ʿAlī, as his close advisor. The appointment is said to have given the Jews great political influence, which they used to fabricate and disseminate hundreds of ḥadīths that falsified the meaning and message of Islam. One writer lamented that under ʿUmar, Jewish influence over the Arabs returned to the same level as before the advent of Islam. Another equated Jewish control over culture in ʿUmar's tenure to Hollywood's role in spreading "Christian-messianic Zionism" in the present age.[96] A few Shīʿī writers even gave ʿUmar's expulsion of the Jews from the Arabian Peninsula a pro-Jewish twist, claiming that it was not an expulsion but, based on Kaʿb's advice, a fulfillment of the Jewish dream to return to their holy land and establish a de facto Israel.[97]

---

94 For an example in Sunnī sources, see Aḥmad ibn Ḥanbal, *Musnad Aḥmad ibn Ḥanbal* (Cairo: Dār al-Maʿārif, 1985) vol. 3, 387. The ḥadīth compendium *Biḥār al-anwār* contains quite a few traditions on ʿUmar relations with the Jews.

95 Ilāhī, Yazdānī, and Kāẓimzādeh, *Mahār-i inḥirāf*, 112; "Ahl-i Sunnat neveshtehānd ʿUmar bin Khaṭṭāb va-dokhtaresh ʿalāqa-i shadīdī beh torat dāshtand," http://www.antishobhe.blogfa.com/post/124; "ʿAlāqa-i ʿUmar bā dīn Yahūd," http://tarikhislam1400.blogfa.com/post/24; "ʿUmar wal-Yahūd, yahūdiyat-i ʿUmar bin al-Khaṭṭāb va-taʾāmurihi maʿa al-Yahūd," http://marwan1433143.blogspot.co.il/2014/10/blog-post.html; "Naqsh-i Yahūd dar taḥrīf-i ḥādithat-i Ghadīr Khumm;" "ʿUmar bin Khaṭṭāb sutūn-i panjom-i Yahūdiyān-i Medīna," 25 Dey 1393/January 15, 2015, http://amīremomenin.persianblog.ir/post/942.

96 "Ahl-i Sunnat va-Yahūd"; "Kaab Interfered in the Caliphate," *A Shiʿite Encyclopedia*, 942–945; "Naqsh-i Yahūd dar taḥrīf-i ḥādithat-i Ghadīr Khumm;" "Dast-i Yahūd va-Naṣārā dar āsatīn-i saqīfa-i nashīnān," http://www.bonyad-mahdi.blogfa.com/cat-45.aspx; al-Ṭāʾī, *Faḍāʾiḥ-i Yahūd mutalabbisūn bil-Islām*, 60–100; "ʿUmar wal-Yahūd dirāsa nafsiyya fī khalfiyat ʿUmar al-dīnīyya (pt. 2)," http://izapilla.blogspot.com/2013/0h9/id00137.html; "ʿUmar bin al-Khaṭṭāb al-khalīfa al-thānī/Muʾāmarat al-Muslimīn ʿalā al-nabī Muḥammad," http://marwan1433.blogspot.co.il/2013/07/5.html; "Dawr al-Yahūd fī al-muʾāmara/Muʾāmarat al-Muslimīn ʿalā al-nabī Muḥammad;" Ṭabāṭabāʾī, "Naqsh-i jarayān-i Masīḥī-Yahūdī dar tarbiyat-i Yazīd." These charges appear also in official textbooks such as the Grade 11 Religion and Life textbook, cited in Saeed Paivandi, *Discrimination and Intolerance in Iran's Textbooks* (Washington, DC: Freedom House, 2008), 43.

97 Mahdīpūr, *Taʾrīkh-i Islām bā rūyikard-i dushman shināsī*, 58; "ʿUmar wal-Yahūd/Yahūdiyat ʿUmar b. al-Khaṭṭāb wa-taʾāmurihi maʿa al-Yahūd;" "Dawr al-Yahūd fī al-muʾāmara."

According to this narrative, the Jews remunerated ʿUmar for his friendship. Although they did not, as a rule, allow gentiles to study with them, they made an exception with ʿUmar, thus proving their close friendship. ʿUmar had doubts about his eligibility for the caliphate, but the Jews convinced him that his appointment had been foretold in their scriptures. Most significantly, the Jews "with their funds, craftiness, and alliance with the Umayyad's," brought him to Muḥammad's throne, thereby isolating ʿAlī, the rightful heir. Finally, it was the Jews were named ʿUmar "al-Fārūq," namely, the one who distinguishes between truth and falsehood, which became his honorary title among the Sunnīs.[98]

The third motif explaining Jewish actions against Shīʿīsm attributes Jewish ancestry to leading Sunnī figures. Such attribution of Jewish ancestry to rivals was widespread among Muslims (both Sunnīs and Shīʿīs) and Christians during the medieval period. It reflected the notion of Jews as a metaphor of evil but also served as a mechanism of self-defense, by presenting the accusers themselves as innocent of the charge.[99]

The most prominent example is the claim that "several" of the fourteen leading villains against ʿAlī (presumably a counter trope to the "fourteen pure ones" of the Shīʿa) are *Yahūdīzadegan*.[100] According to Mahdī Ṭāʾib, Abū Bakr did not only install a Jewish system in Medina following the Prophet's death but was in fact himself of Jewish descent. Similarly, the pejorative term "*Yahūdīzade*" is often applied to ʿUmar.[101]

---

98 "ʿUmar al-Yahūd/yahūdiyat ʿUmar;" "ʿUmar wal-Yahūd: dirāsa nafsiyya fī khalfiyat ʿUmar al-dīnīyya (pt. 2)."

99 Nirenberg, *Anti-Judaism*, 231.

100 The fourteen "villains" are: Abū Bakr, ʿUmar, ʿUthmān, Muʿāwiya, ʿAmru b. al-ʿĀṣṣ, Ṭalḥa, Saʿad b. Abī Waqāṣ, ʿAbd al-Raḥman b. ʿAwf, Abū ʿUbaydah b. Jarrāḥ, Abū Mūsā al-Ashʿarī, Abū Hurayra, Mughīra b. Shuʿba, Maʿādh b. Jabl, and Sālim Mawlā Abi Ḥadīfa. "Naqsh-i Yahūd dar vaqāyiʿ-i taʾrīkh-i Islām." The fourteen Shīʿī pure ones are the Prophet, his daughter Fāṭima, and the twelve imāms. For more on this theme see also, "Poshtībānī-i Yahūd az saqīfa-i gerāyān."

101 "Ḥujjat al-Islām Ṭāʾib: naḥwa beh qudrat rasīdan-i Abū Bakr baʿd piyāmbar akram (s)," 26 Bahman 1389/January 15, 2011, http://tabiin.blog.ir/1389/11/26; Dashtī, *Rahāvard-i mubārazat-i ḥażrat-i Zahrāʾ*, 128; "ʿUmar va-Abū Bakr;" "Yahduizādehgān musalmān-nemā;" "Naqsh-i Yahūd dar shahādat-i Imāmān;" "Naqsh-i Yahūd dar shahādat-i ahl-i bayt." ʿUmar's case reflects the change from the traditional to the modern popular discourse. A ḥadīth attributed to Imām Jaʿfar al-Ṣādiq, speaks of Qunfudh (lit. hedgehog), ʿUmar's slave (*ghulām*), who struck Fāṭima and caused her death (cited in Majlisī's *Biḥār al-anwār*, 43:170). The popular sources today have omitted the term slave and attached the term *qunfudh* this time as a pejorative to ʿUmar, while also adding the adjective "*Yahūdīzādeh*" to him.

Another prominent case of Judaizing the enemies of the Shīʿa is the alignment of the Umayyad dynasty – the ultimate villains in the Shīʿī worldview – with the Jews. This charge is based on a tradition that Umayyah, the founder of the family, had married a Jewish slave girl from Sepphoris in northern Palestine.[102] The Shīʿīs endorsed this tradition early on and depicted the whole Umayyad dynasty as descendants of Jews. Thus, *Nahj al-Balāgha*, the revered collection of sermons, letters, exegeses, and narrations attributed to ʿAlī, refers to the future Umayyad caliph, Marwān b. al-Ḥakm (d. 685), as a Jew.[103] The contemporary discourse expanded the Umayyad family's Jewish connection beyond genealogy and into broad collaboration. Accordingly, the doctrinal and cultural deviations in Islam – allegedly the outcome of Jewish falsifications of ḥadīths, as discussed earlier – paved the way for the Umayyad seizure of power.[104] In the words of Ḥujjat al-Islam and former Minister of Intelligence Ḥaydar Musliḥī, the Jewish-Zionist falsification of pure Islam and the actions of the Umayyads are the "same accursed tree."[105] Formerly, the Umayyads headed the Shīʿī ranking of evil. In a significant shift between pre-modern and contemporary priorities, a writer from the Mouood Cultural Institute in Qom placed the Jews above them as he explained that "the link of the Umayyads with the party of Satan [the Jews] is … the greatest proof of the satanic essence of this family."[106]

In the modern narrative, Kaʿb al-Aḥbār is the one who advised ʿUmar to appoint Muʿāwiya (d. 680) as governor of Syria and who lit in Muʿāwiya's mind "the fire of ambition and determination" to assume power. According to various stories, Kaʿb foretold ʿUmar about his imminent murder and predicted the rise of the Umayyads to power following two other caliphs succeeding ʿUmar.

---

102 For an analysis of the tradition, see Seth Ward, "Muḥammad Said: 'You Are Only a Jew from the Jews of Sepphoris': Allegations of the Jewish Ancestry of Some Umayyads," *Journal of Near Eastern Studies* 60, no. 1 (2001): 31–42.

103 Ḥabībollah Hāshimī Khoʾī, *Manhaj al-barāʿa fī sharḥ nahj al-balāgha* (Beirut: Muʾassasat al-Wafaʾ, 1953), sermon no. 72, vol. 5, 218, which refers to Marwān's hand as "the hand of a Jew." See also Majlisī, *Biḥār al-anwār* vol. 31, 458. Among the modern attributions, see "Naqsh-i Yahūd dar vaqāyiʿ-i taʾrīkh-i Islām;" "Naqsh-i Yahūd va-Naṣārā dar āsatīn-i saqīfa-i nashīnān;" "Naqsh-i Yahūd dar vāqiʿa-i ʿĀshūrāʾ va-shahādat-i Sayyid al-Shuhadāʾ ʿalayhi al-salām," – http://intiqam.blogfa.com/post-27.aspx; A Tebyān article "Teknīkhā-i dushman shināsī az manẓar-i Imām ʿAlī," added an explanation to Marwān's Jewish nature as "treacherous and unscrupulous," 27 Abān 1388/November 18, 2009, https://article.tebyan.net/107858/.

104 Mahdīpūr, *Taʾrīkh-i Islām bā rūyikard-i dushman shināsī*, 10, 50–55.

105 "ʿUżvū hayʾat-i raʾīsa-i bonyād-i ḥafẓ va-nashr-i athār va-arzeshhā-i difāʿ muqaddas," http://www.nedayeurmia.ir/index.aspx?fkeyid=&siteid=8&pageid=214&newsview=264860.

106 "Banī Umayya va-Yahūd," 25 Tīr 1395/July 15, 2016, http://www.mouood.org/component/k2/item/36944.

The prediction, which Kaʿb claimed was written in the Jewish scriptures, had a profound effect on ʿUmar and determined his decision to allow the council to nominate his successor, thereby depriving ʿAlī of his rights once again.[107] The Jewish Studies Center, an anti-Semitic institute in Tehrān, projects Kaʿb's guilt on the Jews as a whole. Since Kaʿb knew about ʿUmar's murder in advance, the Jews as a collective must also have known. Another writer ascribes Kaʿb an important role in the sedition that led to the murder of the third caliph, ʿUthmān in 656, as he knew that it would advance Muʿāwiya's rise to power. Since Sunnīs accused ʿAlī's supporters of the murder, this allegation both exonerated the Shīʿīs of the crime and pinned it on the external enemy. Not surprisingly, Musliḥī concluded that Muʿāwiya was able to assume power thanks to "Jewish-Zionist capital and influence."[108] Once in power, Muʿāwiya is said to have appointed many Jews to key positions in the Umayyad administration, enabling them to erect a complex and secret system akin to the present-day situation in the United States where the Jews wield immense power. Ḥujjat al-Islam Hāmid Kāshānī, for example, described Muʿāwiya as a tool in the exercise of Jewish influence, thereby belittling Umayyad evil and inflating the Jewish aspect.[109]

The participants in the new discourse are divided, however, over the question of whether Muʿāwiya married a Jewish woman who gave birth to Yazīd (d. 683), the evil monarch who was responsible for the tragedy at Karbalāʾ. A few have maintained that Yazīd's mother originated from a Christian tribe; others, like Ayatollah Qarahī, insist that she had been Jewish. One writer even asserted that she conceived Yazīd with a Jewish man in order to preserve the purity of his Jewish blood.[110] The importance of the Jewish motif is such that several writers, conceding that Yazīd was educated by the Christian priest Yūḥānā, have described the priest as a "Crusader-Zionist." The anachronism of this term is two-fold: as Zionism is a modern movement and the Crusaders emerged only in the eleventh century. Interestingly, the term "Crusader-Zionist" is borrowed

---

107 Al-Ṭāʾī, *Faḍāʾiḥ-i Yahūd mutalabbisūn bil-Islām*, 102–103; "Naqsh-i Yahūd dar taḥrīf-i ḥādithat-i Ghadīr Khumm;" "Kaʿb al-Aḥbār, shakhṣī ke dar musalmānan nufūẕ kard."

108 "Iṭṭilāʿ-i Yahūd az terōr-i khalīfa-i dovom," http://jscenter.ir/judaism-and-islam/jewish-intrigue/5549; "Poshtībānī-i Yahūd az saqīfa-i gerāyān;" "ʿUżvū hayʾat-i raʾīsa;" al-Ṭāʾī, *Faḍāʾiḥ-i Yahūd mutalabbisūn bil-Islām*, 86.

109 Mahdī Ṭāʾib, "Yahūd dushman-i dīrīnah-i Islām," *Mowʿūd* 57 (1384/ 2005): 14–19. "Rivāyat-i Ḥujjat al-Islām Ṭāʾib az naqsh-i Yahūd dar dastgāh-i khilāfat-i Muʿāwiya," 22 Dey 1391/ January 11, 2013, http://www.farsnews.com/newstext.php?nn=13911021000692; "Barresī-i nifāq va-khaṭarnaktar az nifāq;" "Yūḥānā muʿallīm-i Yazīd rā beshenāsīd," 19 Abān 1392/ November, 10 2013, http://www.mouood.org/component/k2/item/15236-یوحنا-معلم-یزید-را-بشناسید-.html.

110 Ṭabāṭabāʾī, "Naqsh-i jarayān-i Masīḥī-Yahūdī dar tarbiyat-i Yazīd;" "Ayatollah Qarahī: Abā Sufyān va-Muʿāwiya."

from modern Sunnī Islamists who use it to denote the joint Western-Jewish threat to Islam.[111] These depictions enabled Ḥujjat al-Islam Aḥmad Rahdār and Ismāʿīl Shafīʿī Sarvestānī, managing director of the Mouood Cultural Institute, to break away from the traditional Shīʿī position, which has viewed Yazīd as the epitome of evil, and shift at least part of the blame to the Jews. Pondering why Muslims would go against Imām Ḥusayn, Rahdār's solution was simple: they were influenced by the Jews. Shafīʿī, for his part, asserted that Yazīd was not the source (*aṣl*) of the ʿĀshūrāʾ tragedy but more the "cruel worker (*ʿamala*)" who carried it out, with the true source of ʿĀshūrāʾ being the Jews. Muḥammad Mahdī Ḥamīdī went further by claiming that in carrying out the Karbalāʾ massacre, Yazīd sought to "eliminate and eradicate Islam and thereby fully realize Jewish aspirations."[112] With the Jewish-Umayyad bond in mind, Musliḥī concluded that Imām Ḥusayn rose in rebellion in order to correct the deviation in Islam that was created by the "Zionist Jews," thereby relegating the Umayyads to a secondary role in the camp of evil.[113]

The idea of Jewish complicity in the Karbalāʾ tragedy appeared in early Shīʿī sources. One such tradition is attributed to the sixth imām, Jaʿfar al-Ṣādiq, who stated that the "hand of Jews" was involved in the martyrdom of ʿAlī, Ḥasan, and Ḥusayn.[114] Modern versions have added a few details in order to expand the Umayyad-Jewish link. Ibrāhīm-niyā linked the timing of the tragedy to the Jews, saying that even the *jāhilī* Arabs respected the sanctity of Muḥarram and never fought during that month; however, the Jews, he stated, never had any qualms about shedding blood during holy months, seeing it as an opportunity to get closer to Iblīs (Satan). He explained that although Ḥusayn had arrived in Karbalāʾ on 9 Muḥarram, the Umayyad commander started the battle and massacre a day later, because on 10 Muḥarram, the Jews celebrated their Day of Atonement with great fanfare and he wanted all the people to celebrate and rejoice together. As was the case elsewhere, Jewish origins was also attributed to the Umayyad officer Shimr b. Dhī al-Jawshan, who had dealt the final blow to Ḥusayn.[115]

---

111 Ṭabāṭabāʾī, "Naqsh-i jarayān-i Masīḥī-Yahūdī dar tarbiyat-i Yazīd;" "ʿYūḥānāʾ muʿallīm-i Yazīd rā beshenāsīd."

112 "Naqsh-i Yahūd dar vāqiʿa-i khūnīn Karbalāʾ," https://www.mouood.org/component/k2/item/6417; Ḥamīdī, *Dushmanān-i mahdaviyat cherā? Va-chegūneh?* 115.

113 "ʿUżvū hayʾat-i raʾīsa."

114 Bāqir al-ʿUlūm Institute, *Farhang-i jamīʿ sokhnān-i Imām Ḥusayn ʿalayhi al-salām* (Qom, 1392/2013), 32; Shafīʿī Sarvestānī, "Naqsh-i Yahūd dar vāqiʿa-i Karbalāʾ."

115 "Naqsh-i Yahūd dar vāqiʿa-i ʿĀshūrāʾ va-shahādat-i Sayyid al-Shuhadāʾ ʿalayhi al-salām;" "Ustād-i Rāʾifīpūr: Shimr Yahūdī būd," http://www.aparat.com/v/zZ39R; https://www.instagram.com/p/7GP5uBGRLD/.

In a special seminar dedicated to the Jewish role in the tragedy of Karbalāʾ held by the Mouood Cultural Institute in November 2012, various speakers placed the Karbalāʾ event within the broader theme of Jewish conspiracies against Islam. They highlighted the importance of cursing the Jews as part of the ʿĀshūrāʾ ceremonies, as the mourners are required to curse the enemies and the Qurʾān places the Jews above all other enemies. Not surprisingly, Ibrāhīm-niyā concluded that the elimination of the State of Israel would be the proper revenge for the Karbalāʾ tragedy.[116] Contrary to the allegations raised in the contemporary discourse, the *Islamquest* website expressed doubts that the Jews had played any role in the tragedy. It explained that the status and image of the Jews had been so low at the time that even oppressive rulers like Yazīd took care to keep them at a distance.[117] In other words, the new discourse is not yet fully dominant but may be gaining popularity among mid-ranking spokesmen. At the same time, the argument on *Islamquest* website reflected the low status of the Jews in the writer's eyes.

6 The Jews, the Mahdī, and Their Final Fate

The supposed Jewish animosity and activities against Shīʿīsm culminated in the Jews' efforts to prevent the future apparition (*ẓuhūr*) of the Twelfth Imām. According to this narrative, the Jews will fight him once he rises as the Mahdī, who will redeem the Shīʿīs and the world.[118] Nūrī-Hamadānī, while explaining the grave danger which the Jews pose to the Iranian people and to Islam, concluded that "one should fight the Jews and vanquish them so that the

116 "Imām Ḥusayn va-ifshāʾ kardan naqsh-i Yahūd dar vāqiʿa-i ʿĀshūrāʾ," 26 Abān 1391/November 16, 2012, https://www.farsnews.com/news/13910826000113/; "Naqsh-i Yahūd dar vāqiʿa-i khūnīn Karbalāʾ;" "Barresī-i naqsh-i Yahūd dar vāqiʿa-i khūnīn Karbalāʾ," 24 Abān 1391/November 14, 2012, http://www.598.ir/fa/news/93309. "Naqsh-i Yahūd dar vāqiʿa-i ʿĀshūrāʾ va-shahādat-i Sayyid al-Shuhadāʾ ʿalayhi al-salām."

117 "Āyā Yahūdiyān va-Masīḥiyān dar ʾījād ḥāditha-i ʿĀshūrāʾ va-shahādat-i Imām Ḥusayn (a) naqsh dāshtand?," http://www.islamquest.net/fa/archive/question/fa63714.

118 "Duʿā-i Ayat Allah Qarahī barāye nābūdī-i Masīḥiyat va-Yahūdiyat," 1 Shahrīvar 1395/August 22, 2016, http://ashnaie.com/6318/; "Khamenei Associate Mehdi Taeb," MEMRI, Special Dispatch no. 6759. Some writers describe the Zionists as actively working against the Mahdī and seeking to undermine Shīʿī belief in him, see Rūḥollah Zamānī Musāvī, "Iqdāmāt va-barnāmahhā-i ṣahyūnīsm dar taqābul āmūzeh-i mahdaviyat dar ḥawza-i siyāsat va-ijtimāʿ," http://mahdimag.ir/fa/Magazine/articlemagz/اقدامات وبرنامه های صهیونیزم در تقابل با اموزه مهدویت درحوزه سیاست و اجتماع 13950815.

conditions for the advent of the Hidden Imām is met."[119] This hostility raises the question of the Jews' ultimate fate once the Mahdī emerges victorious and restores justice on earth. The Islamic Republic continues the traditional clerical approach of propagating the belief in the imminent return of the Twelfth Imām as the Mahdī. At the same time, it seeks to manage popular Mahdīsm by focusing messianic attentions toward the distant future, presumably out of fear that imprudent messianism may lead to a crisis of faith if it fails to materialize.[120]

Both Shīʿīs and Sunnīs see the Mahdī as fighting Islam's enemies. In Sunnī tradition, these enemies are the unbelievers, i.e., the Christians, and the Jews. For Shīʿīs, the Mahdī will avenge the enemies of *ahl al-bayt* (the Prophet's family), first and foremost the Umayyads but also the "hypocrites" who betrayed them for generations. The classical sources are unclear whether or not the Mahdī will convert all humankind to Islam, but they are certain that he will punish the establishment clerics, who have failed to establish a just Islamic order.[121]

The Jews play an insignificant role in this apocalyptic literature. But, as was the case in the ʿĀshūrāʾ commemorations during the 1970s when the West replaced the Sunnīs as the major oppressor, a new trend regarding the Mahdī has emerged in recent years. Once again the West and, in particular, the Jews have become the "cardinal" enemies of the Mahdī. The Jews are depicted as one of the peoples who God will specifically send the Mahdī to fight against and defeat.[122] Some writers have regarded the existence of Israel on the Muslim

---

119 Ayatollah Nouri-Hamedani, "Fight the Jews and Vanquish Them so as to Hasten the Coming of the Hidden Imam,'" MEMRI, Special Dispatch no. 897, April 22, 2005, https://www.memri.org/reports/ayatollah-nouri-hamedani-%E2%80%98fight-jews-and-vanquish-them-so-hasten-coming-hidden-imam%E2%80%99.

120 Zeev Maghen, "Occultation in Perpetuum: Shiʿite Messianism and the Policies of the Islamic Republic," *The Middle East Journal* 62, no. 2 (2008): 232–257; Abbas Amanat, "The Resurgence of Apocalyptic in Modern Islam," *Apocalyptic Islam and Iranian Shiʿism* (London: I.B. Tauris, 2009), 67.

121 David Cook, "Messianism in the Shiʿite Crescent," *Current Trends in Islamist Ideology* 11 (April 2011): 94.

122 Ḥamīdī, *Dushmanān-i mahdaviyat cherā va-chegūneh?*; "Yahūd dushman-i aṣlī-i Imām-i Zamān (ʿajala Allah taʿālā farajahu);" "Imām-i Zamān (ʿajala Allah taʿālā farajahu al-sharīf) va-saranjām-i Yahūd," 29 Ordībehesht 1390/May 19, 2011, http://article.tebyan.net/165478; "Gozāresh-i Fars az neshest-i ʿnaqsh-i Yahūd dar vāqiʿa-i khūnīn-i Karbalāʾ;" "Nābūdī-i qawm-i Yahūd dar dowran-i ākhar al-zamān," 24 Dey 1387/January 13, 2009, http://www.shia-news.com/fa/news/11981; excerpts of Ismāʿīl Shafīʿī Sarvestānī, *Dāneshestān-i sarzamīnhā-i dargīr dar vāqiʿa-i sharīf-i ẓuhūr* (Tehrān: Mowʿūd-i ʿaṣr, 1391), http://rasekhoon.net/article/show/846954.

land of Palestine as the fulfillment of the traditional signs (*ʿalāʾim*) of the Jewish destruction of Jerusalem, which foretell the coming of the Mahdī.[123]

Most significant is the new association of the Jews with the Sufyānī, the Sunnī tyrant, who will hail from the region of Syria and will fight the Mahdī. The Sufyānī, as his name tells and as his actions prove, serves as the symbolic apocalyptic reincarnation of the hateful Umayyads. The major battle between his forces and those of the Mahdī will take place in Megiddo (the original site of the Christian Armageddon), where he will be defeated and killed, symbolizing the reversal and rectification of the Shīʿī defeat by the Umayyads. Classical messianic literature says that the Sufyānī's appearance will occur either together with or in close connection with "*al-Rūm*" (the Byzantines) invasions of the Muslim world.[124] As the Byzantines no longer exist, various modern writers have associated the term *Rūm* with the West and the Jews, describing the Sufyānī as not only a close ally of the Jews but operating on their behalf as their proxy.[125] The implications are clear: if the Sufyānī is the epitome of evil and of opposition to the just and divine cause of the Mahdī to redeem humanity, then

123 "ʿAlāmāt ẓuhūr al-Imām al-Mahdī al-kubrā allatī taḥaqqaqat wa-allatī lam tataḥaqqaq li-ḥad al-an," https://groups.google.com/forum/#!msg/alnoorh/z6VDSLPWpW8/3TrgApCwmbIJ; "ʿAlāmāt al-ẓuhūr," http://ar.wikishia.net/view/علامات_الظهور.

124 Muḥammad Ṭūsī, *Kitāb al-ghayba* (Beirut: Muʾassasat ahl al-bayt, 1987), 289; Muḥammad al-Nuʿmānī, *Kitāb al-ghayba* (Qom: Mehr, n.d.), 1187, http://shiaonlinelibrary.com/الكتب/1281_كتاب-الغيبة-محمد-بن-إبراهيم-النعماني-ج-١; Majlisī, *Biḥār al-anwār* vol. 52, 208. None of them mention the Jews in this context. Before the 2003 collapse of the Saddam Hussein regime in Iraq, many messianic writers in both the Sunnī and Shīʿī traditions identified Saddam Hussein as the Sufyānī (Cook, "Messianism in the Shiʿite Crescent," 93). After Saddam's fall, the Sufyānī was identified with other evil figures. ʿAbd al-Karīm al-Zubaydī, *ʿAṣr al-Sufyānī* (Beirut: Dār al-Hādī, 2006), 383 identifies him with the United States.

125 ʿAlī al-Kurānī, *ʿAṣr al-ẓuhūr* (Qom: muʾassasat al-maʿārif al-Islāmiyya, 2006), 23–24, 31, 107. The publication of the book's seventeenth edition by 2006 attests to its widespread popularity. In addition, excerpts were published on numerous websites and blogs; Amīr Reżā Rajāyī, *Asrār-i Yahūd va-ākhar-i zamān*, (electronic edition, 1396/2017), 23–24, 119; "Imām-i Zamān (ʿajala Allah taʿālā farajahu al-sharīf) va-saranjām-i Yahūd;" "Mabāḥīth-i mahdaviyat no. 22: pīmān-i mushtarak beyne sufyānī va-gharbīhā," April 14, 2014, http://www.farhangnews.ir/content/208533#_edn10; "Matā tarānī wa-narāka: silsila-i maqālatī pīrāmūn-i mahdaviyat (pt. 1)," 7 Khordād 1394/May 28, 2015, http://www.ebnolreza.ir/cultural/tahlilvizhe/250-selseleh-maghalat-1.html; Saʿīd Bakhshī and Seyyed Masʿūd Pūr Seyyed Aqāyī, "Muvājahat-i Imām-i zamān (ʿalayhi al-salām) bar qawm-i Yahūd dar ʿaṣr-i ẓuhūr," *Mashriq Mowʿūd* 42 (1396/2017): 39–86; "Pīsh qarāvolān-i sufyānī, yā ʿamalahā-i ṣalīb va-ṣahyūn," 18 Tīr 1393/July 9, 2014, https://article.tebyan.net/281196/پیش-قراولان-سفیانی-یا-عمله-های-صلیب-و-صهیون-. The thirteenth-century book by Ibn Tavoos, *Al-malāḥim va-al-fitan* does not award the Jews an important place in relation to the Imam. But in the contemporary translation, the cleric Seyyed Mahdī Ayatollahī added a poem on the back cover that says that when the Mahdī returns, he will "uproot Jewish

his alliance with the Jews or action on their behalf defines them as equally evil. Interestingly, some writers have highlighted the passages that stress the key role of the Khorāsānis, interpreted to signify all Iranians, in fighting alongside the Mahdī and ensuring his victory. Thus, the future religious clash, in which the Jews will constitute "the axis of falsehood (*bāṭel*) and Islamic Iran will constitute the axis of truth," is endowed with a nationalist tinge while setting the Iranians against the Jews.[126]

The significance of the clash between the Mahdī and the Jews and his expected revenge upon them led various writers to associate it with the Qurʾānīc passage (Qurʾān 17:5) regarding the two occasions that Jews will corrupt the land and their expected final punishment. When the Muslims strayed from Islam, one writer explained, the Jews were able to carry out their second corruption, namely, usurping Muslim Palestine and establishing the State of Israel. Now, when the Muslims return to Islam under Iranian leadership, the time of punishment will have arrived and the Mahdī will be the one to carry it out.[127]

The discussion about the second corruption by the Jews falls within the larger motif of Jewish corruption as a threat to humanity at large. According to Miṣbāḥ Yazdī, most of the centers of corruption in the world belong to the Jews, as they try to corrupt the others and thus rule the world. The charge of Jewish corruption culminates in their depiction as "corruption in the earth" (*fasād fī al-arḍ*),[128] a term coined by Khomeini to refer to anti-regime opposition and

---

Zionists," cited in Mehdi Khalaji, *Apocalyptic Politics: On the Rationality of Iranian Policy* (Washington Institute for Near East Policy: Policy Focus #79, January 2008), 24–25.

126 "Jang bā Yahūd dar ākhar al-zamān dar muḥākamāt-i Qurʾānī ast," 12 Khordād 1394/June 2, 2015, https://urlzs.com/8qqzX; Kurānī, *ʿAṣr al-ẓuhūr*, 31, 100; "Ākhar al-zamān va-naqsh-i Irānīān dar dafʿ-i do fitna-i Yahūd az dīdār-i Qurʾān," https://goo.gl/M8Q2Vf; Markaz-i takhaṣṣusī-i mahdaviyat, "Vażʿiyat-i Iran qabl az ẓuhūr va-naqsh-i ān dar ẓuhūr-i ḥażrat-i Mahdī ʿajala Allah taʿālā farajahu al-sharīf chīst?," *Ufq-i ḥawza* 305, 24 Farvardīn 1390/April 13, 2011, https://hawzah.net/fa/Magazine/View/6435/7830/100737.

127 "Vaʿdah-i ilāhī nisbat beh nābūdī-i Yahūdiyān," 2 Azar 1391/November 22, 2012, http://www.tebyan.net/newindex.aspx/index.aspx?pid=934&articleid=751771; "Vaʿdah-i ilāhī bar nābūdī-i Yahūd," http://imammahdi.ir/1396/07/15/2-وعده-الهی-بر-نابودی-یهود/; "Dō vaʿdeh-i ilāhī dar khuṣūṣ-i sarnevesht-i banī Isrāʾīl," 16 Mordād 1394/August 7, 2015, http://2vade.blogfa.com/post/1; Rajāyī, *Asrār-i Yahūd va-ākhar zamān*, 275; "Nābūdī-i qawm-i Yahūd dar dowran-i ākhar al-zamān;" "Dirāsa ḥawla ẓuhūr wa-burūz wa-ʿaqībat qawm al-Yahūd min manẓar al-Qurʾān al-karīm."

128 "Antisemitism and Holocaust Denial in the Iranian Media," MEMRI, Special Dispatch no. 855; "Ayatollah Miṣbāḥ Yazdī speech on Jews;" https://www.terrorism-info.org.il/en/18156/; Qūrtānī, "Yahūd rā behtar beshenāsīm." For more references on Jewish corruption, see Maḥmūd al-Nujayrī, "Talmūd rīsheh-i fasād va-sharārat-i Yahūd," 3 Ordībehesht 1392/April 23, 2013, http://rasekhoon.net/article/show/699380/; "Mīkveh va-fasād-i akhlāqī-i ḥākhāmhā-i Yahūdī," 18 Esfand 1395/March 8, 2017, http://khabarfarsi.com/u/34721670; "Towtīʾah-i Yahūd barāye javānān-i Irānī."

entered into the Iranian penal code as a crime deserving the death sentence. The broader implication of this term is inferred when Khomeini reminded his readers that when the Jewish tribe of Banu Qurayẓa caused "corruption among the Muslims," the Prophet "eliminated them."[129]

Nonetheless, neither traditional nor modern Shīʿī sources are unanimous regarding the fate of the Jews after the Mahdī establishes his just rule on earth. Three different views can be detected in traditional Shīʿism. One believes that the Mahdī will enable the Jews to live as a protected minority (*ahl al-dhimma*), whereby they will continue to pay the *jizya* (poll tax) and practice their religion freely, while recognizing the superiority and domination of Islam.[130] Another view stipulates that after the Mahdī gains victory, "no Jew, no Christian, and no member of any religious community will remain who has not converted to Islam"; "the *jizya* will be abolished and the cross will be broken." Accordingly, those who do not convert will be killed.[131] The third view manifested in many Shīʿī ḥadīths states that all Jews will be killed. Several writers have adapted the Sunnī ḥadīth of "the promise of the stones and trees" (*waʿd al-ḥajr wal-shajr*) and proclaimed that when "the Mahdī returns he will fight the Jews and kill all of them. Even if a Jew hides behind a rock, the rock will speak and say, 'O Muslim! A Jew is hidden behind me. Kill him!'"[132]

129 Khomeini, *Islam and Revolution*, 89.

130 Jassim M. Hussain, *The Occultation of the Twelfth Imam: A Historical Background* (Tehrān: Bonyād Baʿthat, 1982), 24 and the sources cited there; Thāmir Hāshim ʿAmidī, *al-Mahdī al-muntaẓar fī al-fikr al-Islāmī* (Qom: Markaz al-Risāla, 1417/1996), 8; "Sarneveshet-i aqaliyathā-i maẕhabī dar *ḥukūmat*-i mahdavī," 28 Mordād 1394/August 19, 2015, https://www.mashreghnews.ir/news/455524/سرنوشت-اقلیت-های-مذهبی-در-حکومت-مهدوی.

131 Ṭūsī, *Kitāb al-Ghayba*, 59; Majlisī, *Biḥār al-anwār*, 52:340; Nuṣratollah Āyatī, *Ahl-i kitāb dar dawlat-i Mahdī* (aj) (Tehrān: Bonyād-i farhangī-i ḥażrat-i Mahdī mowʿūd, n.d.), 10, 14, 25; Muḥammad Mahdī Qazvīnī, *Imām-i Mahdī az vilādat tā ẓuhūr* (Markaz-i taḥqīqāt rayāneh'i Qā'imiyya-i Iṣfahān, n.d.), 513, 698–699; Asadollah Hāshimī Shahīdī, "Ikhrāj-i Yahūd az sarzamīnhā-i Islāmī," *Ẓuhūr-i ḥażrat-i Mahdī* (*ʿajala Allah farajahu*) *az dīdgāh-i Islām, maẕāhib va-millal-i jahān* (Qom, 1384/2005), http://www.m-ahdi.com/persian/index.php?page=books&id=13#177/.

132 Sayyid Ibn Tavoos, *Al-Malahim wa al-fitan fī zouhoor-i al-Ghaib al-Muntazar*, trans. Sayed Mahdī Ayatollahī (Tehrān: Intishārāt-i Jahānarā, 1385/2006), 142, 204, 200 and ʿAlī Ibn Hessam al-Dīn Mottaqi Hindi cited in Khalaji, *Apocalyptic Politics*, 4; Ismāʿīl Shafīʿī Sarvestānī cited at http://www.lamia.blogsky.com/1392/11/01/post-211; "Yahūd va-ākhar al-zamān 1," http://alhadid.blogfa.com/post-55.aspx; "Imām-i Zamān va-saranjām-i Yahūd," 18 Azar 1396/December 9, 2017, http://pajoohe.ir/امام-زمان-ع-و-سرانجام-یهود_a-35957.aspx.

A similar plurality of voices continues through the post-1979 period as well.[133] A few conservative clerics, most notably Grand Ayatollah Makārem Shīrāzī and Ayatollah Ibrāhīm Amīnī, endorse a moderate view, stating that in the era of the Mahdī most non-Muslims will accept Islam voluntarily, but the few Jews who do not will live as a protected minority paying the *jizya* poll tax under the Mahdī's just rule.[134] By contrast, quite a few mid-ranking hardline clerics and lay writers have concluded that following the battle the fate of the Jews will be annihilation (*nābūdī, qatl tam*) as the Mahdī "will purify the world from the filth of their existence (*lowth-i vujūdeshān*)."[135] It seems that older and more traditional clerics have greater inhibitions regarding the wholesale killing of another group, even an infidel one, whereas the younger clerics put politics above all else.

7 Conclusion

Modern Shīʿī discourse on Judaism represents both continuity and change. Alongside hostile attitudes toward Jews rooted in the rivalry between the new religion and its predecessors, there were also more complex or positive attitudes in early Shīʿīsm. The modern discourse is based on the early hostility but also draws from contemporary Sunnī Islamism and from Western anti-Semitism. As such, it employs more themes and motifs and has increased in the volume of publications and media of dissemination including also television

133 Um al-Banīn Ḥaydarī and Fāṭima Asgarpūr, "Yahūd va-Yahūdiyān dar ʿaṣr-i ẓuhūr," *Pazhūhesh-i Mahdavī* 25 (2018): 113–134 and Muḥammad Reżā Aqājānī Qonād, "Ḥuqūq-i aqaliyathā-i dīnī dar ʿaṣr-i ẓuhūr," *Majmūʿa-i athār-i sevomīn-i hamāyesh-i beyne almilalī doktrīn-i mahdaviyat bā rūyikard-i siyāsī va-ḥuqūqī* (Qom: Mu'asasa-i āyandeh roshān, 1387/2008), 303–352, which review four different approaches and show that each relies on ḥadīths for support.

134 Nāṣir Makārem Shīrāzī, *Ḥukūmat-i jahānī-i Mahdī* (Qom: Intishārāt-i nisl-i javān, 1380/2001), 288; Aqājānī Qonād, "Ḥuqūq-i aqaliyathā-i dīnī dar ʿaṣr-i ẓuhūr," 338; "Āyā Imām-i Mahdī (aj) hangām-i ẓuhūresh bā Masīḥiyān va-Yahūdiyān ṣulḥ mīkonad va-ba ʿArabhā mījangad?," http://hajj.ir/fa/83858; "Āyā Yahūdiyān dar dowran-i ẓuhūr nābūd mīshavand?," 24 Bahman 1393/February 13, 2015, http://www.farsnews.com/printable.php?nn=13931121000429; Kāmil Sulaymān, *Rūzegār-i Rāhhāyī*, vol. 1 (Tehrān: Afāq, 1386), 297–300, 378.

135 Ḥaydarī and Asgarpūr, "Yahūd va-Yahūdiyān dar ʿaṣr-i ẓuhūr;" "Nābūdī-i qawm-i Yahūd dar dowran-i ākhar al-zamān;" Kurānī, *ʿAṣr al-ẓuhūr*, 23–24; "Sufyānī, avvalīn-i neshāneh-i ḥatmī-i ẓuhūr-i Imām-i Mahdī," 12 Khordād 1394/June 2, 2015, http://www.rajanews.com/news/213604; "Maʿrakat al-Imām al-Mahdī ʿalayhi al-salām maʿa al-Yahūd," https://www.ansarh.com/maaref_details_1165_معركة_الإمام_المهدي_عليه_السلام__مع_اليهود.html; Rajāyī, *Asrār Yahūd va-ākhar-i zamān*, 669.

and internet. It has, in addition, become much more politicized, discarding, on the whole, the issue of Jewish impurity but associating the Jews and Zionism with the Western cultural challenge to Islam as a religion, identity, and culture. Another reason for this politicization is the attempt to establish common ground with mainstream Sunnīs against the common enemy in order to ease sectarian animosities within Islam. Thus, Jews or Jewish converts are represented as key players in traumatic historical events for the Shīʿa, thereby somewhat diminishing the guilt of ordinary Sunnīs.

Two major traits that typify the pre-modern Islamic approach can also be found in modern anti-Semitism. The first is the timelessness of Jewish motivations, character, and modes of action, which continue unchanged from the distant past up to the present. This failure to draw distinctions between the past and the present often leads to the usage of modern anachronisms in discussions of earlier historical periods, for example, the term "Zionists" when referring to seventh-century Medina or to the court of the Umayyad caliph Yazīd. Particularly important in this context is the presentation of the Jews as implacable enemies of Shīʿīsm from its inception to the present – a classic case of psychological projection. It is doubtful that Jews had any specific grudge or animosity toward Shīʿīs at times when the Shīʿīs were a persecuted minority in the early Islamic period. While Jews suffered discrimination and sometimes persecutions under the Shīʿī clergy during the Ṣafavīd and Qājār periods, they were too timid to express it outwardly or actually do anything about it.

The second trait is the presentation of the Jews as a calculating and organized monolith, motivated solely by their Jewish character or collective aspirations. Thus, it was "the Jews" and the "Jewish organization" as a collective but not as individuals that supposedly harbored ill toward Imām ʿAlī and worked to rob him of his rightful succession. Likewise, "the Jews" as a collective are identified with modern threats such as capitalism or the Freemasons. The most ominous manifestations of this trait is the myth of *The Protocols of the Elders of Zion* and the presentation of the Jews as the enemies of the future Mahdī who want to prevent humanity and the Shīʿa from attaining salvation at the end of time. As discussed throughout this book, many Shīʿī writers are acquainted with the foreign literature, including Western scholarship, on the subject matters they are debating. Writers about the Jews, on the other hand, rely solely on Islamic sources or on modern anti-Semitic literature and make no visible attempt to address other sources that present a different picture of the Jews. As in the past, they show little interest in using Jewish sources. Apparently, the negative role of the Jews in the Qurʾān and other traditional sources nullifies such a need.

The Shīʿī discourse on Judaism, like Shīʿīsm in general, has never been monolithic. Older Shīʿī sources differed as to the ultimate fate of the Jews once the Mahdī rises and restores justice on earth. In the present-day discourse there are some nuances. It appears that the most active promoters of the vehement anti-Semitic discourse are mid-ranking clerics, functionaries of state-run indoctrination institutes, and semi-official bloggers; in other words, they represent the more politicized sections within the clerical establishment and supporters of the more hardline factions in the Iranian political spectrum. The older grand ayatollahs, while sharing traditional Shīʿī antipathy toward the Jews, are somewhat less vehement, suggesting that generation gaps might be another explanation for this difference. The difference is most striking regarding the issue of the fate of the Jews following the coming of the Mahdī, about which there seem to be barely any references in the writing of the grand ayatollahs, except for Makārem Shīrāzī who speaks of mass conversion to Islam with the remaining Jews allowed to live as a protected minority. By contrast, quite a few of the more vocal anti-Jewish spokesmen write openly about the elimination of the Jews once the Mahdī comes.

A major issue in this context is the measure of acceptance of the anti-Jewish motifs among larger sections of the population. Studies of intellectual history or public discourse in the Middle East face a serious methodological problem of ascertaining reception due to the difficulty of acquiring data on public opinion particularly among the "silent classes" who lack the means to publicize their views. In view of the political situation in the Middle East, the ordinary Shīʿī consumer of religious or political literature is not really exposed to alternative attitudes toward Jews that differ from the dominant discourse. Several factors seem to facilitate widespread acceptance of anti-Jewish arguments: the widespread dissemination of such themes in a variety of media; the Israeli-Palestinian conflict and sympathy for the Palestinians; the use of themes that are deeply rooted in religious tradition; and the linkage of the Jews to other enemies of Shīʿīsm, ranging from the West to the Wahhābīs. Those who are disillusioned by the Iranian government's official ideology may, indeed, be less attracted to this type of discourse. A 2014 survey carried out by the US-based Anti-Defamation League concluded that 56% of adult Iranians hold anti-Semitic attitudes. Despite being a high figure, optimists could argue that it is lower than those surveyed in Arab countries in general and shows that quite a large segment of society is immune to the anti-Jewish discourse.[136]

136 *ADL Global100: An Index of Anti-Semitism 2015*, http://global100.adl.org/#country/iran.

CHAPTER 3

Extending a Hand to "Our Sunnī Brethren"

Shīʿī doctrines and practices were forged largely out of the rivalry with what evolved as the Sunnī majority. The intensity of the Sunnī-Shīʿī split fluctuated over the course of Islamic history but always remained a formative element in Islamic religious and political thought. The growing external threat to the Muslim world in the modern period prompted a counter effort to heal the sectarian rift and enable both groups to confront the common challenge.

This chapter analyzes Shīʿī Iranian attempts from, primarily, the first decade of the Twenty-first century to reach out to the Sunnī mainstream by revising various anti-Sunnī practices. While such efforts began earlier, the unprecedented sectarian violence in the Middle East, particularly after the 2003 shift of power from the Sunnīs to the Shīʿī majority in Iraq, rendered them more pertinent than ever. The new measures caused disagreements within the Shīʿī clerical establishment in and out of Iran as well as certain noncompliance by ordinary believers, thus reflecting tensions between official and popular Islam in Iran. In addition to examining the scholarly and public debate surrounding these measures, I try to assess whether they reflect a fundamental ideological revision regarding the historical and theological divide between Shīʿa and Sunna.

1 Historical Foundations of the Sunnī-Shīʿī Rift

Muslims through the ages award particular significance to the events of the early Islamic period for being the most important, often exclusive, source of reference for understanding or interpreting historical phenomena. The Prophet's lifetime was the golden age of Islam, and the following three generations were the formative period for all subsequent historical and doctrinal developments. The crux of the Sunnī-Shīʿī split, which originated in the struggle over the Prophet's successor, is as much about history as theology. Whereas Sunnīs, particularly modern-day Salafists, see the first generations of Islam as the golden age of religion to whose spirit they wish to return, the Shīʿīs see this period as the source of everything that is wrong in the world. Hence the veneration of the Prophet's Companions (*Sahaba*) by the Sunnīs and their rejection by the Shīʿīs have become an article of faith to both groups.[1]

1 Fanar Haddad, *Sectarianism in Iraq: Antagonistic Visions of Unity* (New York: Oxford University Press, 2011), 23–24.

 | DOI:10.1163/9789004444683_005

Imām, Jaʿfar al-Ṣādiq, who began to systematically articulate the Shīʿī doctrines, posited two intertwined principles which became the central tenets of belief of what later became Twelver Shīʿīsm: *walāya* (Persian *Tavalā*), allegiance to a specific line of male descendants of ʿAlī and Fāṭima as the only true Imāms or leaders of the Muslim community, and, disavowal (*barāʾa*, Persian *tabarrā*) and even enmity (*ʿadāwa*) toward their enemies.[2] In the course of time, *barāʾa* was broadened to include both the usurpers who had deprived ʿAlī of his God-given rights and their supporters. The term is thus applied to the majority of the Prophet's Companions, whom the Shīʿīs accused of having betrayed the Prophet when they sided with ʿAlī's rivals. Particular animosity was leveled at the second caliph, ʿUmar b. al-Khaṭṭāb, for his leading role in robbing ʿAlī of his rights.[3]

As respect for the Prophet's family was widespread among Sunnīs, and because group identity often requires active rejection of the "other," particularly if it is oppressive, Shīʿī doctrine came to regard *walāya* by itself as insufficient and a sign of weak faith if not accompanied with *barāʾa*. *Barāʾa* thus evolved as the "touchstone for allegiance to Imāmi Shīʿīsm" and the crucial boundary between Shīʿīs and Sunnīs.[4] The cursing, deprecation, and vilification of leading Companions became one of the most prominent and popular manifestations of Shīʿī identity throughout medieval Islamic history in contrast to Sunnī reverence for them.[5] Other Shīʿī rituals that developed from the Eighth century, such as visitations (*ziyārāt*) to the tomb of Imām Ḥusayn in Karbalāʾ and the ʿĀshūrāʾ commemorations of his death on the tenth of Muḥarram reinforced Shīʿī sense of victimhood and unique identity as distinguished from the Sunnīs.[6]

At the same time, the Shīʿīs formulated a nuanced spiritual hierarchy between themselves and other Muslims. While only Shīʿīs could be considered "true believers" (*muʾminūn*), non-Shīʿīs were still considered legitimate "Muslims" (*Muslimūn*), enjoying the possibility of salvation that was guaranteed to all Muslims by virtue of their observance of the basic laws and rituals of Islam. However, they could not participate in the powerful and salvific grace

---

2 For a comprehensive analysis of the idea of *walaya* and its sociopolitical ramifications, see Maria Massi Dakake, *The Charismatic Community: Shiʿite Identity in Early Islam* (Albany: SUNY Press, 2007).

3 Etan Kohlberg, "Some Imāmī Shīʿī Views on the Ṣaḥāba," *Jerusalem Studies in Arabic and Islam* 5 (1984): 143–175.

4 Etan Kohlberg, "Barāʾa in Shīʿī Doctrine," *Jerusalem Studies in Arabic And Islam* 7 (1986): 150.

5 Devin J. Stewart, "Popular Shiʿism in Medieval Egypt: Vestiges of Islamic Sectarian Polemics in Egyptian Arabic," *Studia Islamica* 84 (1996): 37.

6 Yitzhak Nakash, "The Visitation of the Shrines of the Imams and the Shīʿī Mujtahids in the Early Twentieth Century," *Studia Islamica* 81 (1995): 154–156; Yitzhak Nakash, "An Attempt to Trace the Origin of the Rituals of ʿĀshūrāʾ," *Die Welt des Islams* 33, no. 2 (1993): 161.

that was only granted to those who accepted and practised *walaya*. In addition, the Shīʿīs considered themselves the "spiritual elite" (*khāṣṣa*) of the Islamic community (*umma*), in contrast to the Sunnī commoners (*ʿāmma*) or "simple people" (*nās*).[7]

The takeover of Iraq by the pro-ʿAlīd Būyīd dynasty (945–1055) marked the full-fledged consolidation of Twelver Shīʿīsm as a system of belief and as a distinct religious community within Islam. The Būyīd Amīr Muʿizz al-Dawla (d. 967) relied on public displays of Shīʿī ideals to promote his religious legitimacy and to strengthen the sense of Shīʿī solidarity in and around Baghdad. Būyīd backing encouraged the appearance of new public manifestations of the Shīʿī creed, namely, the public denigration of the first two caliphs, Abū Bakr and ʿUmar. The new rites in addition to the formation of the separate Shīʿī traditions and jurisprudence served to define the Shīʿa as a distinct community or religious sect. The Muslims of Iraq were thus divided into two increasingly hostile camps, distinguished by peculiar formulas and prescriptions. Processions on Shīʿī holidays served as flash points for occasional sectarian riots in Baghdad, and the conflict encouraged the division of cities into Shīʿī and Sunnī quarters. While the Shīʿīs called themselves "*Imāmiyya*," their rivals termed them "*al-Rāfiḍa*" or "*Rawāfiḍ*," due to their rejection (*rafḍ*) of Abū Bakr, ʿUmar, and most other Companions of the Prophet.[8]

Shīʿī-Sunnī relations, however, were not one-dimensional, and alongside the rivalry, they also encompassed intellectual exchange and borrowings. The weaker minority is usually the one more influenced by the dominant majority, and this was the case with the Shīʿīs. Unlike the *Akhbārī* (Traditionalist) school of Qom and Ray, which developed a more hostile attitude toward Sunnī Islam, Shīʿī scholars in Baghdad interacted more with their Sunnī counterparts. For example, Shaykh al-Mufīd (d. 413/1022), the leader of the Shīʿī community in Baghdad who articulated the doctrine of Imāma, was in continuous contact and an apparently constructive exchange of views with his Sunnī counterparts.[9]

A major turning point in the evolution of the Shīʿī approach toward the Sunnīs was the rise of the Ṣafavīd dynasty in Iran in 1501, followed by their declaration of Shīʿīsm as the state religion and their lavish patronage of the growing Shīʿī clerical establishment. Iran's emergence as an empire and its use

---

7 Dakake, *The Charismatic Community*, 11.

8 Mafizullah Kabir, *The Buwayhid Dynasty of Baghdad (334/946–447/1055)* (Calcutta: Iran Society, 1964), 204; John J. Donohue, *The Buwayhid dynasty in Iraq 334 H./945 to 403 H./1012: Shaping Institutions for the Future* (Leiden: Brill, 2003), 329–334.

9 Ahmad Kāẓimī Mūsavī, "Sunnī-Shīʿī Rapprochement (Taqrīb)," in *Shiʿite Heritage: Essays on Classical and Modern Traditions*, ed. and trans. Lynda Clarke (Binghamton: Binghamton University Press, 2001), 302–303.

of Shīʿīsm as a state instrument, which coincided with the consolidation of the Sunnī Ottoman Empire, deepened the Sunnī-Shīʿī divide, transforming it into an imperial struggle for regional supremacy. This struggle was articulated in religious terms as a war between Sunnīs and Shīʿīs, thus adding new layers of animosity and vehemence to the political and military dimensions.[10]

The attitude of the early Ṣafavīd rulers toward their Sunnī subjects was complex and multifaceted. Sunnī notables continued to feature as courtiers, bureaucrats, and prayer leaders, and as long as they refrained from open displays of their religious affiliation, they were mostly unharmed. The lower strata, however, were the focus of systematic Ṣafavīd efforts at conversion from Sunnīsm to Shīʿīsm. In 1511, Shaykh ʿAlī al-Karakī (d. 1534), the leading Shīʿī scholar who came from Lebanon to Iran at the behest of the Ṣafavīds, wrote an elaborate treatise entitled "Breath of Divinity in Cursing Magic and Idolatry" (*Nafaḥāt al-lāhūt fī laʿn al-jibt wa'l-ṭāghūt*). The treatise denounced the foundations of Sunnī doctrines using the tropes of magic and idolatry as allegorical references to the first two caliphs, Abū Bakr and ʿUmar. Al-Karakī maintained that the defamation and slander of Sunnīs was a complementary part of one's faith and carried great spiritual value and reward. He played a pioneering role in the practice of public cursing, as groups of Shīʿī devotees began roaming the city cursing Abū Bakr and ʿUmar.[11]

Not all scholars approved of the cursing. Ḥusayn ʿAbd al-Ṣamad (d. 1576) for instance, argued in a debate with a Sunnī scholar that "only the fanatical among the laity do so. As for the ʿulamāʾ, none mandated the necessity of cursing them, and their books are clear on that."[12] According to Rula Jurdi Abisaab, occasional and spontaneous Shīʿī cursing of Sunnī Caliphs was different from the institutionalized ritual cursing, which occurred routinely in public and became a defining character of the faith. She maintained that state instigated cursing was less an expression of sectarian hostilities than a function of political conflict. The Ṣafavīds aimed to "denormalize" Sunnīsm and draw sharper lines between Sunnīsm and Shīʿīsm among their subjects. Internally

10 For a review of Sunnī-Shīʿī tensions, see Ofra Bengio and Meir Litvak, "Introduction," in *The Sunna and Shiʿa in History: Division and Ecumenism in Islam*, ed. Ofra Bengio and Meir Litvak (New York: Palgrave-McMillan, 2011), 5–6. For the significance of the Ṣafavīd-Ottoman dispute in this context, see Max Scherberger, "The Confrontation Between Sunnī and Shīʿī Empires: Ottoman-Safavid Relations Between the Fourteenth and the Seventeenth Century," in Ibid., 51–67.

11 Rula Jurdi Abisaab, *Converting Persia: Religion and Power in the Safavid Empire* (London: I.B. Tauris, 2004), 26.

12 Ibid., 34.

and externally, the Ṣafavīds benefited from the maintenance of a rejectionist, militant, and dramatized approach toward Sunnīsm.[13]

2 Attempts at Rapprochement in the Nineteenth and Twentieth Centuries

The growing Western threat to the Muslim world from the Nineteenth century prompted Shīʿīs and Sunnīs to advance Islamic unity against their common adversary. Sulṭān ʿAbdülhamīd II (d. 1918) led this effort on the Ottoman side, while several Iranian intellectuals, such as Mīrzā Yūsuf Khān Mustashār al-Dawla (d. 1895) and Mīrzā ʿAbd al-Raḥman Tālibov Tabrīzī (d. 1911), promoted the idea from the Iranian side. The most active among the Iranians was Abū al-Ḥasan Mīrzā Shaykh al-Raʾīs, (d. 1921), a Qājār prince, political activist, mujtahid, and secret member of the heterodox Bahāʾī faith.[14]

Likewise, during the Twentieth century, various Sunnī and Shīʿī clerics took part in ecumenical efforts, primarily because they saw sectarian divisions as weakening the Muslim world in light of the mounting western threats. Various Shīʿī scholars, most notably the Iraqi mujtahid Muḥammad Ḥusayn Kāshif al-Ghitāʾ (d. 1953) and the Lebanese cleric ʿAbd al-Ḥusayn Sharaf al-Dīn (d. 1957), established relationships with prominent Sunnī figures. Part of their efforts was aimed at reaching common ground with mainstream Sunnīs against the reemergence of violent anti-Shīʿī Wahhābism. While countering anti-Shīʿī polemics, these reformers also introduced a new understanding of the contentious period of early Islam. Kāshif al-Ghitāʾ participated in the World Islamic Congress in Jerusalem in 1931, where he discussed the question of rapprochement with the leading Sunnī reformer Muḥammad Rashīd Riḍḍā. The project failed due to disagreement over fundamental doctrinal points, producing instead mutual acrimonious accusations.[15]

---

13 Ibid., 47.

14 Mehrdad Kia, "Pan-Islamism in Late Nineteenth-Century Iran," *Middle Eastern Studies* 32, no. 1 (1996): 34–35; Juan R.I. Cole, "Shaikh al-Raʾīs and Sulṭān Abdülhamid II: The Iranian Dimension of Pan-Islam," in *Histories of the Modern Middle East: New Directions*, ed. Israel Gershoni, Hakan Erdem, and Ursula Wokock (Bolder: Lynn Rienner, 2002), 167–185. For Ottoman policies, see Jacob M. Landau, *Pan-Islam: History and Politics* (Abingdon: Routledge, 2015), 9–72.

15 Elisheva Machlis, *Shīʿī Sectarianism in the Middle East: Modernisation and the Quest for Islamic Universalism* (London: I.B. Tauris, 2014), 47–48, 52–53; Rainer Brunner, *Islamic Ecumenism in the 20th Century: The Azhar and Shiʿism Between Rapprochement and Restraint* (Leiden and Boston: Brill, 2004), 59–60, 88–89.

Another Shīʿī-led effort in 1947 was the formation in Cairo of Jamāʿat al-taqrīb (the Association of Rapprochement) and Dār al-taqrīb (the Center for Rapprochement), both institutions encouraging the reconciliation of Sunnīsm and Shīʿīsm, under the Iranian Shīʿī scholar Muḥammad Taqī Qommī (d. 1990). Their professed goal was the unification of the various Islamic schools and the legitimization of the Shīʿa as the fifth legal school in Islam, named after the Sixth Imām, Jaʿfar al-Ṣādiq, who is credited with the codification of the Shīʿī legal code. Both institutions came under attack by Sunnī fundamentalists, who claimed they were tools for disseminating Shīʿī propaganda among the Sunnīs.[16] Ayatollah Muḥammad Ḥusayn Boroujerdī (d. 1961), the highest authority in Iran's religious establishment, lent his support to Dār al-taqrīb and sent emissaries to the Arab world promoting closer ties between Shīʿī and Sunnī clerics.[17]

At the other end of the Iranian clerical spectrum, Navāb Ṣafavī (d. 1955), the founder of *Fedaiʾyan-i Islam* (Devotees of Islam), travelled in 1954 to (Jordanian-controlled) East Jerusalem and Cairo in order to promote Islamic unity. After returning to Iran, Ṣafavī began a campaign to promote the Muslim Brotherhood's pan-Islamic ideology in Iran.[18]

The radicalization and shift to activism among younger clerics alongside the emergence of radical, non-clerical religious modernism in Iran during the 1960s, in response to Muḥammad Reżā Shāh's secularized and pro-American policies, generated openness to revivalist Sunnī ideas. It was manifested inter alia in the translation of Muslim Brothers writings into Persian. Most notable was the translation by ʿAlī Khamenei, then a young cleric, of the writings of the Egyptian Sayyid Quṭb (executed 1965), the ideological father of the future jihādī-Salafī movement. The main writings of Abū-l-Aʿlā Mawdūdī (d. 1979) and other Pakistani and Indian Islamists were also translated into Persian. In Mehdi Khalaji's words, these books became the main source of nourishment for the sermons and writings of Iranian militant clerics in the pre-Revolution era.[19]

Khomeini, even prior to the 1979 Revolution, advocated Islamic unity against Western imperialism and urged Sunnīs and Shīʿīs to forget their differences. According to Hamid Enayat, he sought to steer Shīʿīsm closer to Sunnīsm by calling for an Islamic government to be ruled by a just jurist (*faqīh*) and not

16 Ibid., 131–134.

17 Mehrzad Boroujerdi, *Iranian Intellectuals and the West: The Tormented Triumph of Nativism* (Syracuse: Syracuse University Press, 1996), 80–81; Vanessa Martin, *Creating an Islamic State: Khomeini and the Making of a New Iran* (London: I.B. Tauris, 2003), 53.

18 Mehdi Khalaji, "The Dilemmas of Pan-Islamic Unity," *Current Trends in Islamist Ideology* 9 (2009): 69–70.

19 Ibid., 71.

necessarily the infallible Imām.[20] Moreover, in order to provide historical legitimacy for his *vilāyat-i faqīh* concept, Khomeini accepted the Sunnī Caliphate as evidence of the continued existence of an Islamic government after the death of the Prophet. Contrary to the traditional Shīʿī view of Abū Bakr and ʿUmar, he praised them for preserving the Prophet's personal example, adding mildly that "in other matters they committed errors."[21] Still, while Khomeini proclaimed to speak on behalf of all Muslims, all the ḥadīth and clerical authorities that he cited to substantiate his doctrine were Shīʿī.

Following the 1979 Revolution, the Islamic Republic of Iran sought to assume the leadership of the Islamic revival and the Muslim world. However, with the Shīʿīs being the minority in the Muslim world, this goal required the mitigation of the sectarian cleavage and approaching mainstream Sunnī Muslims. Iran presented itself as the only truly Islamic state by offering its guiding principle, the *vilāyat-i faqīh*, as the only appropriate model of government for both Shīʿīs and Sunnīs and by virtue of being the only Muslim country ruled by Sharīʿa law. Iranian calls to the Arab masses to topple their rulers and establish Islamic states only heightened the suspicion, if not animosity, of Sunnī clerical establishments to what they perceived as an attempted Shīʿī takeover of the Muslim world.[22]

Mainstream Sunnī movements initially welcomed the Iranian revolution as a victory for Islamic movements over secularist despotic regimes, as well as over the United States and Israel. Over time, however, enthusiasm gave way to frustration and misgivings due to the perceived Shīʿī and Iranian nationalist posture of the new regime. In addition, the emergence of the radical Sunnī Salafi organizations, which espoused strong anti-Shīʿī ideology, made it more difficult for Iran to advance its goal.[23]

The support of most Arab states for Iraq during the Iran-Iraq war (1981–1989) and the reluctance of the Arab masses to comply with Iranian calls to carry out Islamic revolutions in their countries exposed Iran's failure to reach out to most Sunnī Muslims. Iranian calls for unity did not eliminate sectarian

20 Martin, *Creating an Islamic State*, 113, 115; Hamid Enayat, "Iran: Khumayni's Concept of the 'Guardianship of the Jurisconsult,'" in *Islam in the Political Process*, ed. James P. Piscatori (Cambridge: Cambridge University Press, 1982), 164–167.

21 Mangol Bayat, "The Iranian Revolution of 1978–79: Fundamentalist or Modern?" *Middle East Journal* 37, no. 1 (1983): 36.

22 David Menashri, *Iran: A Decade of War and Revolution* (New York: Holmes & Meier, 1990), 208, 250, 291; Christin Marschall, *Iran's Persian Gulf Policy: From Khomeini to Khatami* (London: Routledge, 2003), 38, 44.

23 For the change in Sunnī attitude, see Meir Hatina, "Debating the 'Awakening Shiʿa': Sunnī Perceptions of the Iranian Revolution," in *The Sunna and Shiʿa in History*, ed. Bengio and Litvak, 203–221.

tensions between Sunnīs and Shīʿīs, which were exacerbated by the strategic and political rivalry between Iran and Saudi Arabia, the champion of Wahhābī Sunnī Islam. According to Martin Kramer, while Sunnīs and Shīʿīs purported to support unity, each declared the other's central practices as deviations from ecumenical Islam.[24] In January 1982 Iran launched the annual celebrations of Unity Week (*hafte-i waḥdat*), deliberately coinciding with the time around the Prophet's birthday – an occasion on which all Muslims, except the Wahhābis, could unite. Unity Week also became the time of the international Islamic congresses calling for unity and denouncing extremism – a clear insinuation of Wahhābism and Salafi Islam.[25]

Following Khomeini's death on June 3, 1989, Iran's new leader Khamenei, intensified the efforts to reach out to mainstream Sunnīs. Under his guidance, Iran launched a massive propaganda campaign designed to promote the ideal of Islamic harmony (*insijām-i Islami*) between Sunnīs and Shīʿīs, which included the publication of books and journals as well as websites and blogs in all Islamic languages.[26] In addition, the Iranian authorities formed organizations promoting the idea of unity of all Islamic schools and legitimizing the Shīʿa as the Jaʿfarī school within a generic Islam that was neither Sunnī nor Shīʿī: in particular, the *Majmaʿ-i jahānī-i ahl-i bayt* (World Forum for the [Prophet's] Family) and the *Majmaʿ-i jahānī taqrīb-i maẕāhīb-i Islāmī* (World Forum for Proximity of Islamic Schools of Thought). Both organizations convene conferences promoting reconciliation between Sunnī and Shīʿī Muslims and organize programs for Sunnī Muslims to study Islam in the seminaries of Qom.[27]

As mentioned above, a series of regional changes enhanced and emboldened the Shīʿa in the Middle East, thereby exacerbating sectarian tensions. Iran's efforts to forge what it called "the axis of resistance" comprising itself, Shīʿī-dominated Iraq, Alawite-dominated Syria, the Lebanese Ḥizballah, and the Sunnī Palestinian Ḥamās, upset the Sunnī Arab elites. Sunnī apprehensions were manifested in various ways, including alarmist statements by rulers about the specter of the rising Shīʿī Crescent stretching from Iran to the Mediterranean, anti-Shīʿī religious rulings, propaganda warfare and, most

24 Martin Kramer, *Arab Awakening and Islamic Revival* (New Brunswick: Transaction, 1996), 161–187.

25 Brunner, *Islamic Ecumenism*, 381–382.

26 Ze'ev Maghen, "Unity or Hegemony? Iranian Attitudes to the Sunnī-Shīʿī Divide," in *The Sunna and Shiʿa in History*, ed. Bengio and Litvak, 184.

27 Wilfrid Buchta, "Teheran Ecumenical Society (Majmaʿ al-taqrīb): A Veritable Ecumenical Revival or a Trojan Horse of Iran?," in *The Twelver Shiʿa in Modern Times: Religious Culture and Political History*, ed. Rainer Brunner and Werner Ende (Leiden: Brill, 2001), 349.

significantly, unprecedented sectarian violence in Iraq initiated by the newly emergent al-Qāʿida organization in Iraq.[28]

In contrast to the governments, public opinion in the various Arab countries was far more ambivalent. On the one hand, the deep-seated reservations against Shīʿīs became increasingly apparent after 2003, manifested in exaggerated press reports of widespread conversions to Shīʿīsm in various Arab countries.[29] A reliable survey of Arab public opinion carried out in 2009 demonstrated that most Muslims believed that the sectarian Sunnī-Shīʿī problem transcended the borders of Iraq and had become "a growing problem in the Muslim world."[30] On the other hand, former president Ahmadinejad, and Lebanese Ḥizballah's leader, Ḥasan Naṣrallah (b. 1960), acquired great popularity in various Sunnī countries thanks to their perceived success and acts of defiance against Israel and the United States. Support for both was also a safe means of voicing protest against Arab governments. Following the 2006 Israel-Lebanon War, the Sunnī Muslim Brothers in Egypt coined the slogan "We are all Naṣrallah."[31]

The rise of the Sunnī jihādī-Salafī organizations, which view the Shīʿīs as apostates, resulted in the death of thousands of Shīʿīs in Iraq and Pakistan. Since the Shīʿīs are a minority in the region, an all-out confrontation was totally unfeasible. Therefore, they adopted two "soft" means to counter the Salafi challenge. The first was the denial of any real doctrinal or political justification for the sectarian rift – as Sunnīs and Shīʿīs have much more in common than differences in both faith and fate – and thus they established a new joint Muslim in-group. The second was an effort to appeal to mainstream Sunnīs in order to create a common front against the jihādī-Salafīsts. This measure involved the revocation of various centuries-old Shīʿī practices that reflected animosity toward Sunnī Islam and elicited Sunnī ire. These changes caused

---

28 *Washington Post*, December 8, 2004; *al-Sharq al-Awsat*, October 14, 2005; http://www.alarabiya.net/articles/2006/04/08/22686.html; *al-Ahram Weekly*, August 2, 2006.

29 Israel Elad-Altman, "The Sunni-Shia Conversion Controversy," *Current Trends in Islamist Ideology* 5 (2007): 1–10; *Washington Post*, October 6, 2006; *al-Sharq al-Awsat*, August 10, 2009.

30 Pew Research Center, *The Pew Global Project Attitude*, February 4, 20104, https://www.pewresearch.org/wp-content/uploads/sites/2/pdf/268.pdf, 4.

31 Dan Murphy, "In War's Dust, a New Arab 'Lion' Emerges: Hizbullah's Nasrallah is Hailed as a Regional Hero," *Christian Science Monitor*, August 29, 2006, https://www.csmonitor.com/2006/0829/p01s02-wome.html; Rachel Shabi, "Palestinians See Naṣrallah as a New Hero," *Al-Jazeera*, August 13, 2006, https://www.aljazeera.com/focus/arabunity/2008/03/2008525125285888o4.html; Khaled Abū Toameh, "Hizballah 'Victory' Boosts Extremists," *Jerusalem Post*, August 13, 2006, https://www.jpost.com/Middle-East/Hizbullah-victory-boosts-extremists; Elad-Altman, "The Sunnī-Shia Conversion Controversy," 5.

heated debates between the dominant and dissident factions within the Shīʿī religious establishment, that is, between those who adhered to the traditional and more doctrinal attitude toward Sunnīs and those with a more modernist approach, which prioritized the political and social considerations guiding Shīʿī-Sunnī relations. The debates also revolved around the question of authority within the clerical establishment as well as clerical authority over ordinary believers and reflected the differences between official and popular religion in Iran.

3 Minimizing the Sectarian Rift

Supreme Leader Khamenei took the lead in minimizing the importance of the doctrinal or ideological roots of the Sunnī-Shīʿī rift. As early as 1989 he stated that excessive preoccupation with past quarrels would preclude Muslim unity. "The past is past," he declared, and nothing can be done about it, but Muslims must focus on their duties before God at the present time if they want to achieve unity.[32] Speaking to clerics from Kurdistan affiliated with both sects in 2009, he conceded that Sunnīs and Shīʿīs disagree on certain doctrinal principles (*uṣūl*) and details of law (*furūʿ*) but insisted that such disagreements were natural and also existed within each of the two schools. He asserted that these differences should not lead to enmity and slander, as what Shīʿīs and Sunnīs shared vastly exceeded their differences, and concluded that those who were enflaming Sunnī-Shīʿī tensions were, even if out of ignorance, serving the enemy.[33]

As the sectarian rift widened, Khamenei bemoaned the fact that, instead of adhering to the Islamic injunction to remain united, Muslims were fighting among themselves. He maintained that the divisions within the Islamic world were not natural but had been imposed and encouraged by the imperialists, headed by the United States and Israel. These enemies knew that

32 "Bayānāt dar dīdār-i jamʿī az ruḥāniyūn-i ḥawza-i ʿulamāʾ-i ahl-i Sunnat," 5 Dey 1368/December 26, 1989, http://farsi.khamenei.ir/newspart-print?tid=3542.

33 "Bayānāt dar dīdār-i ruḥāniyūn va-ṭulāb-i tashayyuʿ va-tasannon-i Kurdistan," 23 Ordībehesht 1388/May 13, 2009, http://farsi.khamenei.ir/speech-content?id=6772. See also "Vaḥdat az manẓar-i rahbar-i muʿaẓẓam-i inqilāb," *IRNA*, 24 Dey 1392/January 14, 2014, http://www.irna.ir/fa/News/80993797; Ali Afshari, "Khamenei Preaches Shiʿite-Sunni Unity Against Islamic State, US," *Al-Monitor*, October 24, 2014, http://www.al-monitor.com/pulse/originals/2014/10/iran-khamenei-sunni-Shiʿite-ghadeer.html#ixzz4CPWxUuQF.

had the Muslim nation been unified it "would have conquered the world."[34] Accordingly, they created al-Qāʿida and ISIS (the Islamic State of Iraq and Shām, *Daʿesh* in Arabīc) and instigated the civil wars in Muslim countries in order to divert the Islamic nation away from the real threat it faced, namely, Zionism. Khamenei criticized Western media for depicting the violence in Iraq as a struggle between Sunna and Shīʿa, when it was in fact a struggle between "humanity and barbarity."[35] In other words, he sought to bridge the sectarian rift or enhance Muslim in-group cohesion by focusing on common external enemies. Unlike the Americans who were said to sow discord, the Iranians presented themselves as motivated by Muslim solidarity and revolutionary commitment to "support the oppressed wherever they are." Thus, Khamenei took pride in the fact that "in our support of the oppressed, we do not look at [their] religious denomination and we have offered the same support that we provided to our Shīʿa brethren in Lebanon to our Sunnī brethren in Gaza."[36] In a similar vein, Iranian President Rouhani stated in his address to the ecumenical conference in 2016 that "Shīʿīs and Sunnīs, different sects and ethnicities, have lived alongside each other for centuries and respected one another. We didn't insult the sanctities of sects, and all Muslims respected the Companions and household of the Prophet." Like Khamenei, Rouhani denied the sectarian nature of the conflict and, citing Khomeini, he framed it as conflict between "American Islam," i.e., Saudi Islam, and "the pure Muḥammadan Islam."[37]

Former president Rafsanjānī went further in seeking to minimize the heavy legacy of early Islamic history on modern political reality. On at least two occasions, when speaking at Islamic Unity conferences of Shīʿī and Sunnī clerics in April 2007 and January 2014, he asked rhetorically, and perhaps even in

---

34 "The Leader's Remarks in a Meeting with a Group of Officials, Ambassadors of Muslim Countries," *Office of the Supreme Leader*, July 18, 2015, http://www.leader.ir/langs/en/index.php?p=bayanat&id=13451.

35 "Bayānāt dar dīdār-i mas'ūlān-i niẓām va-mayhamānān-i conference-i vaḥdat-i Islāmī," 29 Dey 1392/January 19, 2014, http://farsi.khamenei.ir/speech-content?id=25056; "Bayānāt dar dīdār-i afshār-i mukhtalif-i mardom beh munāsabat-i ʿīd ghadīr," 20 Mehr 1393/ October 12, 2014, http://farsi.khamenei.ir/speech-content?id=27896; "Khamenei: lā ḥarb bayna al-Sunna wal-Shīʿa," *Elāph*, June 29, 2014, http://www.elaph.com/Web/News/2014/6/918323.html#sthash.ZnyYpPNh.dpuf.

36 "The Leader: We Will Not Allow the US to Make Economic, Political or Cultural Inroads into Iran," August 15, 2015, http://www.leader.ir/langs/en/index.php?p=contentShow&id=13484.

37 "Rūḥānī: rezhīm-i ṣahyūnīstī va-khūnrīzān-i minṭaqa beh zūdī gereftār ya's khwāhand shod," 25 Azar 1395/ December 15, 2016, https://www.tasnimnews.com/fa/news/1395/09/25/1268404/روحانی-رژیم-صهیونیستی-و-خونریزان-منطقه-به-زودی-گرفتار-یأس-خواهند-شد.

exasperation, "how long are we going to kill each other over who was the first caliph?" Rafsanjānī acknowledged the historical quarrel between Sunnīs and Shīʿīs and their separate development with different religious texts, traditions, and doctrines. But he was willing to challenge the symbolic and emotional importance of these differences and focus on the present and future of the Muslim community, insisting that they should not be the cause of a violent rift in the present era.[38] Considering the centrality of these disagreements over the past in the Sunnī-Shīʿī rift, Rafsanjānī seemed to be looking to transform it from a sectarian dispute based on animosity and mutual exclusion to a denominational difference, as among Christian groups in the West. In other words, he was promoting peaceful coexistence between religious groups that share major tenets of belief and tolerate their differences.[39]

4 Reaching Out to Sunnīs

As part of his effort to defuse sectarian animosity, Khamenei initiated a series of rulings and measures to ban and revoke the practice of disassociation (*tabarrā*) and cursing (*sabb*) of the first three caliphs and the Prophet's Companions. On November 22, 2006, in response to a question by Sunnīs regarding the Shīʿī position on the cursing, Khamenei issued a fatwā saying that "any statement, act, or practice which provides proofs and arguments for the enemy and which produces division and discord among Muslims is strictly forbidden (*ḥarām*) by Sharīʿa."[40] Although the Iranian Foreign Ministry asked for the ruling to be distributed by all media and it was welcomed by the Sunnī International Union

38 "Rafsanjānī: digār mowżūʿiyatī nadārad keh bibīnīm cheh kesī khalīfa avval būdeh ast?," 19 Farvardīn 1386/April 8, 2007, http://www.asriran.com/fa/news/14741; "Towżīḥ-i Hāshimī barāye sokhnānesh dar bārah-i khalīfa-i avval," 7 Bahman 1392/ January 27, 2014, http://www.tabnak.ir/fa/news/374212; "Rafsanjānī ilā matā nataqātalu ḥawla man huwa al-khalīfa al-awwal?," *al-Maṣrī al-Yawm*, December 18, 2014.

39 For an analysis of these terms, see, Russell E. Richey, "Denominations and Denominationalism: An American Morphology," *Reimagining Denominationalism: Interpretive Essays* (1994), ed. Robert Bruce Mullin and Russell E. Richey (Oxford: Oxford University Press, 1994), 74–98. The English version of Khamenei's speeches on his official website often uses the term "denominations" rather than "sects" to describe the Sunnīs. While the translators are not necessarily aware of the sociological definitions, they are apparently aware of the cultural sensitivities of their Western readers.

40 For the full text of the fatwā, see "Fatāwā Shīʿīyya tuḥarrimu sabb al-ṣaḥāba," http://sudaneseonline.com/msg/board/400/msg/1346494097/rn/3.html, November 24, 2006.

for Muslim Scholars headed by Muḥammad Salīm al-ʿAwā, the ruling apparently had little impact on most Shīʿī believers in Iran.[41]

In September 2010, Khamenei published a more explicit ruling, which prohibited slandering "the leaders of our Sunnī brethren, particularly laying charges against the Prophet's wife on any issue that may harm her honor."[42] The ruling came in response to a petition by Shīʿī clerics and laypeople from the Aḥsāʾ province in Saudi Arabia following the broadcasting of a virulent sermon by the London-based Kuwaiti Shīʿī preacher Yāsir Ḥabīb (b. 1979) against ʿAisha, the Prophet's most favored wife. The petition addressed ʿAisha with her Sunnī honorific of "the mother of the believers" (*Umm al*-muʾminīn), and Khamenei's response was particularly significant in view of the deep Shīʿī resentment against her due to her bitter rivalry with Imām ʿAlī.[43] The Lebanese cleric ʿAlī Faḍlallah was quick to note on his Facebook page that Khamenei was following the line set by his father, Grand Ayatollah Muḥammad Ḥusayn Faḍlallah (d. 2010), in the early 1990s.[44] Faḍlallah had, at that time, been subjected to vehement attacks by the Qom school for his conciliatory approach toward the Prophet's Companions; circumstances were now forcing Khamenei to follow suit.[45] The Iranian media was candid about the reasons for the ruling, explaining that Shīʿī communities in the Arab Gulf countries were under intense pressure following Ḥabīb's diatribe.[46]

---

41 "Fatāwā Shīʿīyya tuḥarrimu sabb al-ṣaḥāba," *al-Ahrām*, November 23, 2006.

42 "Al-Murshid al-aʿlā lil-thawra al-Islāmiyya ʿAlī al-Khamenei yaqūlu: yuḥarram al-nayl min rumūz ikhwāninā al-Sunna," *Mehr News*, September 30, 2010, http://www.mehrnews.com/mehr_media/image/2010/09/576469_orig.jpg/.

43 Ḥabīb's most famous book is *al-Fāḥisha: al-wajh al-ākhar li-ʿAisha* (Prostitute: The Other Face of ʿAisha) whose sixth edition was published in 2013. In 2016 Khamenei went further in revising Shīʿī attitudes toward ʿAisha when he stated that no harm should be done to any of the Prophet's pure wives, as they are all respected. He pointed to ʿAlī as the model in this case, by asserting that ʿAlī had treated ʿAisha with respect, even though she led the war against him, because she had been the Prophet's wife, *al-Raʾy* (Iraq), June 12, 2016.

44 "Baʿd al-marjaʿ faḍlallah, al-sayyid ʿAlī al-Khameneʾ yuḥarrimu al-isāʾa li-rumūz ikhwāninā al-sunna zawjāt al-nabī wal-ṣaḥāba," September 28, 2010, https://urlzs.com/2XrHt.

45 For Faḍlallah's statements and clash with the Qom establishment, see Stephan Rosiny, "The Tragedy of Fatima al-Zahraʾ in the Debate of Two Shiʿite Theologians in Lebanon," in *The Twelver Shia in Modern Times: Religious Culture and Political History*, ed. Werner Ende and Rainer Brunner (Leiden: Brill, 2001), 207–219.

46 "Shādī-i ahl-i Sunnat az fatvā-i rahbarī dar bārah-i ʿAisha," *Mashreq News*, 10 Mehr 1389/ October 2, 2010, https://www.mashreghnews.ir/news/8338; "Nigāhī beh fatvā-i taʾrīkhī-i valī-i amr al-Muslimīn dar bārah-i ahl-i Sunnat," *Fars News*, 20 Mehr 1389/ October 12, 2010, https://www.farsnews.com/news/8907191487.

Quite a few writers pursued the same course, which reflected an instrumentalist approach to the whole issue rather than a genuine ideological change of heart. Ḥujjat al-Islam Mahdī Masā'ilī explained that the curses against the first three caliphs helped extremist Sunnīs to spread anti-Shīʿī propaganda and that Shīʿīs had, throughout history, been subjected to persecution because of this charge. Masā'ilī asserted that, aside from a small group of ignorant extremists who serve imperialism, most Sunnīs support a rapprochement between the Islamic schools and it was therefore necessary to appeal to these Sunnīs who fight against the extremists. However, it should be understood that no Sunnī, even the most moderate, will accept these curses, which will result in pushing moderate Sunnīs to the extremist camp against Shīʿīsm.[47] Another example of this instrumentalist approach was Grand Ayatollah Vaḥīd Khorāsānī's statement that "public cursing" is prohibited, implying that cursing in other forms was not, as it did not harm Shīʿī lives.[48] The Arab media in the Gulf publicized Khamenei's ruling and Shaykh al-Azhar Aḥmad al-Ṭayyib (2010–) praised it as reflecting deep understanding of the danger posed by the actions of the "people of sedition" (*ahl al-fitna*) and concern for unity among Muslims.[49] Dozens of Shīʿī clerics condemned any expression of disrespect against Sunnīs; none, however, did it in the form of an official ruling.[50]

The principle of *tabarrā* is deeply entrenched in Shīʿī doctrines and practice, and therefore its reversal or transformation requires the reinterpretation and rearticulation of its meaning and target. While all those addressing the problem agreed that *tabarrā* means disassociation from God's enemies, the issue now was the precise identity of these enemies and the proper way to demonstrate disassociation from them. Masā'ilī, for example, distinguished between three ways of practicing *tabarrā*: in one's heart, conduct, and words. Disassociation from God's enemies should, first and foremost, come from the

47 Mahdī Masā'ilī, *Laʿnhā-i nāmuqaddas* (2014) cited in "Barresī-i yek mas'ala-i muhim dunyā-i Islām dar kitāb-i Laʿnhā-i nāmuqaddas," *Fars News*, 29 Mordād 1393/August 20, 2014, http://www.farsnews.com/newstext.php?nn=13930528001308 (Last accessed June 9, 2015); "Laʿnhā-i nāmuqaddas dar tabyīn 'tabarrā' muntashir shod," 31 Mordād 1393/August 22, 2014, http://www.teribon.ir/archives/270668/; "Kitāb-i laʿnhā-i nāmuqaddas muntashir shod," 29 Mordād 1393/August 20, 2014, http://www.fetan.ir/home/2196.

48 "Ayatollah al-ʿuzma Vaḥīd Khorāsānī: Laʿn-i ʿalanī jāyiz nīst + film," 27 Dey 1393/January 17, 2015, http://www.fetan.ir/home/4247.

49 "Istiqbāl shaykh al-Azhar az fatvā-i maqām-i muʿaẓẓam-i rahbarī," 2 Khordād 1391/May 22, 2012, https://fa.alalamtv.net/news/328564.

50 Ḥamīd Rustamī Najafabādī, "Barresī-i mavāżiʿ va-fatāvā-i rahbarī dar pīshbord-i taqrīb va-vaḥdat-i Islāmī," 11 Azar 1391/December 1, 2012, https://www.farsnews.com/news/13910908000501.

believer's heart and mind, and it should be based on knowledge of God. If genuine, this is far more important than any external manifestation of *tabarrā*. Second and equally important is daily conduct, in other words, keeping one's distance from God's enemies. Third and less significant is showing disassociation by public cursing. *Tabarrā* has clear rules according to time and place, and those who fail to adhere to them commit grave religious sins, even though they may think they are acting properly.[51] One such rule is public cursing of the Prophet's Companions and the first two caliphs, which, Masā'ilī argued, violates the instructions of the Imāms. Masā'ilī tried to walk a fine line between two types of cursing. The first, *dashnām*, carried a certain magical force and was so inappropriate to the believer's pure soul that numerous passages and traditions banned it completely. The second type was *la'n* and *nafrīn* (abuses and invectives), meaning, in the present political context, being disparaging of Sunnī sanctities and, thus, it too violates the instructions of the Imāms.

The emphasis on *tabarrā* in the heart over public cursing may have stemmed from the desire to distinguish between genuine belief and superficial and outward manifestations of religiosity. Alternatively, it may have originated from the desire to curb public cursing by employing more noble arguments of spirituality rather than appeals to political expediency or fear of Sunnīs. One writer thus explained that *tabarrā* means the eschewal of evil, i.e., disassociation from the enemies of God and their friends, but not vulgar curses and invectives against Sunnīs. The Shīʿī Imāms, he explained, never favored *tabarrā* in its popular manner, and "we should therefore ask ourselves whether we curse out of personal hatred and jealousy or in order to follow the Imāms' instructions for the sake of God." The former lacks any value, and he suggests instead following the wish of the Imāms and, in the present day, the instructions of the "full-fledged *faqīh*," who draws his legitimacy from the Hidden Imām and who declared the desistance from disrespecting the Sunnī sanctities as expedient.

This same writer presented the avoidance of cursing not as dissimulation (*taqiyya*), which had been necessary in the past, but as moderation toward the Sunnīs. Another writer, however, argued that cursing and expressing hatred toward the oppressors (*ẓālimīn*) are natural and condoned many times in the Qur'ān, but he qualified that such cursing is prohibited if it harms Muslim unity and leads to bloodshed among Muslims.[52]

---

51 Mahdī Masā'ilī, "*La'nhā-i ke nāmuqaddasand*," http://azadpajooh.com/161. The treatise received a warm welcome and positive reviews by quite a few clerical journals and websites (see note 47).

52 "Hame-i chīz dar bārah-i nohom-i Rabīʿ al-awwal va-bidʿat ʿīd al-Zahrā' (s)," 29 Azar 1394/ December 20, 2015, http://javanenghelabi.ir/news/24241.html; Hādī Qoṭbī, "Rabīʿ al-awwal, jashn-i shādī barāye ahl-i bayt ast yā?," *Kheima* 12–13 (Ordībehsht-Khordād 1383/

The new interpretation of *tabarrā* pointed to the West rather than the Sunnīs as the enemy from which to disassociate. This shift of enemies resembled the above-mentioned change of the 'Āshūrā' commemorations during the 1970s. It reflected the transformation of Shī'īsm from a traditional minority facing Sunnīs into a modern politicized movement that seeks to bring all Muslims together against the West. Various writers explained that the subjects of disassociation and curses were the leaders of polytheism and apostasy (*shirk va-kufr*), a category which applies to the West or to jihādī-Salafīsts but not to ordinary Sunnīs who recite the Islamic *Shahada*.[53] Khamenei's office defined the "enemy" as those who are hostile to the Prophet's family but explained that ordinary Sunnīs regard love and affection for the Prophet's family as a religious obligation and thus presented them as well-meaning Muslims. These arguments contravened numerous past statements by great Shī'ī luminaries who advocated such cursing. However, the proponents of the new approach chose to ignore their predecessors rather than engage in an open scholarly or historical debate with them. Presumably they did not wish to concede that their approach was an innovation that broke away from a centuries-long tradition and were unwilling to challenge illustrious scholars who enjoyed greater historical prestige and stature than themselves.

The rulings against cursing seem to have had little impact on many ordinary believers, however, as public cursing of the Prophet's Companions continued. On January 21, 2013, on the occasion of Unity Week, the official Iranian news agency, IRNA, published a special collection of opinions issued by the *marāji' taqlīd*, which condemned "cursing and disrespect for the sanctity of other religions and sects" for increasing the tension and divisions among Muslims.[54] Similarly, when groups of Iraqi Shī'īs marched in the predominantly Sunnī al-Adhamiyah neighborhood of Baghdad on October 7, 2013 chanting insults and curses against Sunnī historical figures, all Shī'ī leaders in Iraq, headed by Grand Ayatollah 'Alī Sistānī condemned the move as contrary to the instructions of the Shī'ī Imāms.[55] In January 2015, several leading Shī'ī clerics

April–May 2004): 57–58; "bid'at-i 'īd al-Zahrā' be-munāsabat-i nohom Rabī' al-awwal," http://asheqi.parsiblog.com/Posts/118 (n.d.).

53 "Nohom Rabī' al-awwal rūz-i bay'atī dō bāreh bā Imām-i zamān ast," 11 Dey 1393/ December 22, 2015, http://www.farsnews.com/newstext.php?nn=13931010001385; "Hame-i chīz dar bārah-i nohom-i Rabī' al-awwal;" "Tavalā va-tabarrā chīst?," 6 Khordād 1392/ May 27, 2013, http://www.soalcity.ir/node/2075.

54 "Dīdgāh-i marāji' taqlīd-i Shī'a dar bārah-i a'māl-i khorāfī-i rūz-i nohom-i Rabī' al-awwal," 2 Bahman 1391/ January 21, 2013, http://www.irna.ir/fa/News/80508765.

55 "Sabb al-ṣaḥāba jarīma wal-qatl bi-'ism al-ṣaḥāba jihād," October 10, 2013, http://burathanews.com/arabic/articles/214324; "Sistani Issues Fatwa Against Sectarian Violence

reiterated the ban in compliance with the renewed and angry demand by Shaykh al-Azhar al-Ṭayyib that Shīʿī authorities in Iran and Iraq issue rulings strictly forbidding the hurling of insults at Sunnī figures and their sanctities. Khamenei too restated his ruling as late as June 2016, claiming that Imām ʿAlī had respected ʿAisha, even though she had fought against him.[56] The need to keep on issuing such rulings indicates that popular compliance was far from perfect.

5 Nullifying the ʿUmarkoshān Celebrations

Another popular practice which the Iranian authorities sought to revise was the celebration known as ʿĪd al-Zahrāʾ (holiday of Fāṭima, the Prophet's daughter) or more popularly ʿUmarkoshān, which is held annually on the ninth of Rabīʿ al-Awwal marking the murder of the second caliph, ʿUmar b. al-Khaṭṭāb, in 644 by the Persian slave Fīrūz Abū Lūʾlūʾ Nahāvandī. ʿUmar aroused particular animosity among Shīʿīs for his central role in denying ʿAlī his rightful succession and for his mistreatment of Fāṭima after the Prophet's death. According to popular belief, the assassin fled to Kāshān after the deed and became very influential among the local population. He was nicknamed "Bābā Shujāʿ al-Dīn," the hero of religion, and a shrine was erected in his honor when he died.[57] Shīʿī tradition traces the celebration to the period of the Tenth Imām, ʿAlī al-Hādī (d. 254/868) and claims it was held in secret due to the ʿAbbāsid persecutions.[58]

Under the Ṣafavīds, Shīʿī scholars incorporated the day of ʿUmar's death into the Shīʿī eschatological order. In two tracts, Mīr Seyyed Ḥusayn verified the date of ʿUmar's death and explained how Shīʿī believers should commemorate it. He told his readers that the Prophet had predicted that on 9 Rabīʿ God would destroy Imām ʿAlī's enemies, fulfill Fāṭima's prayers, and accept the deeds of loyal Shīʿīs.[59] Years later, the powerful Shaykh al-Islam of Iṣfahān, Muḥammad Bāqir Majlisī (d. 1698), collected in *Biḥār al-anwār* a large number of traditions

---

in Iraq," October 11, 2013, monitor.com/pulse/en/contents/articles/originals/2013/10/iraqi-moderates-manage-sectarianism.html##ixzz3OomGSvl2.

56 ʿAli Mamuri, "Shiite Leaders Forbid Insults Against Sunnīs," *al-Monitor*, January 13, 2015; "Khamenei: al-isāʾa li-zawjāt al-nabī taʿnī al-isāʾa lil-rasūl nafsihi," June 12, 2106, http://www.alraimedia.com/ar/article/foreigns/2016/06/12/686602/nr/iran.

57 Rosemary Stanfield Johnson, "Sunnī Survival in Safavid Iran: Anti-Sunnī Activities During the Reign of Tahmasp I," *Iranian Studies* 27(1994): 1–4, 127n.

58 Abū Lūʾlūʾ's popularity dates back to at least the Fourteenth century, as Ibn Taymiyya (d. 1328) criticizes the Shīʿīs on this point in his *Manhaj al-Sunna*, cited in "Ḥaqīqat qabr qātil ʿUmar b. al-Khaṭṭāb fī Iran," http://alburhan.com/Article/index/7688.

59 Abisaab, *Converting Persia*, 47.

linking 'Umar's death to 9 Rabīʿ and stressed the importance of sharing the joy of the Imāms and, especially, of Fāṭima over the demise of the evil caliph who had tormented her.[60] The 'Umarkoshān celebrations continued well into the 1979 Revolution, though their popularity and scope are not documented.

Following the Revolution, the Iranian authorities banned the celebrations but without much success, as popular animosity toward 'Umar remained intense.[61] The matter assumed new urgency with the rise of sectarian tensions in the region, and the celebrations became an effective Salafī weapon to attack Shīʿīsm as a whole. In January 2007, during a joint Sunnī-Shīʿī conference held in Qatar, which convened to address the escalating sectarian violence in Iraq, the Sunnī participants addressed the visits to Abū Lū'lū''s tomb. Shortly after, a delegation from the International Association of Muslim Scholars came to Iran requesting that the tomb be shut down. In a letter to the association, Ayatollah Muḥammad 'Alī Taskhīrī, the then secretary general of the World Forum for Proximity of Islamic Schools described Abū Lū'lū' as a criminal who had been executed and buried in Medina. He dismissed the grave in Kāshān as a meaningless and invented site that no one visits and dismissed the talk of a shrine as totally absurd. Yet, as visitations continued, the Iranian authorities complied with the request and, in June 2007, ordered the shutdown of the mausoleum. On announcing its closure, Taskhīrī designated it the grave of a local Ṣūfī, which some ignorant people had erroneously turned into a place of significance, and expressed hope that such false practices would totally disappear.[62] These allegations, which were aimed at Sunnī audiences, did not pass smoothly even within clerical circles closely affiliated with the government. Ḥujjat al-Islam Nāṣir Aḥmadī, a spokesperson for Ayatollah Nūrī

60 For many of these traditions taken from other sources as well, see "'Id al-Zahrā': bidʿat yā sunat?," 14 Bahman 1393/ February 3, 2015, http://antifetan.blog.ir/post/7.

61 "Marāsim-i 'Umarkoshūn va-ḥukm-i in marāsim az dīdār-i Imām-i Khamenei," http://rezazamani1375.blogfa.com/post/19; "Taḥqīqāti-i kāmil dar bārah-i nohom Rabīʿ al-awwal," http://sraj.ir/fa/index.php/2015-12-12-16-28-27/416-2015-12-20-14-44-10; "Nohom-i Rabīʿ-i avval va-jashn-i mamnūʿ-i 'Umarkoshān," http://www.socio-shia.com/index.php/sociology-of-shia-fields/shia-rituals/187-9rabi-note. Zeev Maghen maintained that years after the 1979 Revolution, "when Iranian Shīʿī children receive new shoes, they will often scrawl Abū Bakr's name on the sole of one shoe, 'Umar's name on the sole of the other, and then walk through manure." Maghen, "Unity or Hegemony?," 190. 'Umarkoshūn is the colloquial term of 'Umarkoshān. It is used in this chapter whenever it appears in the Persian language sources.

62 "Iran tughliqu mazār Abū Lū'lū' al-majūsī qātil 'Umar b. al-Khaṭṭāb," June 13, 2007, http://www.26sep.net/news_details.php?lng=arabic&sid=28845.

Hamadānī, for example, confirmed the authenticity of the grave and stated that he personally attended it regularly.[63]

The ban did not put an end to the ʿUmarkoshān celebrations, and it is unclear whether they even declined in scope. Iranian concern over the negative effect of the celebrations, particularly after the outbreak of the Arab upheaval, is evident in Khamenei's decision to lead the campaign against them. In his speech on the Day of Ghadīr Khumm, December 17, 2008, Khamenei criticized the ignorant people who think they make Fāṭima happy by celebrating 9 Rabīʿ. In fact, he stated, "Fāṭima is dissatisfied (*rāżū nīst*)" with this practice, because it harms the Revolution, which is the fruition of her struggle. He lambasted those who falsely believe that they were defending the Shīʿa by fomenting the fire of enmity between Shīʿīs and non-Shīʿīs. "This is not defense of the Shīʿa; this is not defense of *valāyat* (belief in the Imāms), if you want [to know] its secret meaning (*bāṭin*) this is defense of America, this is defense of the Zionists," he declared.[64]

A plethora of publications and statements ranging from senior clerics to semi-independent bloggers followed Khamenei's cue, using as their major argument the harm caused by the celebrations to Shīʿīs throughout the region, and the state media published joint condemnations of the celebrations by leading *marājiʿ taqlīd*. The statements reflected the deeply ingrained sense of Shīʿī vulnerability and victimhood vis-à-vis the Sunnī majority. This was particularly salient when they emphasized that the celebrations were taking place at the time when the Wahhābī camp was waging a war against Shīʿī minorities, accusing them of apostasy and killing them. According to the statements, the celebrations provoked unnecessary sedition (*fitna*) between Sunnīs and Shīʿīs and thus contributed to the bloodshed of thousands of innocent Shīʿīs from Indonesia, Pakistan, Iraq, and Lebanon. "The Pure Imāms urged the respect of the sanctities of other sects and even other religions," the joint call argued. Performing such *munkarāt* (wrongdoings) and "innovations" is not only "deviation" from the line of the Imāms but is in fact "oppression (*ẓulm*) and treason" against the Shīʿī religion.[65] The declaration included an earlier statement by Grand Ayatollah Muḥammad Taqī Bahjat (d. 2009), which stressed the need

63 Reżā Mahdavī, "Cherā maqbara-i Abū Lūʾlū' baste shod," 27 Khordād 1386/June 17, 2007, http://fararu.com/fa/news/93.

64 "Bayānāt dar dīdār-i jamʿī az mardom dar rūz-i ʿīd ghadīr," 27 Azar 1387/December 17, 2008, http://farsi.khamenei.ir/speech-content?id=5025.

65 "Dīdgāh-i marājiʿ taqlīd-i Shīʿa dar bārah-i khorāfa-i benām-i ʿīd al-Zahrāʾ," 20 Bahman 1391/February 8, 2013, http://www.farsnews.com/newstext.php?nn=13911030001465; "Khorāfāt-i 9 Rabīʿ dastmāyeh barāye ḥamla beh abrūyī-i tashayyuʿ," 20 Bahman 1391/February 8, 2013, http://www.tasnimnews.com/fa/news/1391/11/02/14537.

to refrain from any action that provokes Sunnīs to act against Shīʿīs, explained that if the celebrations cause the shedding of even one drop of blood, then those who condone them become responsible or at least accomplices in the crime.[66] Ḥujjat al-Islam ʿAlī Yūnesī, former minister of intelligence and advisor to President Rouhani, was more adamant and declared that any person who takes part in such ceremonies against the Sunnīs should know that they are accomplices to the bloodshed of Shīʿīs in Pakistan and Iraq and are thus assisting the Salafi criminals.[67] On November 10, 2014, Rafsanjānī, who was always bolder than others in his readiness to challenge religious conventions, lamented that acts like ʿUmarkoshān, cursing the Prophet's Companions, and sowing discord among Muslims resulted in the birth of al-Qāʿida, ISIS, and the Ṭālibān.[68]

In his earlier address, Ayatollah Bahjat reiterated the importance of *taqiyya* in actions and speech, implying perhaps that he did not oppose the religious motivation behind these celebrations but only their form and timing. His comments echoed those of Grand Ayatollah Vaḥīd Khorāsānī regarding the ban on public cursing. In the appendix of his booklet promoting the celebrations, London-based Shaykh Abū al-Ḥusayn al-Khoʾīnī published signed statements by the same leading Ayatollahs who had signed the petition: Javād Tabrīzī (d. 2006), Luṭfallah Ṣāfī Golpāygānī (b. 1919), Bahjat, Muḥammad Fāżil Lankarānī (d. 2007), and even Khamenei, who preached respect for Abū Lūʾlūʾ and approved visitations to the shrine in Kāshān as a manifestation of love for the Prophet's family. Their changes of mind seem to have come from political considerations rather than a genuine change of hearts toward their former Sunnī enemies. Khoʾīnī's book was banned in Iran because it contravened the official line but also, perhaps, in order to spare these scholars undue embarrassment.[69] Other clerics complained that the celebrations received excessive publicity because of the media and video clips that were distributed in

66 "Naẓar-i Ayatollah Bahjat dar bārah-i nohom Rabīʿ al-awwl," 21 Dey 1392/January 11, 2014, http://aghigh.ir/fa/news/19525.

67 "ʿAlī Yūnesī: aqaliyathā bāyad ostāndār va-farmandār va-vazīr shavand," 21 Mehr 1392/October 13, 2013, http://www.entekhab.ir/fa/news/132846. See a similar assertion that ʿUmarkoshān helps the Wahhābīs in "Bidʿathā-i ʿUmarkoshān va-Shīʿakoshān! (khorāfa-i nohom Rabīʿ)," http://forum.hammihan.com/thread58463.html.

68 "Rafsanjānī: laʿn al-ṣaḥāba wal-iḥtifāl bi-maqtal al-khalīfa ʿUmar awṣalanā ilā Dāʿesh," *al-Quds* (London), November 10, 2014.

69 "Naẓar-i Ayatollah Bahjat dar bārah-i khorāfāt nohom Rabīʿ al-awwal;" "Ayatollah Vaḥīd Khorāsānī: Laʿn-i ʿalanī jāyiz nīst;" "Khorāfāt-i 9 Rabīʿ dastmāyeh barāye ḥamla beh abrūyī-i tashayyuʿ"; Abū al-Ḥusayn al-Khoʾīnī, *Shahādat al-athr fī qātil ʿUmar* (Beirut: hay'at khādim al-Mahdī, 2006).

large numbers by mercenaries. In other words, they appear to have been more upset by the harmful publicity than by the celebrations themselves.[70]

In order to curb the ʿUmarkoshān celebrations, in September 2013, the Iranian Ministry of Intelligence and Security (VIVAK) ordered the security forces to prevent them from taking place and a ministry spokesperson described them as immoral and divisive. The move came as part of a wider crackdown on religious groups and media outlets within Iran that were accused of whipping up hatred against Sunnīs in the wake of ISIS's success in Iraq and Syria. According to some reports, up to twelve s offices belonging to radical satellite channels were shut down for "spreading sectarian sentiments between Shi'ites and Sunnīs."[71]

6 Redefining the Nine Rabīʿ Celebrations

There are quite a few writers who, aware of the difficulty of abolishing a popular holiday, sought to preserve 9 Rabīʿ as a Shīʿī holiday but detach it from ʿUmar's death by two means. The first means was refuting the validity of various details associated in popular Shīʿī imagination with the assassin or with the act of murder in order to deprive them of any significance for the Shīʿa. The second was offering a new meaning to 9 Rabīʿ. Other writers criticized the vulgar nature of the celebrations which, they claimed, negated Shīʿī traditions and values, thereby revealing gaps or differences between official and popular religion. Some of those who sought to preserve ʿĪd al-Zahrāʾ but to separate it from the ʿUmarkoshān celebrations sought to set the historical record straight. They cited leading classical chroniclers, such as al-Masʿūdī and al-Yaʿqūbī, or past prominent Shīʿī authorities, such as Shaykh Mufīd and Ibn Idrīs al-Ḥīllī (d. 1201), who had maintained that there was no historical basis to the claim that ʿUmar was killed on 9 Rabīʿ but that he actually died at the end of Ẕī Ḥijjah or the first of Muḥarram; the ḥadīth attributed to the Prophet of praising the killing of one of the hypocrites (*munāfiqīn*) did not, therefore, refer to him at

70 "Khorāfāt-i 9 Rabīʿ dastmāyeh barāye ḥamla beh abrūyī-i tashayyuʿ;" "Hame-i chīz dar bārah-i nohom-i Rabīʿ al-awwal."

71 "Iran's Intelligence Ministry Bans Anti-Sunnī celebrations," *Al-Sharq al-Awsat*, September 5, 2014, http://english.aawsat.com/2014/09/article55336253/irans-intelligence-ministry-bans-anti-sunni-celebrations. Salafi websites claim that the visitations to Abū Lūʾlūʾ's tomb continue without any government interference, but the reliability of these websites is not beyond doubt.

all. There are also writers who maintained that 9 Rabīʿ marked the killing of the Umayyad commander ʿUmar b. Saʿad by al-Mukhtār's army around 686–687.[72]

Another approach sought to debunk the popular myth that Abū Lūʾlūʾ was a Shīʿī who killed ʿUmar for ideological reasons and that he had enjoyed Imām ʿAlī's support.[73] In 2012, the World Forum for Proximity of Islamic Schools published a booklet called *Abū Lūʾlūʾ: From Truth to Delusion* whose main purpose was to refute these popular myths.[74] In a similar vein, Dr. Islām Mālikī Maʿāf denied any religious or ideological justification for the murder and asserted that the true instigators of the murder had been notables of Quraysh or the Jew Kaʿb al-Aḥbār. ʿAlī, Maʿāf maintained, did not support the murder, as he had sworn his allegiance to ʿUmar, even though he knew that he, ʿAlī, deserved the Caliphate. Moreover, ʿAlī saw no harm in assisting the first three caliphs in matters of importance to Islam despite the usurpation of the Caliphate and could not have supported an assassination that took place inside a mosque, as that would have meant its desecration.[75]

The Umayyad family, or Muʿāwiya specifically, with their close links to the Jews have been singled out by some as the real instigators of the murder as part

72 "Khorāfāt-i 9 Rabīʿ dastmāyeh-i barāye ḥamla beh abrūyī-i tashayyuʿ"; "Naẓar-i Ayatollah Khamenei dar mowred-i khorāfāt-i nohom Rabīʿ," 1 Bahman 1391/January 20, 2013, http://www.farsnews.com/newstext.php?nn=13911101000500; Islām Mālikī Maʿāf, "ʿĪd al-zahrāʾ chīst?/ Abū Lūʾlūʾ kīst?/hameh āncheh keh bāyad dar bārah-i yek jashn-i Inḥirāfī bedānīm," 1 Azar 1396/November 22, 2017, http://www.8deynews.com/249061/عیدالزهرا-چیست؟-ابولولو-کیست؟-همه-آن/#print; Musallam Najafī and Hādī Vakīlī, "Taʾammulātī-i taʾrīkhī dar bārah-i nohom-i Rabīʿ," *Muṭālaʿāt-i Islāmī: taʾrīkh va-farhang* 42, no. 85/4 (Fall-Winter 1389/2010–2011): 53–63.

73 See, for example, al-Khoʾīnī, *Shahādat al-athr fī qātil ʿUmar*, who glorifies Abū Lūʾlūʾ as a devout and pious Muslim (187–189), the "breaker of the greatest effigy in human history" (13, 27). Al-Khoʾīnī claimed that ʿAlī ordered Abū Lūʾlūʾ to carry out the assassination (187) and provided numerous proofs why his place in heaven was assured. Al-Khoʾīnī even praised the visitation to his grave as equal to visiting the graves of the Imams (202–203).

74 ʿAbbās ʿAlī Mishkānī Sabzivārī, *Abū Lūʾlūʾ az ḥaqīqat tā tavahhum* (Majmaʿ-i jahānī-i taqrīb-i maẕāhib-i Islāmī, 2012); Najafī and Vakīlī, "Taʾammulātī-i taʾrīkhī dar bārah-i nohom-i Rabīʿ" (64–65) cited various earlier sources which describe him as either Christian or Zoroastrian.

75 Maʿāf, "ʿĪd al-zahrāʾ chīst?/Abu Lūʾlūʾ kīst?/" citing Jaʿfar Shahīdī, *Taʾrīkh-i taḥlīlī-i Islām* (Markaz nashr dāneshgāhī, 1371/), 129–130. For a similar attribution of responsibility, see "Kaʿb al-Aḥbār va-khalīfa-i dovom," *Majmaʿ jahānī-i Shīʿa shināsī*, 18 Mordād 1395/August 8, 2016, http://shiastudies.com/fa/12608/; "Chegūnegī-i koshte shodan ʿUmar," 24 Tīr 1392/July 15, 2013, https://www.porseman.com/article/چگونگی-کشته-شدن-عمر/127306; Najafī and Vakīlī, "Taʿāmolatī-i *taʾrīkhī* dar bārah-i nohom-i Rabīʿ," 68–69, 77.

of their broader scheme to assume power.[76] As mentioned earlier, the identification of the instigator as a Jew who hated Islam and looked to implant the idea of assassination of caliphs among the Muslims[77] was part of a broader trend, also prevalent among Sunnīs, of blaming the Sunnī-Shīʿī split on Jewish machinations. Shifting the blame to an outsider – in this case a Jew – reflected the Muslims' difficulty with assuming responsibility for splits and failures within the Muslim community. Pointing to a common enemy also served to build a common bridge, just as Khamenei blamed the modern-day sectarian rift on the United States and Zionism. Accordingly, Jews and their present-day Zionist heirs have thus not only remained enemies but continue to scheme against the Muslims.

The popular myth around Abū Lū'lū', explaining his motivation partly as revenge for ʿUmar's conquest of Iran, associated him with certain ethnic or proto-nationalist sentiments.[78] The establishment writers sought to counter these feelings by stressing his loyalty to his Arab master, al-Mughīra b. Shuʿba, a subsequent ally of the Umayyads, but, more importantly, by claiming that Iranians who resided in Medina had been "subject to bashing and attacks," because an Iranian had killed ʿUmar.[79] They reiterated that ʿUmar's assassination resulted in the much worse rule of ʿUthmān and the total takeover of the early Muslim state by the depraved Umayyads. In other words, in the broader scheme of things, Abū Lū'lū' only harmed the Shīʿī cause.[80]

76 Ḥusayn Ilāhī, ʿAlī Yazdānī, Ḥasan Kāẓimzādeh, *Mahār-i inḥirāf: Bāzgavī-i ḥavādith pas az riḥlat-i piyāmbar akram* (s) (Qom: muʿasasa-i *ta'rīkh*-i taṭbīqī, 1393), 228–233; "Banī Umayya va-Yahūd," 25 Tīr 1395/15 July 2016, http://www.mouood.org/component/k2/item/36944; "Iṭṭilāʿ-i Yahūd az terōr-i ʿUmar," http://jscenter.ir/judaism-and-islam/jewish-intrigue/5549.

77 "Muta'asefāne dīrūz ham rokh dād/bargozārī marāsim-i gheyr-i akhlāqī; noh-i Rabīʿ al-awwal khorāfa-i tashayyuʿ-i londonī," December 22, 2015, https://urlzs.com/4P14C. Ironically, the Qom "Questions and Answers" website describes the same Kaʿb as a close advisor for ʿUmar, thereby attributing some of the latter's misdeeds to Jewish influence. See "Mushāvir-i aʿẓam-i khalīfa-i dovom yek Yahūdī tāzeh-musalmān būdeh," http://www.vahabiat.porsemani.ir/content/مشاور-اعظم-خلیفه-ی-دوم-یک-یهودی-تازه-مسلمان-بوده.

78 Hamid Enayat elaborated on ʿUmar's "high place in Iranian folk demonology" already by the Tenth century CE for his role in conquering Iran and the charges leveled against him for discriminating against Iranians and his prohibition of Arab-Iranian intermarriage. *Modern Islamic Political Thought* (London: I.B. Tauris, 2005), 33.

79 "Naqsh-i Irāniān dar terōr-i ʿUmar," November 6, 2007, http://oskarimbns.blogfa.com/post-1.aspx; "Koshte shodan ʿUmar b. Khaṭṭāb beh dast-i Fīrūz Abū Lū'lū' Irānī – sāl 23 hijrī qamarī/27 Ẕū al-Ḥijjah," http://abulolo.persianblog.ir/tag/قتل_عمر.

80 "Ta'rīkh-i daqīq-i marg-i ʿUmar bin Khaṭṭāb," http://belagh1.blogfa.com/post-1130.aspx.

A bolder argument reflecting an openness to self-criticism was that the celebrations were a late invention, a product of political expediency, and therefore could not have been endorsed by the Imāms. Ḥujjat al-Islam Muḥammad Ḥusayn Rajabī Davānī a lecturer in the Qom seminary, for example, explained that in the earlier Islamic period the Shīʿīs were persecuted and kept under such tight surveillance that even holding gatherings, let alone such celebrations, was impossible. It is thus highly probable that the celebrations were devised during the Ṣafavīd or even Qājār period when Shīʿīsm became the official state religion.[81] Dr. Maʿāf explained that the Ṣafavīds initiated the celebrations as part of a broader effort to rally the population behind them against their Sunnī enemies at a time of political distress. In doing so, the Ṣafavīds ignored the consensus among Shīʿī and Sunnī historians as well as the doubtful reliability of the ḥadīth in question. Ḥujjat al-Islam Yūsufī Gharavī of the Qom seminary took a harsher view of the Ṣafavīds for attaching ʿUmar's death to 9 Rabīʿ. The Ṣafavīds could not, he claimed, celebrate ʿUmar's death on its true date, 26 Ẕī Ḥijjah as it was too close to the commemorations of Imām Ḥusayn in ʿĀshūrā'. By attaching ʿUmar's death to 9 Rabīʿ, they could have used dissimulation if threatened, claiming that the celebrations marked the death of ʿUmar b. Saʿad.[82] Regardless of its historical veracity, attributing ʿUmarkoshān to the Ṣafavīds or blaming them for it is highly significant; it reflects a historicized perception and understanding of Shīʿīsm as a dynamic historical phenomenon, which may even be subject to manipulations. While common among scholars, this understanding is rare among believers, particularly clerics, who all too often espouse essentialist and ahistorical views of their own religions.

The criticism of the Ṣafavīds reflects an interesting ambivalence; they are often praised for having transformed Shīʿīsm into the dominant state religion, but their being a monarchical dynasty contradicts the Islamic Republic's fundamental doctrine of *vilāyat-i faqīh*. Moreover, such criticism, which is also directed at Majlisī, whose writings played an important role in the promotion of anti-Sunnī activities, demonstrates this same readiness for self-criticism within the religious establishment itself, as well as an implicit acknowledgement of the politicization of religion in the past, and an almost secular approach to

81 "Naẓar-i Rahbarī dar bārah-i khorāfāt-i 9 Rabīʿ al-awwal," 1 Bahman 1391/January 20, 2013, https://www.mashreghnews.ir/news/187473/-9--نظر-رهبری-درباره-خرافات-ربیع-الاول http://www.lorestankhabar.com item no. 63037. See also Najafī and Vakīlī, "Taʿāmulatī-i ta'rīkhī dar bārah-i nohom-i Rabīʿ," 61.

82 Maʿāf, "ʿĪd al-zahrā' chīst?/ Abu Lū'lū' kīst?/"; Muḥammad Hādī Yūsufī Gharavī, "Naqsh-i maṭāʿin-i biḥār al-anwār dar khorāfa-i nohom Rabīʿ al-awwal," 24 Dey 1392/January 14, 2014 – http://dinonline.com/doc/news/fa/3188/.

religious texts. Significantly, such self-criticism was not applied by these mainstream writers to more modern religious doctrines.

7 The Nine Rabīʿ Celebrations: Popular vs. Official Islam

An important aspect of the debate revolved around the question of authority over the definition of "correct Shīʿism" (*tashayyuʿ-i ṣaḥīḥ*), which also reflected a gap between the official and supposedly more refined Islam and the uncouth, superstitious religiosity of the "common people" (*khorāfāt-i ʿawwām al-nās*). This tension produced condescending descriptions of the ʿUmarkoshān celebrations as a "groundless and foolish tradition of the ignoramuses of the Shīʿa," an expression of "the culture of common Shīʿa," and a "vulgar issue which Shīʿī values and beliefs cannot accept."[83] Indeed, in his response to Shaykh al-Azhar's protest over the persistent cursing of the Companions, Grand Ayatollah Makārem Shīrāzī distinguished between the religious authorities, who condemn such practices, and the actions of the "common" people, who should not be taken into consideration.[84] The celebrations were manifested, it was claimed, in "numerous burlesque plays, carnivals and festivities."[85] According to one testimony:

---

83 "ʿUmarkoshūn!! Yek rasm-i khorāfī va-aḥmaqāne az sūye barkhī jahhāl-i Shīʿa!," 11 Azar 1393/ December 2, 2014, http://313muslims.blog.ir/post; "Khāṭira-i tekān-dehande Ayatollah Marʿashī dar mowred-i ʿUmarkoshūn," http://balatarazbalatarin.blogfa.com/post/237/ خاطره-تکان دهنده-آیت الله-مرعشی-در-مورد-عمر-کشون; "Khorāfāt-i 9 Rabīʿ dastmāyeh-i barāye ḥamla beh arbrūyi-i tashayyuʿ;" "Vīrāyishī jadīd az ʿnohom Rabīʿ, jahālathā, khiṣārathā muntashir mīshavad," 11 Dey 1393/January 1, 2015, http://aghigh.ir/fa/news/44604; "Barresī-i mustanadāt yek jashn-i inḥirāfī," 15 Dey 1393/January 5, 2015, http://www.fetan.ir/home/4016; "bidʿat ʿīd al-Zahrāʾ beh munāsabat-i nohom Rabīʿ al-awwal;" "Nohom Rabīʿ; rūzī ke dushman khōshḥāl ast," 2 Dey 1394/December 23, 2015, http://www.tabnakesfahan.ir/fa/news/150317/; "Naẓar-i ṣarīḥ-i rahbar-i inqilāb dar khuṣūṣ-i ʿUmarkoshūn," 1 Bahman 1391/January 20, 2013, http://www.harfeno.com/vdcf.cdmiw6doygiaw.html.

84 "Naqd va-barresī-i sokhnān-i shaykh al-azhar, bar żede mabānī-i iʿtiqādi-i tashayyuʿ," 24 Shahrīvar 1394/September 15, 2015, http://www.valiasr-aj.com/persian/shownews.php?idnews=8040.

85 Enayat, *Modern Islamic Political Thought*, 33. See similar descriptions in Qoṭbī, "Rabīʿ al-awwal, jashn-i shādī barāye ahl-i bayt ast yā?" See pictures of the ceremony in Qom in which a person (presumably representing ʿUmar) dressed like a clown is seated on a donkey in "Rāhpīmāyi ʿalayh-i seh khalīfa va-ijrā-i marāsim-i ʿUmarkoshān' dar Qom," 20 Dey 1393/January 10, 2015, https://urlzs.com/JPwR6; "Talāsh barāye nābūdī-i Islām dar shahr-i Qom + taṣāvīr," 20 Dey 1393/ January 10, 2015, https://urlzs.com/hM9oV.

> Immediately after Muḥarram, the month of religious mourning, the women start sewing clothes of all colors, particularly red. Some dye their hair and nails with henna, others make for the hairdresser, and when the ceremony finally begins, everyone is dressed up in a bright and colorful way. At the ceremony, which takes place at people's homes, women and men are invited to separate gatherings: the women sing, dance, and recite lewd poetry ("ya Zahrāʾ, yā Zahrāʾ * Zahrāʾ is another name for Fāṭima*, congratulations, your husband's enemy has gone off to hell, etc."). Tambourines, pots, and pans are used to beat the rhythm. A small, colorful doll is prepared for the occasion, representing ʿOmar, which is placed in the middle of the room for the women to dance around and burned at the end of the ceremony.[86]

Hādī Qoṭbī conceded that the celebrations had been originally intended as a commendable act of professing loyalty to the Prophet's family and disassociation from its enemies. But he lamented that in recent years they have become acts of frivolity, parody, and clowning with the disrespectful chanting of profanities and dancing. Such partying is a far cry from the celebrations' original intent and the culture of the Prophet's family and thus degrades the Shīʿa.[87] Not surprisingly, the celebrations have led to scathing criticism of their deviationist (*inḥirāfī*) nature and the prevalence of *khorāfāt* (practices that have no foundation in the Shīʿa) and *taḥrīfāt* (distortions).[88]

Ḥujjat al-Islam Masʿūd Diyānī, who attended the ʿUmarkoshān celebration in Iṣfahān, described it as the "most abhorrent experience" that made him want to cry and throw up in disgust. He described the ceremony as filled with expressions of "blasphemy ... frivolity ... sexual gestures ... undignified acts ... foolishness, and fanaticism": "I wanted to apologize to my Sunnī brothers and sisters as a human being, as a Muslim, and as a Shīʿī religious student."[89] The religious preacher Muḥammad Hādī Meyhandūst urged those eager to participate in the ʿUmarkoshān celebrations to make sure they preserve the

---

86 Cyrus Shahmiri post, April 10, 2006 in "The Baba Shuja-e-din aka Abu lulu, Mausoleum," http://www.allempires.com/forum/printer_friendly_posts.asp?TID=10804.

87 Qoṭbī, "Rabīʿ al-Awwal, jashn-i shādī barāye ahl-i bayt ast yā?"

88 See the sources in note 44.

89 "Iẓhārātī ṣarīḥ dar bārah-i marāsim ʿUmarkoshūn," 23 Dey 1392/January 13, 2014, http://alef.ir/vdccmsqim2bqsm8.ala2.html?211777.

reputation of the Shīʿa: "In the name of the Prophet's family, do not dance … do not involve the Prophet's family in your sins."[90]

A common justification for the unrestrained conduct of participants in the celebrations is the popular interpretation of the "ḥadīth rafʿ al-qalam." Accordingly, God ordered the angels not to register the acts that the believers carry out that day, thus releasing them from religious obligations and allowing them to behave however they please as part of the duty to rejoice over the death of ʿUmar and to make Fāṭima happy.[91] This brings to mind the term Carnivalesque, coined by the literary critic Mikhail Bakhtin in order to analyze the social and cultural ramifications of various social practices associated with the medieval carnival in Europe. Such practices, which entailed free interaction between people and eccentric and even sacrilegious behavior, temporarily challenge the structure of authority and power and provide the subordinate groups with a sense of freedom and liberty, however brief or illusionary. It is thus conceivable that some believers, rather than seeking to challenge the prevalent religious power structure in Iran, regard the ʿUmarkoshān celebrations as an outlet for joy and celebration, at a remove from the more somber or mournful Shīʿī repertoire of holy days and the regime's restrictions on personal conduct.[92]

Not surprisingly, the clerical elite abhorred both aspects of the celebrations: the free conduct and the subtle challenge to established authority. In addition to denouncing and banning these practices, all the *marājiʿ taqlīd* denied the legal validity behind the "rafʿ al-qalam" ḥadīth, claiming that it was unreliable according to the classification rules of the literature which examined the chain of transmitters.[93] They also rejected the popular interpretation of the ḥadīth on the basis that it contradicted the Qurʾān and the pronouncements of all Imāms as well as the principles of logic and Shīʿī theology. Shīʿīs are, they asserted, obligated to carry out their religious duties every day, and forbidden matters (*ḥarām*) and sins are not permitted at any time. The clerics maintained

90 Muḥammad Hādī Meyhandūst, "Beh nām-i ahl-i bayt nāraqṣīd, luṭfan," 7 Bahman 1388/ February 27, 2010, http://1001talangor.blogfa.com/post-59.aspx.

91 "Khorāfāt-i 9 Rabīʿ dastmāyeh-i barāye ḥamla beh abrūyī-i tashayyuʿ."

92 For an analysis of this idea, see Lynn E. Cohen, "Bakhtin's Carnival and Pretend Role Play: A Comparison of Social Contexts," *American Journal of Play* 4, no. 2 (2011): 176–203. See the reference to the dress and conduct of various women in the ʿUmarkoshān celebrations as "carnevalesque outfits," in "The Baba Shuja-e-dīn aka Abū lulu, Mausoleum."

93 "Dīdgāh-i marājiʿ taqlīd-i Shīʿa dar bārah-i aʿmāl-i khorāfī-i rūz-i nohom-i Rabīʿ al-awwal."

that the ḥadīth's true meaning was the enhancement of true repentance by the believer on that particular day.[94]

Alongside the legalistic and political arguments advanced by the Shīʿī establishment against the ʿUmarkoshān celebrations, they were also aware of the unfeasibility of uprooting such a popular practice without offering an appealing alternative. Hence, they opted to preserve 9 Rabīʿ as a joyous day but with a new cause for celebration: "the coronation of the Imām of the Age," in other words, the beginning of the mission and authority (vilāyat) of the Twelfth Imām, the Mahdī.[95] As Ḥujjat al-Islam Jaʿfar Musāvī Nasab Director of the Cultural Foundation of Mashhad explained, the original purpose of 9 Rabīʿ had been to enhance the adherence of Shīʿīs to the principles of *Imāmat* and the *vilāyat* of the Mahdī; the dating of ʿUmar's assassination to this particular day was a conspiracy by the enemies of Islam to distance Shīʿīs from these principles.[96]

While the ʿUmarkoshān celebrations projected animosity toward Sunnī Islam, quite a few leading scholars inverted them by claiming that 9 Rabīʿ should actually highlight the unity of Muslim sects in the face of their common enemies, i.e., Zionism and the West.[97] In contradiction to these efforts, however, on May 2, 2016 the Iranian parliament declared the eighth of Rabīʿ al-Awwal and not the ninth as the official holiday for commemorating the martyrdom of Ḥasan al-ʿAskarī and the beginning of the *Imāmat* of the Twelfth

94 "Ḥaqīqat nohom-i Rabīʿ al-awwal chīst?," http://ahlulbaytclub.com/HtmlFiles/Art0002286_Content.htm; "Hame-i chīz dar bārah-i nohom Rabiʿ al-awwal;" "Khorāfāt-i 9 rabi dastmāyeh-i barāye ḥamla beh abrūyī-i tashayyuʿ."

95 "Naẓar-i Ayatollah Makārem Shīrāzī dar mowred-i marāsim-i ʿīd al-Zahrāʾ," 19 Dey 1392/June 9, 2013, http://www.hawzah.net/fa/News/View/96429; "Nohom Rabīʿ al-awwal, jashn-i aghāz-i Imāmat-i Imām-i zamān ast yā jashn-i ʿīd al-Zahrāʾ?" 11 Bahman 1391/January 30, 2013, https://urlzs.com/beL7P; "Pāyān-i ṣafar va-tikrār khorāfa-i 'daq albāb masājid' aʿmāl muṣṭaḥab nakhostīn rūz-i Rabīʿ al-awwal," 21 Azar 1394/December 12, 2015, https://www.mashreghnews.ir/news/660793; "Hame-i chīz dar bārah-i nohom Rabīʿ al-awwal va-bidʿat ʿīd al-Zahrāʾ (s);" "Piyāmakhā-i tabrīk-i sālrūz-i aghāz-i Imāmat va-vilāyat-i imām-i zamān (AJ)," 10 Dey 1393/December 31, 2014, http://www.yjc.ir/fa/news/5087415.

96 "Nohom Rabīʿ al-awwal, sālrūz aghāz-i Imāmat-i Imām zamān (aj), zamānī barāye shādī muntaẓirān," Dāneshgāh-i Āzād Islāmī Vāḥid Hamedan, 1 Bahman 1391/January 20, 2013, http://www.iauh.ac.ir/about-university/news-archive/45-farhangi/846-9rabiolaval.html (last accessed March 13 2016).

97 "Naẓar-i Ayatollah Bahjat dar bārah-i khorāfāt nohom Rabīʿ al-awwal"; "Nohom Rabīʿ al-awwal, jashn-i aghāz-i imāmat imām-i zamān yā jashn-i ʿīd al-Zahrāʾ."

Imām.[98] Presumbaly, they recoiled at giving the official stamp on such a blatanat political play with an entrenched popular tradition.

8 Reinterpreting Rabīʿ Ninth: Ideology and Tactics

The repeated emphasis on Islamic unity and the rejection of practices that would cause friction with the Sunnī majority did not mean, however, that the Iranian clerical establishment intended to revise the doctrines that defined the distinction of Shʿism from Sunnī Islam or had changed its ideological position toward the Prophet's Companions and, in particular, the Caliph ʿUmar. Khamenei's office sought to allay Shīʿī fears and, possibly, also to discourage Sunnī hopes by making it clear that the ideal of Islamic unity did not mean that Shīʿīs or Sunnīs had to endorse the beliefs of the other. At the same time, they tried to calm Sunnī suspicions by insisting that the emphasis on unity was not concealing Shīʿī ambitions to convert Sunnīs to Shīʿīsm. Both Sunnīs and Shīʿīs should remain who they are, and any Sunnī wanting to become a Shīʿī should do so only through learning and scholarly debates; likewise, neither side should listen to the "whispering" (a clear allusion to Satan's whispering in the Qurʾān) of the enemies to promote mutual animosity but instead should cooperate with each other.[99] In a similar vein, Grand Ayatollahs Ṣāfī Golpāygānī and Lankarānī distinguished between the necessity for Islamic unity and the loss of Shīʿī identity and explained that while it was essential to pursue unity, the essence, truth, and teachings of Shīʿīsm should be firmly sustained. Shīʿīs should not be expected to abandon their allegiance to the Prophet's family or to now think well of those whom they regard as enemies of the Prophet's family and hypocrites. Rather, Shīʿīs and Sunnīs should stand together against the unbelievers and the enemies of Islam.[100]

---

98 "Sālrūz-i aghāz-i imāmat-i valī-i ʿaṣr (ʿaj) taʿṭīl-i rasmī mīshavad," 13 Ordībehesht 1395/ May 2, 2016, http://www.mehrnews.com/news/3614339.

99 "Bayānāt-i rahbar-i inqilāb dar dīdār-i shirkat-konandegān dar dovomīn Hamāyesh buzurgdasht Ibn Maytham Baḥrānī," 25 Dey 1385/January 15, 2007, http://kalameimam.persianblog.ir/post/496/; "Vaḥdat az manẓar-i rahbar-i muʿaẓẓam-i Inqilāb."

100 "Nemūneh-i az taḥrīf-i taʾrīkhī-i nohom Rabīʿ al-awwal/ Sīrat Amīr al-muʾminīn (a) dar ittiḥād-i Islāmī," 29 Azar 1394/December 20, 2015, https://www.farsnews.ir/news/13940925001299/نمونه-ای-از-تحریف-تاریخی-نهم-ربیع-الاول-سیره-امیرالمؤمنین-ع-در; "Ayatollah Ṣāfī-Golpāygānī: Ḥaqīqat-i vaḥdat ʾīn nīst ke shīʿa va-sunnī az ʿaqāyed-i khōd dast bardārand," 29 Dey 1392/January 19, 2014, http://shiayan.ir/3826; "Naẓar-i ʿulamāʾ va-marājiʿ-i ʿuẓām bar vaḥdat miyān Shīʿa va-sunnī," 14 Dey 1393/ January 4, 2015, http://dana.ir/News/206483.html. Rafsanjānī made the same point when explaining his

As an indication of the persistence of the traditional Shīʿī outlook alongside the recurring condemnation of public disrespect toward the Companions, various media outlets of the clerical establishment continued to attack ʿUmar b. al-Khaṭṭāb. Quite a few of these publications appeared in blogs in which the identity of writers as either clerics or laypeople could not be verified. One theme of these writings was the charge that ʿUmar had demonstrated a poor understanding of Islam, for example, his refusal to accept the Prophet's death, and had introduced harmful innovations (*bidʿat*).[101] A more flagrant tactic of these writings was to highlight his supposedly immoral conduct and personality, particularly his duplicitous conduct toward the Prophet or occasional opposition to the Prophet's policy. Accordingly, the Ḥażrat-i Valī-i ʿAṣr Institute published a long article describing ʿUmar's systematic abuse of women during the Prophet's lifetime, which inevitably culminated in his mistreatment of Fāṭima.[102] Other publications, which sought to refute the assertion that ʿUmar had married ʿAlī's daughter Umm Kulthūm as that might have implied that ʿAlī had cooperated with him, elaborated on Umm Kulthūm's brave condemnation of his shameful conduct toward her.[103]

---

statements on the caliphate, see "Towżīḥ-i Hāshimī barāye sokhnānesh dar bārah-ye khalīfa-i avval." In 2006 Ṣāfī Golpāygānī still referred to the caliphate of Abū Bakr and ʿUmar as the *niẓām-e-ghāsib*, "the regime of the usurpers," see Maghen, "Unity or Hegemony?," 190.

101 "Bidʿathā va-iʿtirāżāt-i Abū Bakr va-ʿUmar nisbat beh dīn," http://ama14.blogfa.com/cat-8.aspx; "Yahūdiyān beh ʿUmar bin Khaṭṭāb laqab Fārūq dādand," http://www.lamia.blogsky.com/1392/10/25/post-183; "Rajabī Davānī barresī kard: ʿāmil-i aṣlī-i ghasb-i khilāfat Abū Bakr būd noh ʿUmar," 16 Farvardīn 1391/April 4, 2012, http://www.snn.ir/detail/News/179019/1070. Although Rajabī Davānī elaborated on ʿUmar's improper conduct after the Prophet's death, he insisted that Abū Bakr and not ʿUmar was the key person in usurping ʿAlī's rightful succession. Such a description can be seen to preserve the negative attitude toward ʿUmar but mitigates it so as not to justify the joy over his death.

102 "Shīʿa va-Sunnī, pāsokh beh shubhāt-i barādarān-i Sunnī," http://shiaanswering.blogfa.com/; "Buzurgtarīn-i khiyānat-i ʿUmar dar ḥaqq-i Islām va-muslimīn," http://shiaanswering.blogfa.com/post/130 (accessed March 23, 2019); "Khiyānathā-i ʿUmar beh Islām (2)," http://sedayeshia.blogsky.com/1391/11/04/post-161/; "Istidlāl beh 'ghayrat-i ʿarab' barāye inkār shahādat Zahrāʾ salām Allah ʿalayhā," 5 Farvardīn 1392/March 25, 2013, http://www.valiasr-aj.com/fa/page.php?bank=maghalat&id=146; "ʿUmar bin Khattāb, khalīfa-i dovom keh būd va-cheh khuṣūṣiyat-i raftārī dasht?," http://www.islamquest.net/fa/archive/question/fa34625; "Naqsh-i Abū Bakr va-ʿUmar dar terōr-i rasūl akram ṣala Allah ʿalayhi va-Ālihi," https://amīremomenin.persianblog.ir/QL366j4aoWibxqb11wrQ--نقش-ابوبکر-و-عمر-در-ترور-رسول-اکرم-صلی-الله-علیه-و-آله.

103 "Barresī-i shubha-i izdivāj-i ʿUmar bā Umm Kulthūm," http://morajeat.blogfa.com/post-16.aspx; "Izdivāj-i Umm Kulthūm," 18 Ordībehesht 1388/May 18, 2009, http://porseman.org/showarticle.aspx?id=633; "ʿIllat-i izdivāj-i Umm Kulthūm bā ʿUmar," 13 Dey 1389/January 3, 2011, http://www.hawzah.net/fa/Question/View/63562.

Perhaps the worst insult was linking ʿUmar to another despised "other," namely, the Jews, and several writers maintained that the Jews were those who had originally given him his honorific al-Fārūq – the one who distinguishes between truth and falsehood. Others accused him of collaborating with the Jews while the Prophet was fighting them, thus depicting him as the agent of the Jews, a "fifth column" inside the nascent Muslim community.[104]

It is only natural that the campaign to revise centuries-long popular attitudes and practices encountered opposition within the clerical establishment and among ordinary believers. Moreover, the changing attitude toward some of the most vilified figures in Shīʿī historical memory threatened to challenge the very foundations of Shīʿīsm. For example, if ʿUmar and ʿAisha cease to be villains, this challenges the very notion of the injustice they committed against ʿAlī.[105]

While it is impossible to gauge the exact scope of popular reception or opposition to new religious ideas anywhere, especially in non-democratic countries, several indicators regarding reactions in Iran can be discerned. The repeated publication of rulings by Khamenei and the other leading *marājiʿ taqlīd*, banning the cursing of the Prophet's Companions and the ʿUmarkoshān celebrations, as well as the large number of other publications over several years denouncing these practices, indicate their continued existence. Indeed, quite a few of the official publications conceded that while the scope of these acts may have declined, they were still far from negligible.[106] Anecdotal evidence also points to the persistence of both the cursing and the celebrations.[107] Another indicator is the continued operation of websites and blogs glorifying

104 "Yahūdiyān beh ʿUmar bin Khaṭṭāb laqab Fārūq dādand;" "ʿAlāqa-i ʿUmar bin Khaṭṭāb beh dīn-i Yahūd," 4 Azar 1391/ November 24, 2012, http://tarikhislam1400.blogfa.com/post/24; "Naqsh-i Yahūd dar intikhāb ʿunwān barāye ʿUmar bin Khaṭṭāb," 4 Esfand 1391/ February 22, 2013, http://armanemahdaviyat.ir/?p=158\; "ʿUmar wal-Yahūd, yahūdiyat ʿUmar bin al-Khaṭṭāb wa-taʾāmurihi maʿa al-Yahūd," October 5, 2014, http://marwan1433143.blogspot.co.il/2014/10/blog-post.html; "ʿUmar bin Khaṭṭāb sutūn-i panjom-i Yahūdiyān-i Medīna," 25 Dey 1393/January 15, 2015, http://amīremomenin.persianblog.ir/post/942; "Naqsh-i Yahūd dar vaqāyiʿ-i taʾrīkh-i Islām," 7 Bahman 1386/January 27, 2008, http://www.farsnews.com/printable.php?nn=8609240312. See also Chapter 2.

105 See, for example, the question raised on the official *Islamquest* website that if ʿAlī had accepted ʿUmar's caliphate, how could he be regarded as *maʿṣūm* in "Āyā Shīʿa Abū Bakr va-ʿUmar rā kāfir mīdānad?," 22 Khorad 1397/June 12, 2018, http://www.islamquest.net/fa/archive/question/fa2982.

106 ʿAbd al-*Raḥīm* Abāẓarī, "Iẓhārāt Hāshimī dar bārah-i khalīfa-i avval; hamsū yā mukhālif bā rahbarī?," 9 Bahman 1392/January 29, 2014, http://www.asriran.com/fa/news/317578.

107 See for example: "Bidʿathā-i ʿUmarkoshān va-Shīʿakoshān!," which speaks of "prevalent deviations (*khorāfa-i rāyij*) that take place on Rabīʿ ninth"; "khiyānat beh Islām dar libās maḥabbat beh ahl-i bayt (ʿalayhim al-salām)," http://sahebnews.ir/164612 that laments

Abū Lū'lū' and promoting visitations to his tomb in Kāshān.[108] It is unclear whether this is a result of negligence or incompetence by the authorities or whether they enjoy the protection of powerful patrons within the clerical establishment.

Responses and talkbacks on the internet are, in general a problematic source; it is impossible to estimate how representative they are, and too often opinions found online seem to represent more radical elements than the mainstream. The authenticity of these responses is also often questionable, as various interested parties manufacture responses in order to manipulate public opinion. Thus, while the argument repeated in many of those responses, supporting the official position that one should follow the instructions and teachings of the religious authorities and the Supreme Leader, may represent the true convictions of their writers, they may also be part of the regime's efforts at socialization. On the other hand, the views opposing the official line seem to be more authentic, as it is difficult to see any ulterior motive behind them. To cite just one example: of the seventy-six responses to an article on Ayatollah Marʿashī's discussion of cursing and disrespect toward the Companions, forty approved the new position and thirty-six adhered to the traditional approach. The most common argument among the former was the need to obey the Supreme Leader and the *marājiʿ taqlīd*, who had a better understanding of Shīʿīsm and the needs of the age. The latter were more emotional, occasionally expressing visceral hatred of ʿUmar for the suffering he had inflicted upon ʿAlī and Fāṭima and even naming him *ḥarāmzādeh* (bastard). Some rejected the argument that the cursing fuels the killing of Shīʿīs and asserted that the cursing was simply an excuse for the Sunnīs and that the Shīʿīs had always been the victims of Sunnī animosity. Others dismissed the argument that the Sunnīs should be respected because they too believed in Allah and the Qur'ān, remarking that next the Shīʿīs would be expected to respect the Jews because they too believed in one God and Jerusalem had been the direction of prayer for both religions.[109]

Conservative opponents of the new approach pointed to the ample references in the Shīʿī sources such as ḥadīth given by various imāms and writings

the prevalence of the ceremonies; and "Az kāravānhā-i laʿn va-sabb tā ḥużūr gostardeh dar shabakahā-i mujāzī," 2 Dey 1394/December 23, 2015, – https://qademon.ir/?p=1856.

108 See for example: "Ḥażrat-I Shujāʿ al-Dīn Fayrūz Abū Lū'lū' raḥmat Allah ʿalayhi," https://yazahrajan.blogsky.com/1391/11/07/post-177/; "Weblag takhaṣṣuṣī ḥażrat-i Abū Lū'lū' ʿalayhi al-salām," http://abalolo.blogfa.com/; "Angīzeh-i Abū Lū'lū' dar qatl khalīfa-i dovom cheh būd?," http://shahramrasti.blogfa.com/post-82.aspx.

109 "Khaṭira-i tekān-dehande Ayatollah Marʿashī dar mowred-i ʿUmarkoshūn."

of earlier Shīʿī scholars praising *tabarrā*.[110] Others protested the overreadiness to discard fundamental Shīʿī doctrines for the sake of accommodating Sunnīs. Ḥujjat al-Islam Ravānbakhsh, a supporter of the arch conservative Miṣbāḥ Yazdī, lashed out at Rafsanjānī's willingness to gloss over the dispute over the Prophet's succession. He argued that the identity of the first caliph is not merely an academic point that concerns only historians; rather, the entire Shīʿī doctrine of legitimate government, including the foundations of the *vilāyat-i faqīh* system in the Islamic Republic, depends on the belief that ʿAlī was the rightful successor.[111]

Most prominent among those upholding the traditional view was Ayatollah Muḥammad Ḥusaynī Shāhrūdī (d. 2019), who published an article on his personal website titled "The Day of Nine Rabīʿ al-Awwal: The Killing of ʿUmar b. Khaṭṭāb God's Curse upon Him." This article, which reiterates the standard Shīʿī charges against ʿUmar, described 9 Rabīʿ as a joyous day of celebrations and of thanking God by answering the "curse" of Fāṭima with the killing of ʿUmar.[112] Shāhrūdī 's dissension from the official position is significant not only because of his senior position in the Qom seminary, but also because it did not arouse any sharp response, presumably because of his respected status.

In April 2011, students in Grand Ayatollah Vaḥīd Khorāsānī's senior class protested aloud when he added the common Sunnī phrase, "may Allah be pleased with him," after mentioning ʿUmar's name. The elderly sage reprimanded the students, saying he would not allow such disrespect in his class. However, when asked by the media about the incident, he had to explain that the phrase was not his, he was merely citing Fakhr al-Dīn Rāzi's *Tafsīr*, and that one must distinguish between scholarly criticism and the expression of religious views.[113] The students' response was indicative of their true opinions, and the Grand Ayatollah's need to justify himself by resorting to technical rather than

---

110 See for example, "Naqd-i kitāb-i 'laʿnhā-i nāmuqaddas' barresī-i kitāb-i 'laʿnhā-i nāmoqaddas' athr-i aqā-i Mahdī Masāʾilī," http://naghdobarresi2.blogfa.com; and Masāʾilī's response "Pāsokhī kūtāh beh naqd-i kitāb-i 'laʿnhā-i nāmoqaddas'" December 13, 2016, http://azadpajooh.com/category/پاسخ-به-نقدها.

111 "Naqdī bar pāsokh-i aqā-i Rafsanjānī beh yek iddiʿāʾ," 26 Bahman 1392/February 17, 2014, http://ravanbakhsh.blogfa.com/post-42.aspx; "Āyā behtar nīst bejāyi barāʾat az dushmanān-i aʾīmah ḥisāb-i ānhā rā beh khodā vāgoẕār konīm?," http://www.rahejanat.blogfa.com/post/32.

112 Seyyed Muḥammad Ḥusaynī Shāhrūdī, "Rūz-i nohom-i māh-i Rabīʿ al-awwal: qatl-i ʿUmar bin Khaṭṭāb laʿanahu Allah," http://www.shahroudi.com/Portal.aspx?pid=71309&Culture=Persian&CaseID=4822.

113 "Naẓar-i Ayatollah Vaḥīd dar bārah-i bī iḥtirāmī beh khulafāʾ-i ahl-i Sunnat," 4 Ordībehesht 1390/April 24, 2011, http://www.shia-online.ir/article.asp?id=17770.

ideological reasoning shows his sensitivity toward public opinion on such an emotionally charged issue.

Another difference appeared between state clerics and popular "panegyrists" (*madāḥān*) and between the clerics and the "common people." Madāḥān activity is sponsored by the state, and they play a significant role mediating between the more scholarly section of the clerical establishment and society at large.[114] The madāḥān are not a monolithic group and identify with different political trends within the ruling elite. Yet, due to their role and status, they are probably closer to ordinary believers than their more scholarly colleagues and feel sufficiently confident to follow their constituents and defy the official line. A writer from Kāshān, for example, complained that some madāḥāns take part in the ʿUmarkoshān celebrations despite the explicit bans issued by the *marājiʿ taqlīd* and, particularly, the Supreme Leader. He denounced their sermons as exceeding the bounds of culture, civility, and morality and even displaying some irreverence toward the Prophet's family. The same writer also expressed his dismay at the "Filtering Committee," which has shut down numerous immoral websites but stands idle in the face of websites that regularly publish derogatory video clips against ʿUmar.[115]

9 Clerical Power Struggle or Sectarian Rapprochement

The sharpest dispute over these issues broke out between the Iranian establishment and the dissident Shīrāzī faction, which had moved from Karbalāʾ to Qom but later settled in London. In London they set a mini-media empire overseeing nineteen satellite channels that broadcast in Persian, Arabic, English, and Turkish. The larger issues at stake included: the question of central authority in Shīʿīsm; adherence to a more traditional outlook or adaptation to change; the perpetuation of traditional Shīʿī animosity toward the majority Sunnī world; and the tension between popular and elitist forms of religion.[116]

114 For a broader analysis of the Madāḥān phenomenon, see Raz Zimmt, "The Return of the Eulogists," *Spotlight on Iran*, October 24, 2013, http://www.terrorism-info.org.il/en/articleprint.aspx?id=20587.

115 "Āyā marāsimī-i mawsūm beh ʿUmarkoshūn' muṭābiq sharʿ ast?," 24 Dey 1392/January 14, 2013, http://kashannews.net/1392/10/24/. See also Qoṭbī, "Rabīʿ al-Awwal, jashn-i shādī barāye ahl-i bayt ast yā?"

116 Khomeini championed the doctrine of the absolute guardianship of one jurist (*vilāyat-i faqīh muṭlaq*), whereas the Shīrāzī's proposed the "council of jurists" (*shūrat al-fuqahāʾ*), which gave more clerics a say in political decision-making. For the background of this dispute, see Edith Szanto, "Beyond the Karbala' Paradigm: Rethinking Revolution and Redemption in Twelver Shiʿa Mourning Rituals," *Journal of Shiʿa Islamic Studies* 6, no. 1

Unlike the Iranian establishment, the Shīrāzīs not only upheld the traditional hostile approach toward Sunnīs but even reinforced it; for example, they pronounced official Iranian Unity Week as Disassociation Week in order to highlight their anti-Sunnī position. In response to Khamenei's ban on cursing the Companions, they argued that "cursing the criminals, disavowing them and shaming them are a collective duty (*farḍ kifāya*)" in Islamic law and insisted on upholding the ʿUmarkoshān celebrations. The Shīrāzīs also lent their support to the radical anti-Sunnī preacher Yāsir Ḥabīb.[117]

The Iranian authorities waged an intense media campaign against the Shīrāzīs, branding them "Shīʿī extremists," "London Shīʿīsm," "English Shīʿīsm," and even "MI6 Shīʿīs." Covering the entire polemics against the Shīrāzīs requires a separate study, but for the current purpose, several points should be highlighted. The first anti-Shīrāzī charge was concerned with broader doctrinal or ideological matters than with the Sunnī-Shīʿī dispute. It accused the Shīrāzīs of holding outdated reactionary views which fail to understand that "Islam in its entirety is politics" and support the separation between politics and religion. Dr. Ḥusayn Kachuyān, a member of the Supreme Council of the Cultural Revolution, presented the Shīrāzīs alongside the Takfīrīs (code name for the Sunnī jihādī-Salafīsts) as the two threats within Islam that emerged as responses to the 1979 Revolution in Iran. At the same time, he equated the Shīrāzīs with "Ṣafavīd Islam," a euphemism that the late thinker ʿAlī Sharīʿatī had used for the conservative clerical establishment before the Revolution. Such Islam did not deal with political questions or with the important issues of managing society and state but focused solely on matters of ritual and dry legalism. Kachuyān conceded that while this "Ṣafavīd Islam" had legitimate roots in historical Shīʿīsm, it had ignored the developments that had taken place in Shīʿīsm during the previous century, which culminated in Ayatollah Khomeini's revolution.[118] The charge has much broader ramifications and touches upon

(2013): 75–77; Laurence Louër, *Transnational Shia Politics: Religious and Political Networks in the Gulf* (New York: Columbia University Press, 2008), 88–98, 120–128. See also Arash Azizi, "Iran targets 'MI6 Shiites'," May 4, 2015, https://www.al-monitor.com/pulse/originals/2015/04/iran-shia-shirazi-movement-secterian.html.

117 "Nemūneh-i az taḥrīf-i ta'rīkhī-i nohom Rabīʿ al-awwal;" "Radd fatāwā al-Imām al-sayyid ʿAlī al-Khamenei bi-taḥrīm sabb al-ṣaḥāba," 5 Shahrīvar 1389/August 27, 2010, http://www.alshirazi.com; Azizi, "Iran targets 'MI6 Shiites'." Ḥabīb also attacked Khamenei personally as a heretic in 2009 and on many subsequent occasions: http://www.israj.net/vb/archive/index.php/t-8439.html; https://www.youtube.com/watch?v=nPEZ15w30uk; https://www.youtube.com/watch?v=9z2k6spwQdc.

118 "Tashayyuʿ-i Inglīsī va-Islām Amrīkā'ī hadaf vāhidī dārand," 6 Bahman 1393/January 26, 2015, http://www.mehrnews.com/news/2472433; "Żuʿufhā-i inqilāb manshā 'ījād tashayyuʿ-i Inglīsī shod," 18 Bahman 1393/February 7, 2015, http://www.jahan

what seems to be the root cause of the conflict between the Iranian establishment and the Shīrāzīs, namely, the centrality of politics in religion and its primacy over traditional doctrines however sacrosanct. These issues have topped the agenda of the Iranian religious establishment ever since the Revolution.

On a more practical level, there have been various charges against the Shīrāzīs for providing radical Sunnīs with excuses to kill Muslims. Not only, it is claimed, do they increase hatred of the Shīʿa, but they make the Shīʿa look like heretics, thereby serving the Wahhābī cause. Some have even described Saudi Arabia as the Shīrāzīs' "maternal home."[119] As part of the rhetorical ploy of linking various "others" together, Khamenei charged that "certain radio and television channels" that insult and curse "the great personalities of Sunnī Islam" in the name of the Shīʿa "are funded by the English Treasury," and he dubbed the Shīrāzī trend "English Shīʿīsm." Moreover, he linked the extremism (*ifrāṭgarī*) of "English Shīʿīsm" (i.e., the Shīrāzīs) with "American Sunnīsm" or "American Wahhābism," the code name for the Saudis and jihādī-Salafī organizations, viewing them as two collaborating trends that are serving to deepen the sectarian rift in the Muslim world and thus acting in contrast to true Muslims. In January 2015 Khamenei declared that "neither the Shīʿa Muslims allied with the British MI6 are Shīʿa, nor the Sunnī mercenaries of the American CIA are Sunnīs, as they are both anti-Islamic (mercenaries)."[120]

---

news.com/interview/405574; "Shiʿa Inglīsī dar pay mutawaqqif sākhtan Islām siyāsī ast," 9 Esfand 1393/February 28, 2015, https://www.tasnimnews.com/fa/news/1393/12/09/668383.

119 "Sukūt dar berāber firqa-i Shīrāzīhā jāyīz nīst," 8 Esfand 1393/February 27, 2015, https://rasanews.ir/fa/news/249273; "Ayatollah Arākī: tashayyuʿ-i londonī buzurgtarīn-I khaṭar barāye Islām va-Shīʿa ast," 5 Esfand 1393/February 24, 2015, http://hajj.ir/fa/51467; "Shīʿīyānī keh faqaṭ chend rūz-i sāl Shīʿa-and!," 21 Dey 1392/January 11, 2014, http://www.dana.ir/News/47164.html.

120 "Leader: Shias Allied with MI6, Sunnīs Tied with CIA All Enemies of Islam," January 9 2015, http://www7.irna.ir/en/News/81457345/; "Tashābuh-i tashayyuʿ-i Inglīsī bā tasannon-i Amrīkāʾī/ agar marjaʿiyat rā az shīʿa begīrand, cheh chīzī bāqī mīmānad?," 7 Ordībehesht 1394/April 27, 2015, https://snn.ir/fa/news/405406; "Tashayyuʿ-i Inglīsī va-tasannon-i Amrīkāʾī, dō tighe yek qīchī," 8 Ordībehesht 1395/April 27, 2016, http://qademon.ir/2196-2/; "Provoking the Feelings of Sunnīs is a Plot Funded by the English Treasury'," September 20, 2016, http://english.khamenei.ir/news/4167/Provoking-the-Feelings-of-Sunnīs-is-a-Plot-Funded-by-the-English.

As was the case elsewhere, here too the inevitable link with the other despised enemy, the Jews, appeared. An article that addressed the Shīrāzī support of self-injuries in the ʿĀshūrāʾ commemorations showed a picture of Ayatollah Ṣādiq Shīrāzī with a big Jewish Star of David in the background. Elsewhere the Shīrāzīs were depicted as the product of the "Jews' revenge against Islam" and the "Zionist Muslims."[121] The internal rival is thus associated with external enemies, thereby creating a clear boundary between proper Muslims and the hostile "others." In an argument revealing a deep sense of insecurity, there were expressions of fear that such extremism as espoused by the Shīrāzīs would cause the "severance of Shīʿīsm from the ranks of Islam."[122] In other words, in order to prevent the exclusion of mainstream Shīʿīsm from the broader Muslim in-group, it was essential to exclude the Shīrāzīs and link them with other out-groups.

10 Conclusion

The Shīʿī effort to build bridges with the Sunnī mainstream since the beginning of the Twenty-first century has differed from previous efforts at communal reconciliation and ecumenism in Islam. As in the past, the motivation was political, namely, the need to form a common Muslim front against an external threat. But unlike the past, the massive shedding of Shīʿī blood rendered it more urgent. The Western and Zionist threat has been used to enhance the bond among Muslims in the face of a common enemy and to link the jihādī-Salafīs with this enemy. Put differently, in order to lower the boundaries between mainstream Sunnīs and Shīʿīs, it has been deemed necessary to build up the common wall against the external "other."

Unlike the previous attempts inspired by individual clerics, the driving force behind the reconciliation effort was the Iranian government as part of its broader foreign policy strategy. As a government, it went further than previous rounds of ecumenical discussions when it forced the annulment of

121 https://www.facebook.com/Montaghedane.SadeghShirazi/posts/900825776678113:0; "Tashayyuʿ-i Inglīsī intiqām-i Yahūd az ahl-i bayt (ʿalayhim al-salām) ast," 28 Mehr 1394/October 20, 2015, http://qademon.ir/تشیع-انگلیسی-انتقام-یهود-از-اهل-بیت-علی (accessed April 25, 2016); "Muqtaḍā Ṣadr khāṭaba beh Shīrāzīhā: taklīf-i khōd rā mushakhaṣ konīd," 8 Esfand 1393/February 27, 2015, http://www.fetan.ir/home/4767; "Poshtībānī-i Yahūd az bānd-i Shīrāzīhā," 11 Dey 1394/January 1, 2016 – https://aghigh.ir/fa/news/68925.

122 "Raʾīs-i dāneshgāh-i adyān va-maẕāhib: Khaṭar tashayyuʿ-i Inglīsī jedāsāzī Shīʿa az ṣufūf jahān Islām ast," 16 Ordībehesht 1394/May 6, 2015, https://khabarfarsi.com/u/2865991.

well-established practices that alienated mainstream Sunnīs. Such unprecedented measures and the discourse employed to justify them reveal the contrast between a deep sense of Shīʿī insecurity and victimhood vis-à-vis the Sunnīs and the emergence of Iran as a major regional power that sees itself destined to lead the Muslim world.

The justification for the new approach toward *tabarrā* was openly practical and political, but there was a concerted effort to build scholarly or historical arguments against the ʿUmarkoshān celebrations. Most significant was the assertion that these celebrations had been a Ṣafavīd invention designed to serve political needs. Such an approach reflects a deeper understanding of religion as a dynamic historical phenomenon which evolves in response to challenges and is the product of a specific historical context. While this may seem obvious to historians, it is in fact a very bold assertion when it comes from spokespeople of a religious establishment who tend to endorse historical views of their religion or to backdate religious traditions to the earliest period possible in order to enhance their authenticity. This conciliatory approach toward the Sunnīs encountered reservation within the Iranian clerical establishment, reflecting the difficulty of discarding deeply entrenched religious axioms and traditions for the sake of political expediency and the gap between traditional and more politicized versions of religion. It also confronted outright opposition from the London-based Shīrāzī faction. The latter dissent elicited a wave of polemical attacks in various media, presumably due to the challenge they posed to the authority of the Iranian leadership.

Similarly significant in this discussion is the gap between official and popular religion, as manifested in the persistence of the old practices despite repeated governmental and clerical exhortations. The disregard for the rulings of Khamenei and the other *marājiʿ taqlīd* on the anti-Sunnī practices points to more than just a gap between elite and popular religious conduct. It may also indicate that for ordinary believers these ceremonies represent far more than simple acts of devotion; rather, they represent a cultural identity that is different not only from the Sunnīs but also perhaps from the state.

It is unclear as yet whether the new approach reflects a profound revision of doctrines that define the Shīʿa and serve as its raison d'etre. There are some indications, such as the allusion to *taqiyya*, that so far this change is more an outward gesture than a genuine transformation. However, it seems that both Khamenei and Rafsanjānī went further than mere superficial gesturing when they spoke about the need to draw a distinction between the past and the present in order to put an end to intra-Muslim fights over past events – even when both insist that they adhere to the traditional Shīʿī views regarding that very past. In a sense, both realize that Sunnīs and Shīʿīs cannot agree on the interpretation of these events due to their ramifications for the overall belief systems of the two communities. Therefore, they advocate the idea that Shīʿīs and Sunnīs should acknowledge their differences and accept each other, disagreements notwithstanding. The question remains whether this approach will move Iranian Shīʿīsm closer to the situation that exists among the various Protestant denominations in the United States and Europe, that is, religious groups that maintain their own beliefs but accept the legitimacy of other religious groups to adhere to their own different beliefs.

At the time of writing, it seems that Iran is not there yet. While the religious leadership reiterates the need to respect Sunnī beliefs and practices, Sunnīs in Iran still suffer discrimination and restrictions in practicing their religion.[123] On the international front, Iran's support for the atrocities committed by the Syrian Assad regime demonstrates little regard for the suffering of the civilian Sunnī population. Similarly, Iran's sponsorship of the Shīʿī militias in Iraq, not only in the fight against ISIS since 2014 but also as active players in the Iraqi political arena, shows the power of sectarian allegiances and preferences in the leadership's mindset. In other words, rhetoric notwithstanding, they still view the Sunnīs as "others."

123 According to Mehdi Khalaji the Iranian authorities destroyed Sunnī mosques and seminaries in the politically restive southeastern provinces of Sistan and Baluchistan and exercises a comprehensive discriminatory policy against Sunnī Kurds in Iranian Kurdistan. Khalaji, "The Dilemmas of Pan-Islamic Unity," 76. See also Abbas William Samii, "The Nation and Its Minorities: Ethnicity, Unity, and State Policy in Iran," *Comparative Studies of South Asia, Africa and the Middle East* 20, no. 1 (2000): 128–137; Fatima Aman, "Iran's Uneasy Relationship with its Sunnī Minority," *Middle East Institute*, March 21, 2016, http://www.mei.edu/content/article/iran%E2%80%99s-uneasy-relationship-its-sunni-minorities; David A. Graham, "Iran's Beleaguered Sunnīs," *The Atlantic Magazine*, January 6, 2016.

CHAPTER 4

Anti-Wahhābī and Jihādī-Salafī Polemics: from Apologetics to Denunciation

Of all rival "others" discussed in this book, the traditionalist Sunnī Wahhābī movement and the more modern jihādī-Salafī organizations espouse deep-seated animosity towards Shīʿīsm and regard it as their ultimate "other" to be vanquished. In many ways Wahhābism and Shīʿīsm stand at the two ends of the Islamic and Islamist ideological spectrum. This doctrinal rivalry was also manifested in violence, primarily from the Wahhābī and jihādī-Salafī side against the Shīʿīs, from the early nineteenth century and well into the twenty-first century.[1] Consequently, Shīʿī discourse on Wahhābism and jihādī-Salafīsm has always harbored an element of fear and distress, reflecting a centuries-old sense of vulnerability vis-à-vis their powerful rivals.

Nonetheless, a significant change has been visible in both volume and content of this discourse since, in particular, the turn of the twenty-first century. Shīʿī polemics were formerly mostly defensive when seeking to refute Wahhābī charges of Shīʿī apostasy and to prove that the Shīʿīs had always been loyal Muslims who adhered to the principles of Islam. However, the growing self-confidence of the Islamic Republic manifested itself in an increasing volume of anti-Wahhābī and anti-jihādī-Salafī publications and a shift toward open attacks on the doctrines and practices of these two movements.[2] These attacks culminated in statements that depicted these ideologies as un-Islamic and their adherents as not being Muslims at all and in rulings that declared jihād against them. Such depictions not only presented Shīʿīsm as the complete opposite of these deviant groups but also intended to establish a consensual formulation of Islam that could bring together mainstream Sunnīs and Shīʿīs against the common enemy. To use Rusi Jaspal's terms, the Shīʿī polemicists sought to establish a joint Muslim mainstream Sunnī and Shīʿī in-group against the Wahhābī out-group. An important rhetorical ploy used in

1 For the categorization of jihādī-Salafīsm within the broader Salafi movement, see Quintan Wiktorowicz, "Anatomy of the Salafi Movement," *Studies in Conflict & Terrorism* 29, no. 3 (2006): 207–239 and Guilain Denoeux, "The Forgotten Swamp: Navigating Political Islam," *Middle East Policy* 9, no. 2 (2002): 56–81.

2 ʿAlī Aṣghar Riżvānī, *Salafīgarī (Vahhābiyat) va-pāsokh beh shubuhāt* (Iṣfahān: Markaz taḥqīqāt r rayāneh-i qāʾimiyya, n.d.), 132–138 provides a list of 266 books against Wahhābīsm and jihādī-Salafism published prior to April 2018.

 | DOI:10.1163/9789004444683_006

this effort linked the Wahhābīs with other hostile out-groups such as the West and the Jews.[3]

1 Wahhābism and the Shīʿa: the Historical Background

From its inception in the mid-eighteenth century, Wahhābism targeted Shīʿīsm as the extreme manifestation of heretic distortions of true Islam, or, in the words of one writer, "the struggle against the thoughts and ideas of pure Twelver Shīʿīsm" topped the Wahhābī ideological program.[4] In particular, the Wahhābīs denounced the Shīʿī practice of the intercession (*shafāʿa*) of the twelve imāms between believers and God, the visitations to their graves (*ziyārat al-qubūr*), and the invocation of God by referring to the rank of the Prophet or pious men to gain access to him (*tawassul*). According to the Wahhābīs, these practices detracted from the unity of God and were tantamount to polytheism (*shirk*). Since the Shīʿīs claimed to be good Muslims, the Wahhābīs viewed their conduct as conscious apostasy in defiance of true Islam, therefore deserving death. In a statement reflecting both the depth of his animosity to the Shīʿa as well as the status of Jews as synonymous with evil, Muḥammad b. ʿAbd al-Wahhāb, founder of the Wahhābī movement, described the Shīʿa as "the greatest harm" (*ashaddu al-ḍarar*) to religion, more so even than the Jews and the Christians.[5]

Wahhābī anti-Shīʿīsm was manifested in action as well as words. In 1801, the Wahhābīs attacked the Shīʿī shrine city of Karbalāʾ in Iraq, massacring hundreds, if not thousands, of Shiʿis and desecrating the shrine of Imām Ḥusayn, the martyred grandson of the Prophet Muḥammad.[6] Likewise, the

3 Rusi Jaspal, "Anti-Semitism and Anti-Zionism in Iran: The Role of Identity Processes," *Israel Affairs* 19, no. 2 (2013): 4–5.

4 ʿAbbās Jaʿfarī, "Firqa-i Vahhābiyat va-ʿamalkard-i ān dar taʾrīkh-i muʿāṣir," *Maʿrifat* 12, no. 1 (1381/2002), https://library.tebyan.net/fa/Viewer/Text/78318/1; ʿAbbās Naṣīrī-Fard, Vakāvī-*i seh firqa: barresī va-taḥlīl Vahhābiyat, Bahāʾiyat shayṭān-parastī* (Tehrān: Rāh-i Nīkān, 1392/2013), 212–215. See also "Ahdāf-i istiʿmār az ʾījād firqa-i Vahhābiyat va-nīz rābiṭa beyne Vahhābiyat va-Yahūd," http://www.vahabiat.porsemani.ir/content/اهداف-استعمار-از-ایجاد-فرقهٔ-وهابیت-و-نیز-رابطه-بین-وهابیت-و-یهود.

5 For a succinct analysis of Muḥammad b. ʿAbd al-Wahhāb's views on Shīʿīsm, see Guido Steinberg, "The Wahhabiyya and Shiʿism, from 1744/45 to 2008," in *The Sunna and Shiʿa in History: Division and Ecumenism in the Muslim Middle East*, ed. Ofra Bengio and Meir Litvak (New York: Palgrave-McMillan, 2011), 165–168 and Hamid Algar, *Wahhabism: A Critical Essay* (Oneonta: Islamic Publications of America, 2002), 1–77.

6 Meir Litvak, *Shīʿī Scholars of Nineteenth Century Iraq: The ʿUlamaʾ of Najaf and Karbalaʾ* (Cambridge: Cambridge University Press, 1998), 120–122.

Shīʿī population of al-Aḥsāʾ in Eastern Arabia suffered severe repression and, occasionally, outright persecution after its conquest by ʿAbd al-ʿAzīz b. Saʿūd (d. 1954), founder of the third Saudi state.[7]

The first Shīʿī response to Wahhābism was polemical, reflecting their military weakness as a minority in the Sunnī Ottoman Empire. Shaykh Jaʿfar Kāshif al-Ghitāʾ (d. 1812), the most prominent mujtahid at the time, who organized the defense of Najaf from Wahhābī raids, composed in 1795 the tract *Manhaj al-rashshād li-man arāda al-sadād* (the path of guidance to whoever wanted the right course) and dispatched it to the Wahhābī leader, Amīr ʿAbd al-ʿAzīz bin Saʿūd (d. 1803). The gist of the tract was the argument that the Shiʿ is had always been bona fide Muslims alongside a plea to remove the threat of declaring them *kuffār* (infidels). Kāshif al-Ghitāʾ's main contention was that various Shīʿī practices, such as seeking the aid of imāms (*istighātha*) or *ziyārat al-qubūr*, which the Wahhābīs rejected as polytheism, did not detract from the unity and transcendence of God but were merely ways to reach him. He also asserted that the Shīʿī practice of *shafāʿa* was in fact a recognition of God's omnipotence and claimed that Sunnīs too used metaphorical epithets to describe ʿAlī or his son Ḥusayn, thus implying that their conduct was not essentially so different from the Shīʿī attitude to the two imāms. In a move typical of minorities, Kāshif al-Ghitāʾ advocated the legitimacy of conflicting interpretations of the Qurʾān and emphasized the importance of pluralism in religious practices, as long as all aspire to God. He implicitly criticized the Wahhābī practice of declaring their rivals apostates and, by showing how the founders of Sunnī legal schools avoided doing this, he inferred that the Wahhābīs were deviating from the standard Sunnī path.[8] Kāshif al-Ghitāʾ's treatise served as the prototype for the hundreds of books and essays that Shīʿī clerics and scholars published well into the present in defense of Shīʿī doctrines and rites against Wahhābī charges. The two central themes of all were the assertions that Shīʿī doctrines and practices were thoroughly Islamic and that the charge of apostasy levied against the Shīʿa therefore contradicted the tenets of Islam.

The Saudi takeover of the Ḥijāz in 1925, which was followed by the destruction of the domes of the Meccan and Medinese graves of the Second, Fourth,

---

7 Guido Steinberg, "The Shiʿites in the Eastern Province of Saudi Arabia (al-Aḥsāʾ), 1913–1953," in *The Twelver Shia in Modern Times: Religious Culture and Political History*, ed. Rainer Brunner and Werner Ende (Leiden: Brill, 2001), 236–254.

8 *Manhaj al-rashshād li-man arāda al-sadād*, full text in Muḥammad Ḥusayn Kāshif al-Ghitāʾ, *al-ʿAbaqāt al-ʿinbariyya fī al-ṭabaqāt al-Jaʿfarīyya taḥqīq Jawdat al-Qazwīnī* (Beirut: Bīsān, 1998), 503–587. For a short analysis of the treatise, see Meir Litvak "Encounters between Shiʿi and Sunni ʿUlamaʾ in Ottoman Iraq," ed. Bengio and Litvak, *The Sunna and Shiʿa in History*, 74–77.

Fifth, and Sixth Shīʿī Imāms as well as strong anti-Shīʿī statements by Wahhābī theologians, prompted a spate of Shīʿī polemical responses.[9] The most important tract during the interwar period was Muḥsin al-Amīn's *Kashf al-Irtiyāb fī atbāʿ Muḥammad b. ʿAbd al-Wahhāb*. In addition to defending Shīʿī rites, Amīn's book was probably the first to launch a comprehensive attack on Wahhābī doctrines and practices as illogical and excessive and therefore as deviating from the correct path of Islam.[10]

2 Exacerbation of the Sunnī-Shīʿī Rift: the Islamic Republic vs. the Jihādī-Salafī Challenge

The 1979 Revolution in Iran, which emboldened the Shīʿīs throughout the Middle East, added new strategic and political state-centered dimensions to the religious dispute between the two groups, who represented two opposing religiopolitical models of Islamic government: the Iranian clerical-based *vilāyat-i faqīh* system versus the Saudi monarchy, which is based on an alliance with the Wahhābī clergy. Both claimed the mantle of the leadership of the Muslim world. The official title of Iran's supreme leader is *valī amr al-muslimīn* or leader of the Muslims, while the Saudi king assumed the title, *khādim al-ḥaramayn al-sharīfayn* or custodian of the two holy sanctuaries.[11] Politically, the Islamic Republic of Iran sees itself as the natural regional power in view of its size, population, historical legacy, and advanced culture, while Saudi Arabia regards itself as the natural leader of the Arab side of the Gulf. Thus, during the first years after the Revolution, Iran's leader, Ayatollah Khomeini, repeatedly disparaged the Arab Gulf monarchies and often called for their removal.[12] Fear of Iran pushed the Saudis to support Iraq in its war against Iran (1980–1988), and this support adds to the Iranian grudge against them.

---

9 Rainer Brunner, *Islamic Ecumenism in the 20th Century: The Azhar and Shiʿism between rapprochement and restraint* (Leiden: Brill, 2004), 91.

10 Muḥsin al-Amīn, *Kashf al-Irtiyāb fī atbāʿ Muḥammad b. ʿAbd al-Wahhāb* (Beirut: Dār al-kitāb al-Islāmī, 2006).

11 For analyses of Iranian Saudi strategic rivalry, see Frederic Wehrey et al., *Saudi-Iranian Relations Since the Fall of Saddam: Rivalry, Cooperation, and Implications for U.S. Policy* (Santa Monica: Rand Corporation, 2009); Ariel Jahner, "Saudi Arabia and Iran: The Struggle for Power and Influence in the Gulf," *International Affairs Review* 20, no. 3 (2012): 37–49.

12 David Menashri, *Iran: A Decade of War and Revolution* (New York: Holmes & Meier, 1990), 208, 250, 291; Christin Marschall, *Iran's Persian Gulf Policy: From Khomeini to Khatami* (London: Routledge, 2003), 38, 44.

At the same time, the 1979 Soviet invasion of Afghanistan gave a boost to the jihādī-Salafī organizations in the Arab world. These organizations endorsed many of the anti-Shīʿī attitudes of Ibn Taymiyya and of the Wahhābīs. The shift of power from the Sunnīs to the Shīʿīs following the 2003 US invasion of Iraq generated Sunnī fear of losing their domination in the Middle East and exacerbated Salafī animosity towards Shīʿīsm. As was the case with the Wahhābīs, the jihādī-Salafists resorted to violence, killing thousands of Shīʿī civilians in Iraq and Pakistan. The first commander of al-Qāʿida forces in Iraq, Abū Muṣʿab al-Zarqāwī, called for an all-out war against the Shīʿīs, which was tantamount to calling for their elimination.[13]

The outbreak of the Arab upheaval since 2011 has exacerbated the Sunnī-Shīʿī rift in the Middle East to unprecedented levels of violence and bloodshed. The temporary rise of ISIS, which culminated in the June 2014 capture of the Iraqi city of Mosul and the declaration of the caliphate, increased Shīʿī anxieties. The ISIS pledge to settle its differences with the Shīʿa "not in Sāmarrāʾ or Baghdad but in Karbalāʾ, the filth-ridden city, and in Najaf, the city of polytheism," implied its intention to massacre the Shīʿī population of these two holy shrine cities.[14] In addition, the Iranian government apparently feared the potential appeal of jihādī-Salafī ideology to local Sunnīs in Iran, many of whom lived in the country's poorest regions of Baluchistan and Kurdistan.[15] The attack carried out by Kurdish members of ISIS on June 7, 2017 only added to these fears.[16]

In addition to military measures against the jihādī-Salafī threat, Iran and various Shīʿī organizations launched a massive campaign of polemics and propaganda against jihādī-Salafī doctrines and conduct, reiterating and improving many of the arguments used against Wahhābism. Overall, they presented

---

13 Emily Hunt, *Zarqawi's "Total War" on Iraqi Shiʿites Exposes a Divide among Sunnī Jihadists*, Washington Institute Policy Watch #1049, November 15, 2005; Meir Litvak, "'More Harmful than the Jews': Anti-Shīʿī Polemics in Modern Radical Sunnī Discourse," in *Le Shiʿisme Imamite quarante ans après: Hommage à Etan Kohlberg*, ed. Muhammad ʿAli Amīr-Moezzi, Meir M. Bar-Asher, and Simon Hopkins (Paris: Brepols Publishers, 2008), 285–306.

14 "Baghdad Launches Air Strikes on Insurgents in Mosul," *Financial Times*, June 12, 2014, https://www.ft.com/content/09bf97c2-f200-11e3-9015-00144feabdco.

15 See the warning by Ḥujjat al-Islām ʿAlī Ramażānī Bīrjandī about 5000 Wahhābī websites operate in order to lead Iranian youth astray in "5 hizār sayt Vahhābiyat barāye munḥarif kardan javānān-i Irānī faʿāliyāt dārand," 3 Tīr 1391/June 23, 2012, http://www.farsnews.com/newstext.php?nn=13910603000400; and about actions to counter Wahhābīsm in Zāhidān, capital of the Baluchistan province, in "Musābaqa-i ṣad suʾāl az Vahhābiyat dar Zāhidān," 14 Tīr 1391/July 4, 2012, http://www.farsnews.com/printable.php?nn=13910616000173.

16 Ahmad Majidyar, "Terror Attacks and Cross-Country Arrests Point to Growing Terrorism Problem in Iran," *Iran Observed*, June 9, 2017, http://education.mei.edu/content/io/terror-attacks-and-cross-country-arrests-point-growing-terrorism-problem-iran.

jihādī-Salafīsm as the illegitimate child of Wahhābism or its modern incarnation and, as such, the enemy of true Islam and Muslims. The targeted audiences of the Shīʿī polemics were not only Shīʿīs, who needed to be reassured about their just cause, but also mainstream Sunnīs. The main aim of this campaign was to draw a wedge between these Sunnīs and the jihādī-Salafists in order to build a common cause with them against the radicals. The Shīʿī discourse rarely used the term Salafi to denote their rivals since it had positive connotations for almost all Sunnīs, who cherish the golden age of the righteous forefathers (*al-salaf al-ṣāliḥ*) of the first three generations of Islam. Rather, they used the term Wahhābīs, which portrays these groups as a distinct (and deviant) sect within Islam; the Saudis, on the other hand, call themselves *muwaḥḥdun* (worshippers of the one God). The Shīʿī polemicists also referred to the jihādī-Salafī organizations as *takfīrī*, that is, those who declare all others as apostates, playing on Sunnī historical aversion to loose declarations of apostasy and the connotations between the modern-day Takfīrīs and the Khawārij sect in early Islam.[17] By portraying their enemies as the deviant sect, the Shīʿīs thus become ipso facto integral members, if not the main representatives, of "true" Islam. Since various Arab governments also used the pejorative *khawārij* to depict the jihādī-Salafīsts, the Shīʿīs could portray themselves as standing alongside mainstream Sunnīs to confront the common enemy.

3 Shīʿī Deconstruction of Wahhābī Doctrines

By conflating the Wahhābīs and the jihādī-Salafīsts, Shīʿī efforts to deconstruct Wahhābī doctrine and practices focused on several interrelated themes: the presentation of Wahhābism as an unsophisticated and crude distortion of Islam that is rejected by most mainstream Sunnīs; the denunciation of the Wahhābī concept of *takfīr* and its manifestation in Wahhābī brutality toward other Muslims, particularly the Shīʿīs; and, finally, the linking of Wahhābism to other historical and modern enemies of Islam. In their search for the origins and sources of Wahhābī savagery, Shīʿī polemicists start with the birthplace of Muḥammad ibn ʿAbd al-Wahhāb, the Najd in Eastern Arabia. They note that the Prophet himself, even according to Sunnī ḥadīths, refrained from blessing the Najd when he described it as the area where "seditions and tremors" would take place and where "Satan's horn will rise." Indeed, according to this view, the

17 For the Khawārij in early Islamic history and modern applications of this term, see Jeffrey T. Kenney, *Muslim Rebels: Kharijites and the Politics of Extremism in Egypt* (Oxford and New York: Oxford University Press, 2006).

Najd was the source of extremist deviant movements throughout Islamic history. The false prophet Musaylima appeared there during the Prophet's time, and following the Prophet's death, many Najd inhabitants reneged on Islam. Not surprisingly, they claim, many of the Khawārij, who betrayed ʿAlī in his wars against Muʿāwiya, also came from the Najd, as did the radical Qarmaṭi sect of the ninth–tenth centuries. Similarly, Ibn Taymiyya's harsh and intolerant ideas spread in the Najd, which was "devoid of civilization and lacking culture."[18] It was, accordingly, only natural that Ibn ʿAbd al-Wahhāb, who grew up in the Najd, would have developed such a narrow-minded doctrine, as he had never known the wealth and depth of Islamic culture; while most Sunnī clerics rejected his views and marginalized him, the backward people of the Najd, who lacked any true scholars, accepted his ideas wholeheartedly.[19]

This problematic background explains the two greatest faults of Wahhābism in Shīʿī eyes: the charge of apostasy against all those who do not adhere to its distorted interpretation of Islam and the brutality employed against all Muslims, particularly the Shīʿa, who disagree with them. The major Shīʿī claim over the past two centuries, which reflected their status as a minority, was that any Muslim who had uttered the two declarations of faith (*shahādatayn*), accepted the Muslim direction of prayer, and performed the Muslim prayers was a genuine Muslim. They therefore asserted that Wahhābī intolerance contradicted the Qurʾān and the consensus among all Muslim scholars, particularly the Sunnīs. Like Kāshif al-Ghitāʾ two centuries earlier, they preached pluralism in Islamic interpretation and practice and insisted that all Muslims agree on several major principles, especially that true Islamic government comes from God alone. Islam has, they claimed, always accepted differing readings of the scriptures, but the idea that conflicting interpretations of religious texts should lead to a declaration of apostasy had been inconceivable in Islamic tradition and history. They concluded that were any group to declare all others

---

18 Seyyed Muḥammad Ḥusaynī Qazvīnī, *Vahhābiyat az manẓar-i ʿaql va-sharʿ* (Qom: Muʾassasa-i taḥqīqāti-i ḥażrat-i valī-i ʿaṣr, 1392/2013), 76; ʿAbd al-Raḥman Akhund Tangalī, *Taḥẕīr al-ikhwān ʿan makāyid ḥizb al-shaytān yā taʾrīkhcheh-i Vahhābiyat* (Gorgan: Naʿīm, 1393/2014), 53; ʿAlī Aṣghar Riżvānī, *Raftār-i vahhābiyān bā musalmānān* (Iṣfahān: Markaz taḥqīqāt-i rayāneh'-i qāʾimiyya, 1341/1962), 32–37; "Shabāhathā va-tafāvothā-i tafakkur-i Dāʿesh bā Vahhābiyat chīst?," 28 Tīr 1393/July 19, 2014, https://www.mashreghnews.ir/news/325090.

19 Daftar-i Tablīghāt-i Islāmī, *Darsnāmah-i ashnāʾī va-naqd-i Vahhābiyat: tabārshināsī va-jarayānshināsī-i Vahhābiyat* (Qom: Daftar-i Tablīghāt-i Islāmī ḥawza, 1389/2010), 54–55; Riżvānī, *Raftār-i vahhābiyān bā musalmānān*, 39–40.

apostates, Muslims would be drawn into an endless vicious circle of violence and persecutions.[20]

Grand Ayatollah Makārem Shīrāzī went the furthest in advocating pluralism and tolerance within Islam as the right response to *takfīr*. He criticized the Wahhābīs for imposing their views on other Muslims, particularly on issues deriving from *ijtihād* and *istinbāṭ*, and for refusing to acknowledge that other Muslims had clerics and mujtahids who understand and interpret Islam. More importantly, he claimed, neither the Wahhābīs nor any other group have the right to impose their views on others, and they should instead respect the views of other Muslims. These statements, which reflected the minority's fears of the majority's intolerance, also presented the Shīʿa as advancing pluralism and tolerance not only compared with the Wahhābīs but in Islam in general.[21] Khamenei added a modernist twist to this argument by asserting that the recourse to *takfīr* stemmed from the ignorance of the new understanding of the Islamic intellectual and scholarly legacy.[22] It should be noted, however, that while preaching pluralism vis-à-vis Sunnīs and attacking the Wahhābī and jihādī-Salafī recourse to *takfīr*, the clerical establishment in Iran showed little tolerance toward its domestic dissidents.[23]

In order to bolster their position, particularly among Sunnī audiences who would not accept Shīʿī sources and authorities, the Shīʿī polemicists used to quote extensively from the Companions of the Prophet, most notably his wife ʿAisha (who had been famous for her opposition to ʿAlī), as well as leading Sunnī scholars. Most important among the latter were Abū Ḥanīfa (d. 767) and al-Shāfiʿī (d. 820), the eponyms of the two leading Sunnī legal schools, who ruled that the life and property of all who recognized the unity of God and the Prophet's message must be guaranteed and protected. Moreover, the Shīʿī polemicists contended that in a series of doctrinal matters, such as *shafāʿa*, *ziyārat al-qubūr*, and *tawassul*, mainstream Sunnīs parted ways with the Wahhābīs

20 "Shabāhathā va-tafāvothā-i tafakkur-i Dāʿesh bā Vahhābiyat chīst?"; "Jarayān shināsī-i salafīgarī-i muʿāṣir + taṣāvīr," 17 Dey 1391/January 6, 2013, https://www.mashreghnews.ir/news/176522; Riżvānī, *Salafgarī (Vahhābiyat) va-pāsokh beh shubuhāt*, 42.

21 Nāṣir Makārem Shīrāzī, *Vahhābiyat bar sar dō rāhī* (Qom: Intishārāt-i Madrasat al-Imām ʿAlī ibn abī Ṭālib, 1384/2005), 51–54.

22 "Bayānāt dar dīdār-i shirkat-i konandegān dar ijlās-i jahānī-i asātīd-i dāneshgāh-i jahān-i Islām va-bīdārī-i Islāmī vīzhegīhā-i jarayān-i takfīrī," 21 Azar 1391/December 11, 2012, http://farsi.khamenei.ir/speech-content?id=21741.

23 For a scathing criticism of this contradiction or hypocrisy, see Akbar Ganjī, "Paradox takfīrihā-i żede takfīrī," 2 Azar 1393/November 22, 2012, https://www.radiozamaneh.com/189163.

and were much closer to the Shīʿīs.[24] A few Shīʿī writers tried to emphasize this point further by presenting an idealized picture of Sunnī-Shīʿī relations in a past when the two sects had lived harmoniously side by side. Accordingly, animosity toward Shīʿīsm had no roots in mainstream Sunnī Islam, and it was only Wahhābism that had sowed sectarian discord.[25]

Furthermore, the Shīʿī writers highlighted the contrasts between Wahhābism and mainstream Sunnī Islam in order to frame them, instead of the Shīʿīs, as the true outsiders of Islam. The Wahhābīs claim to be Sunnīs, they asserted, but in fact they divide the Sunna, just as they have denigrated clerics and Ṣūfīs, and have attacked most other Sunnī groups including the Muslim Brothers and the quietist Salafī group Jamāʿat al-tablīgh. The writers went on to accuse the Wahhābīs of systematically distorting or forging the writings of prominent Sunnī scholars, even accusing Sayyid Quṭb, the founder of the modern jihādī-Salafī trend, of being an apostate despite having views not very different from theirs; Quṭb, unlike the Wahhābīs, never declared the apostasy of the entire Muslim community, they stated.[26] Even a leading Sunnī Islamist such as Abū-l-Aʿlā Mawdūdī denied the claim that his views resembled Wahhābism, which he described as "narrow-minded, hardheaded, fanatic, and rigid."[27] The Shīʿī writers maintained that most Sunnī clerics came out against Wahhābism from its inception; they highlighted (almost gleefully) that Muḥammad Ibn ʿAbd al-Wahhāb's father and brother, described as highly respectable and righteous clerics, were the first to come out against him.[28] Majīd Fāṭimīnezhād a researcher at Madrasat Ahl al-Bayt, for example, cited Sulaymān Ibn ʿAbd

---

24 Qazvīnī, *Vahhābiyat az manẓar-i ʿaql va-sharʿ*, 76, 141–42, 154; Riżvānī, *Salafīgarī (Vahhābiyat) va-pāsokh beh shubuhāt*, 172–178; "Chegūnegī beh vujūd āmadan-i firqa-i Vahhābiyat va-tafāvot-i ān bā digār-i maẕāhib-i ahl-i tasannon," http://www.adyan.porsemani.ir/node/1690.

25 "Vahhābiyat beh Sunnat nazdīktar ast yā modernīte?," 19 Esfand 1395/March 9, 2017, http://ferghenews.com/fa/news/15359/وهابیت-به-سنت-نزدیک‌تر-است-یا-مدرنیته.

26 "Vahhābiyat dar khidmat-i dushmanān-i Islām," http://almazhab.org/?p=282; Riżvānī, *Salafīgarī (Vahhābiyat) va-pāsokh beh shubuhāt*, 127–128; Majīd Fāṭimīnezhād, "Naqd va-barresī-i takfīr az dīdār-i salafī-i vahhābī va-salafī-i jihādī," 19 Bahman 1395/ February 7, 2017, http://rasekhoon.net/article/show/1257768/; *Maslak-i Vahhābiyat: chegūnegī beh vujūd āmad?* (Tehrān: Rāh-i Nīkān, 1393/2014), 59–61, 125–126.

27 ʿAbbās Najafī Fīrūzjāyī, "Bonyādhā-i fikrī-i al-qāʿida va-Vahhābiyat," *Rāhbord* 27 (1382/ 2003): 240.

28 Akhund Tangalī, *Taḥẕīr al-ikhvan ʿan makāyid ḥizb al-shaytān*, 54; "Chegūnegī beh vujūd āmadan-i firqa-i Vahhābiyat"; Daftar-i tablīghāt-i Islāmī, *Darsnāmah-i ashnāʾī va-naqd-i Vahhābiyat*, 88; "Chegūnegī-i shikl gīrī Vahhābiyat va-tafāvot-i ān bā ahl-i Sunnat," 12 Khordād 1393/June 2, 2014, https://rasekhoon.net/article/show/903822; "Pīshīneh va-kārnāmah-i Vahhābiyat (pt. 1) – Vahhābiyat va-tafrīqa," 7 Mehr 1386/September 29, 2007, http://www.farsnews.com/newstext.php?nn=8607010023.

al-Wahhāb, who supposedly stated that his brother Muḥammad invented a "sixth pillar (*rukn*) of Islam" that declared anyone who disobeyed him an apostate.[29]

While the Shīʿīs have always been the major victims of Wahhābī brutality, many polemicists sought to present Wahhābī actions as aimed against Muslims in general. An article on *Mashreq News*, for example, explained that Ibn ʿAbd al-Wahhāb gave the Saʿūd clan permission to shed the blood of all Muslims whom they regarded as apostates. Similarly, the emphasis on the destruction of the graves of members of the Prophet's family in Medina and the description of the Wahhābīs setting important libraries on fire was most likely an appeal to the respect for the Prophet's family felt by ordinary Sunnīs in an attempt to turn them against Wahhābīs.[30] The underlying idea was that the extremist Wahhābī approach threatened mainstream Sunnī Islam as much as it threatened the Shīʿīs and, therefore, the Wahhābīs, and not the Shīʿīs, were those who had deviated from normative Islam and estranged themselves from all other Muslims. By pursuing this line and playing to Sunnī sensitivities, various Shīʿī writers equated the Wahhābī approach with the hated Khawārij of the early Islamic period. The historical Khawārij had disappeared, but their mode of thinking had survived and resurfaced in the Wahhābī movement, insisted a contributor to the Qom-affiliated *Rasekhoon* website. In addition to declaring takfīr against all other Muslims, both the Khawārij and the Wahhābīs are typified by excessive displays of piety and zealotry, which, in fact, reflect rigidity, fanaticism, and stagnation in their understanding of religion.[31] Others have claimed that the Wahhābīs are worse than the Khawārij, since the latter focused on questions that all Muslims unanimously regarded as major sins

29 Fāṭimīnezhād, "Naqd va-barresī-i takfīr az dīdār-i salafī-i vahhābī va-salafī-i jihādī."

30 For a few examples among many, see Qazvīnī, *Vahhābiyat az manẓar-i ʿaql va-sharʿ*, 89–114; ʿAlī Aṣghar Riżvānī, Shenākht-*i Salafīhā* (*Vahhābiyat*) (Iṣfahān: Markaz-i taḥqīqāt-i rayāneh-i qaʾamiyya, 1341/1962); "Pīshīneh va-kārnāmah-i Vahhābiyat (pt. 3) – ʿaqāyed va-ʿamalkard," 8 Mehr 1386/September 30, 2007, https://basirat.ir/fa/news/13511/پیشینه-و-کارنامه-وهابیت-عقاید-و-عملکرد; Group of Authors, *Dānestanīhā-i Vahhābiyat* (Iṣfahān: Markaz taḥqīqāt rayāneh-i qaʾimiyyia, n.d.), 48–63; Riżvānī, *Raftār-i vahhābiyān bā musalmānān*, 90–97; ʿAlī Aṣghar Faqīhī, *Taʾrīkh-i Vahhābiyat* (Iṣfahān: Majmaʿ jahānī-i ahl al-bayt, 1385/2006), 24–36; "Shabāhathā va-tafāvothā-i tafakkur-i Dāʿesh bā Vahhābiyat chīst?" See also Muḥammad Jawād Mughniyya, *Hadhihi hiyya al-Wahhābiyya* (Muʾassasat dar al-kitāb al-Islāmi, 1426h/2006), 130–135.

31 Mujtabā Ṣabūrī, "Barresī-i irtibāṭ-i khawārij bā Vahhābiyat," 19 Tīr 1393/July 10, 2014, http://rasekhoon.net/article/show/918275; "Chegūnegī-i shikl gīrī Vahhābiyat va-tafāvot-i ān bā ahl-i Sunnat"; Riżvānī, *Salafīgarī* (*Vahhābiyat*) *va-pāsokh beh shubuhāt*, 126–127; Muḥammad Niʿma al-Samāwī, *al-ʿAṣr al-wahhābi: qirāʾāt fī adab al-taṭṭaruf* (Beirut: Dār al-kutub al-taʾrīkhiyya, 1436/2010), 7.

(*kabā'ir*) and determined that anyone who committed one of these acts was a heretic. The Wahhābīs, on the other hand, attack Muslims who have committed minor offences that are not considered sins (*ẕunūb*) and even those who have performed preferred actions (*mustaḥabbāt*) that the Companions and their followers also performed. Moreover, the Khawārij were active mainly in Kūfa, whereas the Wahhābīs dominate the two holy cities of Mecca and Medina and therefore cause much greater harm to Islam. Worse still, the Khawārij did not befriend the enemies of the Muslims in their time, while the Wahhābīs are allies of Islam's greatest enemies: the British, the Americans, and the Zionists.[32]

A similar argument criticizes Wahhābism for undermining Islamic unity against the Prophet's wishes. The angry responses of leading Iranian clerics to the statement by the Friday prayer leader in the Grand Mosque in Mecca in 2009 that Shīʿīs are infidels reflected both the Shīʿī fear of exclusion and an attempt to turn the tables on the Wahhābīs. Grand Ayatollah Luṭfollah Ṣāfī Golpāygānī accused the Wahhābīs of creating sedition (*fitna*) among the Muslims that had led to the shedding of Muslim blood in Iraq, Pakistan, Afghanistan, and India. Likewise, according to the *Rasekhoon* website, the fanatical Wahhābī approach destroyed Islamic unity when it declared 1.5 billion Muslims apostates.[33]

Numerous Shīʿī writers have pointed to the massacre of Shīʿīs in Karbalā' in 1801 and Sunnīs in Tā'if in 1924 and the destruction of the Shīʿī sanctities in Medina as the obvious outcome of the exclusionary Wahhābī doctrines. These actions prove, Makārem Shīrāzī maintained, that violence and aggression are inherent in Wahhābī teachings and stand in contradiction to the essence of Islam as a "kind" (*laṭīf*) religion which should rule only with affection (*maḥabba*). The Wahhābīs harm the image of Islam as a peaceful and compassionate religion and thus serve American and Zionist propaganda.[34] Such a blow to the peaceful nature of Islam has no precedence in Islamic history, Ayatollah Ṣāfī Golpāygānī added.[35] Others have charged that the Wahhābī claim of fighting apostates and infidels was often a pretext for more

---

32 Ṣā'ib ʿAbd al-Ḥamīd, *al-Wahhābiyya fī ṣūratihā al-ḥaqīqiyya*, http://www.mezan.net/radalshobohat/21Whabi.htm; Ṣabūrī, "Barresī-i irtibāṭ-i khawārij va-Vahhābiyat."

33 Jaʿfar Subḥānī, *Vahhābiyat mabānī-i fikrī va-kārnāmah-i ʿamalī* (Qom: Mu'asasa-i Imām Ṣādiq, 1388/2009), 11; "Vakonesh beh ihānat-i rūḥānī-i vahhābī beh Shīʿīyān," *Akhbār-i Shīʿīyān* 43 (1388/ 2009), http://www.hawzah.net/fa/Magazine/View/5658/6891/82959/; "Chīstī va-cherāyī shikl gīrī-i jarayānhā-i takfīrī va-dalāyil-i qudratyābī-i ān dar deheh-i akhīr," 3 Shahrīvar 1395/August 24, 2016, http://rasekhoon.net/article/show/1202440.

34 Makārem Shīrāzī, *Vahhābiyat bar sar dō rāhī*, 17, 30, 40.

35 "Vakonesh beh ihānat-i rūḥānī-i vahhābī beh Shīʿīyān."

mundane motivations such as territorial expansion and pillage in the service of the Saʿūd family.[36]

4 Wahhābī Obscurantism vs. Shīʿī Rationalism

One major reason for Wahhābī brutality, according to the Shīʿī critics, is its primitive and unsophisticated nature and relentless hostility to reason and intellect. In addition to this boorish Najd heritage, another factor was the anti-rationalist and reactionary intellectual climate that shaped the world view of Ibn Taymiyya, the forefather of Wahhābī thought. This intellectual climate caused by the destruction of Islamic civilization following the thirteenth-century Mongol invasion contrasted sharply with the rationalist Muʿtazila doctrine that influenced Shīʿīsm, tilting it toward a literal reading of the Qurʾān and uncritical reliance on the ḥadīth. His faults notwithstanding, Shīʿī writers have acknowledged that Ibn Taymiyya was a scholar possessing great knowledge of Islamic law and jurisprudence. Ibn ʿAbd al-Wahhāb, on the other hand, was ignorant of *ijtihād*, theology, philosophy, and logic; nor did he have any knowledge or command of the principles of jurisprudence. His education was confined to the ḥadīth, as shown by his uncritical acceptance of the Isrāʾīliyyāt and reliance on Ibn Taymiyya for all his major rulings.[37] According to the Shīʿī narrative, while Ibn Taymiyya accepted reason as an auxiliary tool in the interpretation of the law, Ibn ʿAbd al-Wahhāb rejected it completely. The Wahhābīs thus rely only on transmitted traditions (*naql*) and on the outward dimensions (*ẓāhir*) of the scriptures, and they reject and abhor the use of rational reasoning to prove God's existence and attributes. Consequently, anti-rationalism and a lack of logic have, the Shīʿa claim, become major features of Wahhābism.[38] Grand Ayatollah Jaʿfar Subḥānī stated that this approach ignores many Qurʾānic passages which explicitly stipulate the use of reason in the interpretation of the law, which therefore does not detract from God's omnipotence and deviates from his wishes. Interestingly, he cited Rousseau's statement about the necessity of the ideal legislator to be of "a superior intelligence who saw all of

---

36 Daftar-i Tablīghāt-i Islāmī, *Darsnāmah-i ashnāʾī va-naqd-i Vahhābiyat*, 101–102.

37 "Vahhābiyat va-ʿaql setīzī," https://farsi.al-shia.org/وهابيت-و-عقل-ستيزي; Muḥammad ʿAlī Rajāyī Borūjnī, "ʿAql gerīzī va-ʿadālat setīzī-i Vahhābiyat dar taqābul bā ʿaql gerāyī va-ʿadālat jūyī-i muʿtazila," June 26, 2015, http://maliradjaee.blogfa.com/post/66.

38 "Vahhābiyat va-naqsh-i ʿaql dar shenākht-i maʿārif-i dīnī," 10 Bahman 1394/January 30, 2016, http://www.adyannet.com/fa/news/17615; Daftar-i Tablīghāt-i Islāmī, *Darsnāmah-i ashnāʾī va-naqd-i Vahhābiyat*, 66–67; "Vahhābiyat va-ʿaql setīzī."

man's passions and experienced none of them," as the basis of all laws.[39] Such characterization fits the Shīʿī concept of the collective capabilities of the clergy, and particularly of the just jurist, who stands at the helm. In other words, even a Western philosopher identified with the European enlightenment has a better understanding than the Wahhabis regarding the importance of the use of reason, and the qualifications of the right type of clergy in implementing it.[40]

The Wahhābī approach, which abhors reason and relies exclusively on the earlier generations, creates an "absurdity," according to Dr. ʿAbbās Najafī Fīrūzjāyī of the Strategic Studies Center. It denies the believers' ability to understand and grasp Islam and limits understanding to only the early generation of the Muslims, while there are, in his opinion, clear criteria and principles which enable all people to acquire the true knowledge of Islam at any time.[41] His criticism is aimed not only at the Wahhābīs or Salafists but at Sunnīs in general, who glorify the generation of *al-salaf al-ṣāliḥ* as the epitome of virtue, while the Shīʿīs resent them for betraying ʿAlī's right to succeed the Prophet. In addition, it elevates the status of the Shīʿī clerics, who possess the keys to a true understanding of Islam and to adapting it to changing needs in contrast to their seemingly backward-looking Sunnī counterparts, who are more bound by precedents.

Among the most glaring manifestations of the Wahhābī anti-rationalist and simplistic approach and their literal reading of the Qurʾān is the endorsement of anthropomorphism (*tajsīm*) in their reading and understanding of God's attributes (*al-ṣifāt al-ilāhīyya*). Shīʿī writers seem to enjoy ridiculing the Wahhābī understanding and descriptions of God as having a physical body, including eyes, hands, and fingers, though not a beard. They noted with irony that God, in Wahhābī eyes, laughs and cannot be everywhere at the same time. They contrast Wahhābī understanding with Shīʿīsm, which regards God as transcendental above any physical or corporeal being, and here too they enlist Sunnī critics of Wahhābī views in order to present the Wahhābīs as those standing outside the boundaries of true Islam.[42]

---

39 Jean-Jacques Rousseau, *The Social Contract and Other Later Political Writings*, trans. Victor Gourevitch (Cambridge: Cambridge University Press, 1997), 68.

40 Subḥānī, *Vahhābiyat Mabānī-i fikrī*, 39–40.

41 Fīrūzjāyī, "Bonyādhā-i fikrī-i al-qāʿida va-Vahhābiyat," 239.

42 "Vahhābiyat va-ʿaql setīzī"; Subḥānī, *Vahhābiyat mabānī-i fikrī*, 11, 17; Muḥammad Javād Āhangar, "Vahhābiyat: taʾrīkhcheh va-naqd-i andīshehā (pt. 1)," *Golbarg* 98 (1387/2008): 49–58; Mughniyya, *Hadhihi hiyya al-Wahābiyya*, 165–168; Rajāyī Borūjnī, "ʿAql gerīzī va-ʿadālat setīzī-i Vahhābiyat dar taqābul bā ʿaql gerāyī va-ʿadālat jūyī-i muʿtazila"; "Pīshīneh va-kārnāmah-i Vahhābiyat (pt. 3) – ʿaqāyed va-ʿamalkard"; "Salafiyya cheh kesānī hastand? Aṣlītarīn-i ʿalāyim-i salafiyya chīst?," 4 Mordād 1392/July 26, 2014, http://shiayan.ir/2901/; Riżvānī, *Salafīgarī (Vahhābiyat) va-pāsokh beh shubuhāt*, 155–157; ʿAlī Aṣghar

Deserving equal criticism, according to the Shīʿī point of view, is the Wahhābī insistence that God is not bound by reason or by his nature to act justly, as that would diminish his omnipotence as well as their claim that whatever God does is just. This was the subject of a heated theological debate between the rationalist Muʿtazila and their traditionalist rivals during the ninth century over God's attributes and whether God is the source of moral principles or bound by them.[43] It seems that in addition to presenting Wahhābī doctrines as primitive, the Shīʿī polemicists seek to portray them as denigrating God's standing in contrast to the Shīʿīs themselves, who hold God in a higher regard.

In order to further disparage the Wahhābīs, various writers have described them as *ghulāt* (those who exaggerate). Historically, the term *ghulāt* was used to refer to extremist Shīʿī sects that deified ʿAlī; now, however, the Shīʿīs are applying it to the Wahhābīs for anthropomorphizing God.[44] This trope served to distance Twelver Shīʿīsm from the heterodox groups which had historically opposed the clergy. The description of the Wahhābīs as *ghulāt* is significant, as modern Salafists often use the term Ṣafavīds, who were originally *ghulāt*, to denote Arab Shīʿīs as a whole. As is the case with the charge of being Jewish hurled at them by Sunnīs, the Shīʿī writers turn the charge against them into a weapon against their rivals.

The Wahhābī anti-rationalist approach is, according to their Shīʿī critics, also the source of their misreading of the term *bidʿa* (unlawful innovation) as referring to anything that did not exist during the Prophet's lifetime. This approach, the Shīʿī writers state, drove the Wahhābīs to oppose not only new technologies such as the radio, telephone, or television but everything that other Muslims practice. They even resorted to violence against other Muslims for endorsing these alleged innovations.[45] According to Subḥānī, the Wahhābī

Riżvānī, *Khodāyī mujassam-i Vahhābiyat* (Iṣfahān: Markaz taḥqīqāt rayāneh-i qāʾimiyya, n.d.), 35–44; Qazvīnī, *Vahhābiyat az manẓar-i ʿaql va-sharʿ*, 119–120; ʿAbdollah ʿAlī Bakhshī, *Vahhābiyat az nigāhī digār* (Tehrān: Rāh-i Nīkān, 1390/2011), 28–30.

43 Rajāyī Borūjnī, "ʿAql gerīzī va-ʿadālat setīzī-i Vahhābiyat dar taqābul bā ʿaql gerāyī va-ʿidālat jūyī-i muʿtazila."

44 Cited in Isaak Hasson, *Contemporary Polemics Between Neo-Wahhabis and Post-Khomeinist Shiʿites* (Washington DC: Hudson Institute, 2009), 7; Khalīl ʿAlī Ḥaydar, "al-Shīʿa wa-ghulāt al-salaf wa-mudākhalat abā al-khīl," July 15, 2008, http://www.middleeasttransparent.com/article.php3?id_article=4153; "Ghulat al-Wahhābiyya yadʿūna ilā manʿ al-Muslimīn min irtiyād al-mawāqiʿ al-Islāmiyya al-mashhūra wa-tahdīmihā wa-tasayyujihā," January 5, 2009, http://burathanews.com/arabic/news/57083; ʿAbd al-Ḥamīd, *al-Wahhābiyya fī ṣūratihā al-ḥaqīqiyya*. On the *ghulāt*, see Heinz Halm, "Ğolāt," *Encyclopaedia Iranica*, http://www.iranicaonline.org/articles/golat and Matti Moosa, *Extremist Shiʿites: The Ghulāt Sects* (Syracuse: Syracuse University Press, 1988).

45 Fīrūzjāyī, "Bonyādhā-i īfikrī-i al-qāʿida va-Vahhābiyat," 237, 240.

position has no basis in either the Qur'ān or the Sunnī ḥadīth, as Islam had never opposed technological or scientific improvements and modernization but was, in fact, in harmony with human nature that strove toward such improvements. Makārem Shīrāzī asserted that the Wahhābīs fail to understand that the progress of civilization is not a *bid'a*. A true *bid'a* refers to intervention in divine matters or to legislation that either adds or subtracts from religion or was attributed to God even though it had no religious basis, which, he added, is what the Qur'ān had accused the Jews and Christians of doing.[46] Ayatollah Seyyed Muḥammad Ḥusaynī Qazvīnī of the Qom seminary explained that only an innovation to which there is no specific or general reference in the scriptures can be called *bid'a*; issues to which the scriptures allude in a general way or which can be deduced from the scriptures are legitimate and should therefore not fall in this category. He takes pains to prove that all the Shī'ī practices that the Wahhābīs abhor have a sound Qur'ānic basis, and therefore should not be counted as *bid'a*.[47] This argument is no different from the more traditional Shī'ī apologetics vis-à-vis Wahhābī attacks on Shī'īsm.[48]

As proof of the alleged absurdity of the Wahhābī approach to innovations, Shī'ī writers have highlighted Wahhābī opposition to a series of religious practices that are highly popular among both Sunnīs and Shī'īs. Most important among these are the celebration of the Prophet's birthday, praising God after completing the reading of the Qur'ān, and mourning ceremonies over the death of the Prophet and righteous historical figures. Their aim in listing these practices was not only to legitimize Shī'ī practices such as the 'Āshūrā' commemorations but also to present the Wahhābīs as anti-Muslim. Similarly, by ridiculing Wahhābī opposition to family celebrations of the birth of new babies, they seek to portray the Wahhābīs as inhumane. The Qom affiliated *adyan.net* website criticized the Wahhābī clerics for excessive prohibitions and equated them with the Jews and Christians "who banned what was allowed and allowed what had been banned."[49]

As part of this criticism, various writers have charged the Wahhābīs with duplicity or with failing to abide by their own principles: they profess hatred toward other Muslims but befriend all the polytheists (*mushrikān*) of other countries; they rejected bicycles as "the vehicle of Satan" but now drive the latest models of American, Japanese, and German cars; they claim to adhere to

46 Makārem Shīrāzī, *Vahhābiyat bar sar dō rāhī*, 69–70.

47 Qazvīnī, *Vahhābiyat az manẓar-i 'aql va-shar'*, 191–194, 202–204.

48 Subḥānī, *Vahhābiyat, mabānī-i fikrī*, 41–43; Naṣīrī-Fard, Vakāvī-*i seh firqa*, 216–218.

49 Qazvīnī, *Vahhābiyat az manẓar-i 'aql va-shar'*, 183–189; "Tashābuh-i pīrūwān-i Vahhābiyat bā Yahūd va-Naṣārā," 4 Khordād 1393/May 25, 2014, http://www.adyannet.com/fa/news/11407; Bakhshī, *Vahhābiyat az nigāhī digār*, 31–38.

the pure ways of the past, but modern and capitalist features such as luxurious office buildings and hotels have been built all over the city of Mecca, destroying many historical sites. Moreover, while Wahhābī clerics in Saudi Arabia oppose Shīʿī mourning ceremonies as a *bidʿa*, they have legitimized the invented Saudi National Day on the basis of public interest (*maṣlaḥat*). Fīrūzjāyī, for example, described this as "neo-Wahhābism," namely, employing severity, intolerance, and rigidity toward others but surrendering to the necessities of life, which suit them. Their talk about adhering to tradition and the ways of the Salaf, he continued, are mere rhetorical devices and a tool, blindly endorsed by various radical groups in the Muslim world, for getting Saudi money.[50]

The overall conclusion of this Shīʿī criticism of Wahhābī narrow-mindedness is that Wahhābism belongs to the age of regression and backwardness. It is based on a mechanistic and misguided reading of texts and suffers from intellectual stagnation. It is distinct from the civilized and cultured spirit and rich, intellectual legacy of true Islam and is incapable of persuading people through rational arguments, successful only among simple, intellectually inferior people and those who are attracted by money. With thinly disguised condescension, Ḥujjat al-Islam Muḥsin Qirāʾatī, a senior functionary in the H.Q. of organizing prayers, wrote that Shīʿī clerics have been urging the Wahhābīs for over twenty years to hold live debates with them on television. The latter decline, he asserted, because they know that their claims are totally groundless and they cannot contend with rational arguments. In view of its intellectual inferiority, Wahhābism resorts to violence as the only way of winning over people's minds.[51]

These depictions of Wahhābī fanaticism, obscurantism, and rigidity serve to highlight Shīʿīsm in a particularly positive light. The most salient features of Shīʿīsm, in stark contrast to Wahhābism, are rationalism, theological sophistication, and pluralism. These distinctions are also applied to the founding figures of both groups. For example, Philosophy expert Muḥammad ʿAlī Rajāyī Borūjnī contrasted Ibn ʿAbd al-Wahhāb with Muḥammad Bāqir Bihbihānī

50 Makārem Shīrāzī, *Vahhābiyat bar sar dō rāhī*, 40–41; Fīrūzjāyī, "Bonyādhā-i īfikrī-i al-qāʿida va-Vahhābiyat," 253; Qazvīnī, *Vahhābiyat az manẓar-i ʿaql va-sharʿ*, 205–206; "Vahhābiyat beh Sunnat nazdīktar ast yā modernīte?"

51 Samāwī, *al-ʿAṣr al-wahhābī: qirāʾāt fī adab al-taṭṭaruf*, 7, 9, 14; Daftar-i Tablīghāt-i Islāmī, *Darsnāmah-i ashnāʾī va-naqd-i Vahhābiyat*, 113; "Jumūd-i fikrī dar tafakkur-i vahhābīyyat, ānhā rā dar gamrāhī va-żalālāt qarār dādeh ast," 15 Abān 1392/November 6, 2013, http://www.farsnews.com/printable.php?nn=13920813000982; "Vahhābiyat va-ʿaql setīzī"; Fāṭima Pūrshafīʿ, "Jumūd-i fikrī va-qashrī va-taḥajjurī-i Vahhābiyat," 28 Ordībehesht 1395/May 17, 2016, http://yadbiza.mahdiblog.com/article-67.html; "Qirāʾatī: muftīhā-i vahhābī tavān-i munaẓara bā ʿulamāʾ-i Shīʿa rā nadārand," 29 Dey 1392/January 19, 2014, http://shiayan.ir/3818/.

(d. 1791), the founder of the new Shīʿī rationalist Uṣūli school: the former produced an obscurantist and backward-looking doctrine and sought to impose it by force, the latter renovated a rationalist approach that enabled Shīʿīsm to address new challenges by exercising reason.[52] Likewise, present-day Wahhābī clerics are portrayed as narrow-minded people familiar with only Ḥanbalī jurisprudence and lacking any knowledge of the major Sunnī theologians. "Wahhābīs are a tribe who publish the findings of their religious sciences and scientific experiences after 100 years solely in the form of dissertations on what is ḥalāl and what is ḥarām (forbidden), marriage, privy parts of man and women, sexual intercourse and copulation and other similar subjects," wrote Saber al-Daghamseh sarcastically in the *Iran Daily*. The Shīʿī polemicists, on the other hand, highlight the wide knowledge of their own clerics in Shīʿī and Sunnī jurisprudence and methodology of the law.[53]

According to Makārem Shīrāzī, Wahhābī narrow-mindedness and refusal to be exposed to other Islamic views is the reason for their intellectual stagnation, but it also reflects their lack of confidence and fear of the challenge of opposing ideas. By contrast, the libraries of the Shīʿī seminaries contain the books of all Sunnī schools as well as criticisms of Shīʿīsm, so why, he asked rhetorically, are the Wahhābīs so afraid of other views, while we are not?[54] The answer, although not given, is clear. Wahhābī fear stems from intellectual weakness and their inability to contend with intellectual challenges, particularly when compared with the Shīʿīs, who are confident of the righteousness and intellectual superiority of their cause.

5 Wahhābism and the Other Enemies of Islam

Alongside the critique of Wahhābī doctrines and their resultant conduct, another Shīʿī polemical device is to link the Wahhābīs with other external rivals, most prominently the British and the Jews when referencing the past and the West, personified by the United States and Israel in the present day. As mentioned above, these charges are a result of the traditional Muslim tendency to

52 Rajāyī Borūjnī, "ʿAql gerīzī va-ʿadālat setīzī-i Vahhābiyat." For a valuable analysis of the two men and their opposed paths to modernity, see Zack Heern, *The Emergence of Modern Shiʿism: Islamic Reform in Iraq and Iran* (London: Oneworld, 2015).

53 "Gozāresh-i kitāb-i juẕūr-i Dāʿesh qirāʾa fī turāth al-wahhābiyya wa-ʿulamāʾ al-saʿūdiyya," http://takfir.ir/modules/smartsection/item.php?itemid=1494; Saber al-Daghamseh, "What's the Reason for All the Blind Hatred Against Iran?," *Iran Daily*, June 18, 2018, https://en.irna.ir/news/82945555/What-s-the-reason-for-all-the-blind-hatred-against-Iran.

54 Makārem Shīrāzī, *Vahhābiyat bar sar dō rāhī*, 60.

attribute the emergence of perceived heresies to outsiders, particularly Jews.[55] It also reflects the proclivity toward conspiracy theories in modern Iranian and Arab political culture, manifested in particular in the "paranoid style" of Iranian historiography, which inflates the British as the source of most evils in modern times.[56] The charge places the Shīʿīs as the foremost defenders of Islam against the common Western/Jewish enemy and presents their rivals as those who have undermined the Islamic cause and unity from the Mongol invasion until today. It also serves to refute accusations against the Shīʿīs by modern Wahhābīs and Salafist of serving the foreign enemies of Islam.

5.1 *Wahhābism's Jewish Origins*

The attribution of Jewish ancestry to the Wahhābīs was a response to counter accusations by Wahhābī polemicists against the Shīʿīs as well as to Wahhābī charges that placed the Shīʿīs in the same line with the Americans and the Jews or describing them as "more harmful than the Jews."[57] As elsewhere, the natural response of turning these charges against the Wahhābīs serves, in David Nirenberg's words, as a mechanism of self-defense by presenting the accuser as innocent of that charge.[58] While in both cases the Jews serve as a metaphor for all evil, the internal Muslim rival (the Shīʿīs for Wahhābīs and the Wahhābīs for Shīʿīs) is regarded as more dangerous because it claims to represent true Islam. As is often the case, radicals give higher priority to fighting the internal enemy, against whom they compete for the souls of believers, over the external one, who does not pose such a challenge.

A popular theme along these lines has been the attribution of Jewish ancestry to Ibn ʿAbd al-Wahhāb as a way of explaining his rancor against most Muslims. One version traces his origins to a fifteenth-century Jewish family from Baṣra; another claims that his grandfather (or great-grandfather depending on the source) had been an Anatolian Jew who converted to Islam. More significant is the attribution of descent from the crypto-Jewish Dönme sect in

---

55 Steven Wasserstrom, *Between Muslim and Jew: The Problem of Symbiosis under Early Islam* (Princeton: Princeton University Press, 2014), 157.

56 Houchang E. Chehabi, "The Paranoid Style in Iranian Historiography," in *Iran in the 20th Century: Historiography and Political* Culture, ed. Touraj Atabaki (London: I.B. Tauris, 2009), 155–176.

57 "Pīshīneh va-kārnāmah-i Vahhābiyat (pt. 3) – ʿaqāyed va-ʿamalkard"; "Taktīkhā-i Shīʿa setīzī-i Vahhābiyat," http://mouood.org/index.php?option=com_k2&view=item&id=8542:سس; Bakhshī, *Vahhābiyat az nigāhī digār*, 52–53. For Salafi charges against Shīʿīsm, see Isaac Hasson, "Les Šiʿites vus par les neo-wahhabites," *Arabica* 53 (2006): 299–330; Litvak, "More Harmful than the Jews," 285–306.

58 David Nirenberg, *Anti-Judaism: The Western Tradition* (New York: W.W. Norton, 2013), 231.

the Ottoman Empire.[59] This supposed Dönme ancestry tapped into the conspiracy theory popular among Middle Eastern Sunnī Islamists regarding the sect's central role in the collapse of the Ottoman Empire following the 1908 Young Turks (Committee of Union and Progress) revolution, which toppled the pious Sulṭān ʿAbd al-Ḥamīd II. Linking the Wahhābīs with the Dönme was perhaps another means used by the Shīʿīs of turning against two common enemies, the Wahhābīs and the Jews, in order to forge a common cause against them with mainstream Sunnīs.[60] Ironically, this Jewish ancestry was not applied to Ibn ʿAbd al-Wahhāb's father or brother, whom the Shīʿī writers describe as pious clerics.

This charge of Jewish ancestry also targeted the Saʿūd clan, Ibn ʿAbd al-Wahhāb's protectors, claiming they were related to a Jewish clan in Najrān or to Jewish clans of the ʿAnaza tribal confederation.[61] However, as the bloodshed between Sunnīs and Shīʿīs grew worse following the outbreak of the 2011 Arab upheaval, two other charges became increasingly prevalent. The first maintained that the Saʿudis had descended from the Jewish tribe of Banu Qaynuqāʿ, defeated by the Prophet Muḥammad in Medina, and the second that their ancestors had been the Jews of the Khaybar oasis, defeated by ʿAlī in 628.[62] The Saudis have been even accused of apparently boasting of their

59 "Muḥammad bin ʿAbd al-Wahhāb va-Yahūdiyat," 30 Bahman 1393/February 19, 2015, http://daesh93.rasekhoonblog.com/show/369903; "Ahdāf-i istiʿmār az ʾījād firqa-i Vahhābiyat va-nīz rābiṭa beyn Vahhābiyat va-Yahūd"; "Nigāhī beh zindigī-i Muḥammad bin ʿAbd al-Wahhāb," 4 Esfand 1394/Febuary 23, 2016, http://www.adyannet.com/fa/news/18016; "Vahhābiyat va-Yahūd niyākān-i Āl Saʿūd va-Muḥammad bin ʿAbd al-Wahhāb," 25 Mordād 1394/August 16, 2015, http://313-nafar.rozblog.com/61.

60 Ṭalʿat Pasha, one of the three Young Turk leaders, was reputedly descended from the Dönme. For more on the conspiracy theory, see Marc David Baer, "An Enemy Old and New: The Dönme, Anti-Semitism, and Conspiracy Theories in the Ottoman Empire and Turkish Republic," *The Jewish Quarterly Review* 103, no. 4 (2013): 523–555; Rıfat N. Bali, *A Scapegoat for All Seasons: The Dönmes or Crypto-Jews of Turkey* (Istanbul: Isis Press, 2008).

61 "Ahdāf-i istiʿmār az ʾījād firqa-i Vahhābiyat va-nīz rābiṭa beyn Vahhābiyat va-Yahūd"; "Rīshehhā-i Yahūdī-i Āl Saʿūd," 8 Abān 1391/October 29, 2012, http://salafi-vahabi.blogfa.com/post/88; "Yā AL Saʿūd Yā Āl Yahūd," http://www.vahabiat.porsemani.ir/content/«آل-سعود»-يا-«آل-يهود».

62 "Fars: ajdād-i Āl Saʿūd Yahūdiyān-i khaybar hastand," 9 Farvardīn 1394/March 29, 2015, http://www.parsine.com/fa/news/232655/; "Āl Saʿūd Yahūd wa-yantasibūna ilā banī Qaynuqāʿ: al-taʾrīkh yuthbitu yahūdiyat Āl Saʿūd, pt. 1," June 9, 2014, http://aljamahir.amuntada.com/t27969-topic. The claim that the Saudis were originally Jews goes back at least to the early 1980s, see Martin Kramer, "Khomeini's Messengers: The Disputed Pilgrimage of Islam," in *Religious Radicalism and Politics in the Middle East*, ed. Emmanuel Sivan and Menachem Friedman (New York: SUNY Press, 1990), 192.

Jewish origins.[63] This Saudi connection to Jews is evident in the chant "*Yā ĀL Saʿūd yā ĀL Yahūd*" (Oh the family of Saʿūd, Oh the family of Jews) which has been heard at various anti-Wahhābī gatherings.[64] Other denigrating rhetorical devices have included the use of the term "Āl Saʿyūn," a combination of the name Saʿūd with Zion (Ṣahyūn), to refer to the Saudi clan or the term "Āl Saʿūd Āl Juhud," the colloquial pejorative term for the Jews in Iran.[65] Linking the Saudis with these two historical enemies of Islam reinforces their evil nature and provides a partial explanation of their hatred of the Shīʿa as belated revenge for their earlier defeats, while also offering a prediction that they will meet the same fate.

More important than this alleged Jewish genealogical link, however, is the charge that the Jews "had a hand in creating Wahhābism" as the distortion of Islam, which they perpetrated in its early days paved the way for the emergence of Wahhābism centuries later. Even a leading Saudi cleric has confirmed, they claim, that the *Isrāʾīliyat* ultimately conceived Wahhābism, especially their emphasis on the rejection of reason and the application of anthropomorphism regarding God's attributes.[66] It has been said that the Wahhābīs, unlike all other Muslims, exonerate the Jews for distorting the scriptures that God gave to Moses.

According to the hardline *JavānNews*, there is a wide resemblance between Jewish and Wahhābī doctrines, as both groups believe they are superior to

---

63 "Āl Saʿūd beh Yahūdī būdan-i khōd iftikhār mīkonad," June 13, 2016, http://www.shia-news.com/fa/news/120325/; "Rīsheh-i Vahhābiyat va-Yahūd beh gofteh-i khōd Vahhābiyat+pazhūhesh," http://fadaeyane-velayat.persianblog.ir/post/1505.

64 "Yā ĀL Saʿūd yā ĀL Yahūd al-waʿd al-waʿd," April 21, 2015, https://www.youtube.com/watch?v=f-KQbyQITeg; "Al-mawt yā ĀL Saʿūd yā ĀL Yahūd," https://www.youtube.com/watch?v=EkO5IJX8-1Q; "Yā ĀL Saʿūd yā ĀL Yahūd sawfa nantaqimu minkum sharr intiqām sayyid Amīr Ḥusaynī," https://www.youtube.com/watch?v=eaI_mf4r4Qo.

65 See Ṣāliḥ Qāsimī, Āl *Saʿyūn: taʾrīkhcheh peydāyesh va-jināyat-i Āl Saʿūd* (Tehrān: Shomārgān, 1395) and favorable reviews of the book in "Kitāb Āl Saʿyūn muntashir shod," 17 Mordād 1395/ August 7, 2016, https://www.mehrnews.com/news/3734153; "Nigāhī beh kitāb ʿĀl Saʿyūn," 19 Shahrīvar 1395/September 9, 2016, http://www.farsnews.com/newstext.php?nn=13950618000671 and "Kitāb Āl Saʿyūn bā hadaf-i tabyīn jināyat-i Āl Saʿūd rivāneh bāzār shod," 24 Shahrīvar 1395/September 14, 2016, http://www.rasanews.ir/detail/News/449582/52. See also a talkback on "Vīzhegīhā-i mushābih beyn Vahhābiyat va-Yahūd," 4 Ordībehesht 1387/April 23, 2008, http://valiasr-aj.com/fa/page.php?bank=shobheh&id=34.

66 "Goftegū: Nufūẕ-i Yahūd dar miyān-i musalmānān-i ṣadr-i Islam," 18 Farvardīn 1399/April 6, 2020, http://tarikh.org/1399/01/18/گفت-وگوی-اختصاصی-نفوذ-یهود-در-بین-مسلمانان-در-صدر-اسلام; "Rīsheh-i Vahhābiyat va-Yahūd beh gofteh-i khōd Vahhābiyat + pazhūhesh."

all others and are therefore justified in killing those who disagree with them. More ominously, the Wahhābīs, Kāẓimyan-pūr of ʿAlāma Ṭabāṭabāʾī University maintains, have inherited their hatred for other Muslims and their cruelty from the Jews, with both groups regarding the killing of Shīʿīs as a value and therefore putting it at the top of their agendas. The evil Jewish character has, apparently, taken over the Saudi dynasty and turned it into a group of murderers and traitors against the Muslims and Arabs, while the Wahhābī killing of Shīʿīs is a manifestation of their servitude to the Jews.[67] The Shīʿī writers therefore conclude that Wahhābism is the "child of the illegitimate Jewish people," Wahhābī Islam is "Zionist Islam," and, even worse, Wahhābīs are in fact "Jews who put on makeup" in order to disguise their true identity. A clear proof of these charges is seen in the Saudi wars against Arabs and Muslims but never against the Jews.[68]

According to the Shīʿī narrative, the impact of Jewish descent and Wahhābī attachment to the Jews was also evident in the conduct and policies of the Saʿūd dynasty in the twentieth century. While they destroyed the graves of the Shīʿī Imāms and of the Companions in Mecca and Medina, they allegedly preserved Jewish graves in Khaybar.[69] In addition, the Saudi monarch ʿAbd al-

67 Qazvīnī, *Vahhābiyat az manẓar-i ʿaql va-sharʿ*, 131; "Ishtirākāt-i ʿaqīdatī-i Vahhābiyat va-Yahūdiyat," 20 Esfand 1393/March 11, 2015, http://www.jahannews.com/sound/411939; "Vīzhegīhā-i mushābih beyn Vahhābiyat va-Yahūd"; Ghulām Reżā Kāẓimyan Pūr, "Taṭābuk va-hamāhangī-i Vahhābiyat va-Yahūdiyat dar teʾōrī va-ʿamal," 25 Abān 1393/ November 16, 2014, http://www.x-shobhe.com/shobhe/5571.html; "Vahhābiyat dar khidmat-i dushmanān-i Islām"; "Yahūdiyat va-Vahhābiyat naqsh-i koshtan-i Shīʿīyān rā dar sar dārand," 26 Dey 1392/January 16, 2014, http://www.diyarebaran.ir/50026; "Muḥammad bin ʿAbd al-Wahhāb va-Yahūdiyat"; "Āl Saʿūd Yahūd wa-yantasibūna ilā banī qaynuqāʿ pt. 1."

68 "Karshinās-i masāʾil-i dushman shināsī: Vahhābiyat farzand-i qawm-i nāmashrūʿ-i Yahūd ast," 16 Ordībehesht 1393/May 6, 2014, http://www.snn.ir/detail/News/312753/164; "Vahhābiyat dast-i parvardeh-i yahūdiyat ast," 16 Mordād 1393/August 7, 2014, http://www.rasanews.ir/detail/news/215610/23; "Nufūẕ-i Yahūdiyān dar Islām barāye taghyīr-i dādan masīr-i dīn," 10 Esfand 1395/February 28, 2017, http://ferghenews.com/fa/news/15317; Kāẓimyan Pūr, "Taṭābuk va-hamāhangī-i Vahhābiyat va-Yahūdiyat dar teʾōrī va-ʿamal"; "Āl Saʿūd Yahūd wa-yantasibūna ilā banī Qaynuqāʿ: al-taʾrīkh yuthbitu yahūdiyat Āl Saʿūd pt. 1"; "Vahhābiyat dar khidmat-i dushmanān-i Islām."

69 "Al-taʾrīkh yuthbitu yahūdiyat Āl Saʿūd," May 30, 2013, http://burathanews.com/news/196926.html; "Bil-barāhīn nasab Āl Saʿūd al-Yahūdī," https://www.youtube.com/watch?v=ah8eI1ksYRc; Saʿūd al-Sabʿānī, "Aṣl-i Āl Saʿūd al-majhūl wa-yahūdiyat nasabihim," http://altaghyeer1.3abber.com/post/156225; "Al-Uṣūl al-Yahūdiyya li-Āl Saʿūd wa-tadmīrihim li-athār al-nabī wal-ṣaḥāba bi-Makka wal-muḥāfaẓa ʿalā athār al-Yahūd bi-Khaybar (pt. 2)," June 9, 2014, https://ar-ar.facebook.com/notes/673051039417372/.

ʿAzīz bin Saʿūd is said to have supported "handing over Palestine to the Jews."[70] The Shīʿī sources use as proof a photograph of a letter purportedly written by him in 1915 in which he stated to Percy Cox, Britain's resident in the Persian Gulf, that his country "has no objection to presenting Palestine to the Jews or to others, as Britain sees fit."[71] He also allegedly refrained from helping the Palestinian revolts against the British and the Zionists in 1929 and 1935 and refused to send his army to fight the Jews in 1948. The Jews in turn helped him take over the entire Arabian Peninsula at the end of World War I.[72] The anger at this supposed Wahhābī-Jewish complicity increased with the exacerbation of Sunnī-Shīʿī sectarian strife, particularly after the 2006 Israel-Lebanon War when Saudi clerics banned prayers in support of the Shīʿī Ḥizballah due to their being heretics.[73] Ḥujjat al-Islam Qirāʾatī asked in response to this why the Wahhābīs, who justify the killing of Shīʿīs for being infidels, don't consider the Israelis infidels that should be killed.[74]

5.2 *Wahhābism as Protégé of British Imperialism*

Alongside the Jews, the Shīʿī polemicists assigned a major role in the emergence of Wahhābism to the British, the erstwhile villain in the Iranian historical repertoire. In Khomeini's words, Islam has long withstood the machinations of foreign foes and their agents. At one time, the enemies of Islam "invented religions" and "propagated Bābīsm, Bahāʾīsm, and Wahhābism" to protect their "colonial interests" and "destroy the unity of Islam."[75] According to this nar-

70 "Kodām pādishāh-i Saʿūdī felestīn rā beh Yahūdiyān bakhshīd + sanad taʾrīkhi," 24 Farvardīn 1390/April 13, 2011, http://www.shia-news.com/fa/news/20538.

71 "Vahhābiyat-i Āl Saʿūd va-Yahūd," 7 Farvardīn 1392/March 27, 2013, https://rasekhoon.net/forum/thread/731244.

72 "Estrātizhī-i Āl Saʿūd dar bārah-i rezhīm-i ṣahyūnīstī," 1 Mordād 1394/July 23, 2015, https://www.teribon.ir/archives/267190; "Khiyānat-i Āl Saʿūd li-felestīn wal-muslimīn," https://www.youtube.com/watch?v=WlluzFtH1NI; Daftar-i Tablīghāt-i Islāmī, *Darsnāmah-i ashnāʾī va-naqd-i Vahhābiyat*, 102–105. While ʿAbd al-ʿAzīz did not send his army against the new state of Israel in 1948, the Saudi dynasty espoused strong anti-Zionist and anti-Jewish views, see Meir Litvak and Esther Webman, *From Empathy to Denial: Arab Responses to the Holocaust* (New York: Columbia University Press, 2009), 37 and William B. Quandt, *Saudi Arabia in the 1980s: Foreign Policy, Security, and Oil* (Washington DC: The Brookings Institution, 1981), 31.

73 ʿAbdallah ibn Jibrīn, "Naṣrat ḥizballah al-rāfiḍī wal-inḍiwāʾ taḥt amrihim wal-duʿāʾ lahum bil-naṣr wal-tamkīn," http://www.ibn-jebreen.com/fatwa/vmasal-4174-.html; ʿAbdallah ibn Jibrīn, "Al-radd ʿalā al-fatwā al-khāṣṣa bi-naṣrat ḥizballah al-lubnānī al-mansūba li-faḍilat al-shaykh ibn Jibrīn," http://ibn-jebreen.com/fatwa/vmasal-15294-.html.

74 "Qirāʾatī: muftīhā-i vahhābī tavān-i munaẓara bā ʿulamāʾ-i Shīʿa rā nadārand"; "Vakonesh beh ihānat-i rūḥānī-i vahhābī beh Shīʿīyān."

75 *Ṣaḥīfa-i nūr: majmūʿa-i rāhnimūdhā-i ḥażrat-i Imām-i Khomeini quddisa sirruhu al-sharīf* Vol. 17 (Tehrān: Vizārat-i farhang va-irshād-i Islāmī, 1370–1373/1991–1993), 203–204.

rative, the British implanted the "cancerous tumor" of Wahhābism as part of their broader imperialist design against Islam.[76] An essential element in their scheme to seize control of the Persian Gulf was to break down Islamic unity by fomenting rebellions in the Ottoman Empire and destroy Sunnī-Shīʿī peaceful and almost harmonious coexistence. The British agent Hempher found in Ibn ʿAbd al-Wahhāb the suitable tool and collaborator to carry out this ploy.[77]

Subḥānī presented a picture of a besieged Muslim world in order to highlight Wahhābī harm to Islamic unity, conflating a series of events that spanned a century before and after the advent of Wahhābism. Chief among them are the British and Dutch siege of the straits of Hurmuz, the British invasion of India, Russian efforts to take over the Caucasus and Iran in order to reach the Persian Gulf, Habsburg attacks on the Ottomans, and the American attempt to seize North Africa through their 1803 raid on Tangier. During such harsh times for Islam, Ibn ʿAbd al-Wahhāb decided that *ziyārat al-qubūr* and *tawassul* were the greatest threats to Islam and justified the declaration of apostasy and war. Instead of supporting Muslim unity against the Western threat, he was bent on sowing discord and launched a series of internal wars.[78] Interestingly, one Shīʿī writer enlisted the Ṣūfīs in order to attack the Wahhābīs. He maintained that the British and the Jews, as "the parents of Wahhābism," sought to hinder the expansion of Islam, in which the Sunnī Ṣūfī orders played a key role at the time, by creating Wahhābism and unleashing it against the Ṣūfīs.[79] As the Shīʿī clergy had fought against organized Ṣūfīsm during the late eighteenth and early nineteenth centuries,[80] this myth is one more indication of their need to form as wide alliance as possible against Wahhābism including the rehabilitation and enlistment of former rivals.

Wahhābī collaboration with and subservience to the British reached a new height (or low) under ʿAbd al-ʿAzīz ibn Saʿūd, who allegedly declared that he

---

76 "Vahhābiyat dar khidmat-i dushmanān-i Islām."

77 Akhund Tangalī, *Taḥẕīr al-ikhvan ʿan makāyid ḥizb al-shaytān*, 55–58; Mīrzā Ṣāliḥ Iqtiṣād Marāghī, *ʾĪqāẓ, yā bīdārī dar kashf-i khiyānat-i dīnī va-vaṭanī-i Bahāʾīyān* (Qom: Bonyād-i farhangī-i ḥażrat-i Mahdī Mowʿūd (ʿaj), 1390/2011), 8; "Chegūnegī-i shikl gīrī Vahhābiyat va-tafāvot-i ān bā ahl-i Sunnat"; "Ahdāf-i Inglīs az āfarīnesh-i firqa-i Vahhābiyat," http://bcir.pchi.ir/show.php?page=contents&id=9619; "Naqsh-i Inglīshā dar tashkīl-i Vahhābiyat," 15 Mordād 1393/August 6, 2014, https://www.mashreghnews.ir/news/333231; "Inglistān va-ẓuhūr-i Vahhābiyat va-Āl Saʿūd," 27 Azar 1392/December 18, 2013, http://alwahabiyah.com/fa/Article/View/2627; "Ahdāf-i istiʿmār az ʾījād firqa-i Vahhābiyat va-nīz rābiṭa beyn Vahhābiyat va-Yahūd"; Fīrūzjāyī, "Bonyādhā-i fikrī-i al-qaʿida va-Vahhābiyat," 244–245.

78 Subḥānī, *Vahhābiyat mabānī-i fikrī*, 21.

79 "Vahhābiyat dar khidmat-i dushmanān-i Islām."

80 Litvak, *Shiʿi Scholars of Nineteenth Century Iraq*, 47–48.

would never "until Judgment Day" disobey Britain.[81] To prove their point, the Shīʿī writers charge that the Wahhābīs never fought the Jews or the British but only other Muslims. Moreover, they claimed that Wahhābīs always opened their gates to the West to enable it to take control of the Muslim countries. The British reciprocated by helping the Wahhābīs to build their state. Likewise, the Americans, as part of their policy of "devouring" the wealth and oil resources of the Arab countries, extended their support for the Wahhābīs, who subsequently adopted a pro-American policy.[82] Tying the Jewish and Western themes together, Ṣāʾib ʿAbd al-Ḥamīd depicted the Wahhābīs as "the malignant bacteria that prepared the ground for the West to plant Israel ... in the heart of this nation and they are the malignant bacteria working today to consolidate the West's hold at the heart of the Muslim world."[83] The denunciation and ridiculing of the Jewish-Zionist-Western ancestry of Wahhābism appeared also in caricatures. For Grand Ayatollah Fāżil Lankarānī the conclusion was clear: Wahhābism was the creature of infidelity and the Jews and thus stood completely outside the boundaries of Islam.[84]

As in other cases discussed here, the Shīʿī-Iranian discourse depicted the 1979 Revolution as the turning point in the historical encounter with various "enemies." Accordingly, the Revolution dealt a decisive blow to Wahhābism, as Iran has become the epicenter and flag bearer of true Islam as well as the focus of the Muslims' hopes. Thus, the Revolution played a key role in refuting and isolating the false Wahhābī doctrine. Yet, as the semi-official *Rasekhoon* website conceded, the resentment that many Sunnīs felt toward the empowerment of the Shīʿa, which they viewed as doctrinally unacceptable, enhanced their support for radical jihādī-Salafī groups.[85]

6 The Wahhābīs and Jihadi Salafists

Like the Wahhābīs before them, some of the jihādī-Salafī organizations, most notably the al-Qāʿida branch in Iraq, which later evolved into ISIS, and the

81 Jawād Ḥusayn Al-Daylamī, *"Shubuhāt al-Salafiyya"* (*Suspicions [Regarding] the Salafiyya*) cited in Isaak Hasson, *Contemporary Polemics Between Neo-Wahhabis and Post-Khomeinist Shiites* (Washington DC: Hudson Institute, 2009), 9, 19.

82 "Inglistān va-ẓuhūr-i Vahhābiyat va-Āl Saʿūd"; Daftar-i Tablīghāt-i Islāmī, *Darsnāmah-i ashnāʾī va-naqd-i Vahhābiyat*, 89–91.

83 ʿAbd al-Ḥamīd, *al-Wahhābiyya fī ṣūratihā al-ḥaqīqiyya*.

84 Qazvīnī, *Vahhābiyat az manẓar ʿaql va-sharʿ*, 20.

85 Daftar-i Tablīghāt-i Islāmī, *Darsnāmah-i ashnāʾī va-naqd-i Vahhābiyat*, 101; "Chīstī va-Cherāyī shikl gīrī-i jarayānhā-i takfīrī va-dalāyil-i qudratyābī-i ān dar deheh-i akhīr."

former al-Nuṣra Front in Syria, espoused deep animosity against Shīʿīsm as a major pillar of their ideology and identity. However, unlike in the past, the Shīʿī response to the jihādī-Salafī threat integrated political and military efforts together with polemics; it is the latter which will be discussed here.

As mentioned above, a major goal of Shīʿī-Iranian policy was to forge a common front with mainstream Sunnīs against the jihādī-Salafists and the Saudis. As part of this effort, Iran organized joint conferences of Shīʿī and Sunnī clerics, each attended by hundreds of clerics and scholars, most of them Sunnīs, from forty different countries.[86] The messages emerging from these conferences and from numerous other publications were as follows: the gap in doctrine and practice between jihādī-Salafists and mainstream Sunnīs was much greater than Sunnī-Shīʿī differences; the jihādī-Salafists pose a major threat to all Muslims and not just Shīʿīs;[87] and finally, the United States and Israel stand behind jihādī-Salafī actions and benefit from them.

Similar to the anti-Wahhābī polemics, the Shīʿī discourse portrayed the jihādī-Salafists as a deviant trend that distorts the true Islam espoused by both Sunnīs and Shīʿīs, calling them Takfīrīs and playing on the deep-seated Sunnī disapproval of rash declarations of apostasy against other Muslims, including sinners. Occasionally, the Shīʿīs use the term Wahhābīs in order to link these groups with their Saudi adversaries and to depict them as a radical sect that all sound Muslims should renounce. As mentioned above, the Shīʿīs refrain from using the term Salafī to denote their rivals due to the term's positive connotation among all Sunnīs. Moreover, the Shīʿīs challenged the very construct of the Salaf as a legitimate religious category in order to prove that the jihādī-Salafī claim to follow the early Islamic precedence is groundless and to thus deprive them of the status of an ideological school.

Subḥānī, in a book addressed to Arabic-language readers, explained that the Prophet's Companions and their immediate followers had never constituted a coherent legal or doctrinal school as they had been divided on many issues. Moreover, in a reflection of the traditional Shīʿī grudge against those Companions who rejected ʿAlī, he denied the basic Sunnī premise that the

86 For this practice, see Zeev Maghen, "Unity or Hegemony: Iranian Attitudes Towards the Sunnī-Shīʿī Divide," ed. Bengio and Litvak, *The Sunna and Shiʿa in History*, 183–202. See also the website of the *Majmaʿ-i jahānī taqrīb-i maẓāhib-i Islāmī* (The World Forum for Proximity of Islamic Schools of Thought), http://taghrib.org/farsi/pages/moetamar.php.

87 See, for example, the statements of Ḥasan Naṣrallah, leader of the Lebanese Ḥizballah, *al-Akhbār*, August 15, 2014, http://english.al-akhbar.com/content/hezbollah-leader-warns-isis-growing-threat-region-must-be-defeated; Nour Samaha, "Hezbollah Chief Urges Middle East to Unite Against ISIL," February 16, 2015, http://www.aljazeera.com/news/2015/02/hezbollah-hassan-nasrallah-isil-150216214845193.html.

Salaf were preferable in faith or religious knowledge over succeeding generations. Regarding the subsequent evolution of legal and theological schools, Subḥānī maintained that each of the four legal schools of Sunnī Islam as well as the field of Kalām (scholastic theology), i.e., the rationalists whose views the Shīʿīs adopted, had distinct principles which defined their identity and doctrine. Conversely, the Traditionists (*ahl al-ḥadīth*), who the present-day Salafists claim to follow, had lacked any unifying doctrines on questions of faith or clear or precise foundations on matters of jurisprudence.[88]

The 2014 International Conference on Radical and Takfīrī Movements, in which both Sunnī and Shīʿī clerics participated, took a more inclusionary approach toward the historical Salaf, reflecting Shīʿī readiness to soften their grudge against them in light of the present-day enemy. It asserted that, unlike the Takfīrīs, all four legal Sunnīs schools of law have emulated the Shīʿī Imāms as members of the Salaf. In other words, the Takfīrī claim to be Salafist, that is, genuine followers of the Salaf, is totally groundless.[89]

Pursuing this line, Subḥānī maintained that present-day jihādī-Salafī movement constituted a gross distortion of the nineteenth-century Salafiyya, which mainstream Sunnī Islamists held in high esteem. He added that Jamal al-Dīn Asadabādī (known outside Iran as al-Afghani) and his disciple Muḥammad ʿAbduh did not promote the idea of Salafiyya in order to "slander, discriminate, and declare other Muslims as apostates." Rather, their Salafiyya was a "return to the Qurʾān and to the spirit of religious zeal of the early generations against the aggressive enemies of Islam" and to "awaken the nation to adhere to Islam and stay away from the imperialist cultural project."[90] This description was probably intended to show the great similarity between the Iranian *vilāyat-i faqīh* system and the nineteenth-century Salafiyya as two anti-imperialist movements fighting for genuine Islamic regeneration, thereby placing the Shīʿīs on the same side as mainstream Islamists while positioning the jihādī-Salafīsts beyond the boundaries of normative Islam.

88 Jaʿfar Subḥānī, *al-Salafiyya: taʾrīkhān mafhūman hadafan* (Qom: Muʾassasat Imām Ṣādiq, 1388/2009), 10, 22, 27–30. See similar arguments in Riżvānī, *Salafīgarī (Vahhābiyat) va-pāsokh beh shubuhāt*, 56; Syed ʿAli Shahbaz, "The Heretical Cult of Wahhabi Takfīrī Salafis," http://www.imamreza.net/eng/imamreza.php?id=11318.

89 "Al-Mīthāq al-ʿilmī: al-muʾtamar al-ʿālamī lil-tiyārāt al-mutashaddida wal-takfīriyya min wujhat naẓar-i ʿulamāʾ al-Islām," 1 Azar 1391/November 21, 2012, http://dinpajoohan.com/ ararticle13102.html.

90 Subḥānī, *al-Salafiyya: taʾrīkhān mafhūman hadafan*, 50.

7 The Takfīrī Trend: the Child of Wahhābism

Rather than being the heirs of genuine revivalist Islam, the Shīʿī polemicists branded the Takfīrī movements the child of Wahhābism. Accordingly, the jihādī-Salafī terrorist organizations were the product of the Saudi propaganda machine and of widespread financial spending carried out in order to advance the Saudi royal family's quest for domination. The *Ṣubḥ-i Ṣādiq* daily even published an article entitled, "The Takfīrī Terrorism is a Wahhābī Gift to the Arrogance [i.e., the United States]." By linking these three villains – the Takfīrīs, Wahhābīs, and Americans – together, Ayatollah Ṣādiq Āmolī Lārījānī, then head of the Iranian judiciary, charged that Wahhābism, the product of imperialism, was the moving force behind the Takfīrī groups, since true Islam could not have produced "rubbish" (*zebālahhā*) like ISIS.[91] The link between ISIS and Wahhābism is self-evident, the Qom official website explained. One only needs to look at the beliefs and attitudes toward other Muslims and the crimes committed in order to prove that ISIS is a Wahhābī terrorist group.[92]

Most important among the similarities between the two trends is, according to the Shīʿī writers, their intolerant and exclusionary doctrines regarding numerous Islamic practices and declarations of apostasy that denied the faith of most Muslims but were aimed particularly against the Shīʿīs. They claim that jihādī-Salafīsts regard themselves as superior to all other Muslims and seek to impose their views upon them by "employing the sword of *takfīr*." Subḥānī reflected this general view in his depiction of takfīr as "totally condemned in Islam" and as a "disaster, tragedy, and disease that has emerged in Muslim societies."[93]

---

91 Samāwī, *al-ʿAṣr al-wahhābī: qirāʾāt fī adab al-taṭṭaruf*, 27–28; *Sobh-i Ṣādiq*, January 26, 2014 cited in A. Savyon, Yossi Mansharof, E. Kharrazi and Y. Lahat, "Iran Calls For Violent Shiʿite Reaction Against Saudi Arabia," Memri, Inquiry & Analysis Series no. 1068, February 12, 2014, https://www.memri.org/reports/iran-calls-violent-shiite-reaction-against-saudi-arabia; "Imkān nadārad Islām vāqiʿī zebālahā-i mithl-i Dāʿesh towlīd konad," 16 Azar 1394/ December 7, 2015, https://www.tasnimnews.com/fa/news/1394/09/16/936971.

92 "Dāʿesh chehre-i digār-i Vahhābiyat," http://andisheqom.com/fa/Article/view/1100078. See also "Tamām āncheh keh bāyad dar mowred-i gurūh-i terrōristī-i Dāʿesh bedānīm," 1 Mordād 1393/July 23, 2014, http://hawzahnews.com/TextVersionDetail/335334; Riżvānī, *Salafīgarī (Vahhābiyat) va-pāsokh beh shubuhāt*, 50.

93 Seyyed Aḥmad Sādāt, "Vahhābiyat pedar-i Dāʿesh, yār-i ṣahyūnīsm," 30 Khordād 1394/ June 20, 2015, http://parstoday.com/fa/iran-i81226; Aḥmad Muṣṭafā and ʿAlāʾ Ḥasan Muṣṭafā, "Tafāvot miyān-i jonbeshhā-i inqilābī va-jarayānāt-i takfīrī va-terōristī," *Javān-i Irānī*, 6 Mordād 1395/July 27, 2016, https://khabarfarsi.com/u/22640089; Riżvānī, *Salafgarī (Vahhābiyat) va-pāsokh beh shubuhāt*, 42; "Takfir is Totally Condemned in Islam: Grand Ayatollah Subhani," November 26, 2014, http://sachtimes.com/en/world/around-the-world/1813-takfir-is-totally-condemned-in-islam-grand-ayatollah-subhani.

The 2014 Conference equated jihādī-Salafī conduct with that of the Khawārij because, Ḥujjat al-Islam Javād Abūl-Qāsimī explained, they regard the internal enemy as worse than the external one. Makārem Shīrāzī and Subḥānī, however, viewed the Takfīrīs as worse than the Khawārij. They maintained that in earlier times the Khawārij operated out of ignorance and mistaken beliefs, whereas the conduct of present-day Takfīrīs is the outcome of the planning and organizations of the enemies of Islam. Furthermore, the original Khawārij did not perpetrate the same atrocities as the present-day Takfīrīs, such as mass killings of civilians, selling women as sex slaves, and mass destructions of holy sites. Not surprisingly, others equated Takfīrī conduct with the Mongols – the epitome of cruelty and barbarism in Islamic historical imagery.[94]

As in their anti-Wahhābī discourse, the Shīʿī writers argued that the jihādī-Salafī conduct was a *bidʿa* that deviated from the path of the Prophet, for whom any Muslim who had uttered the *shahādatayn* could never be declared an apostate. Subḥānī, who denied the special virtues of the Salaf, pointed to their restraint in declaring other Muslims as apostates in order to ridicule the jihādī-Salafīsts, who claim to follow these Salaf but take the opposite approach on such a crucial issue.[95] The implication was quite clear, not only did the jihādī-Salafīsts invent new practices that have no precedent in normative Islam, but they are also hypocritical liars when they claim to follow the original Salaf. Contrary to the jihādī-Salafī bigotry, the Shīʿī writers present their own group as the champions of tolerance and pluralism within Islam.

A major cause of Takfīrī misreading of the Qurʾān and of true Islam, according to the Shīʿī view, is their rejection of reason and rationalism like the Wahhābīs. Likewise, their understanding of the principle of *towḥīd* (unity of God) is simplistic and confined to opposition to *shafāʿa* while ignoring its spiritual and philosophical aspects. The Salafists are the enemies of philosophy, of Kalām, and of rational principles of jurisprudence as well as being completely ignorant of other religions, of modern political thought, and of philosophy. Not surprisingly, the 2014 Conference found them partially responsible for the

---

94 "Pīsh qarāvolān-i sufyānī, yā ʿamālahā-i ṣalīb va-ṣahyūn," 18 Tīr 1393/July 9, 2014, https://article.tebyan.net/281196-; "Salafiyya cheh kesānī hastand? Aṣlītarīn-i ʿalāʾim-i salafiyya chīst?"; "Nigāhī beh abʿād-i mukhtalif-i kongreh-i jahānī-i jarayānhā-i ifrāṭī va-takfīrī az dīdār-i ʿulamāʾ-i Islām," 2 Azar 1393/November 23, 2014, http://www.farsnews.com/news text.php?nn=13930901000989.

95 "Ayatollah Makārem Shīrāzī: ʿulamāʾ-i Islām bā ṣedā-i boland az takfīr barāʾat jūyand," 8 Bahman 1394/January 28, 2016, http://hajj.ir/84/65199; "al-Mīthāq al-ʿilmī: al-muʾtamar al-ʿālamī lil-tiyārāt al-mutashaddida wal-takfīriyya min wujhat naẓar-i ʿulamāʾ al-Islām"; Subḥānī, *al-Salafiyya: taʾrīkhān wa-mafhūman wa-hadafan*, 110–111.

backwardness of various parts of the Muslim world,[96] portraying the Shīʿīs as the champions of reason and of Islamic progress.

A blatant expression of Takfīrī ignorance and distortion of Islamic law is, according to the Shīʿī writers, their encouragement and practice of "sexual jihād" (*jihād al-nikāḥ*), namely, encouraging Sunnī women to travel to Syria in order to serve sexual comfort roles by marrying jihādī-Salafī fighters, repeatedly and temporarily, in order to boost their morale.[97] Not only is this practice, as well as ISIS's general abuse of women, contrary to the Qurʾān and Islamic law, the Shīʿī writers stated, but it proved that the major motivation of the jihādī-Salafīsts was not fighting for the sake of Islam but selfish reasons.[98] Despite their ignorance of Islam, the Takfīrīs take the liberty of practicing so-called *ijtihād* and issuing rulings on crucial matters such as apostasy and killings, which sow discord among Muslims.[99]

7.1 *The Takfīrīs and Islamic Unity*

Indeed, a major harm caused by the Takfīrīs is fomenting a split between Sunnīs and Shīʿīs, while the dominant Shīʿī narrative contends that there is no real conflict between the two sects. Both Khamenei and Subḥānī asserted that at a time when the Islamic nation faces numerous threats and challenges from external enemies, the Takfīrīs provoke hatred among Muslims and aggravate minor disagreements in order to incite deep animosity between Sunnīs and

---

96 "Al-Mīthāq al-ʿilmī: al-muʾtamar al-ʿālamī lil-tiyārāt al-mutashaddida wal-takfiīriyya min wujhat naẓar-i ʿulamāʾ al-Islām"; Subḥānī, *al-Salafiyya taʾrīkhān wa-mafhūman wa-hadafan*, 107–110; "Salafī kīst va-cheh mīgūyad?/cherā salafīgarī buzurgtarīn-i khaṭar pīshrū-i jahān-i Islām ast?," 16 Dey 1391/January 5, 2013, https://www.mashregh news.ir/news/176518; "Jarayān shināsī salafīgarī-i muʿāṣir + taṣāvīr"; Riżvānī, *Salafīgarī (Vahhābiyat) va-pāsokh beh shubuhāt*, 47–48.

97 "Chegūnegī-i shikl gīrī Vahhābiyat va-tafāvot-i ān bā ahl-i Sunnat"; "Dāʿesh va-idīʾūlūzhī gezīnesh nīrū," April 12, 2014, http://www.farsnews.com/newstext.php?nn=13931022001323. On sexual jihād, see "Tunisia's 'Sexual Jihad' – Extremist Fatwa or Propaganda?," October 27, 2013, http://www.bbc.com/news/world-africa-24448933; B. Chernitsky and R. Goldberg, "Tunisian Daily Al-Shurouq's Campaign Against 'Sexual Jihad'," Memri Inquiry & Analysis Series no. 1062, February 1, 2014, https://www.memri .org/reports/tunisian-daily-al-shurouqs-campaign-against-sexual-jihad.

98 "Tashābuh-i pīrūwān-i Vahhābiyat bā Yahūd va-Naṣārā"; Muṣṭafā and Muṣṭafā, "Tafāvot miyān-i jonbeshhā-i inqilābī va-jarayānāt-i takfīrī va-terōristī"; "Jināyat-i shibh-i sufyānī: ṣaḥnehā-i ke ʾīn zan nemītavānad farāmūsh konad," 2 Dey 1393/December 23, 2014, https://www.porseman.com/article/جنایات-شبه-سفیانی-صحنه هایی-که-این-زن-نمی تواند-فراموش-کند/160194; "al-Mīthāq al-ʿilmī: al-muʾtamar al-ʿālamī lil-tiyārāt al-mutashaddida wal-takfīriyya min wujhat naẓar-i ʿulamāʾ al-Islām."

99 "Chīstī va-cherāyī-ī shikl gīrī-i jarayānhā-i takfīrī va-dalāyil-i qudratyābī-i ān dar deheh-i akhīr."

Shīʿīs. Subḥānī highlighted the Takfīrī efforts to foil all ecumenical efforts of Sunnī and Shīʿī clerics by fueling doctrinal and ideological controversies and seditions. He even accused them of causing internal ruptures in Muslim countries in preparation for the Crusader (i.e., Western) and Zionist offensive on the Muslims.[100]

The escalation of the 2011 Arab upheaval toward sectarian violence dashed Iran's hope for the emergence of a new Islamic Middle East under its leadership.[101] The key role of the jihādī-Salafīst organizations in this change, particularly in its most aggressive manifestations of mass killings and atrocities against civilians, served as a major motif in Shīʿī writings. According to Khamenei, the Takfīrī groups penetrated all countries that had experienced true Islamic awakening in order to distort it and divert it from its correct path. Originally, this awakening had been an anti-American movement, but the Takfīrī orientation "turned it into a war between Muslims and into fratricide" and caused severe economic destruction which would hamper the progress of these countries for years to come. The crimes against humanity perpetrated by the Takfīrīs revealed their "satanic essence," stated a report on the 2014 Conference, while Makārem Shīrāzī concluded in the same conference that the bloodshed among Muslims, which the Takfīrīs had caused, had brought Islam to its worst crisis in 1400 years.[102] However, for Khamenei, the "unforgettable crime committed by the Takfīrī movement," was shifting the frontline of the Islamic struggle from the borders of occupied Palestine to the streets of Iraq, Syria, Pakistan, and Libya. Others complained that the Takfīrīs refrained from attacking Israel, fighting instead the Shīʿa. Ḥujjat al-Islam Seyyed Muḥammad Ḥusaynī Shāhrūdī Khamenei's personal representative in Kurdistan added that the greatest crime that the Takfīrī groups committed by fighting in Iraq and

100 "Hasht neshāneh az khidmat-i takfīrihā beh jarayān-i istikbār," 14 Dey 1393/June 4, 2014, http://farsi.khamenei.ir/others-note?id=28548; Subḥānī, *al-Salafiyya: ta'rīkhān mafhūman wa-hadafan*, 8–9, 111–113.

101 For statements on the new Islamic Middle East, see Semira N. Nikou, "Iranians Split on Egypt's Turmoil," *The Iran Primer*, February 3, 2011, http://iranprimer.usip.org/blog/2011/feb/03/iranians-split-egypt%E2%80%99s-turmoil; Babak Rahimi, "How Iran Views the Egyptian Crisis," Jamestown Foundation, February 3, 2011, https://jamestown.org/program/special-commentary-how-iran-views-the-egyptian-crisis/.

102 "Supreme Leader's Full Speech in International Congress," November 26, 2014, http://www.miu-lb.org/details.php?id=591&cid=484; "Hasht neshāneh az khidmat-i takfīrihā beh jarayān-i istikbār"; "Nigāhī beh abʿād-i mukhtalif-i 'kongreh-i jahānī-i jarayānhā-i ifrāṭī va-takfīrī az dīdār-i ʿulamāʾ-i Islām"; Nāṣir Makārem Shīrāzī, "al-Āliyāt al-munāsiba fī muwājahat al-tiyārāt al-takfīriyya, arāʾ al-marjaʿ Makārem Shīrāzī," February 29, 2016, https://www.makarem.ir/main.aspx?lid=2&typeinfo=1&catid=45227&pageindex=0&mid=394969.

Syria was breaking the siege on Israel, which was, by implication, worse than killing Muslims.[103]

Leading clerics have grieved that the "Takfīrīs represent an [image of] Islam that is completely violent," whereas true Islam "is known for its mercy, reason, and logic."[104] Makārem Shīrāzī accused the Takfīrīs of tarnishing the image of Islam by committing atrocities in its name that had nothing to do with Islam. He also blamed the Salafists, with the help of the Zionist media, for the addition of the adjective "Islamic" to the concepts of terrorism and brutality in the minds of most people around the world, and for the shift of the term "Wahhābī terrorism" to "Islamic terrorism," thereby tarnishing the image of Islam all over the world in the service of Zionism. The poet Muḥammad Niʿma al-Samāwī included non-Muslims among the victims of Takfīrī terrorism and charged al-Qāʿida's terrorist acts with the emergence of Islamophobia worldwide; Ayatollah Seyyed Hāshim Ḥusaynī Būshehrī even went as far as to claim that the Takfīrīs were actually trying to promote Islamophobia around the world.[105]

8 ISIS as Harbingers of the Mahdī

Using the common Shīʿī polemical device discussed earlier of conjoining diverse enemies including those from different historical epochs, Ḥujjat al-Islam Muḥammad ʿAlī Sālārī of the Mahdaviyat Center in Mashhad and others have accused the Wahhābīs of paving the ground for the rise of the Sufyānī – the Sunnī tyrant who will hail from the region of Syria and fight the awaited Shīʿī Mahdī – and equated his crimes with their doctrines.[106] This practice as well as the regional upheaval caused by the Salafi-Shīʿī rift led to the association

---

103 "Supreme Leader's Full Speech in International Congress"; "Tashayyuʿ-i Inglīsī beh jāy-i faḥāshī bā manṭiq az Shīʿa difāʿ conand," http://shabestan.ir/detail/News/442258; "Takfīrīhā nemād-i ʿaynī-i inḥirāf-i sufyānī hastand," 23 Khordād 1393/June 13, 2014, http://www.farsnews.com/printable.php?nn=13930323000380.

104 "Ayatollah Makārem Shīrāzī: ʿulamāʾ-i Islām bā ṣedā-i boland az takfīr barāʾat jūyand."

105 "Takfiris Misrepresent Islam as Violent Religion: Ayatollah Subḥānī," November 25, 2014, http://theiranproject.com/blog/2014/11/25/takfiris-misrepresent-islam-as-violent-religion-ayatollah-sobhani/; "al-Mīthāq al-ʿilmī: al-muʾtamar al-ʿālamī lil-tiyārāt al-mutashaddida wal-takfīriyya min wujhat naẓar-i ʿulamāʾ al-Islām"; "Ahdāf-i istiʿmār az ʾījād firqa-i Vahhābiyat va-nīz rābiṭa beyn Vahhābiyat va-Yahūd"; Samāwī, *al-ʿAṣr al-wahhābī: qirāʾāt fī adab al-taṭṭaruf*, 12; "Takfiris are Trying to Promote Islamophobia: Ayatollah Hussaini Boshehri," November 26, 2014, http://en.shabestan.ir/search/Hussaini%20Boshehri.

106 "Jināyat-i sufyānī besiyār mushābih ʿaqāʾid Vahhābiyat ast," 11 Dey 1392/January 1, 2014, https://www.mehrnews.com/news/2205919/.

of ISIS with the Sufyānī. A debate on this started and spread in the Iranian social media following the speedy conquest of Mosul in June 2014 and the subsequent atrocities that ISIS carried out in the region. A few clerics, most notably Ayatollah ʿAlī Kurānī, who has written a very popular book on the appearance of the Mahdī,[107] and Ayatollah Seyyed Muḥammad ʿAlī Musāvī Jazāyīrī, the Supreme Leader's representative in the Khuzistān province, were initially carried away on this tide. Jazāyīrī even agreed that the presence of ISIS and the followers of the Umayyads in Iraq as well as the sedition in both countries are signs of the appearance of the Mahdī and rise of the Sufyānī.[108] The scale and intensity of the online debate prompted official organizations and media to provide an authoritative response, demonstrating the anxiety of the clerical establishment about the uncontrolled messianic expectations of ordinary believers. Such expectations pose numerous threats: they encourage believers to carry out irresponsible actions that may harm the Shīʿa in general; they generate a potential crisis of belief should they fail to materialize; and they challenge the authority of the clergy as the sole representatives of the Hidden Imām.[109]

Leading scholars, most notably Grand Ayatollah ʿAlī Sistānī, the foremost Shīʿī legal authority in Najaf and probably in the entire Shīʿī world, flatly rejected any link between the rise of ISIS and the coming of the Sufyānī. Kurānī, presumably due to pressure from his peers, reversed his previous position and joined the effort to calm the messianic talk by pointing to the textual sources on the matter.[110] Official clerical spokesmen sought to prove that the rise and actions of ISIS do not conform to the 119 detailed and clearly defined indicators enumerated by the Shīʿī Imāms to denote the coming of the Mahdī and the Sufyānī. For instance, the real Sufyānī would boast of his Umayyad ancestry, while ISIS leader Abū Bakr al-Baghdādī falsely claims to be a descendant of the

---

107 ʿAlī al-Kurānī, *ʿAṣr al-ẓuhūr* (Qom: muʾassasat al-maʿārif al-Islāmiyya, 2006).

108 "Ẓuhūr-i 'Dāʿesh' neshāneh-i nazdīk shodan-i ẓuhūr-i ḥażrat-i Mahdī ast," n.d., http://www.alvadossadegh.com/fa/article/mahdaviat/mahdavi-6/82559; "Nemāyandeh-i valī-i faqīh dar Khūzistān: Dāʿesh az neshānehhā-i khurūj-i sufyānī ast," 24 Khordād 1393/June 14, 2014, https://www.mashreghnews.ir/news/317921.

109 For explicit concern over the spread of the debate, see "Āyā Dāʿesh hemān sufyānī ast?," 26 Dey 1393/January 15, 2015, https://www.farsnews.com/news/13931024001094/ایا-داعش-همان-سفیانی-است; "Ḥamla-i Dāʿesh neshāneh-i ẓuhūr ast?," 22 Khordād 1393/June 12, 2014, https://article.tebyan.net/279563/حمله-داعش-نشانه-ظهور-است-; "Pīsh qarāvolān-i sufyānī, yā ʿamālahā-i ṣalīb va-ṣahyūn."

110 "Ayatollah Sistānī: ẓuhūr-i `Dāʿesh' hīch rabṭī beh sufyānī nadārad," 29 Mordād 1393/August 20, 2014, http://iusnews.ir/fa/news-details/139581; "Dāʿesh irtibāṭi beh qiyām-i 'Sufyānī' nadārad/taṭbīq-i rivāyat-i ẓuhūr-i Imām-i Zamān (ʿaj) bā zamān-i muʿāṣir khilāf sharʿ ast," 12 Mordād 1393/August 3, 2014, http://fa.abna24.com/cultural/archive/2014/08/03/628736/story.html.

Prophet; the Sufyānī is supposed to raise a red flag (the Umayyad color), while ISIS raises black flags; the Sufyānī would conquer the entire Shām (Greater Syria) in six months and proceed directly to Mecca, while ISIS failed to do so and was about to lose its territorial gains; the people of Syria are supposed to follow the real Sufyānī, while at present they support their government and oppose ISIS; and, most importantly, the Sufyānī's emergence should coincide with rather than precede the appearance of the Mahdī.[111] The emphasis on these text-based arguments to refute messianic expectations was intended not only to calm these hopes but also to highlight the centrality of the clergy as the sole interpreters of religious truth. Genuine belief in the elaborate Shīʿī apocalyptic scheme should not be discounted as well.

Various official spokesmen highlighted the adoption of Umayyad symbols and titles by jihādī-Salafī organizations as an indication of their identification with the Sufyānī. They contended that ISIS activists publicly addressed the Shīʿī ḥadīth regarding the signs foretelling the coming of the Mahdī and the Sufyānī (thereby implicitly acknowledging their validity) and boasted that their path is the "Umayyad path."[112] Others denied that ISIS was the Sufyānī but pointed to glaring similarities between the two, such as hatred of the Shīʿa and brutality.[113] Ḥusaynī Shāhrūdī proposed a new interpretation for the concept of the Sufyānī and its manifestation by ISIS. Accordingly, the advent of the Sufyānī at the end of time does not refer to an actual person but to the emergence of a deviationist ideology. ISIS, with its deviations and, in particular, its aspiration to cause sedition in the service of the "Arrogance" (i.e., the United

111 "Rābiṭa-i Dāʿesh bā rivāyat-i sufyānī, dajjāl va-parchamhā-i siyāh," 29 Mordād 1396/August 20, 2017, http://www.hawzah.net/fa/Discussion/View/44809/رابطه-داعش-با-روایات-سفیانی-دجال-و-پرچم-های-سیاه; "Ḥamla-i daʿesh neshāneh-i ẓuhūr ast?"; "Āyā Dāʿesh hemān sufyānī ast?," 26 Dey 1393/January 16, 2015, http://www.farsnews.com/newstext.php?nn=13931024001094.

112 "Nemāyandeh-i valī-i faqīh dar Khūzistān: Dāʿesh az neshānehhā-i khurūj sufyānī ast"; "Dāʿesh parchamdārān-i siyāh pūsh ākhar al-zamān?"; "Badl sāzī-i Dāʿesh bā sufyānī va-ghiflat az dushman-i aṣlī," 25 Khordād 1393/June 15, 2014, https://www.tasnimnews.com/fa/news/1393/03/25/401992; "Pīsh qarāvolān-i sufyānī, yā ʿamālahā-i ṣalīb va-ṣahyūn," who refer to the names "Amīr al-muʾminīn Yazīd" and "Sufyānī" given to Jabhat al-Nuṣra's units in Syria; "Āyā Dāʿesh hemān sufyānī ast?," 9 Khordād 1394/May 30, 2015, https://mouood.org/component/k2/item/29783.

113 "Shabāhat va-tafāvothā-i Dāʿesh va-sufyānī bar asās rivāyat-i ākhar al-zamānī," 14 Mehr 1393/October 6, 2014, https://www.tasnimnews.com/fa/news/1393/07/14/520096/شباهت-ها-و-تفاوت-های-داعش-و-سفیانی-بر-اساس-روایات-اخرالزمانی; "Pīsh qarāvolān-i sufyānī, yā ʿamālahā-i ṣalīb va-ṣahyūn"; "Rābiṭa beyne shūresh-i sufyānī va-ḥavādith-i Sūriya," 20 Mehr 1393/October 12, 2014, https://www.mashreghnews.ir/news/353477/شباهت-ها-و-تفاوت-های-داعش-و-سفیانی.

States) and Zionism, is therefore a "tangible manifestation" of the Sufyānī.[114] With ISIS' military defeat in Iraq, the debate subsided completely.

9 The Jihādī-Salafists, the Jews, and the West

Once again, the harm caused by the jihādī-Salafists serves the Shīʿī rhetorical device of linking them with the two major external enemies of Islam: the West and the Zionists. Khamenei accused the Takfīrīs of reaching a "compromise with the Zionists so that they would fight Muslims" rather than Israel.[115] However, while Khamenei blamed world arrogance for creating ISIS, quite a few clerics and some of the Iranian media have blamed Israel for creating ISIS, and they speak of ISIS as a "Zionist project." Others have noted "the Zionist-American essence," of these groups, which are trying, "in line with the general Zionist approach," to weaken Iranian efforts to promote unity among Muslims. The brutality practiced by ISIS against Muslim – which has no basis in the traditions of Islam, Christianity, or any other religion – is, they have claimed, rooted in the Jewish Torah and Talmud. ISIS is implementing ideas that the Zionists dictated but have not yet been able to carry out, they concluded.[116]

The *Mashreq* news agency, affiliated with the Revolutionary Guards, endorsed a story, citing the pro-Nazi *Veterans Today* website, that ISIS leader and self-proclaimed caliph, Abū Bakr al-Baghdādī, had been an Israeli Mossad officer named Simon Elliot.[117] With these ideas in mind, a report by the *Iranian Students News Agency*, employing a play of words in Arabic, interpreted the

114 "Takfīrīhā nemād-i ʿaynī-i inḥirāf-i sufyānī hastand"; "Badl sāzī-i Dāʿesh bā sufyānī va-ghiflat az dushman-i aṣlī."

115 "Supreme Leader's Full Speech in International Congress."

116 Rasoul Souri and Jahan Heidari, "Iran and the Threat of Salafism," August 31, 2016, http://www.iranreview.org/content/Documents/Iran-and-the-Threat-of-Salafism.htm; "Dāʿesh parchamdārān-i siyāh pūsh ākhar al-zamān?," 18 Shahrīvar 1393/September 9, 2014, https://article.tebyan.net/284586; "Hasht neshāneh az khidmat-i takfīrihā beh jarayān-i istikbār"; "Ahdāf-i prōzhe-i ṣahyūnīstī-i Dāʿesh cheh būd? + film va-mustanadāt," 30 Ābān 1396/November 21, 2017, https://www.yjc.ir/fa/news/6329019; "Tashkīl-i Dāʿesh zayr sāyeh ḥimāyat ʿibrī, ʿarabī va-gharbī," http://www.empireoflies.ir/تشکیل-داعش-حمایت-عبری-عربی/; "Khoshūnat-i Dāʿesh va-rīshehhā-i ān dar kitāb-i muqaddas-i Yahūd," http://erfaneha.parsiblog.com/Posts/389/خشونت+داعش+و+ریشه+هاي+آن+در+کتاب+مقدس+یهود/.

117 "Veterans Today: Rahbar-i Dāʿesh Yahūdī va-jāsūs mossad ast," 16 Mordād 1393/August 7, 2014, https://www.mashreghnews.ir/news/333465/رهبر-داعش-یهودی-و-جاسوس-موساد-است. The semi-official *Iranian Students News Agency* published the same story at https://www.isna.ir/news/93051607502/.

ISIS Arabic acronym to mean "the Israeli State of Iraq and Sham" (*Dowlat-i Isrā'īlī Irāq va-Shām*). Another conspiratorial mind attributed the name ISIS to the ancient deity Isis, which, it claimed, is shared by the ancient Pharaonic culture and the Jewish Kabbalistic "ancient spirit of Zionism." ISIS which, they claimed, was established by neo-conservative circles in Washington in order to further divide the region, was thus designed to serve as the guardian of Israel.[118]

This theme of the Takfīrīs as products of Western plots enjoyed a prominent place in Khamenei's discourse. On various occasions he stated that although the "Takfīrī orientation is not new and although it has a historical background … these criminal organizations like al-Qaeda and ISIS … were manufactured and created" by the imperialist enemies, America, Britain, and the Zionist regime, in order to "pit nations against one another." The Takfīrī orientation is Islamic in appearance, he added, but, in practice, these groups and the governments which protect them (meaning the Saudis) are at the service of "Arrogance" (i.e., the United States), the European imperialists, and the Zionists.[119] Other officials and media followed suit, asserting that the Takfīrī groups were the "handiwork of the intelligence services of Britain, the Zionist regime and the United States."[120]

The West's main goals in establishing the Takfīrī groups were to "ruin the real image of Islam," weaken the Islamic nation, and fight the "Islamic awakening." ISIS also served to divert world attention from the crimes that "global arrogance" and the Zionists were perpetrating against the Muslims.[121] This

118 "Ayatollah Sistānī: ẓuhūr-i `Dā'esh' hīch rabṭī beh sufyānī nadārad," "I'tirāf-i Abū Bakr al-Baghdādī," http://www.atabatkh.com/646/اعتراف-ابوبكر-البغدادي-به-شكست-داعش/; "Dā'esh negahbān-i Isrā'īl; Isrā'īl Dā'eshī digār," 15 Mordād 1393/August 6, 2014, http://www.shia-news.com/fa/news/76416.

119 "Supreme Leader's Full Speech in International Congress"; "The Leader's Remarks in a Meeting with a Group of Officials, Ambassadors of Muslim Countries," July 18, 2015, http://www.leader.ir/langs/en/index.php?p=bayanat&id=13451; "Hasht neshāneh az khidmat-i takfīrihā beh jarayān-i istikbār"; "Bayānāt dar marāsim-i bīst-o-panjomīn-i sālgard-i riḥlat-i Imām-i Khomeini (rh)," 14 Khordād 1393/June 4, 2014, http://farsi.khamenei.ir/newspart-index?id=26615&nt=2&year=1393&tid=989#49962.

120 "Takfiris Handiwork of US, UK, Israel," November 27, 2014, http://www.islamicinvitationturkey.com/2014/11/27/takfiris-handiwork-of-us-uk-israel/; Ayatollah Nouri Hamedani cited in *Mehr*, January 19, 2014 in Savyon, Mansharof, Kharrazi, and Lahat, "Iran Calls For Violent Shi'ite Reaction Against Saudi Arabia."

121 "Nigāhī beh ab'ād-i mukhtalif-i kongreh-i jahānī-i jarayānhā-i ifrāṭī va-takfīrī az dīdār-i 'ulamā'-i Islām"; Muṣṭafā Musliḥzādeh, "Dā'esh Shī'a rā dushman-i aṣlī-i khōd mīdānad," 6 Mehr 1393/September 29, 2014, http://www.farsnews.com/newstext.php?nn=13930705001759; "Iranian Judiciary Chief: West Seeking to Promote Shi'itophobia to Stir Differences among Muslims," November 27, 2014, http://www.14masoomeen.org/News-Detail-mod-Iranian-Judiciary-Chief-West-Seeking-to-Promote-Shi'itophobia-to

enabled Khamenei to posit Shīʿī Iran as the positive opposite pole to ISIS in the struggle for Islam's soul and future, and therefore as the main target of western machinations.

Having supposedly established the close ties of the Wahhābīs and Takfīrīs with the United States, Khamenei addressed them as "American Islam" or "American Sunnīsm" in order to further denigrate them.[122] Originally, the term American Islam referred to a compromising Islam practiced by establishment Sunnī clerics who collaborated with the semi-secular Middle Eastern rulers. But Khamenei incorporated into this category an opposite type of Islam, namely, jihādī-Salafīsm, and contrasted it with the "pure Muḥammadan Islam" represented by revolutionary Shīʿīsm. Accordingly, Khamenei's office contrasted "principlist (*uṣūl gerā*), moderate, and rational Islam" (that is Shīʿī Islam) with "the Islam of barbarity and ignorance," in other words, a combination of "secular Westernized Islam" together with "violent Takfīrī" Islam.[123] The term "American" in this context thus seems to resemble the attributes "Jew" or "Jewish" used as a criterion for evil in early Islamic contexts.

The alleged jihādī-Salafī-Western-Zionist triangle revealed differences regarding who was considered the greatest threat to Islam. The official *Islamquest* website conceded that while the Jews had been Islam's worst enemy in the early Islamic period, the Wahhābīs had now overtaken them.[124] Makārem Shīrāzī went further to depict the Takfīrīs as the greatest problem

-Stir-Differences-among-Muslims-id.html; "ʿIllat-i ḥamla-i Dāʿesh beh Iraq dar ʾīn borhahā-i zamānī chīst?," 26 Khordād 26, 1393/June 13, 2014, http://adyannews.com/4573; "Hasht neshāneh az khidmat-i takfīrihā beh jarayān-i istikbār."

122 See Khamenei's twitter of May 9, 2014, "Takfiri & #AlQaeda Movement that Tolerates Enemies of Islam but Acts Brutally Against Shia & Sunni Muslims is an American Islam 2/3/12," *Khamenei.ir @khamenei_ir*. See also "Imām-i Jumʿa-i Tabrīz: tafrīqa-i hadaf-i aṣlī-i tashayyuʿ-i Inglīsī va-tasannon-i Amrīkāʾī," 3 Dey 1395/December 23, 2016, ttps://www.mehrnews.com/news/3857704/; "Taʾammolī dar mushtarakāt-i `tashayyuʿ-i Inglīsī va-tasannon-i Amrīkāʾī'," 14 Mordād 1395/August 4, 2016, https://www.fardanews.com/fa/news/552052.

123 See detailed contrast published by Khamenei's office, "Tafāvothā-i Islām nāb Muḥammadī va-Islām Amrīkāʾī," 26 Abān 1393/November 17, 2014, http://farsi.khamenei.ir/print-content?id=28198; "Khurūjī neshest-i mushtarak-i dawlat va-majlis bāyad ḥall mushkilāt-i mardom bāshad," 19 Mehr 1393/October 11, 2014, http://www.hawzah.net/fa/News/View/98018.

124 "Buzurgtarīn-i dushman-i idīʾūlūzhīk-i Islām, Amrīkā ast, yā Inglīs, yā vahhābiyān va-salafiyān?," 29 Ordībehesht 1393/May 19, 2014, http://www.islamquest.net/fa/archive/question/fa29589. See a similar statement by Ḥujjat al-Islām Javād Fāżil Lankarānī in "Vahhābiyat mūriyāneh'i ast keh beh jān-i Islām oftādeh va-samī ast barāye az bīn bordan-i Shīʿa va-ahl Sunnat," 5 Shahrīvar 1386/August 27, 2007, https://www.isna.ir/news/8606-02487.

facing not only the Muslims but the world at large.[125] Ayatollah Muḥammad Muḥammadī-Golpāygānī, the director of Khamenei's office, agreed with this diagnosis and associated the Takfīrī threat with their rulings which "proclaim Shīʿīs to be inferior to the Jews and Christians" and their efforts to incite Muslim infighting.[126] The concluding statement of the 2014 Conference, on the other hand, regarded the Takfīrīs and the "external enemies" as equally dangerous to Islam.[127] Khamenei himself placed the Takfīrīs within a broader context of the threats confronting the Muslim world due to their divisive doctrine and harmful actions.[128] Yet, based on his assessment of the long-term challenge to the raison d'etre of the Islamic Republic and to Islam in general, he ordered the threats differently. Khamenei argued that although the Takfīrī, Wahhābī, and Salafi groups fight Iran and the Shīʿa and have perpetrated crimes, they are not the "principal enemy" (*dushman-i aṣlī*). The principal enemy is instead those who conceived, sustained, and incite them and who created the rift between these "ignorant and uninformed groups and the oppressed Iranian nation," namely, the West and the Americans.[129] The logic behind Khamenei's statements was clear. Wahhābīs and jihādī-Salafīsts shed Shīʿī blood, but they cannot defeat the Shīʿa or Iran nor can their ideology appeal to Iranian youth. Concurrently, while he believed in the ultimate defeat of the West, he was much more concerned with the appeal of Western culture to Iranian youth and its threat to the foundations of the Iranian political and ideological system.

10 The Takfīrīs as Non-Muslims

The subordination of the Wahhābīs and jihādī-Salafīsts to the West served to justify a more serious judgement: their exclusion from Islam altogether. Makārem Shīrāzī, for example, contrasted true Islam, which is based on "prayers and submission to God, the compassionate and merciful," with the

125 "Ayatollah Makārem Shīrāzī: Takfīrīhā buzurgtarīn-i tahdīd barāye jahān-i Islām hastand," 15 Shahrīvar 1395/September 5, 2015, https://www.mehrnews.com/news/3770245; "ʿUlama' bā ṭard-i takfīrihā, abrūyī Islām rā ḥafẓ konand/ ṣulḥ va-arāmesh rā beh Muslimīn bargardanīm," 28 Mehr 1395/October 19, 2016, http://hawzahnews.com/detail/News/396493.

126 *Fars* (Iran), January 30, 2014, cited in Savyon, Mansharof, Kharrazi, and Lahat, "Iran Calls for Violent Shiʿite Reaction Against Saudi Arabia."

127 "Al-Mīthāq al-ʿilmī: al-muʾtamar al-ʿālamī lil-tiyārāt al-mutashaddida wal-takfīriyya min wujhat naẓar-i ʿulamāʾ al-Islām."

128 "Hoshdār-i rahbar-i muʿaẓẓam-i inqilāb-i Islāmī nisbat beh khaṭar-i buzurg-i jarayānhā-i takfīrī," 29 Dey 1392/January 19, 2014, https://www.isna.ir/news/92102916491.

129 "Bayānāt dar marāsim-i bīst-o-panjomīn-i sālgard-i riḥlat-I Imām-i Khomeini (rh)."

Takfīrī religion, which is based on the shedding of blood, destruction, and intimidation. This religion, he proclaimed, "is not Islam."[130] During a conference of Sunnī and Shīʿī clerics against extremism on March 24, 2016, he stated that the Takfīrīs were "neither Sunnīs nor Shīʿīs" but merely a political trend with no connection to the two major schools of Islam. Makārem Shīrāzī, who spoke of the need to distinguish between the Wahhābīs and true Sunnīs, described the former as the "greatest calamity of the world" who endangered the Muslims not only physically but also spiritually as they targeted the very foundation of Islam. All the clerics of Islam, he stated elsewhere, should stand together and affirm that the Wahhābīs are not Muslims and have nothing to do with Islam.[131]

Turning to another rhetorical device of exclusion, Khamenei adopted the trope of "neo-jāhiliyya," coined by the Sunnī Salafī thinkers Abū-l-Aʿlā Mawdūdī of India and Sayyid Quṭb of Egypt, and applied it to ISIS. Originally, "neo-jāhiliyya" referred to Muslim societies that had reverted to the pre-Islamic reality as, having adopted Western ideas and way of life, they no longer abided by Islamic law.[132] Khamenei highlighted the original meaning of the word *jāhiliyya* (barbarity), as he spoke of the prevalence of "illogical and unrestrained wanton and cruelty" and "unrestricted killings" caused by the Takfīrī organizations. He saw present-day *jāhiliyya* as worse than its earlier version, not just because of the more lethal modern weaponry but, primarily, because the modern jihādī-Salafīsts lack the minimal moral restraints that even the "Meccan polytheists" had respected during the Prophet's lifetime: for example, the "Meccan polytheists" did not fight during holy months, whereas their modern successors violate even such basic principles.[133]

---

130 "Sayyid Ḥasan Naṣrallah: dīn-i takfīrihā Islām nīst," 15 Dey 1391/January 4, 2013, https://shafaqna.com/persian/services/other-news/item/31824; "Nigāhī beh abʿād-i mukhtalif-i kongreh-i jahānī-i jarayānhā-i ifrāṭī va-takfīrī az dīdār-i ʿulamāʾ-i Islām"; "Ayatollah Makārem Shīrāzī: Takfīrihā buzurgtarīn-i tahdīd barāye jahān-i Islām hastand."

131 "Bāyad ḥisāb Vahhābiyat az ahl-i Sunnat jedā shavad," 25 Esfand 1394/March 15, 2016 https://www.hawzahnews.com/news/374778/باید-حساب-وهابیت-از-اهل-سنت-جدا-شود-حوزه-در-جبهه-فکری-و-فرهنگی; "Naẓar-i ʿulamāʾ va-marājiʿ-i ʿuẓām bar vaḥdat miyān-i Shīʿa va-Sunnī," 14 Dey 1393/January 4, 2015, http://www.dana.ir/export/print/206483?module=news; "Al-Āliyāt al-munāsiba fī muwājahat al-tiyārāt al-takfīriyya, arāʾ al-marjaʿ Makārem Shīrāzī"; "ʿUlamaʾ bā ṭard-i takfīrīhā, abrūyī Islām rā ḥafẓ konand/ ṣulḥ va-arāmesh rā beh Muslimīn bargardanīm."

132 Asyraf Haj. A.B. Rahman and Nooraihan ʿAli, "The Influence of Al-Mawdudi and the Jamaʿat Al Islami Movement on Sayyid Qutb Writings," *World Journal of Islamic History and Civilization* 2, no. 4 (2012): 232–236. For Quṭb's concept, see Sayed Khatab, *The Political Thought of Sayyid Qutb: The Theory of Jahiliyya* (London: Routledge, 2006). Khamenei was the one who translated Quṭb's book into Persian.

133 "Hoshyārāneh bāyad bā jāhiliyat-i modern muqābala kard," 26 Ordībehesht 1394/May 16, 2015, http://farsi.khamenei.ir/video-content?id=29735; "Raqṣ-i shamshīr-i jāhiliyat-i

Both the equation of the jihādī-Salafists with the pre-Islamic pagan Arabs and the contention that their conduct rendered them un-Islamic were tantamount to declaring them apostates. The daily *Jumhūrī-i Islāmī*, which is close to the religious seminaries of Qom, urged jurisprudents from the various Islamic schools to issue a joint fatwā that would declare the Takfīrī trend officially heretical and explain in detail the fate of "those who have turned to the weapon of takfīr."[134] However, the leading Shīʿī scholars refrained from issuing rulings that explicitly declared the jihādī-Salafists apostates. Historically, Shīʿī clerics had never declared Sunnīs as apostates but, instead, had viewed the Sunnīs as misguided Muslims who should be drawn into the Shīʿī fold through propagation of Shīʿī literature. They were aware that it would be politically unwise for a minority to raise the ire of the majority in such a confrontationist way. They probably also feared that declaring apostasy based on conduct alone might be used as a weapon against the Shīʿīs themselves, as Sunnī Salafists condemned various Shīʿī practices. Since the jihādī-Salafists did not reject the Qurʾān or the principle tenets of Islamic belief, contemporary Sunnī clerics, first and foremost al-Azhar in Egypt, refused to declare them apostates.[135] The Shīʿī clerics acted similarly, most likely fearing that a ruling of apostasy would thwart their efforts to forge an alliance with mainstream Sunnīs against the jihādī-Salafists and leave them alone in the confrontation. Instead, they chose to label the jihādī-Salafists as non-Muslims, that is, those who had stood in the first place completely outside the realm of Islam, an approach that enabled leading clerics to issue rulings declaring a jihād against the jihādī-Salafists. This is similar to the Iranian decision to depict Saddam Ḥusayn as an idolatrous tyrant (*ṭāghūt*) during the Iran–Iraq war and thus overcome the Sharīʿa ban on waging jihād against fellow Muslims.[136]

---

modern dar konār jāhiliyat-i qabīlagī rā hajū konīd," 21 Khordād 1396/June 11, 2017, https://www.tasnimnews.com/fa/news/1396/03/21/1432910/رقص-شمشیر-جاهلیت-مدرن-در-کنار-جاهلیت-قبیلگی-را-هجو-کنید. See also Shahbaz, "The Heretical Cult of Wahhabi Takfīrī Salafis." For more references to this equation and an equation with the pre-Islamic tribes, see "Dāʿesh va-jarayān-i takfīrī bar athr-i taʿrīf-i ifrāṭī-i jāhiliyat beh vujūd āmad," Azar 28, 1393/December 19, 2014, https://www.tasnimnews.com/fa/news/1393/09/28/593677.

134 *Jumhūri-i Islāmī*, January 25, 2014, cited in Savyon, Mansharof, Kharrazi, and Lahat, "Iran Calls For Violent Shiʿite Reaction Against Saudi Arabia."

135 See "Egypt's Al-Azhar Stops Short of Declaring ISIS Apostates," December 13, 2014, https://eng-archive.aawsat.com/theaawsat/news-middle-east/egypts-al-azhar-stops-short-of-declaring-isis-apostates; "Why Does Egypt's Largest Muslim Beacon, Al-Azhar, Refuse to Declare IS 'Apostate'?" April 14, 2017, http://www.egyptindependent.com/why-does-egypt-s-largest-muslim-beacon-al-azhar-refuse-declare-apostate/.

136 Saskia Gieling, *Religion and War in Revolutionary Iran* (London: I.B. Tauris, 1999), 44, 76.

Ayatollah Kāẓim Hā'irī was the first to issue such a fatwā on November 18, 2013, which described the struggle of the Lebanese Ḥizballah against the Sunnī rebels in Syria as a confrontation against disbelief and a defense of Islam or, in other words, a religious duty.[137] In June 2014, following Mosul's capture by ISIS, Grand Ayatollah Sistānī issued a fatwā calling on all able-bodied men to enlist and join the struggle against the ISIS "terrorists" in defense of Iraqi territory, the nation, and religious sanctities. His fatwā stated that, according to the law of jihād, whoever is killed in the fight will be regarded as a martyr (*shahīd*). Muqtaḍā Ṣadr, whose religious standing was much lower than Sistānī's, followed suit and issued his own fatwā against ISIS a few months later.[138]

While Khamenei did not issue a formal ruling declaring a jihād against jihādī-Salafīsts, he continued to call for an all-out struggle and combat against them. He labeled ISIS a "cancerous tumor" created by the enemies – a term he also employed toward Israel, signifying not only the supposed links between these two enemies of the Shīʿa but also, as such tumors must be eradicated, their appropriate end.[139] The circle was thus closed. A discourse that had been motivated largely by the fear and anger of being excluded and branded as apostates ended in the declaration of the Wahhābī-Salafi adversary as an un-Islamic enemy that must be fought and eliminated.

11 Conclusion

Shīʿī polemics against Wahhābism and jihādī-Salafīsm or the Takfīrī orientation in Shīʿī parlance reflect a duality of anxiety and fear alongside growing self-confidence and assertiveness. The anxiety stems not only from Wahhābī and jihādī-Salafī violence against Shīʿīs in the past and present but also from

137 "Fatvā-i Ayatollah Kāẓim Hā'irī barāye iʿẓām beh Sūriye," http://www.teribon.ir/archives/246396/.

138 "Ayatollah Sistānī fatvā-i jihād ṣādir kard," 23 Khordād 1393/June 13, 2014, https://hawzah.net/fa/News/View/97209; "Fatvā-i jihād Muqtaḍā Ṣadr ʿalayh-i Dāʿesh," http://www.trt.net.tr/persian/mntqh/2014/12/11/ftwy-jhd-mqtdy-sdr-lyh-d-sh-145270.

139 "Bringing U.S. to Its Knees, in the Region, is a Miracle of the Islamic Revolution," November 22, 2017, http://english.khamenei.ir/news/5289/Bringing-U-S-to-its-knees-in-the-region-is-a-miracle-of-the Revolution. For other expressions of this term by Shīʿī spokesmen, see Ayatollah Muḥammad Ḥasan Akhtarī, *IRNA*, February 2, 2014, cited in Savyon, Mansharof, Kharrazi, and Lahat, "Iran Calls For Violent Shiʿite Reaction Against Saudi Arabia"; "Ayatollah Qabalān: Takfīr ghīdeh-i sarṭānī-i minṭaqa," 24 Dey 1394/January 14, 2016, http://www.shia-news.com/fa/news/109817; "Muʿāvin-i dabīr-i kull ḥizballah Lubnān: terōrism-i takfīrī ghīdeh-i sarṭānī ast keh bāyad rīsheh kon shavad," 7 Farvardīn 1395/March 26, 2016, http://www.jamnews.com/detail/News/648891.

its potential impact on mainstream Sunnī Islam, which might lead to the total exclusion of the Shīʿa from Islam and its branding as a form of apostasy. At the same time, Shīʿī self-confidence emanates from a deep-seated belief in the justness of its cause and ultimate salvation at the end of time, like all other religious groups, but also from regional developments that bolstered the Shīʿī and Iranian strategic positions in Iraq, Lebanon, Syria, and Yemen. Another possible cause for this duality is the need to appeal to both Shīʿī believers, reassuring them about their beliefs when facing hardships and suffering, and mainstream Sunnīs, with the aim of forging a common cause with them by presenting the two radical violent groups as enemies of all Muslims and not just the Shīʿa.

The duality is evident in a major shift in the Shīʿī polemics against their rivals. Formerly, these writings were apologetic, seeking to prove the Shīʿa's genuine Islamic credentials and advocating pluralism in the interpretation of the scriptures. They sought to prove that Wahhābī and jihādī-Salafī inclination to declare their rivals, particularly the Shīʿa, as apostates contradicted true Islam. While apologetic writings have not disappeared, the new self-confidence transforms the discourse into open attacks on Wahhābī and jihādī-Salafī fundamental doctrines and practices. The new polemics portray Wahhābism and jihādī-Salafīsm as a crude, duplicitous, and intellectually inferior interpretation of Islam. Whatever success they have achieved is attributed to foreign support, material remunerations to unsophisticated audiences, and their resort to violence. As such, the two movements are portrayed as the negative mirror image of Shīʿīsm, which is represented as rationalist, intellectually sophisticated, and prudent. Whereas Wahhābī thought and practices lead to stagnation, Shīʿīsm maintains the right balance between adherence to the correct principles of Islam and the adaptation of various legal practices to modern needs and circumstances thanks to the use of *ijtihād*.

The Wahhābīs and jihādī-Salafīsts are charged of undermining Islamic unity by regarding the vast majority of Muslims, both Shīʿīs and Sunnīs, as apostates for failing to follow their own deformed version of Islam. This divisiveness is particularly harmful in modern times when foreign forces threaten Islam from the outside. By contrast, the Shīʿīs portray themselves as the true champions of Islamic unity and the vanguard of the struggle against these external threats. They claim that the pervasive and brutal violence perpetrated by the Wahhābīs and jihādī-Salafīsts contradicts and misrepresent the true essence and image of Islam, transforming it from a kind and peaceful religion to a violent and inhumane one.

A noteworthy rhetorical feature in Shīʿī writings is the frequent use of modernist terms such as reactionary (*bargesht gerāʾī*) and fundamentalist (*qashrī*) to describe the Wahhābīs. The adoption of these terms, which are borrowed, consciously or not, from the West, reflects the modernity of the new polemical discourse, which endorses the view, implied here by way of contrast, that being dynamic and progressive are the symbols of Shīʿī virtue.

Perhaps a more powerful rhetorical device is the association of the Wahhābīs and jihādī-Salafsts with other enemies of Islam, namely, the West and the Jews/Zionists, and their portrayal as the "handiwork" and tools of these external enemies. This connection vilifies the "other" as a traitor to Islam and exonerates the Shīʿīs from similar counter-charges raised by the jihādī-Salafīsts. Thus, the Wahhābīs and Saudis, who opened the region's gates to the imperialist British, American, and Zionist intrusion, replace or overshadow the Shīʿī Vizier Ibn al-ʿAlqami, who, according to the Salafists, and opened the gates of Baghdad to the invading Mongols in 1258. The new discourse thus portrays the Shīʿīs not as the much-maligned traitors of the past but as standing at the forefront of the struggle against the external enemies of Islam. These charges underline the fallacy or tragedy of the Sunnī-Shīʿī rift and open the door to cooperation with mainstream Sunnīs against this threat to Islam. The portrayal of the Wahhābīs and jihādī-Salafīsts as the tools of the West not only denigrates them by denying their authenticity, but it downplays their force and the long-term threat they pose to Islam compared with the more formidable Western threat. From a purely ideological point of view, the jihādī-Salafī actions against the lives of Shīʿī believers are less harmful than the negative evil impact of the West to their souls. A more practical approach regards the jihādī-Salafī threat as more manageable in the long run, since it does not endanger Shīʿī communities, particularly the Islamic Republic, from within and can be defeated on the battlefield, as was the case in Syria and Iraq between 2016 and 2019. Conversely, the Western cultural impact may be much more difficult to contain and could challenge the Islamic Republic's political foundations.

Like all other Islamist writings, the Shīʿīs invoke images from the early Islamic past in order to describe present-day reality. In the present case, it is the equation of the Wahhābīs and jihādī-Salafīsts with the Khawārij of early Islamic history and, in a few cases, the pre-Islamic jāhilī Arab tribes. This approach reflects the perception of the past, especially the earliest formative period, as the "originating paradigm"[140] which shaped Islam and has determined Islamic history ever since as well as defining the inseparability between past and present, a common theme among modern fundamentalist movements in all religions. Equally important, this equation serves to present the Wahhābīs and jihādī-Salafīsts as un-Islamic or as apostates in practice if not in the full

140 Douglas Pratt, "Muslim–Jewish Relations: Some Islamic Paradigms," *Islam and Christian–Muslim Relations* 21, no. 1(2010):12.

legal sense of the word and thereby legitimizes an all-out war against them. Yet, while mobilizing tens of thousands of volunteers to fight the jihādī-Salafī organizations in Iraq and Syria, the clerical establishment took care to deny any eschatological meaning to this struggle and disassociate it from the coming of the awaited Mahdī and the derided Sufyānī. Invoking messianic themes in the context of the conflict with the West or the Jews presumably seemed less problematic as these referred to a more distant future. Conversely, the imminent victory over these enemies in the short run required the diminution of the messianic element lest it lead to a crisis of belief if failing to materialize. In other words, while completing a circle, from helplessness in the face of violence and the fear of being excluded to mobilizing troops and declaring their rivals as un-Islamic, the clerical establishment has been careful to preserve the othering of the Wahhābīs and jihādī-Salafīsts within the pragmatic theological and political realm and to avoid sliding into the dangerous messianic realm.

CHAPTER 5

Liberty and Its Boundaries vis-à-vis Dissent and Apostasy

On December 19, 2016 President Ḥasan Rouhani unveiled the Citizens' Rights Charter (*mashrūʿ-i ḥuqūq-i shahrvandī*), thereby fulfilling an important election campaign pledge. The Charter, which contains 120 articles, guaranteed inter alia "freedom of speech, protest, fair trials, and privacy." In the lively debate that ensued media critics outside Iran maintained that most of the rights promised in the Charter have been routinely violated in the Islamic Republic. Reformists inside the country complained that although Iran had proper laws, the problems lay in their implementation. Hardliners, on the other hand, ridiculed the measures as diverting public attention away from Iran's real problems, i.e., the economy.[1]

The debate reflected the continued importance of the question of liberty in modern Iranian political and cultural discourse, particularly the meaning and scope of liberty within a religious framework and the connection between liberty and democracy and the latter's compatibility or conflict with religion. The current discourse is rooted in the contradiction found in the Iranian Constitution between democratic concepts and the doctrine of *vilāyat-i faqīh*, which serves as the foundation of the Islamic Republic, and between various guarantees of civil liberties and their subordination to Islamic principles.[2] In the context of the present study, the debate also pertains to the boundary separating permitted or tolerated personal or collective conduct and activities within the Iranian religious and political community from those that lead to exclusion with all its consequences: in other words, the boundary between insiders and outsiders, or enemies, from the regime's point of view.

1 "Rohani Officially Launches Iranian Citizens' Rights Charter," December 19, 2016, http://www.rferl.org/a/iran-rohani-launches-citizens-rights-charter/28184867.html; Rohollah Faghihi, "Can Rouhani's Citizens' Rights Charter Be Enforced?," December 20, 2016, http://www.al-monitor.com/pulse/originals/2016/12/iran-rouhani-citizens-rights-charter-conservative-criticism.html; Reza Haghighatnejad, "What Good is Rouhani's Citizens' Rights Charter?," December 20, 2016, https://iranwire.com/en/features/4271; *Armān* editorial cited in *MidEast Mirror*, December 20, 2016; *Mardom Sālārī*, December 21, 2016.

2 For a detailed analysis of the contradictions in Iran's constitutional system, see Asghar Schirazi, *The Constitution of Iran: Politics and the State in the Islamic Republic* (London: I.B. Tauris, 1998), 1, 8–15, 19.

 | DOI:10.1163/9789004444683_007

Unlike the contemporary debate, the concept of liberty never acquired great importance in traditional Islamic thought, which subordinates human beings to God by the imposition of laws that guide their conduct in almost all aspects of life. In Islamic medieval tradition, therefore, the concept of *ḥurriyya* (freedom) did not refer to political and civil liberties but was instead used to denote the legal status that contrasted with slavery.[3] Wael Abu-ʿUksa showed that "preoccupation with the subject of freedom became a core issue in the construction of modern ideologies in Arab countries" after the mid-nineteenth century.[4] In Iran, freedom assumed its modern meaning associated with political and civil liberties only toward the end of the century, due probably to the intrusion of Western ideas and the growing sense of threat of Western imperial domination. Yet, even during the 1906–1911 Constitutional Revolution, Shaykh Muḥammad Ḥusayn Na'īnī, the leading clerical spokesman for constitutionalism, still used the term freedom in the traditional sense.[5]

The Shīʿī public debate on freedom has evolved at various levels of intensity ever since the Constitutional Revolution, as the modern meaning of freedom as related to politics and ideology gradually replaced the traditional concept. Liberty, independence, and the Islamic Republic were the three most popular slogans of the 1979 Revolution used to denote both the fight against the Shāh's oppressive regime and the struggle for freedom and independence from Western domination. The debate intensified during the 1990s following Khomeini's death and, in particular, after the 1997 election of the reformist Khātamī as president and his relaxation of the restrictions on ideological and political discussion.

Middle Eastern Islamists throughout the ideological spectrum have discussed the meaning and scope of liberty, but the Shīʿī case study has several unique traits. First is its emphasis on the freedom of choice given to Muslim believers, which is rooted in the rationalist Muʿtazilī theology that the Shīʿa adopted in the tenth century CE. Second, the Muʿtazilī influence is also discernable in the effort of all Shīʿī writers to ground their case on both rationalist

3 For a broad discussion of the meaning of freedom in traditional Islamic thought, see Frantz Rosenthal, *The Muslim Concept of Freedom* (Leiden: Brill, 1960), 29ff. For a discussion of freedom in pre-Revolution Iranian thought, see Farough Jahanbakhsh, *Islām, Democracy and Religious Modernism in Iran (1953–2000): From Bazargan to Soroush* (Leiden: Brill, 2001), 94–98.

4 Wael Abu-ʿUksa, *Freedom in the Arab World: Concepts and Ideologies in Arabic Thought in the Nineteenth Century* (Cambridge: Cambridge University Press, 2016), 2.

5 Ali Gheissari, "Constitutional Rights and the Development of Civil Law in Iran, 1907–1941," in *The Iranian Constitutional Revolution*, ed., Vanessa Martin and Houchang Chehabi (London: I.B. Tauris, 2010), 69–80.

arguments and texts, in accordance with the tradition of *ijtihād* that is practiced in Shīʿī seminaries. This logical construction of arguments stands in sharp contrast to the modern Sunnī-Salafi mode of argument, which relies almost exclusively on citations from the scriptures.[6] Third, while the mainstream Shīʿī writers are neither liberal nor tolerant, they are more reluctant to resort to declarations of apostasy (*takfīr*) against their opponents than the Sunnī Salafists. Finally, the Shīʿī discourse reflects, as always, a broad range of views, regardless of the forty-two years of authoritarian Islamic government.

The contemporary Shīʿī discourse recognizes the multiple meanings of the concept of liberty, which have been largely shaped by social and cultural circumstances including foreign influences. Hence, the Shīʿī debate, particularly since the 1990s, continues to grapple with Western liberal concepts of freedom in view of their influence on and appeal to large segments of Iranian society. The debate thus has two contradictory characteristics. The first is the presentation of a sharp, almost essentialist, dichotomy between East and West in an effort to demonstrate the superiority of Islamic concepts over Western ones like the UN Universal Declaration of Human Rights. The second is the attempt to show the similarity between the ideas of certain leading Western thinkers, such as John Locke and Immanuel Kant, and various Shīʿī concepts, in order to convince Iranians that they need not look outside their country for inspiration. Consequently, all current Iranian leaders pay lip service to the idea of freedom to prove that the Revolution and regime do not oppose it but merely give it a different and highly superior interpretation. Another Iranian characteristic is the status of Khomeini, who established the contours and limitations of the debate such that any deviation from his views is possible only as part of a much deeper opposition to the foundation of the Islamic regime.

All participants in the debate speak about liberty in glowing terms. They describe it as a natural human right, an important element of the human essence, since humanity can only be realized by being free. It is a necessary precondition for the prosperity of humanity, since decline is rooted in the denial of liberty. Liberty is, they assert, also one of the greatest Islamic values, since Islam itself is the religion of the free.[7] In his first year in power and in response

---

6 Quintan Wiktorowicz, "Anatomy of the Salafi Movement," *Studies in Conflict & Terrorism* 29, no. 3 (2006): 210–211.

7 Markaz Nūn, *al-Ḥurriyya fī fikr al-imām al-Khumaynī* (Beirut: Jamʿiyat al-maʿārif al-Islāmiyya al-thaqāfiyya, 2006), 142–144; "Barresī-i mafhūm-i āzādī dar andīsheh-i shahīd-i Beheshtī," 4 Tīr 1393/June 27, 2014, http://defapress.ir/fa/news/22136; Mahdī ʿAzīzān "Pluralism farhangī az naẓar-i ustād-i Muṭṭaharī," *Maʿārif* 25(1384/2005), 18–21, http://hawzah.net/Hawzah/Magazines/MagArt.aspx?LanguageID=1&id=54746&SearchText=ازادی; Ismāʿīl Salīmī, "Āzādī az dīdār-i ustād-i Muṭṭaharī," pt. 1, *Andisheh-i ḥawza* 60 (1385/ 2006): 101–144.

to the need of large segments of Iranian society, Khomeini issued a series of statements on liberty, some of them contradictory. Like some of the European Enlightenment thinkers, he described freedom as a natural right of the people; he added, however, that only God – and no government – can grant freedom to the people. Since governments do not grant freedom, they cannot take it away from the people but must protect it as a divine commandment.[8] Khomeini also explained that the struggle against oppression (*Ẓulm*) was always a major principle of Shīʿīsm, and therefore Shīʿīsm, unlike other schools in Islam, guarantees the freedom of humanity.[9]

The Shīʿī clerical-intellectual arena has been divided since the Revolution on many issues ranging from gender to economics. Concerning the debate over liberty, three major approaches have been discernable since the 1990s: the dominant group headed by Supreme Leader Khamenei and following Khomeini's path; the reformists represented by Khātamī; and a smaller group of liberal mid-level clerics, most of whom were in prison and who are now in exile. However, with the return to more overt political repression in April 2001, the debate became largely one-sided as the reformist and liberal advocates of freedom were systematically silenced.[10] Still, the Iranian ruling elite has continued to propagate its interpretation of freedom through a large variety of means and media. This continued effort seems to reflect their belief in the need to counter popular pressure for the sake of greater openness and democratization. While quite a few of the scholarly writings grapple with contemporary Western writings on freedom, there is clearly a high degree of continuity and consistency in the dominant concepts and arguments.[11]

1 Critique of Liberal Negative Liberty

The concept of freedom has been hotly contested in modern political and social thought.[12] The most prevalent liberal definition, namely, the distinction between negative and positive liberty, goes back, at least, to Rousseau. It was

8 Rūḥollah Khomeini, *Ṣaḥīfa-i nūr: majmūʿa-i rāhnimūdhā-i Imām-i Khomeini* (Tehrān: Vizārat-i Irshād-i Islāmī, 1995), vol. 2, 67, 100; vol. 9, 128.

9 Ibid., vol. 5, 70.

10 Meir Litvak, "Iran," in *Middle East Contemporary Survey 2000*, ed., Bruce Maddy-Weitzman (Tel Aviv: Moshe Dayan Center for Middle Eastern and African Studies, 2002), 206–245.

11 See, for example, the list of such articles on the website of the Qom community of learning (*ḥawza*), http://www.hawzah.net/fa/article/view/91247.

12 Patrick Day summarized five different definitions and interpretations of the term in "Is the Concept of Freedom Essentially Contestable?" *Philosophy* 61, no. 235 (1986): 116–123.

elaborated by Kant but examined and defended in depth by Isaiah Berlin in the 1950s and 1960s. The concept of negative liberty centers on freedom from interference, an account of freedom that is usually put forward in response to the question: "What is the area within which the subject – a person or group of persons – is or should be left to do or be what he is able to do or be, without interference by other persons?"[13] Liberty can, in other words, be seen as the absence of obstacles external to the agent: you are free if no one is stopping you from doing whatever you might want to do.

Unlike their Sunnī counterparts, mainstream and hardline Shīʿī clerics addressed Berlin's definition at length. They rejected it due to both their opposing approach to the essence of liberty and the perceived moral and political implications deriving from it.[14] In a way, the idea of negative liberty goes against the logic of the law-centered monotheistic religions, which are based on obedience and fulfillment of divine laws. The basic idea of the Islamic Sharīʿa, just like Jewish law, is human obligations toward God and, by implication, toward other human beings and not natural rights spearheaded by freedom.[15]

Various writers have rejected the philosophical foundations of the liberal idea of freedom, presenting instead a sharp, almost essentialist, dichotomy between East and West. For them, the major flaw in the liberal perception of freedom is its human-centered vantage point in place of God. The liberal West puts liberty as the pillar on which society stands, whereas Islam posits God as its central pillar. In other words, in the West, it is "freedom for the sake of freedom" and not for the sake of any lofty moral or spiritual goal. Hence, freedom stands above truth, morality, and reason. As proof, the "Questions & Answers" section of the official website of the Qom learning complex cites French philosopher Jean Paul Sartre as saying that he rejects God because he limits man's freedom.[16] Moreover, the centrality of human dignity as the pillar of liberalism and liberty means that morality is based on human criteria and, therefore, everything is permitted if its suits humans. It also implies, they claim, that morality is inherently relative. Thus, the liberal notion of freedom means acceptance

---

13 Isaiah Berlin, *Four Essays on Liberty* (Oxford: Clarendon Press, 1969), 121–122.

14 Farshād Sharīʿat and Mahdī Nādirī Bābānārī, "Āzādī dar andīsheh-i Ayatollah Murtażā Muṭṭaharī va-Izāyā Berlin," *Tamāshāgah-i Rāz* 1(Spring 1391/2012): 107–130; Qāsim Pūrḥasan, "ʿAql-i āzādī barresī-i taṭbīqī-i arā'-i Murtażā Muṭṭaharī va-Izāyā Berlin," *Maqālāt va-barresīhā* 36, no. 74 (Winter 1382/2003–04): 33–60; Murtażā Afsharī, "Dō mafhūm-i āzādī dar andīsheh-i Izāyā Berlin," *Iʿtimād*, 4 Esfand 1388/February 23, 2010.

15 On the Jewish perception, see Eugene Koron, "Tradition Meets Modernity: On the Conflict of Halakha and Political Liberty," *Tradition* 25, no. 4 (1991): 30–35.

16 "Mafhūm-i āzādī az dīdār-i Islām," 21 Dey 1385/January 11, 2007, http://hawzah.net/Hawzah/Questions/QuestionView.aspx?LanguageID=1&QuestionID=11700&SearchText.

and respect of any belief that people believe in without any regard to its truth or value. In Islam, on the other hand, revelation and even reason stand above freedom, with all the inevitable repercussions.[17]

Reżā Dāvarī, the "philosophical spokesman of the regime," belittled the importance of liberty; unlike religion, which is as old as humankind, it is a product of modernity, which he rejected vehemently elsewhere.[18] Similarly, former president, Rafsanjānī, presented freedom as a relative term, a product of distinct historical circumstances and not a universal value. Accordingly, the principle and ideal of liberty in the West emerged as a response to the dark period of the Middle Ages, the Inquisition, and the French Revolution with its mass killings. Conversely, in an Islamic society one must "look in the Qurʾān and in Islamic teachings for correct, effective, constructive, and harmless freedoms."[19]

A major flaw in the liberal interpretation of liberty according to the mainstream Shīʿī view is the absence of prohibitions, restrictions, and limitations due to the assumption that this is the primary and natural will of all humans. According to Ayatollah Muḥammad Beheshtī (d. 1981), who served as Khomeini's right-hand during the Revolution, if freedom means the ability to do as we wish, the result is enslavement to our desires and whims, which are mainly materialistic and selfish. Khomeini denounced such subservience as the ultimate submission and warned that it would degrade us from the level of humanity to that of animals. Material power can liberate humans from external restrictions and hurdles, Beheshtī added, but cannot secure real liberty.[20] The severe moral and social consequences of such liberty have been regarded as equally bad. Dr. Hādī Vakīlī, for example, noted that even the most foul and immoral acts such as homosexuality are defended and sanctified as a natural

17 "Naẓar-i shahīd-i Beheshtī dar bārah-i āzādī," 24 Ordībehesht 1393/May 14, 2014, http://www.jahannews.com/analysis/360232; Markaz Nūn, *al-Ḥurriyya fī fikr al-imām al-Khumaynī*, 22; "Mafhūm-i a̱zādī dar falsafa-i gharb?," www.siasi.porsemani.ir/content/مفهوم-آزادی-در-فلسفه‌ی-غرب؟; "Tafāvot-i āzādī-i Islāmī va-āzādī-i gharbī," 1 Mehr 1391/September 22, 2012, http://article.tebyan.net/221126.

18 Reżā Dāvarī Ardakānī, "ʿIlm va-āzādī," *Farhang* (1379/2000), http://bashgāhandishe.info/fa/content/show/9140. For his views on modernity, see Chapter 1.

19 *Jumhūrī-i Islāmī*, June 21, 2000.

20 Sharīf Lakzāʾī, "Sāz va-kārhā-i āzādī dar andīsheh-i ayatollah Beheshtī," *ʿUlūm-i siyāsī* 4, no. 13 (Spring 1380/2001), 163; Muḥammad Ṣādiq Shahbāzī, "Āzādī az dīdār-i Imām-i Khomeini," 24 Tīr 1391/July 14, 2012, http://www.teribon.ir/archives/114286; Markaz Nūn, *al-Ḥurriyya fī fikr al-imām al-Khumaynī*, 10, 20; "Dīn va-āzādī dar goftegū bā Ayatollah Muḥammad ʿAlāmī Hashtrūdī," *Kayhān*, December 8, 1998.

human right.[21] Not surprisingly, Khomeini denounced the liberal notion of liberty as the means used by the West to lead the young people of Iran to moral corruption and oblivion.[22] Miṣbāḥ Yazdī went further and denounced the Western notion of freedom as an idol (*batt*) that must be broken. He further complained that "the greatest betrayals of Islam and of Islamic culture have taken shape in the name of the sacred term of freedom."[23]

Part of this criticism was directed against the UN Universal Declaration of Human Rights. Grand Ayatollah ʿAbdollah Javādī Āmolī attacked the declaration as seeking to impose the Western notion of human rights on the tremendous diversity of humanity while ignoring the true unifying force that is God. He claimed that its founders consequently denounce a genuine defense of rights as terrorism and legitimize true terrorism in defense of rights. Grand Ayatollah Jaʿfar Subḥānī charged that the Declaration did not guarantee true freedom of faith but only those liberties that harmed true human happiness, in other words, those leading to moral corruption. Khomeini, for his part, dismissed the hypocrisy of the signatory countries, stating that Iran "had suffered and continued to suffer" at "the hands of governments who have signed the Declaration of Human Rights and who loudly proclaim the human right to freedom."[24] In addressing the Declaration, Miṣbāḥ Yazdī stressed that the meaning of rights (*ḥaqq*) in Islam also refers to truth in contrast to falsehood. Hence, the criteria for human rights should be rights whose validity is absolute and eternal, that is, God's laws, instead of the transient criteria that change according to shifting political interests, as manifested in the UN document.[25]

---

21 Hādī Vakīlī, "Naqd-i mabānī-i umanīstī-i ḥuqūq-i bashar-i gharbī," *Kitāb-i naqd* 36 (1384/2005): 134; Maḥmūd Ḥakīmī, "Gharb bīmār ast (10): Āzādī-i jinsī, fājiʿa-i buzurg-i gharb," *Darshā-i az maktab-i Islām* 11, no. 1 (1348/ 1970): 27–30; ʿAbbās Nīkzād, "Āzādīhā-i ijtimāʿī az dīdār-i Islām," *Riwāq-i andīsheh* 25 Dey 1382/December 2003: 7–25.

22 Rūḥollah Khumaynī, *al-Kalimāt al-qiṣār mawaʿiẓ wa-ḥukm min kalām al-imām al-khumaynī* (*qudisa sirruhu*) (Beirut: Dār al-Wasīla, 1995), 143; *Minhajiyat al-thwara al-Islāmiyya: muqtaṭafāt min afkār wa-arāʾ al-Imām al-Khumaynī* (Tehrān: muʾassasat tanẓīm wa-nashr turāth al-Imām al-Khumaynī (S) 1996), 360.

23 Muḥammad Taqī Miṣbāḥ Yazdī, *Buzurgtarīn-i farīża* (Qom: Intishārāt-i Muʾasasa-i amūzeshi va-pazhūheshī-i Imām-i Khomeini, 1389/2010), 186–187.

24 "Ayatollah Javādī Āmolī: Amrīkāʾīhā ʿaql nadārand," October 21, 2012, http://www.asriran.com/fa/news/237623; Jaʿfar Subḥānī, "Irtidād va-āzādī-i andīsheh," http://www.shafaqna.com/persian/services/religious-questions/item/20252-ارتداد-و-آزادی-اندیشه?tmpl=component&print=1; Ruhollah Khomeini, *Islam and Revolution: Writings and Declarations of Imam Khomeini*, trans. Hamid Algar (Berkeley: Mizan Press, 1981), 220. Some writers, however, have cited the Declaration to prove that respect for freedom of belief in Islam is essentially identical, see Mahdī Hadhadī, "Az āzādī-i bayān tā irtidād," 25 Esfand 1382/February 14, 2004, http://article.tebyan.net/5472.

25 "Misbah Yazdī Comments on Islamic Human Rights," *IRNA*, April 21, 2000 (FBIS); Muḥammad Mojtahed-Shabestarī, "Yā ḥuqūq-i bashar yā ḥuqūq-i khodā, mughālaṭa

All the regime's spokespeople rejected the ideal of absolute liberty implicit in the notion of the absence of obstacles. No person, not even the "sinless" (*maʿṣūm*) Imāms had absolute liberty, Ayatollah Muḥammad ʿAlāmī Hashtrūdī of the Qom seminary stated. According to *Kayhān*, the newspaper published by the Leader's office, absolute freedom is an imaginary concept that can never exist. Such freedom is self-destructive, as it inevitably leads to anarchy and the denial of freedom of others.[26] Those who advocate absolute freedom forget, maintained Seyyed Ḥusayn Ishāqī, a lecturer at the IRGC, that people are not only rational beings but are also influenced by whims and impulses that can destroy any solid foundation of society. Liberty is like a knife, he stated, a useful tool in the hands of one person and very dangerous in the hand of another or like electricity, which is very beneficial but can kill when too strong.[27] Hence, another concluded, we must sacrifice minimal liberties in order to preserve the maximal liberty that will enable people to achieve their true spiritual destiny in life. Miṣbāḥ Yazdī pointed out that even in Western societies with their liberal ideas, women are not allowed to walk naked in the street in order to protect the sensitivities of others. Why, then, should Islamic restrictions on liberty be viewed as less valid?[28] Another prevalent argument for limiting freedom was rooted in the Hobbesian worldview of many Islamic thinkers (Shīʿī and Sunnī alike) who feared a descent into chaos in the absence of a strong government.[29]

This reading of negative liberty as freedom without restriction is, however, incorrect. Not only is it conditioned upon avoiding harm to others, but once it is applied universally, it in fact sets considerable restrictions on the liberty of each individual. In addition, while classical liberalism advocated the removal of as many legal restraints as possible, it did not oppose law itself and regarded law and government as necessary for the maintenance of peace and security. Nonetheless, many Shīʿī writers criticized these liberal restrictions on

---

ast," 17 Mehr 1386/October 9, 2007 http://www.islahweb.org/content/2007/10/665/ محمد-مجتهد-شبستری-یا-حقوق-بشر-یا-حقوق-خدا،-مغالطه-است.

26 "Dīn va-āzādī dar goftegū bā Ayatollah Muḥammad ʿAlāmī Hashtrūdī."

27 Seyyed Ḥusayn Ishāqī, "Ḥudūd-i āzādī-i bayān dar Islām," *Shamīm yās* 46 (1385/2007): 18–22.

28 Muḥammad Taqī Miṣbāḥ Yazdī, "Dīn va-āzādī (2): goftegū bā Ayatollah Miṣbāḥ Yazdī;" *Mublighān* 23 (1380/2001), 145–150; Ayatollah Muḥammad Yazdī in *Voice of the Islamic Republic of Iran*, February 27, 1998 (BBC Monitoring); "Āzādī az cheh? barāye cheh?" *Didār-i Āshinā* 20 (1380/2002), http://www.hawzah.net/fa/Magazine/View/114/4444/31323.

29 Seyyed Ḥusayn Ḥusaynī Kārnāmī, "Āzādī-i ʿaqīda va-āzādī-i bayān bā takiya bar vakāvī-i tafsīrī-i āya ʿlā ikrāh fī al-dīn,'" *Maʿārif Qurʾānī* 19 (1393/2014): 82–83; Jaʿfar Subḥānī, "Irtidād va-āzādī-i bayān," https://rasekhoon.net/article/show/670338/; "Āyā Āya sharīfa lā ikrāh fī al-dīn, bā ḥukm-i iʿdām barāye murtad munāfat nadārad?," http://www.andisheqom.com/public/application/index/viewData?c=11028&t=qa; "Irtidād (2) āzādī (8)," *Ḥawza* 42 (1369/1991), http://www.hawzah.net/fa/Magazine/View/4518/4555/32889.

liberty, as highly deficient. The compilers of Khomeini's statements on liberty explained that such an approach would lead to constant feuds between people without any justification; people are not free, they claimed, to demean or degrade themselves morally, even if this does not harm others.[30]

Miṣbāḥ Yazdī raised several arguments against the liberal concept of restrictions on freedom. First, he posited moral principles as superior to liberty via the example that allowing a person to commit suicide may respect their liberty and certainly does not harm others, but it contradicts the moral principle of preserving life. Second, the criterion of not harming others is too vague. Islam, he claimed, offers clear principles regarding such offenses, while Western liberalism does not.[31] Miṣbāḥ Yazdī criticized the liberal criteria of addressing only this-worldly issues and privileging material concerns over spiritual well-being. Using the example of laws on drugs, he noted that Western societies ban the use of drugs because they are harmful to one's body and jeopardize one's financial interest, but they neglect the spiritual harm: "Shouldn't we ban poisons that take away the health of the soul and rob humans of their faith? Isn't this action anything but harm to the humanity of humans? … We believe in laws that protect the spiritual interests of people … [which] are above material interests.… Laws must protect both … those who transgress moral laws must [also] be restrained."[32]

A prevalent criticism, part of the broader rejection of Western civilization, was the failure of the liberal West to adhere to its own pretensions. Khamenei dismissed Western ideas of liberty, which the Shīʿī reformists wish to import to Iran, as inferior to the authentic Islamic principles. He insisted that only capitalists enjoyed true freedom in the West.[33] Likewise, the West might pretend to practice freedom of religion, but it bans Muslim women from wearing the veil, not out of moral considerations but in order to curb Islam. Conversely,

30 Markaz Nūn, *Al-Ḥurriyya fī fikr al-Imām al-khumaynī*, 22.

31 Miṣbāḥ Yazdī, "Dīn va-āzādī (2): goftegū bā Ayatollah Miṣbāḥ Yazdī," 145.

32 Miṣbāḥ Yazdī, *Silsila-i mabāḥith: Islām, siyāsat va-ḥukūmat*, 50 cited in Sussan Siavoshi, "Ayatullah Misbah Yazdi: Politics, Knowledge, and the Good Life," *The Muslim World* 100 (2010): 124–144. See similar argument in Nīkzād, "Āzādīhā-i ijtimāʿī az dīdār-i Islām," 7–25.

33 "Matn-i kāmil-i bayānāt-i maqām-i muʿaẓẓam-i rahbarī dar khuṭbahā-i namāz jumʿa-i Tehrān," 23 Ordībhehesht 1379/May 12, 2000, https://www.leader.ir/fa/speech/1903/ اقامه -نماز-جمعه -تهران -به -امامت -رهبر-معظم -انقلاب -همزمان -با-میلاد - امام -موسي - کاظم-(ع); Khamenei, "Freedom of Media in the U.S. means freedom of speech for the mogul-capitalists," May 3, 2019, http://english.khamenei.ir/news/6675/Freedom-of-Media-in-the-U-S-means-freedom-of-speech-for-the.; See also "Pīsh-bīnī-i suqūṭ-i gharb tavassoṭ-i maqām-i muʿaẓẓam-i rahbarī," http://siasi.porsemani.ir/node/1806.

Muslim countries enforce the veil in order to prevent moral corruption.[34] Moreover, even though the West asserts that people are its highest priority and the pursuit of human happiness is a supreme value, it refuses to set limits to freedom, even for the sake of people, as proved by economic liberalism, which is totally unrestricted despite its threat to the preservation of society.[35]

Overall, Shīʿī writers reject the ideological foundations of the liberal concept of liberty as "freedom from" (*āzādī az cheh*), which revolves around human dignity or even more problematically from their point of view, "freedom for the sake of freedom." By contrast, they all agree that freedom is not an end in itself but rather a means to achieve much loftier goals, which are the true objective or destiny of human life. These include, first and foremost, the attainment of perfection (*takāmul, kamāl-i adamī*) and the ultimate happiness of humanity" (*saʿādat-i nihāʾī-i bashar*). Human dignity will be achieved by the aspiration toward perfection, which can be attained only by total adherence to the laws of Islam. According to Khomeini, freedom that does not lead to spiritual perfection is false and should be abhorred. In addition, two other God-given blessings stand alongside human liberty in Islam: reason and revelation. Both commandments stand above liberty, since God stands above liberty.[36]

2 Spiritual Liberty as True Liberty

Unlike liberal freedom, which subordinates and enslaves people to its whims and desires, the path paved by the prophets for the liberation of humanity is the internal revolution in the human spirit. This revolution enables people to control these human desires and overcome their personal ambitions, which lead them to oppress and enslave others. The prophets wanted to liberate humans from this low state, so that they might ascend the steps to perfection. Religion is, therefore, the greatest liberating revolution in history. True and sublime freedom, according to Ayatollah Muṭṭaharī, is internal and spiritual:

---

34 "Ḥijāb va-ʿifāf dar kalām-i maqām-i muʿaẓẓam-i rahbarī," https://hawzah.net/fa/Article/View/94793.

35 "Āzādī-i ʿaqīda va-bayān va-ḥuqūq-i bashar va-ḥukm-i irtidād chegūneh bā ham jamʿ mīshavad," http://masjedaliasghar.ir/?p=3003; "Āzādī az cheh? Barāye cheh?"

36 "Āzādī az cheh? Barāye cheh?"; Murtażā Muṭṭaharī, *Insān-i kāmīl* (Tehrān: Intishārāt-i Ṣadrā, 1373/1994), 346; "Barresī-i mafhūm-i āzādī dar andīsheh-i shahīd-i Beheshtī;" Khomeini, *Ṣaḥīfa-i nūr*, vol. 13, 72; Khomeini, *al-Kalimāt al-qiṣār*, 144; Vakīlī, "Naqd-i mabānī-i umanīstī-i ḥuqūq-i bashar-i gharbī"; Manṣūr Mīr-Aḥmadī, "Mafhūm-i āzādī dar fiqh-i siyāsī-i Shīʿa," *ʿUlūm-i siyāsī* 1, no. 1 (1377/1998): 80; Ghulām Reżā Khāje-Servī and Mahdī Nādirī, "Āzādī dar goftemān-i faqāhatī-i inqilāb-i Islāmī-i Iran," *Jastarhā-i siyāsī-i muʿāṣir* 4, no. 2 (1392/2013): 36.

freedom from the shackles of the self and true devotion to God and the truth. Freedom is, he added, essential for the attainment of perfection.[37]

Khomeini added a mystical angle to this approach, claiming that liberty is a duty (*taklīf*), and the duty of humans is not to be a slave to doctrinal deviations or internal passions. Spiritual liberty, which enables people to extricate themselves from such enslavement to passions and delusions, materializes through true piety and renouncing this world. As proof, Khomeini pointed to the Jews, who are among the wealthiest peoples in the world as far as money is concerned but who, throughout history, have spent their lives "in misery, distress, and humiliation" because of their spiritual poverty and emptiness.[38] Beheshtī, who adopted the Islamic philosophical principle of liberty as the product of knowledge and reason, claimed that real liberty can be attained only when people apply their spiritual and moral power to overcoming the shackles of human nature, i.e. desire, society's norms, and history through the power of reason and higher morality.[39] The logical conclusion for Khomeini and the others is that the only way to attain true liberty is by total submission and voluntary enslavement to God and his laws. In fact, freedom can prosper only within the framework of true religious piety. Or, in Beheshtī's words, the higher the level of people's enslavement to God, the greater liberty they attain.[40]

The idea of servitude to God as true liberty is not so different from the traditional Jewish view.[41] It can be seen as a perception shared by most religions,

37 ʿAzīz al-Ḥamdānī, "ʿUqdat al-dīmuqrāṭiyya," *al-Munṭalaq* 115 (1996): 70; Lakzāʾī, "Sāz va-kārhā-i āzādī," 160–163; Seyyed Nūr al-Dīn Sharīʿatmadārī Jazāyīrī, "Mabānī-i āzādī dar kalām va-fiqh-i Shīʿī," *ʿUlūm-i siyāsī* 3 (1377/1999), 3–4; Murtażā Muṭṭaharī, *Pānzdah goftār* (Tehrān: Intishārāt-i Ṣadrā, 1380/2001), 274.

38 Markaz Nūn, *Al-Ḥurriyya fī fikr al-Khumaynī*, 29, 31. Khamenei followed suit and added that Western notions of liberty emphasize the role of external forces in inhibiting freedom whereas Islam adds the internal obstacles such as corrupt morality, self-indulgence, hatred, and desires that prevent people from attaining true freedom, cited in Khāje-servī and Nādirī, "Āzādī dar goftemān-i faqāhatī," 53.

39 Lakzāʾī, "Sāz va-kārhā-i āzādī," 163; Muḥammad Ḥusayn Pazhūhande, "Nisbat-i dīn va-āzādī az dīdār-i shahīd-i Ayatollah Dr. Beheshtī va-digār-i andīshmandān-i muʿāṣir-i dīnī," https://sarcheshmeh.org/news/ID/554/. See also ʿAlī Akbar Ẓākīrī, "Dīn va-āzādī az dīdār-i shahīd-i Muṭṭaharī," *Ḥawza* 97 (1377/2000): 112–144.

40 Cited in Pezhūhande, "Nisbat-i dīn va-āzādī;" Mu'asasa-i Farhangī-i Tebyān, "Naẓar-i Islām dar bārah-i āzādī chīst? Va-ayā taqvā mukhālif-i āzādī ast?," http://library.tebyan.net/fa/Viewer/Text/145417/1.

41 See, for example, the tractate Ethics of the Fathers (Chapter 6:2), "there is no free individual, except for he who occupies himself with the study of Torah" or the medieval Jewish poet Yehuda Halevi who wrote: "Servants of time are servants of servants; only God's servant alone is free," "Servants," in Franz Rosenzweig, *Ninety Two Poems and Hymns of Yehuda Halevi*, trans. Thomas Kovach et al. (Albany: SUNY Press, 2000), 124. The original Hebrew word is "slave" and not servant.

which regards the liberation of human beings from their desires as true liberty and the attainment of spiritual liberty as the loftiest goal. The problem is the transfer of this notion of inner spiritual freedom into civil and political spheres or, put differently, using spiritual freedom to dismiss or deny the meaning of political and civil liberties. Liberty as submission to God has clear conclusions for Shīʿī thinkers. First, liberation from the self and total submission to God means the elimination of all other types of subjugation to other human beings. For Miṣbāḥ Yazdī it meant first and foremost freedom from subjugation to imperialism. Muṭṭaharī added a social aspect, maintaining that true freedom means that human beings will not be exploited, subjugated, or enslaved by others, what he termed, "social liberty."[42]

3 Islam as the Guarantor of Liberty

In the political realm, the idea of true liberty as submission to God means the rejection of democratic rule where human laws formulated by an accidental majority, impose laws and restrictions on society and the submission to divine law. Such submission to God and liberation from subjugation to other human beings is the reason for Khomeini's statement that Islamic rule cannot be despotic, and therefore dictatorship in Islam "has not been, is not and never shall be" possible.[43] Consequently, freedom can neither be summed up through or be dependent on the legal provisions that human beings create. Freedom in Islam will not be attained unless people rid themselves of the legal restrictions that they or others have imposed upon them and fully subject themselves to God through his divine directives manifested in Islamic law.[44]

According to Khamenei, "Islam has come for the liberation of humankind both from the chains and cuffs of arrogance and from the pressure of oppressive systems ... and thus to establish a just government for humankind and to liberate [humankind] from wrong thoughts, ideas and illusions ruling their lives." Our duty, he concluded, is to strive to attain the liberty of the Islamic worldview.[45] Former head of the judiciary, Ayatollah Muḥammad Yazdī, argued

---

42 ʿAzīzān, "Pluralism farhangī az naẓar-i ustād-i Muṭṭaharī." See a similar idea by ʿAlāma Muḥammad Ḥusayn Ṭabāṭabāʾī cited in Nīkzād, "Āzādī-i ijtimāʿī az dīdār-i Islām."

43 Khomeini, *Ṣaḥīfa-i nūr*, vol. 9, 128; Mīr-Aḥmadī, "Mafhūm-i āzādī dar fiqh-i siyāsī-i Shīʿa," 7–8.

44 Dāvarī cited in Mehran Kamrava, *Iran's Intellectual Revolution* (Cambridge: Cambridge University Press, 2008), 67.

45 Khamenei, "Bayānāt dar dīdār-i masʾūlān-i niẓām va-mayhamānān-i vaḥdat-i Islām," 29 Dey 1392/January 19, 2014, http://farsi.khamenei.ir/speech-content?id=25056.

that before the advent of Islam, freedom had been non-existent; it had been trampled on and destroyed and people were exploited as slaves. But Islam revived freedom and granted freedom to all social strata, particularly to women, children and other weaker members of society.[46]

Thus, true liberty does not mean the absence of law or restrictions. Rather, Shīʿī thinkers seem to agree with Locke's statement that liberty is conditional upon the law or Kant's view which presents liberty as voluntary obedience to laws that are based on reason.[47] However, whereas Locke spoke of laws that were "established by consent in the commonwealth," the Shīʿī writers reject human laws since no legislator has the knowledge and understanding of human beings and their needs like God. Likewise, whereas Kant spoke of laws based on human reason, these Shīʿī thinkers believe that Islamic law is based on reason, but they reject human reason, since people are often subject to irrational whims and desires; the law that reflects pure reason is, rather, the divine law manifested in the Sharīʿa. Moreover, the most suitable law for the application of liberty, the law that liberates human beings from their desires and from the prison of their nature is the law of Islam.[48]

These views are similar to those espoused by mainstream Sunnī thinkers,[49] however, unlike the latter, the Shīʿīs emphasize the importance of the institution of *vilāyat-i faqīh* as the interpreter and executor of God's laws. As is well known, according to Khomeini, a necessary condition for fully implementing the monotheistic principle is the establishment of an Islamic government led by *vilāyat-i faqīh*. The existence of the state is essential in order to prevent both anarchy and chaos and the oppression and fear of people by others. In other words, the state has two duties or functions: the implementation of God's laws and the preservation of people's liberties. The only system that ensures both goals is the Islamic Republic.[50]

---

46 Yazdī, *Voice of the Islamic Republic of Iran*, September 25, 1998 (SWB), May 5, 2000 (DR).

47 Richard Ashcraft, "Locke's Political Philosophy," in *The Cambridge Companion to Locke*, ed. Vere Chappell (Cambridge: Cambridge University Press, 1994), 232.

48 Sharīʿatmadārī Jazāyīrī, "Mabānī-i āzādī dar kalām va-fiqh-i Shīʿī."

49 See Ḥasan al-Turābī, "al-Shūrā wal-dīmuqrāṭiyya: al-muṣṭalaḥ wal-mafhūm," *al-Mustaqbal al-ʿArabī* 75 (1985): 22–23; Fahmi Huwaydī, "al-Dīmuqrāṭiyya min al-manẓūr al-mashrūʿī al-ḥaḍārī," *al-Mustaqbal al-ʿArabī* 269 (2001): 141; Muḥammad ʿAlī Dīnāwī, *Kubrā al-ḥarakāt al-Islāmiyya fī al-taʾrīkh* (Cairo: al-Jamāʿa al-Islāmiyya bi-jāmiʿat al-Qāhira, 1976), 123–124.

50 Khomeini, *Ṣaḥīfa-i nūr*, vol. 10, 22; ʿAbd al-Wahhāb Furātī, "Āzādī dar andīsheh-i Imām-i Khomeini," *Ḥukūmat-i Islāmī* 12 (1378/1999), 124–137. Furātī went further in asserting that in this formulation Khomeini actually combines Hobbes' concept of achieving security (*kasb-i amniyat*) with Locke's idea of guaranteeing liberty (*taẓmīn-i āzādī*) as well as Plato's concept of the state.

Khomeini argued that true freedom is communal rather than individual, and individuals receive their freedom by performing duty to the community rather than demanding rights from it. But this freedom does not come easily to people and requires a special leader who knows God's laws and can faithfully implement them. The leader becomes the embodiment of the rational will of the faithful nation and, therefore, its deliverer and liberator. Khomeini rejected the danger that *vilāyat-i faqīh* might lead to tyranny by claiming that the constitutional qualifications for becoming the supreme leader "prevent him from going astray."[51] Ḥujjat al-Islām Manṣūr Mīr-Aḥmadī of Shahīd-i Beheshtī University conceded that absolute *vilāyat-i faqīh*, which awards the ruling jurist widespread authority, restricts freedom. But, he minimized the effect of such limitations by arguing that they relate more to "false freedom" (*āzādī-i kāẕib*). Where actual freedom (*āzādī-i vāqiʿī*) is concerned, however, the institution of *vilāyat-i faqīh* is in fact the best guarantor of true liberty, since it saves people from falling into corruption and becoming enslaved to their desires.[52]

These views are reminiscent of the monologue of the Grand Inquisitor of Seville in Dostoyevsky's celebrated novel *The Brothers Karamazov*. Speaking to Christ who was shackled in the Inquisition's dungeon after revealing himself to the people of Seville, the Inquisitor explains that the Church's responsibility in preserving the purity of the believers' soul arises from the great burden which "Liberty, Freedom of Thought and Conscience, and Science" imposes upon ordinary believers. And he added, "we will take good care to prove to them that they will become absolutely free only when they have abjured their freedom in our favor and submit to us absolutely."[53]

4 Positive Liberty and Its Application

As mentioned above, Isaiah Berlin developed the concept of positive liberty alongside negative liberty. Positive liberty is the possibility of acting – or the fact of acting – in such a way as to take control of one's life and realize one's fundamental purposes. While negative liberty is usually attributed to individual agents, positive liberty is sometimes attributed to collectivities or to individuals considered primarily as members of certain collectivities. In

---

51 Sussan Siavoshi, "Ayatollah Khomeini and the Contemporary Debate on Freedom," *Journal of Islamic Studies* 18, no. 1 (2007): 35; Khomeini, "The Religious Scholars Led the Revolt (January 2, 1980)," interview cited in *Islam and Revolution*, 342.

52 Manṣūr Mīr-Aḥmadī, "Āzādī va-vilāyat dar fiqh-i siyāsī-i muʿāṣir-i Shīʿa," *ʿUlūm-i siyāsī* 3 (1377/1999): 94.

53 Fyodor Dostoyevsky, *The Brothers Karamazov* (Toronto: Aegitas, 2016), 539.

its political form, positive freedom has often been thought of as necessarily achieved through a collectivity. Perhaps the clearest case is Rousseau's theory of freedom, according to which individual freedom is achieved through participation in the process whereby the community exercises collective control over its own affairs in accordance with the "general will."[54]

Berlin, who developed this concept during the Cold War under the shadow of Communism, was wary of the potential abuse of positive liberty. He explained that positive theories of freedom, or perversions of them, have been more frequently used as instruments of oppression than negative ones. These positive theories typically rely on a split between a "higher" and a "lower" self, that is, the self of the passions, unreflecting desires, and irrational impulses. People are free when their higher, rational selves are in control and they are not slaves to their passions or to merely their empirical selves. A problem occurs, however, when some individuals claim or believe that they are more rational than others and therefore know best what is in their own and others' rational interests. This allows them to assert that by forcing people less rational than themselves to do the rational thing and thus realize their true selves, they are in fact liberating them from their merely empirical desires. Coercion is justified on the grounds that it leads to a realization of the aims of the higher self. Berlin posits that positive theories of freedom have historically been used to justify various kinds of oppression, and that saying that freedom involves self-mastery is only a short step away from justifying all kinds of state interference in the lives of individuals on the grounds that, in Rousseau's words, there are some circumstances in which it is right to be "forced to be free."[55]

The Shīʿī discourse on the religious principle of "commanding right and forbidding wrong" (*al-amr bi'l-marʿrūf wa'l-nahy ʿan al-munkar*) confirms Berlin's apprehensions about the pitfalls of positive liberty almost verbatim. Historically, "commanding right" refers to the exercise of legitimate authority, either by holders of public office or by individual Muslims who are legally competent, with the purpose of encouraging or enforcing adherence to the requirements of Islamic law.[56] In Iran, it refers mostly to the imposition of Islamic

54 "Positive and Negative Liberty," *Stanford Encyclopedia of Philosophy*, http://plato.stanford.edu/entries/liberty-positive-negative/.

55 "The Paradox of Positive Liberty," *Stanford Encyclopedia of Philosophy*, http://plato.stanford.edu/entries/liberty-positive-negative/.

56 Michael Cook, "Al-Nahy ʿan al-Munkar," *Encyclopaedia of Islam*, http://referenceworks.brillonline.com/entries/encyclopaedia-of-islam-2/al-nahy-an-al-munkar-COM_1437. See also Michael Cook's magisterial analysis *Commanding Right and Forbidding Wrong in Islamic Thought* (New York: Cambridge University Press, 2000).

codes of dress and public conduct by the state. Shīʿī thinkers emphasize two points in this context. The first, as mentioned above, is that true freedom means liberty from personal desires or wishes and total voluntary submission to God and his rules in order to achieve spiritual perfection. The second is that Islam, unlike Western society, promotes the interest and good of society as a whole and not just that of the individual. In Islam, society is like a big family and each person is responsible for serving and realizing its collective needs and benefits. The duty of "commanding right" is, in this context, a crucial means of helping and guiding the individual and society to attain true liberty and perfection. It is society's duty to remove and eliminate all those obstacles that stand in the way of achieving perfection. Consequently, attaining this superior liberty for society as a whole by enforcing Islamic laws and codes of conduct has precedence over individual liberty. Hence, coercion for the right cause is the key to true liberty. In addition, since humans are social beings, any deviation or misdeed by the individual is likely to harm society as a whole. Individuals cannot use the excuse of practicing their own personal liberty to harm the general good, just as no ship passenger or crew member has the right to dig a hole in their cabin, claiming that they are free to do as they wish while risking the lives of all others.[57]

Grand Ayatollah Nāṣīr Makārem Shīrāzī explained that moral deviations – such as not conforming to the Islamic dress code – are like infectious diseases, and it is the moral duty of society to fight them just as physicians fight the spread of diseases. The pretext of protecting individual liberty should not be used to avoid fulfilling the important social mission of protecting society.[58]

---

57 J' Bābāmīr, "Amr beh maʿrūf va-nahyi az munkar dar taʿāmul bā āzādī-i fardī va-ijtimāʿī," 21 Esfand 1396/March 12, 2018, https://bit.ly/2FXEkna; Aḥmad Ḥaydarī, "Amniyat, āzādī, difāʿ az żaʿīf va-amr beh maʿrūf va-nahyi az munkar," *Payām-i zan* 17 (1385/ 2006): 6–10; Ḥusnī Pāsokh-dād, "Jāygāh-i maṣlaḥat-i ijtimāʿī dar amr beh maʿrūf kojāst/ayā nahyi az munkar bā āzādī sāzgarī dārad," 13 Bahman 1392/February 2, 2014, http://www.farsnews.com/newstext.php?nn=13941110000662; Shūrā-i amr beh maʿrūf va-nahyi az munkar shahrdārī-i Mashhad, "Amr beh maʿrūf va-nahyi az munkar chīst?," https://marouf.mashhad.ir/portal_content/1042556-امر-معروف-نهی-منکر-چیست.html.

58 "Āyā amr beh maʿrūf va-nahyi az munkar bā aṣl āzādī dar taʿāruż nīst?," http://rasekhoon.net/faq/show/485765/; Nāṣir Makārem Shīrāzī, "Munāfat-i nahyi az munkar bā āzādī-i insān!," http://makarem.ir/main.aspx?lid=0&typeinfo=42&catid=29470&pageindex=0&mid=322195. See the same argument in Pāsokh-dād, "Jāygāh-i maṣlaḥat-i ijtimāʿī dar amr beh maʿrūf kojāst."

5 Limits on Freedom under Islam

The Shīʿī-Iranian interpretation of the two concepts of liberty, negative and positive, entails certain limitations or restrictions in their implementation. Regime spokesmen take pride in the institutionalization of freedom in the Iranian Constitution, seeing it as a major achievement of the Revolution. But, as mentioned above, they renounce non-restricted freedom as leading to anarchy, chaos, or corruption and therefore reject the argument that subordination to Sharīʿa law means infringement of liberty. In defining subordination to the law, Khomeini distinguished between the private sphere, where the government is not supposed to intervene, and the public sphere, where liberty can be restricted as part of protecting the laws of Islam.[59] Khomeini's disciples argue that since he saw liberty as a primary principle (*aṣl awwalī*) in Islam, he restricted it only in those cases where there was an explicit prohibition in the scriptures. A major justification for such restrictions was the well-being of society as a whole, which was based on the premise that Islam bans only what is harmful to society and that Islam, unlike Western society, promotes the interest and good of society as a whole and not just of the individual.[60] Thus, Khomeini and others emphasized that within the Islamic system no one tells the individual where to reside or what job to do.[61]

On the other hand, Grand Ayatollah Muḥammad Ḥusayn Faḍlallah of Lebanon conceded that one can argue that Islam does not recognize the liberty of individuals since it interferes with their food, dress, and relations with the opposite sex in a way that makes the state punish transgressions in these areas or pushes society to do so in the absence of the state. But, he explained, since people are not only materialistic creatures but also have spiritual and moral needs, they need to be protected from the negative inclinations that will violate their own and society's stability. Just as no person has the right to harm themselves physically, neither should the state nor society allow them to harm their own spiritual fulfillment and health as determined by Islamic law. Allowing freedom in these areas will turn individuals into people "paralyzed intellectually, extremist in disposition, aggressive in their conduct, and

---

59 Khomeini, *Ṣaḥīfa-i nūr*, vol. 7, 18–19; vol. 9, 89.

60 Rūḥollah Musāvī Khomeini, *al-Makāsib al-muḥarrama* vol. 1 (Qom, 1381/2002–2003), 32; Markaz Nūn, *al-Ḥurriyya fī fikr al-Imām al-Khumaynī*, 23, and Jaʿfar Subḥānī, *Tahdhīb al-uṣūl: taqrīrāt dars al-Imām al-Khumaynī* (Qom, 1363/1984–1985), 139, 212–213 cited in Furātī, "Āzādī dar andīsheh-i Imām-i Khomeini"; "Dīn va-āzādī dar goftegū bā Ayatollah Muḥammad ʿAlāmī Hashtrūdī;" Nīkzād, "Āzādīhā-i ijtimāʿī az dīdār-i Islām."

61 See Oriana Fallaci's interview with Khomeini in *Ṣaḥīfa-i nūr*, vol. 9, 88. See also Nīkzād, "Āzādīhā-i ijtimāʿī az dīdār-i Islām."

selfish in their personal relationships" and will negatively affect individuals and society alike. The harm done by restricting individual freedom is less than the harm done to individuals and society if individuals are permitted to do as they wish.[62]

The outcome of this approach has been a long list of limitations and restrictions, which empties these lofty words of any meaning. Moreover, in discussing the various categories of freedoms and their limitations, the Shīʿī writers have considered the intentions of those who wish to exercise their freedom as an important criterion and whether or not such liberties should be allowed. Of the wide spectrum of liberties, only three will be discussed here.

Political Freedom. Political freedom, according to Shīʿī mainstream writers, is the participation of the people in the political process: the more influence people have on political sovereignty, the freer society is. They have explained that freedom cannot be imposed on society, but rather society must evolve and mature until it can realize its own liberty. In addition, since the majority of people in Iran are Muslims, it is obvious that their true will cannot be anything except "in accordance with Islamic principles," which are determined by the clergy.[63] Ayatollah Ibrāhīm Amīnī, member of the Assembly of Experts thus clarified that freedom does not mean total permiscuity but has limits, which, determined by the supreme leader, entail the harm done to people's faith and beliefs as well as to the state.[64] Khomeini, he claimed, allows people various liberties, but with one reservation, namely, that no activity endangers the nation's interest or contradicts the principles of chastity.[65] This idea was enshrined in Article 26 of the 1979 Constitution:

> The formation of parties, societies, political or professional associations, as well as religious societies, whether Islamic or pertaining to one of the recognized religious minorities, is permitted provided they do not violate the principles of independence, freedom, national unity, the criteria of Islam, or the basis of the Islamic Republic.[66]

---

62 Muḥammad Ḥusayn Faḍlallah, "al-Ḥurriyya wal-dīmuqrāṭiyya fī al-ru'ya al-Islāmiyya," in *Madkhal ilā al-fikr al-siyāsī*, trans. Khalīl al-ʿIṣāmī (Tehrān: Maktab al-dirāsāt al-thaqāfiyya al-duwaliyya, 2001), 289, 303–305. See also al-ʿAlāma Muḥammad Sayyid al-Amīn, "Ḥawla al-dīn wa-ḥaqq al-ikhtilāf," *al-Munṭalaq* 15 (1996): 11.

63 Radio Iran, March 20, 1998, March 31, 2000 (DR); IRNA, July 31, 1998, October 4, 1998; *Jumhūrī-i Islāmī*, June 21, 2000; Mahdī Muntaẓir Qā'im, "Āzādī-i siyāsī," *Ḥukūmat-i Islāmī* 3 (1376/1997), http://www.ensani.ir/fa/content/81279/default.aspx.

64 IRNA, July 31, 1998, October 4, 1998.

65 See also, Markaz Nūn, *Al-Ḥurriyya fī fikr al-imām al-Khumaynī*, 22.

66 *Iran (Islamic Republic of)'s Constitution of 1979 with Amendments through 1989*, www.constituteproject.org/constitution/Iran_1989.pdf?lang=en.

Khomeini acknowledged the people's right to rebel, provided it was against oppressive rulers who deviate from the truth, violate the law, and harm the people's rights. Naturally, this permissive approach does not apply to the Islamic Republic, where such ills do not exist, and therefore the people are obliged to support the government. Another restriction on liberty was on all kinds of "corruption," as determined by the Islamic government, such as the absence of the hijab.[67]

For Muḥammad Yazdī, political freedom means that human beings are free to express their views about the management of their country: they are free to form political parties or other organizations and cannot be forced to participate in a particular political party. He cautioned, however, that if such freedoms were without limits or boundaries, they could bring about chaos which would damage this very freedom, since human beings differ in their views and thus have disputes and quarrels with one another. This could lead to anarchy and a violation of the boundaries of freedom. He maintained that the Islamic Revolution supported the principle of freedom in accordance with Islamic instructions and enshrined it in many laws. The government was duty bound to provide political and social freedoms but also to limit and streamline them via certain legal regulations. In order to avoid unnecessary disputes, Muḥammad Yazdī stressed that the only people who can determine whether an action conforms to Islamic principles are the jurisconsults of the Council of Guardians, who are appointed by the Supreme Leader. He further explained that in the Islamic Republic of Iran, freedom, independence, unity, and territorial integrity are inseparable, and freedom cannot be used to undermine the unity of the people or the country's independence and territorial integrity.[68]

Similarly, Miṣbāḥ Yazdī conceded that the scope of freedom in Islam was narrower than in the West; freedom in Islam is based on the spiritual and material interests of society, while in the West only material interests determine its boundaries. Liberal ideology puts the individual on top, whereas religion gives priority to communal over individual interests. In addition, he argued, the three slogans of the Revolution, "Independence, Liberty and Islamic Republic," were inspired by the Qur'ān. Hence liberty implied liberation from the "claws of arrogance," i.e., the United States, and not "from religion, God and common sense," (an idea which is not so different from the secular Ba'th party's conceptualization of liberty as freedom from imperialism).[69] In other words, Miṣbāḥ Yazdī, as a staunch advocate of the absolute *vilāyat-i faqīh* and a thinker who

67 Khomeini, *Ṣaḥīfa-i nūr*, vol. 3, 48, 159; vol. 4, 259; vol. 5, 247; vol. 22, 160, 201.

68 Yazdī, *Voice of the Islamic Republic of Iran*, September 25, 1998 (SWB), May 5, 2000 (DR).

69 *Iran*, May 6, 1999; IRNA, April 21; *Risālat*, May 16; *Jumhūrī-i Islāmī*, June 21, 2000.

denied the people any role in governing society, rejected the notion of political liberty within the framework of the Islamic Republic.[70]

In October 2000, in the midst of the hardline offensive against the reformists, Ḥujjat al-Islām Rūḥollah Ḥusayniyān, a judge in the special court for clerics, complained, in an interesting reversal of roles, that the reformists "promote suppression in the name of freedom" and asked:

> What kind of freedom is it that allows people to show their hair, allows boys and girls to sit beside each other in expensive cars, and allows their music to disturb the hearts of the believers?… Is it correct that in this country everyone should be free except those who have really made great efforts for religion and the revolution? What kind of freedom is it in which religious youngsters are not allowed to defend religion?

The reformists, he concluded, "create suppression in the name of freedom."[71]

Freedom of thought. The question of the freedom of belief (*ʿaqīda*) and thought is seen as more delicate than political freedom. All Shīʿī clerics and mainstream intellectuals agree that God gave people the ability and right to choose what to think and believe. As proof, they point to the Qurʾānic passage, "there is no compulsion in religion" (*Lā ikrāh fī al-dīn*, 2:256), which bans forced conversions to Islam.[72] However, alongside these rights come certain "duties" (*takālīf*) stipulated by Sharīʿa, which guide people in choosing the right path and reward or punish them accordingly. The questions at stake, therefore, are whether or not people have the right not to believe, the right to freedom from religion, the right to conduct themselves according to whatever belief they choose, and the inherent tension between freedom of belief and charges of apostasy, which, in Islamic law, entail the death sentence.

All mainstream clerics highlight Islam's acceptance of the freedom of belief. They insist that imposing beliefs forcibly is impossible and undermines the whole purpose of religion. Muṭṭaharī explained that all past attempts to supervise and control thoughts had harmed Islam and warned that attempts to do so might bring about the fall of the Islamic Republic. He expressed confidence,

---

70 For more on Miṣbāḥ Yazdī's views of democracy, see Siavoshi, "Ayatullah Misbah Yazdī," 129–130.

71 "They Promote Suppression in the Name of Freedom," *Risālat*, October 5, 2000 (FBIS).

72 For a thorough analysis of this issue, see Yohanan Friedmann, *Tolerance and Coercion in Islam: Interfaith Relations in the Muslim Tradition* (Cambridge: Cambridge University Press, 2003), 100–106; Patricia Crone, "No Pressure, Then: Religious Freedom in Islam," November 7, 2009, https://www.opendemocracy.net/patricia-crone/no-compulsion-in-religion.

however, that Islam possessed the doctrinal and ideological strength to logically refute any opposing or antagonistic views; thus, he maintained, freedom of thought poses no danger to Islam. Despite this insistence that all are free to think whatever they want, Shīʿī thinkers clarify that freedom of belief is not unrestricted. Islam, they insist, cannot accept or respect beliefs based on false premises, just as a teacher cannot accept mathematical mistakes as correct, and because Islam regards itself superior to all other beliefs, it cannot accept false ideas. What they are concerned about, therefore, is the dissemination of "false" or "corrupt" opinions and beliefs.[73] In other words, freedom of belief is permitted provided each person keeps their beliefs to themselves.

Freedom of expression. A critical corollary of political freedom and a subject of intensive debate in Shīʿī discourse is freedom of expression. The training of the clerical elite in the seminaries has always been based on religious texts and the traditional means of communication with constituents has been preaching, as was evident in the important role of sermons and audio cassetes in mobilizing the people during the 1979 Revolution. Hence, the clerics have always appreciated the power of the written and spoken word and have given much thought to the question of the scope or limits of freedom of expression. It elicited widespread discussion following the conservative shutdown of dozens of reformist newspapers in mid-2000 and, later, after the 2009 demonstrations. As with political freedom, the criterion for restricting freedom was the vague concept of violating Islamic or revolutionary principles as defined by the authorities.

Khomeini sought to present his position in positive terms by stating that the freedom of expression, as prescribed by Islam, aims to benefit the people and promote comradeship. The limits of such freedom should be the will of the nation, and it should not allow conspiracies, the spread of corruption, the promotion of chaos, or the raising of questions that may lead the people toward deviation.[74] In addition to this moralist perspective, Khomeini justified these restrictions as the necessary response to the "conspiring pens" of "the

73 Subḥānī, "Irtidād va-āzādī-i andīsheh;" Salīmī, "Āzādī as dīdār-i ustād-i Muṭṭaharī"; Mahdī Muntaẓir Qā'im, "Āzādī-i andīsheh," *Ḥukūmat-i Islāmī* 7 (1377/1999): 39–40; "Āzādī-i ʿaqīda dar Islām," 15 Mordād 1388/August 6, 2009, https://article.tebyan.net/98833/آزادی-عقیده-در-اسلام; Wahba al-Zuhaylī, "Āzādī-i andīsheh va-goftār az manẓar-i adyān va-farhanghā," *Ḥawza* 128–129 (1384/2005), http://jh.isca.ac.ir/article_1055.html; Kārnāmī, "Āzādī-i ʿaqīda va-āzādī-i bayān;" ʿAbbās Nīkzād, "Āzādī-i ʿaqīda va-maẕhab dar Islām," *Riwāq-i andīsheh* 18 (1382/2003), http://ensani.ir/fa/article/48368/.

74 Jamʿiyyat al-maʿārif al-Islāmiyya al-thaqāfiyya, *Durūs min khaṭ al-Imām al-Khumaynī, silsilat al-durūs al-thaqāfiyya* (Beirut, 2007), 69; Muḥammad Ṣādiq Shahbāzī, "Āzādī az dīdār-i Imām-i Khomeini," 24 Tīr 1391/July 14, 2012, http://www.teribon.ir/archives/114286.

mercenaries" of America, the former Shāh, and Zionism, who endeavor to take advantage of the liberalism and tolerance permitted by the Revolution.[75]

All mainstream clerics followed suit in defining the scope and limits of freedom of expression, often using the charge of conspiracies and bad intentions to restrict it. Rafsanjānī argued that the Islamic government guarantees numerous basic liberties, such as the freedom for people to take part in shaping their fate and to express their views. Freedom, discussion, debate, and argument are all good and constructive, he asserted, and society would not progress if not for political criticism; however, such criticism should respect limits and boundaries so as not to be misused by "the many enemies who are lying in ambush."[76]

Both Muṭṭaharī and Miṣbāḥ Yazdī pointed to Imām ʿAlī – who did not banish his greatest critics, the Khawārij, from society but allowed them to express their views – as the ideal model of free speech in Islam. Miṣbāḥ Yazdī went even further and justified criticism of Islamic principles that was done in good faith and for the sake of Islam. Yet, both scholars added that ʿAlī permitted everything except the spread of corruption, sedition, and misguidance of the people, and thus they added the proviso that harboring conspiracies and bad intentions or the desire to drive people away from the correct religious path was totally unacceptable. Others likened subversive speech to a drug that poisons the soul and should therefore be banned like drugs that poison the body.[77] In other words, freedom of expression is confined to "correct" beliefs alone.

During the brief window of cultural openness in the later 1990s, Muḥammad Yazdī attacked journalists for interpreting freedom to mean that they could write about whatever they liked. He complained that they considered it their right to resort to sophistry, create doubt, mislead young people, and question even the most fundamental Islamic principles about which there is consensus among Islamic scholars. Muḥammad Yazdī distinguished between legitimate freedom – i.e., freedom as defined by the regime which the judiciary is bound to support – and the anarchic freedom advocated by elements of the press. Both he and Ayatollah Aḥmad Jannatī, head of the powerful Council of the Guardians, threatened journalists, stating that their tongues would be cut out

---

75 Markaz Nūn, *Al-Ḥurriyya fī fikr al-Imām al-Khumaynī*, 20.

76 *Voice of the Islamic Republic of Iran*, March 20, 1998 (BBC Monitoring); *Jumhūrī-i Islāmī*, June 21, 2000 (DR).

77 Ẕākīrī, "Dīn va-āzādī as dīdār-i shahīd Muṭṭaharī"; Miṣbāḥ Yazdī, "Dīn va-āzādī (2) goftegū bā Ayatollah Miṣbāḥ Yazdī." See also Muntaẓir Qāʾim, "Āzādī-i Andīsheh"; and Ishāqī, "Ḥudūd-i āzādī-i bayān dar Islām," 19–22.

should they continue to write against Islam, the Revolution, and the people's sacred values.[78]

Various clerics in Qom, who did not hold official positions, distinguished between freedom of expression for ordinary people and the freedom of thought reserved for clerics. For example, Ayatollah Yūsuf Ṣāneʿī and ʿAbd al-Karīm Mūsavī Ardabīlī (d. 2016) defended the rights of the liberal Ḥujjat al-Islām Muḥsin Kadīvar to come out against the *vilāyat-i faqīh* doctrine, claiming that a *mujtahid* (a cleric qualified to issue independent rulings) was entitled to deal with legal and philosophical question without interruption. Likewise, a petition of 385 clerics supporting Ayatollah Ḥusayn ʿAlī Montaẓerī (d. 2009), Khomeini's deposed designated heir, was submitted in March 1998, calling for the recognition of the right of the *marājiʿ taqlīd* to express their views freely in matters of religion. Similarly Ḥujjat al-Islām Muḥammad Taqī Fāżil Maybudī, lecturer at Mufīd University in Qom, insisted on the right of clerics to think independently, even if their views are unacceptable to the mob. However, many of these clerics distinguished between keeping freedom of thought and expression within the seminary and bringing it to the wider public whose superficial religious knowledge could be harmed by exposure to the doubts and internal debates of the clergy. This difference corresponds with the age-old Shīʿī tradition of distinguishing between exoteric knowledge (*ẓāhir*), which is accessible to all believers, and esoteric knowledge (*bāṭin*), which is confined to the knowledgeable few. Even Muṭṭaharī and Muḥammad Yazdī accepted theoretical scholarly debates within the religious seminaries, where some might even deny the existence of God, the Prophet, and imāms, but why, Muḥammad Yazdī asked, raise such issues in public and among students who had no political experience?[79]

Legislation constraining the freedom of expression was passed and implemented, and Article 24 of the Iranian Constitution thus stipulated that: "Publications and the press have freedom of expression except when it is

---

78 Yazdī cited in *Voice of the Islamic Republic of Iran* September 25, 1998 (SWB), May 5, 2000 (DR). See similar threats to use force in *Risālat*, December 3, 1998; January 11, 1999.

79 AFP, March 11, 1998; *Iṭṭilāʿāt*, December 22, 1998; *Voice of the Islamic Republic of Iran Radio*, May 1, 5, 2000 (DR); "No System Would Permit Some People to Abuse Freedom in Order to Effect an Overthrow," *Risālat*, August 21, 2000 (FBIS); Salīmī, "Āzādī az dīdār-i ustād-i Muṭṭaharī"; Ḥabīb Ḥaydarī and Mahdī ʿAzīzān, "Irtidād: Āzādī-i andīsheh va-āzādī-i bayān," *Kalām-i Islāmī* 43 (1381/2002): 74–85. An historical example of this approach is the struggle of the mainstream clerics against Shaykh Aḥmad Ahsāʾī, the founder of the Shaykhiyya movement, at the beginning of the nineteenth century. They accused him, among other things, of "bringing down" esoteric knowledge to the masses when it should have been confined to the clergy, see Meir Litvak, *Shīʿī Scholars of Nineteenth Century Iraq: The ʿUlamaʾ of Najaf and Karbalaʾ* (Cambridge: Cambridge University Press, 1998), 54–55, 58–60.

detrimental to the fundamental principles of Islam or the rights of the public." The Press Law went further and banned "publishing atheistic articles or issues which are prejudicial to Islamic codes or promoting subjects which might damage the foundation of the Islamic Republic" and "propagating obscene and religiously forbidden acts."[80] The most famous case of implementing this approach was the 1989 fatwā in which Khomeini sentenced to death the British-Indian author Salman Rushdie and all those involved in the publication of his book *The Satanic Verses* on the basis of blasphemy and "opposition to Islam, the Prophet, and the Qur'ān."[81]

When the reformist-dominated parliament sought to modify the Press Law and allow greater freedom of expression in August 2000, Khamenei blocked it, stating, in a letter to Speaker Mahdī Karrūbī, that the current press law was capable of preventing the takeover or infiltration of the press by the enemies of Islam and the Revolution. Any amendment of the law would "threaten the security, unity, and faith of the people." Obeying Khamenei's instruction, Karrūbī adjourned the parliamentary session and ended the affair.[82]

The Iranian judiciary subsequently shut down dozens of reformist newspapers and sought to restrict such liberties on the local internet scene as well. According to various human rights observer organizations, "since June 2009, the authorities have cracked down on online activism through various forms of judicial and extra-legal intimidation," and an increasing number of bloggers have been threatened, arrested, tortured, kept in solitary confinement, and denied medical care, while others have been formally tried and convicted.[83]

6 Freedom, Apostasy, and Treason

On setting the various restrictions on liberty, many could not ignore their apparent contradiction to the Qur'ānīc principle "there is no compulsion in religion." Most glaring was the contradiction between freedom of belief and expression

80 "Iran (Islamic Republic of): Press Law (as amended on April 18, 2000)," http://www.wipo.int/wipolex/en/text.jsp?file_id=248969.

81 For analyses of the affair, see Marty M. Slaughter, "The Salman Rushdie Affair: Apostasy, Honor, and Freedom of Speech," *Virginia Law Review* 79, no. 1 (1993): 153–204; Anthony Chase, "Legal Guardians: Islamic Law, International Law, Human Rights Law, and the Salman Rushdie Affair," *American University International Law Review* 11, no. 3 (1996): 375–435.

82 IRNA, August 6, 2000.

83 Freedom House, "Freedom on the Net 2012: A Global Assessment of Internet and Digital Media," http://www.freedomhouse.org/report/freedom-net/freedom-net-2012; "Human Rights Watch World Report 2017: Iran Events 2016," *Human Rights Watch*, https://www.hrw.org/world-report/2017/country-chapters/iran.

and the punishment of death for apostasy (*irtidād*) or the renunciation of Islam. Sunnī jurists have historically been very cautious in declaring someone an apostate; modern, radical Sunnī jihādī-Salafīsts, on the other hand, are much more willing to call those who disagree with their strict interpretation of religion apostates who deserve death.[84] Shīʿī scholars, who represent a minority within the Muslim community, have not declared Sunnīs as apostates, both because they feared a violent backlash and because they sought to draw the Sunnīs into the Shīʿī fold. At the same time, declaring rivals to be apostates became an increasingly important tool in internal ideological struggles within Shīʿīsm from the late eighteenth century. The Islamic Republic's penal code does not explicitly prohibit apostasy. Nevertheless, it states that in accordance with Article 167 of the Iranian Constitution, Sharīʿa law must be applied in instances where the penal code is silent regarding a particular crime. This provision enables the judiciary to prosecute cases of apostasy, even though there is no codified provision defining such a crime.

Indeed, only a few clerics and intellectuals, most notably Ḥasan Yūsufī Eshkivarī (October 2000) and Hāshim Aghājarī (November 2002), were tried under this charge, but their death sentences were commuted to imprisonment. In addition, Iran's revolutionary court sentenced eighteen Christian converts to long prison terms for apostasy. The evolving ideological discourse in the Islamic Republic has expanded the definition of apostasy from the outright rejection of religion to disrespect (*ihānat*) toward Islamic sanctities or rejection of the doctrine of *vilāyat-i faqīh*, the basis of the Islamic Republic's political system. Similarly, various hardline clerics declared the leaders and activists of the Green Movement as committing apostasy following their 2009 protest.[85] While this increasing intolerance did not lead to the same conduct as radical jihādī-Salafīsts, it has enabled greater suppression of religious and political dissent.

---

84 For legal and historical analyses of apostasy in Sunnī Islam, see Rudolph Peters and Gert J.J. De Vries, "Apostasy in Islam," *Die Welt des Islams*, New Series 17, no. 1/4 (1976–1977): 1–25; Sherazad Hamit, "Apostasy and the Notion of Religious Freedom in Islam," *Macalester Islam Journal* 1, no. 2 (2006): 31–38; Abdullah Saeed and Hassan Saeed, *Freedom of Religion, Apostasy and Islam* (Burlington, VT: Ashgate, 2002).

85 Iran Human Rights Documentation Center, *Apostasy in the Islamic Republic of Iran*, July 2014, http://www.iranhrdc.org/english/publications/reports/1000000512-apostasy-in-the-Islamic-Republic-of-Iran.html#1.3. See the statement by ʿAlī Miṣbāḥ Yazdī to IRGC officers on Khordād 24, 1389/ June 14, 2010 that any person who knowingly rejects *vilāyat-i faqīh* is an apostate, http://www.farsnews.com/newstext.php?nn=8903240252; "Ayatollah Khōshvaqt: Mūsavī va-Karrūbī, murtad va-kāfirand," January 2, 2013, http://rahedigar.net/1391/10/13/7577/.

Mainstream writers have addressed the contradiction between the principle of "no compulsion in religion" and the growing intolerance toward dissent by drawing the distinctions between freedom of belief and freedom of expression or conduct or between silent and public apostasy. Accordingly, apostates are free to think or believe whatever they like; provided they keep their ideas to themselves, they need not be punished on earth and will be judged by God alone. However, the moment they express themselves in public, they must be punished due to the consequences of their deeds. Subḥānī limits apostasy to public challenges on the essential principles of religion and excludes the questioning of less prominent matters of law or belief. Some go further and differentiate between so called "scholarly" (*ʿilmī*) and practical (*ʿamalī*) apostates. In other words, and as mentioned above, they are willing to tolerate the questioning of major theological issues if done as part of a scholarly or theological debate; those questioning deserve an appropriate intellectual response and should only be punished if they insist on spreading their views in public.[86]

A prevalent view confines the principle of "no compulsion in religion" to the right of non-Muslims to practice their religions freely but does not free Muslims from their religious duties or allow them to leave Islam. According to this principle, a person should only adopt Islam voluntarily. But, since Islam is a comprehensive and unified system, it must be accepted as a whole, including the provision which bans Muslims from renouncing it and converting to another religion. Just as those who adopt Islam cannot reject the prohibition on drinking wine and on immoral sexual conduct, neither can they oppose this ban on leaving Islam. The story of a group of Jews who sought to join Islam and subsequently retracted their action in order to undermine the beliefs of other Muslims is used to justify this ban.[87] Freedom of religion is thus accepted, but they deny Muslims the right of freedom from religion.

Several writers have used the liberal limitation on freedom to depict the act of apostasy as the greatest infringement and violation of the rights of others. In discussing the various categories of those whose rights should be respected and protected from the apostate, Scholars Ḥabīb Ḥaydarī and Mahdī ʿAzīzān placed God on top as the worthiest of respect and consideration. Preventing apostates from disseminating their views, they argued, is not a deprivation of

---

86 Kārnāmī, "Āzādī-i ʿaqīda va-āzādī-i bayān;" Ḥaydarī and ʿAzīzān, "Irtidād: Āzādī-i andīsheh va-āzādī-i bayān;" Subḥānī, "Irtidād va-āzādī-i andīsheh."

87 Muḥammad Bāqir Sharīʿatī Sabzivārī, "Irtidād," *Maʿārif-i Islāmī* (1384/2005–2006): 56–59; "Āzādī va-irtidād," *Maʿārif* 47 (1386/2007): 32–35; "Āyā Āya sharīfa lā ikrāh fī al-dīn, bā ḥukm-i iʿdām barāye murtad munāfat nadārad?"; "Āzādī-i ʿaqīda va-bayān va-ḥuqūq-i bashar va-ḥukm-i irtidād chegūneh bā ham jamʿ mīshavand?"; "Ganjīnah-i Maʿārif: Āzādī-i ʿaqīda," 9 Azar 1389/November 30, 2010, http://www.hawzah.net/fa/Article/View/91773.

liberty but, rather, a protection of the rights of others: first and foremost, God, who is followed closely by Muslim society at large.[88] In fact, apostasy constitutes the most heinous crime against society, since it undermines social peace, projects blatant disrespect toward the beliefs and feelings of the Muslims, destabilizes the faith of the community, and thereby threatens the "eternal and true happiness (*sa'ādat*)" of society.[89]

Adherence to faith and religion are among the most basic rights of the individual believer and community, which are subverted by apostates when they disseminate their views. One writer even cited Article 19 of the 1966 UN International Covenant on Civil and Political Rights, which subordinates freedom of expression to "the protection of national security or of public order (ordre public), or of public health or morals," as a legal universal justification for protecting society from the apostate. Therefore, just as society does not allow people to share their beliefs about committing suicide, so too it cannot allow apostates to spread views which promote society's spiritual death. Moreover, just as every country has the right to protect its territory, its natural resources, or even "stone sculptures and pieces of ancient gold," so every society has the right to protect its religion as well as its spiritual and cultural heritage from apostates who seek to undermine it. The fear of the impact of apostates' ideas on society has led some to equate them with AIDS or a pestilence (*tā'ūn*) that threatens society. Even a relative moderate like Ayatollah Montaẓerī equated the apostate who "starts questioning the sanctity of religious elements" with "a cancerous tumor that will gradually spread to the other healthy parts of the body."[90] In the same way that any normal society protects itself from such diseases and eliminates a cancerous tumor, Muslim society should do the same to those who threaten its spiritual health, which is more important than its physical condition. Since Islam, unlike Western liberalism, prioritizes the interests of the community over the individual, preventing the one from harming the many is the correct implementation of liberty.[91] This is stated very clearly on

88 Ḥaydarī and 'Azīzān, "Irtidād: Āzādī-i andīsheh;" "Āzādī va-irtidād."

89 "Āzādī-i bayān va-i'dām-i murtad," http://www.adyan.porsemani.ir/content/آزادی-بیان-و-اعدام-مرتد.

90 Muḥammad Sorūsh, "Āyā irtidād kīfar 'ḥadd' dārad? (Ta'ammolī bar mahiyat-i kīfar irtidād)," *Ḥukūmat-i Islāmī,* 19 (1380/2001), http://ensani.ir/fa/article/83786/آیا-ارتداد-کیفر-حدّ-دارد-تأملی-بر-ماهیت-کیفر-ارتداد-.

91 Ja'far Subḥānī in *Risālat,* 30 Tīr 1389/June 30, 2010; Kārnāmī, "Āzādī-i 'aqīda va-āzādī-i bayān;" "Cherā dar Islām murtad rā mīkoshānd? Āyā 'īn kār mukhālif-i āzādī-i 'aqīda ast?," http://www.islamquest.net/fa/archive/question/fa289; "Āyā Āya sharīfa lā ikrāh fī al-dīn, bā ḥukm-i i'dām barāye murtad munāfat nadārad?;" "International Covenant on Civil and Political Rights," https://treaties.un.org/doc/publication/unts/volume%20999/

the website of the ʿAlī Aṣghar Mosque: "Freedom of belief, yes; freedom of destruction, never!"[92]

When discussing the challenge the so-called apostates posed to Muslim society, Khamenei emphasized the duty of Islam to protect the faith of the "weak people" (*mardom-i żaʿīf*), who may not be strong enough to withstand this challenge by themselves.[93] The numerous references to the threat that apostates pose to Muslim society reflect a deep sense of insecurity among fundamentalists of all religions concerning the inability of the masses to stand up to the challenge of modernity.[94] However, whereas fundamentalists outside the government opt for self-imposed seclusion as the solution to this threat, spokesmen for the Islamic Republic prefer to take action against agents of the supposed threat. The mainstream discourse goes further than simply justifying the restrictions on apostates' liberties and advocates executing them as those who "wage war against God and His Prophet" (al-Māʾida 33).[95] Most writers realize or fear that the mere citation of the Qurʾānīc passages regarding apostasy may not suffice.[96] Hence, they resort to harsh depictions of the threat of apostates and their crimes against Islam.[97] Such depictions reflect the prevalent fundamentalist view of history "as a cosmic struggle between good and evil using stark binary dichotomies to describe the opposing camps." Accordingly,

---

volume-999-i-14668-english.pdf; Ḥusayn ʿAlī Montaẓerī, "Dar bāb-i tazāḥum: dīn, modārā va-khoshūnat," https://amontazeri.com/book-index/didgaha/475.

92 "Āzādī-i ʿaqīda va-bayān va-ḥuqūq-i bashar va-ḥukm-i irtidād chegūneh bā ham jamʿ mīshavad."

93 "Ḥifāẓāt va-ḥirāsāt az imān-i mardom, vaẓīfa-i niẓām-i Islāmī," 15 Esfand 1365/March 6, 1987, http://farsi.khamenei.ir/newspart-print?id=21492&npt=7&nt=2&year=1365. See similar apprehensions in Kārnāmī, "Āzādī-i ʿaqīda va-āzādī-i bayān," 83; "Āzādī-i ʿaqīda va-bayān va-ḥuqūq-i bashar va-ḥukm-i irtidād chegūneh bā ham jamʿ mīshavad."

94 See the discussion on the Western cultural offensive in Chapter 1.

95 ʿAbdollah Javādī Āmolī, "Irtidād va-āẕādī (2)," *Pāsdār-i Islām* 282 (1382/2003–2004), http://ensani.ir/fa/article/138408/2-ارتداد-و-ازادی-.

96 Although apostasy is mentioned in thirteen verses of the Qurʾān, nowhere is a specific earthly penalty delineated. The Qurʾān penalizes apostates with eternal damnation in the afterlife but neglects to specify a penalty here on earth. A Sunnī ḥadīth, however, cited the Prophet as saying that whoever changes their Islamic religion must be killed. At present, the death penalty has been adopted by many countries with Sharīʿa law to punish apostasy. See David A. Jordan, "The Dark Ages of Islam: Ijtihad, Apostasy, and Human Rights in Contemporary Islamic Jurisprudence," *Washington and Lee Journal of Civil Rights and Social Justice* 9, no. 1 (2003): 61–62.

97 Kārnāmī, "Āzādī-i ʿaqīda va-āzādī-i bayān" 82–83; "Āzādī va-irtidād"; "Āzādī-i bayān va-iʿdām-i murtad;" "Ganjīnah-i Maʿārif: Āzādī-i ʿaqīda;" "Az āzādī-i bayān tā irtidād;" Seyyed Ibrāhīm Ḥusaynī, "Irtidād dar āyīnah-i falsafa-i ḥuqūq-i Islāmī," *Maʿrifat* 70 (1382/2003): 47–58.

apostates are seditious warmongers and traitors, who consciously conspire and fight against Islam in order to destroy it.[98]

Subḥānī, for example, maintained that while apostasy was formerly a Jewish plot against the Prophet, today it is a Zionist plot against Islam. Moreover, as Islam as a system and the Islamic Republic in particular are subject to "the psychological and propaganda war" waged by the West, apostates commit a conscious act of treason (*khiyānat*) against both by actively assisting the enemy in this war. Under such circumstances, executing apostates does not contradict the principle of freedom of belief, since every country, even the more liberal ones, executes traitors and spies during wartime as an act of self-defense.[99] Ishāqī used a certain Orwellian logic to conclude that since Islam provides the only path to true liberty, that is spiritual perfection and happiness, then "the execution of the apostate is in essence the preservation of the liberty of the others."[100]

7 The Reformist and Liberal Approach

Unlike the dominant mainstream, the reformists, who were largely silenced after the crackdown in 2000, had sought a more genuine reconciliation between the regime's ideology and liberal concepts of freedom, believing that this was essential for the long-term survival of the regime and the country's prosperity. Prior to the crackdown, Khātamī maintained that "religion and freedom should not oppose each other. Freedom should not be held back in the name of religion, or religion in the name of freedom." At the same time, however, he asserted that freedom without religion was "the reason for the fall of humanity." For Khātamī, there was no contradiction between Islam and individual rights and the Islamic Republic embodies the ideal combinations of both Islam and freedom: "Religion complies with human rights and civil rights; freedom complies with Islamic cultural values. The Islamic Republic was created for the sake of this combination." He criticized his conservative

98 David Zeidan, "The Islamic Fundamentalist View of Life as a Perennial Battle," *MERIA Journal* 5, no. 4 (2001), http://www.rubincenter.org/2001/12/zeidan-htm-2001-12-02/.

99 "Ayatollah Subḥānī: Taftīsh ʿaqāyid dar dīn mamnūʿ ast," 30 Tīr 1389/July 21, 2010, https://www.isna.ir/news/8904-16421/آیت-الله-العظمي-سبحاني-تفتيش-عقايد-در-دين-ممنوع-است-ارتداد; Subḥānī in *Risālat*, 30 Tīr 1389/July 21, 2010.

100 Seyyed Ḥusayn Ishāqī, "Āzādī-i ʿaqīda dar Islām," *Riwāq-i andīsheh* 29 (1383/2004), https://hawzah.net/fa/Article/View/82409/آزادی-عقیده-در-اسلام. This statement was repeated in quite a few channels. See also Kārnāmī, "Āzādī-i aqīda va-āzādī-i bayān."

rivals, who were using religion as a cover to work against freedom which they equated with anarchy, and charged that the practice of religion without freedom disguised bigotry and the selfish lust for power by religious hardliners in the name of God. Such views, he asserted, were detrimental to Islam, and Iran must strive for freedom or face the risk of more violence.[101]

Khātamī also stressed the importance of diverse trends and ideas and the opportunity to express them. He favored such pluralism not only as a necessity – he was aware that oppression would fail – but also as positive value. If we do not allow the expression of other views, he stated, we insult humanity and a free Islamic society, and he thus concluded that no group should be able to impose its opinions on society.[102] Khātamī went further than the dominant conservative faction in advocating freedom even for those who opposed the regime:

> Freedom does not mean freedom [only] for those who support us.... It means freedom even for those who oppose us. In an Islamic society people should have the freedom to think, and our opponents should be allowed to express their views. We do not have the right to accuse anyone who criticizes us of apostasy and blasphemy. Even if we succeed in stopping criticism for a while, we will not be able to avoid the consequences of such an action.[103]

This, however, is where Khātamī's ideas encounter difficulties. Seeking to harmonize between religion and freedom, he contended that it is impossible to "have freedom in all its legal, philosophical, and political implications without the law.... You cannot endanger security for the sake of freedom, and you cannot endanger freedom for the sake of security.... This is a delicate balance," he admonished impatient students. He emphasized that freedom should come "with responsibility," which is stipulated by the Constitution. Therefore, he said elsewhere, freedom "should not be against the tenets of Islam and the rights of the public." Anyone who accepts the law has rights and these political rights must be defended. But, he warned, those who seek to overthrow the

---

101 Muḥammad Khātamī, *Muṭālaʿāt fī al-dīn wal-Islām wal-ʿaṣr* (Beirut: Dār al-jadīd, 1988), 190–191; *Time*, January 12, 1998; *Iran News*, May 12, 1998; IRIB Television, May 14, 1998 (DR); Voice and Vision of the Islamic Republic of Iran Network 1, July 25, 1999 (SWB); *Mideast Mirror*, May 24, 1999; AFP, February 10, 2001.

102 Khātamī interview to *Middle East Insight* 13, no. 1 (1997): 27; IRIB Television, December 30, 1997, May 14, 1998 (DR); *Time*, January 12, 1998; Voice and Vision of the Islamic Republic of Iran Network 1, July 25, 1998 (SWB), November 26, 2000 (DR).

103 *Radio Free Europe/Radio Liberty IRAN REPORT* 2, no. 21, May 24, 1999.

system are a different matter altogether. They must be guided as far as possible, but, if they do not accept logic, they must be addressed in a different language. In other words, while Khātamī went further than his counterparts, his views still put major constraints on the meaning and scope of freedom, since the criteria were still those defined by the Islamic regime and he ignored the option of freedom from religion.[104]

The position on freedom advanced by ʿAbdollah Nūrī, who served briefly as minister of interior under Khātamī, in his 1999 trial served as a bridge between the reformists and the more liberal clerics. Facing his judges in a political trial, Nūrī argued that the Revolution led by Khomeini had been a golden opportunity for liberating the people from suppression, tyranny, and despotism, and although this had not been attained, Iranians now had another opportunity to achieve this goal. He stated that it was only by acknowledging and preserving the rights of their opponents that they could ensure the longevity and independence of the regime; the abrogation of the liberties of those opposed to the government was an indication not of the regime's power and strength but rather of its feebleness.[105] Nūrī cited Muṭṭaharī's statement that the Qur'ān sought to liberate humans from the enslavement and subjugation by others and added that this social freedom was one of its greatest lessons. Reciting verse 58 of Sūrat Āl ʿImrān, which calls the people of the book to "worship none but God," he told his judges that there could not be a "more lively and more exciting passage, neither in the eighteenth nor the nineteenth centuries when the philosophers' ideas of human liberty were realized and freedom evolved from mere expressions of faith to reality."[106] Taking into consideration the constraints that Nūrī was facing when he made this statement, it may indeed imply that he regarded the freedom to worship God and the spiritual unity of believers as the greatest liberty available. However, he apparently could not fathom or bring himself to say that freedom *from* worship was also a possibility.

Ḥujjat al-Islam Muḥsin Kadīvar acquired fame after showing that the *vilāyat-i faqīh* doctrine not only completely contradicted genuine democracy but also had never enjoyed the exclusive status in Shīʿīsm that its adherents claimed. His equation of the *vilāyat-i faqīh*'s broad powers with those of the previous monarchy earned him eighteen months in prison, and he was later forced to leave Iran. Kadīvar's starting point was the absolute need for freedom

---

104 IRIB Television First Program Network, December 30, 1997 (DR); IRNA, August 7, 2000; *Tehran Times*, August 23, 2000; *New York Times*, September 8, 2000; AFP, February 12, 2001; Voice and Vision of the Islamic Republic of Iran Network May 2, 28, June 2, 2001 (DR).

105 ʿAbdollah Nūrī, *Showkārān-i iṣlāḥ difāʿiyat-i Abdollah* Nūrī *dar dādgāh-i vīzheh-i rūḥāniyat* (Teheran: Tarh-i now, 1999), 197; *Iran News*, November 14, 1999.

106 Nūrī, *Showkaran-i iṣlāḥ*, 159.

of belief and the rejection of any coercion in religion regarding not just forced conversion to Islam but, more importantly, the practice of religion. He argued that obeying Islamic ordinances under duress rather than from genuine belief was meaningless from a religious point of view and would harm religion in the long run. Presumably as an argumentative ploy against his hardline adversaries, Kadīvar added practical reasons to his more principled position, explaining that in the age of modern communications no society could shut out external ideas, and pluralism of thought was therefore inevitable. Furthermore, the lack of freedom would lead to deceit and hypocrisy, which would ultimately lead to both the destruction of faith and the stagnation of religion and society. Hence, society should accept or even welcome criticism on the principles of religion in order to remain vibrant and dynamic.[107] Kadīvar went further than all other clerics when he maintained that in cases of divergence between religious precepts and the will of the people, popular will should prevail and only peaceful persuasion be employed and never coercion. The "people should not be dragged to paradise by chains and shackles," he insisted.[108]

Kadīvar accepted the liberal notion of "the right to choose and adhere to any idea; the right to think, believe, express, teach, promote, and act on one's beliefs, so long as the rights of others are not obstructed." However, he also added the caveat "so long as … public peace and order is not disrupted,"[109] a qualification which could be and has been used by authoritarian governments to suppress and silence any opposition or ideological dissent. It is unclear whether Kadīvar was aware of this problem. In view of his public defense of dissidents and Bahāʾis, it is conceivable that he leaned toward the position of "defensive democracy" adopted by some European governments in order to combat radical right-wing extremists.

Significantly, Kadīvar rejected the dominant Shīʿī doctrine on apostasy as incompatible with freedom and with a true reading of the Qurʾān. He argued that the death penalty for those choosing to leave Islam contradicts the "no compulsion in religion" principle; freedom of religion, he claimed, meant "freedom

107 Mohsen Kadivar, "The Freedom of Religion and Belief in Islam," in *The New Voices of Islam: Reforming Politics and Modernity – A Reader*, ed. Mehran Kamrava (London: I.B. Tauris, 2006), 129–131; *Aftāb-i Yazd*, December 30, 2000.

108 Muḥsin Kadīvar, "Mardomsālārī-i dīnī," www.kadivar.com; *Bahār*, July 11, 2000 (DR); Muhsin Kadīvar to *Frankfurter Allgemeine Zeitung*, August 21, 2000 (DR); Muḥsin Kadīvar to *Jāmiʿa-i madanī*, cited in www.payvand.com, October 23 and 25, 2000. See a similar approach by President Rouhani, "Let people choose their own path to heaven. We cannot send people to heaven by force or the lash," Golnaz Esfandiari, "Dispute Over Heaven Rages in Iran," RFE/RL June 4, 2014, https://www.rferl.org/a/iran-rohani-religion-dispute/25410189.html.

109 Kadivar, "The Freedom of Religion and Belief in Islam," 122.

in both matters: freedom in bringing religion and freedom in leaving it." In a bold statement that could have earned him the charge of apostasy among hardliners, he agreed that God can punish the apostate in the next world. He concluded, however, that "there is no doubt that death sentence and life imprisonment for the apostate or making an infidel choose between Islam and death are obviously clear examples of duress in religion." Moreover, he equated the persecution of apostates and implicitly those condemned by the regime as apostates with the "the attitude of the tyrants and the pharaohs," which God condemns.[110] True to his words, Kadīvar relied on the Universal Declaration of Human Rights to oppose the suppression of Bahā'īs in Iran.

Kadīvar's teacher, Montaẓerī, softened his position on apostasy over time, presumably in response to the misuse of the term by the regime and its supporters as a weapon against political dissidents. In 2005 he ruled that converting as a result of intellectual endeavor and without open hostility to Islam ("the Truth,") and rejection of the essentials of religion (*ḍarāriyyāt*) were not apostasy provided they did not lead to the negation of Prophethood and should not be punished. According to Montaẓerī, the rejection of Islam (i.e., apostasy) is dependent upon enmity and hostility.[111] In other words, Montaẓerī expanded the freedom of religion and even allowed, in practice, freedom from religion, but he conditioned it on the basis of refraining from any open criticism or attack on religion.

While Kadīvar approached the question of freedom from the discipline of jurisprudence, Ḥujjat al-Islam Muḥammad Mojtahed-Shabestari addressed it from a theological point of view.[112] He made an important contribution to the Shīʿī intellectual debate by pointing out the limited nature of religious knowledge and Islamic jurisprudence. He dismissed any assertion that human beings could ever come into direct possession of God's absolute truth; our knowledge of God and his commandments is always mere human knowledge, and as such it is mutable and never absolute. Mojtahed-Shabestari maintained that one can never really understand texts, including the Qur'ān, and therefore

---

110 Kadivar, "The freedom of thought and religion in Islam -II-," https://nawaat.org/portail/2005/02/03/the-freedom-of-thought-and-religion-in-islam-ii/.

111 Mohsen Kadivar, "Introduction," in *Apostasy, Blasphemy, & Religious Freedom in Islam: A Critique Based on Demonstrative Jurisprudence* (Islam and Human Rights Series no. 2), e-book, http://en.kadivar.com/2014/07/23/an-introduction-to-apostasy-blasphemy-religious-freedom-in-islam/.

112 On this distinction between the two, see Mahmoud Sadri, "Sacral Defense of Secularism: The Political Theologies of Soroush, Shabestari, and Kadivar," *International Journal of Politics, Culture and Society* 15, no. 2 (2001): 266. Between 1970 and 1979, Mojtahed-Shabestari was the director of the Islamic Center in Hamburg, where he became acquainted with German philosophy as well as Catholic and Protestant theology.

he insisted that "our understanding of revelation must be viewed in terms of a hermeneutic exercise and that this understanding is not a fixed category" as "every text is a hidden reality that has to be revealed through interpretation."[113] Relying on Jurgen Habermas, he cautioned that all interpreters have particular epistemological interests when reading texts and their hypotheses are based on those interests. The text answers only those questions put to it, and everyone finds in the Qur'ān the answers they seek. This is also, he claimed, what allows for a democratic interpretation of Islam. In other words, the key to the hermeneutic conception of Islam is that it is capable of different readings and interpretations.[114] The official reading (*qirā'at*) of Islam is historically contingent and only one of its many possible readings. However, he continued, the official reading of Islam in Iran has, over time, been undermined by a crisis of legitimacy since it advocated non-participation, theorized violence, and lacked scientific validity.[115] Mojtahed-Shabestari was thus asserting that freedom of thought and beliefs and pluralism were crucial for preserving true faith.

Like the mainstream clerics, Mojtahed-Shabestari sees faith as resting on free will, one of the key traits characterizing humanity. The faithful must continually reflect upon what is part of their faith and what is not. This means that they must distinguish between behavior based on a freely made inner decision, which is the result of a spiritual or religious experience, and conduct, which is ultimately a purely superficial imitation of religious acts and truisms. He believes that in order to achieve such awareness, one must seriously and openly come to terms with contemporary criticisms of religious thinking – whether they derive from Muslim or non-Muslim sources. Likewise, true understanding and an embracing of God is possible primarily as a result of a critical attitude and of liberating one's thought from any form of dogmatism. Mojtahed-Shabestari thus combines highly self-critical and emancipatory aspirations with the concept of faith.[116] Therefore, in the desired Islamic society even external critiques of religion, such as those of Marx and Feuerbach, are not only tolerated but are even welcomed to some extent as they can help the

---

113 Vahdat, "Post-revolutionary discourses of Muḥammad Mojtahed Shabestari and Mohsen Kadivar: Reconciling the terms of mediated subjectivity," *Critique: Critical Middle Eastern Studies*, 16 (Spring 2000): 36–37.

114 Naser Ghobadzādeh, "Religious Secularity: A Vision for Revisionist Political Islam," *Philosophy and Social Criticism* 39, no. 10 (2013): 1016.

115 Mojtahed-Shabestari, *A Critique of the Official Reading of Religion* (2000) cited in Said A. Arjomand, *After Khomeini: Iran under his Successors* (Oxford: Oxford University Press, 2009), 80–81.

116 Roman Seidel, "Portrait Muḥammad Shabestari: Faith, Freedom, and Reason," http://en.qantara.de/content/portrait-Muḥammad-shabestari-faith-freedom-and-reason.

faithful refine their conceptions of religion and thus achieve purer forms of religiosity. In such a society, if books against religion are not published and a critique of religion is not allowed, faith loses its main characteristic and would no longer be a conscious act of choosing.[117] Furthermore, he claimed, "in the society of the faithful there are no 'red lines' to demarcate the limits of critique. The critics must have all the space to engage in critique without any red lines."[118] In the eyes of some hardliners, such statements could be perceived as condoning apostasy.

Mojtahed-Shabestari rejected the call by the arch-conservative Miṣbāḥ Yazdī to "break the idols of freedom," stating that liberty was in fact the true "idol-breaker" (*bat shekān*). The core of liberty in the modern age, he explained, is the unquestionable knowledge of the right to freedom of thought, belief, and expression together with moral responsibility for all members of society without any exception: "If we consider liberty to be an idol and ban it, how would people be able to discern what is an idol and what is God? and how would they be able to keep away from idols and adhere to God?" he stated.[119] In other words, for Mojtahed-Shabestari, freedom was essential for genuine religious belief and practice.

Mojtahed-Shabestari, like the mainstream clerics, posited that true freedom is internal, namely, the liberation of humans from internal shackles. Unlike them however, he maintained that as far as the attributes and components of liberty were concerned, Islam never went beyond general principles, and these remained subject to human interpretation. Moreover, in sharp contrast to the mainstream, he insisted that the people's choice of inner freedom must correspond with external freedom, because the inner belief in God cannot be forced upon people from the outside. He yearned for a free and tolerant atmosphere that respected the sanctity of individuals and allowed them to live true religious lives; religious dogmas that prescribe what people should or should not believe are not, he claimed, guideposts to true faith but rather barriers that hinder the free development of faith. He criticized the dominant interpretation of the Qur'ānic passage "there is no compulsion in religion" as referring to only non-Muslims and argued that "this compulsion, this lack of freedom, creates an irreligious society, one that no longer has any sense of what religion is,

---

117 Amīr Rowshan and Muḥsin Shafīʿī Sayfabādī, "Tafsīr-i dīn va-ta'thīr-i ān bar mafhūm-i āzādī dar andīsheh-i siyāsī-i Ayatollah Muḥammad Taqī Miṣbāḥ Yazdī va-Muḥammad Mojtahed Shabestari," *Pazhūhesh-i siyāsat-i naẓarī* 6 (Winter 1389/2010 & Spring 1390/2011): 32.

118 Vahdat, "Post-Revolutionary Discourses," 52–53.

119 Muḥammad Mojtahed-Shabestari, "Āzādī bat nīst, bat shekān ast!," May 13, 2014, http://www.cgie.org.ir/fa/news/12362.

treats religion with indifference."[120] Therefore, human rights and democracy, in his view, are in keeping with Islam, not because they have been dictated by the Qur'ān or the prophetic tradition but because their realization enables people to create the basic political and social conditions under which a free and, therefore, true faith can be fostered. Democracy and human rights thus serve Islam much better than any Islamic, yet authoritarian, system.[121]

AbdolKarim Soroush, who turned from a revolutionary into a prominent intellectual critic of the Islamic Republic, approached the question of freedom from two complementary vantage points: first, the philosophical compatibility and interdependence between reason and freedom and second, his own distinction between religion as revealed by God and religion as understood by humans. Like Mojtahed-Shabestari, he perceived religion as divine, eternal, immutable, and sacred. He maintained, however, that the understanding of religion is a human endeavor like any other. Religious knowledge (*maʿrifat-i dīnī*) is not sacred and is affected by and in constant exchange with all other fields of human knowledge, and it is thus in flux, relative, and time-bound. In other words, Soroush rejected the idea of one correct interpretation of religion and dismissed the attempts to formulate an official Islamic political ideology, advocating instead pluralism in the interpretation of religion, similar to Mojtahed-Shabestari's approach to hermeneutics. Freedom of thought and expression is, accordingly, essential for religion.[122] This logic culminates in Soroush's position on apostasy which resembles Mojtahed-Shabestari's and Kadīvar's: freedom of religion does not end once a person has chosen a religion, and he rejected the imposition of belief on Muslims.[123] In his essay "Reason and Freedom," Soroush emphasized the interdependence between freedom and reason as well as the correspondence between freedom and

120 "Interview with Muḥammad Mojtahed Shabestari (Part 1): 'Islam Is a Religion, Not a Political Agenda,'" https://en.qantara.de/content/interview-with-Muḥammad-mojtahed-shabestari-part-1-islam-is-a-religion-not-a-political-0.

121 Vahdat, "Post-Revolutionary Discourses," 46; Seidel, "Portrait Muḥammad Shabestari" Rowshan and Shafīʿī Sayfabādī, "Tafsīr-i dīn," 33–35.

122 Soroush has been the subject of numerous studies. The passages on him are taken from Kamrava, *Iran' s Intellectual Revolution*, 157; Jahanbaksh, *Islam, Democracy and Religious Modernism in Iran, 1953–2000*, 148; Valla Vakili, "Debating Religion and Politics in Iran: The Political Thought of Abdolkarim Soroush," Council on Foreign Relations, January 1996, http://www.drsoroush.com/PDF/E-CMO-19960100-Debating_Religion_and_Politics_in_Iran-Valla_Vakili.pdf; David Menashri, *Post-Revolutionary Politics in Iran: Religion, Society, and Power* (Portland: F. Cass, 2001), 33–34.

123 Abdolkarim Soroush, *Reason, Freedom, and Democracy in Islam: The Essential Writings of Abdolkarim Soroush*, ed. and trans. Mahmoud Sadri and Ahmad Sadri (New York: Oxford University Press, 2000), 141–142.

truth. Since religion is, in essence, the epitome of truth, he suggested that religion should not contradict freedom. He used this premise to criticize those who are afraid of freedom, arguing that: "freedom might upset personal convictions, but it cannot possibly offend the truth except for those who presume to personify the absolute truth," i.e. those clerics who claim to monopolize the truth and thereby deprive others of freedom.[124] He also criticized the conservatives who "make the mistake of resenting freedom because it may allow the forces of darkness and corruption to surround righteousness." Rather, he argued that freedom provides "a range and dynamism for the truth that is absent in unfreedom."[125]

Soroush, like most other religious thinkers, highlighted the great value of internal freedom as "liberating oneself from the rein of passion and anger." But, contrary to the mainstream clerics and similar to Mojtahed-Shabestari, he also emphasized the importance of external freedom which emancipated people "from the yoke of potentates, despot, charlatans, and exploiters." The prerequisite for achieving external freedom was participation "in the contest of freedom," namely participation in a political democratic process. Moreover, in a true democratic fashion, he concluded that one "must tolerate the enemies, except the enemies of tolerance."[126] Unsurprisingly, in July 2013, the Qom's Society of Seminary Teachers declared Soroush himself an apostate.[127]

8 Conclusion

The Shīʿī Iranian discourse on freedom evolved in response to pressure from below for greater liberties and from an awareness of the wide social appeal of Western liberal interpretations of freedom. Contributors to the discourse on freedom formulate a religious Islamic concept, not unlike that of other religions, of internal spiritual freedom, which purports to liberate people from enslavement to material desires and subjugation to other human beings by a voluntarily submission to God and his rules. It subordinates freedom to the nobler goal of attaining spiritual perfection and "ultimate happiness." The traditional concept of internal freedom might have suited minorities who lacked any political power or mystics who focused more on otherworldly spiritual

124 Soroush, "Reason and Freedom," in *Reason, Freedom, and Democracy in Islam*, 89, 91.

125 Ibid., 91–92.

126 Ibid., 99.

127 "Irtidād ʿAbd al-Karīm Sorūsh iʿlām shod," 23 Mehr 1392/October 15, 2013, http://adyannews.com/fa/news/5914/.

salvation than on managing society and state. However, in the specific Iranian case, it means the laws of Islam as interpreted by the ruling clergy and, in particular, acceptance and subordination to the *vilāyat-i faqīh* system and the denial of liberty from political dissidents.

The belief that submission to God or to religious laws facilitates true liberty reflects an essentialist view of religion which stands independent of the people who interpret and implement it. This approach ignores the historical reality of the Islamic Republic, where interpretation has often been an instrument designed to serve the various interests of the interpreters, i.e., the ruling clergy or factions within it. In other words, this approach facilitates oppression in the name of Islamic freedom.

The Iranian writers discussed here reject the liberal interpretation of negative liberty as opening the floodgates to moral degeneration and social anarchy. Yet, contrary to their basic argument it may be said that liberal thought originally focused more on the relationship between the individual and the state and the threat of state-imposed restrictions on liberty and less on the moral aspects of individual conduct. In denying the liberal notion of negative liberty, they emphasize that absolute liberty does not exist in any society. Yet, advocates of negative liberty recognize this notion and accept various restrictions on liberty. The questions at stake, therefore, concern scope and authority: what are the criteria restricting liberty, who sets them, and what are the limits of their power? In a functioning liberal democracy, the limits on liberties are subject to the continuous criticism of elected bodies and public debate. Their faults notwithstanding, liberal democracies have, in addition, demonstrated a greater degree of tolerance toward deviant views, including those of groups that essentially reject democracy. In the Iranian case, the guardians of liberties are unelected clerics whose power is not subject to popular scrutiny, and the criteria they employ to restrict liberties have often been used to silence critics.

The Shīʿī writers take various liberal arguments and skillfully turn them around in order to justify the denial of liberties according to their narrower definition of liberty. One such argument is that the idea of not harming others should apply to religious and cultural sensitivities and not just physical damage. This point is used to accept the principle of "no compulsion in religion," which allows all people to think and believe freely, while preventing them from disseminating ideas that could supposedly harm others. A second relates to the placing of the communal good above the individual and states that freedom should not endanger the nation's interests, as these are defined by the ruling elites. This line of argumentation culminates in the justification for suppressing and even eliminating apostates whose views and activities are presented as threatening the spiritual and religious sensitivities of the Muslim community and serving the enemies of the Islamic Republic. A third argument transforms the idea of positive liberty into an instrument of suppression by employing the principle and practice of "commanding right and forbidding wrong." It maintains that enabling believers to attain perfection even by coercively enforcing Islamic laws and codes of conduct is the fulfillment of true liberty and therefore has precedence over individual liberty.

The Shīʿī debate on liberty, comparable to debates in religious Judaism, presents a complex picture of the compatibility or contradiction between monotheistic religions based on law, such as Islam and Judaism, and liberty. Clerics and religious thinkers should not be required to tolerate views which reject religion; such blatantly secular views are sinful and prevent the collective from attaining spiritual salvation. In other words, allowing the opponents of religion free action against a religious government is not only politically problematic but also has serious moral and spiritual ramifications. Undoubtedly, the modern Islamist – both Sunnī and Shīʿī – concept stands in sharp contrast to Western liberal thought in general, particularly as far as liberty is concerned, and sees itself as the antithesis of Western liberalism. It can, of course, be said that all religions based on law are inherently opposed to the idea of negative liberty since their main goal is to restrict various human characteristics in order to mold a certain type of believer.

At the same time, Shīʿī political thought contains genuine efforts to reconcile religious obligations with true liberty. The arguments raised by Kadīvar, Mojtahed-Shabestari, and Soroush regarding the importance of religious criticism for ensuring the vitality of religion – which are almost identical to the statements of Rabbi Judah Loew, "the Maharal of Prague" (d. 1609) – show that there is a way in both Islam and Judaism to integrate religion with essential principles of freedom.[128] Both cases, however, represent a minority – be it within the ruling clerical establishment in Iran or among spokesmen for a Jewish minority within a Christian majority – and that may partially explain their attitudes, as their views are subject to censorship and persecution.

The attitude of the Shīʿī mainstream toward liberty is in essence similar to that of the Sunnī mainstream, except for the former's more extensive and sophisticated grappling with contemporary Western liberal thought. There nonetheless appears to be more pluralism within the Shīʿīs clerical establishment than among their Sunnī counterparts. One reason for this might be the greater role of philosophy and rational theology in Shīʿīsm in comparison to orthodox

128 For more on the Maharal's view, see Aviezer Ravitsky, "The Question of Tolerance: Between Pluralism and Paternalism," in *Freedom on the Billboards: Other Voices of Religious Thought* (Tel Aviv: Am Oved, 1999), 121 [Hebrew].

Sunnīsm. Another might be the historical experience of political suppression under an Islamic regime, where the question of liberty was not merely a theoretical issue but had a serious impact on peoples' lives. A third reason might be the realization among Shīʿī liberals that liberty is essential for the preservation of religion and that oppression drives people away.

Finally, both mainstream Sunnī and Shīʿī clerics have loosened the definition of apostasy to include disrespect to religious sanctities. In Iran they added opposition to the dominant doctrine of *vilāyat-i faqīh*, thereby placing political dissidents as outsiders or hostile "others" who need to be suppressed and even eliminated. Still, unlike the radical jihādī-Salafīsts, the Shīʿīs have so far refrained from executing those convicted of apostasy inside Iran. While thoughts and ideas within the two schools of Islam are similar to some extent, their practice is different.

CHAPTER 6

The Deviationist and Misguided Bahāʾī Sect

Bahāʾīsm, which emerged as an independent religion in the 1860s from the heterodox Shīʿī sects of Shaykhism and Bābism, and was named after its founder Ḥusayn ʿAlī Nūrī Bahāʾullah (1817–1892), may be regarded as the ultimate internal "other" for modern Shīʿīsm.[1] Bahāʾīsm promoted a cosmopolitan worldview which stood in contrast to Islam's claim to universality and Shīʿīsm's ethos as a persecuted minority.[2] Its doctrine challenged Shīʿīsm on three major issues: the belief in continued revelation after the Prophet Muḥammad; the substitution of the Qurʾān by Bahāʾī scriptures; the abrogation of the Islamic Sharīʿa and its replacement by Bahāʾī ordinances. These three issues were sufficient doctrinally to brand it as a form of apostasy, which threatened Islam.[3] The ideological challenge was augmented by Bahāʾīsm's success in convincing a large number of Muslims to abandon Islam and embrace it.[4] The fusion of these two elements meant a direct threat to the authority of the Shīʿī clergy both as flag bearers of Islam but also as communal and political leaders. It was therefore only natural that the clerical establishment marked the Bahāʾīs as "waging war against God (*muḥārib*) and his religion" and deserving the death penalty. To make matters worse, the Bahāʾīs, as the internal out-group have been inextricably linked, in the Shīʿī discourse, with two more vilified external

1 On the emergence and evolution of Bahāʾīsm and its doctrines, see Peter Smith, *The Babi and Bahāʾī Religions* (Cambridge: Cambridge University Press, 1987); Michael McMullen, *The Bahāʾī: The Religious Construction of a Global Identity* (New Brunswick: Rutgers University Press, 2000); Denis MacEoin, "Bahāʾīsm," *Encyclopædia Iranica*, http://www.iranicaonline.org/articles/bahaism-index.

2 Margit Warburg, "Bahāʾīs of Iran: Power, Prejudice and Persecutions," in *Religious Minorities in the Middle East: Domination, Self-Empowerment, Accommodation*, ed. Anh Nga Longva and Anne Sofie Roald (Leiden: Brill, 2011), 197.

3 "Āyā Bahāʾiyat murtad ast?," http://adyan.porsemani.ir/content/ارتداد-بهائیت; ʿAlī Reżā Muḥammadī, "Bahāʾiyat/taʾrīkhcheh, iʿtiqādāt va-važʿiyat-i konūnī (qismat-i dovom)," *Maʿārif* 70 (1388): 20–24; "Bahāʾiyat, maẕhab-i istiʿmār sākhte barāye muqābala bā Islām," *Jumhūrī-i Islāmī*, 26 Bahman 1382/February 5, 2004.

4 As the Bahāʾīs are not recognized as an official minority in Iran, government statistics ignore them. According to Peter Smith's, "A Note on Babi and Bahāʾī Numbers in Iran," *Iranian Studies* 17, no. 2–3 (1984): 296, their numbers in Iran rose to nearly 350,000 on the eve of the 1979 Revolution. According to the US "Iran 2017 International Religious Freedom Report," the Bahāʾīs in Iran numbered at least 300,000 by 2017, https://www.state.gov/documents/organization/281226.pdf. The stagnation in numbers was probably due to emigration.

 | DOI:10.1163/9789004444683_008

others: Western imperialism and the Jews/Zionism.[5] In their polemics against the Bahāʾīs, Shīʿī writers indeed employ the same tactic used with the Jews. Accordingly, Bahāʾīs are never individuals motivated by genuine beliefs or by innocent wishes to improve their situation; rather, they all seek to achieve sinister goals on behalf of the Bahāʾī collective. In addition, they project the activities of each individual Bahāʾī on the entire community, thereby presenting it as a collective conspiracy operating as a monolith and in complete unison, exactly like the Jews.

Yet, as Abbas Amanat observed, the legal ground for issuing rulings on Bahāʾī apostasy was not always concomitant with actualizing such potentials and enforcing the invested judicial power by ordering executions.[6] Rather than mass executions, the Bahāʾīs in Iran suffered recurring waves of random and organized violence, discrimination, and persecutions against their adherents and institutions. In all, it is estimated that 300 to 400 Bahāʾīs were killed in Iran from the inception of the movement until the 1979 Revolution.[7] During the Pahlavī period (1925–1979), the Bahāʾīs enjoyed periods of relative tolerance. However, during this period, physical attacks gave way to general civil and religious discrimination, representing a broader consensus of anti-Bahāʾī feeling at all levels of society. As Bahāʾīs were generally better educated than the average Iranian and were politically quietists, many of them enjoyed upward social mobility. Some even gained high posts in business and state administration. Many Bahāʾīs emphasized their support for Reżā Shāh's attacks on the clergy and his various programs of modernization. However, this failed to win them sympathy from secular modernists and merely served to further alienate them from conservative and religious elements in Iranian society. This was to prove disastrous for the Bahāʾīs in later years, as the Pahlavī reforms in the 1960s came to be more widely criticized and the Bahāʾīs found themselves identified (as sometimes they had identified themselves) as bearers of Western values within an Islamic context.[8]

---

5 Abbas Amanat, "The Historical Roots of the Persecution of Babis and Bahāʾīs in Iran," in *The Bahāʾīs of Iran: Socio-Historical Studies*, ed. Dominic Parviz Brookshaw and Seena B. Fazel (London: Routledge, 2012), 174.

6 Amanat, "The Historical Roots of the Persecution of Babis and Bahāʾīs in Iran," 174. It is possible that the ambiguity whether or not converts from Zoroastrian or Jewish background were regarded as apostates in terms of Islamic law was another reason for this gap.

7 For a careful analysis of the conflicting figures and conclusion, see Denis MacEoin, "From Babism to Bahāʾism: Problems of Militancy, Quietism, and Conflation in the Construction of a Religion," *Religion* 13, no. 3 (1983): 236–237.

8 Warburg, "Bahāʾīs of Iran: Power, Prejudice and Persecutions," 204; Eliz Sanasarian, *Religious minorities in Iran* (Cambridge: Cambridge University Press, 2000), 52–53; Houchang E. Chehabi, "Anatomy of Prejudice: Reflections on Secular Anti-Bahāʾism in Iran,"

The period from Reżā Shāh's abdication in 1941 to the 1955 pogrom (see below) marked a turning point in anti-Bahā'ī discourse and action. It ushered in a period of relative political and cultural opening (until the 1953 coup) and saw a resurgence of religion and, particularly, the emergence of a much more politicized Shīʿīsm which sought to construct an Islamic future for Iran and developed in direct conflict with the Bahā'ī religion. One of its manifestations was the proliferation of religious associations whose main goal was anti-Bahā'ī propagation.[9] The most radical among them was the Ḥojjatiya, which was founded in the aftermath of the 1953 coup d'état with the explicit goal of training cadres for the "scientific defense" of Shīʿī Islam in the face of the Bahā'ī theological challenge and became known as the Anti-Bahā'ī Society.[10]

The increasing politicization of Shīʿīsm also produced a shift in the anti-Bahā'ī discourse from religious polemics to a presentation of the Bahā'īs as foreign agents and traitors. The most prominent example of the new trend was the publication and widespread popularity of *The Confessions of Dolgoruki*, a forged memoir attributed to the nineteenth-century Russian ambassador to Iran, Dimitry Ivanovich Dolgorukov, which supposedly revealed that the Bābī and Bahā'ī movements were creations of Russian imperialism. The publication took place when Iranians were suffering the shock of the 1941 Allied invasion and the forced abdication of a monarch whom most believed had been both brought to power and overthrown by foreign imperialists. The perception that these events were orchestrated by foreign powers (the powerful external "other") and the suspicion that such events were signs of their heinous ulterior motives toward the Iranian nation heightened popular receptivity of conspiratorial theories, especially those concerning traditionally hated minority groups, the internal "other."[11] It reflected a tendency in Iranian nationalism and in many other societies to portray the internal "other" as linked with or a tool of external "others." Following the establishment of the State of Israel in

---

in Brookshaw and Fazel (eds.), *The Bahā'īs of Iran*, 188–190; Denis MacEoin, "BAHAISM vii. Bahā'ī Persecutions," *Encyclopædia Iranica*, http://www.iranicaonline.org/articles/bahaism-vii.

9 Mohamad Tavakoli-Targhi, "Anti-Bahā'īsm and Islamism in Iran," in Brookshaw and Fazel (eds.), *The Bahā'īs of Iran*, 201, 204–210; Mina Yazdānī, "The Islamic Revolution's Internal Other: The Case of Ayatollah Khomeini and the Bahā'īs of Iran," *Journal of Religious History* 36, no. 4 (2012): 594.

10 Mahmoud Sadri, "Ḥojjatiya," *Encyclopædia Iranica*, http://www.iranicaonline.org/articles/hojjatiya; Tavakoli-Targhi, "Anti-Bahā'īsm and Islamism in Iran," 206.

11 Mina Yazdani, "*The Confessions of Dolgoruki*: The Crisis of Identity and the Creation of a Master Narrative," in *Iran Facing Others*, ed. Abbas Amanat (New York: Palgrave Macmillan, 2012), 53.

1948, a new element was added to the otherization of the Bahāʾīs, namely, their depiction as agents of Zionism.

In 1955, the unpopular Muḥammad Reżā Shāh sought to gain clerical support in his efforts to crush the communist movement and the militant Fidāʾiyān-i Islām, both of which were clamoring against Western influence in the country, by turning against the Bahāʾīs. Following a series of anti-Bahāʾī speeches by Shaykh Muḥammad-Taqī Falsafī, which were broadcasted throughout Iran in Ramaẓān/April 1955, the Iranian army occupied the national Bahāʾī headquarters in Tehrān, after which Minister of the Interior Asadollah ʿAlam announced that orders had been issued for the suppression of Bahāʾīsm. With official sanction, the clergy instigated an anti-Bahāʾī pogrom across the country, in which many Bahāʾīs were murdered, property (including holy sites) was confiscated and destroyed, women were raped, Bahāʾīs in government service were dismissed, and other measures were taken to harass the Bahāʾīs both individually and collectively.[12]

After the 1955 pogrom, charges against the Bahāʾīs shifted from heresy to an emphasis on immorality and sexual excess as well as allegations of spying and subservience to foreign powers. According to Amanat, it was as though the branding of the heretical "other" in earlier years transformed into an act of reaffirming a threatened and confused Shīʿī self at a time when social dislocations, acculturation, and political oppression under the Shāh left little else for the Shīʿī majority to rally behind.[13]

The ascendance of Khomeini to national prominence in the early 1960s, thanks to his confrontational stance against Muḥammad Reżā Shāh, marked an escalation in the anti-Bahāʾī rhetoric in Iran. Compared to other senior clerics, Khomeini made more frequent and direct references to the Bahāʾī "danger," calling the Bahāʾīs traitors, Zionists, economic plunderers, and enemies of Islam. In 1963, when the First Bahāʾī World Congress convened in London, Khomeini dubbed it an "anti-Islamic" gathering in betrayal of the Iranian homeland and inspired by "satanic" thoughts and plans. He also equated the "the party of Bahāʾīsm" (*ḥizb-i Bahāʾīyyat*) with "the party of the Jews" (*ḥizb-i Yahūd*).[14]

12 Tavakoli-Targhi, "Anti-Bahāʾīsm and Islamism in Iran," 210–220; Shahrough Akhavi, *Religion and Politics in Contemporary Iran: Clergy-State Relations in the Pahlavi Period* (Albany: State University of New York Press, 1980), 76–90; Iran Human Rights Documentation Center, *A Faith Denied: The Persecution of the Baháʼís of Iran* (New Haven, December 2006), 7–12.

13 Amanat, "The Historical Roots of the Persecution of Babis and Bahāʾīs in Iran," 171–172.

14 Yazdani, "The Islamic Revolution's Internal Other," 596–600.

The 1979 Revolution and the establishment of the Islamic Republic elevated the otherization of the Bahāʾīs into an integral component of the official state ideology and policy. Although the Shīʿī clergy now dominated a powerful state apparatus, they still regarded the small Bahāʾī minority as both an ideological and political threat to Iran and Islam. Article 13 of the Constitution of the Islamic Republic recognized only Zoroastrians, Jews, and Christians – the Peoples of the Book – as legitimate religious minorities. Government officials, headed by Khomeini, explicitly excluded the Bahāʾīs from this category, denouncing them as a harmful political faction whose religious activities were not to be tolerated.[15] In fact, from the earliest days of the Islamic Republic, official and semi-official institutions and media waged relentless propaganda campaigns against Bahāʾī doctrines and alleged practices, deeming them inimical and threatening to Islam and the Iranian nation.[16] The campaign was organized around several major motifs: Bahāʾīsm as a form of heresy or apostasy; Bahāʾīsm as a deviant sect and cult; and, finally, Bahāʾīsm as a political movement working in conjunction with royalist, Zionist, American, British, or other agencies for the subversion of Islam and the Iranian nation.[17]

By order of the government all Bahāʾī holy places, endowments, and properties were confiscated; Bahāʾī institutions at the national and local levels ceased to function; thousands of Bahāʾīs were arrested, tortured, and imprisoned, and more than 180 were executed. Dozens of others Bahāʾīs were kidnapped or disappeared without a trace. Thousands of Bahāʾīs lost their private property to government expropriation. Since the social, economic, and cultural persecution of the Bahāʾīs in Iran has been the subject of numerous studies, it will not be dealt with in this chapter, which instead, focuses on anti-Bahāʾī religious discourse.[18]

---

15 Sanasarian, *Religious Minorities in Iran*, 20–22; Iran Human Rights Documentation Center, *A Faith Denied*, 20; Nazila Ghanea-Hercock, *Human Rights, the UN and the Baháʾís in Iran* (Leiden: Martinus Nijhoff Publishers, 2002), 102–103.

16 The *Bāzār Kitāb* website provides a list of over 350 books published against the Shaykhism, Bābīsm, and Bahāʾīsm prior to 2018. See http://www.ghbook.ir/index.php?option=com_k2&view=item&id=348:&lang=fa.

17 It should be noted, as MacEoin stated, that no convincing evidence has ever been presented for Bahāʾī involvement with British, Israeli, or American intelligence or with SAVAK (the state security agency), "BAHAISM vii. Bahāʾī Persecutions."

18 Firuz Kazimzadeh, "The Bahāʾīs in Iran: Twenty Years of Repression," *Social Research* 67, no. 2 (2000): 537–558; Reza Afsharī, "The Discourse and Practice of Human Rights Violations of Iranian Bahāʾīs in the Islamic Republic of Iran," in Brookshaw and Fazel (ed.), *The Bahāʾīs of Iran*, 232–277.

1 A Deviationist Sect – Not a Religion

While Supreme Leader Khamenei did not address Bahāʾīsm as frequently as Khomeini, he maintained a similar exclusionary approach toward them. In several religious rulings, the latest one issued on July 29, 2013, he declared that "all members of the misguided Bahāʾī sect" are guilty of infidelity and impurity (*nejāsat*) as they are the enemies of religion. He urged believers to confront the "craftiness and corruption of this perverse sect" and prevent others from following their deviation. Referring to daily encounters with Bahāʾīs, Khamenei stressed the need to adhere to the ordinances of ritual purity and to avoid any exchange of food or merchandise that have "contagious humidity" with them.[19] Adopting a fatherly tone he advised his "dear children" to avoid fraternizing with Bahāʾīs and to keep a distance from them.[20] Likewise, Grand Ayatollahs Nāṣir Makārem Shīrāzī and Muḥammad Reżā Golpāygānī declared the Bahāʾīs apostates (*murtad*) and impure and banned any contact with them. Due to their impurity, Grand Ayatollah Ḥusayn Nūrī Hamadānī declared all marriages with Bahāʾīs null and void.[21] While the ban on associating with the Bahāʾīs comes from the dominant and oppressive establishment against a small and defenseless minority, the *Porseman* website, which is affiliated with the Supreme Leader's Office, presented it as a defensive measure necessary for preserving the ideological, social, and political independence of the nation in the struggle against menacing foreign influence. In other words, internal purity is essential for defense against the external "other." Moreover, it described the ban as the most humane way for a nation to protect its existence and independence and to reform and guide this depraved sect.[22] Various mid-level clerics took these calls literally and sought to implement them fully. Against the backdrop of increasing economic pressure, Ḥujjat al-Islam ʿAbbās Ramażānī-Pūr, the Friday prayers leader of Rafsanjān, for example, demanded the expulsion of the "unclean" Bahāʾīs from the city in compliance with "the rightful wishes

---

19 According to Shīʿī doctrines, ritual impurity, like various diseases, passes by physical contact via liquids or humid substances. Hence, drinks or humid foods are ritually "contagious" while dry food is not.

20 Ayatollah al-ʿUzma Hajj ʿAlī Khamenei, *Risāla-i ajvibat al-istiftāʾāt* (Tehrān: Sāzimān-i tablīghāt-i Islāmī, 1388/2009), 45–46; Niẓām al-Dīn Mīthāqī, "Nejāsat yā pākī-i Bahāʾīyān: bohāneh-i barāye ḥaẓf," December 8, 2014, https://iranwire.com/fa/news/215/6061.

21 "Bahāʾiyat az naẓar-i marājiʿ ʿuẓẓām-i taqlīd," 26 Ordībehesht 1395/ May 15, 2016, http://www.qomefarda.ir/news/186298.

22 "Āyā irtibāṭ-i musalmānān bā Bahāʾiyat jāyiz ast?," http://www.porseman.org/q/vservice.aspx?logo=images/right.jpg&id=89512.

of the people." It is unclear whether his statements presaged a concerted effort to drive Bahā'īs out of Rafsanjān.[23]

The continued use of the ritual impurity motif against the Bahā'īs is highly significant, particularly when it was dropped from use, at least by Khamenei, in reference to Iranian Jews. Khamenei seems to have realized that maintaining this provision regarding the Jews was politically inexpedient when claiming to distinguish between anti-Semitism and anti-Zionism. However, he probably felt he could ignore external criticisms or protests regarding the Bahā'īs due to the greater domestic political benefit of playing on popular anti-Bahā'ī sentiment. In addition to the persistent emotional power of the traditional notions and practices of impurity, the stress on Bahā'ī ritual impurity, which required their exclusion from society, reflected the ongoing fear and anxiety about the appeal of their ideas among ordinary Shī'īs. One writer described Bahā'īsm as "a kind of ideological and political sickness (*bīmārī*)" which necessitated placing its carriers under quarantine and strict supervision in order to prevent the spread of this infection throughout the body of Muslim society.[24] The use of this metaphor resembles the description of homosexuals and Jews in various pre-World War II European nationalist ideologies.[25] As in those cases, here too it implied the need for harsher measures against the supposed apostates, the carriers of such infections, from seclusion all the way to elimination.

With encouragement from the highest religious authorities, the various official media exerted considerable efforts explaining why Bahā'īsm was not a legitimate religion. One problem they faced was that Bahā'īsm appeared to correspond to some of the definitions of religion that had been formulated by leading Shī'ī scholars, namely, a system of beliefs based on holy scriptures and prophecy. The official *Adyān* website raised various arguments on the matter which would only appeal to those already convinced by the veracity of their own religion and which could be applied against Shī'īsm by its detractors. It argued that religion should, first and foremost, be based on truth and attributed to truth. Furthermore, one of the central prerequisites for the truth of any religion is that it be heavenly and divine and not earthly and man-made and that

23 "Imām jum'a Rafsanjān khastār-i ikhrāj-i Bahā'īyān az 'īn shahr shod," December 4, 2014, http://www.bbc.com/persian/iran/2014/12/141202_u04_iran_bahais; "Bahā'īs See Regime Toughening," *International Iran Times*, December 26, 2014, http://www.bbc.com/persian/iran/2014/12/141202_u04_iran_bahais.

24 'Alī Nāṣirī, *Bahā'īyat va-taḥrīf-i ta'rīkh* (Abridged electronic edition) (Iṣfahān: Markaz-i taḥqīqāt rayāneh'ī-i qā'imiyya, 1386/2007), 9.

25 See this theme in George Mosse, *Nationalism and Sexuality: Respectability and Abnormal Sexuality in Modern Europe* (New York: H. Fertig, 1985). For such perceptions of apostates, see Chapter 5.

its laws reflect God's will. Therefore, all the earlier religions mentioned in the Qur'ān have a common basis and can be considered legitimate religions, and Islam can accept them due to the principle of supersession (*naskh*). Bahā'īsm, on the other hand, is different from other religions because its principles do not reflect God's will but are man-made ideas, which are thus false. The writer pointed out that contrary to all true prophets, the founders of Bahā'īsm had never experienced any miracles – a major proof that they lack any grace from God. Likewise, Bahā'ullah's knowledge of Arabic, the language of the Qur'ān, God's eternal word, was deficient, and he showed ignorance of well-known and basic historical and scientific facts. Another proof used to contrast Bahā'īsm with all other heavenly religions was its rejection of the fundamental principles of the resurrection of the dead at the end of time.[26]

'Alī Reżā Muḥammadī acknowledged that Bahā'īsm fitted the definition of religion as a system of values that keeps society together that was stipulated by Émile Durkheim, one of the founding fathers of modern sociology. But, citing the Prophet's statement to the polytheists "To you be your religion, and to me my religion" (Qur'ān 109:6), he argued, that even if Bahā'īsm complies with this definition, it is still no different from any other polytheist religion and hence it is false.[27]

Other than religion, the term that was most frequently employed against Bahā'īsm, was "the deviationist and misguided Bahā'ī sect" (*firqa-i munḥarif-i żālla-i Bahā'iyat*) or simply "the misguided sect" (*firqa-i żālla*). While this pejorative denigrated the adherents of *Bahā'*īsm and justified their persecution, it also absolved the authorities of the duty to physically eradicate them as apostates. By classifying Bahā'īsm as a sect, the Shī'ī writers were distinguishing between two types of sects in Islam. The first are groups that share with mainstream Islam beliefs in the principal doctrines, such as the unity of God (*towḥīd*) and prophecy, but differ from it in various details of the law and in nuances of practices. Such a definition actually applies to Shī'īsm when contrasted

26 "Islām va-shubhāt-i Bahā'iyat chīst?," http://adyan.porsemani.ir/content/-اسلام-و-شبهات-بهائیت; "Radd va-ibṭāl firqa-i Bahā'iyat," 10 Tīr 1385//July 1, 2006, https://hawzah.net/fa/Question/View/2644/; 'Alī Reżā Rūzbehānī, *Taḥlīl va-naqd-i Bahā'iyat* (Qom: Markaz-i pazhūheshhā-i Islāmī ṣedā va-simāyī jumhūrī-i Islāmī Iran, 1389/2010), 123–124; 'Alī Reżā Muḥammadī, "Jarayān-shināsī-i Bahā'iyat: qismat-i sevom (daftar 35 porseshhā va-pāsokhhā)," http://www.porseman.org/showarticle.aspx?id=1244; Muḥammadī, "Bahā'iyat/ta'rīkhcheh, i'tiqādāt va-vaż'iyat-i konūnī (qismat-i dovom)"; 'Abd al-Ḥusayn Khosrō-panāh, "Sayr-i intiqādī dar ta'rīkh va-bāvarhā-i Bahā'iyat," *Kitāb-i naqd* 12, no. 52–53 (1388/2009): 40; "Tafāvot-i 'aqā'id-i Bahā'iyat bā 'aqā'id-i adyān-i asmānī dar chīst?," http://rwgn.net/index.aspx?siteid=1&pageid=319.

27 'Alī Reżā Muḥammadī, "Jarayān-shināsī-i Bahā'iyat: qismat-i sevom (daftar 35 porseshhā va-pāsokhhā)."

with Sunnī Islam. The second are groups like the Ishāqīyya and Ḥurūfiyya that may regard themselves as Muslim but due to the extremist conduct and practices of their leaders, can no longer be counted as part of Islam. Various Shīʿī writers acknowledged that Bahāʾīsm originated from Shīʿī Islam and evolved in a Muslim environment. However, after it had seceded and denounced the Muslim consensus on questions such as *Imāmat*, prophecy, and God's nature, Bahāʾīsm could no longer be regarded as a sect within Islam but rather as a totally alien group.[28] Hence, they maintained, Bahāʾīsm has all the sociological attributes of a modern sect or cult: for example, the internal structure of a political organization, heavy indoctrination, total control of its members, blind obedience to the leader, methods of intimidation, and a ban on leaving the group.[29] As proof, the official *Fars News Agency* published the charges of the former Bahāʾī Francesco Ficicchia that the "extremist political beliefs" of the Bahāʾī leadership "are drawn from Fascist predispositions." According to these charges, members of Bahāʾī organizations face expulsion if they raise any kind of critical thinking, initiative, advocacy of freedom of opinion, or disapproval of harsh regulations and censorship.[30]

2 Critiquing Bahāʾī Doctrines

A major point in the Shīʿī attacks on Bahāʾīsm as a legitimate religion is the Bahāʾī concept of progressive revelation, which is the basis of Bahāʾullah's claim to prophecy, in contradiction to the Muslim doctrine of the finality of Muḥammad's prophecy. Acceptance of this principle would mean the end of the Islamic belief system and its entire worldview. The threat to the clergy's social and political role is obvious, although the clergy's fear and opposition to Bahāʾīsm cannot be belittled to mere questions of power while ignoring genuine belief. This central Bahāʾī concept, the Shīʿī polemicists have argued, is false because it contradicts the explicit and unequivocal words of the Qurʾān and the eternal world of God and the ḥadīth. However, some polemicists seem to have sensed the possible weakness of this argument which, in proving a Qurʾānic

28 "Āyā Bahāʾiyat firqa būdeh va-az firqahā-i Islāmī maḥsūb mī-shavad?" http://rasekhoon.net/faq/show/782603; Naṣīrī-Fard, Vakāvī-*i seh firqa*, 35–64.

29 Muḥammadī, "Jarayān-shināsī-i Bahāʾiyat: qismat-i sevom (daftar 35 porseshhā va -pāsokhhā);" Sharīfī, "Bahāʾiyat va-siyāsat," 141.

30 "ʿAqāʿid-i siyāsī-i Bahāʾiyat mutaʾthir az gerāyeshāt fāshīstī ast," 28 Mehr 1387/October 19, 2008, https://www.farsnews.com/news/8707160379, which was also published as "Fāshīsm-i zīrbināʾī-i Bahāʾiyat," in the Shīʿa Studies World Assembly, http://shiastudies.com/fa/14850.

statement by citing the Qurʾān itself, may seem tautological. Therefore, they have tried to show that Bahāʾīsm contradicts itself on this issue. First, some have contended (relying only on Shīʿī secondary sources) that Bahāʾullah himself had recognized the finality of Muḥammad's prophecy and had referred to him as the "seal of the Prophets."[31] Others have, in addition, argued that the doctrine and institution of the *Imāmat*, namely, the continued divine guidance of humanity through the Imām, is a proof of the eternity of (Shīʿī) Islam. Likewise, the practice of *ijtihād* enables the adaptation of Islamic law to changing circumstances, thereby denouncing the idea and need for new divine revelations as both superfluous and false.[32] Moreover, this supposed Bahāʾī inconsistency reveals something much more sinister, namely, the Bahāʾī acknowledgement of Muḥammad's final prophecy came with the declaration of Bahāʾullah's appearance (*ẓuhūr*) as "the Promised One," thereby placing him above the Prophet. The claim of Bahāʾullah's prophecy was so absurd, one writer added, that even many Bābīs came out against it and resorted to violence to refute it.[33]

Even worse, according to the Shīʿī writers, was the claim by both the Bāb and Bahāʾullah that God had manifested himself through them, as they had both boasted to have reached the highest level of truth. Based on this notion, the Shīʿī writers accuse Bahāʾullah of equating himself with God.[34] However, these writers seem to have interpreted Bahāʾullah's claim of attaining the ultimate mystical experience of spiritual elevation to equate him with the controversial ninth-century Baghdad mystic al-Ḥallāj, who was executed after having claimed "I am the truth," implying that he had united with God.[35]

Another polemical device used by the Shīʿī writers was to point to internal contradictions or supposed absurdities in Bahāʾī doctrines and laws in order

31 "Islām va-shubhāt-i Bahāʾiyat chīst?"; Khosrō-panāh, "Sayr-i intiqādī dar taʾrīkh va-bāvarhā-i Bahāʾiyat," 43–45; Rūzbehānī, *Taḥlīl va-naqd-i Bahāʾiyat*, 98–101, 163; Muḥammadī, "Jarayān-shināsī-i Bahāʾiyat: qismat-i sevom (daftar 35 porseshhā va-pāsokhhā);" Muḥammadī, "Bahāʾiyat/taʾrīkhcheh, iʿtiqādāt va-važʿiyat-i konūnī (qismat-i dovom)."

32 "Islām va-shubhāt-i Bahāʾiyat chīst?"

33 "Radd va-ibṭāl-i firqa-i Bahāʾīat;" Rūzbehānī, *Taḥlīl va-naqd-i Bahāʾiyat*, 78.

34 "Āyā Bahāʾiyat murtad ast?"; "Cherā Bahāʾiyat rā nejes mīdānīm va-farq beyne mā va-ānhā dar chīst?," http://old.aviny.com/occasion/jang-narm/bahaeiat/bahaeian-najesand.aspx; "Āyā iʿtiqādāt-i Bahāʾiyat bā mavāzin-i ʿilmī va-ʿaqlī munṭabiq ast?," http://andisheqom.com/fa/Question/View/9171 – last accessed April 11, 2018; ʿIzz al-Dīn Reżānezhād, "Naqd va-barresī-i āyīn-i Bahāʾiyat," *Intiẓār-i mowʿūd* 4, no. 12–13 (1383/2005): 533–546; "Ashnāʾī va-iṭṭilāʿāṯī dar Bahāʾiyat," http://www.adyan.porsemani.ir/content/اشنايي-و-اطلاعاتى-در-بهائيت.

35 For more on al-Ḥallāj, see Louis Massignon, *The Passion of Al-Hallaj: Mystic and Martyr of Islam* (Princeton: Princeton University Press, 1982).

to detract from its potential appeal as a modern or progressive religion. Their basic argument is that a true divine religion, unlike a false, man-made religion, cannot contain internal contradictions.[36] According to historian Luṭfallah Luṭfī, the Bahāʾī scripture *Kitāb-i Aqdas* is a compilation of incomprehensible and strange laws originating from the ancient East. Some of these laws regarding punishments (*ḥudūd*), women's inheritance, and polygamy even go so far as to ignore basic social freedoms, and this is why, he claimed, the Bahāʾīs refrained from publishing them in Western countries.[37] Ḥujjat al-Islām ʿAlī Reżā Rūzbehānī of the Kalām Institute in Qom, likewise, highlighted the advocacy of monogamy by the Bahāʾī leader Shoghi Effendi (d. 1957) despite the fact that Bahāʾullah himself had four wives. He asserted that this disparity – Shoghi Effendi's change was apparently introduced in order to curry favor with the West – proves Bahāʾī inconsistency.[38] Furthermore, while the Bahāʾīs accept the Qurʾān as a holy book, they reject its explicit statements on the finality of Muḥammad's prophecy. Similarly, both the Bāb and Bahāʾullah raised contradictory claims regarding their own status. The Bāb first described himself as the precursor of the Hidden Imām, next declared himself as the Imām, later claimed prophecy, and finally pretended to be a manifestation of the divine. Similarly, Bahāʾullah first asserted that he experienced revelations from God and next claimed to be a manifestation of God. According to the Shīʿī writers, Bahāʾī leaders are fully aware of the many contradictions in their doctrines and therefore often change their texts and scriptures.[39] For some, the apparent contradictions are proof of Bahāʾullah's hypocrisy. He rejected the principle of *taqiyya* (dissimulation) but practiced it himself when in exile. Worse still, he declared all human beings to be equal but later described non-Bahāʾīs as no different from animals in their relations to God and equated black Africans with cows. In addition, despite the Bahāʾī claim to advocate equality between men and women, no women serve in their leadership bodies.[40]

---

36 ʿAbbās Naṣīrī-Fard, Vakāvī-*i seh firqa: Barresī va-taḥlīlī-i Vahhābiyat, Bahāʾiyat, shayṭān-parastī* (Tehrān: Rāh-i Nīkān, 1392/2013), 95–96, 142–148; Muḥammadī, "Jarayān-shināsī-i Bahāʾiyat: qismat-i sevom (daftar 35 porseshhā va-pāsokhhā)."

37 Luṭfallah Luṭfī, "Bahāʾiyat: Fāshīsm-i jadīd: goftārī az franchesco fichikia (pazhūheshgar suʾīsī)," *Iran*, 7 Abān 1387/October 28, 2008; Muḥammadī, "Bahāʾiyat/taʾrīkhcheh, iʿtiqādāt va-važʿiyat-i konūnī (qismat-i dovom)."

38 Rūzbehānī, *Taḥlīl va-naqd-i Bahāʾiyat*, 129, 131.

39 "Āyā iʿtiqādāt-i Bahāʾiyat bā mavāzin-i ʿilmī va-ʿaqlī munṭabiq ast?"; "Tanaqużāt dar āʾīn-i Bahāʾiyat," https://www.tebyan.net/newindex.aspx?pid=934&articleID=843884; Muḥammadī, "Bahāʾiyat: taʾrīkhcheh, iʿtiqādāt va-važʿiyat-i konūnī (qismat-i dovom)"; "Islām va-shubhāt-i Bahāʾiyat chīst?"; Rūzbehānī, *Taḥlīl va-naqd-i Bahāʾiyat*, 101.

40 "Islām va-shubhāt-i Bahāʾiyat chīst?"; Rūzbehānī, *Taḥlīl va-naqd-i Bahāʾiyat*, 134–135; "Az nā-barābirī-i ḥuqūq-i zanān-i Bahāʾī tā ʿadam-i riʿāyat-i ḥuqūq-i insānī dar

Since Bahāʾī ideas regarding faith are, according to Shīʿī discourse, an inarticulate and incomprehensible amalgam, Bahāʾīsm lacks an independent harmonious and defensible intellectual and ideological structure – the prerequisite for a genuine religion. As it cannot provide answers to the knowledgeable and astute, it can appeal only to ignorant and simpleminded people.[41] Moreover, Bahāʾīsm claims to be a rationalist religion, presenting the compatibility between reason and religion and science and religion as one of its major principles and rejecting any contradiction between the two as a flaw in proper understanding of religion. Shīʿī writers responded to these claims in two ways. First, they dismissed the Bahāʾī claim for exceptionalism on this point by insisting that all divine religions and Shīʿīsm in particular are compatible with reason.[42] Second, they insisted that Bahāʾī doctrines actually contain many logical contradictions, which ipso facto prove the fallacy of their claim to be a true religion. According to the *Adyān* website, this incompatibility stands in direct contrast to Shīʿī Islam, in which the harmony between reason and faith is one of its major attributes.

The Q&A section of the *Adyān* website continues equating Islam with reason, while ridiculing Bahā'ullah's alleged flawed knowledge of basic science and denouncing Bahāʾī principles as opposed to this equation. Many of the Bāb's and Bahā'ullah's very actions are portrayed as defying reason and logic.[43] As an example of Bahāʾīsm's primitive and fanatical nature, the Shīʿī polemicists cited Bahāʾī alleged belief in the sanctity of the earth of ʿAkkā, Bahā'ullah's burial place, and the prevalent custom among many Bahāʾīs of carrying a handful of this earth with them wherever they go.[44] Typical of the self-other dichotomy where the same practice is regarded as positive when attributed to the self and negative when attributed to the "other," the charge ignores the

Bahā'iyat," http://bahairesearch.org/article/از-نابرابری-حقوق-زنان-بهائی-تا-عدم-رعایت-حقوق-انسانی-در-بهائیت.

41 Muḥammadī, "Bahā'iyat/ta'rīkhcheh, iʿtiqādāt va-vażʿiyat-i konūnī (qismat-i dovom)."

42 Naṣīrī-Fard, Vakāvī-*i seh firqa*, 109–113; "ʿAql-i setīzī va-ʿilm-i setīzī dar Bahā'iyat," 26 Dey 1394/January 16, 2016, http://ferghenews.com/fa/news/4926/-عقل-ستیزی-و-علم-ستیزی-در-بهائیت; "Naqd va-barresī-i uṣūl-i iʿtiqādi-i Bahā'iyat," http://www.hazrate-ghaem.blogfa.com/post/41/نقد-و-بررسي-اصول-اعتقادي-بهائيت.

43 "Islām va-shubhāt-i Bahā'iyat chīst?"; see also "Radd va-ibṭāl-i firqa-i Bahā'iyat."

44 Muḥammadī, "Jarayān-shināsī-i Bahā'iyat: qismat-i sevom;" "Islām va-shubhāt-i Bahā'iyat chīst?"; Muḥammadī, "Bahā'iyat/ta'rīkhcheh, iʿtiqādāt va-vażʿiyat-i konūnī (qismat-i dovom);" "Rad va-ibṭāl-i firqa-i Bahā'iyat;" ʿAlī Būrūnī, "Ta'rīkhcheh peydāyesh Bābiyat va-Bahā'iyat (bakhsh-i sevom)," *Ḥawza-i Iṣfahān* 3 (1379/2000–2001): 178–179.

popular Shīʿī practice of producing rosaries and necklaces for the deceased, rings on their forefingers and armlets all made of the sacred clay of Karbalāʾ.[45]

Several writers also condemned the Bahāʾī approach toward other religions. Ḥujjat al-Islam ʿAbd al-Ḥusayn Khosrō-panāh a philosophy lecturer at the Qom seminary, for example, criticized Bahāʾullah's advocacy of religious pluralism as granting validity to all religions when Islam is the only true religion. He deemed such an approach illogical, as it legitimizes ideological opposites and contradicts the Islamic principle of superseding (*tanāsukh*) all previous religions. In a similar vein, Rūzbehānī castigated the Bahāʾī call for world peace. Global unity is, he acknowledged, highly desired provided it is based on faith, but the Bahāʾī call, which disregards incongruities in doctrine and conduct, is unacceptable as it defies Islam and human conscience. Not only does Islam reject this kind of unity, but it regards "black-hearted infidels" as worse than animals.[46]

Others dismissed the Bahāʾī idea of world peace as simplistic and shallow. Dr. Muḥammad ʿAlī Khanjī (d. 1972), alluding to the contrast between the *ẓāhir* (pure external) and *bāṭin* (pure internal) in Shīʿīsm, asserted that the Bahāʾī notion of world peace focused on external dimensions and aspects but ignored any deep internal meaning. The Bahāʾīs do not, he claimed, examine the reasons for conflicts nor offer any scientific way of bringing about peace except for denying the real differences between peoples. Similarly, Saʿīd Sharīfī accepted that peace is a noble value but maintained that just as violence cannot bring about peace neither can pacifism or collaboration with oppressive regimes. Distorted pacifism against tyrants stands in contrast to the revolutionary spirit and to the struggle against oppression, which are the foundations of the Shīʿa, he concluded.[47]

One of Bahāʾīsm's major flaws, which has also been a reason for the great threat it poses to Islam, is seen as its association with Western modernity. Indeed, Bahāʾīsm posed a great challenge to the Shīʿī clergy by offering a path to modernity that stems from the indigenous culture of Shīʿīsm itself and is

45 For such practices, see Meir Litvak, "The Finances of the ʿUlamāʾ Communities of Najaf and Karbalāʾ, 1796–1904," *Die Welt des Islams*, New Ser. 40, no. 1 (2000): 60.

46 Khosrō-panāh, "Sayr-i intiqādī dar taʾrīkh va-bāvarhā-i Bahāʾiyat," 49–50; Rūzbehānī, *Taḥlīl va-naqd*, 109.

47 "Barresī-i intiqādī chend shiʿār-i Bahāʾiyat az dīdār-i doktor Muḥammad ʿAlī Khanjī," http://rasekhoon.net/article/show/753374; Saʿīd Sharīfī, "Bahāʾiyat va-siyāsat," *Faṣlnāmah-i muṭālaʿāt-i taʾrīkhi* 32 (1390/2011):144.

thus free from almost instinctive opposition to changes that come from the outside, particularly the West.[48]

As was the case of the Bābī doctrine, the concept of renewed revelations entailed the idea of religious renewal and the adaptation of religion to new circumstances.[49] By addressing modernity in indigenous terms, Bahāʾīsm was far more threatening than Bābīsm, especially when many Bahāʾīs in the pre-1979 period seemed to successfully embrace modernity yet remain embedded in Iranian culture and society.

The Shīʿī writers addressed this challenge by portraying Bahāʾīsm as either a conscious emulation of Western culture or an invented Western religion designed to spread and disseminate Western culture in the East and in Iran. Various writers described Bahāʾīsm as part of the reformist movement that had emerged in Iran in response to the crises and defeats suffered in the nineteenth century which sought to alter its "national" culture and adopt Western culture in its place.[50] Conversely, Ibrāhīm Fayāż, a writer in *Mowʿūd*, described Bahāʾīsm as the religion of Iranian modernism, a religion with Western characteristics that was invented by the West and brought to Iran by Europeans in order to disseminate Western culture. As proof, he pointed to many similarities between Bahāʾī and Protestant doctrines, particularly the emphasis on religious individualism and divorcing religious knowledge from the clergy.[51] An *Adyān* writer sought to belittle Bahāʾīsm by dismissing ʿAbd al-Bahā's ideas as an eclectic replication and adaptation of prevalent nineteenth-century Western ideas such as enlightenment, modernism, and humanism. As a result, "Bahāʾī universalism and advocacy of religious pluralism was the most modern means in the complete cultural, political, and economic absorption and assimilation by the Iranian people and other nations in the globalized culture, politics, and economy of the West."[52]

---

48 Denis MacEoin has attempted to develop an analysis based on the parallel between Western and Bahāʾī perceptions of Bahāʾīsm as a positive bearer of "progressive" Western values on the one hand and Iranian perceptions of the faith as a negative bearer of foreign, anti-Islamic influences on the other. See "The Bahāʾīs of Iran: The Roots of Controversy," in *BRISMES Proceedings of the 1986 International Conference on Middle Eastern Studies* (Oxford, 1986) 207–215.

49 Denis MacEoin, "Orthodoxy and Heterodoxy in Nineteenth-Century Shiʿism: The Cases of Shaykhism and Babism," *Journal of the American Oriental Society* 110, no. 2 (1990): 328–329.

50 ʿAlī Akbar ʿĀlimiyān, "Pahlavīhā dar khidmat-i Bahāʾiyat," *Pūyā* 7 (1386/ 2008): 91–92; Murtażā Ashrāfī, "Bahāʾiyat va-bāvarsāzīhā-i kāẕib," *Pegāh-i ḥawza* 303 (1390/2011): 26–27.

51 Ibrāhīm Fayāż, "Bahāʾiyat-i jadīd," *Mowʿūd* 60 (1384/2005): 26–27.

52 "Islām va-shubhāt-i Bahāʾiyat chīst?"; ʿAlī Reżā Muḥammadī, "Jarayān-shināsī-i Bahāʾiyat: qismat-i yekom (daftar 35 porseshhā va-pāsokhhā)," http://www.porseman.org/showarticle.aspx?id=1242.

The Bahāʾī adoption of Western ideas on liberalism and feminism is particularly problematic for many Shīʿī writers. Khomeini even attributed calls for equality between men and women to Bahāʾī cultural influence. The website *Adyān* criticized the removal of the veil and the abolition of various Islamic prohibitions on marriage as a symptom of Bahāʾīsm's "unbridled promiscuity." Likewise, the relaxation of various injunctions regarding women's modesty was seen as compliance with imperialist schemes to undermine Islamic morality.[53] Grand Ayatollah Jaʿfar Subḥānī warned of a joint Christian-Bahāʾī and counter-revolutionary plot to spread "improper veils" in Iranian cities as a means to undermine the Revolution's ideology.[54] The general apprehensiveness of conservative men toward the more egalitarian Bahāʾī attitude on issues such as equality between sons and daughters in inheritance law, for example, was both an important reason to oppose it and a useful rhetorical ploy for mobilizing popular opinion against it.[55] A complementary way of minimizing the threat of Bahāʾī-mediated modernity was to present Bahāʾīsm as much less progressive than it claims to be: for example, highlighting Bahāʾullah's marriage to four wives, the permission he granted to marry two sisters, the distinction he made between the rights of urban and rural women, and the absence of women in the Bahāʾī higher administrative bodies. Politicized Shīʿīsm, on the other hand, is presented as the true champion of positive values wrongly associated with the West.[56]

In addition to the critique of alleged Bahāʾī doctrinal fallacies, quite a few writers pointed to disagreements and splits among the various leaders of the Bahāʾī community or between the leadership and the followers as proof that power and money were the driving forces within Bahāʾīsm rather than genuine

53 Khosrō-panāh, "Sayr-i intiqādī dar taʾrīkh va-bāvarhā-i Bahāʾiyat," 50; ʿĀlimiyān, "Pahlavīhā dar khidmat-i Bahāʾiyat;" "Tasāhul va-tasāmuḥ dar Bahāʾiyat," http://www.adyan.porsemani.ir/content/تساهل-و-تسامح-در-بهاییت; Mīrzā Ṣāliḥ Iqtiṣād Marāghī, *ʾĪqāẓ, yā bīdārī dar kashf-i khiyānat-i dīnī va-vaṭanī-i Bahāʾīyān* (Qom: Bonyād-i farhangī-i ḥażrat-i Mahdī Mowʿūd (ʿaj), 1390/2011), 56n; Nādim Bahāʾīzādeh and Amīr Mostowfiyān, *Bāriqa-i ḥaqīqat dar shenākht-i Bahāʾiyat* (Tehrān: Rāh-i Nīkān, 1387/2008), 33–38.

54 "Ayatollah Subḥānī hoshdār dād: barnāmah vīzheh-i Masīḥiyat, Bahāʾiyat va-żede inqilāb barāye tarvīj-i badḥijābī," May 1, 2012, https://www.farsnews.com/news/13910212001099.

55 For an emphasis on these points, see "khashm-i serrān-i Bahāʾiyat az bī tavvajuhī-i jahānīyān beh ānān," 25 Khordād 1388/June 15, 2007, http://rasekhoon.net/article/show/135799; Luṭfī, "Bahāʾiyat: Fāshīsm-i jadīd;" Ḥujjat al-Islām Reżā Beranjkār, "Mahdaviyat va-firqa-hā (2)," *Mowʿūd* 22 (1379/2000–2001), http://www.ensani.ir/fa/content/61425/default.aspx; Naṣīrī-Fard, Vakāvī-*ye seh firqa*, 198–199.

56 Muḥammadī, "Bahāʾiyat/taʾrīkhcheh, iʿtiqādāt va-vażʿiyat-i konūnī (qismat-i dovom);" Rūzbehānī, *Taḥlīl va-naqd-i Bahāʾiyat*, 129, 131; Naṣīrī-Fard, Vakāvī-*ye seh firqa*, 176; "Islām va-shubhāt-i Bahāʾiyat chīst?"

belief. Examples include the bitter rivalry between Bahāʾullah and his older brother, Yaḥyā ʿAlī Nūrī Ṣubḥ-i Azāl (d. 1912), the leader of the Bābī community, and the struggle between Bahāʾullah's sons over succession and leadership. Similarly, Bahāʾullah's aforementioned claim to be "the Promised One" was so fallacious and absurd that many Azālī Bābīs challenged him, leading to bloodshed between the Bābīs and the Bahāʾī's. Moreover, following the death of Shoghi Effendi, many members left the movement claiming that the International House of Justice, which succeeded him as the leadership body, lacked any legitimacy.[57] Ignoring the fact that disagreements and splits took place in every religion, including Islam and Shīʿīsm itself, the Shīʿī writers' obvious conclusion was that such conduct and practices preclude the possibility of Bahāʾīsm being a religion, a sect, a philosophical school, or even a creed.[58]

Still, despite their derision, the Shīʿī polemicists nonetheless acknowledged the Bahāʾī past and even present-day appeal. In describing the spread of Bahāʾīsm in the Qājār period, a *Jumhūrī-i Islāmī* article conceded that the "structures and pillars of belief, moral values, and spiritual fidelity of Islamic society were shaken; the unity and solidarity of the Muslims of Iran was broken." Furthermore, the "incomparable power of the Shīʿī religion, of the centers of learning and jurisprudence ... of the *marājiʿ taqlīd* and of the awakening clergy," which were "the fortified strongholds of defense of religious identity, independence and honor," was reduced.[59] As for the present day, official spokespeople boasted, as they had with other ideological enemies, that the 1979 Revolution had dealt a major blow to the Bahāʾīs and their supporters both inside and outside Iran. They claimed somewhat disingenuously that thanks to the use of cultural and ideological means the Islamic Republic had succeeded in thwarting the spread of the misguided Bahāʾī beliefs and their negative activities in the service of imperialism.[60]

Yet, at the same time, various media and clerical spokesmen continued to express fear of Bahāʾī subversion that would "sap the people's energy" and of the impact of Bahāʾī propagation on ordinary believers. They warned that

57 Ismāʿīl Rāʾīn, *Inshiʿāb pas az marg-i Showqī Rabbānī* (Tehrān: muʾasasa-i taḥqīqī-i Rāʾīn, 1978); Rūzbehānī, *Taḥlīl va-naqd-i Bahāʾiyat*, 122, 167; Khosrō-panāh, "Sayr-i intiqādī dar taʾrīkh va-bāvarhā-i Bahāʾiyat," 28; ʿAlī Būrūnī, "Taʾrīkhcheh peydāyesh Bābiyat va-Bahāʾiyat (bakhsh-i pāyānī)," *Ḥawza-i Iṣfahān* 6 (1380/2001):186.

58 A letter dated July 29, 1979 from the provincial government of Sirjan, cited in Warburg, "Bahāʾīs of Iran: Power, Prejudice and Persecutions," 208.

59 "Bahāʾiyat, maẕhab-i istiʿmār sākhte barāye muqābala bā Islām."

60 Muḥammadī, "Jarayān-shināsī-i Bahāʾiyat: Qismat-i dovom (daftar 35 porseshhā va-pāsokhhā)"; ʿAlī Reżā Muḥammadī, "Bahāʾiyat/taʾrīkhcheh, iʿtiqādāt va-vażʿiyat-i konūnī (qismat-i sevom)," *Maʿārif* 71 (1388/2009): 29–34.

the Bahāʾīs were using their immense financial resources to spread their false ideas among poor and ignorant peasants, uninformed youth, and even children in day-care centers.[61] According to sociologist Misagh Parsa, conversion to Christianity and Bahāʾīsm became a form of resistance to the Islamic Republic. Fear of such conversions led Khamenei to issue a warning in Qom in October 2010, stating that the enemies of Islam were plotting to weaken religion by promoting carelessness in religion and conversion to false religions such as Bahāʾīsm and Christianity. Following suit, Subḥānī emphasized the Bahāʾī threat to young people and contended that the danger of Bahāʾīsm had been less tangible before the Revolution but was now particularly difficult. He put Bahāʾī propagation on a par with devil worshiping cults as seeking to lead young people away from Islam.[62]

3 Bahāʾīsm as a Political Enemy

As mentioned above, the 1940s marked the emergence of a new type of anti-Bahāʾī polemics, which emphasized politics and branded Bahāʾīsm a political sect rather than simply a deviationist religious one. While denying the religious essence of Bahāʾīsm, the official Iranian discourse nonetheless often charged the Bahāʾīs with heresy and denounced them as *mushrikān* (polytheists). This inconsistency seems to reflect the politicization of Shīʿīsm rather than a lack of clarity in viewing Bahāʾīsm. Alternatively, the shift to political charges and the appeal to nationalist sentiments by associating Bahāʾīsm with foreigners might have stemmed from the apprehension that purely religious arguments on doctrinal matters were losing their appeal among growing segments of the population.

Shīʿī writers, from Khomeini onward, increasingly conceived of religion and all religious phenomena as essentially political and positioned politics as the

61 “Faʿāliyat-i zīr zamīnī-i Bahāʾiyat bā shināsāyī-i sarshākhe-i ān kāmilān motavvaqif shod,” 25 Abān 1389/November 16, 2010, https://www.farsnews.com/news/8908250336/فعاليت-زيرزميني-بهائيت-باشناسايي-سرشاخه -ان- كاملاً-متوقف-شد; “Cherāyī ḥasāsiyat-i ʿulamāʾ va-buzurgān dar rābiṭa bā Bahāʾiyat,” 8 Khordād 1395/May 28, 2016, http://hawzahnews.com/TextVersionDetail/380910; “Naqd-i Bahāʾiyat, beh kam-i Bahāʾiyat,” 20 Dey 1389/January 10, 2011, https://www.mashreghnews.ir/news/23703/; “Bahāʾiyat yek tahdīd-i jeddī barāye javānān ast,” 13 Azar 1390/November 4, 2012, http://www.farsnews.com/printable.php?nn=13900912001424; Muḥammadī, “Bahāʾiyat/taʾrīkhcheh, iʿtiqādāt va-vażʿiyat-i konūnī (qismat-i sevom).”

62 Misagh Parsa, *Democracy in Iran: Why It Failed and How It Might Succeed* (Cambridge: Harvard University Press, 2016), 19–20; “Bahāʾiyat az naẓar-i marājiʿ ʿuẓẓām-i taqlīd”; “Bayānāt-i Ayatollah Subḥānī (zayyida ʿizzuhu) dar khuṣūṣ-i Bahāʾiyat,” 11 Esfand 1394/March 1, 2016, https://www.adyannet.com/fa/news/18146.

central pillar of religion.[63] They thus seemed to have projected their understanding of their own belief system on their rivals. Therefore, they dubbed the Bahāʾī a political sect whose main goal is to deceive "the young and the old" and to distort the image of pure Islam. They are accused of using Shīʿī symbols and ideas in order to simulate Muslims as a means of disseminating their false beliefs in the service of imperialism. When considering the central role of imperialism in the initial formation of Bahāʾīsm, the Shīʿīs claim that it is impossible to regard it as anything but a political group. The best indicator of the political essence of this group that seeks to eliminate Islam is its alleged use of "Jewish tactics" to harm the Islamic Republic.[64]

While depicting Bahāʾīsm as a political sect, the Shīʿī polemicists present the Bahāʾī principle of non-intervention in politics as intellectually invalid. It is seen to oppose the essence of genuine religions, particularly Islam, which is a comprehensive system that guides all aspects of life including politics, economics, culture, and morality. Just as all religious people know that their cultural and economic proclivities are guided by their religion, so they should understand that their political conduct is shaped by their cultural and religious outlook. It is impossible to separate politics from all other activities; therefore, the Bahāʾī call to refrain from politics is untenable. Equally unsustainable is the Bahāʾī call for clerical non-intervention, aimed at preventing the clergy from fulfilling their crucial religious and social role of leading the community and opposing oppression.[65] In light of the prevalence of anti-Bahāʾīsm in society, contrasting their restraint from politics with the political activism of the clergy seemed a good way of enhancing popular support for the latter.

At the same time, the Shīʿī polemicists argued that non-intervention in politics is essentially a political strategy, as it actually means indirect support of all governments including the dictatorial and oppressive. Citing ʿAbd al-Bahāʾ's statements on the need to refrain from political activity and obey rulers, Khanjī dismissed this idea as outdated and backward since it denied the people any political rights and viewed only the rulers as eligible to rule. Others charged

63 See, for example, Khomeini's famous dictum from December 1987 and January 1988 that "the government (state) which is a part of the absolute vice-regency of the Prophet of God is one of the primary injunctions (*aḥkām-i avvaliyya*) of Islam and has priority over all other secondary injunctions, even prayers, fasting and Hajj," *Iṭṭilāʿāt*, January 8, 1988; and Article 109 of the revised 1988 Constitution, which gave precedence to political acumen over learning in the criteria for electing the supreme leader.

64 Reżānezhād, "Naqd va-barresī-i āyīn-i Bahāʾiyat (1);" Khosrō-panāh, "Sayr-i intiqādī dar taʾrīkh va-bāvarhā-i Bahāʾiyat," 36, 54; "Bahāʾiyat az naẓar-i marājiʿ ʿuẓẓām-i taqlīd."

65 Seyyed Muṣṭafā Taqavī, "Bahāʾiyat va-siyāsat, ʿadam mudākhala dar siyāsat," *Faṣlnāmah-i muṭālaʿāt-i taʾrīkhī* 17 (1386/2007): 179–188; Reżānezhād, "Naqd va-barresī-i āyīn-i Bahāʾiyat"; Muḥammadī, "Jarayān-shināsī-i Bahāʾiyat: qismat-i yekom (daftar 35 porseshhā va-pāsokhhā)."

the Bahāʾīs with being indifferent to people's suffering under political oppression and contrasted this with Shīʿīsm, presented as the champion of people's rights and, by clear implication, far more modern and progressive.[66]

Various polemicists denounced the call for non-intervention as hypocritical, asserting that the Bahāʾīs themselves engaged in politics whenever it suited them but never admitted it. ʿAbd al-Bahā's visits to Europe were a political act as was Bahāʾī support of Zionism. Likewise, the seemingly benign calls for the unity of humanity and world peace enabled the Bahāʾīs to cooperate with various governments in order to advance their political ambitions. One prominent example was their support of Muḥammad ʿAlī Shāh's policies during the Constitutional Revolution and, even worse, their collaboration with the Pahlavī monarchs.[67] Few writers conflated the Bahāʾīs and the Azālī Bābīs, who were engaged in radical politics, in order to accuse the Bahāʾīs of perpetrating acts of political terrorism while claiming to oppose politics.[68] Perhaps the most paradoxical charge against the Bahāʾīs, which might have been inspired by the notorious anti-Semitic tract *The Protocols of the Elders of Zion*, contended that the Bahāʾī advocacy of non-intervention in politics was, in fact, a cover for the conspiratorial activities of their organizations all over the world.[69]

Most prevalent among Shīʿī writers is the contrast between Bahāʾī advocacy of non-intervention in politics and the national and religious duty to defend Iran and Islam against foreign intruders. In light of the imperialist Western onslaught on Iran, this Bahāʾī position is equated with shirking the struggle of the freedom fighters and defenders of the homeland and instead fulfilling one of the basic goals of imperialism. Indeed, this has been seen as an important part of the service that Bahāʾīsm renders to Western imperialism.[70] The reason for this supposed service is clear, considering the prevalent charge that Bahāʾīsm

66 Muḥammad Bāqir Najafī, *Bahāʾīyān* (Qom: shiʿr mashʿar, 1383/2004), 737, 745–746; Taqavī, "Bahāʾiyat va-siyāsat, ʿadam mudākhala dar siyāsat," 178; "Barresī-i intiqādī chend shiʿār-i Bahāʾiyat az dīdār-i doktor Muḥammad ʿAlī Khanjī;" Rūzbehānī, *Taḥlīl va-naqd-i Bahāʾiyat*, 114–115; "Idīʾūlūzhī-i Bahāʾiyat – Bahāʾiyat va-siyāsat," 14 Abān 1390/November 5, 2011, https://www.porseman.com/article/145286/ايدئولوژي-بهائيت-بهائيت-و-سياست.

67 Bahrām Afrāsiyābī, *Bahāʾiyat beh rivayat-i taʾrīkh* (Tehrān: pūrustash, 1366/1987–1988), 235–244; Sharīfī, "Bahāʾiyat va-siyāsat," 127, 141; Būrūnī, "*Taʾrīkhcheh* peydāyesh Bābiyat va-Bahāʾiyat (bakhsh-i sevom)," 179–183.

68 Muḥammadī, "Jarayān-shināsī-i Bahāʾiyat: qismat-i sevom (daftar 35 porseshhā va-pāsokhhā)"; "Farāmāsōnarī chegūneh sāzimānī ast? Cheh nowʿ irtibāṭi bā Bahāʾiyat dārad?" http://www.siasi.porsemani.ir/node/1112; Ashrāfī, "Bahāʾiyat va-bavarsāzīhā-i kāẕib."

69 Luṭfī, "Bahāʾiyat: Fāshīsm-i-i jadīd."

70 Najafī, *Bahāʾīyān*, 737; "Tasāhul va-tasāmuḥ dar Bahāʾiyat;" Taqavī, "Bahāʾiyat va-siyāsat, ʿadam mudākhala dar siyāsat," 40; Khosrō-panāh, "Sayr-i intiqādī dar taʾrīkh va-bāvarhā-i Bahāʾiyat," 36.

was created, groomed, and protected by British and Russian intelligence services in the nineteenth century and subsequently supported by the Americans and Israelis. In fact, according to this narrative, the Bahāʾīs were one among several heretical groups, such as the Wahhābīs in the Middle East and the Aḥmadiyya in India, created by the British in order to divide the Muslims, undermine their belief, and break the power of Islam. It should be noted that these charges also appear in official school textbooks.[71] The specific claim is that, with the Shīʿī clergy at the forefront of the struggle against Western imperialism, the British were looking for the means to break the power of Islam, especially Shīʿīsm. They realized that the Shīʿī culture of ʿĀshūrāʾ, that is, of sacrifice and martyrdom, would never allow submission to foreigners and understood the power of the Shīʿī belief in the Mahdī and his future return as a means of mobilizing against Western imperialism. The British, determined to break the power of the Shīʿa, of its centers of learning and jurisprudence, and of the clergy, the true leaders of Islam, and therefore created Bābīsm and Bahāʾīsm with their false messianic ideas and claims of prophecy in order to turn people away from Islam.[72] Various writers have used the protection that the Russian Embassy gave to Bahāʾullah as a way of building a larger case, with the Bahāʾīs as instruments of Russian imperialism in Iran alongside the British.[73] Some of them even extended this support to the Bolshevik intelligence services.[74]

---

71 Iqtiṣād Marāghī, *ʾĪqāẓ, yā bīdārī dar kashf-i khiyānat-i dīnī va-vaṭanī-i Bahāʾīyān*, 8; Reżānezhād, "Naqd va-barresī-i āyīn-i Bahāʾiyat," 537. See also the seven articles in *Taʾrīkh-i muʿāṣir-i Iran* 49 (1388/2009) which are dedicated to alleged Bahāʾī collaboration with and service to Britain, http://www.iichstore.ir/product_info.php/products_id/308/pname/49-فصلنامه-تخصصی-تاریخ-معاصر-ایران،-شماره; Grade 8 History Textbook p. 37 cited in Saeed Paivandi, *Discrimination and Intolerance in Iran's Textbooks* (A Freedom House Publication, 2008), 43–44.

72 Muḥammadī, "Jarayān-shināsī-i Bahāʾiyat: Qismat-i yekom (daftar 35 porseshhā va-pāsokhhā)"; "Tasāhul va-tasāmuḥ dar Bahāʾiyat;" Muḥammadī, "Bahāʾiyat/taʾrīkhcheh, iʿtiqādāt va-važʿiyat-i konūnī (qismat-i dovom);" Naṣīrī, *Bahāʾiyat va-taḥrīf-i taʾrīkh*, 8; Muẓaffar Nāmdār, "Istiʿmār va-ẓuhūr-i maslakhā-i shibh-i dīnī," https://rasekhoon.net/article/show/136454/.

73 Bahrām Afrāsiyābī, *Taʾrīkh-i jāmiʿ-i Bahāʾiyat* (Tehrān: Mehrfam, 1382/2003), 217–229; Bahrām Afrāsiyābī, *Bahāʾiyat beh rivāyat-i taʾrīkh*, 123–131; Rūzbehānī, *Taḥlīl va-naqd-i Bahāʾiyat*, 75; "Radd va-ibṭāl-i firqa-i Bahāʾiyat." See also the seven articles in *Taʾrīkh-i muʿāṣir-i Iran* 49 which are dedicated to alleged Russian support and protection of Bahāʾīsm.

74 Muʾasasa-i firaq va-adyān-i Zāhidān, "Bahāʾīgarī va-sāzimānhā-i iṭṭilāʿātī va-amniyatī shūrāvī," 30 Shahrīvar 1396/September 21, 2017, http://mafaz.ir/content/bahaiiat_shorvi; Muʾasasa-i muṭālaʿāt-i va-pazhūheshhā-i siyāsī, "*Irtibāṭāt*-i Bahāʾiyat bā servīshā-i jāsūsi-i sharq va-gharb," http://zionism.pchi.ir/show.php?page=contents&id=5172.

According to this narrative, the Bābīs and Bahā'īs assisted imperialism and actively sought to undermine Iran's national identity by presenting Western influence as a vehicle for renewal and progress, advocating the separation of religion from politics, and implanting Westernizers in senior positions in the government.[75] Historian Muḥammad Bāqir Najafī acknowledged that the animosity and loathing of the Iranians and other Muslims toward the Bahā'īs played a certain role in pushing them to serve imperialism. Nonetheless, he insisted that the major reason for Bahā'ī collaboration with the imperialists was their opposition to the ideas of homeland (*vaṭan*) and patriotism (*vaṭan-dūstī*). He contrasted this with the dynamic patriotism of the Iranian nation and explained it by highlighting the Bahā'ī rejection of the Islamic principle that love of homeland is a religious belief due to their belief in supersession (*naskh*) and serving foreigners. Using arguments that are highly reminiscent of those used against the Jews in Europe, he asserted that Bahā'īs have never been loyal to any country but only to their own religion; even their views on the equality of humanity and their advocacy of non-violence are an outcome of their lack of patriotism. When Iran was being subjected to Russian and British attacks and invasions during the Constitutional Revolution and during the First and Second World Wars, the Bahā'ī leaders, who lived outside the country, instructed their followers not to oppose the invaders.[76] The Qom Ḥawza organ, *Hawza.net*, even asked whether anything supported by imperialism can conceivably be a heavenly religion that can offer felicity (*saʿādat*) to humanity.[77]

As with all conspiracy theories, the Shīʿī narrative links the Bahā'īs with another favorite enemy of authoritarian movements, the Freemasons, who are depicted as a key tool of British imperialism in Iran.[78] Bahā'īsm was, accordingly, a product of the Masonic scheme to spread Western humanistic ideas through the Muslim world under the guise of new religions. Moreover, the Freemasons provided the context for the link between the Bahā'īs and Jewish capitalists and Zionist organization. Rūzbehānī concluded that "there are not enough words to describe the criminal Masonic activity in Iran as an

---

75 Maḥbūba Ismāʿīlī, "Naqsh-i Inglistān dar shikl gīrī va-tadāvum-i firqa-i Bahā'iyat dar Iran," 20 Bahman 1392/February 9, 2014, http://rasekhoon.net/article/show/863393; Nāmdār, "Istiʿmār va-ẓuhūr-i maslakhā-i shibh-i dīnī."

76 Najafī, *Bahā'īyān*, 720, 723–725. See also Muḥammadī, "Bahā'iyat/ta'rīkhcheh, iʿtiqādāt va-vażʿiyat-i konūnī (qismat-i dovom)."

77 "Radd va-ibṭāl-i firqa-i Bahā'iyat."

78 The international and semi-secretive nature of the Freemasons made them "natural suspects" for many authoritarian regimes all over the world. See Christopher Campbell Thomas, *Compass, Square and Swastika: Freemasonry in the Third Reich* (Texas: A&M University, 2011); Howard Spier, "'Zionists and Freemasons' in Soviet Propaganda," *Patterns of Prejudice* 13, no. 1 (1979): 1–5.

instrument of Western imperialism"; similarly, a whole book is needed to describe Masonic-Bahāʾī collaboration in this context.[79]

Likewise, their alleged close association with the Jews became a central proof of Bahāʾī evil and a powerful means of further demonizing Bahāʾīsm.[80] Various writers have endorsed the allegation that Seyyed ʿAlī Muḥammad Shīrāzī, founder of the Bābī religion, worked in his youth in the service of wealthy Jewish merchants in Būshehr who were engaged in the opium trade (a morally reprehensible commodity) and that he had been heavily influenced by them. They added that a "network of powerful and wealthy Jewish families" had been among his early supporters.[81] Others turned the conversion of many Jews to Bahāʾīsm on its head: rather than being a manifestation of the crisis of the Jewish community and the desire of Jews to fully integrate in Iranian society, the conversions were presented as a Jewish conspiracy designed to infiltrate and manipulate Islam from within. An emphasis on the role of the Jews, particularly those disguised as Muslims, in spreading Bahāʾīsm in Iran, serves to minimize the guilt of ordinary Muslims. Khomeini, for example, invented the appellations "Jews disguised as Bahāʾīs" and "the Bahāʾī Jews" in order to highlight the intermingling of the two groups.[82] Some writers, looking to stress the Jewish influence on Bahāʾīsm, have claimed that Bahāʾīsm started as a "Jewish exegesis of Shīʿī Islam" and insist that the Jewish impact is also evident

---

79 ʿAlī Rajabī, "Farāmāsūnarī, Bahāʾiyat, istiʿmār: ḥużūr-i Bahāʾiyat dar anjumanhā-i māsōnī va-shibh-i māsōnī," http://rasekhoon.net/article/show-84986.aspx; Ismāʿīlī, "Naqsh-i Inglistān dar shikl gīrī va-tadāvum-i firqa-i Bahāʾiyat dar Iran;" "Farāmāsōnarī chegūneh sāzimānī ast? Cheh nowʿ irtibāṭi bā Bahāʾiyat dārad?"; Rūzbehānī, *Taḥlīl va-naqd-i Bahāʾiyat*, 177. Afrāsiyābī in his *Taʾrīkh-i Jāmiʿ-i Bahāʾiyat* pointed to an alleged similarity between Bahāʾī and Masonic organizational structure as proof of their close collaboration, 507–508, 529–581; Ashrāfī, "Bahāʾiyat va-bavarsāzīhā-i kāẕib." See also "Vaqtī Bahāʾiyat pāygāh-i istiʿmār dar Iran mīshavad," 29 Ordībehesht 1393/May 19, 2014, https://www.mashreghnews.ir/news/310619.

80 The cover of many of the books on Bahāʾīsm listed in the digital catalogue carry the Star of David, even though their titles address many aspects of Bahāʾīsm, which have nothing to do with Judaism, http://73ferghe.blog.ir/post/66/-کتابخانه-بهاییت-شناسی-دانلود-بیش-از-صد-کتاب.

81 ʿAbdollah Shahbāzī, "Justārīhā az taʾrīkh-i bahāyīgerāʾī dar Iran," *Taʾrīkh-i muʿāṣir-i Iran*, 27 (1382/2003): 21–23; Mikāʾil Javāhirī, *Bahāʾiyat pād jonbesh-i tajdīd ḥayāt-i millat-i Iran* (Tehrān: Muʾasasa-i muṭālaʿāt va-pazhūheshhā-i siyāsī, 1393/2014), 241–290; "Firqa-i inḥirāfī-i Bahāʾiyat," http://rasekhoon.net/article/show/187889/فرقه-انحرافی-بهائیت/; Khosrō-panāh, "Sayr-i intiqādī dar taʾrīkh va-bāvarhā-i Bahāʾiyat," 38; "Dar mowerd-i naqsh-i Yahūd va-ṣahyūnīsm dar jarayān-i Bahāʾiyat," http://bahaismiran.net/index.php/مقالات-بهائیت/item/952-/952.

82 Rāʾīn, *Inshiʿāb dar Bahāʾīat pas az marg-i Showqī* Rabbānī, 208; "Dar mowred-i naqsh-i Yahūd va-ṣahyūnīsm dar jarayān-i Bahāʾiyat;" Yazdani, "The Islamic Revolution's Internal Other," 603.

in the devious tactics used by the Bahāʾīs to expand their influence over Iran. The claim of similarity and even the influence of the devilish Jewish practices enumerated in *The Protocols of the Elders of Zion* on Bahāʾī tactics has led to an identical demonization between the Bahāʾīs and the Jews.[83]

An even harsher accusation in this respect is the link made between Bahāʾīsm and Zionism and the presentation of Bahāʾīsm as both an ally and instrument of Zionism and Israel. The link is rooted in Bahāʾullah's exile in 1867 and his stay during the last twenty-four years of his life first as a prisoner in ʿAkkā (known as ʿAkko in present-day Israel) and later as an exile in a nearby village. On visiting the nearby town of Haifa, Bahāʾullah endowed Mount Carmel with special sanctity and stipulated that the Bāb should be buried there. Bahāʾullah's mausoleum in ʿAkkā and the dome in Haifa are regarded as the two holiest sites for Bahāʾīs. The Bahāʾī central leadership and administrative institutions are located in Haifa. The Bahāʾīs are free to practice their religion in Israel but voluntarily refrain from any proselytizing.[84]

As religion and state are intertwined in the Islamic Republic, the Shīʿī polemicists applied the same model to the Bahāʾī open presence in Israel and used it to link together the two enemies or, in their words, the two "cancerous tumors." The similarity between symbols, the Bahāʾī star and the Jewish Star of David, serve them as another proof of the collaboration between the two hostile 'others.' According to this narrative, the Bahāʾīs already supported Zionism under the Ottomans. In 1948, they actively supported the establishment of Israel, realizing that had the "Muslim people of Palestine" won in 1948, their fate in Palestine would have been the same as in all Arab countries, namely, exclusion and persecution.[85] Hence they saw no other way but to betray the

83 Ashrāfī, "Bahāʾiyat va-bavarsāzīhā-i kāẕib;" Khosrō-panāh, "Sayr-i intiqādī dar taʾrīkh va-bāvarhā-i Bahāʾiyat," 55.

84 Chehabi, "Anatomy of Prejudice: Reflections on Secular Anti-Bahāʾīsm in Iran," 193–194 emphasized the accidental link between Bahāʾullah and Palestine/Israel. Moshe Sharon, *The Bahāʾī Faith and its Holy Writ: The Most Holy Book* (*al-Kitāb al-Aqdas*) (Jerusalem: Carmel Publishing, 2005,) 121–129 (Hebrew) highlighted the mystical aura surrounding Mt. Carmel dating back to the Bible with its echoes of Christianity and Islam and its impact on Bahāʾullah. He maintains that Bahāʾullah regarded the Carmel as "his Mount Sinai" and as associated with his revelation.

85 The Bahāʾīs recognized the Jewish attachment to the Holy Land and accepted the return of the Jews to their ancestral homeland, though they officially declared their neutrality regarding the desired political and territorial solution of the country in 1947–1948. See, for instance, the statement by Bahāʾullah's son and spiritual heir, ʿAbd al-Bahāʾ: "Zionists must work with other races.… There is too much talk today of what the Zionists are going to do here. There is no need of it. Let them come and do more and say less," *Star of the West*, September 8, 1919, https://bahai.works/Star_of_the_West/Volume_10/Issue_10#pg196.

Muslims and serve their enemies. After 1948 the Bahāʾīs turned from being supporters to being a tool in the service of Zionism and American imperialism.[86] As mentioned above, Khomeini took the lead in propagating this motif as early as 1962. In response to a local elections bill allowing non-Muslims to compete, Khomeini charged that "the Zionists who have appeared in Iran as the Bahāʾī party … have endangered the economy and independence of the country, will soon overtake the economy through the support of their agents." He accused the Bahāʾīs of spying for Israel and described Iranian TV, whose director, Ḥabīb Thabet Pasal, was a Bahāʾī, as an Israeli espionage center in Iran. The Bahāʾīs regard spying for Israel against Iran as a source of pride, Ḥujjat al-Islam Ḥusayniyān explained.[87]

The Bahāʾī-Zionist threat culminated, according to Shīʿī writers, in their alleged alliance with the Pahlavī regime and the joint effort to destroy Islam and subjugate Iran to their control.[88] This charge of a Bahāʾī-Pahlavī understanding does, in fact, have some factual basis. The 1955 pogrom notwithstanding, many Bahāʾīs enjoyed upward social mobility thanks to Pahlavī secularizing and modernizing policies, and some were even integrated in the upper echelons of Iranian bureaucratic and business circles. Many Bahāʾīs, having faced relentless clerical animosity, preferred the Pahlavīs over the religious opposition. The Shīʿī polemicists, however, see this as an alliance driven by evil motivations. They accuse the Bahāʾīs of actively helping the Pahlavīs to seize power and, later, consolidate their domination over Iran. According to this narrative, the Bahāʾī Ḥabībollah ʿAyn al-Molk, father of the future prime minister Amīr ʿAbbās Hoveida, served as the British liaison to Reżā Khān in facilitating the 1921 coup that brought the latter to power. Reżā Shāh reciprocated by secretly helping the Bahāʾīs after gaining power.[89] Under Muḥammad Reżā Shāh the

86 Rūzbehānī, *Taḥlīl va-naqd-i Bahāʾiyat*, 143–149; Afrāsiyābī, *Taʾrīkh-i jāmiʿ-i Bahāʾiyat*, 464–472; Najafī, *Bahāʾīyān*, 656–691; Ibrāhīm Anṣārī, "Bahāʾīhā va-isrāʾīl," *Faṣlnāmah-i muṭālaʿāt-i taʾrīkhī*, 17 (Summer 1386/2007): 201–207; "Dar mowerd-i naqsh-i Yahūd va-ṣahyūnīsm dar jarayān-i Bahāʾiyat;" Ashrāfī, "Bahāʾiyat va-bavarsāzīhā-i kāẕib."

87 ʿAlī Davānī, *Nahzat-i Rawhaniyun-i Iran*, vol. 3 (Tehrān: Muʾasasa-i Khayriya va-Farhangī-i Imām Reżā, 1979/1980), 114 cited in Mina Yazdani, "The Islamic Revolution's Internal Other," 597–598; ʿĀlimiyān, "Pahlavīhā dar khidmat-i Bahāʾiyat;" Ḥujjat al-Islām Rūḥollah Ḥusayniyān, "Bahāʾiyat, rezhīm-i Pahlavī va-mavāżiʿ-i ʿulamāʾ," *Faṣlnāmah-i muṭālaʿāt-i taʾrīkhī* 4, no. 17 (1386/2007): 22.

88 Ḥusayniyān, "Bahāʾiyat, rezhīm-i Pahlavī va-nahżatʿ-i ʿulamāʾ," 11, 20; "Inqilāb-i Islāmī va-muqābala bā nufūẕ-i Bahāʾiyat dar Irān," 30 Azar 1396/December 21, 2017, http://basijnews.ir/fa/news/8964916.

89 ʿAlī Ḥaqīqatjū, "Bahāʾiyat va-kūdetā-i Reżā Khān," 5 Esfand 1386/November 26, 2007, https://www.farsnews.com/printable.php?nn=8612050168; Javāhirī, *Bahāʾiyat pād jonbesh-i tajdīd ḥayāt-i millat-i Iran*, 291–321; Muḥammadī, "Jarayān-shināsī-i Bahāʾiyat:

alliance is said to have expanded, and many Bahā'īs served in high state positions to the detriment of the Iranian nation. Most notable among them was Amīr ʿAbbās Hoveida, who served as prime minister from 1965 to 1977 and was executed shortly after the 1979 Revolution. The Shīʿī writers claim that during his tenure he advanced the evil goals of Zionism and imperialism.[90] According to Sharīfī and others, the Bahā'īs regarded the Pahlavī "pseudo-modernization" policy as the fulfillment of their doctrines and as a means of disseminating their ideas that served imperialism. Their large presence in powerful positions in the Iranian regime was not, therefore, just the manifestation of personal motivations but the overall ideological policy of the Bahā'ī community as a whole to gain influence and control.[91]

Other polemicists have gone further and asserted that the Bahā'īs "managed to overrun political, cultural, social, economic, military, judicial sovereignty," in Iran, control "all affairs," and exploit all the institutions, means, and powers of the state in order to realize their goals. They accuse the Bahā'īs of attempting to transform Iran into a Bahā'ī monarchy with Bahā'īsm as the official religion. In an unconscious projection of the Islamic Republic's aspirations to lead the Muslim world, Rūzbehānī claimed that Iran was then to have served as the center of a universal Bahā'ī state. Muḥammad Reżā Shāh was, according to this line of thinking, a prisoner and puppet of the Bahā'ī and the Pahlavī state became a Bahā'ī rather than a Shīʿī state. The land reform of the early 1960s, for example, was a conspiracy to rob Muslim owners of their land and transfer it into Bahā'ī hands. Similarly, the Bahā'īs were accused of arranging refuge for themselves outside of Iran during the latter months of Pahlavī rule and transferring billions of dollars that belonged to "the oppressed nation of Iran" to the laps of the Americans, British, and Zionists. The writer goes on to ponder how

---

Qismat yekom (daftar 35 porseshhā va-pāsokhhā);" Sharīfī, "Bahā'iyat va-siyāsat," 132. In fact, Reżā Shah closed all Bahā'ī schools in Iran, as he did to all other independent sectarian schools.

90 Ḥujjat al-Islām Muḥammad Reżā Nasūrī, "Peyvand va-hamkārī-i Bahā'iyat bā rezhīm-i Pahlavī," *Intiẓār-i Mowʿūd* 27 (1387/2008–2009), 195–222. Ashrāfī, "Bahā'iyat va-bavarsāzīhā-i kāẕib;" "Farāmāsōnarī chegūneh sāzimānī ast? Cheh nowʿ irtibāṭi bā Bahā'iyat dārad?" See also Javāhirī, *Bahā'iyat pād jonbesh-i tajdīd ḥayāt-i millat-i Iran*, 322–420, which provides lists and details of alleged Bahā'īs who served in high positions under Muḥammad Reżā Shah. For more on Hoveyda, see Abbas Milani, *The Persian Sphinx: Amir Abbas Hoveyda and the Riddle of the Iranian Revolution: A Biography* (London: I.B. Tauris, 2000).

91 Sharīfī, "Bahā'iyat va-siyāsat," 132–140; "Inqilāb-i Islāmī va-muqābala bā nufūẕ-i Bahā'iyat dar Iran;" Shādāb ʿAsgarī, *Bahā'īyān-i niẓāmī dar ḥukūmat-i Pahlavī dovom* (Tehrān: Markaz-i asnād-i inqilāb-i Islāmī, 1396); Afrāsiyābī, *Bahā'iyat beh rivāyat-i ta'rīkh*, 236–269; Rūzbehānī, *Taḥlīl va-naqd Bahā'iyat*, 152–156.

many crimes were later committed against the poor nations of Palestine and Iraq thanks to these Bahāʾī funds.[92] Not surprisingly, the Shīʿī writers assert, when the Iranian people as a whole rose up against Muḥammad Reżā Shāh, only the Bahāʾīs stood by his side.[93]

As was the case with the opposition to imperialism, the Shīʿī clergy were the vanguard in defending Islam and Iran against the Bahāʾī menace as well. The hostile attitude toward Bahāʾīs of leading traditionalist clerics, most notably Grand Ayatollah Muḥammad Ḥusayn Boroujerdī, receives high praise among the Shīʿī polemicists.[94] But, it is Khomeini who is praised as having fully understood the true scope and gravity of the Bahāʾī threat and who mobilized the clergy and people against them.[95] Some writers have acknowledged the anti-Bahāʾī activity of the Ḥojjatiya association, but, in view of its subsequent break with the authorities under the Islamic Republic, they deny it any positive recognition. The Ḥojjatiya, they claim, erred completely in its opposition to political activism under the Pahlavīs and were probably influenced by the Bahāʾīs in their call for the separation of religion and politics. Typical of conspiracy theorists, these writers speculate that the Ḥojjatiya was created or at least activated by the Pahlavī regime in the 1950s in order to divert clerical attention and efforts against the Bahāʾīs instead of against the oppressive monarchy. What the Ḥojjatiya supposedly failed to understand was the broader context of Bahāʾīsm, i.e., its links with imperialism, Zionism, and the Pahlavīs, and the fact that the removal of the Pahlavīs would be the decisive blow to

92 ʿAlī Reżā Aqāyī, "Naqsh-i rezhīm-i Pahlavī dar taḥkīm-i firqa-i Bahāʾiyat," 21 Farvardīn 1385/April 10, 2006, https://www.farsnews.com/news/8501200597; Ḥusayn Fardūst, *Ẓuhūr va-suqūṭ-i salṭanat-i Pahlavī* Vol. 1 (Tehrān: Intishārāt-i iṭṭilāʿāt, 1370/1991), 202; ʿĀlimiyān, "Pahlavīhā dar khidmat-i Bahāʾiyat;" Ḥusayniyān, "Bahāʾiyat, rezhīm-i Pahlavī va-nahżat-i ʿulamāʾ," 14; Khosrō-panāh, "Sayr-i intiqādī dar taʾrīkh va-bāvarhā-i Bahāʾiyat," 32; Muḥammadī, "Jarayān-shināsī-i Bahāʾiyat: Qismat-i yekom (daftar 35 porseshhā va-pāsokhhā)"; Muḥammadī, "Jarayān-shināsī-i Bahāʾiyat: Qismat-i dovom (daftar 35 porseshhā va-pāsokhhā)"; Rūzbehānī, *Taḥlīl va-naqd-i Bahāʾiyat*, 151–152.

93 "Inqilāb-i Islāmī va-risvāʾī-i firqa-i Bahāʾiyat," http://kanoonhend.ir/fa/news/2459/انقلاب-اسلامی-و-رسوائی-فرقه-بهائیت.

94 For a few examples, see "Ayatollah Bourūjerdī va-mubāraza bā Bahāʾīhā," http://www.broujerdi.ir/index.php/2016-03-22-09-01-51/2016-03-22-09-05-56/260-2016-03-26-04-19-40; "Ayatollah Ṭāliqānī Bahāʾiyat rā shikl-i digār-i ṣahyūnīsm dar keshvar mīdānest," http://zionism.pchi.ir/show.php?page=contents&id=5252.

95 For a few examples among many, see Maryam Rafīʿī, *Imām-i Khomeini va-Bahāʾiyat* (Tehrān: muʾasasa jām-jām, 1387/2008); Seyyed Muṣṭafā Taqavī, "Imām-i Khomeini va-shāgerdhā-i imperialism," *Zamāneh* 61 (1386/2007), 179–188; "Imām-i Khomeini (rh) va-Bahāʾiyat," http://siasi.porsemani.ir/node/1109; Muʾasasa-i muṭālaʿāt-i va-pazhūheshhā-i siyāsī, "Jumlatī az imām-i Khomeini (rh) dar bārah-i peyvand Israʾīl va-Bahāʾiyat," http://revolution.pchi.ir/show.php?page=contents&id=4973.

this "misguided sect."[96] Just as the Bahā'īs served the British by fabricating and disseminating a false religion, so did the Ḥojjatiya seek to "break the foundations of pure Muḥammadan Islam," a *FarsNews* writer explained. The writer even suggested that members of the Ḥojjatiya disguised as Bahā'īs disseminated their association's "degenerate ideas" and concluded that there was no real difference between these two groups who were simply "two sides of the same coin."[97]

According to this Shīʿī discourse, the Bahā'ī betrayal got worse after the victory of the Revolution. While many Bahā'īs fled to the West, those who stayed in Iran, the official media explained, continued their "destructive and hypocritical" activities in subverting the revolution, as their leaders maintained constant contact with the American "den of spies" (the American embassy in official Iranian parlance). During the war with Iraq, the Bahā'īs allegedly served as a fifth column of the foreigners. Under the slogan of "non-intervention in politics," they spared no effort to help the enemies and passed information to the International House of Justice in Haifa, that is, to Israel. The Bahā'īs who were arrested and executed were not innocent victims who were persecuted for their beliefs, Muḥammadī explained, but rather traitors who had spied against their own country.[98] After the war, the Bahā'īs continued in their anti-Iranian propaganda and played an active and central role in the growing international pressure to prevent Iran from acquiring "peaceful" nuclear knowledge and capabilities.

The Bahā'īs have also been accused of looking to distort the history of Iran via, in particular, *Encyclopaedia Iranica*, whose founding editor, Ehsan

96 Rasūl Jaʿfariyān, *Jarayānhā va-sāzimānhā-i maẕhabi-siyāsī-i Iran: az rū-i kārāmadan-i Muḥammad Reżā Shah tā pīrūzī-i inqilāb-i Islāmī, sālhā-i 1320–1357* (Tehrān: Markaz-i Asnād-i Inqilāb-i Islāmī, 2004), 377; Maryam Ṣādiqī, "Naẓar-i Imām dar mowred-i anjuman-i Ḥojjatiya," *Kayhān*, 4 Mehr 1391/September 25, 2012; "Pāsokh beh chend shubha-i muhim-i ta'rīkhī dar bārah-i anjuman-i Ḥojjatiya/bakhsh-i dovom," 11 Mehr 1396/October 3, 2017, http://ferghenews.com/fa/news/15985/; Muḥammadī, "Jarayān-shināsī-i Bahā'iyat: qismat-i yekom (daftar 35 porseshhā va-pāsokhhā)."

97 "Anjuman-i Ḥojjatiya va-Bahā'iyat; do rūye yek sekeh!" May 30, 2016, https://www.parsnews.com/بخش-سیاسی-3/369584-انجمن-حجتیه-بهائیت-دو-روی-یک-سکه.

98 "Inqilāb-i Islāmī va-risvā'ī-i firqa-i Bahā'iyat;" "Jarayān-shināsī-i Bahā'iyat: Qismat sevom (daftar 35 porseshhā va-pāsokhhā);" Muḥammadī, "Bahā'iyat/ta'rīkhcheh, iʿtiqādāt va-važʿiyat-i konūnī (qismat-i sevom)." A public letter of then Minister of Intelligence, Ayatollah Qorban-ʿAlī Dorri Najafabādī to the Chief Prosecutor charged the Bahā'īs of continued close contacts and collaboration with external enemies, particularly Israel, as a reason for banning their activities. "Faʿāliyathā-i firqa-i żalla-i Bahā'iyat gheyr qānūnī va-mamnūʿ ast," February 15, 2009, https://www.farsnews.com/news/8711271271/فعالیتهاي-فرقه-ضاله-بهائیت-غیر-قانوني-و-ممنوع-است.

Yarshater, was a Bahāʾī, funding is American, and ideas are Zionist.[99] Likewise, they have been held accountable by the daily *Kayhān*, published by the Supreme Leader's Office, for the 2009 mass protests which followed the rigged presidential elections.[100] This was a clear attempt to leverage the widespread antipathy toward the Bahāʾīs, even among non-Islamists, in order to slander the popular protest movements as a whole.

In view of such supposed treasonous activity, it was only natural that Grand Ayatollah Makārem Shīrāzī explained that the Bahāʾīs did not deserve the status of Dhimmīs (protected minorities) as they serve foreign interests and are protected by foreign countries. In other words, they do not seek to live in peace with the Muslims but are in fact "waging war against God." Therefore, he concluded, there is no prohibition against expropriating their money and property.[101]

4 Liberal Voices

Considering the intensity of anti-Bahāʾī emotions, rhetoric, and activities, which were also shared by non-Islamists, dissident voices were few and far between, emerging only as part of a broader reassessment or questioning of the basic foundations of the official state ideology. The first and most prominent dissident voice was Ayatollah Montaẓerī the deposed designated heir to Khomeini. Toward the end of his life and despite his disdain for Bahāʾīsm as a religion, Montaẓerī argued for protection of the Bahāʾīs rights as citizens. In a fatwā signed on May 14, 2008, he stated that:

99 Muḥammadī, "Jarayān-shināsī-i Bahāʾiyat: qismat-i dovom (daftar 35 porseshhā va-pāsokhhā)"; Muḥammadī, "Bahāʾiyat/taʾrīkhcheh, iʿtiqādāt va-vażʿiyat-i konūnī (qismat-i dovom)."

100 *Kayhān*, 21 Dey 1388/January 11, 2010. See also the collection of documents published by the Islamic Revolution Documents Center purporting to prove the prominent Bahāʾī role in these riots, Markaz-i asnād-i Inqilāb-i Islāmī, *Naqsh-i Bahāʾiyat dar fitna-i 1388* (Tehrān, 1390/2011).

101 "Bahāʾīyān: Ayatollah al-ʿuzma Makārem," http://portal.anhar.ir/node/2171#gsc.tab=0. See a similar declaration by a court in 1993 in Kazimzadeh, "The Baha'is in Iran: Twenty Years of Repression," 551. The punishment for *muḥārib*, according to the Iranian judiciary spokesman, Ghulām-Ḥusayn Muḥsinī-Ejeʾī, ranges from leg amputation to execution, "Iran: Judiciary Spokesperson Says Punishment For Mohareb 'Waging War With God' Varies From Execution To Leg Amputation," Iran Human Rights Monitor, https://iran-hrm.com/index.php/2017/06/22/mohareb-punishment/.

> Not having a heavenly book like the Jews, Christians, and Zoroastrians, according to the Constitution [of Islamic republic of Iran], Bahāʾīs are not considered one of the religious minorities. However, since they are the citizens of this country, they have the rights of citizenship. Furthermore, they must benefit from Islamic compassion which is stressed in the Qurʾān and by the religious authorities.[102]

As Sussan Siavoshi noted, Montaẓerī's fatwā was noteworthy not only because it was the first but because it reflected a new view regarding the innate dignity of all humans regardless of their creed, which contrasted with his own earlier and strong anti-Bahāʾī attitude. The change in Montaẓerī's position was not purely theological, as he never accepted Bahāʾīsm as a legitimate religion. Nor did he change in any profound way his views on the unequal legal status of the other religious minorities that Islam recognizes as legitimate "people of the book."[103] Rather, his shift was political, relating to his revised views on the political aspects of Shīʿīsm, in particular his reservations about direct and overbearing clerical rule. In a way, Montaẓerī was advocating here a certain separation between religion and state, whereby religious ordinances would not encompass all aspects of state policy, and between religion and civic identity.

The liberal Ḥujjat al-Islam Muḥsin Kadīvar advanced Montaẓerī's view on three major points. First, he relied on the Universal Declaration of Human Rights to state that no one should be deprived of their civic and human rights because of their religious beliefs. Not only did he use a source of authority that was external to Islam, but he also used it to incorporate the broader term of human rights and apply it to the Bahāʾīs. Second, he addressed the Bahāʾīs as integral members of the Iranian people on a par with the Shīʿīs and the officially recognized religious minorities, Zoroastrians, Christians, and Jews. Third, he sought to minimize their "guilt" of association with Zionism (which he vehemently denounced) by pointing out that Bahāʾullah arrived in Palestine fifty years before the establishment of the Israeli state. He further insisted that any charges of collaboration with Israel should be leveled against individuals

---

102 The original version issued on Montaẓerī's personal website is no longer available. This version is taken from Sussan Siavhoshi, "Human Rights and the Dissident Grand Ayatullah Hussain ʿAli Montaẓerī," *The Muslim World* 106, no. 3 (2016): 621. For Persian versions, see Muḥsin Kadīvar "Ḥuqūq-i shahrvandī-i Bahāʾiyat az manẓar-i ustād," https://kadivar.com/?p=8284.

103 Siavhoshi, "Human Rights and the Dissident Grand Ayatullah Hussain ʿAli Montaẓerī," 621. In his second fatwā (June 14, 2008), which expanded on the issue of their civic rights, Montaẓerī referred to the Bahāʾīs with the prevalent pejorative, "the misguided sect" (*firqa-i żālla*) (Kadīvar, "Ḥuqūq-i shahrvandī-i Bahāʾiyat az manẓar-i ustād.").

based on clear evidence and not as a collective charge on the community as a whole. In other words, he opposed the traditional approach, which regarded all Bahāʾīs as one monolithic bloc, exclusively guided by their religious beliefs; he saw them, instead, as individuals.[104]

In 2013 Kadīvar went further and tackled the theological issue as well. He distinguished between two meanings of the term *kāfir* (disbeliever) in Shīʿīsm. The first applied to non-Muslims, such as Christians and Jews, who, while not equal to Muslims, enjoyed certain rights in Islam. The second referred to secularists and atheists who rejected God altogether. Kadīvar claimed that the first definition applied to the Bahāʾīs, who he recognized as monotheists (*muwaḥḥidūn*) as they believed in God. Even though they reject the finality of Muḥammad's mission, he highlighted their acceptance of his prophecy as a further mitigating element, in contrast to Jews and Christians who rejected the Prophet completely. Departing from the traditional Shīʿī position regarding the laws of religious impurity, he concluded that in the case of monotheists (*ahl-i towḥīd*), the invalidation of religion and belief does not necessarily lead to impurity. The call for the impurity of monotheists and those who believe in the prophecy is problematic, and he concluded that the Bahāʾīs are, therefore, ritually pure.[105]

A few dissidents chose public gestures over words to pronounce a different attitude toward Bahāʾīsm. In January 2014, Muḥammad Nūrizād, a former conservative journalist who became a dissident, paid a public visit to a Bahāʾī home, accepting tea in cups handled by his Bahāʾī hosts in blatant disregard of the taboos regarding ritual uncleanliness. He also kissed a Bahāʾī child whose parents had been imprisoned for their faith. Similarly, in May 2016, Ayatollah ʿAbd al-Ḥamīd Maʿṣūmī Tehrānī joined a gathering of human rights activists commemorating the sixth anniversary of the incarceration of the seven-person leadership group of the Bahāʾī community of Iran.[106] The gesture that aroused

104 Muḥsin Kadīvar, *Ḥaqq al-nās* (*Islām va-ḥuqūq-i bashar*) (Tehrān: Intishārāt-i Kvir, 1388/2009), 163; Muḥsin Kadīvar, "Ẓulm beh Bahāʾīyān," 5 Shahrīvar 1390/August 27, 2011, https://kadivar.com/?p=8202; Muḥsin Kadīvar, "Maḥrūmiyat-i Bahāʾīyān az ḥuqūq-i shahrvandī fāqid-i vujahat-i sharʿī va-qānūnī ast," 2 Dey 1393/December 23, 2014, https://kadivar.com/14211.

105 Muḥsin Kadīvar, "Āyā Bahāʾīyān kāfirand?," 5 Farvardīn 1392/March 25, 2013, https://kadivar.com/?p=10412; Muḥsin Kadīvar, "ʿAdam-i nejāsat-i Bahāʾiyat," 23 Shahrīvar 1392/September 14, 2013, https://kadivar.com/?p=12743.

106 Winston Nagan, "An Ayatollah in Iran Takes an Unorthodox Step in Support of Bahāʾīs," *International Policy Digest*, June 1, 2014, https://masoumitehrani.wordpress.com/tag/abdol-hamid-masoumi-tehrani/; "Ayatollah ʿAbd al-Ḥamīd Maʿṣūmī Tehrānī: khuṣūmat bā Bahāʾīyān ṟā ḵonār begoẕārīm," 1 Ordībehesht 1393/April 21, 2014, https://www.peace-mark.org/آيت-الله-عبدالحميد-معصومى-تهرانى-خصوم.

the harshest reactions was the public visit in April 2016 of Fā'iza Hāshimī, daughter of the former president Rafsanjānī, and former member of the Majlis, to the temporarily paroled Bahā'ī leader, Farībā Kamālabādī, with whom she had shared a prison cell in 2009. Kamālabādī, along with six other members of the ad hoc seven-person Iranian Bahā'ī administration known as the *hay'at-i Yārān* (the Council of Friends), had been tried and sentenced to ten-years imprisonment on charges of espionage and spying for Israel. Conservative figures and media chided Fā'iza Hāshimī for "counter-revolutionary conduct" when visiting "the Bahā'ī band ... sworn enemies of the Islamic Republic" and ritually impure people who wage a struggle against the Islamic Republic. They also seized the event as an opportunity to lash out against the former president, a leading member of the reformist camp, demanding that he denounce his daughter's move. The bold gesture and the subsequent pressure proved too strong for him, as he reportedly stated that "she has committed a wrong deed and should be ashamed of herself."[107] Kadīvar, on the other hand, when asked following the visit how Bahā'īs should be treated, responded sharply "as human beings."[108]

5 Conclusion

The Bahā'īs have been the only internal collective "other" in Shī'īsm against which widespread polemics as well as physical repression have been applied. The polemics may be divided into two major categories. The first criticizes Bahā'ī doctrines and beliefs in order to prove that Bahā'īsm is tantamount to apostasy and should not be recognized as a legitimate (though false) religion like Christianity or Zoroastrianism. Many of the arguments in this category, particularly regarding questions such as the finality of the Muḥammad's

---

107 "Vākoneshhā beh dīdār-i Fā'iza Hāshimī bā mudīr-i jāmi'a-i Bahā'īyān," May 14, 2016, – http://www.bbc.com/persian/iran/2016/05/160514_l57_fariba_kamalabadi_meetup_reax; "Fā'iza Hāshimī az dīdār-i khōd bā mudīr-i jāmi'a-i Bahā'īyān difā' kard," May 14, 2016, https://bit.ly/2HA6XHH; "Fā'iza Hāshimī bā kodām bānd ṣahyūnīstī peyvand khōrd?," 26 Ordībehesht 1395/May 15, 2016, https://www.mashreghnews.ir/news/574056; "Tanaqużhā-i Hāshimī pedar va-Hāshimī dokhtar," 26 Ordībehesht 1395/May 15, 2016, http://sobheqazvin.ir/news/183717-newscontent.

108 Muḥsin Kadīvar, "Ba Bahā'īyān chegūneh barkhōrd konīm?," 25 Ordībehesht 1395/May 14, 2016, http://kadivar.com/?p=15243; Thomas Erdbrink, "An Ayatollah's Daughter Prompts a Debate on Religious Persecution in Iran," *The New York Times*, May 18, 2016, https://www.nytimes.com/2016/05/19/world/middleeast/iran-bahais-kamalabādī-hashemi-meeting.html.

prophecy or the coming of the Mahdī, are based on textual reasoning that attempts to refute Bahāʾī precepts. Their main thrust is that Bahāʾī doctrine contradicts clear and irrefutable Islamic or Shīʿī doctrines and, therefore, must, by definition, be false. This approach aims, first and foremost, to bolster the belief and conviction of ordinary Shīʿīs, who are already convinced in the veracity of their own beliefs and scriptures; it is unlikely to affect those who harbor doubts or opposite views. Some of the claims use logical argumentation such as the attempt to prove internal contradictions within Bahāʾī doctrines or contradictions between Bahāʾī claims and practices; others strive to disparage Bahāʾī ideas, such as universal human equality, as shallow or impractical or as reactionary and supportive of oppressive regimes. These arguments present Shīʿīsm as the complete opposite of Bahāʾīsm, based on the correct balance between revelation and reason and as the champion of the oppressed in the struggle against injustice, thus applying the prevalent dichotomous juxtaposition of the (positive) "self" and the (negative) "other." As in other cases of the self-other contrast, these arguments ignore the potential existence of such traits within Shīʿīsm itself.

The second category of polemics attacks alleged Bahāʾī practices and links to the other enemies of Shīʿīsm and Iran. Their most prominent theme is the portrayal of Bahāʾīsm as a creature and tool of Western imperialism well into the present. Of particular importance in this context is the juxtaposition of the Bahāʾīs as the direct enemies and total opposite of the Shīʿī clergy – the authentic leaders of the people and the defenders of Islam and Iran. Added to this are the charges of the Bahāʾī-Jewish and later Bahāʾī-Zionist connection and, finally, Bahāʾī collaboration with Iraq in its war with Iran during the 1980s. The Bahāʾīs are thus depicted as foreign agents and traitors to their country who deserve to be punished more severely than how they are already treated.

Domestically, the Bahāʾīs have been portrayed as the closest allies of the Pahlavīs and even as the powerful force behind them, aiming to undermine Islam and spread Western culture and way of life in the service of imperialism. Here too, the sharpest dichotomy is made between the Bahāʾīs and the clergy, most prominently Khomeini, who stood at the forefront of the struggle for Islam and the people.

Overall, it seems that the one element that connects the two categories of anti-Bahāʾī charges is their association as representatives or agents of Westernized modernity. It is this element which may explain the great fear they arouse among the Shīʿī clergy despite being a small, weak, and repressed minority. At the same time, the repeated warnings of the Bahāʾī ideological and political threat have served several more practical goals, especially as the likelihood of large-scale conversions to a persecuted minority is not great. Every revolutionary regime needs, as mentioned earlier, to constantly highlight the specter of enemies in order to stem the waning of ideological ardor among its constituents, and alleged Bahāʾī activity can be used to explain such a decline and absolve regime supporters from a painful soul-searching process to analyze the true reasons. Likewise, inflating the threat of Bahāʾīsm or other religious dissidents helps justify the continued repression of political dissidents, e.g., feminists, by promoting a siege mentality and portraying them as Bahāʾī allies or tools. Magnifying the Bahāʾī threat also serves the clergy's corporate interests, as manifested in the large number of clerics and other writers who are engaged in anti-Bahāʾī propagation and in reports about the training of 3500 religious seminary students to fight Bahāʾī propaganda.[109] Anti-Bahāʾī propaganda also serves the regime's anti-Western policy, as many of its arguments play on popular nationalism and on the anti-Western attitudes shared by larger segments of society.[110] Interestingly, the Iranian authorities have not followed the Soviet model under Stalin and have not blamed imaginary Bahāʾī "saboteurs" for its economic failures, preferring instead to blame the West. This was probably out of concern for inflating alleged Bahāʾī influence inside Iran.

Historian Mina Yazdani has pointed to the strong resemblance between Khomeini's anti-Bahāʾī rhetoric and Nazi redemptive anti-Semitism, for example, in Khomeini's assertion that the Muslim nation of Iran would not be saved unless purged of Bahāʾīs.[111] While Khomeini did introduce harsh repressive measures against the Bahāʾīs after assuming power in 1979, he fell short of actually exterminating them or expelling them en masse; the West, particularly the United States, became instead the greatest threat. The Islamic Republic's handling of the Bahāʾīs, especially under Khamenei, seems, therefore, to have more in common with Christian anti-Semitism as practiced in the past by the Catholic Church. This entails socioeconomic discrimination and measured persecution and includes violence but not extermination. The Catholic Church needed the Jews as a symbol of the victory of Christianity over Judaism which would culminate in their mass conversion. Similarly, the Bahāʾīs serve as a useful "other" to be demonized as a source of trouble to the Shīʿīs, to be associated with other enemies, to serve as scapegoats, and to be suppressed but not to be killed; if eliminated, they can no longer serve as a useful "other."

---

109 "Naqd-i Bahāʾiyat, beh kam-i Bahāʾiyat."

110 Warburg, "Baha'is of Iran: Power, Prejudice and Persecutions," 208. For elaboration of this point, see Chehabi, "Anatomy of Prejudice: Reflections on Secular Anti-Baha'ism in Iran."

111 Yazdani, "The Islamic Revolution's Internal Other," 603.

CHAPTER 7

Feminism: The "Gift" of the West to Islam

The statements that feminism is the West's "gift" to Islam[1] and the "greatest enemy" of the family reflect two aspects of the broad and extensive orthodox Shīʿī polemics against this movement and ideology. Gender relations have been a major preoccupation of all monotheistic religions throughout history not only because of their significance for private and public morality but also because of the centrality of gender in the configuration of social and political power. The changing role of women in society in the modern period and, particularly, their conduct and dress in the public sphere has occupied an increasingly prominent place in the discourse of modern Islamist movements the world over. Modern scholarship has made significant progress in studying the various aspects of gender relations in Iran and in Shīʿī communities in the Arab world including the legal status of women and women's access to education, employment, and property through their participation in politics and representation in the media and popular culture.[2] The purpose of this chapter, therefore, is to focus only on attitudes toward feminist ideology and movements as both internal and external threats to Shīʿī Islam. The importance of this issue can be seen in Karim Sajjadpour's observation that the ideological edifice of the Islamic Republic is built on three important pillars: the ḥijāb for women, opposition to the United States, and opposition to Israel.[3]

All modern Islamist movements, Sunnī and Shīʿī alike, view feminism as a major manifestation of Western cultural imperialism and an assault on Islamic culture and way of life. Leila Ahmed maintained that women were the centerpiece of the Islamist agenda, in part because they were used as a key feature in the colonial critique of Islam and Arab culture.[4] Janet Afary went on to explain that the strength of fundamentalism lies in its creation of the illusion that a return to traditional, patriarchal relations is the answer to the social

1 Abūl-Ḥasan Ḥusaynzādeh and Ḥusayn ʿAbbāsiyān, "Naqd va-barresī-i mabānī-i fikrī va-shākheṣhā-i feminism-i Islāmī," *Pazhūheshī-i insānī pazhūheshī-i dīnī* 34 (1394/2015): 210.

2 The literature on gender in the Islamic Republic is too vast to be listed here. For more on gender questions in Iraqi Shīʿīsm, see Noga Efrati, *Women in Iraq: Past Meets Present* (New York: Columbia University Press, 2012), 163–174.

3 Karim Sajjadpour, *Reading Khamenei* (Washington DC: Carnegie Endowment, 2009), 14.

4 Margot Badran, *Feminism in Islam: Secular and Religious Convergence* (Oxford: Oneworld, 2001), 1; Leila Ahmed, *Women and Gender in Islam: Roots of a Modern Debate* (New Haven: Yale University Press, 1992), 236–237.

and economic problems that both Western and non-Western societies face in the era of late capitalism.[5] It can be argued that by associating feminism with the Western cultural offensive, Islamists hoped to mobilize a broader struggle against Western culture and gain the support of men who, having been stripped of their old identities as patriarchs, were keen to preserve the prevalent patriarchal social and cultural system.[6] Feminism has come to epitomize Western culture and, therefore, criticizing it has become a useful Islamist tool for attacking Western culture as a whole. Furthermore, the feminist struggle for gender equality and the empowerment of women is seen to challenge or even threaten the three pillars of Islam: the centrality and stature of Sharīʿa law; the family as the bastion of proper religious life; and the monopoly of the male clerics over the interpretation of religion.

Shīʿī criticism of feminism predates the 1979 Revolution and has been developing ever since. A comparison of the views of Khomeini before and after the Revolution and with those of his disciples is clear evidence of this process. Khomeini had addressed gender issues extensively in a variety of forms, but he had never referred to feminism in name or as a concept prior to the Revolution. It is, in fact, unclear whether he was acquainted with feminist theories at all, as his discourse on the issue remained rooted in traditional Shīʿīsm. His discussion and rulings on women underwent significant change between the 1960s, when he opposed women's suffrage in 1962–1963 and rejected the 1968 Family Protection Law, and the 1980s, when he was in power and forced to respond to the pleas of Islamist women. According to Haleh Afshar, Khomeini's early writings reflected his belief in women's "inferiority, not only physically and psychologically but also morally and intellectually." He thus regarded the idea of gender equality as "blasphemy" and a "Western plot" and believed that by encouraging women's involvement in social and political activities, the Western enemy was trying to bring women out of the home and block their "sacred national function of rearing pious children." He also accused "intellectuals" of using the concept of women's rights to fight Islam.[7] In his famous

5 Janet Afary, "The War Against Feminism in the Name of the Almighty: Making Sense of Gender and Muslim Fundamentalism," *New Left Review* 224 (1997): 89–110, https://newleftreview.org/issues/I224/articles/janet-afary-the-war-against-feminism-in-the-name-of-the-almighty-making-sense-of-gender-and-muslim-fundamentalism/.

6 Fatima Mernissi, *Islam and Democracy: Fear of the Modern World* (Wokingham: Basic Books, 1992), 165.

7 Haleh Afshar, "Khomeini's Teachings and Their Implications for Women," *Feminist Review*, 12 (1982): 64; Haideh Moghissi, *Populism and Feminism in Iran: Women's Struggle in a Male-Defined Revolutionary Movement* (New York: St. Martin, 1994), 61. For an analysis of the evolution of Khomeini's views, see Azādeh Kian, "Gendered Khomeini," in *A Critical Introduction to Khomeini*, ed. Arshin Adib-Moghaddam (Cambridge: Cambridge University

1963 Fayżiyya speech Khomeini urged the Shāh to acknowledge that the ideas of gender equality and universal compulsory education belonged to the Bahā'ī leader, 'Abd al-Bahā'.[8] In this way, he sought to vilify feminism by associating it with a particularly abhorred "other," which has been linked in the public eye with modernity and foreign conspiracies that supposedly threatened the integrity of Iranian Muslim society. Following the Revolution, Khomeini somewhat mitigated his discourse. He rejected the charge that Islam kept women in the home and argued that the active participation of women in the Revolution was one of the wonders of Islam, which had transformed women spiritually and mentally and brought them into the streets against the Shāh. In contrast to his earlier opposition, Khomeini even supported women's suffrage in the 1979 Constitution.[9]

Unlike Khomeini, his disciples, most notably Muṭṭaharī disputed feminism directly or articulated their positions on gender with feminist arguments on their mind. By the late 1980s, leading clerics such as Aḥmad Azarī-Qommī, Yūsuf Ṣāne'ī, 'Abdollah Javādī Āmolī, and Ibrāhīm Amīnī were addressing the "woman question" in their scholarship. In 1992, the Islamic Propagation Office of the Qom Seminary (*Daftar-i tablīghāt-i ḥawza-i 'ilmīyya-i Qom*) began publishing a women's journal called *Payām-i Zan* (women's message), which aimed to find an Islamic solution to the "woman question." The journal, which was run by young male clerics, contains, in Ziba Mir-Hosseini's words, "state-of-the-art" clerical thinking on women's rights and maps the evolution of the Islamic Republic's official discourse on gender.[10]

Mir-Hosseini maintained that this official discourse was, however, never monolithic, encompassing three broad Islamic perspectives and debates on women and gender: traditionalist, neo-traditionalist, and modernist. A prominent voice among the modernists, who advocated the concept of dynamic jurisprudence (*fiqh-i pūyā*) that would offer new legal solutions to modern problems, was the cleric Seyyed Muḥsin Sa'īdzādeh, a frequent contributor to the Islamic feminist journal *Zanān*, who took issue with the premises of the official discourse on women and exposed its inherent gender bias. Sa'īdzādeh's articles, written in the language and mode of argumentation of jurisprudence,

---

Press, 2014), 170–192; Rūḥollah Khomeini, *Ṣaḥīfa-i nūr: majmū'a-i rāhnimūdhā-i imām-i Khomeini* Vol. 10 (Tehrān: Vizārat-i Irshād-i Islāmī, 1995), 86–88.

8 Cited in Mina Yazdani, "The Islamic Revolution's Internal Other: The Case of Ayatollah Khomeini and the Bahā'īs of Iran," *Journal of Religious History* 36, no. 4 (2012): 600.

9 Khomeini, *Ṣaḥīfa-i nūr*, vol. 9, 230, Vol. 18, 263.

10 Ziba Mir-Hosseini, "Religious Modernists and the 'Woman Question': Challenges and Complicities," in *Twenty Years of Islamic Revolution: Political and Social Transition in Iran since 1979*, ed. Eric Hooglund (Syracuse: Syracuse University Press, 2002), 74.

conveyed *Zanān*'s message to the heart of the clerical seminaries.[11] While advancing a moderate feminist agenda, these modernists were cautious enough not to openly identify as feminists. The foremost spokesperson of this liberal trend, Muḥsin Kadīvar, described gender equality as one of the main pillars of a human rights regime and a democratic order. Gender equality and women's autonomy have also been central to the work of other clerics among the modernists. Most notable was ʿAbdollah Nūrī (minister of interior under President Khātamī), who took a strong stance on the issue of the veil – a central issue for Islamists worldwide – arguing that it should be voluntary.[12]

Over the years, particularly since the early 1990s, the anti-feminist discourse has expanded considerably in scope and sophistication both in printed and electronic media. Many of the anti-feminist arguments that Shīʿī writers (both male and female) have raised are similar to those advocated by Sunnī Islamists. However, the Shīʿī discourse goes beyond the mere rejection of feminist calls for gender equality or criticism of various manifestations of female conduct in the public sphere. Rather, it grapples with and confronts feminist ideology from a place of extensive familiarity with modern feminist literature and the historical development and evolution of feminism and skillful manipulation of the disputes among the different feminist trends.[13] The scope of this anti-feminist literature and, particularly, the efforts to study feminist history and arguments reflect the establishment's fear of the appeal of feminism and the challenge it poses to the dominant ideology. Ḥujjat al-Islam Muḥammad Āsef Muḥsinī of the Bishārat Cultural Institute in Ghazna (Afghanistan), for example, explained the importance of presenting Islam's true position on gender lest the tenets of feminist thought appeal to people with limited education.[14]

---

11 Ziba Mir-Hosseini, "Beyond 'Islam' vs 'Feminism,'" *IDS Bulletin* 42, no. 1 (2011): 71; Mir-Hosseini, "Religious Modernists and the 'Woman Question,'" 75.

12 Shahra Razavi, "Islamic Politics, Human Rights and Women's Claims for Equality in Iran," *Third World Quarterly* 27, no. 7 (2006): 1228.

13 For a few examples, see Narjes Rūdgār, *Feminism: Taʾrīkhcheh, naẓariyat, gerāyeshhā, naqd* (Qom: Daftar-i muṭālaʿāt va-taḥqīqāt-i zan, 1388); Aḥmad Reżā Towḥīdī, "Barresī-i jonbesh-i feminism dar gharb va-Iran," in *Hamāyesh-i Islām va-feminism* Vol. 1, ed. Hādī Vakīlī (Tehrān: daftar-i nashr-i maʿārif, 1381/2002), 161–188; Hamīrā Mushīrzādeh, "Zamīnhā-i ẓuhūr-i feminism dar gharb," in Vakīlī (ed.), *Hamāyesh-i Islām va-feminism* Vol. 2, 505–547; Hālā Lājvardī, "Feminism muthbat feminism manfī," *Pazhūhesh-i zanān* 35, no. 3 (1386/2008): 83–107; Sorūr Esfandiyār, "Ravand-i ẓuhūr-i feminism dar chahār-i qarn-i akhīr," *Payām-i zan* 138 (1387/2009): 25–40.

14 "Muṣāḥaba-i majala-i nigāh bā dabir hamāyesh Ḥujjat al-Islām wal-Muslimīn Muḥammad Āsif Muḥsinī (Ḥikmat)," Mīzān 29, 1496/October 21, 2017, http://www.bsharat.com/id/9/6.html. See a similar argument in Ḥusayn ʿAlī Raḥmanī, "Cherāyī va-chegūnehgī naqd-i falsafa-i akhlāq-i femīnīstī," *Pazhūhesh-i zanān*, 6, no. 4 (1387/2009): 109–126.

The ongoing efforts of spokespersons and writers years after the 1979 Revolution to prove that Islam has never discriminated against women indicate, according to Dr. Mahdī Lakzā'ī of Adyān University, a subconscious endorsement of the feminist premise while rejecting it as an ideology.[15] At the same time, and as will be discussed below, the Shī'ī mainstream flatly rejected the effort of activist women – both supporters of the regime inside Iran and various female scholars in the West – to develop Islamic feminist ideology. The general Shī'ī criticism against feminism focuses on several interrelated issues: feminism as part of the Western onslaught on Islam, the challenge feminism poses to Islamic law, and feminism's negative ramifications on society as a whole.

1 Feminism and the West

Both Sunnī and Shī'ī Islamists view feminism as a new and sophisticated extension of older colonial policies and as part of the Western plot to undermine Muslim culture and way of life.[16] The mainstream view portrays it as an aspect of the broader phenomenon of Western secularist and materialistic modernity which threatens religion. Feminism is, they have claimed, a product of the "cultural and conceptual disarray of the West" and a crucial element in the "soft war" which the West wages against Islam in order to impose its values and culture on Islamic countries, particularly Iran. A *Farsnews* writer equated the feminists with missionaries operating on behalf of the West against Islam. Likewise, other writers have described feminism as an aggressive expansionist movement, reflecting the broader essence of the West and expressing Western cultural imperialism, which seeks to obliterate all other cultures. The West is even accused of using feminism as a propaganda weapon against the Islamic Revolution immediately after its victory.[17]

---

15 "Rūyikard-i femīnīstī beh dīn; bā ta'kīd bar Yahūdiyat va-Masīḥiyat," 19 Ordībe hesht 1395/April 30, 2016, https://urd.ac.ir/fa/cont/5966/«روی- کرد-فمینیستی-به-دین؛ -با-تاکید-بر-یهودیت-و-مسیحیت».

16 Ziba Mir-Hosseini, "Beyond 'Islam' vs 'Feminism,'" 69.

17 Seyyed Ḥusayn Ishāqī, "Feminism towṭi'ah-i gharb 'alayh-i zanān (pt. 1)," *Mublighān* 72 (1384/ 2005): 76–79; "Ashnā'ī bar jarayānhā-i aṣlī-i femīnīstī dar Iran," 16 Mehr 1390/ October 8, 2008, www.farsnews.com/newstext.php?nn=13900716000477; Mowlūd A'ẓamyān Bīdgolī, "Barresī-i taṭbīqī-i feminism va-jāygāh-i zan dar gharb va-Islām," November 2015, http://emamemobin.com/index.php/thought/2014-09-23-16-15-08/2015-11-15-06-26-29/537-2015-11-15-07-34-28; Farībā 'Alāsavand, *Naqd konvension-i raf'-i kulīye-i ashkāl-i tab'īż 'alayh-i zanān* (Qom: Intishārāt-i markaz-i mudīriyat-i ḥawza-i 'ilmiyya Qom, 1382/2003), 28.

Andisheqom, the official website of the Qom community of learning, has traced the origins of feminism to the Constitutional period (1906–1911) and asserted that those who worked for women's rights were influenced by Western ideas and became part of the Western project. Feminism in the Islamic Republic therefore constitutes direct continuity from the period of the Shāh, when it was imported by intellectuals who had opposed religion. Its main features, both then and now, are hostility to the piety of women and to the practice of women's rights within the framework of Islamic jurisprudence, demanding instead Western-style rights.[18] Ḥujjat al-Islam Zībāyī-nezhād, among others, distinguished between the legitimate struggle to improve various aspects of women's rights during the Constitutional Revolution and feminism, which he described as an upper-class phenomenon inspired by Western-minded intellectuals.[19] A semi-official blogger asserted that although the efforts to spread Western culture were made openly and unscrupulously prior to the 1979 Revolution, today they are carried out in a subtle way under the guise of defending women's rights. The overall consensus among clerical mainstream writers is that feminism in Iran is not an indigenous movement but, rather, is at odds with the local culture because it borrows so heavily from the West. This excessive borrowing explains the eclectic character of the feminist movement in Iran and its internal disparities and contradictions.[20] The Western origins of feminism as well as the alleged uncritical and flawed reading of Western feminist writings led Ibrāhīm Shafīʿī Sarvestānī to conclude that there is no

18 "Feminism taʿrīf kardeh va-athār-i mukharrib ʾīn jonbesh rā bayān konīd," http://www.andisheqom.com/fa/Question/View/1113 (accessed November 2, 2017); "Tafāvot-i jawharī-i iḥyāʾ-i ḥuqūq-i zanān dar Islām va-jonbesh-i feminism," 18 Bahman 1390/February 7, 2012, http://www.hawzah.net/fa/News/View/91073; Shihāb Zamānī, "Naqd va-barresī-i feminism va-payāmadhā-i ān (pt. 1)," 17 Khordād 1391/June 6, 2012, http://basirat.ir/fa/print/238441; Shihāb Zamānī, "Naqd va-barresī-i feminism va-payāmadhā-i ān (pt. 7)," 21 Khordād 1391/June 10, 2012, http://basirat.ir/fa/news/241074; "Konkāshī dar kalām-i Imām (rh) bar irtijāʿ-i feminism," *Shūrā-i farhangī va-ijtimāʿī-i zanān* 5 (1378/1999), http://www.hawzah.net/fa/Article/View/88684; ʿAlī Reżā Anūshīrvānī, "Uṣūl va-naẓarīyyahā-i feminism dar gharb," in Vakīlī (ed.), *Hamāyesh-i Islām va-feminism* Vol. 1, 83–92.

19 Muḥammad Reżā Zībāyī-nezhād, "Khāstgāh-i feminism dar Iran," *Howrāʾ* 38 (1388/2009–2010), http://ensani.ir/fa/article/112010.

20 "Az feminism-i jahānī tā feminism-i Irānī/ nigāhī-i kul girāyāneh beh jonbesh va-naẓariyya-i feminism dar Iran va-jahān," *Howrāʾ* 27 (1387/2008), http://www.hawzah.net/fa/Magazine/View/6432/6664/78751. For the emphasis on the internal contradictions in feminism, see "Feminism va-tanāquż dar rāhbordhā," *Howrāʾ* 17 (1384/ 2005), http://www.hawzah.net/fa/Magazine/View/6432/6446/73692/; Muḥammad Āsif Ḥikmat, "Barresī va-naqd-i naẓariyat-i tarbiyatī-i feminism," *Islām va-pazhūheshhā-i tarbiyatī* 4, no. 1 (2012), http://eslampajoheshha.nashriyat.ir/node/69.

such thing as an Iranian feminism that addresses specific Iranian issues and problems and is suitable to Iranian society.[21]

A major flaw of feminism, according to the Shīʿī discourse, is its humanistic and rationalist basis, which is rooted in its Western origins and stands in contrast to the Islamic spiritual and religious worldview. Islam is based on divine revelation and metaphysics and regards God as the source of humanity's well-being. Humanism, on the other hand, places human beings at the center as the source of intellect, moral values, and legislation.[22] This humanist, materialist, and secularist perspective drives feminist women to fight religion. However, it is, the Shīʿī writers claim, harmful to society and to the women themselves; by focusing on women's rights, the humanistic worldview disregards their duties toward family and society. The emphasis on material equality contradicts the Islamic ideal of cooperation and partnership between men and women in the realms of values and spirituality. Moreover, the secular foundation of feminism prevents women from attaining human perfection (kamāl), which is the ultimate goal of religion and humanity.[23]

Ironically, considering the overall Islamist rejection of Western rationalism, a few writers used arguments raised by radical feminists, attributing them to all feminists, to accuse feminists in general of ignoring human reason and rationality altogether. They charged the feminists with emphasizing the importance of feminine emotions in the process of knowledge production and denying the distance between reason and emotions. Consequently, the ideas of feminist science and epistemology are not used to seek truth but merely to prove their point of view and enhance their position vis-à-vis men.[24] This

21 Muḥammad Reżā Zībāyī-nezhād and Ibrāhīm Shafīʿī Sarvestānī, "Goftemān-i femīnīstī dar Iran: negāreshhā va-taḥlīlhā," *Howrāʾ* 27 (1387/2008), http://ensani.ir/fa/article/111302.

22 Rūdgār, *Feminism: "Taʾrīkhcheh, naẓariyat, gerāyeshhā, naqd*, 188–227; Muḥammad Reżā Zībāyī-nezhād and Muḥammad Taqī Subḥānī, *Darāmadī bar niẓām-i* shakhṣiyat*-i zan dar Islām* (Tehrān: Daftar-i Muṭālaʿāt va-taḥqīqāt-i zanān, 1381/2002), 20; "Rābiṭa-i Islām va-feminism," http://www.andisheqom.com/public/application/index/viewData?c=11344&t=article; "Āyā Islām bā naẓarāt-i maktab-i feminism movāfiq ast?," http://www.porseman.org/q/show.aspx?id=130250; Seyyeda Maʿṣūma Ḥasanī, "Tafāvothā-i jinsiyatī az dīdār-i Islām va-feminism," *Muṭālaʿāt-i rāhbordī-i zanān* 23 (1383/2004), https://www.noormags.ir/view/en/articlepage/212042.

23 Ismāʿīl Chirāghī Kutiyānī, "Feminism va-kār kard khānevādeh," *Maʿrifat* 8, no. 131 (1387/ 2008), 108; Muḥammad Ḥusayn Bīdgolī, "Naqd va-barresī-i falsafa-i akhlāq-i femīnīstī – akhlāq-i zanāneh negār," 30 Abān 1396/November 21, 2017, http://moralphilosophy.ir/اخلاق-فمینیستی-اخلاق-زنانه; "Jonbesh-i feminism, maʿnāyī-i feminism," http://www.porseman.org/q/vservice.aspx?id=98942; ʿAlāsavand, *Naqd konvension-i rafʿ-i kulīye-i ashkāl-i tabʿīż ʿalayh-i zanān*, 10.

24 Ismāʿīl Chirāghī Kutiyānī, "Barresī-i intiqādī-i rūsh-shināsī-i femīnīstī az manẓar-i realism Ṣadrāyī," *Maʿrifat-i Farhangī Ijtimāʿī* 2, no. 3 (1390/2011), http://ensani.ir/fa/article/322403.

flawed feminist "other" is, of course, presented in stark contrast to the Shīʿīs, who combine reason with belief.

An even greater problem is what they see as the link between feminism and capitalism. According to this narrative, feminism originally emerged as a reaction to the cultural and social oppression of women in Western societies but has become an arena for realizing the goals of the Western power system and capitalism. The capitalists sought to deprive women of their humanity and transform them into a workforce in order to consolidate the capitalist system. Quite a few of the achievements claimed by feminists are, in fact, gains of the capitalist system with all its negative ramifications. Thus, according to the Shīʿī discourse, women were the first victims of Westernized modernism.[25] Rather than being an appropriate response to the oppression of women, feminism has, instead, become its cause. The mixing of men and women in the workplace increased the competition and animosity between them, and while claiming to make women economically independent, it has actually increased the suffering of poor women. Ḥasan Raḥīm-pūr Azghadī, a member of the Supreme Council of the Cultural Revolution, concluded that feminism is the "oppression of the secular man upon the Western woman."[26] Feminism is thus portrayed by the Shīʿī writers as one aspect of the broader reality of Western-dominated humanist, liberal, and capitalist culture; not only does it not favor or support women but in fact victimizes them, and one of its worst outcomes is the spread of prostitution as a global industry.[27]

This capitalist connection prompted various writers to link feminism with another external threat: the Jews and world Zionism. One writer built a series

---

25 "Tafāvot-i jawharī-i iḥyā'-i ḥuqūq-i zanān dar Islām va-jonbesh-i feminism;" Bīdgolī, "Barresī-i taṭbīqī-i feminism va-jāygāh-i zan dar gharb va-Islām;" Zaynab Niyāzī, "Feminism va-mabānī-i tafakkur-i ṣahyūnīsm (pts. 1 + 2)," http://zionism.blogfa.com/post-866.aspx; Rūdgār, *Feminism: ta'rīkhcheh, naẓariyat, gerāyeshhā, naqd*, p. 236–237; Rāmīn Mehrāyīnī, "Ta'mmolī dar feminism yā maktab-i iṣālat-i zan dar gostāresh-i fasād-i ijtimāʿī va-furūpāshī-i khānevādeh," 3 Esfand 1389/February 22, 2011 – http://www.aftabir.com/articles/view/applied_sciences/social_science/c12_1298375749p1.php/; "Az feminism-i jahānī tā feminism-i Irānī/ nigāhī-i kul girāyāneh beh jonbesh va-naẓariyya-i feminism dar Iran va-jahān;" Muḥammad Bāqir Ẕū al-Qadr, *Qiṣṣa-i ghurbat-i gharbī: goftārī dar mabānī-i farhang va-tamaddun-i gharb* (Tehrān: Dāneshgāh-i farmāndehī va-setād dowra-i ʿālī-i jang, 1381/2002), p. 111.

26 "Islām dar bārah-i feminism cheh mīgūyad? Barāberī-i zan va-mard dar Islām;" ʿAlāsavand, *Naqd konvension-i rafʿ-i kulīye-i ashkāl-i tabʿīż ʿalayh-i zanān*, p. 28; Ẕū al-Qadr, *Qiṣṣa-i ghurbat-i gharbī*, p. 111; Ḥamīda Amīnī-fard, "Feminism, ẓulm-i insān-i sekūlār beh zan-i gharbī ast," *Iran*, 5 July 2007 – http://vista.ir/article/265702.

27 ʿAlāsavand, *Naqd konvension-i rafʿ-i kulīye-i ashkāl-i tabʿīż ʿalayh-i zanān*, 28.

of logical inferences whereby Zionism was the source of secularism and was, therefore, just the same as the other ills of modernity that bred feminism, that is, humanism, liberalism, capitalism, and individualism. Using fabricated citations, the author presented the Talmud as a source of moral and sexual corruption and argued that the sexually immoral foundations of feminism are tantamount to Zionist principles. Feminism was, he asserted, closely linked to the "secret undercurrent" that was running throughout history, namely, the Jews and, consequently, all women in the world are under attack by the Zionists.[28] In a similar vein, a conference held in early July 2007 and attended by Zahrāʾ Ṭabībzādeh Nūrī, then advisor to President Ahmadinezhad on women and family affairs, devoted a special session to the link between feminism and Zionism. The gist of the discussion was that feminism was a "gift" which Zionism supposedly awarded Western women but through which the modern *jāhiliyya* (age of barbarity) has plagued all women in industrial societies. The major goal of the Zionists, in cooperation with the Freemasons and the Bahāʾīs, has been to use feminism in order to undermine the family and thus control the various disintegrating societies.[29] The speakers cited as proof the notorious *Protocols of the Elders of Zion*, which elaborated on the need to destroy the family. Not surprisingly, Ḥujjat al-Islam Amīn Fāṭimī of Loristan University, among others, diagnosed two types of women that had evolved in the West: those who serve humanity, and those who follow *The Protocols of the Elders of Zion*, who are divided between the feminists and the corrupt.[30]

---

28 Niyāzī, "Feminism va-mabānī-i tafakkur-i ṣahyūnīsm (pts. 1 + 2);" "Towṭiʿah-i family yā tablīghāt-i feminism," 13 Tīr 1390/July 4, 2011, http://www.ghatreh.com/news/nn7813132. See also "Naqsh-i feminism va-ṣahyūnīsm dar żāyiʿ kardan jins-i zan," 6 Mordād 1396/ July 28, 2018 – https://www.yjc.ir/fa/news/6613218/.

29 ʿAlī Reżā Muḥammadī, "Jarayān-shināsī Bahāʾiyat: Qismat-i dovom (daftar 35 porseshhā va-pāsokhhā)," http://porseman.org/ShowArticle.aspx?id=1243; ʿAlī Akbar ʿĀlimiyān, "Pahlavīhā dar khidmat-i Bahāʾiyat," *Pūyā* 7 (Esfand 1386/March 2008): 91–96; Zībāyī-nezhād, "Khāstgāh-i feminism dar Iran."

30 Amīnī-fard, "Feminism, ẓulm-i insān sekūlār beh zan-i gharbī ast;" "Feminism va-ṣahyūnīsm," 20 Tīr 1386/July 11, 2007, http://banoo.blogfa.com/post-82.aspx; "Ṣahyūnīsm va-andīsheh-i farāmāsūnarī-i ḥuqūq-i doghūrīn-i zanān," 14 Mehr 1392/ October 16, 2013, http://mouood.org/component/k2/item/14159; "Feministha va-pīshtāzān harzahgerāʾī pīrū prōtokol ṣahyūnīsm hastand," 31 Farvardīn 1393/ April 20, 2013, https://www.isna.ir/news/93013113406. See a similar conference in Bojnūrd, "Neshest-I hamandīshī 'ṣahyūnīsm, feminism, umānīsm,' dar Bojnūrd bargozār shod," 8 Khordād 1391/May 28, 2012, https://iqna.ir/fa/news/1018945/-نشست-هم اندیشی صهیونیسم-فمینیسم-و-اومانیسم-در-بجنورد-برگزار-شد.

2 The Feminist Challenge to Islamic Law

The portrayal of feminism as part of the broader Western plot against Islam derived, in part, from the real challenge that the central feminist principle of gender equality posed to central Islamic legal principles, which were accused of discriminating against women. In his seminal text, *Women's Rights in Islam* (*Niẓām-i ḥuqūq-i zan dar Islām*), Murtażā Muṭṭaharī framed the argument that became the basis of the official gender discourse of the Islamic Republic. Originally published in response to the Shāh's 1968 Family Protection Law, Muṭṭaharī rejected gender equality as a Western concept and "mere propaganda" with no place in Islam. Instead, he raised the notion of the complementarity of gender rights and duties, arguing that the apparent disparity in rights and duties between men and women as mandated in Islamic laws is, if properly understood, the essence of divine justice. It cannot be perceived as discriminatory against women, because the Sharīʿa is in harmony with the law of nature and embodies God's design for men, women, and society as a whole. Muṭṭaharī did not deny that women had suffered discrimination but maintained that the true awakening of women would not be achieved by "blind emulation of the Western peoples" that would "cause them thousands of misfortunes." Rather, the solution lies in returning to the correct interpretation and implementation of Islam, and thus "reviving the numerous overlooked women's rights in Islam."[31]

Seeking to counter the feminist demand for gender equality, Muṭṭaharī distinguished between two categories: "equality" (*tasāvī*) and "sameness" (*tashābuh*). Accordingly, men and women are equal as humans, as they constitute two types of the same species. They are equal in their proximity to God, in their ability and duty to distinguish between right and wrong, and, therefore, in most religious duties. Yet, they are not the same due to biological differences and therefore should not be treated the same or have the same laws applied to them. If, he stated, women want to have equal rights and enjoy an equal fate with men, then the "sameness" of rights must be removed so that men and women acquire the rights they each deserve. He insisted that the dissimilarity of men's and women's rights due to the limits set by nature is compatible not

31 Ziba Mir-Hosseini, "Debating Women: Gender and the Public Sphere in Post-Revolutionary Iran," in *Civil Society in the Muslim World Contemporary Perspectives*, ed. Amyn B. Sajoo (London: I.B. Tauris, 2002), 111; Murtażā Muṭṭaharī, *Niẓām-i ḥuqūq-i zan dar Islām* (Tehrān: Intishārāt-i Ṣadrā, 1357/1979), 122.

only with justice and natural laws but also with the well-being of the family and society.[32]

A host of writers have criticized the feminist claim to gender equality and its accompanying charge of discriminatory Islamic law. Khomeini, for example, stated that while Islam takes care of women's rights, absolute equality is not obligatory as the Qur'ān contains explicit laws for men and others for women. He, therefore, described the Pahlavī policy of imposing gender equality as one of the acts of oppression they committed against Islam and against women.[33] Likewise, Ayatollah ʿAbdollah Javādī Āmolī's *Women in the Mirrors of Glory and Beauty* (*Zan dar āyīnah-i jalāl va-jamāl*) was for years the most important post-Revolutionary text on women. While concurring with Muṭṭaharī's thesis on the complementarity of gender rights and duties, he placed the issue on the spiritual plane, where the real destinies of men and women lie.[34] One writer maintained that the feminists themselves acknowledge the physiological differences between men and women but deny the impact, which, he claimed, is absurd considering the implication of such differences on childbirth and child rearing. The feminists, he went on, exaggerate the impact of social gender construction; the differences between men and women are in their functions but not in their spirituality, piety, purpose in life, and religious calling. According to Farībā ʿAlāsavand, of the Women and Family Research Center, Islam emphasizes gender differences on questions of law and morality, while regarding this distinction as the foundation of proper conduct.[35]

---

32 Muṭṭaharī, *Niẓām-i ḥuqūq-i zan dar Islām*, 123; Ziba Mir-Hosseini, *Islam and Gender: The Religious Debate in Contemporary Iran* (Princeton: Princeton University Press, 1999), 117.

33 Mu'asasa-i tanẓīm va-nashr athār-i Imām-i Khomeini, *Jāygāh-i zan dar andīsheh-i Imām-i Khomeini* (S) (Qom, 1374/1995), 248–250.

34 Mir-Hosseini, *Islam and Gender*, 84. See similar views in Ḥamīd Reżā Aqā Muḥammadīan and Reżā Pūr Ḥusayn, "Tafāvothā-i raftārī-i zan va-mard (pāye-i fīzyūlūzhīk va-gheyr-i fīzyūlūzhīk)," in Vakīlī (ed.), *Hamāyesh-i Islām va-feminism* Vol. 1, 51–83; Muḥammad Rabbānī, "Negārshī bar tafāvothā-i biyūlūzhīk-i zan va-mard," in Vakīlī (ed.), *Hamāyesh-i Islām va-feminism* Vol. 1, 271–286; "Feminism-i nafsānī-i gharb yā mushārakāt hame-i jānibeh-i Islām," *Tebyān*, 2 Mordād 1382/July 24, 2003, https://article.tebyan.net/2902.

35 "Āyā Islām bā naẓrat-i maktab-i feminism muvāfiq ast?," http://www.porseman.org/q/show.aspx?id=130250; Ḥasanī, "Tafāvothā-i jinsiyatī az dīdār-i Islām va-feminism;" Shihāb Zamānī, "Naqd va-barresī-i feminism va-payāmadhā-i ān (pt. 6)," 17 Khordād 1391/June 6, 2012, http://basirat.ir/fa/news/239969; Seyyed Ibrāhīm Ḥusaynī, "Feminism, farāz yā furūd?," 11 Esfand 1386/March 1, 2008, https://rasekhoon.net/article/show/10ttps://rasekhoon.net/article/show/109435/فمینیسم-فراز-یا-فرود-قسمت-اول/; Rūḥollah Bāqirī, "Ḥuqūq-i zinashūyī va-mabānī-i ān az manẓar-i Qur'ān," October 16, 2012, http://old.ido.ir/a.aspx?a=1391072511; ʿAlāsavand, *Naqd konvension-i rafʿ-i kulīye-i ashkāl-i tabʿīż ʿalayh-i zanān*, 30.

Unlike the conflictual Western and feminist approach, in the Islamic worldview, all humans are parts of a big, harmonious, and wise whole. Men and women therefore complement rather than oppress each other, and Islam promotes true collaboration between men and women with each fulfilling their role. The perfect example for the Shīʿī writers is Fāṭima, who assisted Imām ʿAlī in his struggles, while he helped her to carry out some of her duties.[36] Still, the Qom website maintained that even in this complementary framework, the Qurʾān is very explicit about the superiority of men over women.[37]

Feminists equate equality with justice, but such a view does not, it is claimed, take into account the differences in human capabilities and needs. The Islamic understanding of justice, on the other hand, means giving each person his or her rights as stipulated by the law. Consequently, true and just equality between men and women corresponds with their natural "biological essence" and the stipulations of Islamic law. Since men are biologically and psychologically different and since women fulfill different social functions than men, their legal rights and duties are also seen to be different.[38] Ayatollah Seyyed Muḥammad Ḥusayn Ḥusaynī Tehrānī (d. 1374/1995) of Mashhad maintained that nature and biology determine people's duties and social rights and, therefore, equality does not mean they are equal in the way they are built and in their strength. Put differently, equality does not mean sameness (*tashābuh*) but rather the preservation of the innate properties and essential vestiges of creation that exist in each person.[39] Others argued that the feminist rejection of natural differences harms women by ignoring their femininity and expecting them to behave like men and compete with men; a woman who wants equality with men must, they claim, give up her femininity. A corollary to this argument is that the goal of complete equality between men and women, which ignores the differences and the inevitable boundaries between them, is neither correct nor feasible. Such an unfounded aspiration will not bring about happiness (*saʿādat*), which is the ultimate goal of humanity, according to which men and women should each proceed along the path dictated by nature and law.[40]

---

36 "Feminism chīst?," 29 Tīr 1395/July 19, 2016, http://www.welayatnet.com/fa/forum/فمینیسم-چیست؟; Bīdgolī, "Barresī-i taṭbīqī-i feminism va-jāygāh-i zan dar gharb va-Islām"; ʿAlāsavand, *Naqd-i konvension-i rafʿ-i kulīye-i ashkāl-i tabʿīż ʿalayh-i zanān*, 89.

37 "Rābiṭa-i Islām va-feminism;" Ḥasanī, "Tafāvothā-i jinsiyatī az dīdār-i Islām va-feminism."

38 "Āyā Islām bā naẓrat-i maktab-i feminism muvāfiq ast?"

39 Muḥammad Ḥusayn Tehrānī, *Risāla-i badīʿa* (Mashhad: Intishārāt-i ʿalāma Ṭabāṭabāʾī, 1418h/1998), 88.

40 Bīdgolī, "Barresī-i taṭbīqī-i feminism va-jāygāh-i zan dar gharb va-Islām;" Zamānī, "Naqd va-barresī-i feminism va-payāmadhā-i ān (pt. 7)"; "Ashnāʾī bar jarayānhā-i aṣlī-i femīnīstī dar Iran."

One of the Shīʿī writers pointed out that leading Western thinkers, such as Locke and Kant, did not accept the idea of gender equality and even the feminists themselves are divided over this issue. Equality in well-being is neither realistic nor possible, he added, due to the conflicting interpretations over its meanings.[41] Khamenei described past efforts in the West to establish equality between men and women as "one of the biggest intellectual mistakes" of the Western world. "Why should a job that is masculine be given to a woman? What kind of honor is it for a woman to do a man's job?," he asked rhetorically in a 2014 speech. Three years later, he stated with confidence that "today Western thinkers and those who pursue issues such as gender equality regret the corruption that it has brought about." Moreover, Khamenei turned feminism itself into the cause and source of women's exclusion in society, and he contrasted it with Islam which "taught us to embrace who we are and live according to the Word set forth.... Women need not to be defined when God made them free.... Women are just as capable of excellence as men are – only differently."[42]

Indeed, feminist hostility to Islamic law has become a prominent theme in Shīʿī writings. Feminists allegedly espouse a secularist and this-worldly (*dunyā-gerāʾī*) point of view, which attacks all religions for supposedly discriminating against women and restricting them. Estrangement from religion and a total disregard for Islamic ordinances are, therefore, major attributes of this movement. A *Farsnews* writer charged Iranian feminists with hypocrisy, as he lumped them all together as one monolithic group and ignored the constraints under which they operate. In the West, he stated, feminists appear avowedly secular and openly disparage Islamic law, but inside Iran they speak in favor of dynamic jurisprudence; either way, they want to enact anti-Islamic legislation but without proper knowledge of *ijtihād* and jurisprudence.[43] In a speech made on July 4, 2007 Khamenei warned against attempts by "some women activists and some men ... to play with Islamic laws ... in order to harmonize them with international conventions relating to women."[44]

---

41 Shihāb Zamānī, "Naqd va-barresī-i feminism va-payāmadhā-i ān (pt. 5)," 17 Khordād 1391/June 6, 2012, http://basirat.ir/fa/print/239938.

42 "Bayānāt dar dīdār-i jamʿī az bānuvān-i bargezīdeh-i keshvar," 30 Farvardīn 1393/April 19, 2014, http://farsi.khamenei.ir/speech-content?id=26155; Catherine Shakdem, "Feminism – Women Are Not Commodities Says Ayatollah Khamenei," March 23, 2017, http://english.khamenei.ir/news/4731/Feminism-Women-are-not-commodities-says-Ayatollah-Khamenei.

43 Ḥikmat, "Barresī va-naqd-i naẓariyat-i tarbiyatī-i feminism"; "Feminism-i nafsānī-i gharb yā mushārakāt hame-i jānibeh-i Islām"; "Feminism taʿrīf kardeh va-athār-i mukharrib in jonbesh rā bayān konīd"; "Ashnāʾī bar jarayānhā-i aṣlī-i femīnīstī dar Iran."

44 "Bayānāt dar dīdār-i bānuvān-i nokhbe astāneh sālrūz-i ḥażrat-i Zahrāʾ (salām Allah ʿalayhā)," 13 Tīr 1386/July 4, 2007, http://farsi.khamenei.ir/speech-content?id=3390.

While rejecting feminist calls for legal equality, many writers insisted that a clear distinction should be made between a proper protection of women's rights, which Islam offers, and feminism. Khomeini amended his views in light of the active role of women during the Revolution and their important contribution to its success. In a series of statements, he maintained that Islamic law had provided women real equality with men in important areas such as the scope of liberties, the right to vote and be elected, and employment opportunities in all economic fields. Most importantly, he asserted, women have equal rights to men in building Islamic society.[45]

Contrary to the Western perspective, according to which religion is the enemy, the official Iranian position insists that Muslim women know Islamic values and laws to be their best friend and protector. In this sense, Islamic law is neither patriarchal nor matriarchal, one writer stated; rather, it is the protector of women's true rights and of the family. At a time when women were oppressed in Arab society, Islam was the standard-bearer for women's rights.[46] The Qom website complained that feminists do not understand the blessing (*niʿmat*) of Islamic laws for women on matters such as ownership of property, inheritance, the right to study, and many others.[47]

While similarly highlighting Islam's benevolence toward women, both Khomeini and Khamenei acknowledged the need to amend certain Islamic precepts relating to women in view of changing social circumstances. They – and following them all establishment writers – insisted that the only way to make such amendments was by applying the Shīʿī Islamic rules of *ijtihād* and *istinbāṭ* (inference).[48] This qualification aimed, first and foremost, at preserving the clerical monopoly over any legal reinterpretation or legislation on women and depriving feminists of any right to intervene or even influence the process. In addition, it restricted the scope of permissible change to the parameters of Islamic texts and precluded conscious or heavy borrowing from

45 *Jāygāh-i zan dar andīsheh-i Imām-i Khomeini* (S), 53–92; "Feminism va-bāztāb-i ān dar Jahān-i Islām," 3 Bahman 1390/January 23, 2012, http://zayeri.blogfa.com/post/97; "Feminism-i nafsānī-i gharb;" Seyyed Muḥammad Shafīʿī Māzanderānī, "Feminism va-jāygāh-i zan dar Islām," *Majala-i payām-i ḥawza* 25 (1379/2000), http://www.hawzah.net/fa/Magazine/View/4210/4231/27770.

46 Louise Lāmyā al-Fārūqī, "Sunnathā-i Islāmī va-jonbesh-i feminism muvājaha yā hamkārī," *Khabarnāmah-i dīn-i pazhūhān* 10 (1381/2002): 33, http://www.hawzah.net/fa/Magazine/View/5427/5441/51046/; "Nigāhī beh feminism-i Islāmī: radd-i feminism-i Islāmī, nafy-i ḥuqūq-i zan dar Islām nīst," 30 Bahman 1390/February 19, 2012, http://snn.ir/fa/news/172554.

47 "Feminism taʿrīf kardeh va-athār-i mukharrib in jonbesh rā bayān konīd;" al-Fārūqī, "Sunnathā-i Islāmī va-jonbesh-i feminism (1)."

48 "Feminism va-bāztāb-i ān dar Jahān-i Islām."

Western cultures. Various writers complained that while feminists claim to aspire to equality, in fact they always favor women over men; ʿAlī Akbar Rashād even asserted that the radical feminists want to replace male domination with female domination.[49]

Shīʿī writers concluded unanimously that there is a general incompatibility between feminism and Islam. In their critiques of the 1994 Convention on the Elimination of All of Discrimination against Women, both Farībā ʿAlāsavand and Maʿṣūma Ṣābirī of Kāshān University concluded that Muslims faced two alternatives: either follow the edicts of religion or accept the conference's resolutions that would lead to the abolition of the laws of Islam, separate the people from the government, and undermine the institutions of government in Muslim societies. Similarly, the website *Javān* stated that feminist thought is based on secular, liberal, and humanist thought and can be envisioned only in the realms of self-indulgence and "absolute freedom"; it therefore has nothing to do with the truth or with religion.[50]

3 The Feminist Threat to Morality

The other major threat that feminism was seen to pose was the promotion of moral laxity and sexual promiscuity among women, which allegedly emanated from its attack on the family – the bastion of proper Islamic society. Numerous spokespersons have highlighted the negative impact of feminism on Western societies and, in particular, on Western women. Khamenei chided the West for pretending to stand on the moral high ground by playing the feminist card while insulting women by treating them as a commodity or in his words as "goods and means of pleasure." This treatment was a sin which, he wrote in a tweet, was "among the Zionists' plots to destroy human community." He went on to state that "harassing women, exerting different sexual pressures, and inflicting psychological harm on women are done far more frequently in

49 Ḥasanī, "Tafāvothā-i jinsiyatī az dīdār-i Islām va-feminism;" "Feminism-i nafsānī-i gharb yā mushārakāt hame-i jānibeh-i Islām;" ʿAlī Akbar Rashād, "Āsīb shināsī-i feminism," *Kitāb-i naqd* 17 (1379/2001): 34–39.

50 ʿAlāsavand, *Naqd konvension-i rafʿ-i kulīye-i ashkāl-i tabʿīż ʿalayh-i zanān*, 31; "Islām dar bārah-i feminism cheh mīgūyad? Barāberī-i zan va-mard dar Islām," *Javān*, 4 Shahrīvar 1392/August 26, 2013, http://www.yjc.ir/fa/news/4523625/اسلام; Maʿsūma Ṣābirī, "Naqd konvension-i rafʿ-i kulīye-i ashkāl-i tabʿīż ʿalayh-i zanān," *Ẓuhūran* 13 (1391/2012): 154; "Ashnāʾī bar jarayānhā-i aṣlī-i femīnīstī dar Iran." See the same conclusion on the conference in "Feminism va-dīdār-i Islām dar mowred-i ān," 11 Azar 1390/December 2, 2012, http://siasi.porsemani.ir/node/2109.

the West than in our own country." He also added that "by dragging men and women into sexual corruption, provoking them into indulging their sexual desires in an unprincipled way, [the West has] betrayed humanity, in general, and women, in particular."[51]

The greatest moral and social damage wreaked by the feminists' aspiration for total freedom for women can be seen in their attacks on the family, the "most important and most sacred" social institution in Muslim society, and in their promotion of "hatred of the family" (*khānevādeh setīzī*). In the "second wave" of feminism (1960s to early 1980s) radical feminists censured the family as a social institution that has oppressed women throughout history and preserved their subservience and inferior status to men.[52] Various writers thus accused the feminists of placing the individual woman above her commitment to the family and society. Islam, they claim, protects the family and takes into consideration society as a whole by establishing a balance between the goals of the individual woman and of the family. According to Islamic thought, the welfare of each member of society depends on the well-being of society at large. Therefore, when women fight for their rights, they should be aware that their well-being depends on the well-being of society as a whole.[53]

The feminists' "most detestable" aspect, as highlighted in the Shīʿī discourse, is their criticism and denigration of motherhood – women's "most noble mission." The leading theoreticians of the feminist "second wave" are accused of not only denying the value of motherhood but actually fighting against it, regarding it as an instrument of male domination over women. The radical

---

51 Khamenei.ir, https://mobile.twitter.com/khamenei_ir/status/843423686963183620, March 19, 2017. See a slightly different wording on his official website, "Feminism – Women Are Not Commodities Says Ayatollah Khamenei," http://english.khamenei.ir/news/4731/Feminism-Women-are-not-commodities-says-Ayatollah-Khamenei, March 23, 2017; "Oppression of Women Can Be Prevented Via Laws and Edification of Men", April 16, 2017, http://english.khamenei.ir/news/4763/Oppression-of-women-can-be-prevented-via-laws-and-edification; "Bayānāt dar dīdār-i bānuvān-i nokhbe astāneh sālrūz-i ḥażrat-i Zahrāʾ (salām Allah ʿalayhā)." In the latter speech as well Khamenei blamed Zionism and colonialism for the distorted and immoral description of women in modern Western literature.

52 Suheylā Ṣādiqī Fasāʾī et al., *Feminism va-khānevādeh* (Tehrān: Shūrā-i farhangī-i ijtimāʿī-i zanān 1386/2007); Niyāzī, "Feminism va-mabānī-i tafakkur-i ṣahyūnīsm (pts. 1 + 2)"; Hamīrā Mushīrzādeh, *Az jonbesh tā naẓariyya-i ijtimāʿī: taʾrīkh-i dō qarn-i feminism* (Tehrān: nashr va-pazhūhesh-i shīrāzeh, 1382/2003), 285; Ḥikmat, "Barresī va-naqd-i naẓariyat-i tarbiyatī-i feminism;" Rashād, "Āsīb shināsī-i feminism"; Maryam Muhājirī, "Āsīb Shināsī-i payāmad-i akhlāqī-i feminism dar gharb va-bāztāb-i ān dar nihād-i khānevādeh," *Pazhūhesh nāmah-i zanān* 2, no. 1 (1390/2011): 100.

53 ʿAlāsavand, *Naqd konvension-i rafʿ-i kulīye-i ashkāl-i tabʿīż ʿalayh-i zanān*, 25; al-Fārūqī, "Sunnathā-i Islāmī va-jonbesh-i feminism muvājaha yā hamkārī," 30, 33.

feminists, various Shīʿī writers charge, regard motherhood as a mere biological fact denying or rejecting its emotional and social importance of rearing the future generations. They also view it as a burden that limits women's freedom. ʿAbdollah Muḥammadī of the Bāqir al-ʿUlūm Research Center asserted that this view stands in sharp contrast to the sayings and traditions of the Imāms, who praised the lofty status of motherhood and described paradise as lying under the feet of mothers. The Imāms even regarded pregnancy and breast-feeding as acts of worship (*ʿibādāt*), which deserved abundant remuneration.[54] Other writers, such as Dr. Suheylā Ṣādiqī Fasāʾī of Tehrān University and Dr. Fāṭima Hamdāniyān, have distinguished between the radical feminists and their liberal counterparts who do not attack motherhood per se but demand gender equality for the task of childrearing. Ṣādiqī Fasāʾī concluded that both radical feminists and the faction of hardline traditionalists among the clergy have betrayed women, thereby presenting the two extremes on an equal footing in contrast to the moderate and benevolent Shīʿī mainstream.[55]

The ramifications of these feminist attitudes and ideology are depicted by the Shīʿī writers as a spiritual and psychological crisis, manifested in the collapse of morality in Western societies and the severe weakening of the family as proved by the sharp increase in the number of unmarried couples, divorce cases, single-parent families, and children born out of wedlock. This alleged promiscuity has not liberated women but rather freed men from any commitment or responsibility for restraining their desire for women's bodies. The final outcome has not been liberated women but ruined marriages, with young women becoming the prize for wealthy men.[56]

Particularly problematic, according to the dominant narrative, is the proliferation of lesbianism – the outcome of the feminist war against what they saw as patriarchy and of their desire for sexual experimentation. Such relationships, one writer asserted, have had negative psychological, medical, and social ramifications, such as the spread of depression and AIDS, the increased

---

54 Ḥujjat al-Islām Ḥamīd Pārsāniyā, "Bar żedd-i feminism," *Kayhān*, 9 Mehr 1384/October 1, 2005; ʿAbdollah Muḥammadī, "Dīn va-feminism," http://pajoohe.net/fa/index.php?Page=definition&UID=37430; Seyyed Ḥusayn Ishāqī, "Feminism towṭiʾah-i gharb ʿalayh-i zanān (pt. 2)," *Mublighān* 74 (1384/2005–2006): 69–79.

55 Suheylā Ṣādiqī Fasāʾī, "Chālesh-i feminism bā mādarī," *Muṭālaʿāt-i Rāhbordī-i Zanān* 28 (1384/2005): 19–43; Fāṭima Hamdāniyān, "Mādarī dar naẓariyat-i femīnīstī," 3 Ordībehesht 1392/April 23, 2013, http://mehrkhane.com/fa/news/6419/مادری-در-نظریات-فمینیستی (last accessed December 23, 2017).

56 Ḥikmat, "Barresī va-naqd-i naẓariyat-i tarbiyatī-i feminism"; "Az feminism-i jahānī tā feminism-i Irānī/ nigāhī-i kul girāyāneh beh jonbesh va-naẓariyya-i feminism dar Iran va-jahān"; Muhājirī, "Āsīb shināsī-i payāmad-i akhlāqī-i feminism dar gharb va-bāztāb-i ān dar nihād-i khānevādeh," 110; "Feminism va-bāztāb-i ān dar Jahān-i Islām."

consumption of medicines and drugs, and the growing number of suicides.[57] The women affected by this promiscuous feminist approach are accused of suffering from a certain type of sexual sadism. Their pursuit of self-gratification and hedonism has undermined their human essence, diminishing if not eradicating the differences between their conduct and that of animals. The most effective way to confront these phenomena is to revert to the religious worldview and morality.[58]

Shīʿī writers also view the proliferation of abortions as the outcome of the feminist attack on the family and childrearing: "millions of fetuses have been mercilessly murdered" because of the feminist view that raising children means the subjugation of women."[59] An article published by the Mouood Cultural Institute concluded that the excess of abortions has made feminism more dangerous than racism because it affects half of humanity; the number of those who lost their lives due to feminist-inspired abortions is hundreds of times higher than those who lost their lives due to racism.[60]

In contrast to all this harm caused by feminist-inspired promiscuity, Islamic law and morality are presented as women's greatest ally. According to Khamenei, a growing number of prominent Western women have acknowledged that Islam protects women from male abuse and violence thanks to the ḥijāb. By following the tradition of ḥijāb, Muslim women can have an active and influential role in a whole array of social activities, demonstrating to the whole world Iranian women's independence and cultural identity.[61]

Ḥujjat al-Islam Ḥamīd Pārsāniyā, writing in *Kayhān*, charged radical feminism with being the most destructive and benighted movement to have emerged in recent decades. Lacking any reformist component, it is imbued with a dictatorial and totalitarian spirit which rejects all values and traditions,

---

57 Zinat Ṭaybī and Maryam ʿAhdī, "Feminism va-hamjinsgerāʾī," 4 Azar 1390/November 25, 2011, http://www.siasatrooz.ir/prtceeqe.2bqoe8laa2.html; Maryam Farahamand, "Feminism va-lezbiyanīsm," *Muṭālaʿāt-i rāhbordī-i zanān* 28 (1384/2006): 125–154; "Az feminism-i jahānī tā feminism-i Irānī/ nigāhī-i kul girāyāneh beh jonbesh va-naẓariyya-i feminism dar Iran va-jahān;" Bahrām Akhavān Kāẓimī, "Feminism-i ifrāṭī va-ufūl-i Amrīkā," 28 Mordād 1391/August 18, 2012, http://www.khabaronline.ir/detail/236979/weblog/akhavankazemi.

58 Muhājirī, "Āsīb Shināsī-i payāmad-i akhlāqī-i feminism dar gharb va-bāztāb-i ān dar nihād-i khānevādeh," 102–104; "Āyā Islām bā naẓrāt-i maktab-i feminism muvāfiq ast?"; Ẓū al-Qadr, *Qiṣṣa-i ghurbat-i gharbī*, 114.

59 Ḥikmat, "Barresī va-naqd-i naẓariyat-i tarbiyatī-i feminism."

60 "*Ṣahyūnīs*m va-andīsheh-i farāmāsūnarī-i ḥuqūq-i doghūrīn-i zanān"; Ṣādiqī Fasāʾī et al., *Feminism va-khānevādeh*, 161–175; "Feminism va-dīdār-i Islām dar mowred-i ān."

61 "Rahbar-i muʿaẓẓam-i inqilāb-i Islāmī dar dīdār-i hizārān-i nafar az shāʿirān va-setāyeshgerān-i ahl-i beyt ʿalayhim al-salām," 17 Esfand 1396/March 6, 2018, http://www.leader.ir/fa/content/20734.

even those respected in Western societies. It misleads women by attributing all their unhappiness and troubles to men and, most despicable of all, it opposes the sacred role of women in the family. Therefore, fighting radical feminism is, Pārsāniyā concluded, a sacred duty that should be carried out by women themselves.[62]

4 Countering Islamic Feminism

Branding radical feminism as the most destructive movement should not come as a surprise considering the overall anti-feminist discourse. More significant, however, was the widespread criticism against the social and intellectual current that stood at the other end of feminist spectrum, i.e., Islamic feminism. The term "Islamic feminism" gained currency in the 1990s as a label for a brand of feminist scholarship and activism seeking a new approach to questions of gender justice and equality in the Islamic context. It is, to use Margot Badran's definition, "a feminist discourse and practice articulated within an Islamic paradigm"[63] that attempted to carry out a synthesis between cultural tradition (including the importance of the role of women within the family), modern values (including the active participation of women in social, political, economic, and cultural life) and gender equality.[64] Many of the Iranian feminists who pursued this approach emerged from the heart of the establishment but gradually came to adopt critical positions in response to some of the doctrinaire measures adopted by the Islamic Republic. They reread the Qur'ān and ḥadīth using the classic Islamic methodologies of *ijtihād* and *tafsīr* (interpretation of the Qur'ān), which they see as guaranteeing social justice including gender equality. Their main aim was to unearth the woman-friendly aspects of Islam, which they claimed have been overlooked over the centuries

62 Parsaniyā, "Bar żedde Feminism."

63 Cited in Fereshteh Ahmadi, "Islamic Feminism in Iran: Feminism in a New Islamic Context," *Journal of Feminist Studies in Religion* 22, no. 2 (2006): 35.

64 Azadeh Kian, "Islamic Feminism in Iran: A New Form of Subjugation or the Emergence of Agency," trans. Ethan Rundell, *Critique Internationale* 46 (2010): 48. For more on Islamic feminism in Iran see: Valentine M. Moghadam, "Islamic Feminism and Its Discontents: Toward a Resolution of the Debate," *Signs* 27, no. 4 (2002): 1135–1171 and the sources cited by her; Afsaneh Najmabadi, "Feminism in an Islamic Republic: Years of Hardship, Years of Growth," in *Islam, Gender, and Social Change*, ed. Yvonne Yazbeck Haddad and John Esposito (Oxford: Oxford University Press, 1999), 59–84; Mir-Hosseini, "Beyond 'Islam' vs 'Feminism,'" 67–77.

by masculinist readings of the holy texts.[65] A major organ for the Islamic feminists was the journal *Zanān* (Women) founded by Shahlā Shirkat in 1992 until its forced closure in 2008. As Afsaneh Najmabadi has shown, *Zanān*'s interpretive work on women's rights was novel, with many of the contributing authors engaging in direct interpretations of canonical texts from the perspective of individual women's lived experiences, demands, and desires. *Zanān*, particularly in its earlier issues, challenged orthodox Islamic teachings on the differential rights and responsibilities of women and men by claiming women's right to equality.[66]

The goals of the Islamic feminists and their methodology posed a dual threat to the cleric-led system. Their reinterpretation of the scriptures and their deconstruction of the Shīʿī exegetes offered a viable alternative to the dominant readings and to age-long religious and social practices. The fact that the new reading was grounded in Islamic terminology enhanced its appeal among those Shīʿīs, male and female, who were apprehensive of an overtly secular and Westernized feminism. Similarly, by engaging in *ijtihād*, the feminists challenged the monopoly of the clergy over religious interpretation of the law and their leadership of the Shīʿī community.

The challenge posed by Islamic feminism is evident in the volume of polemics against it written by establishment writers and media. First, they sought to demean the new phenomenon by describing its protagonists as suffering from an identity crisis, torn between admiration for Western culture and their Islamic roots. As a way out of this predicament, these feminists were allegedly looking to reinterpret the sacred texts and produce a new kind of Islam. Alternatively, they described the Islamic feminists as secular women, many of whom lived in the West, who adhere to Western culture and disseminate materialistic ideas out of a distorted understanding of religion. Scholars Abūl-Ḥasan Ḥusaynzādeh and Ḥusayn ʿAbbāsiyān stated that the Islamic feminists who are either located in the West or inspired by the West lack a proper understanding of the social, economic, and cultural conditions in Iran.[67]

Seeking at first to advance women's rights by secular arguments, these feminists soon realized that Islamic religious beliefs and values are deeply rooted in Iranian society and that no political change could take place unless framed as Islamic. Bushrā Ishārat of the Family and Women News Analysis Center

65 Razavi, "Islamic Politics, Human Rights and Women's Claims for Equality in Iran," 1230–1231.

66 Najmabadi, "Feminism in an Islamic Republic," 59–84; Moghadam, "Islamic Feminism and Its Discontents," 1144, 1155.

67 Ḥusaynzādeh and ʿAbbāsiyān, "Naqd va-barresī-i mabānī-i fikrī va-shākheṣhā-i feminism-i Islāmī," 226.

contended that the Western feminist movement invented the concept of Islamic feminism, having understood that the only way to disseminate secular and liberal ideas among Muslim women was to use the term Islam. The movement was also plotting, she claimed, to use Muslim women to advance its own goals, and thus, out of pure political expediency, adopted the name Islamic feminists as a means to advance their secular agenda. These feminists are not, according to this discourse, looking to protect Islam from radical groups that denounce it as patriarchal; rather they view Islam as a mere guise for protecting feminism. A *Student News Network* article charged that this feminism is not Islamic but feminism wearing an Islamic veil (*niqāb*). The Q&A website *Porseman* went further, accusing the feminists of using Islamic terminology and topics as well as the name "Islamic feminism" in order to wage a political and cultural struggle against the Islamic Republic. This is not the first time that the term "Islamic" is attached to a foreign ideology as a means of disseminating it; as was the case in the past, the slogan of Islamic feminism will disappear, but Islam will remain forever, the *Student News Network* writer concluded.[68]

The root problem of Islamic feminism is, accordingly, its Western origins and source of inspiration. Various writers have censured the Islamic feminists for borrowing Western concepts such as humanism and human rights and reinterpreting the Qur'ān and other Islamic texts to fit them. They thus aim to reformulate the concept of Islamic justice according to Western humanism, and their insistence on legal equality between men and women is similarly based on Western principles. A major problem, Seyyed Ḥusayn Ishāqī railed, is that the pro-Western bias of the Islamic feminists prevents them from addressing the negative social consequences of the feminist struggle in Western societies.[69]

In addition to challenging venerable legal practices regarding women, the efforts of the Islamic feminists to reinterpret Islamic law threatened the clerical monopoly and power based on the practice of *ijtihād*. One writer explained that the Islamic feminists criticize present-day *ijtihād* as inadequate and incompatible with the needs of modern society. They even reinterpret various

---

68 Seyyed Ḥusayn Ishāqī, "Mahiyat va-ahdāf-i feminism Islāmī," *Payām-i zan* 229 (1390/2011): 46–49; Seyyed Ḥusayn Ishāqī, "Ta'ammolī bar paykareh va-payāmadhā-i feminism-i Islāmī," *Riwāq-i andīsheh* 44 (1384/ 2005): 50–75; Bushrā Ishārat, "Murūrī-i ijmālī bar Khāstgāh-i 'feminism Islāmī'," 9 Bahman 1391/January 28, 2013, http://mehrkhane.com/fa/news/5380; "Āyā Islām bā naẓrāt-i maktab-i feminism muvāfiq ast?"; "Nigāhī beh feminism-i Islāmī: radd-i feminism-i Islāmī, nafy-i ḥuqūq-i zan dar Islām nīst;" "Barresī-i jarayānhā-i femīnīstī Islāmī va-khāstgāh-i ān dar Iran (bakhsh-i pāyānī)," 18 Esfand 1395/March 8, 2017, htttp://basijnews.ir/fa/print/8836298.

69 "Ashnā'ī bar jarayānhā-i aṣlī-i femīnīstī dar Iran;" Ḥusayn Ishāqī, "Feminism towṭi'ah-i gharb 'alayh-i zanān (pt. 3)," *Mublighān* 75 (1384/2005): 131–143.

Qur'ānīc passages to suit their own preconceived notions and regard their own reasoning and logic as the sole criterion for interpretation, despite the clear and established ways of interpreting the Qur'ān and ḥadīth. They thus disregard all previous interpretations and ignore explicit warnings of the Shīʿī Imāms against unqualified interpreters of religion; in other words, they see themselves as more qualified than the Imāms and the clergy and therefore endanger the entire system of religious interpretation.[70]

According to a *Farsnews* article, the audacity of the Islamic feminists is compounded by their ignorance of Islam, its true laws, and the correct principles of *ijtihād*. They lack sufficient knowledge of the biographies of the Prophet and the Imāms and resort to selective and superficial readings of a few Qur'ānīc passages and the misapplication of various ḥadīths in order to advance their claims. They also misapply the foundations and principles of *ijtihād* due to their ignorance, which results in unfounded beliefs and views. Finally, the article accuses the feminists of disregarding the authoritative interpretations of the Shīʿī Imāms and past scholars.[71] While this charge of partisan feminist interpretation of religion can be seen to have some validity, the same, ironically, could be said about the politicized interpretation of religion advocated by the dominant mainstream, but typically of the self-other dichotomy, this analogy alludes the critics of feminism.

A major flaw of the Islamic feminist approach, according to the establishment, is its denial of the eternal nature of Islamic laws and its demand to examine the laws of Islam in their historical sociopolitical context. These feminists attribute a disproportionate influence to customary law (*ʿurf*) in the formulation of Islamic laws on women and, in particular, the concept of justice, which is central to the Shīʿī worldview. Consequently, the Islamic feminists contend that these laws and concepts were valid only for the early Islamic period and are inappropriate and untenable in the present day. They are thus seen to be calling for a new type of Islam that would conform to modern Western culture. The establishment spokespeople, however, maintain that

70 Nayreh Sotūdeh, "Feminism-i farāmodern va-feminism-i Islāmī," *Howrā'* 5 (1383/2004), http://www.ensani.ir/fa/content/109004/default.aspx; "Rābiṭa-i Islām va-feminism"; Ishāqī, "Ta'mmolī bar paykareh va-payāmadhā-i feminism-i Islāmī"; Ḥusaynzādeh and ʿAbbāsiyān, "Naqd va-barresī-i mabānī-i fikrī va-shākheṣhā-i feminism-i Islāmī," 212; Jaʿfar Murādī, "'Feminism-i Islāmī' tarkīb-i paradoxical," in Vakīlī (ed.), *Hamāyesh-i Islām va-feminism* Vol. 2, 495–496.

71 "Ashnā'ī bar jarayānhā-i aṣlī-i femīnīstī dar Iran."

the concept of Islamic justice is based on reason and is therefore correct and valid for eternity.[72]

Equally reprehensible in the eyes of the Shīʿī mainstream is the distinction Islamic feminists make between religion and religiosity (*din dārī*) as a private matter, which they favor, and the control or domination of religion (*din madārī*) in society, which they oppose. Since religious domination over the public sphere and politics is the raison d'être of the Islamic Republic, the animosity of the various establishment spokespeople to this approach is inevitable.[73] According to the Qom website, this distinction is the basis for the major contradiction between the Islam of these feminists, which is based on a selective reading of distorted Western texts, and the authentic religion practiced in Iran. Hence, a writer for the Mouood Cultural Institute concluded that "Islamic feminism is the worst type of feminism."[74]

The clerical establishment not only debated Islamic feminism but also took measures to curb its activities and influence. As mentioned above, in 2008 the authorities shut down the journal *Zanān*, the major voice of Islamic feminism, for offering "a somber picture of the Islamic republic" and for publishing "morally questionable information."[75] Shirkat launched a new monthly on May 28, 2014 named *Zanān-i Emrūz* (Today's Women), taking advantage of the changed public environment following the election of Rouhani as president in 2013. However, even before it hit the newsstands, *Zanān-i Emrūz* came under heavy criticism from conservative media outlets, which blasted its publication as a "failure" of President Rouhani's government. A *Mashreqnews* report, for example, charged that the worldview of Shirkat and other *Zanān* editors was shaped by Western views of women, which differed significantly from Islamic teachings.[76] In September 2014 Shirkat was summoned to a special press

72 Ishāqī, "Feminism towṭi'ah-i gharb ʿalayh-i zanān (pt. 3)"; Zībāyī-nezhād and Subḥānī, *Darāmadī bar niẓām-i* shakhṣiyat-*i zan dar Islām*, 181–182.

73 Ishāqī, "Mahiyat va-ahdāf-i feminism-i Islāmī"; "Feminism-i farāmodern va-feminism-i Islāmī"; "Cherā feminism beh vujūd āmad? Āyā in jarayān qābil naqd ast?," http://www.zaviye.net/?p=1944 (accessed October 15, 2017).

74 "Rābiṭa-i Islām va-feminism"; Ḥusaynzādeh and ʿAbbāsiyān, "Naqd va-barresī-i mabānī-i fikrī va-shākheṣhā-i feminism-i Islāmī," 223; "Feminism va-dīdār-i Islām dar mowred-i ān"; "*Ṣahyūnī*sm va-andīsheh-i farāmāsūnarī-i ḥuqūq-i doghūrīn-i zanān."

75 Golnaz Esfandiari, "Iranian Women's Monthly Under Pressure From Hard-Liners," September 1, 2014, https://www.rferl.org/a/iran-womens-monthly-under-pressure/26561137.html.

76 Esfandiari, "Iranian Women's Monthly Under Pressure From Hard-Liners"; "Bāzgesht feminism beh ʿarṣeh-i maṭbūʿāt: Bāzkhwānī-i mavāżiʿ-i iʿtiqādi va-siyāsī-i Shahlā Shirkat + ʿaks," 13 Khordād 1393/June 3, 2014, https://www.mashreghnews.ir/news/314711.

court, but the authorities seemed to have dropped the charges, presumably out of apprehension over the international outcry. By April 2015, however, *Zanān-i Emrūz* was forced to suspend its publication but continued its operation online.[77]

According to a 2016 Amnesty International report, the Iranian authorities summoned more than a dozen women's rights activists in Tehrān to long, intensive interrogations by the Revolutionary Guards and threatened them with imprisonment on national security-related charges. Many of these women had been involved in a campaign launched in October 2015 for the increased representation of women in the February 2016 parliamentary election.[78] It is thus clear that even reform-minded Rouhani could do little to combat the dominant view of Islamic feminism as a threat.

5 Conclusion

The mainstream modern clerical Shīʿī discourse opposes feminism as a manifestation of the Western cultural offensive against Islamic culture and way of life. It also sees it as contesting the male domination embedded in Islamic law and challenging the clerical monopoly over the interpretation of religion. If the West is the ultimate external "other," feminism has become its central offshoot in the domestic arena, thus explaining the effort to link it with other perceived ills of Western culture such as humanism and capitalism and additional foreign threats, first and foremost, Zionism. The perceived danger of feminism has somewhat turned it into a focal point for the broader Western threat to the "authentic" Muslim way of life and, therefore, into a rallying point for the Shīʿī and Sunnī struggle against the broader impact of Western culture.

Typical of the "self-other" dichotomy, the Shīʿī polemicists accuse the feminists of locating gender as the major foundation of society and politics while ignoring its central role in a religious worldview. They stress that Khomeini founded modern Shīʿī political thought, culminating in the *vilāyat-i faqīh* doctrine, according to moral and spiritual values, whereas the feminists regard gender as the cornerstone of the political and social order.[79] Regulating gender

77 "Iran Women's Magazine Forced to Close," *Al-Monitor*, May 18, 2015, http://www.al-monitor.com/pulse/originals/2015/05/iran-womens-magazine-zanān-emrooz-suspended.html#ixzz5YVv9lQw.

78 Amnesty International, "Iran: Women's Rights Activists Treated as 'Enemies of the State' in Renewed Crackdown," August 10, 2016, https://www.amnesty.org/en/latest/news/2016/08/iran-womens-rights-activists-treated-as-enemies-of-the-state-in-renewed-crackdown/.

79 "Feminism-i nafsānī-i gharb yā mushārakāt hame-i jānibeh-i Islām."

relations has, however, always been central to the Shīʿī and Sunnī worldview, based on the notion that the biological differences between men and women determine their different social and political roles. This emphasis on the biological differences resembles the radical feminist perception but leads to totally opposite conclusions. The Shīʿīs claim that, because of these differences, men and women are not the same but instead complement each other, and they contrast the feminist call for legal and material equality with the Islamic ideal of cooperation and partnership in values and spirituality. Aware of the possible weakness of this argument, they resort to several rhetorical devices. First, they emphasize disagreements in feminist theory and political movements about the centrality of the biological differences. Next, they elaborate on the perceived harm that feminism has caused to family and society and, particularly, the charge that feminism has played a key role in oppressing and victimizing women. This then leads them to their counterargument which presents Islam as women's true protector.

Within the broader feminist milieu, Islamic feminism has become a special target of "othering" and demonization. Its attempt to offer a different reading of Islam from within poses a serious challenge to the clerical monopoly of religious interpretation and, therefore, to clerical authority at large. A particularly striking theme of the mainstream discourse is the charge that Islamic feminists adopted their approach as, at best, a way of dealing with their own identity crisis and, at worst, a devious scheme to undermine Islam from within. The vehemence of the rhetoric against Islamic feminism reinforces the view that rigid ideologues oppose those who are closer to them in the ideological spectrum much more than those who are further away due to the competition over their shared constituency.

The Shīʿī discourse on feminism, as on other topics, is not monolithic. Alongside the conservative mainstream are modernists within the clerical establishment who seek to reconcile moderate feminist ideas with the official ideology but were cautious not to openly identify themselves as feminists. Conversely, the foremost spokesperson of the liberal trend, Muḥsin Kadīvar, openly advocated gender equality but could do so only in exile. The constraints on freedom in the wider Shīʿī ideological and political debate were thus found to apply to feminism as well.

Conclusion

The evolution of Shīʿīsm as a minority sect, which was often subjected to discrimination played a crucial role in the formation and articulation of their attitudes toward their external and even internal "others." For centuries, the most important "other" for the Shīʿa was the majority Sunnī Islam. While the articulation of the self–other dichotomy against the Sunnīs was most often defensive, it always emphasized Shīʿī moral and intellectual superiority as an essential way of justifying adherence to Shīʿīsm despite the hardships, which it entailed.

Since the early nineteenth century, Shīʿīs faced a growing number of new formidable "others" who challenged their worldview and identity. First and foremost among them was Western imperialism and Western-inspired modernity in its various manifestations or offshoots, such as modern concepts of liberty and feminism. Within Sunnī Islam, Wahhābīs and later jihādī-Salafists emerged as enemies who threatened Shīʿī lives more than their beliefs. At the same time, as a dominant religious establishment in Iran, Shīʿīs encountered weaker internal "others" such as the Baha'is and Jews. Their othering of the latter two groups involved polemics as well as discrimination and at times even persecution.

Politics have always played an important part in the Shīʿī self–other juxtaposition starting from the dispute over the Prophet's succession to the refutation of modern feminism, as most theological or doctrinal arguments revolved over questions of power as well. Still, with the emergence of Islamism or a highly politicized Islamic ideology and movements, particularly since the 1960s politics acquired a more central role in the evolution and articulation of the Shīʿī self–other dichotomy. This politicization, which was often accompanied by demonization, led to the representation of the various "others" as full-fledged religious and political enemies that need to be fought and vanquished. The 1979 Iranian Revolution and the formation of the Islamic Republic required, but also made possible, new and modern modes of othering in the Shīʿī discourse and action. Unlike the past, the othering process assumed the form of full-fledge organized policy promoted by the Supreme Leader and the politicized clerical elite with state resources at their disposal. This new othering comprised legal measures as well as mass indoctrination carried out by state schools, an array of state-funded religious institutions as well as print and electronic media.

The centrality of politics is evident in the Shīʿī responses to the Wahhābī and jihādī-Salafī threats. One example is the attempt to reach out to mainstream Sunnīs by linking the Wahhābīs and jihādī-Salafists with the West and

 | DOI:10.1163/9789004444683_010

emphasizing the combined threat these enemies pose to Islam as a whole. This approach required the highlighting of beliefs, ideals, and practices common to both Sunnīs and Shīʿīs and, at the same time, the annulment of long-established practices that aroused Sunnī ire. These latter practices, which formerly had played an important role in forging Shīʿī identity in opposition to Sunnī Islam, had to give way to the more urgent needs of confronting more dangerous enemies. Politicization also marked the othering of the Bahāʾīs, generating a shift from religious polemics to the presentation of the Bahāʾīs as foreign agents and traitors, as well as presenting feminism as a Zionist plot. Another example is the marginalization of Jewish ritual impurity coupled with the endorsement of modern anti-Semitic conspiracy theories. Concurrently, one charge raised against the conservative Shīrāzī faction is their reactionary view, which fails to understand that "Islam in its entirety is politics." The Shīʿī clergy, on the other hand, is glorified as the flag carriers of the national struggle against western imperialism.

The representation of the various "others" as enemies is not necessarily a reflection of actual historical reality and enmity to Shīʿīsm. Rather, it is often a product of Shīʿī insecurity born out of centuries of discrimination and the Manichean worldview of radical religious movements throughout the world. The radical ideological vantage point regards any challenge that some of these "others," like liberalism, feminism, and Baha'ism, have posed to Shīʿī doctrines as an outright threat that must be suppressed. In addition, such representations serve the interests of the Iranian regime for whom, similar to any other revolutionary or authoritarian systems, the threat of enemies serves to mobilize the population behind it and to suppress all opposition.

The most glaring example of this development is the representation of the Jews as active enemies of Shīʿīsm from the early days of Islam to the present, which also constitutes a clear case of psychological projection. As a minority in the Muslim world and in Shīʿī Iran, the Jews never developed a particularly anti-Shīʿī worldview, still less acted as a group against Shīʿīsm. Neither did the Jews threaten Shīʿī doctrines, communities, or power. The anti-Jewish discourse is rooted in the numerous anti-Jewish statements in the Qurʾān and ḥadīth literature, which are shared with the Sunnīs. Yet, it was deemed necessary for Shīʿīs in order to refute Sunnī charges regarding the Jewish role in the emergence of Shīʿīsm and the similarity and proximity between Judaism and Shīʿīsm. This discourse became increasingly politicized in the modern period due to the exposure to and borrowing from modern Western anti-Semitism, the association of the Jews with the Western threat to Islam, and the advent of Zionism, which seemed to challenge the Islamic viewpoint on the right historical order. The politicization was evident in the depreciation of Jewish ritual impurity as the major distinction between Shīʿīs and Jews and its replacement by the adoption of modern European anti-Semitic charges against Judaism.

Various aspects of Western culture, among them feminism and liberalism, have posed significant challenges to the Shīʿī worldview, to Islam in general, and to any other conservative religions. Feminism threatened central and deeply entrenched Islamic ordinances and doctrines as well as the authority of the clergy. The liberal notion of freedom also opened the gates to subversive ideas that threatened these religious foundations.

Contrary to these "others," the Wahhābīs and jihādī-Salafīsts have actually targeted the Shīʿīs as their enemies, branding Shīʿī doctrines and practices as un-Islamic. Unlike Western-inspired ideas, their doctrines had little appeal among ordinary Shīʿīs. Rather, their main threat is the violence they have used against Shīʿī communities and the potential appeal of their claims among ordinary Sunnīs, which could result in the further marginalization of the Shīʿīs and their exclusion from Islam as apostates.

While the Shīʿī discourse depicted its various "others" as generic enemies, a clear hierarchy emerged in line with anthropologists Gerd Baumann and André Gingrich's structure of "encompassment."[1] The hierarchy was based on the perceived threat posed by each of these enemies and the scale of differentiation from true Shīʿī Islam. Both Khomeini and Khamenei described "global arrogance," namely, the United States, and the "network of global Zionism" as the most dangerous external enemies, with Khamenei denouncing the United States as the enemy of all of humanity. As for Zionism, the Shīʿī discourse often conflated it with Judaism and the Jews, despite denials by various officials including Khamenei.[2] This depiction was not only a response to Western political and economic imperialism but also reflected apprehensions of the Western "cultural assault" and the potential appeal of Western ideas and culture to modernized Shīʿīs and, therefore, to Islam as a whole. Judaism as a religion never posed any direct challenge to Shīʿī doctrines, and there was no danger of its appeal to Shīʿīs, and Shīʿī clerics in past centuries devoted little attention to religious refutations against it. Rather, it was the perceived success of the Jews in the post-World War II West and the establishment of the State of

1 Gerd Baumann and Andre Gingrich, eds., *Grammars of Identity/Alterity: A Structural Approach* (Oxford/New York: Berghahn, 2004), x, xi.

2 "Dushman shināsī az dīdār-i maqām-i muʿaẓẓam-i rahbarī (1)," 25 Mehr 1388/October 17, 2009, https://rasekhoon.net/article/show/145713/(1); "Dushman shināsī dar kalām Imām va-rahbarī (powerkey)," *Kayhān*, 30 Shahrīvar 1393/September 21, 2014; "The Enemy of Iran and Humanity is the Regime that Separates 1000s of Children from their Mothers," June 20, 2018, http://english.khamenei.ir/news/5757/The-enemy-of-Iran-and-humanity-is-the-regime-that-separates-1000s.

Israel that challenged Muslim doctrine, which regards the Jews as destined to dispersal and humiliation as well as the association of the Jews with modernity. As in the past, the portrayal of the Jews as enemies served to disprove Salafi claims of the Jewish–Shīʿī connection and to mitigate Sunnī–Shīʿī animosities by advocating a unified front against the common foe.

While jihādī-Salafī actions pose a clear threat to the lives of Shīʿī believers, from a purely ideological point of view, they are less harmful than the negative impact of the West on their souls. The depiction of the US as the "Great Satan" attests not only to its power, but also to its perceived threat to the believer's soul. A more practical approach regards the jihādī-Salafī threat as more manageable in the long run, since it does not endanger Shīʿī communities, particularly the Islamic Republic, from within and can be defeated on the battlefield, as was the case in Syria and Iraq between 2016 and 2019. The Western cultural impact, on the other hand, may be more difficult to contain and could challenge the Islamic Republic's political foundations.

The relative ideological and intellectual challenge of each of these enemies is evident in the methods used by the Shīʿī polemicists to contest them. Polemics against the West address modern Western intellectual and scholarly writings ranging from Isaiah Berlin and John Rawls to Samuel Huntington and Francis Fukuyama. Likewise, anti-feminist polemics demonstrate familiarity and mastery of modern feminist thought and the sociological data needed to refute it. Similarly, the Shīʿī discourse has addressed the early and more recent writings and statements by Wahhābī and jihādī-Salafī scholars and thinkers.

Writings against Judaism, on the other hand, have relied almost exclusively on the Qurʾān and early Islamic polemical literature as well as on traditional Jewish sources, albeit often distorted translations. One reason was the large number of anti-Jewish statements in the well-known, highly respected, and easily accessible traditional sources. Equally important, Judaism, contrary to modern Western concepts, had no appeal for younger and modern educated Iranians and therefore did not require similar intellectual efforts to confront or refute it. Interestingly, Shīʿī writers had no problem borrowing themes from modern anti-Semitism, even though it originated in the much-maligned West, but completely ignored modern Jewish writings or modern scholarship on Judaism. This selective borrowing from Western sources was motivated by Shīʿī ferocity against the Jews, reflecting in part a reluctant appreciation of the West as a knowledgeable or highly reliable source on the Jews, and the fact that in the struggle against one enemy all means are legitimate even assistance from another one.

The centrality of the West, and to a similar extent of Judaism-Zionism as the most dangerous "other" has been evident in the powerful rhetorical ploy of the

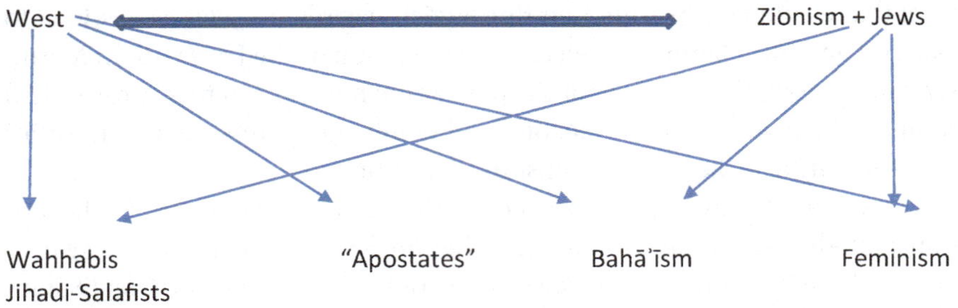

FIGURE 1 The Enemies: Hierarchy and Interaction

othering discourse which linked all enemies of Shīʿīsm with the West or even branded them as its creatures in order to augment their evil nature, as shown in Figure 1.

Thus the Shīʿī discourse, by demonstrating the proclivity toward conspiracy theories in modern Iranian and Arab political culture, attributed key roles in the earlier creation of Wahhābism and Bahāʾīsm to the British and in the more recent creation of jihādī-Salafīsm to the Americans. Wahhābism and the clerical establishments in most Sunnī countries were labeled "American Sunnīsm," while the more conservative Shīrāzī faction within Shīʿīsm was named "English Shīʿīsm." The rejection of the West as the greatest evil was also manifested in the number of references to it in Shīʿī publications, which eclipsed all other "enemies."[3]

Judaism and the Jews too were used as a prevalent denominator of all enemy "others." Accordingly, manufactured Jewish ancestry was the common trait of the Umayyads, of several of the "fourteen evil ones" who conspired against Imām ʿAlī as well as of Muḥammad b. ʿAbd al-Wahhāb and the Saʿūd clan in the modern period. Sunnī Islam had, apparently, been heavily "infected" and distorted by Jewish influence in the distant past, while the Bāb was heavily influenced by wealthy Jews in the nineteenth century. Likewise, feminism was a Zionist invention designed to destroy civilization, and the Bahāʾīs collaborated with Zionism. Many of the covers of the books on the various "others" are decorated with the Star of David, thereby associating them with Judaism. Such transparent symbolism clearly affirms the notion of the Jews as the personification of evil. Sunnīs too have practised this rhetorical ploy throughout history,

3 The *Hawza.net* portal of the Qom learning complex, which contains Q&A sections on numerous religious issues, articles on scholarly journals, book reviews, and abstracts of PhD and MA theses produced as of April 10, 2019, has 24,076 references to the word "West" compared with 6070 references to the word "Jews" and 3588 references to "Wahhābīsm" and "Wahhābīs," https://hawzah.net/fa/Search?SearchText=%u0648%u0647%u0627%u0628%u06CC%u062A; https://hawzah.net/fa/Search?SearchText=%u06CC%u0647%u0648%u062F.

reaching a peak in the Arab upheaval, when charges of Jewish ancestry were hurled against many hated Arab leaders. The depiction of various enemies as creations of the West and/or the Jews had two seemingly contradictory results. While it magnifies the threat they pose to Shīʿīsm, it also denigrates them by denying their authenticity and presenting them as mere instruments of manipulation by more sinister forces. Such depictions also elevate Shīʿī opposition to their enemies as standing up to the West in its various guises.

The transformation of the "others" into enemies entailed a radicalization in the Shīʿī response as well. Such was the case with the declaration of apostasy against jihādī-Salafīsm and the call for jihād against them as well as talks about the wholesale killing of the Jews following the advent of the Mahdī. While Bahāʾīs had always suffered discrimination and often persecution including executions, the clergy refrained from declaring all of them as apostates who deserved death. Rhetoric aside, the clergy appear reluctant to execute tens of thousands of Bahāʾīs either out of expediency or out of psychological inhibitions. Whatever the reason may be, the Bahāʾīs serve the Iranian government as perpetual "others" and enemies and thus justifying the formation of substantial state-funded apparatus to fight them.

Another manifestation of this phenomenon is the use of the "disease" metaphors to describe various "others," which supposedly threaten the healthy body of Muslim society. Thus, "moral deviations" and Bahāʾī beliefs were equated with "infectious diseases," and the "questioning the sanctity of religious elements" with "a cancerous tumor that will gradually spread to the other healthy parts of the body."[4] Similarly, Wahhābism, jihādī-Salafīsm and Zionism were portrayed as "cancerous tumors." The proper response to such threats was evident. Thus, one writer proposed to place the carriers of the Bahāʾī disease "under quarantine and strict supervision in order to prevent the spread of this infection throughout the body of Muslim society." Confronting the supposed "cancerous tumors" entailed the explicit solution of removal and eradication by action and force. The use of the disease metaphor during the twentieth century by radical movements and regimes against perceived enemies and its gruesome outcome attests to its highly problematic significance in the Iranian context.

There are several features common to all the self–other dichotomies discussed above in addition to the obvious representation of Shīʿīsm as the correct or pure Islam. They all reflect a duality between conflicting emotions of

4 Muḥammad Sorūsh, "Āyā irtidād kīfar 'ḥadd' dārad? Ta'ammolī bar mahiyat-i kīfar irtidād," *Ḥukūmat-i Islāmī*, 19 (1380/2001), http://ensani.ir/fa/article/83786/–آیا-ارتداد-کیفر-حدّ-دارد-تأملی-بر-ماهیت-کیفر-ارتداد-.

short-term insecurity and absolute self-confidence in the future success and superiority of Shīʿīsm. The former is based on a strong sense of victimization borne out of past persecutions and discrimination coupled with a sense of vulnerability vis-à-vis modern ideological and cultural challenges. These feelings are also evident in the claim that Shīʿīsm and its political manifestation in the Islamic Republic are the primary targets of the various enemies. The West targets Iran as its foremost enemy, because it stands at the forefront of the struggle of all oppressed nations for justice and against imperialist domination and exploitation. The Jews have nothing against Sunnī Islam but have focused their animosity on Shīʿīsm from the time of the Prophet to the present because Shīʿīsm represents true faith, justice, and compassion. Wahhābī Islam placed Shīʿīsm on top of its agenda, while Bahāʾīsm aimed to undermine and destroy Shīʿīsm from within.

The Shīʿī discourse describes all of these enemies as targeting the Shīʿī clergy as their main rival, while, at the same time, it glorifies the clergy as the defenders of true Islam and the authentic leaders and champions of Iranian nationalism. The implied message of this description is the need to rally behind the clergy in their capacity as the leaders of the oppressed as the only way of standing up to enemy machinations and the association of any opposition to the clergy with betrayal of Iran itself. Thus, the broad phenomenon of othering serves as a political tool to legitimize and bolster clerical rule.

While most of the enemies discussed above are modern, the message of the entire othering discourse is the ongoing struggle of the Shīʿa throughout history. This answers the Shīʿī "need to perceive appropriate levels of self-continuity across time," as discussed by the identity process theory (IPT). Another manifestation of this continuity is the adaptation of early beliefs to suit the present. Thus, the West is seen to represent the Rūm (Byzantines), against whom the Mahdī will fight in the future, ISIS is the modern manifestation of the hated Sufyānī, and Zionism is the modern expression of Jewish animosity against Islam. Typical of all Islamic movements, both Sunnī and Shīʿī, the early period of Islamic history (from the Prophet to Ḥusayn's martyrdom in Karbalāʾ) serves as the predominant and almost exclusive source of reference and repertoire of symbols, images and models of emulation from which to draw lessons.

At the same time, the Shīʿī discourse maintains and even boasts that the 1979 Revolution was the turning point in this global ideological struggle between the forces of good and evil. It inflicted the first defeat upon the enemies of Islam and put an end to Iran's exploitation by and subjugation to the enemies. The Revolution turned the tide against the forces of evil and launched the historical process that will bring Islam to its proper state and glory as the world's leading civilization. Borrowing again from IPT, these types of assertions

299

validate to members of the threatened group, in this case the Shīʿīs, the sense of "competence and control" over their lives and future that are necessary for the formation of group identity.[5] In other words, thanks to the Revolution, Shīʿīs and Iranians ceased to be objects of history and of hostile forces and emerged as assertive masters of their own history and destiny.

While the Revolution still faces threats and challenges from hostile external and internal "others," it boosted confidence in the future and inevitable victory of Shīʿī Islam. Accordingly, the first step is the demise of Western civilization that will pave the way to a universal *vilāyat-i faqīh*. The ultimate victory of Shīʿīsm and the true "end of history" will be the universal rule of the Mahdī. Interestingly, the coming of the Mahdī is portrayed differently depending on the context in which it is discussed and the audience to which it is appealing. Thus, the discussion of future rise of the Mahdī in the context of the struggle against ISIS or the fate of the Jews followed the traditional approach of a violent and bloody struggle against the historical enemies of Shīʿīsm. However, when presented in the context of the universal rule of the Mahdī following the fall of the West – in contrast to Francis Fukuyama's liberal end of history – the description is a very different and is portrayed as peaceful, ecumenical, and harmonious one. Presumably, the different targeted readership, i.e., those exposed to modern Western writings, was a major reason for this difference as this audience is looking for a more humane Islam.

An important element of the criticism or even condemnation of the various "others" was the articulation of a mirror image of Shīʿīsm. The Shīʿī discourse depicts the teachings and ideologies of the various enemies as crude, shallow, often violent, and typified by internal contradictions and despicable morality as well as by the failure to live up to their self-proclaimed ideas or pretensions. By contrast, it emphasizes the combination of Shīʿī spirituality and high morality together with its strong rationalist foundation, superior intellectual sophistication, moderation, and progressive nature. This formulation is reminiscent of Houchang Chehabi's observation regarding Islamic modernism, which contrasts the often purely theoretical Islamic ideals with the most negative aspects of Western reality.[6] The emphasis on rationalism also elevates Shīʿīsm above mainstream Sunnī Islam – an important "other" in the past. While the Shīʿī discourse seeks to reach out to the Sunnīs, it still makes sure to highlight the Shīʿī

---

5   Rusi Jaspal and Marco Cinnirella, "Coping with Potentially Incompatible Identities: Accounts of Religious, Ethnic and Sexual Identities from British Pakistani Men Who Identify as Muslim and Gay," *British Journal of Social Psychology* 49, no. 4 (2010): 849–870.

6   Houchang E. Chehabi, *Iranian Politics and Religious Modernism: The Liberation Movement of Iran under the Shah and Khomeini* (New York: I.B. Tauris, 1990), 74–75.

advantage if not outright superiority. The mirror-imaging of Shīʿīsm vis-à-vis the various "enemies" is also manifested in the opposite evaluation of similar practices that exists in both sides. Various writers ridicule Baha'i veneration of the Bab's burial place in Haifa, while ignoring similar practices regarding Shīʿī holy sites in Karbalāʾ, Najaf or Mashhad. Similarly, they attack Islamic feminists for selective readings and politicized interpretation of the scriptures, while such phenomena exist in all religions including Islam and Shīʿīsm itself. In the Shīʿī case, politicization of religious interpretation is praised as the correct religious approach.

Shīʿī Islam has never been monolithic thanks to both the principle of *ijtihād*, which encourages independent thinking and the informal nature of clerical leadership, which lacked the coercive means to impose unanimity. The establishment of the Islamic Republic created a formal leadership, which formulated a dominant ideological line, and even resorted to repression in order to ensure uniformity. Still, divisions and disagreements over religious interpretation and ideology never disappeared and possibly even grew, as is also evident in the othering discourse. While Khomeini set the contours of the legitimate religious and political debate and Khamenei formulates the official or mainstream line, different views have always been voiced. This was evident in the Shīʿī debate on liberty and feminism and even Bahāʾīsm, as reformists and liberals expressed more tolerant and inclusive views than the mainstream. The same was true regarding efforts to reach out to mainstream Sunnīs, with hardliners or conservatives refusing to endorse the more ecumenical approach of the dominant faction. Even in the debate on Judaism there is some divergence along generational lines over the fate of the Jews at the end of time. This pluralism has narrowed since the turn of the century. Khamenei has never enjoyed the same ideological stature as Khomeini, whose decisions often ended ideological debates although his policy to crush the liberals and marginalize the reformists often produced one-sided intellectual and ideological debates. Most liberal writers went into exile, but their ideas continued to challenge the conservative mainstream, as can be seen in the large number of publications against their arguments.

Reception within society at large is central to any discussion on the articulation and dissemination of a state-sponsored religious and political discourse. Definitive answers are hard to come by, considering both the size and diversity of Shīʿī-Iranian society and the authoritarian nature of the state, which discourages the dissemination and expression of dissident views. However, some observations or sophisticated guesses are possible due to various indicators. For example, the repetition via a variety of means and media of bans of certain practices, such as anti-Sunnī rituals, or of warnings from external threats, such as Western cultural onslaught, point to their popularity within a broad cross-section of society in opposition to the official line. Talkbacks on the internet, with all their inherent problems regarding authenticity and representativeness, may also provide some indicators, particularly if they oppose the official line. For example, numerous expressions against the repeal of anti-Sunnī practices reflect the limitations of an official religious discourse propagated from above in changing entrenched popular traditions. In a similar vein, anti-Jewish expressions in talkbacks attest to the spread of such feelings at large.

Another indication is the scope, volume, and level of sophistication that is exerted in the intellectual effort to debate or combat the various "others" or enemies. When promoters of the Shīʿī discourse sense that rival ideas are more appealing than their own arguments, they are much more likely to increase their efforts to improve their own arguments and present them as more sophisticated. Anti-Jewish or anti-Wahhābī themes do not require the same effort to dispute them as feminism, which has a more obvious appeal among women, or liberalism, which is likely to attract the youth.

An additional factor here is the degree to which various attitudes are already rooted in Shīʿī tradition. Thus, anti-Sunnī feelings play a more important role in the formation of Shīʿī identity than the definition and scope of liberty. Therefore, attempts to change these feelings encounter greater difficulties. At the same time, it is highly likely that the rhetoric and polemics against Wahhābism and jihādī-Salafī groups enjoy widespread reception. The violence used by these groups against Shīʿīs plays as central a role in the reception of the rhetoric against them. Similarly, though for different reasons, anti-Bahāʾī feelings remain rife among large segments of Iranian society; however, the need to resort to political arguments accusing them of being traitors to the nation is a probable indicator of the diminishing effect of the traditional polemics.

Shīʿī attitudes toward "others" have constantly evolved as historical circumstances and contexts change. The picture and analysis presented in this book have sought to reflect these changes while also showing the continuity with the past and to shed light on Shīʿī self-perceptions. These changing feelings complement each other as part of the broader whole of Shīʿī self-perceptions vis-à-vis the surrounding world, including also possible contradictions such as anxieties alongside self-confidence and feelings of isolation and victimhood alongside a sense of increasing empowerment. Shīʿīsm is a dynamic religion, and the future is therefore likely to produce new feelings and perspectives on "others" that will require ongoing investigations and explorations.

List of Sources

Sources in Persian and Arabic

Abāẓarī, ʿAbd al-Raḥīm. "Iẓhārāt-i Hāshimī dar bārah-i khalīfa-i avval; hamsū yā mukhālif bā rahbarī?," http://www.asriran.com/fa/news/317578.

ʿAbd al-Ḥamīd, Ṣāʾib. "Bayna al-Wahhābiyya wal-khawārij," in *al-Wahhābiyya fī ṣūratihā al-ḥaqīqīyya*, http://www.mezan.net/radalshobohat/21Whabi.htm.

ʿAbdollahī, Muḥammad. "Bīst dalīl barāye furūpāshī-i Amrīkā," 23 Mehr 1390/ October 15, 2011, https://www.farsnews.com/news/13900723000034/20.

Afrāsiyābī, Bahrām. *Bahāʾiyat beh rivāyat-i taʾrīkh* (Tehrān: purustash, 1366/1987–1988).

Afrāsiyābī, Bahrām. *Taʾrīkh-i jāmiʿ-i Bahāʾiyat* (Tehrān: Mehrfam, 1382/2003).

Afsā, Muḥammad Jaʿfar. "Naẓariyat-i barkhōrd-i tamaddunhā," *Farhang-i kowthar* 41 (Mordād 1379/August 2000): 17–21.

Afsharī, Murtaẓā. "Dō mafhūm-i āzādī dar andīsheh-i Izāyā Berlin," *Iʿtimād*, 4 Esfand, 1388/23 February 2010.

Āhangar, Muḥammad Javād. "Vahhābiyat: taʾrīkhcheh va-naqd-i andīshehā (pt. 1)," *Golbarg* 98 (1387/2008), 49–58.

Akhavān, Muḥammad. "Mahdaviyat va-jang-i tamaddunhā," *Intiẓār mowʿūd* 16 (1385/2006): 4–5.

Akhavān Kāẓimī, Bahrām. "Feminism-i ifrāṭī va-ufūl-i Amrīkā," 28 Mordād 1391/ August 18, 2012, http://www.khabaronline.ir/detail/236979/weblog/akhavankazemi.

Akhund Tangalī, ʿAbd al-Raḥman. *Taḥẕīr al-ikhwān ʿan makāyid ḥizb al-shaytān yā taʾrīkhcheh-i Vahhābiyat* (Gorgan: Naʿīm, 1393/2014).

Āl-i Aḥmad, Jalāl. *Gharbzedegī* (Tehrān, multiple dates).

ʿAlāsavand, Farībā. *Naqd konvension-i rafʿ-i kulīye-i ashkāl-i tabʿīż ʿalayh-i zanān* (Qom: Intishārāt-i markaz-i mudīriyat-i ḥawza-i ʿilmiyya Qom, 1382/2003).

ʿAlavī, Ḥusayn. "Gharb modern az nowzāyī tā nāzāʾiyī," *Risālat*, 17 Esfand 1391/March 7, 2013.

ʿĀlimiyān, ʿAlī Akbar. "Pahlavīhā dar khidmat-i Bahāʾiyat," *Pūyā* 7 (Esfand 1386/ March 2008), 91–96.

ʿAlī Ḥaydar, Khalīl. "al-Shīʿa wa-ghulāt al-salaf wa-mudākhalat abā al-khīl," 15 July 2008, http://www.middleeasttransparent.com/article.php3?id_article=4153.

ʿAmidī, Thāmir Hāshim. *al-Mahdī al-muntaẓar fī al-fikr al-Islāmī* (Qom: Markaz al-Risāla 1417h/1996).

Al-Amīn, Muhammd Sayyid. "Ḥawla al-dīn wa-ḥaqq al-ikhtilāf," *al-Munṭalaq* 15 (Spring–Summer 1996).

Al-Amīn, Muhsin. *Kashf al-Irtiyāb fī atbāʿ Muḥammad b. ʿAbd al-Wahhāb* (Beirut: Dār al-kitāb al-Islāmī, 2006).

Amīnī Golestānī, Muḥammad. "Intiqām-i Yahūdiyān az Imām ʿAlī (A)," http://ahdema.ir/انتقام-یهودیان-از-امام-علی-ع.

Amīnī-fard, Ḥamīda. "Feminism, ẓulm-i insān-i sekūlār beh zan-i gharbī ast," July 5, 2007, http://vista.ir/article/265702.

Anṣārī, Ibrāhīm. "Bahāʾīhā va-isrāʾīl," *Faṣlnāmah-i muṭālaʿāt-i taʾrīkhī* 17 (Summer 1386/2007), 201–207.

Anūshīrvānī, ʿAlī Reżā. "Uṣūl va-naẓarīyyahā-i feminism dar gharb," in *Hamāyesh-i Islam va-feminism*, editor Hādī Vakīlī (Tehrān: daftar-i nashr-i maʿārif, 1381/2002), Vol. 1, 83–92.

Aqājānī Qonād, Muḥammad Reżā. "Ḥuqūq-i aqaliyathā-i dīnī dar ʿaṣr-i ẓuhūr," *Majmūʿa-i athār-i Sevomīn-i hamāyesh-i beyne almilalī doktrīn-i mahdaviyat bā rūyikard siyāsī va-ḥuqūqī* (Qom: Muʾasasa-i āyandeh roshān, 1387/2008).

Aqā-Muḥammadīyan, Ḥamīd Reżā & Reżā Pūr Ḥusayn. "Tafāvothā-i raftārī-i zan va-mard (pāye-i fīzyūlūzhīk va-gheyr-i fīzyūlūzhīk)," *Hamāyesh-i Islam va-feminism*, editor Hādī Vakīlī (Tehrān: daftar-i nashr-i maʿārif, 1381/2002), Vol. II: 51–83.

Aqāyī, ʿAlī Reżā. "Naqsh-i rezhīm-i Pahlavī dar taḥkīm-i firqa-i Bahāʾiyat," 21 Farvardīn 1385/April 10, 2006, https://www.farsnews.com/news/8501200597.

ʿAsgarī, Shādāb. *Bahāʾīyān-i niẓāmī dar ḥukūmat-i Pahlavī dovom* (Tehrān: Markaz-i asnād-i inqilāb-i Islāmī, 1396/2017).

Ashrāfī, Murtażā. "Bahāʾiyat va-bāvarsāzīhā-i kāẕib," *Pegāh-i ḥawza*, 303 (Khordād 1390/2011), 26–27.

Ashrāfī, Murtażā. "Tahājum-i farhangī (nātū-i farhangī)," 24 Abān 1393/November 15, 2014 http://pajoohe.ir/تهاجم-فرهنگی-ناتوی-فرهنگی__a-44577.aspx.

Āyatī, Nuṣratollah. *Ahl-i kitāb dar dawlat-i mahdī (aj)* (Tehrān: Bonyād-i farhangī-i ḥażrat-i Mahdī mowʿūd, n.d.).

Ayzadī, Fuʾād. "Amrīkā va-abr qudratīʾāsh," May 18, 2013, http://farsi.khamenei.ir/others-note?id=21786.

ʿAzīzān, Mahdī. "Pluralism farhangī az naẓar-i ustād-i Muṭṭaharī," *Maʿārif* 25 (1384/2005), 18–21, http://hawzah.net/Hawzah/Magazines/MagArt.aspx?LanguageID=1&id=54746&SearchText=آزادی.

Bābāmīr, J'. "Amr beh maʿrūf va-nahyi az munkar dar taʿāmul bā āzādī-i fardī va-ijtimāʿī," 21 Esfand 1396/March 12, 2018, https://bit.ly/2FXEkna.

Bahāʾīzādeh, Nādim & Amīr Mostowfiyān. *Bāriqa-i ḥaqīqat dar shenākht-i Bahāʾīyat* (Tehrān: Rāh-i Nīkān, 1387/2008), 33–38.

Bahmand, Shuʿayb, Masʿūd Jaʿfarī-nezhād Alī Reżā Golshānī. "Żarūrathā-i tadvīn-i algū-i Islāmī Irānī pīshraft az manẓar-i rahbar-i muʿaẓẓam-i inqilāb-i Islāmī," *Pazhūheshhā-i inqilāb-i Islāmī* 19 (Winter 1395/2017): 107–129.

Bakhshī, ʿAbdollah ʿAlī. *Vahhābiyat az nigāhī digār* (Tehrān: Rāh-i Nīkān, 1390).

Bakhshī, Saʿīd and Seyyed Masʿūd Pūr Seyyed Aqāyī. "Muvājahat-i Imām-i zamān (ʿalayhi al-salām) bar qawm-i Yahūd dar ʿaṣr-i ẓuhūr," *Mashriq Mowʿūd* 42 (Summer 1396/2017), 39–86.

Bakhtiyārī, Javād. "Dushman shināsī dar Qurʾān bā taʾkīd bar dushmanī-i Yahūd," Muʾasasa-i amūzeshī-i pazhūheshī-i imām Khomeini, http://www.hawzah.net/fa/Seminar/View/78647/دشمن-شناسی-در-قرآن-با-تاکید-بر-دشمنی-یهود/?SearchText=دشمن شناسی&LPhrase=.

Bāqir al-ʿUlūm Institute. *Farhang-i jamīʿ sokhnān-i Imām Ḥusayn ʿalayhi al-salām* (Qom, 1392/2013).

Bāqirī, Rūḥollah. "Ḥuqūq-i zinashūyī va-mabānī-i ān az manẓar-i Qurʾān," October 16, 2012, http://old.ido.ir/a.aspx?a=1391072511.

Bashgāh-i khabar-negārān javān. "Tamaddun-i gharb dar sarʾāshībī suqūṭ," 27 Dey 1391/January 16, 2013, https://www.yjc.ir/fa/news/4234980/تمدن-غرب-در-سراشیبی-سقوط.

Beheshtī, Aḥmad. "Islām va-umanīsm," *Ufq-i ḥawza* 28, 9 Tīr 1382/June 3, 2003, https://hawzah.net/fa/Magazine/View/6435/8078/106170/.

Beranjkār, Reżā. "Mahdaviyat va-firqa-hā (2)," *Mowʿūd*, no 22 (1379/200–2001) http://www.ensani.ir/fa/content/61425/default.aspx.

Bīdgolī, Mowlūd Aʿẓamyān. "Barresī-i taṭbīqī-i feminism va-jāygāh-i zan dar gharb va-Islām," November 2015, http://emamemobin.com/index.php/thought/2014-09-23-16-15-08/2015-11-15-06-26-29/537-2015-11-15-07-34-28.

Bīdgolī, Muḥammad Ḥusayn. "Naqd va-barresī-i falsafa-i akhlāq-i femīnīstī – akhlāq-i zanāneh negār," 30 Abān 1396/November 21, 2017, http://moralphilosophy.ir/اخلاق-فمینیستی-اخلاق-زنانه/.

Būrūmand, Khūshyār & Seyyed Ḥasan Ḥusaynī. "Barresī-i rūyikard Heidegger dar muvājaha bā teknūlūzhī," *Gharb shināsī bonyādī* 5, no. 1 (Spring–Summer 1393/2014): 8–11.

Būrūnī, ʿAlī. "Taʾrīkhcheh peydāyesh Bābiyat va-Bahāʾiyat (bakhsh-i pāyānī)," *Ḥawza-i Iṣfahān*, 6 (1380/2001–2002), 181–198.

Būrūnī, ʿAlī. "Taʾrīkhcheh peydāyesh Bābiyat va-Bahāʾiyat (bakhsh-i sevom)," *Ḥawza-i Iṣfahān*, 3(1379/2000–2001), 172–192.

Chirāghī Kutiyānī, Ismāʿīl. "Barresī-i intiqādī-i rūsh-shināsī-i femīnīstī az manẓar-i realism Ṣadrāyī," *Maʿrifat-i farhangī ijtimāʿī* 2, no. 3 (Summer 1390/2011), http://ensani.ir/fa/article/322403.

Chirāghī Kutiyānī, Ismāʿīl. "Feminism va-kār kard khānevādeh," *Maʿrifat* 8, no. 131 (1387/2008), 87–108.

Daftar-i Tablīghāt-i Islāmī, *Darsnāmah-i ashnāʾī va-naqd-i Vahhābiyat: tebarshināsī va-jarayānshināsī-i Vahhābiyat*, (Qom: Daftar-i Tablīghāt-i Islāmī ḥawza, 1389/2010).

Daḥmān, Būdan. *Wasaṭiyyat al-Islām bayn al-Yahūdiyya wal-naṣrāniyya: dirāsa muqārina* (MA Thesis), https://vb.tafsir.net/tafsir52961/#.W88eknszYkI.

Dashtī, Muḥammad. *Rahāvard-i mubārazat-i ḥażrat-i Zahrāʾ ʿalayhā al-salām* (Iṣfahān: Markaz taḥqīqāt-i rayāneh'ī-i qā'imiyya-i Iṣfahān, n.d.) Electronic edition.

Dāvarī, Bāmdād. "Mojtahed-Shabestari: Yā ḥuqūq-i bashar yā ḥuqūq-i khodā, mughālaṭa ast," 17 Meher 1386/9 October 2007, http://www.islahweb.org/content/2007/10/665/ محمد-مجتهد-شبستری-یا-حقوق-بشر-یا-حقوق-خدا،-مغالطه-است.

Dāvarī Ardakānī, Reżā. "Autopia va-ta'rīkh-i jahān-i jadīd," http://rezadavari.ir/index.php?option=com_content&view=article&id=450:2015-06-14-11-21-38&catid=43:2015-06-13-12-02-50&Itemid=79.

Dāvarī Ardakānī, Reżā. *Dar bārah-i gharb* (Tehrān: Intishārāt-i Hermes, 1390/2011).

Dāvarī Ardakānī, Reżā. "Daʿvat-i dīnī va-tahājum-i farhangī," *Mashriq* nos. 2–3, (January–February 1995/2016), 12–17.

Dāvarī Ardakānī, Reżā. "ʿIlm va-āzādī," *Farhang* (Fall, 1379/2000), http://bashgahandishe.info/fa/content/show/9140.

Dāvarī Ardakānī, Reżā. *Tamaddun va-tafakkur-i gharbī* (Tehrān: Sāqī, 1380/2001).

Dīnāwī, Muḥammad ʿAlī. *Kubrā al-ḥarakāt al-Islāmiyya fī al-ta'rīkh* (Cairo: al-Jamāʿa al-Islāmiyya bi-jāmiʿat al-Qāhira, 1976).

Duke, David. *Bartarī ṭalabī Yahūd* (Tehrān: Amīr Kabir, 1393/2014).

Esfandiyār, Sorūr. "Ravand-i ẓuhūr-i feminism dar chahār-i qarn-i akhīr," *Payām-i zan*, 138 (1387/2008), 25–40.

Faḍlallah, Muḥammad Ḥusayn. "al-Ḥurriyya wal-dīmuqrāṭiyya fī al-ru'ya al-Islāmiyya," *Madkhal ilā al-fikr al-siyāsī*, trans. Khalīl al-ʿIṣamī (Tehrān: Maktab al-dirāsāt al-thaqāfiyya al-duwaliyya, 2001) 185–209.

Faqīhī, ʿAlī Aṣghar. *Ta'rīkh-i Vahhābiyat* (Iṣfahān: Majmaʿ jahānī-i ahl al-bayt, 1385/2006–07).

Farahamand, Maryam. "Feminism va-lezbiyanīsm," *Muṭālaʿāt-i rāhbordī-i zanān* 28 (Winter 1384/2006), 125–154.

Fardūst, Ḥusayn. *Ẓuhūr va-suqūṭ-i salṭanat-i Pahlavī* (Tehrān: Intishārāt-i iṭṭilāʿāt, 1370/1991), Vol. 1.

Al-Fārūqī, Louise Lāmyā. "Sunnathā-i Islāmī va-jonbesh-i feminism," *Khabarnāmah-i dīn-i pazhūhān* 10 (1381/2002), 33, http://www.hawzah.net/fa/Magazine/View/5427/5441/51046/.

Fāṭimīnezhād, Majīd. "Naqd va-barresī-i takfīr az dīdgāh-i salafī-i vahhābī va-salafī-i jihādī," 19 Bahman 1395/February 7, 2017, http://rasekhoon.net/article/show/1257768/.

Fayāż, Ibrāhīm. "Bahā'iyat-i jadīd," *Mowʿūd*, 60 (1384/2005), 26–27.

Furātī, ʿAbd al-Wahhāb. "Āzādī dar andīsheh-i Imām-i Khomeini," *Ḥukūmat-i Islāmī* 12 (Summer 1378/1999), 124–137.

Ganjī, Akbar. "Paradox-i takfīrīhā-i żede takfīrī," 2 Azar 1393/22 November 2012 – https://www.radiozamaneh.com/189163.

Ḥaddādī, Mujtabā. "Ufūl-i gharb-i modern va-talāsh barāye takhrīb-i Islam," *Risālat*, 17 Esfand 1389/March 8, 2011.

Hadhadī, Mahdī. "Az āzādī-i bayān tā irtidād," 25 Esfand 1382/February 14, 2004, http://article.tebyan.net/5472.

Ḥakīmī, Maḥmūd. "Gharb bīmār ast (8): Gharb va-mashīnīzm" Darshā-i maktab-i Islam 10, no. 11 (1348/1969), 777–780.

Ḥakīmī, Maḥmūd. "Gharb bīmār ast (10): Āzādī-i jinsī, fāji'a-i buzurg-i gharb;" *Darshā-i az maktab-i Islam* 11, no. 1 (1348/1970), 27–30.

Al-Ḥamdānī, 'Azīz. "'Uqdat al-dīmuqrāṭiyya," *al-Munṭalaq*, 115 (Spring–Summer 1996).

Hamdāniyān, Fāṭima. "Mādarī dar naẓarīyat-i femīnīstī," 3 Ordībehesht 1392/April 23, 2013, http://mehrkhane.com/fa/news/6419/مادری-در-نظریات-فمینیستی.

Ḥamīdī, Muḥammad Mahdī. *Dushmanān-i mahdaviyat cherā? Va-chegūneh?* (Iṣfahān: Markaz-i taḥqīqāt-i rayāneh-i qā'imiyya Iṣfahān, 1387/2008).

Ḥamīdī, Muḥammad Mahdī. "Yahūd az manẓar-i ta'rīkh," 30 Farvardīn 1396/19 April 2017, http://www.bonyadmahdi.com/sysnews/cid/373.

Ḥaqīqatjū, 'Alī. "Bahā'iyat va-kūdetā-i Reżā Khān," 5 Esfand 1386/November 26, 2007, https://www.farsnews.com/printable.php?nn=8612050168.

Ḥasanī, Ma'ṣūma. "Tafāvothā-i jinsīyatī az dīdgāh-i Islām va-feminism," *Muṭāla'āt-i rāhbordī-i zanān* 23 (Spring 1383/2004), https://www.noormags.ir/view/en/article page/212042.

Hāshimī Shahīdī, Asadollah. "Ikhrāj-i Yahūd az sarzamīnhā-i Islāmī," *Ẓuhūr-i ḥażrat-i Mahdī ('ajala Allah farajahu) az dīdgāh-i Islām, maẕāhib va-millal-i jahān* (Qom, 1384/2005), http://www.m-ahdi.com/persian/index.php?page=books&id=13#177/.

Ḥaydarī, Aḥmad. "Amniyat, āzādī, difā' az ża'īf va-amr beh ma'rūf va-nahyi az munkar," *Payām-i zan* 17 (1385/2006), 6–10.

Ḥaydarī, Ḥabīb and Mahdī 'Azīzān. "Irtidād: Āzādī-i andīsheh va-āzādī-i bayān," *Kalām-i Islāmī* 43(1381/2002), 74–85.

Ḥaydarī, Um al-Banīn and Fāṭima Asgarpūr. "Yahūd va-Yahūdiyān dar 'aṣr-i ẓuhūr," *Pazhūhesh-i mahdavī*, 25 (Summer 2018), 113–134.

Ḥażratī, Ḥasan and Nafīse Falāḥpūr. "Muqāyasa-i andīsheh-i mahdaviyat-i Shī'a ithnā-'asharī va-naẓarīyat-i pāyān-i ta'rīkh-i Fūkūyāmā," *Ta'rīkh-i Islām* 83 (Summer 1388/2009), 161–186.

Ḥikmat, Muḥammad Āsif. "Barresī va-naqd-i naẓarīyat-i tarbiyatī-i feminism," *Islām va-pazhūheshhā-i tarbīyatī*, 4:1 (Spring & Summer 2012), http://eslampajoheshha .nashriyat.ir/node/69.

Ḥusayn Abādī, Muẓaffar Hājiyān. "Dushman shināsī żarūrat-i millī" 29 Mehr 1396/21 October 2017, http://eskimia.ir/دشمن-شناسی،-ضرورتی-ملی/.

Ḥusaynī, Seyyed Ibrāhīm. "Feminism, farāz yā furūd?," 11 Esfand 1386/March 1, 2008, https://rasekhoon.net/article/show/109435/فمینیسم-فراز-یا-فرود-قسمت-اول/.

Ḥusaynī, Seyyed Ibrāhīm. "Irtidād dar āyīnah-i falsafa-i ḥuqūq-i Islāmī," *Maʿrifat*, 70 (1382/2003), 47–58.

Ḥusaynzādeh, Abūl-Ḥasan & Ḥusayn ʿAbbāsiyān. "Naqd va-barresī-i mabānī-i fikrī va-shākheṣhā-i feminism-i Islāmī," *Pazhūheshī-i insānī pazhūheshī-i dīnī* 34 (Fall–Winter 1394/2015), 207–228.

Ḥusayniyān, Rūḥollah. "Bahāʾiyat, rezhīm-i Pahlavī va-mavāżiʿ-i ʿulamāʾ," *Faṣlnāmah-i muṭālaʿāt-i taʾrīkhī*, 4:17 (Summer 1386/2007), 11–23.

Huwaydī, Fahmī. "Al-Dīmuqrāṭiyya min al-manẓūr al-mashrūʿī al-ḥaḍārī," *al-Mustaqbal al-ʿArabī* 269 (July 2001), 132–148.

Ibn ʿAbd al-Wahhāb, Muḥammad. *Risāla fī al-radd ʿalā al-rāfiḍa* (Sanʿā: Dār al-athār, 2006).

Ibn Ḥanbal, Aḥmad. *Musnad Aḥmad ibn Ḥanbal* (Cairo: Dār al-Maʿārif, 1985).

Ibn Jibrīn, ʿAbdallah. "Naṣrat ḥizballah al-rāfiḍī wal-inḍiwāʾ taḥt amrihim wal-duʿāʾ lahum bil-naṣr wal-tamkīn," http://www.ibn-jebreen.com/fatwa/vmasal-4174-.html.

Ibn Jibrīn, ʿAbdallah. "Al-radd ʿalā al-fatwā al-khāṣṣa bi-naṣrat ḥizballah al-lubnānī al-mansūba li-faḍilat al-shaykh ibn Jibrīn," http://ibn-jebreen.com/fatwa/vmasal-15294-.html.

Ibrāhīm-niyā, Muḥammad. "Naqsh-i Yahūd dar shahādat-i ḥażrat-i Zahrāʾ salām Allah ʿalayhā," http://intiqam.blogfa.com/post-24.aspx.

Ijrāʾī, Ḥasan. "Fūkūyāmā va-mahdaviyat: az afsāneh tā vāqiʿiyat," *Sāʿat-i ṣifr* 16, December 9, 2002, http://www.parsine.com/fa/news/58818.

Ilāhī, Ḥusayn, ʿAlī Yazdānī, Ḥasan Kāẓimzādeh. *Mahār-i inḥirāf-i: Bāzgavī-i ḥavādith pas az riḥlat-i piyāmbar-i akram (s)* (Qom: Muʾasasa-i taʾrīkh-i taṭbīqī, 1393/2014).

Iqtiṣād Marāghī, Mīrzā Ṣāliḥ. *ʾĪqāẓ, yā bīdārī dar kashf-i khiyānat-i dīnī va-vaṭanī-i Bahāʾīyān* (Qom: Bonyād-i farhangī-i ḥażrat-i Mahdī Mowʿūd (ʿaj), 1390/2011).

ʿIsā-zādeh, ʿAbbās & Seyyed Ḥusayn Sharaf al-Dīn. "Naẓariyat-i barkhōrd-i tamaddunhā chahārchūb-i mafhūm-i dark-i Islām harāsī," *Gharb shināsī bonyādī* 8, no. 2 (1395/2016): 47–52.

Ishāqī, Seyyed Ḥusayn. "Āzādī-i ʿaqīda dar Islām," *Riwāq-i andīsheh*, 29 (1383/2004), https://hawzah.net/fa/Article/View/82409/ازادی-عقیده-در-اسلام.

Ishāqī, Seyyed Ḥusayn. "Feminism towṭiʾah-i gharb ʿalayh-i zanān (pt. 1)," *Mublighān* 72 (1384/2005), 76–79.

Ishāqī, Seyyed Ḥusayn. "Feminism towṭiʾah-i gharb ʿalyah-i zanān (pt. 2)" – *Mublighān*, 74 (1384/2005–2006), 69–79.

Ishāqī, Seyyed Ḥusayn. "Feminism towṭiʿah-i gharb ʿalayh-i zanān (pt. 3)," *Mublighān*, 75 (1384/2005), 131–143.

Ishāqī, Seyyed Ḥusayn. "Ḥudūd-i āzādī-i bayān dar Islām," *Shamīm yās* 46 (1385/2007): 18–22.

Ishāqī, Seyyed Ḥusayn. "Mahiyat va-ahdāf-i feminism Islāmī," *Payām-i zan* 229 (1390/2011), 46–49.
Ishāqī, Seyyed Ḥusayn. "Ta'ammolī bar paykareh va-payāmadhā-i feminism-i Islāmī," *Riwāq-i andīsheh* 44 (1384/2005), 50–75.
Ishārat, Bushrā. "Murūrī-i ijmālī bar khāstgāh-i 'feminism Islāmī," 9 Bahman 1391/ January 28, 2013, http://mehrkhane.com/fa/news/5380.
Ismā'īlī, Maḥbūba. "Naqsh-i Inglistān dar shikl gīrī va-tadāvum-i firqa-i Bahā'iyat dar Iran," 20 Bahman 1392/February 9, 2014, http://rasekhoon.net/article/show/863393.
Ja'farī, 'Abbās. "Firqa-i Vahhābiyat va-'amalkard-i ān dar ta'rīkh-i mu'āṣir," *Ma'rifat* 12:1 (1381/2002), https://library.tebyan.net/fa/Viewer/Text/78318/1.
Ja'fariyān, Rasūl. *Jarayānhā va-sāzimānhā-i maẕhabi-siyāsī-i Iran: az rū-i kārāmadan-i Muḥammad Reżā Shāh tā pīrūzī-i inqilāb-i Islāmī, sālhā-i 1320–1357* (Tehrān: Markaz-i Asnād-i Inqilāb-i Islāmī, 2004).
Jam'iyyat al-ma'ārif al-Islāmiyya al-thaqāfiyya, *Durūs min khaṭṭ al-Imām al-Khumaynī, silsilat al-durūs al-thaqāfiyya* (Beirut, 2007).
Jamshīdī, Muḥammad Ḥusayn. "Tahājum-i farhangī: Tahājum-i farhangī chīst?," *Muṭāla'āt-i rāhbordī-i basīj* 3–4 (Summer–Fall 1373/1994), 75–112.
Jamshīdī, Muḥammad Ḥusayn. "Tahājum-i farhangī (3): mabānī-i niẓām-i farhangī-i gharb," *Muṭāla'āt-i rāhbordī-i basīj* 7–8 (1374/1995): 21–48.
Jamshīdī, Muḥammad Ḥusayn. "Tahājum-i farhangī (4);" *Muṭāla'āt-i rāhbordī-i basīj* 9–10 (1996): 56–79.
Javādī, 'Alī. "Umanīsm: inḥiṭāṭ ma'navī va-fasād-i akhlāqī-i gharb," *Risālat*, March 5, 2009.
Javādī Āmolī, 'Abdollah. "Irtidād va-āzādī (2)," *Pāsdār-i Islām* 266 (1382/2003–04).
Javāhirī, Mikā'il. *Bahā'iyat pād jonbesh-i tajdīd ḥayāt-i millat-i Iran* (Tehrān: Mu'asasa-i muṭāla'āt va-pazhūheshhā-i siyāsī, 1393/2014).
Kadīvar, Muḥsin. "'Adam-i nejāsat-i Bahā'iyat," 23 Shahrīvar 1392/14 September 2013, https://kadivar.com/?p=12743.
Kadīvar, Muḥsin. "Āyā Bahā'īyān kāfirand?" 5 Farvardīn 1392/March 25, 2013, https://kadivar.com/?p=10412.
Kadīvar, Muḥsin. "Ba Bahā'īyān chegūneh barkhōrd konīm?" 25 Ordībehesht 1395/ 14 May 2016, http://kadivar.com/?p=15243.
Kadīvar, Muḥsin. *Ḥaqq al-nās* (*Islām va-ḥuqūq-i bashar*), (Tehrān: Intishārāt-i Kvir, 1388/2009).
Kadīvar, Muḥsin. "Ḥuqūq-i shahrvandī-i Bahā'iyat az manẓar-i ustād," https://kadivar.com/?p=8284.
Kadīvar, Muḥsin. "Maḥrūmiyat-i Bahā'īyān az ḥuqūq-i shahrvandī fāqid-i vujahat-i shar'ī va-qānūnī ast," 2 Dey 1393/December 23, 2014, https://kadivar.com/14211.
Kadīvar, Muḥsin. "Mardomsālārī-i dīnī," www.kadivar.com.

Kadīvar, Muḥsin. "Ẓulm beh Bahā'īyān," 5 shahrīvar 1390/August 27, 2011, https://kadivar.com/?p=8202.

Karīmyān, Aḥmad. "ʿAvāmīl-i nifrat az Yahūd (7)," http://rasekhoon.net/article/show/750799/.

Karīmyān, Aḥmad. *Yahūd va-ṣahyūnīsm: taḥlīl-i ʿanāṣir-i qawmī, ta'rīkhī va-dīnī-i yek fājiʿa* (Qom: Bustān, 1389/2010).

Kārnāmī, Seyyed Ḥusayn Ḥusaynī. "Āzādī-i ʿaqīda va-āzādī-i bayān bā takiye bar vakāvī-i tafsīrī-i āya ʿlā ikrāh fī al-dīn'," *Maʿarif Qur'ānī* 19 (Winter 1393), 71–90.

Kāshif al-Ghitā', Muḥammad Ḥusayn. *Al-ʿAbaqāt al-ʿinbariyya fī al-ṭabaqāt al-Jaʿfarīyya taḥqīq Jawdat al-Qazwīnī* (Beirut: Bisan, 1998).

Kāẓimyan-Pūr, Ghulām Reżā. "Taṭābuk va-hamāhangī-i Vahhābiyat va-Yahūdiyat dar te'ōrī va-ʿamal," 25 Abān 1393/November 16, 2014, http://www.x-shobhe.com/shobhe/5571.html.

Khāje-Servī, Ghulām Reżā and Mahdī Nādirī. "Āzādī dar goftemān-i faqāhatī-i inqilāb-i Islāmī Iran," *Jastarhā-i siyāsī-i muʿaṣir* 4, no. 2 (1392/2013): 27–55.

Khāliqī Afkand, ʿAlī. *Imām Khomeini va-goftemān-i gharb* (Tehrān: Anjuman-i maʿārif-i Islāmī, 1379/2000), http://www.ghadeer.org/Book/15/2336.

Khamenei, Seyyed ʿAlī. "Bayānāt dar dīdār-i afshār-i mukhtalif-i mardom beh munāsabat-i ʿīd ghadīr," 20 Mehr 1393/12 October 2014, http://farsi.khamenei.ir/speech-content?id=27896.

Khamenei, Seyyed ʿAlī. "Bayānāt dar dīdār-i a'īmah-i masājid-i astān-i Tehrān," 21 Mordād 1395/August 11, 2016, http://farsi.khamenei.ir/speech-content?id=34109.

Khamenei, Seyyed ʿAlī. "Bayānāt dar dīdār-i bānuvān-i nokhbe astāneh sālrūz-i ḥażrat-i Zahrā' (salām Allah ʿalayhā)," 13 Tīr 1386/July 4, 2007, http://farsi.khamenei.ir/speech-content?id=3390.

Khamenei, Seyyed ʿAlī. "Bayānāt dar dīdār-i jamʿī az bānuvān-i bargezīdeh-i keshvar," 30 Farvardīn 1393/April 19, 2014, http://farsi.khamenei.ir/speech-content?id=26155.

Khamenei, Seyyed ʿAlī. "Bayānāt dar dīdār jamʿī az madāḥān," 11 Ordībehesht 1392/May 1, 2013, http://farsi.khamenei.ir/speech-content?id=22443.

Khamenei, Seyyed ʿAlī. "Bayānāt dar dīdār-i jamʿī az mardom dar rūz-i ʿīd ghadīr," 27 Azar 1387/December 17, 2008, http://farsi.khamenei.ir/speech-content?id=5025.

Khamenei, Seyyed ʿAlī. "Bayānāt dar dīdār-i jamʿī az rūḥāniyān," 11 Mordād 1368/August 2, 1989, http://farsi.khamenei.ir/speech-content?id=2151.

Khamenei, Seyyed ʿAlī. "Bayānāt dar dīdār-i jamʿī az ruḥāniyūn-i ḥawza-i ʿulamā'-i ahl-i Sunnat," 5 Dey 1368/December 26, 1989, http://farsi.khamenei.ir/newspart-print?tid=3542.

Khamenei, Seyyed ʿAlī. "Bayānāt dar dīdār-i javānān-i astān-i Khorāsān-i shimālī," 23 Mehr 1391/October 14, 2012, http://farsi.khamenei.ir/speech-content?id=21252.

Khamenei, Seyyed ʿAlī. "Bayānāt dar dīdār-i mas'ūlān-i niẓām," 30 Tīr 1392/July 21, 2013, http://farsi.khamenei.ir/speech-content?id=23175.

Khamenei, Seyyed ʿAlī. “Bayānāt dar dīdār-i mas’ūlān-i niẓām va-mayhamānān-i conference-i vaḥdat-i Islāmī,” 29 Dey 1392/January 19, 2014, http://farsi.khamenei.ir/speech-content?id=25056.

Khamenei, Seyyed ʿAlī. “Bayānāt dar dīdār-i ruḥāniyūn va-ṭulāb-i tashayyuʿ va-tasannon-i Kurdistan,” 23 Ordībehesht 1388/13 May 2009, http://farsi.khamenei.ir/speech-content?id=6772.

Khamenei, Seyyed ʿAlī. “Bayānāt dar dīdār-i shirkat konandegān dar ijlās-i jahānī-i asātīd-i dāneshgāhhā-i jahān-i Islam va-bīdārī-i Islāmī vīzhegīhā-i jarayān-i takfīrī,” 21 Azar 1391/December 11, 2012, http://farsi.khamenei.ir/speech-content?id=21741.

Khamenei, Seyyed ʿAlī. “Bayānāt dar dīdār shirkat konandegān dar ʿkongreh-i jahānī-i jarayānhā-i ifrāṭī va-takfīrī az dīdgāh-i ʿulamā’-i Islam,” 4 Azar 1393/November 25, 2014, http://farsi.khamenei.ir/speech-content?id=28278.

Khamenei, Seyyed ʿAlī. “Bayānāt dar dīdār-i ṭulāb va-asātīd-i madrasa-i ʿilmī-i ayatollah mujtahidī” 21 Khordād 1383/June 10, 2004, http://farsi.khamenei.ir/speech-content?id=1138.

Khamenei, Seyyed ʿAlī. “Bayānāt dar dīdār-i zā’irān va-mujāvirān-i ḥaram-i muṭahhar-i rażavī,” 1 Farvardīn 1389/March 21, 2010, http://www.ghadeer.org/BsnText/13260.

Khamenei, Seyyed ʿAlī. “Bayānāt dar marāsim-i bīst-o-panjomīn-i sālgard-i riḥlat-i Imām Khomeini (rh),” 14 Khordād 1393/June 4, 2014, http://farsi.khamenei.ir/newspart-index?id=26615&nt=2&year=1393&tid=989#49962.

Khamenei, Seyyed ʿAlī. *Bayānāt-i Imām Khamene’ī dar bārah-i tahājum-i farhangī*, http://toorenamaree.blogfa.com/post/8.

Khamenei, Seyyed ʿAlī. “Bayānāt-i maqām-i muʿaẓẓam-i rahbarī beh munāsabat-i rūz-i mubāraza bā istikbār-i jahānī,” 9 Aban 1375/October 30, 1996, http://www.leader.ir/fa/speech/1346.

Khamenei, Seyyed ʿAlī. “Bayānāt-i rahbar-i inqilāb dar dīdār-i shirkat-konandegān dar dovomīn hamāyesh buzurgdasht Ibn Maytham Baḥrānī,” 25 Dey 1385/January 15, 2007, http://kalameimam.persianblog.ir/post/496/.

Khamenei, Seyyed ʿAlī. “Boḥrān-i gharb,” http://farsi.khamenei.ir/keyword-print?id=2236.

Khamenei, Seyyed ʿAlī. “Dīdār-i aʿżā’-i shūrā-i ʿāli-i inqilāb-i farhangī bā rahbar-i inqilāb,” 23 Khordād 1390/June 13, 2011, http://farsi.khamenei.ir/news-content?id=12693.

Khamenei, Seyyed ʿAlī. “Dushman shināsī,” farsi.khamenei.ir/keyword-print?id=1022.

Khamenei, Seyyed ʿAlī. *Felestīn az manẓar-i* ḥażrat-i *Ayat Allah al-ʿuzmā Khamenehi* (Tehrān: Inqilāb-i Islāmī, 1391/2013).

Khamenei, Seyyed ʿAlī. “Hasht neshāneh az khidmat-i takfīrīha be jarayān-i istikbār,” 14 Dey 1393/June 4, 2014 http://farsi.khamenei.ir/others-note?id=28548.

Khamenei, Seyyed ʿAlī. “Ḥifāẓāt va-ḥirāsāt az imān-i mardom, vaẓīfa-i niẓām-i Islāmī,” 15 Esfand 1365/March 6, 1987, http://farsi.khamenei.ir/newspart-print?id=21492&npt=7&nt=2&year=1365.

Khamenei, Seyyed ʿAlī. "Ḥijāb va-ʿifāf dar kalām-i maqām-i muʿaẓẓam-i rahbarī," https://hawzah.net/fa/Article/View/94793.

Khamenei, Seyyed ʿAlī. "Hoshyārāneh bāyad bā jāhiliyat-i modern muqābala kard," Ordībehesht 26, 1394/May 16, 2015, http://farsi.khamenei.ir/video-content?id=29735.

Khamenei, Seyyed ʿAlī. "Khaṭar al-ghazw al-thaqāfī," *Tebyān* n.d., https://library.tebyan.net/fa/Viewer/Text/141579/0.

Khamenei, Seyyed ʿAlī. "Matn-i kāmil-i bayānāt-i maqām-i muʿaẓẓam-i rahbrī dar khuṭbahā-i namāz jumʿa-i Tehrān," Ordībhehesht 23, 1379/May 12, 2000, https://www.leader.ir/fa/speech/1903/اقامه-نماز-جمعه-تهران-به-امامت-رهبر-معظم-انقلاب-همزمان-با-میلاد-امام-موسی-کاظم-(ع).

Khamenei, Seyyed ʿAlī. "Nufūẕ-i dushman," http://farsi.khamenei.ir/newspart-index?tid=6592.

Khamenei, Seyyed ʿAlī. "Rahbar-i muʿaẓẓam-i inqilāb-i Islāmī dar dīdār-i hizārān-i nafar az shāʿirān va-setāyeshgerān-i ahl-i bayt ʿalayhim al-salām," 17 Esfand 1396/March 6, 2018, http://www.leader.ir/fa/content/20734.

Khamenei, Seyyed ʿAlī. *Risāla-i ajvibat al-istiftāʾāt* (Tehrān: Sāzemān-i tablīghāt-i Islāmī, 1388).

Khamenei, Seyyed ʿAlī. "Sibk zindigī," Mehr 24, 1391/October 15, 2012, http://farsi.khamenei.ir/speech-content?id=21293.

Khamenei, Seyyed ʿAlī. "Tafāvothā-i Islām nāb Muḥammadī va-Islām Amrīkāʾī," Abān 26, 1393a/November 17, 2014, http://farsi.khamenei.ir/print-content?id=28198.

Khātamī, Aḥmad. "Dushman shināsī az dīdgāh-i Imām ʿAlī," *Pāsdār-i Islām* 209 (1378/1999), https://hawzah.net/fa/Magazine/View/89/3409/15864.

Khātamī, Muḥammad. *Muṭālaʿāt fī al-dīn wal-Islām wal-ʿaṣr* (Beirut: Dār al-jadīd, 1988).

Khazʿalī, Mahdī. "Poshtbordeh ānūsīhā," Mordād 15, 1389/August 6, 2010, http://k4t8u2.blogspot.com/2010/10/blog-post_7023.html.

Khoʾī, Ḥabībollah Hāshimī. *Manhaj al-barāʾa fī sharḥ nahj al-balāgha*, (Beirut: Muʾassasat al-Wafaʾ, 1953).

Al-Khoʾīnī, Abū al-Ḥusayn. *Shahādat al-athr fī qātil ʿUmar* (Beirut: hayʾat khādim al-Mahdī, 2006).

Khomeini, Rūḥollah Musāvī. *al-Makāsib al-muḥarrama* Vol. 1 (Qom 1381/2002).

Khomeini, Rūḥollah Musāvī. *Ṣaḥīfa-i nūr: majmūʿa-i rāhnemūdhā-i imām-i Khomeini* (Tehrān: Vizārat-i Irshād-i Islāmī, 1995).

Khosrō-panāh, ʿAbd al-Ḥusayn. "Sayr-i intiqādī dar taʾrīkh va-bāvarhā-i Bahāʾiyat," *Kitāb-i naqd* 12, nos. 52–53 (Fall–Winter 1388/2009), 13–60.

Khumaynī Rūḥollah Musāvī. *Al-Ḥukūma al-Islāmiyya*, (Beirut: Dār al-Ṭalīʿa, 1979).

Khumaynī Rūḥollah Musāvī. *Al-Kalimāt al-qiṣār mawāʿiẓ wa-*ḥukm *min kalām al-imām al-Khumaynī* (*qudisa sirruhu*) (Beirut: Dār al-wasīla, 1995).

Khumaynī Rūḥollah Musāvī. *Al-Qaḍiyya al-filasṭīniyya* fī *kalām al-imām* al-Khumaynī (Beirut: Dār al-wasīla, 1996).

Kowthari, ʿAlī Aṣghar. "Zavāl-i tamaddun-i gharb," May 2, 2013, http://kosari113.mihanblog.com/post/543.

Al-Kurānī, ʿAlī. *ʿAṣr al-ẓuhūr* (Qom: mu'assasat al-maʿārif al-Islāmiyya, 2006).

Kūshkī, Muḥammad Ṣādiq. "Ravand-i furūpāshī-i tamaddun-i gharb az pīrūzī-i inqilāb-i Islāmī aghāz shodeh ast," 17 Azar 1390/December 8, 2011, https://www.mehrnews.com/news/1485518.

Lājvardī, Hālā. "Feminism muthbat feminism manfī," *Pazhūhesh-i zanān* 35:3 (Winter 1386/2008), 83–107.

Lakzā'ī, Sharīf. "Sāz va-kārhā-i āzādī dar andīsheh-i ayatollah Beheshtī," *ʿUlūm-i Siyāsī*, 4, no. 13 (Spring 1380/2001), 159–179.

Lankarānī, Javād Fāżil. "Vahhābiyat mūriyāneh'i ast keh beh jān-i Islam oftādeh va-samī ast barāye az bīn bordan-i Shīʿa va-ahl Sunnat," 5 Shahrīvar 1386/August 27, 2007, https://www.isna.ir/news/8606-02487.

Maʿāf, Islām Mālikī. "ʿĪd al-zahrā' chīst?/ Abū Lū'lū' kīst?/hameh āncheh keh bāyad dar bārah-i yek jashn-i inḥirāfī bedānīm," 1/9/1396/November 22, 2017, http://www.8deynews.com/249061/عيدالزهرا-چيست؟-ابولولو-کيست؟-همه-آن/#print.

Mahdavī, Reżā. "Cherā maqbara-i Abū Lū'lū' baste shod," 27 Khordād 1386/June 17, 2007, http://fararu.com/fa/news/93.

Mahdavī Zādehgān, Da'ūd. "Rīshe-yābī-i naẓariyat-i barkhōrd-i tamaddunhā," *Ḥukūmat-i Islāmī* 11 (1378/1999): 182–201.

Mahdīpūr, ʿAlī Akbar. *Ta'rīkh-i Islam bā rūyikard-i dushman shināsī* (Qom: Naghmat, 1390/2012).

Majīdī, Keyvān. "Vāqiʿiyat-i Yahūd setīzī: protokolhā-i zuʿamā'-i ṣahyūn," pt. 1 + 2 18 Dey 1389/January 8, 2011, http://basij-ganjnameh.persianblog.ir/post/84/ (Last accessed March 10, 2013).

Majlisī, Muḥammad Bāqir. *Biḥar al-anwār* (Beirut: Dār iḥyā' al-turāth al-ʿArabī, 1983).

Makārem Shīrāzī, Nāṣir. "Al-Āliyāt al-munāsiba fī muwājahat al-tiyārāt al-takfīriyya, arā' al-marjaʿ Makārem Shīrāzī," February 29, 2016, https://www.makarem.ir/main.aspx?lid=2&typeinfo=1&catid=45227&pageindex=0&mid=394969.

Makārem Shīrāzī, Nāṣir. *Ḥukūmat-i jahānī-i Mahdī* (Qom: Intishārāt-i nisl javān, 1380/2001).

Makārem Shīrāzī, Nāṣir. "Munāfat-i nahyi az munkar bā āzādī insān!," http://makarem.ir/main.aspx?lid=0&typeinfo=42&catid=29470&pageindex=0&mid=322195.

Makārem Shīrāzī, Nāṣir. *Vahhābiyat bar sar dō rāhī* (Qom: Intishārāt-i Madrasat al-Imām ʿAlī ibn abī Ṭālib, 1384/2005).

Maqām-i muʿaẓẓam-i rahbarī. *Pāyān-i Gharb: Justārī dar bayānāt-i rahbar-i muʿaẓẓam-i inqilāb* (*madda ẓilluhu al-ʿālī*) *pīrāmūn niẓām sarmāyeh-dārī* (Tehrān: Kitāb-i Farda, 1390/2011).

Maqām-i muʿaẓẓam-i rahbarī. "Zavāl va-ufūl tamaddun-i gharb dar kalām rahbarī," May 1, 2013, http://mkhb.r98.ir/post/114.

Markaz-i asnād-i Inqilāb-i Islāmī, *Naqsh-i Bahāʾiyat dar fitna-i 1388* (Tehrān, 1390/2011).

Markaz-i millī-i pāsokhgūyi-i beh suʾālāt-i dīnī. "Nejes-i būdan ahl-i kitāb," 30 Mordād 1389/21 August 2010, http://www.pasokhgoo.ir/node/17135.

Markaz Nūn. *al-Ḥurriyya fī fikr al-imām al-Khumaynī* (Beirut: Jamʿiyat al-maʿārif al-Islāmiyya al-thaqāfīyya, 2006).

Markaz takhaṣṣusī-i mahdaviyat. "Vażʿiyat-i Iran qabl az ẓuhūr va-naqsh-i ān dar ẓuhūr-i ḥażrat-i mahdī ʿajala Allah taʿālā farajahu al-sharīf chīst?," *Ufq-i ḥawza* 305, 24 Farvardīn 1390/April 13, 2011, https://hawzah.net/fa/Magazine/View/6435/7830/100737.

Masāʾilī, Mahdī. "*Laʿnhā-i ke nāmuqaddasand*," http://azadpajooh.com/161.

Masāʾilī, Mahdī. "Pāsokhī kūtāh be naqd-i kitāb-i 'laʿnhā-i nāmuqaddas'" December 13, 2016, http://azadpajooh.com/category/پاسخ-به-نقد-ها.

Mehrāyīnī, Rāmīn. "Taʾammolī dar feminism yā maktab-i iṣālat-i zan dar gostāresh-i fasād-i ijtimāʿī va-furūpāshī-i khānevādeh," 3 Esfand 1389/February 22, 2011, http://www.aftabir.com/articles/view/applied_sciences/social_science/c12_1298375749p1.php/.

Meyhandūst, Muḥammad Hādī. "Beh nām-i ahl-i bayt nāraqṣīd, luṭfan," 7 Bahman 1388/February 27, 2010, http://1001talangor.blogfa.com/post-59.aspx.

Mīr-Ahmadi, Manṣūr. "Āzādī va-vilāyat dar fiqh-i siyāsī-i muʿāṣir-i Shīʿa," *ʿUlūm-i siyāsī* 3 (Winter 1377/1999), 75–107.

Mīr-Ahmadi, Manṣūr. "Mafhūm āzādī dar fiqh-i siyāsī-i Shīʿa," *ʿUlūm-i siyāsī* 1, no. 1 (Summer 1377/1998), 70–88.

Mīr-Bāqirī, Muḥammad Mahdī. "Boḥrān-i idīʾūlūzhīk-i tamaddun-i gharb ʿāmil ʾījād boḥrān-i Iqtiṣādī shod ast," 30 Farvardīn 1393/April 19, 2014 http://www.hamandishi.ir/news/216675/.

Miṣbāḥ Yazdī, Muḥammad Taqī. *Buzurgtarīn-i farīża* (Qom: Intishārāt-i Muʾasasa-i amūzeshī va-pazhūheshī-i Imām-i Khomeini, 1389/2010).

Miṣbāḥ Yazdī, Muḥammad Taqī. "Dīn va-āzādī (2): goftegū bā Ayatollah Miṣbāḥ Yazdī," *Mublighān* 23 (1380/2001), 139–158.

Mīthāqī, Niẓām al-Dīn. "Nejāsat yā pākī-i Bahāʾīyān: bohāneh-i barāye ḥaẕf," December 8, 2014, https://iranwire.com/fa/news/215/6061.

Mishkānī Sabzivārī, ʿAbbās ʿAlī. *Abū Lūʾlūʾ az ḥaqīqat tā tavahhum*, (Majmaʿ-i jahānī-i taqrīb-i maẕāhib-i Islāmī, 2012).

Mojtahed Shabestari, Muḥammad. "Āzādī bat nīst, bat shekan ast!" May 13, 2014, http://www.cgie.org.ir/fa/news/12362.

Montaẓeri, Ḥusayn ʿAlī. "Dar bāb-i tazāḥum: dīn, modārā va-khoshūnat," https://amontazeri.com/book-index/didgaha/475.

Mu'asasa-i farhangī va-iṭṭilāʿ-i rasānī-i Tebyān. *Yahūdā dīnī ke dar rāh-i shaytān qadam bar mīdārad* (Qom, 1395/2016).

Mu'asasa-i firaq va-adyān-i Zāhidān. "Bahā'īgarī va-sāzemānhā-i iṭṭilāʿātī va-amniyatī shūrāvī," 30 Shahrīvar 1396/September 21, 2017, http://mafaz.ir/content/bahaiiat_shorvi.

Mu'asasa-i muṭālaʿāt-i va-pazhūheshhā-i siyāsī. "*Irtibāṭāt*-i Bahā'iyat bā servīshā-i jāsūsī-i sharq va-gharb," http://zionism.pchi.ir/show.php?page=contents&id=5172.

Mu'asasa-i muṭālaʿāt-i va-pazhūheshhā-i siyāsī. "Jumlatī az imām-i Khomeini (rh) dar bārah-i peyvand Isrā'īl va-Bahā'iyat," http://revolution.pchi.ir/show.php?page=contents&id=4973.

Mu'asasa-i muṭālaʿāt-i va-taḥqīqāt-i beyne almilalī. *Az afsāneh-i Yahūdī setīzī tā vāqiʿiyat-i Islam setīzī* (Qom, 1394/2015).

Mu'asasa-i ta'rīkh-i taṭbīqī, "Barresī-i ikhlālgarī va-nufūẕ-i farhangī-i Yahūd pas as riḥlat-i piyāmbar-i Islām (a) dar goftegū bā Ḥujjat al-Islām Saʿādatī," 31 Mordād 1395/August 21, 2016, shorturl.at/inuwL, (accessed August 13, 2018).

Mu'asasa-i ta'rīkh-i taṭbīqī. "Goftegū: Nufūẕ-i Yahūd dar miyān-i musalmānān-i ṣadr-i Islām," 18 Farvardīn 1399/ April 6, 2020, http://tarikh.org/1399/01/18/گفت-وگوی-اختصاصی-نفوذ-یهود-در-بین-مسلمانان-در-صدر-اسلام.

Mu'asasa-i tanẓīm va-nashr athār-i Imām Khomeini. *Jāygāh-i zan dar andīsheh-i Imām-i Khomeini* (S) (Qom, 1374/1995).

Mu'assasat tanẓīm wa-nashr turāth al-Imām al-Khumaynī. *Minhajiyat al-thawra al-Islāmiyya: muqtaṭafāt min afkār wa-arā' al-Imām al-Khumaynī* (Tehrān: (S) 1996).

Mudarrisī (Ṭabāṭabā'ī), Seyyed Muḥammad ʿAlī. *Tamaddun-i mādī gerāyāne mā gharbīhā: dīdgāh-i jamʿī az dāneshmandān-i gharbī dar naqd-i tamaddun-i gharb* (Qom: Intishārāt Shafaq, 1382/2003).

Mughniyya, Muḥammad Jawād. *Hadhihi hiyya al-Wahhābiyya* (Mu'assasat dar al-kitāb al-Islami, 1426h/2006).

Muhājirī, Maryam. "Āsīb Shināsī-i payāmad-i akhlāqī-i feminism dar gharb va-bāztāb-i ān dar nihād-i khānevādeh," *Pazhūhesh-i nāmah-i zanān* 2, no. 1 (Spring–Summer 1390/2011), 99–115.

Muḥammadī, ʿAbdollah. "Dīn va-feminism," http://pajoohe.net/fa/index.php?Page=definition&UID=37430.

Muḥammadī, ʿAlī Reżā. "Bahā'iyat/ta'rīkhcheh, iʿtiqādāt va-vażʿiyat-i konūnī (qismat-i dovom)," *Maʿārif* 70 (1388/2009), 20–24.

Muḥammadī, ʿAlī Reżā. "Bahā'iyat/ta'rīkhcheh, iʿtiqādāt va-vażʿiyat-i konūnī (qismat-i sevom)," *Maʿārif* 71 (1388/2009), 29–34.

Muḥammadī, ʿAlī Reżā. "Jarayān-shināsī Bahā'iyat: Qismat-i dovom (daftar 35 porseshhā va-pāsokhhā)," http://porseman.org/ShowArticle.aspx?id=1243.
Muḥammadī, ʿAlī Reżā. "Jarayān-shināsī Bahā'iyat: qismat-i sevom (daftar 35 porseshhā va-pāsokhhā)," http://www.porseman.org/showarticle.aspx?id=1244.
Muḥammadī, ʿAlī Reżā. "Jarayān-shināsī Bahā'iyat: qismat-i yekom (daftar 35 porseshhā va-pāsokhhā)," http://www.porseman.org/showarticle.aspx?id=1242.
Muḥammadī, Muḥsin. "Muvājaha-i Islām bā ṣahyūnīsm, tamaddunī ast neh siyāsī," 15 Azar 1395/December 5, 2016, https://www.farsnews.com/news/13950915000103.
Muḥammadpūr, ʿAlī. "Fūkūyāmā ham iʿtirāf mīkonad," *Amān*, 5 (1386/2007), http://www.hawzah.net/fa/magazine/magart/6024/6029/63103.
Mukhtārī, Majīd Mūsā. "Ufūl-i gharb va-ilzāmāt barpāyī tamaddun-i Islāmī," Javandaily.com, June 13, 2009.
Muntaẓir Qā'im, Mahdī. "Āzādī-i andīsheh," *Ḥukūmat-i Islāmī* 7 (1377/1999), 37–69.
Muntaẓir Qā'im, Mahdī. "Āzādī-i siyāsī," *Ḥukūmat-i Islāmī* 3 (Spring 1376/1997), http://www.ensani.ir/fa/content/81279/default.aspx.
Murādī, Jaʿfar. "'Feminism Islami' tarkīb-i paradoxical," in *Hamāyesh-i Islam va-feminism*, editor Hādī Vakīlī (Tehrān: daftar-i nashr-i maʿārif, 1381/2002), Vol. 2: 495–496.
Mushīrzādeh, Hamīrā. *Az jonbesh tā naẓariyya-i ijtimāʿī: ta'rīkh-i dō qarn-i feminism* (Tehrān: nashr va-pazhūhesh-i shīrāzeh, 1382/2003).
Mushīrzādeh, Hamīrā. "Zamīnhā-i ẓuhūr-i feminism dar gharb," in *Hamāyesh-i Islam va-feminism*, editor Hādī Vakīlī (Tehrān: daftar-i nashr-i maʿārif, 1381/2002), Vol. II, p. 505–547.
Musliḥzādeh, Muṣṭafā. "Dāʿesh Shīʿa rā dushman-i aṣlī-i khōd mīdānad," Mehr 6, 1393/September 29, 2014, http://www.farsnews.com/newstext.php?nn=13930705001759.
Muṣṭafā, Aḥmad & ʿAlā' Ḥasan Muṣṭafā. "Tafāvot miyān-i jonbeshhā-i inqilābī va-jarayānāt-i takfīrī va-terōristī," *Javān-i Irani*, 6 Mordād 1395/July 27, 2016, https://khabarfarsi.com/u/22640089.
Muṣṭafavī, Reżā. *Al-Tiyām: farjam shināsī-i jarayānhā-i ta'rīkh* (Tehrān, 1395/2016).
Muṭṭaharī, Murtażā. *Insān-i Kāmil* (Tehrān: Intishārāt-i Ṣadrā, 1373/1994).
Muṭṭaharī, Murtażā. *Niẓām-i ḥuqūq-i zan dar Islām* (Tehrān, Intishārāt-i Ṣadrā, 1357/1979).
Muṭṭaharī, Murtażā. *Pānzdah goftār* (Tehrān: Intishārāt-i Ṣadrā, 1380).
Muṭṭaharī, Murtażā. *Yāddāshtahā-i ustād-i Muṭṭaharī* (Tehrān: Intishārāt-i Ṣadrā, 1377/1998), vol. 2.
Al-Muẓaffar, Muḥammad Riḍā. *Saqīfa* (Beirut: Mu'assasat al-aʿlamī lil-maṭbūʿāt, 1973).
Muẓaffarī, Āyat. *Rāhbordhā-i dushman shināsī* (Qom: Zamzama-i Hidāyat, 1392/2013).
Naḥawī, Muḥammad Bāqir (ed.). *Maslak-i Vahhābiyat: chegūnehgī beh vujūd āmad?* (Tehrān: Rāh-i Nīkān, 1393/2014).

Najafabādī, Ḥamīd Rustamī. "Barresī-i mavāżiʿ va-fatāvā-i rahbarī dar pīshbord-i taqrīb va-vaḥdat-i Islāmī," 11 Ordibehehst 1392/May 1, 2013, https://defapress.ir/fa/news/205083.

Najafī, Muḥammad Bāqir. *Bahā'īyān* (Qom: shiʿr mashʿar, 1383/2004).

Najafī, Mūsā. "Falsafa-i takāmul-i bīdārī-i Islāmī va-jawhar-i ufūl-i yābande-i tamaddun-i gharb," *Justārhā-i siyāsī-i muʿāṣir* 2, no. 2 (Fall-Winter 1390/2011), 73–90.

Najafī, Mūsā. *Naẓariyat-i tamaddun-i jadīd-i Islāmī: Falsafa-i takāmul-i tamaddun-i Islāmī va-jawhar-i ufūl-i yābande-i tamaddun-i gharb* (Iṣfahān: Armā, 1392/2013).

Najafī, Musallam & Hādī Vakīlī. "Ta'ammulatī-i ta'rīkhī dar bārah-i nohom-i Rabīʿ," *Muṭālaʿāt-i Islāmī: ta'rīkh va-farhang* 42, no. 85/4 (Fall–Winter 1389/2010–2011), 53–63.

Najafī Fīrūzjāyī, ʿAbbās. "Bonyādhā-i fikrī al-qāʿidah va-Vahhābiyat," *Rāhbord* 27 (Spring 1382/2003), 232–256.

Najafpūr, Shahriyār. "Muṭālaʿa-i taṭbīqī-i naẓarīyat-i pāyān-i ta'rīkh-i Fūkūyāmā," https://rasekhoon.net/article/show/120494/.

Nāmdār, Muẓaffar. "Istiʿmār va-ẓuhūr-i maslakhā-i shibh-i dīnī," https://rasekhoon.net/article/show/136454/.

Naqdī, Jaʿfar. *Al-Anwār al-ʿalawiyya wa-al-asrār al-murtaḍawiyya fī aḥwāl amīr al-mu'minīn wa-faḍā'ilihi wa-manāqibihi wa-ghazawātihi* (Najaf: al-Maṭbaʿa al-Ḥaydarīyya, 1962).

Nāṣirī, ʿAlī. *Bahā'īyat va-taḥrīf-i ta'rīkh* (Abridged electronic edition) (Iṣfahān: Markaz-i taḥqīqāt rayāneh-i qā'imiyya, 1386/2007).

Nāṣirī, Mahdī. *Islam va-Tajaddud* (Tehrān: Ṣubḥ, 1380/2001).

Naṣīrī-Fard, ʿAbbās. Vakāvī-*i seh firqa: barresī va-taḥlīl Vahhābiyat, Bahā'īyat shayṭān-parastī* (Tehrān: Rāh-i Nīkān, 1392/2013).

Nasūrī, Muḥammad Reżā. "Peyvand va-hamkārī-i Bahā'iyat bā rezhīm-i Pahlavī," *Intiẓār-i Mowʿūd* 27 (Winter 1387/2008–2009), 195–222.

Nīkzād, ʿAbbās. "Āzādī-i ʿaqīda va-maẕhab dar Islam," *Riwāq-i andīsheh* 18 (Khordād 1382/June 2003), http://ensani.ir/fa/article/48368/.

Nīkzād, ʿAbbās. "Āzādīhā-i ijtimāʿī az dīdgāh-i Islam," *Riwāq-i andīsheh* 25 (Dey 1382/January 2004), 7–25.

Niyāzī, Aḥmad ʿAlī. "Pāyān-i ta'rīkh dar andīsheh-i Fūkūyāmā va-naẓarīyat-i mahdaviyat," *Sangar Sāybarī*, November 22, 2010, http://cyberbunker.blogfa.com/post/127.

Niyāzī, Zaynab. "Feminism va-mabānī-i tafakkur-i ṣahyūnīsm (pts. 1 + 2)," http://zionism.blogfa.com/post-866.aspx.

Al-Nujayrī, Maḥmūd. "Talmūd rīsheh-i fasād va-sharārat-i Yahūd," 3 Ordībehesht 1392/April 23, 2013 – http://rasekhoon.net/article/show/699380/.

Al-Nuʿmānī, Muḥammad. *Kitāb al-ghayba* (Qom: Mehr, n.d.), http://shiaonlinelibrary.com/1281/كتاب-الغيبة-محمد-الكتب-بن-إبراهيم-النعماني-ج-١.

Nūrī, ʿAbdollah. *Showkārān-i iṣlāḥ difāʿiyat-i ʿAbd Allah* Nūrī *dar dādgāh-i vīzheh-i rūḥāaniyat* (Tehrān: Tarh-i now, 1999).

Omīdī, Fāṭima. *Āyīn-i Pāsdārī pīrāmūn vaḥdat, basīj, dushman shināsī* (Tehrān: Nashr-i Shahīd, 1392/2013).

Pārsāniyā, Ḥamīd. "Bar żedd-i feminism," *Kayhān*, 9 Mehr 1384/October 1, 2005.

Pāsokh-dād, Ḥusnī. "Jāygāh-i maṣlaḥat-i ijtimāʿī dar amr beh maʿrūf kojāst/ayā nahyi az munkar bā āzādī sāzgarī dārad," 13 Bahman 1392/2 February 2014, http://www.farsnews.com/newstext.php?nn=13941110000662.

Pazhūhande, Muḥammad Ḥusayn. "Nisbat-i dīn va-āzādī az dīdgāh-i shahīd-i Ayatollah Dr. Beheshtī va-digār-i andīshmandān-i muʿāṣir-i dīnī," https://sarcheshmeh.org/news/ID/554/.

Pūrḥasan, Qāsim. "ʿAql-i āzādī barresī taṭbīqī-i arāʾ-i Murtażā Muṭṭaharī va-Izāyā Berlin," *Maqālāt va-barresīhā* 36, no. 74 (Winter 1382/2003–04), 33–60.

Pūrshafīʿ, Fāṭima. "Jumūd-i fikrī va-qashrī va-taḥajjurī-i Vahhābiyat," 28 Ordībehesht 1395/May 17, 2016, http://yadbiza.mahdiblog.com/article-67.html.

Qarahī, Rūḥollah. "Vīlāyat; kelīd-i uṣūl-i dīn/ramz-i maṣūniyat-i iʿtiqādāt az nufūẕ-i Yahūd chīst?" 26 Mehr 1394/October 18, 2015, http://www.mehrnews.com/news/2942890/.

Qāsimī, Ṣāliḥ. *Āl Saʿyūn: taʾrīkhcheh peydāyesh va-jināyat-i Āl Saʿūd* (Tehrān: Shomārgān, 1395/2016).

Qāsimī, Salmān. *Yahūdiyān banī Isrāʾīl va-farāmāsōnarī* (Iṣfahān: Kiyārād, 1391/2012).

Qazvīnī, Seyyed Muḥammad Ḥusaynī. *Vahhābiyat az manẓar-i ʿaql va-sharʿ* (Qom: Muʾassasa-i taḥqīqāti-i ḥażrat-i valī-i ʿaṣr, 1392/2013).

Qazvīnī, Muḥammad Mahdī. *Imām Mahdī az vilādat tā ẓuhūr* (markaz-i taḥqīqāt-i rayāneh-i qāʾimiyya Iṣfahān, n.d.).

Qommī, ʿAbbās. *Muntahī al-amāl fī tawārīkh al-nabī wal-āl ʿalayhim al-salām* (Tehrān: Bāqir al-ʿulūm, 1384/2005).

Qoṭbī, Hādī. "Rabīʿ al-Awwal, jashn-i shādī barāye ahl-i bayt ast yā?" *Kheima*, nos. 12–13 (1383/2004), 57–58.

Qūrtānī, Seyyed ʿAlī Ḥusaynī. "Yahūd rā behtar beshenāsīm," 7 Khordād 1391/27 May 2012 http://rasekhoon.net/article/print/213036/.

Rabbānī, Muḥammad. "Negārshī bar tafāvothā-i biyūlūzhīk-i zan va-mard," in *Hamāyesh-i Islam va-feminism*, editor Hādī Vakīlī (Tehrān: daftar-i nashr-i maʿārif, 1381/2002), Vol. 1, 271–286.

Rafīʿī, Maryam. *Imām Khomeini va-Bahāʾiyat* (Tehrān: muʾasasa jam-jam, 1387/2008).

Rahbar, Muḥammad Taqī. "Tamaddun-i gharb dar sarʾāshībī suqūṭ," pt. 1 *Pāsdār-i Islām*, 324 (1387/2008), 1–3.

Rahbar, Muḥammad Taqī. "Tamaddun-i gharb dar sarʾāshībī suqūṭ," pt. 2, *Pāsdār-i Islām*, 326, (1387/2009), 12–15.

Rahdār, Aḥmad. "Barresī-i panj-i naẓariyya dar bāb-i pāyān-i modernīte," *Maʿrifat* 68 (May 16, 2010): 43–59, http://www.hawzah.net/fa/article/articleview/89074.

Raḥmanī, Ḥusayn ʿAlī. "Cherāyī va-chegūnegī naqd-i falsafa-i akhlāq-i femīnīstī," *Pazhūhesh-i zanān* 6, no. 4 (Winter 1387/2009), 109–126.

Raḥmat, Bahār. "Naẓar-i Fūkūyāmā jāponī al-aṣl va-tabaʿ-i Amrīkā dar mowred-i vilāyat-i faqīh," 19 April 2011, http://baharrahmat.mihanblog.com/post/40.

Rāʾifī-Pūr, ʿAlī Akbar. "Vāʿqiʿiyat-i Yahūd setīzī 1," 24 Bahman 1387/12 February 2009, http://antisemitism.blogfa.com/post-1.aspx.

Rāʾīn, Ismāʿīl. *Inshiʿāb pas az marg Showqī Rabbānī* (Tehrān: Muʾasasa-i taḥqīqī-i Rāʾīn, 1978).

Rajabī, ʿAlī. "Farāmāsūnarī, Bahāʾiyat, istiʿmār: ḥużūr-i Bahāʾiyat dar anjumanhā-i māsōnī va-shibh-i māsōnī," http://rasekhoon.net/article/show-84986.aspx.

Rajablū, Ibrāhīm. "Jang-i Ravānī-i ṣahyūnīsm, mafāhīm va-mażamīn," *Ḥawza*, 189, 28 Mordād, 1385/August 19, 2006.

Rajāyī, Amīr Reżā. *Asrār-i Yahūd va-ākhar-i zamān*, (electronic edition, 1396/2017).

Rajāyī Borūjnī, Muḥammad ʿAlī. "ʿAql gerīzī va-ʿadālat setīzī-i Vahhābiyat dar taqābul bā ʿaql gerāyī va-adālat jūyī-i muʿtazila," June 26, 2015, http://maliradjaee.blogfa.com/post/66.

Ranjīr, Maqṣūd. "Falsafa va-siyāsat-i gharb dar andīsheh-i Dāvarī," *Pegāh-i Ḥawza*, 317, (Dey 1390/December 2011), 8–16.

Rashād, ʿAlī Akbar. "Āsīb shināsī-i feminism," *Kitāb-i naqd* 17 (Winter 1379/2001), 34–39.

Rashād, ʿAlī Akbar. "Mowj-i Islam-gerāʾī dar jahān gharb," http://rashad.ir/category/آثار/غرب شناسی/.

Rashād, ʿAlī Akbar. "Tajdīd ḥayāt-i dīnī va-maʿnavīgarāʾi dar gharb muʿāṣir," July 15, 2014, http://rashad.ir/2017/09/13/تجدید-حیات-دینی-و-معنویت‌گرایی-در-غرب/.

Rażavī, Seyyed ʿAbbās. "Shahīd Muṭṭaharī va-ruʾya-iʾ digār tamaddun gharb," *Ḥawza* 105–106 (1380/ 2001): 342–383.

Rażavī, Masʿūd. *Pāyān-i taʾrīkh: Suqūṭ-i gharb va-aghāz-i ʿaṣr-i sevom* (Tehrān: Shafīqī, 1381/2002).

Reżāʾi, Muḥammad Ḥusayn (ed.). *Dushman Shināsī dar Kalām-i Imām-i Khamenei* (Muʾasasa-i farhangī valāʾ-i muntaẓar (aj), 1392/2013).

Reżānezhād, ʿIzz al-Dīn. "Naqd va-barresī-i āyīn-i Bahāʾiyat," *Intiẓār-i mowʿūd* 4 nos. 12–13 (Spring–Summer 1383/2005), 533–546.

Riżvānī, ʿAlī Aṣghar. *Raftār-i Vahhābiyān bā Musalmānān* (Iṣfahān: Markaz-i taḥqīqāt-i rayāneh-i qāʾimiyya, 1341/1962).

Riżvānī, ʿAlī Aṣghar. *Khodāyī mujassam-i Vahhābiyat* (Iṣfahān: Markaz taḥqīqāt rayāneh-i qāʾimiyya, n.d.).

Riżvānī, ʿAlī Aṣghar. *Salafīgarī (Vahhābiyat) va-pāsokh beh shubuhāt* (Iṣfahān: Markaz-i taḥqīqāt-i rayāneh-i qāʾimiyya, n.d.).

Riżvānī, ʿAlī Aṣghar. *Shenākht-i Salafīhā (Vahhābiyat)* (Iṣfahān: Markaz-i taḥqīqāt-i rayāneh-i qāʾimiyya, 1341/1962).
Roknī, Seyyed Muḥammad Bāqir. *Akhlāq-i Yahūdī va-tamaddun-i gharb* (Tehrān: Nashr, 2010).
Rowshan, Amīr & Muḥsin Shafīʿī Sayfabādī. "Tafsīr-i dīn va-taʾthīr-i ān bar mafhūm-i āzādī dar andīsheh-i siyāsī-i ayatallah Muḥammad Taqī Miṣbāḥ-i Yazdī va-Muḥammad Mojtahed Shabestari," *Pazhūhesh-i siyāsat-i naẓarī* 6 (Winter 1389/2010 & Spring 1390/ 2011), 21–43.
Rūdgār, Narjes. *Feminism: taʾrīkhcheh, naẓarīyat, gerāyeshhā, naqd* (Qom: Daftar-i muṭālaʿāt va-taḥqīqāt-i zan, 1388/2009).
Rūḥānī, Ḥusayn. "Furūpāshī-i Amrīkā vāqiʿiyatī-i maḥtūm," *Kayhān*, 6 Khordād 1393/ May 27, 2014.
Rūḥānī, Ḥusayn. Ḥusayn. "Dāneshgāh-i farāmūshī inḥiṭāṭ-i gharb," *Kayhān*, 4 Shahrīvar 1393/August 26, 2014.
Rūzbehānī, ʿAlī Reżā. *Taḥlīl va-naqd-i Bahāʾiyat* (Qom: Markaz-i pazhūheshhā-i Islāmī ṣedā va-simāyī jumhūrī-i Islāmī-i Iran, 1389/2010).
Al-Sabʿānī, Saʿūd. "Aṣl-i Āl Saʿūd al-majhūl wa-yahūdiyat nasabihim," http://altaghyeer1.3abber.com/post/156225.
Ṣābirī, Maʿṣūma. "Naqd konvension-i rafʿ-i kulīye-i ashkāl-i tabʿīż ʿalayh-i zanān," *Ẓuhūran* 13 (Summer 1391/2012), 145–168.
Ṣabūrī, Mujtabā. "Barresī-i irtibāṭ-i khavārij bā Vahhābiyat," 19 Tīr 1393/July 10, 2014, http://rasekhoon.net/article/show/918275.
Sādāt, Seyyed Aḥmad. "Vahhābiyat pedar-i Dāʿesh, yār-i ṣahyūnīsm," 30 Khordad 1394/ June 20, 2015, http://parstoday.com/fa/iran-i81226.
Ṣādiqī, Maryam. "Naẓar-i Imām dar mowred-i anjuman-i Ḥojjatiya," *Kayhān*, 4 Mehr 1391/September 25, 2012.
Ṣādiqī Fasāʾī, Suheylā. "Chālesh-i feminism bā mādarī," *Muṭālaʿāt-i rāhbordī-i zanān* 28 (1384/2005), 19–43.
Ṣādiqī Fasāʾī, Suheylā et al. *Feminism va-khānevādeh* (Tehrān: Shūrā-i farhangī-i ijtimāʿī-i zanān 1386/2007).
Ṣadrā, ʿAlī Reżā. "Āsīb-i shināsī-i jahānī-shodan va-jahānīsāzī bā model jahānīgerāʾī-i mahdaviyat," *Qabasāt*, 33 (Spring 1383/2004): 155–176, http://ensani.ir/fa/article/7278/.
Ṣadrā, ʿAlī Reżā & Muḥammad Muḥsin Sharʿī. "Mafhūm-i sharq va-gharb dar Fardīd," *Siyāsat* 40, no. 2 (Summer 1389/2010).
Ṣadūq, Shaykh. *Kamāl al-dīn wa-tamām al-niʿma* (Qom: Muʾassasat al-nashr al-Islāmī, 1363/1984).
Sajjādī, ʿAbd al-Quyūm. "Jahānī-shodan va-mahdaviyat: dō nigāh beh āyandeh," *Qabasāt* 33 (Spring 1383/2004): 129–142.

Salīmī, Ismāʿīl. "Āzādī az dīdgāh-i ustād-i Muṭṭaharī," pt. 1, *Andisheh-i ḥawza*, 60 (1385/2006), 101–144.

Salmānpūr, Muḥammad Javād. "Dushman shināsī va-dushman setīzī az dīdgāh-i Imām (rh)," *Miṣbāḥ* 7:30 (1378/1999), 59–83.

Ṣamadī, Qanbar ʿAlī. "Doktrīn-i mahdaviyat va-naẓarīyat-i pāyān-i ta'rīkh: vīzhegīhā va-tafāvothā," 19 Mordād 1390/August 10, 2011, http://www.intizar.ir/vdcgrq934ak93.pra.html (Last accessed June 11, 2012).

Al-Samāwī, Muḥammad Niʿma. *Al-ʿAṣr al-Wahhābī: qirā'āt fī adab al-taṭṭaruf* (Beirut: Dār al-kutub al-ta'rīkhiyya, 1436h/2010).

Samīʿī Iṣfahānī, ʿAlī Reżā & Yaʿqub Karīmī Menjarmuʿe. "Pāyān ta'rīkh yā boḥrān-i idī'ūlūzhī," *Dānesh Siyāsī va-beyn milalī* 1 (Spring 1391/2012), 1–27.

Sanchūlī, Zaynab. "Tabyīn-i mahiyat-i algū-i Islāmī Irānī pīshraft," *Alguyi pīshraft Islāmī Irānī* 2, no. 3 (1392/2013): 79–104.

Shafīʿī Māzanderānī, Muḥammad. "Feminism va-jāygāh-i zan dar Islam," *Majala-i payām-i ḥawza* 25 (Spring 1379/2000), http://www.hawzah.net/fa/Magazine/View/4210/4231/27770.

Shafīʿī Sarvestānī, Ismāʿīl. *Dāneshestān-i sarzamīnhā-i dargīr dar vāqiʿa-i sharīf-i ẓuhūr* (Tehrān: 1391/2012).

Shafīʿī Sarvestānī, Ismāʿīl. "Gharb va-ākhar al-zamān," (2002), http://www.iec-md.org/farhangi/gharb_aakherozzamaan_shafiei-sarvestaani.html.

Shafīʿī Sarvestānī, Ismāʿīl. "Naqsh-i Yahūd dar vāqiʿa-i Karbalā'," 13 Mehr 1395/October 4, 2016, https://www.ourpresident.ir/analysis/report/-مهم-نقش-یهود-در-واقعه-کربلا-2.

Shahbāzī, ʿAbdollah. "Justārīhā az ta'rīkh-i bahāyīgerā'ī dar Iran," *Ta'rīkh-i muʿāṣir-i Iran* 27 (1382/2003): 1–54.

Shahbāzī, Muḥammad Ṣādiq. "Āzādī az dīdgāh-i Imām-i Khomeini," 24 Tīr 1391/July 14, 2012, http://www.teribon.ir/archives/114286.

Shāhdīn, Ḥamīd Javādānī. "Darāmadī bar shenākht-i abʿād-i tahājum-i farhangī va-naḥwa-i muqābala bā ān," *Rūsh shināsī-i ʿulūm-i insānī* 35 (1382/2003): 85–104.

Shāhrūdī, Seyyed Muḥammad Ḥusaynī. "Rūz-i nohom-i māh-i Rabīʿ al-awwal: qatl-i ʿUmar bin Khattāb laʿanahu Allah," http://www.shahroudi.com/Portal.aspx?pid=71309&Cultcure=Persian&CaseID=4822.

Sharīʿat, Farshād and Mahdī Nādirī Bābānārī. "Āzādī dar andīsheh-i Ayatollah Murtażā Muṭṭaharī va-Izāyā Berlin," *Tamāshāgah-i Rāz* 1 (Spring 1391/2012): 107–130.

Sharīʿatī Sabzivārī, Muḥammad Bāqir. "Irtidād," *Maʿārif-i Islāmī* (Azar-Dey-Bahman va-Esfand 1384/December 2005, January–March 2006), 56–59.

Sharīʿatmadārī Jazāyirī, Seyyed Nūr al-Dīn. "Mabānī-i āzādī dar kalām va-fiqh-i Shīʿī," *ʿUlūm-i siyāsī* 3 (Winter 1377/1999): 3–4.

Sharīfī, Saʿīd. "Bahā'iyat va-siyāsat," *Faṣlnāmah-i muṭālaʿāt-i ta'rīkhī* 32 (Spring 1390/2011): 121–147.

Shīrūdī, Murtażā. "Inqilāb-i Islāmī va-chīstī niẓām-i āyandeh-i jahānī," *Ḥuṣūn* 11 (Spring 2007): 42–65, http://www.ensani.ir/fa/content/122667/default.aspx.

Shūrā-i amr beh maʿrūf va-nahyi az munkar shahrdārī-i Mashhad. "Amr beh maʿrūf va-nahyi az munkar chīst?," https://marouf.mashhad.ir/portal_content/1042556 -امر-معروف-نهی-منکر-چیست.html.

Subḥānī, Jaʿfar. "Irtidād va-āzādī-i andīsheh," http://www.shafaqna.com/persian/services/religious-questions/item/20252-ارتداد-و-آزادی-اندیشه?tmpl=component&print=1.

Subḥānī, Jaʿfar. "Irtidād va-āzādī-i bayān," https://rasekhoon.net/article/show/670338/.

Subḥānī, Jaʿfar. *Al-Salafiyya: taʾrīkhān mafhūman hadafan* (Qom: Muʾassassat Imām Ṣādiq, 1388/2009).

Subḥānī, Jaʿfar. "Taftīsh ʿaqāyid dar dīn mamnūʿ ast," 30 Tīr 1389/July 21, 2010, https://www.isna.ir/news/8904-16421/آیت-الله-العظمي-سبحاني-تفتيش-عقايد-در-دين-ممنوع-است-ارتداد.

Subḥānī, Jaʿfar. *Tahdhīb al-uṣūl: taqrīrāt dars al-Imām al-Khumaynī* (Qom, 1363/1984).

Subḥānī, Jaʿfar. *Vahhābiyat mabānī-i fikrī va-kārnāmah-i ʿamalī* (Qom: Muʾasasa-i Imām Ṣādiq, 1388/2009).

Sorūsh, Muḥammad. "Āyā irtidād kīfar 'ḥadd' dārad? (Taʾammolī bar mahiyat-i kīfar irtidād)," *Ḥukūmat-i Islāmī*, 19 (1380/2001), http://ensani.ir/fa/article/83786/آیا-ارتداد-کیفر-حدّ-دارد-تأملی-بر-ماهیت-کیفر-ارتداد.

Sotūdeh, Nayreh. "Feminism-i farāmodern va-feminism-i Islāmī," *Howrāʾ* 5 (1383/2004), http://www.ensani.ir/fa/content/109004/default.aspx.

Sulaymān, Kāmil. *Rūzegār-i Rāhhāyī* (Tehrān: Afāq, 1386/2007).

Sulṭān-Shāhī, ʿAlī Reżā. *Yahūd setīzī (anti Semitism) vāqiʿiyat yā dastavīz-i siyāsī* (PhD dissertation, Dāneshgāh-i Āzād Islami, 1381/2002).

Ṭabāṭabāʾī, Muḥammad Reżā. "Naqsh-i jarayān-i Masīḥī-Yahūdī dar tarbiyat-i Yazīd," 15 Abān 1393/November 6, 2014, http://www.farsnews.com/printable.php?nn=13930812000133.

Ṭāhirzādeh, Aṣghar. *ʿIlal-i tazalzul-i tamaddun-i gharb* (Iṣfahān: Lub al-Mīzān, 1388).

Al-Ṭāʾī, Najāḥ. *Faḍāʾiḥ-i Yahūd mutalabbisūn bil-Islām* (Beirut-London: Dār al-hudā li-iḥyāʾ al-turāth, 1422/2001).

Ṭāʾib, Mahdī. "Yahūd dushman-i dīrīnah-i Islam," *Mowʿūd* 57 (1384/2005), 14–19.

Ṭāʾib, Mahdī et al. *Tabār-i inḥirāf: pazhūheshī dar dushmanʾshināsī-i taʾrīkhī* (Qom: Muʾasasa-i farhangī valāʾ-i muntaẓar, 1390/2011).

Ṭālib-nezhād, ʿAlī Aṣghar, Seyyed Muḥammad ʿAlī Taqavī, and Ranjkesh, Muḥammad Javād. "Vakāvī-i dīdgāh-i ayatollah Muṭṭaharī dar mowred-i tamaddun-i modern-i gharb va-chegūnegī taʾamol bā ān," *Pazhūheshī naẓariyahā-i ijtimāʿī mutafakkirān-i musalmān* 8, no. 2 (1397/2018): 109–130.

Taqavī, Seyyed Muṣṭafā. "Bahāʾiyat va-siyāsat, ʿadam mudākhala dar siyāsat," *Faṣlnāmah-i muṭālaʿāt-i taʾrīkhī* 17 (Summer 1386/2007), 179–188.

Taqavī, Seyyed Muṣṭafā. “Imām Khomeini va-shāgerdhā-i imperialism,” *Zamāneh* 61 (1386/2007).

Tavānā, Muḥammad ʿAlī. “Islam va-naẓarīyat-i pāyān-i taʾrīkh,” *Taʾrīkh dar āyīnah-i pazhūhesh* 8, no. 3 (2011): 71–86.

Ṭaybī, Zinat & Maryam ʿAhdī. “Feminism va-hamjinsgerāʾī,” 4 Azar 1390/November 25, 2011, http://www.siasatrooz.ir/prtceeqe.2bqoe8laa2.html.

Tehrānī, Muḥammad Ḥusayn. *Risāla-i badīʿa* (Mashhad: Intishārāt-i ʿalāma Tabātabāʾi, 1418h/1998).

Towḥīdī, Aḥmad Reżā. “Barresī-i jonbesh-i feminism dar gharb va-Iran,” in *Hamāyesh-i Islam va-feminism* Vol. 1, editor Hādī Vakīlī (Tehrān: daftar-i nashr-i maʿārif, 1381/2002): 161–188.

Al-Turābī, Ḥasan. “Al-Shūrā wal-dīmuqrāṭiyya: al-muṣṭalaḥ wal-mafhūm,” *al-Mustaqbal al-ʿArabī* 75 (May 1985): 4–23.

Ṭūsī, Muḥammad. *Kitāb al-ghayba* (Beirut: Muʾassasat ahl al-bayt, 1987).

Vāʿizī, Ḥasan. “Shikl gīrī-i ṭarḥ-i furūpāshī-i shūrāvī hazīnehā-i khārijī va-dākhilī,” 7 Esfand 1386/February 26, 2008, http://www.rasekhoon.net/article/show-2934.aspx.

Vakīlī, Hādī. “Naqd-i mabānī-i umanīstī-i ḥuqūq-i bashar-i gharbī,” *Kitāb-i naqd* 36 (1384/2005): 129–154.

Vakīlī, Hādī (ed.). *Hamāyesh-i Islām va-feminism*, Vols. I & II, (Tehrān: daftar-i nashr-i maʿārif, 1381/2002).

Valīzādeh, Ismāʿīl. “Tahājum-i farhangī va-rāhhā-i muqābala bā ān,” *Maʿārif,* 69 (1388/2009) https://hawzah.net/fa/Magazine/View/5211/7149/87155.

Vīlāyatī, ʿAlī Akbar. *Irān wa-*falasṭīn *(1867–1937), judhūr al-ʿalāqa wa-taqallubāt al-siyāsa* (Beirut: Dār al-Ḥaqq, 1997).

Yaḥyā, Hārūn. “Dāstān-i ḥaqīqī-i Qābāla,” *Mowʿūd*, 62 (1385/2006), 34–39.

Yāqūt, Mājida Aḥmad Sulaymān. *Fatḥ al-bārī fī sharḥ Ṣaḥīḥ al-Bukhārī: dirāsa fī al-manhaj wa-al-maṣādir* (Alexandria: Dār al-Maʿrifah al-Jāmiʿīyah, 2014), Vol. 15.

Yūsufī Gharavī, Muḥammad Hādī. “Naqsh-i maṭāʿin-i biḥār al-anwār dar khorāfa-i nohom Rabīʿ al-awwal,” 24 Dey 1392/January 14, 2014, http://dinonline.com/doc/news/fa/3188/.

Zāhidī, Muḥammad Taqī. “Taʾrīkhcheh tharwat andūzī-i zarsālārān-i Yahūd,” 22 Azar 1392/13 December 2013, http://www.mashreghnews.ir/news/270442.

Zamānī, Maḥmūd. “Gharb az aghāz tā pāyān,” http://rasekhoon.net/article/show/764209.

Zamānī, Shihāb. “Naqd va-barresī-i feminism va-payāmadhā-i ān (pt. 1),” 17 Khordād 1391/June 6, 2012, http://basirat.ir/fa/print/238441.

Zamānī, Shihāb. “Naqd va-barresī-i feminism va-payāmadhā-i ān (pt. 5),” 17 Khordād 1391/June 6, 2012, http://basirat.ir/fa/print/239938.

Zamānī, Shihāb. “Naqd va-barresī-i feminism va-payāmadhā-i ān (pt. 6),” 17 Khordād 1391/June 6, 2012, http://basirat.ir/fa/news/239969.

Zamānī, Shihāb. "Naqd va-barresī-i feminism va-payāmadhā-i ān" (pt. 7), 21 Khordād 1391/June 10, 2012, http://basirat.ir/fa/news/241074.

Zamānī Musāvī, Rūḥollah. "Iqdāmāt va-barnāmahhā-i ṣahyūnīsm dar taqābul āmūzeh-i mahdaviyat dar ḥawza-i siyāsat va-ijtimāʿ," http://mahdimag.ir/fa/Magazine/articlemagz/اقدامات وبرنامه های صهیونیزم در تقابل با آموزه مهدویت درحوزه سیاست و اجتماع13950815.

Zarshenas, Shāhriar. "Mahiyat-i modernīte," http://enzargroup.blogfa.com/post-43.aspx.

Zībāyī-nezhād, Muḥammad Reżā. "Khāstgāh-i feminism dar Iran," *Howrāʾ* 38 (1388/2009–2010), http://ensani.ir/fa/article/112010.

Zībāyī-nezhād, Muḥammad Reżā and Ibrāhīm Shafīʿī Sarvestānī. "Goftemān-i femīnīstī dar Iran: negāreshhā va-taḥlīlhā," *Howrāʾ* 27 (1387/2008), http://ensani.ir/fa/article/111302.

Zībāyī-nezhād, Muḥammad Reżā and Muḥammad Taqī Subḥānī. *Darāmadī bar niẓām-i shakhsiyat-i zan dar Islam* (Tehrān: Daftar-i muṭālaʿāt va-taḥqīqāt-i zanān, 1381/2002).

Zorgān, Farukhandeh. "Dushman shināsī az manẓar-i Imām ʿAlī "alayhi al-salām,'" *Kayhan*, 15 Mordad 1385/August 6, 2006.

Al-Zubaydī, ʿAbd al-Karīm. *ʿAṣr al-Sufyānī* (Beirut: Dār al-Hādī, 2006).

Al-Zuʿbī, al-Arqam. "Ḥaqāyiqī dar bārah-i Yahūdiyat," *Maʿrifat* 74 (1382/2004), 57–65.

Al-Zuhaylī, Wahba. "Āzādī-i andīsheh va-goftār az manẓar-i adyān va-farhanghā," *Ḥawza* 128–129 (Spring 1384/2005), http://jh.isca.ac.ir/article_1055.html.

Ẕākīrī, ʿAlī Akbar. "Dīn va-āzādī az dīdgāh-i shahīd-i Muṭṭaharī," *Ḥawza* 97 (1377/2000), 112–144.

Ẕū al-Qadr, Muḥammad Bāqir. *Qiṣṣa-i ghurbat-i gharbī: goftārī dar mabānī-i farhang va-tamaddun-i gharb* (Tehrān: Dāneshgāh-i farmāndehī va-setād dowra-i ʿālī-i jang, 1381/2002).

Anonymous Authors

"Aghāz-i intiẓār-i taʾrīkh," http://karbarayezohor.blogfa.com/post/39.

"Ahdāf-i Inglīs az āfarīnesh-i firqa-i Vahhābiyat," http://bcir.pchi.ir/show.php?page=contents&id=9619.

"Ahdāf-i istiʿmār az ʾījād firqa-i Vahhābiyat va-nīz rābiṭa beyne Vahhābiyat va-Yahūd," http://www.vahabiat.porsemani.ir/content/اهداف-استعمار-از-ایجاد-فرقۀ-وهابیت-و-نیز-رابطه-بین-وهابیت-و-یهود.

"Ahdāf-i keshvarhā-i gharbī az tahājum-i farhangī," 16 Dey 1391/January 11, 2013 – http://www.siasi.porsemani.ir/node/1738.

"Ahdāf-i prōzhe-i ṣahyūnīstī-i Dāʿesh cheh būd? + film va-mustanadāt," 30 Abān 1396/November 21, 2017, https://www.yjc.ir/fa/news/6329019.

"Ahl-i Sunnat neveshtehānd ʿUmar bin Khaṭṭāb va-dokhtaresh ʿalāqa-i shadīdī beh torat dāshtand," http://www.antishobhe.blogfa.com/post/124.

"Ahl-i Sunnat va-Yahūd," http://fa.tarikh.org/index.php/نکات-ناب/معاونت-علمی/ITEM/1751-اهل-سنت-و-یهود.

"Ākhar al-zamān va-naqsh-i Irāniān dar dafʿ-i dō fitna-i Yahūd az dīdgāh-i Qurʾān," https://goo.gl/M8Q2Vf.

"Āl Saʿūd beh Yahūdī būdan-i khōd iftikhār mīkonad," June 13, 2016, http://www.shia-news.com/fa/news/120325/.

"Āl Saʿūd Yahūd wa-yantasibūna ilā banī Qaynuqāʿ: al-taʾrīkh yuthbitu yahūdiyat Āl Saʿūd, pt. 1," June 9, 2014. http://aljamahir.amuntada.com/t27969-topic.

"ʿAlāmāt al-ẓuhūr," http://ar.wikishia.net/view/علامات_الظهور.

"ʿAlāmāt ẓuhūr al-Imām al-Mahdī al-kubrā allatī taḥaqqaqat wa-allatī lam tataḥaqqaq li-ḥad al-an," https://groups.google.com/forum/#!msg/alnoorh/z6VDSLPWpW8/3TrgApCwmbIJ.

"ʿAlāqa-i ʿUmar bin Khaṭṭāb beh dīn-i Yahūd," 4 Azar 1391/November 24, 2012, http://tarikhislam1400.blogfa.com/post/24.

"ʿAlī Miṣbāḥ Yazdī: har kes dāneste vilāyat-i faqīh rā inkār konad murtad ast," 24 Khordād 1389/June 14, 2010, http://www.farsnews.com/newstext.php?nn=8903240252.

"ʿAlī Yūnesī: aqaliyathā bāyad ostāndār va-farmandār va-vazīr shavand," 21 Mehr 1392/13 October 2013, http://www.entekhab.ir/fa/news/132846.

"Aligārshī-i Yahūdī va-usṭūra-i inkīzīsion," – 25 Tīr 1395/July 15, 2015, http://www.mouood.org/component/k2/item/36945.

"ʿAmaliyāt-i Yahūd barāye muqābala bā piyāmbar (S) (radpāy-i Yahūd dar ḥavādith-i ṣadr-i Islam)," https://hawzah.net/fa/Article/View/97206.

"Amrīkā va-asāsān 'gharb' rū be-sūye furūpāshī pīsh mīravad," 10 May 2011, http://u313yasin.blogfa.com/post-100.aspx.

"Angīzeh Abū Lūʾlūʾ dar qatl khalīfa-i dovom cheh būd?," http://shahramrasti.blogfa.com/post-82.aspx.

"Anjuman-i Ḥojjatiya va-Bahāʾiyat; dō rūye yek sekeh!" May 30, 2016, https://www.parsnews.com/بخش-سیاسی-3/369584-انجمن-حجتیه-بهائیت-دو-روی-یک-سکه.

"Ānūsī chīst va-cherā bāyad muslimīn ānūsīhā rā beshenāsad," 31 Mehr 1389/October 23, 2010, http://www.andishehha.com/view/6048.

"ʿAqāʾid-i siyāsī-i Bahāʾiyat mutaʾthir az gerāyeshāt fāshīstī ast," 28 Mehr 1387/October 19, 2008, https://www.farsnews.com/news/8707160379.

"ʿAql-i setīzī va-ʿilm-i setīzī dar Bahāʾiyat," 26 Dey 1394/January 16, 2016, http://ferghenews.com/fa/news/4926/عقل-ستیزی-و-علم-ستیزی-در-بهائیت.

"Ashnāʾī bar jarayānhā-i aṣlī-i femīnīstī dar Irān," 16 Mehr 1390/October 8, 2008, http://www.farsnews.com/newstext.php?nn=13900716000477.

"Ashnā'ī va-iṭṭilā'ātī dar Bahā'iyat," http://www.adyan.porsemani.ir/content/-آشنایی-و-اطلاعاتی-در-بهائیت.
"Āsīb shināsī-i ta'rīkh-i Islām va-naqsh-i Yahūd dar ān," http://analytichistory.blogfa.com/post-3.aspx.
"Asl-i āzādī-i 'aqīda," 14 Dey 1395/January 3, 2017, http://www.andisheqom.com/public/application/index/viewData?c=51&t=shobhe.
"Asrār-i farāmāsōnhā: Yahūdiyān farāmāsōn chegūneh jahān rā idāra mīkonand?" 18 Khordād 1396/8 June 2017, http://www.historywonders.ir/2017/06/08/.
"Āyā amr beh ma'rūf va-nahyi az munkar bā aṣl āzādī dar ta'āruż nīst?" http://rasekhoon.net/faq/show/485765.
"Āyā Āya sharīfa lā ikrāh fī al-dīn, bā ḥukm-i i'dām barāye murtad munāfat nadārad?," http://www.andisheqom.com/public/application/index/viewData?c=11028&t=qa.
"Āyā Bahā'iyat firqa būdeh va-az firqahā-i Islāmī maḥsūb mīshavad?," http://rasekhoon.net/faq/show/782603.
"Āyā Bahā'iyat murtad ast?," http://adyan.porsemani.ir/content/ارتداد-بهائیت.
"Āyā behtar nīst bejāyi barā'at az dushmanān-i a'īmah ḥisāb-i ānhā rā beh khodā vāgoẕār konīm?," http://www.rahejanat.blogfa.com/post/32.
"Āyā Dā'esh hemān sufyānī ast?" 26 Dey 1393/January 15, 2015, https://www.farsnews.com/news/13931024001094/آیا-داعش-همان-سفیانی-است.
"Āyā Da'esh hemān sufyānī ast?," 9 Khordād 1394/May 30, 2015, https://mouood.org/component/k2/item/29783.
"Āyā gharb az ban-bast idī'ūlūzhīk khārij mīshavad?," December 24, 2012, https://www.bultannews.com/fa/news/116796/.
"Āyā ibn Muljam Yahūdī būd?" 28 Tīr 1393/July 19, 2014, https://www.farsnews.com/printnews/13930427000047.
"Āyā Imām-i Mahdī (aj) hangām-i ẓuhūresh bā Masīḥiyān va-Yahūdiyān sulḥ mīkonad va-ba 'Arabhā mījangad?," http://hajj.ir/fa/83858.
"Āyā irtibāṭ-i musalmānān bā Bahā'iyat jāyiz ast?," http://www.porseman.org/q/vservice.aspx?logo=images/right.jpg&id=89512.
"Āyā Islam bā naẓrat-i maktab-i feminism muvāfiq ast?," http://www.porseman.org/q/show.aspx?id=130250.
"Āyā i'tiqādāt-i Bahā'iyat bā mavāzin-i 'ilmī va-'aqlī munṭabiq ast?," http://andisheqom.com/fa/Question/View/9171 – last accessed April 17, 2017.
"Āyā marāsimī-i mawsūm be "Umarkoshūn' muṭābiq shar' ast?" 24 Dey 1392/January 14, 2013, http://kashannews.net/1392/10/24/.
"Āyā Shī'a Abū Bakr va-'Umar rā kāfir mīdānad?" 22 Khordād 22, 1397/June 12, 2018, http://www.islamquest.net/fa/archive/question/fa2982.
"Āyā Yahūdiyān dar dowran-i ẓuhūr nābūd mīshavand?" 24 Bahman 1393/February 13, 2015, http://www.farsnews.com/printable.php?nn=13931121000429.

"Āyā Yahūdiyān va-Masīḥiyān dar ʾījād ḥāditha-i ʿĀshūrāʾ va-shahādat-i Imām Ḥusayn (a) naqsh dāshtand?," http://www.islamquest.net/fa/archive/question/fa63714.

"Ayatollah ʿAbd al-Ḥamīd Maʿṣūmī Tehrānī: khuṣūmat bā Bahāʾīyān rā konār begoẕārīm," 1 Ordībehesht 1393/April 21, 2014, https://www.peace-mark.org/آیت‌الله-عبدالحمید-معصومی-تهرانی-خصوم.

"Ayatollah Arākī: tashayyuʿ-i londonī buzurgtarīn-i khaṭar barāye Islām va-Shīʿa ast," 5 Esfand 1393/February 24, 2015, http://hajj.ir/fa/51467.

"Ayatollah Bourūjerdī va-mubāraza bā Bahāʾīhā," http://www.broujerdi.ir/index.php/2016-03-22-09-01-51/2016-03-22-09-05-56/260-2016-03-26-04-19-40.

"Ayatollah Jaʿfar Subḥānī: mushkil-i Isrāʾīliyyāt dar ḥadīth, bekhāṭir-i bidʿathā-i ṣadr-i Islam ast," 27 Tīr 1390/January 17, 2012, http://www.hawzah.net/fa/News/View/88892-آیت-الله-سبحانی-مشکل-اسرائیلیات-در-حدیث-بخاطر-بدعت-های-صدر-اسلام-است/?SearchText=اسرائیلیات&LPhrase=.

"Ayatollah Javādī Āmolī: Amrīkāʾīhā ʿaql nadārand," October 21, 2012, http://www.asriran.com/fa/news/237623.

"Ayatollah Khōshvaqt: Mūsavī va-Karrūbī, murtad va-kāfirand," January 2, 2013, http://rahedigar.net/1391/10/13/7577/.

"Ayatollah Makārem Shīrāzī: Takfīrīhā buzurgtarīn-i tahdīd barāye jahān-i Islam hastand," 15 Shahrīvar 1395/September 5, 2015, https://www.mehrnews.com/news/3770245.

"Ayatollah Makārem Shīrāzī: ʿUlamāʾ-i Islam bā ṣedā-i boland az takfīr barāʾat jūyand," 8 Bahman 1394/January 28, 2016, http://hajj.ir/84/65199.

"Ayatollah Qabalān: Takfīr ghīdeh-i sarṭānī-i minṭaqa," 24 Dey 1394/January 14, 2016, http://www.shia-news.com/fa/news/109817.

"Ayatollah Qarahī: Abā Sufyān va-Muʿāwiya musalmān na-būdand/Barresī-i ʿilal-i ʿĀshūrāʾ va-taʾrīkh-i Karbalāʾ," 29 Mehr 1394/October 21, 2015, http://www.mehrnews.com/news/2946109.

"Ayatollah Ṣāfī-Golpāygānī: Ḥaqīqat-i vaḥdat in nīst ke Shīʿa va-sunnī az ʿaqāyed-i khōd dast bardārand," 29 Dey 1392/19 January 2014, http://shiayan.ir/3826.

"Ayatollah Sistānī fatvā-i jihād ṣādir kard," 23 Khordād 1393/June 13, 2014, https://hawzah.net/fa/News/View/97209.

"Ayatollah Sistānī: ẓuhūr-i 'Dāʿesh' hīch rabṭī beh sufyānī nadārad"; 29 Mordād 1393/August 20, 2014, http://iusnews.ir/fa/news-details/139581.

"Ayatollah Subḥānī: farzand-i kamtar zindigī behtar, shiʿārī Yahūdī va-bar khīlāf-i Islām ast," 15 Shahrīvar 1389/September 6, 2010, http://www.irna.ir/fa/NewsPrint.aspx?ID=2000621401.

"Ayatollah Subḥānī hoshdār dād: barnāmah vīzheh-i Masīḥiyat, Bahāʾiyat va-żede inqilāb barāye tarvīj-i badḥijābī," May 1, 2012, https://www.farsnews.com/news/13910212001099.

"Ayatollah Ṭāliqānī Bahā'iyat rā shikl-i digār-i ṣahyūnīsm dar keshvar mīdānast," http://zionism.pchi.ir/show.php?page=contents&id=5252.

"Ayatollah al-ʿuzma Vaḥīd Khorāsānī: Laʿn ʿalanī jāyiz nīst + film," 27 Dey 1393/January 17, 2015, http://www.fetan.ir/home/4247.

"Ayatollah Vaḥīd Khorāsānī: Qur'ān, bashar rā as ifrāṭ wa-tafrīṭ dar mowred-i ʿĪsā najāt mīdahad," 24 Farvardīn 1390/April 13, 2011, https://www.isna.ir/news/9001-09767/آیت-الله-وحید-خراسانی-قرآن-بشر-را-از-افراط-و-تفریط-در-مورد.

"Az feminism-i jahānī tā feminism-i Irānī/ nigāhī-i kul girāyāneh beh jonbesh va-naẓariyya-i feminism dar Irān va-jahān," *Howrā'* 27 (1387/2008), http://www.hawzah.net/fa/Magazine/View/6432/6664/78751.

"Az kāravānhā-i laʿn va-sabb tā ḥużūr gostardeh dar shabakahā-i mujāzī," 2 Dey 1394/December 23, 2015, https://qademon.ir/?p=1856.

"Az nā-barābirī-i ḥuqūq-i zanān-i Bahā'ī tā ʿadam-i riʿāyat-i ḥuqūq-i insānī dar Bahā'iyat," http://bahairesearch.org/article/از-نابرابری-حقوق-زنان-بهائی-تا-عدم-رعایت-حقوق-انسانی-در-بهائیت.

"Āzādī-i ʿaqīda va-bayān va-ḥuqūq-i bashar va-ḥukm-i irtidād chegūneh bā ham jamʿ mīshavad," http://masjedaliasghar.ir/?p=3003.

"Āzādī-i ʿaqīda dar Islām," 15 Mordād 1388/August 6, 2009, https://article.tebyan.net/98833/آزادی-عقیده-در-اسلام.

"Āzādī-i bayān va-iʿdām-i murtad," http://www.adyan.porsemani.ir/content/آزادی-بیان-و-اعدام-مرتد.

"Āzādī az cheh? barāye cheh?" *Dīdār-i Āshinaā* 20 (1380/2002), http://www.hawzah.net/fa/Magazine/View/114/4444/31323.

"Āzādī az dīdgāh-i Imām-i Khomeini," 24 Tīr 1391/July 14, 2012, http://www.teribon.ir/archives/114286\.

"Āzādī va-irtidād," *Maʿārif*, 47 (1386/2007), 32–35.

"Baʿd al-marjaʿ faḍlallah, al-sayyid ʿAlī al-Khamene' yuḥarrimu al-isā'a li-rumūz ikhwāninā al-sunna zawjāt al-nabī wal-ṣaḥāba," September 28, 2010, https://urlzs.com/2XrHt.

"Badl sāzī-i Dāʿesh bā sufyānī va-ghiflat az dushman-i aṣlī," 25 Khordād 1393/June 15, 2014, https://www.tasnimnews.com/fa/news/1393/03/25/401992.

"Bahā'īyān: Ayatollah al-ʿuzma Makārem," http://portal.anhar.ir/node/2171#gsc.tab=0.

"Bahā'iyat az naẓar-i marājiʿ ʿuẓẓām-i taqlīd," 26 Ordībehesht 1395/May 15, 2016 http://www.qomefarda.ir/news/186298.

"Bahā'iyat, maẕhab-i istiʿmār sākhte barāye muqābala bā Islam," *Jumhūrī-i Islāmī*, Bahman 26, 1382/February 5, 2004.

"Bahā'iyat yek tahdīd-i jeddī barāye javānān ast," 13 Azar 1390/4 November 2012, http://www.farsnews.com/printable.php?nn=13900912001424.

"Banī Umayya va-Yahūd," 25 Tīr 1395/July 15, 2016, http://www.mouood.org/component/k2/item/36944.

"Barresī-i intiqādī chend shiʿār-i Bahā'iyat az dīdgāh-i doktor Muḥammad ʿAlī Khanjī," http://rasekhoon.net/article/show/753374.

"Barresī-i jarayānhā-i femīnīstī Islāmī va-khāstgāh-i ān dar Iran (bakhs-i pāyānī)" – 18 Esfand 1395/March 8, 2017, http://basijnews.ir/fa/print/8836298.

"Barresī-i mafhūm-i āzādī dar andīsheh-i shahīd-i Beheshtī," 4 Tīr 1393/June 27, 2014, http://defapress.ir/fa/news/22136.

"Barresī-i mustanadāt yek jashn-i inḥirāfī," 15 Dey 1393/January 5, 2015, http://www.fetan.ir/home/4016.

"Barresī-i naqsh-i Yahūd dar vāqiʿa-i khūnīn Karbalā'," 24 Abān 1391/November 14, 2012, http://www.598.ir/fa/news/93309.

"Barresī-i nifāq va-khaṭarnaktar az nifāq," 4 Abān 1394/October 26, 2015, http://iusnews.ir/fa/news-details/183224/معاويه-راه-باز-كن-يهود-در-اسلام|-كعب
الاحبار-يار-غار-خليفه-دوم-بود|-قيام-سيدالشهدا-مانع-پا-گرفتن-جريان-خطرناكتر-از-نفاق-
صوت+/.

"Barresī-i shubha-i izdivāj-i ʿUmar bā Umm Kulthūm," http://morajeat.blogfa.com/post-16.aspx.

"Barresī-i yek mas'ala-i muhim-i dunyā-i Islam dar kitāb 'Laʿnhā-i nāmuqaddas'," 29 Mordād 1393/August 20, 2014, http://www.farsnews.com/newstext.php?nn=13930528001308 (Last accessed June 9, 2015).

"Bāyad ḥisāb Vahhābiyat az ahl-i Sunnat jedā shavad," 25 Esfand 1394/March 15, 2016 https://www.hawzahnews.com/news/374778/-بايد-حساب-وهابيت-از
اهل-سنت-جدا-شود-حوزه-در-جبهه-.

"Bayānāt-i Ayatollah Subḥānī (zayyida ʿizzuhu) dar khuṣūṣ Bahā'iyat," 11 Esfand 1394/March 1, 2016, https://www.adyannet.com/fa/news/18146.

"Bāzgesht feminism be ʿarṣeh-i maṭbūʿāt: Bāzkhwānī mavāżiʿ-i iʿtiqādi va-siyāsī-i Shahlā Shirkat + ʿaks," 13 Khordād 1393/June 3, 2014, https://www.mashreghnews.ir/news/314711.

"Begīrad farzand-i zan-i Yahūdī rā," http://masaf.ir/View/Contents/29817/.

"Bidʿat ʿĪd al-Zahrā' be-munāsabat-i nohom Rabīʿ al-awwal," http://asheqi.parsiblog.com/Posts/118 (n.d.).

"Bidʿathā-i ʿUmarkoshān va-Shīʿakoshān! (khorāfa-i nohom Rabīʿ)," http://forum.hammihan.com/thread58463.html.

"Bidʿathā va-iʿtirāżāt-i Abū Bakr va-ʿUmar nisbat beh dīn," http://ama14.blogfa.com/cat-8.aspx.

"Bil-barāhīn. nasab Āl Saʿūd al-Yahūdī," https://www.youtube.com/watch?v=ah8eI1ksYRc.

"Buzurgtarīn-i dushman-i idī'ūlūzhīk-i Islam, Amrīkā ast, yā Inglīs, yā vahhābiyān va-salafiyān," http://www.islamquest.net/fa/archive/question/fa29589.

"Buzurgtarīn-i khiyānat-i ʿUmar dar ḥaqq-i Islām va-muslimīn," *Shīʿa va-Sunnī, pāsokh beh shubhāt-i barādarān-i Sunnī*, http://shiaanswering.blogfa.com/post/130 (accessed 23 March 2019).

"Cheh kesī Yahūdī ast? M'uasses-i Shī'a yā muḥaddith-i sunni?!" http://bedat.blogfa.com.

"Chegūnegī beh vujūd āmadan-i firqa-i Vahhābiyat va-tafāvot-i ān bā digār-i maẕāhib-i ahl-i tasanon," http://www.adyan.porsemani.ir/node/1690.

"Chegūnegī-i koshte shodan 'Umar," 24 Tīr 1392/July 15, 2013, https://www.porseman.com/article/چگونگی- کشته-شدن-عمر/127306.

"Chegūnegī shikl gīrī Vahhābiyat va-tafāvot-i ān bā ahl-i Sunnat" 12 Khordād 1393/June 2, 2014, https://rasekhoon.net/article/show/903822.

"Cherā Bahā'iyat rā nejes mīdānīm va-farq beyne mā va-ānhā dar chīst?," http://old.aviny.com/occasion/jang-narm/bahaeiat/bahaeian-najesand.aspx.

"Cherā dar Islām murtad rā mīkoshānd? Āyā īn kār mukhālif-i āzādī-i 'aqīda ast?," http://www.islamquest.net/fa/archive/question/fa289.

"Cherā feminism beh vujūd āmad? Āyā in jarayān qābil naqd ast?" – http://www.zaviye.net/?p=1944 (accessed October 15, 2017).

"Cherā ibn Muljam qātil Imām 'Alī ('a) shod," 25 Tīr 1394/July 16, 2015, http://snn.ir/fa/news/425891.

"Cherāyī ḥasāsiyat-i 'ulamā' va-buzurgān dar rābiṭa bā Bahā'iyat," 8 Khordād 1395/May 28, 2016, http://hawzahnews.com/TextVersionDetail/380910.

"Chīstī va-cherāyī-i shikl gīrī-i jarayānhā-i takfīrī va-dalāyil-i qudratyābī-i ān dar deheh-i akhīr," 3 Shahrīvar 1395/August 24 2016, http://rasekhoon.net/article/show/1202440.

"Dā'esh chehre-i digār-i Vahhābiyat," http://andisheqom.com/fa/Article/view/1100078.

"Dā'esh irtibāṭi beh qiyām-i 'Sufyānī' nadārad/taṭbīq-i rivāyat-i ẓuhūr-i Imām-i Zamān ('aj) bā zamān-i mu'āṣir khilāf shar' ast," 12 Mordād 1393/August 3, 2014, http://fa.abna24.com/cultural/archive/2014/08/03/628736/story.html.

"Dā'esh negahbān-i Isrā'īl; Isrā'īl Dā'eshī digār," 15 Mordād 1393/August 6, 2014, http://www.shia-news.com/fa/news/76416.

"Dā'esh parchamdārān-i siyāh pūsh ākhar al-zamān?," 18 Shahrīvar 1393/September 9, 2014, https://article.tebyan.net/284586.

"Dā'esh va-idī'ūlūzhī gezīnesh nīrū," April 12, 2014 – http://www.farsnews.com/newstext.php?nn=13931022001323.

"Dā'esh va-jarayān-i takfīrī bar athr-i ta'rīf-i ifrāṭī-i jāhiliyat beh vujūd āmad," 28 Azar 1393/December 19, 2014, https://www.tasnimnews.com/fa/news/1393/09/28/593677.

"Dar mowerd-i naqsh-i Yahūd va-ṣahyūnīsm dar jarayān-i Bahā'iyat," http://bahaismiran.net/index.php/مقالات-بهائیت/item/952-/952.

"Dar mowred-i nufūẕ-i Yahūd dar Islām towżīḥ bedīn," ttp://www.porseshkadeh.com/mob-question/25952.

Group of Authors. *Dānestanīhā-i Vahhābiyat* (Iṣfahān: Markaz-i taḥqīqāt-i rayāneh-i qā'imiyya, n.d.).

Group of Authors. *Darsnāmah-i ta'rīkh-i taḥlīlī-i dushman shināsī* (Qom: Mu'asasa-i Iṭilāʿ rasānī va-Muṭālaʿāt-i Farhangī-i Lawḥ va-Qalam, 1383/2004).

"Dast-i Yahūd va-Naṣārā dar āsatīn-i saqīfa-i nashīnān," http://www.bonyad-mahdi .blogfa.com/cat-45.aspx.

"Dawr al-Yahūd fī al-mu'āmara/Mu'āmarat al-Muslimīn ʿalā al-nabī Muḥammad," September 15, 2013, http://marwan1433.blogspot.co.il/2013/09/11.htm.

"Dīdgāh-i marājiʿ taqlīd-i Shīʿa dar bārah-i aʿmāl-i khorāfī-i rūz-i nohom-i Rabīʿ al-awwal," 2 Bahman 1391/January 21, 2013, http://www.irna.ir/fa/News/80508765.

"Dīdgāh-i marājiʿ taqlīd-i Shīʿa dar bārah-i khorāfa-i benām-i ʿīd al-Zahrā'," 20 Bahman 1391/February 8, 2013, http://www.farsnews.com/newstext.php?nn=13911030001465.

"Dīn va-āzādī dar goftegū bā ayatollah Muḥammad ʿAlāmī Hashtrūdī," *Kayhān*, December 8, 1998.

"Dirāsa ḥawla ẓuhūr wa-burūz wa-ʿaqībat qawm al-Yahūd min manẓar al-Qur'ān al-karīm," September 22, 2009, http://iqna.ir/ar/news/1828520.

"Dō vaʿdeh-i ilāhī dar khuṣūṣ-i sarnevesht-i banī Isrā'īl," 16 Mordād 1394/August 7, 2015, http://2vade.blogfa.com/post/1.

"Dunyā bāzīcheh dast-i Yahūd," http://montazer-mousa.blogfa.com/post/14.

"Duʿā-i Ayatollah Qarahī barāye nābūdī-i Masīḥiyat va-Yahūdīyat," 1 Shahrīvar 1395/ August 22, 2016, http://ashnaie.com/6318/.

"Dushman-i bīrūnī va-durūnī-i inqilāb-i Islāmī," 1 Shahrīvar 1394/August 23, 2015, https://www.farsnews.com/news/13940529000720/.

"Dushman shināsī," http://www.masjed.ir/fa/article/2816/دشمن-شناسی.

"Dushman shināsī az dīdgāh-i maqām-i muʿaẓẓam-i rahbarī (1)," 25 Mehr 1388/ October 17, 2009, https://rasekhoon.net/article/show/145713/(1).

"Dushman shināsī az dīdgāh-i maqām-i muʿaẓẓam-i rahbarī (2)," 25 Mehr 1388/ October 17, 2009 http://rasekhoon.net/article/show/145714-دشمن-شناسی-از/ دیدگاه-مقام-معظم-رهبری-(2).

"Dushman shināsī az manẓar-i maqām-i muʿaẓẓam-i rahbarī," *Maʿārif* 64 (1387/2009), https://hawzah.net/fa/Magazine/View/5211/6900/83079.

"Dushman shināsī va-rāhkārha-i muqābala bā ān az manẓar-i Qur'ān chīst?" http:// www.islamquest.net/fa/archive/question/fa35070.

"Dushmanī-i Yahūd va-bī tavajjuhī-i musalmānān beh takālif-i ijtimāʿī. Baʿith-i ʿadam-i tashkīl-i ḥukūmat-i Islāmī dar dowra-i ghaybat ast," 3 Abān 1394/October 25, 2015, http://vasael.ir/fa/print/1239/-دشمنی-یهود-و-بی-توجهی-مسلمانان-به-تکالیف-اجتماعی، باعث-عدم-تشکیل-حکومت-اسلامی-در-دوره-غیبت-است/.

"Estrātizhī-i Āl Saʿūd dar bārah-i rezhīm-i ṣahyūnīstī," 1 Mordād 1394/July 23, 2015, https://www.teribon.ir/archives/267190.

"Faʿāliyathā-i firqa-i żalla-i Bahā'iyat gheyr qānūnī va-mamnūʿ ast," February 15, 2009, https://www.farsnews.com/news/8711271271/-فعاليتهاي-فرقه-ضاله-بهائيت غير-قانوني-و-ممنوع-است.

“Faʿāliyat-i zīr zamīnī-i Bahā’iyat bā shināsāyī-i sarshākhe-i ān kāmilān motavvaqif shod,” 25 Abān 1389/November 16, 2010, https://www.farsnews.com/news/8908250336 /فعالیت-زیرزمینی-بهائیت-با-شناسایی-سرشاخه‌آن-کاملاً-متوقف-شد.

“Fā’iza Hāshimī az dīdār-i khōd bā mudīr-i jāmiʿa-i Bahā’īyān difāʿ kard,” May 14, 2016, https://bit.ly/2HA6XHH.

“Fā’iza Hāshimī bā kodām bānd ṣahyūnīstī peyvand khōrd?” 26 Ordībehesht 1395/May 15, 2016, https://www.mashreghnews.ir/news/574056.

“Falsafa-i ikhtilāf-i Yahūdiyān bā Shīʿīyān,” 13 Dey 1393/January 3, 2015, http://www.welayatnet.com/fa/news/51395.

“Farākhwān-i rahbar-i inqilāb barāye takmīl va-irtiqāyi algūyī pāyeh-i Islāmī Irānī pīshraft,” 22 Mehr 1397/October 14, 2018, http://farsi.khamenei.ir/news-content?id=40693.

“Farāmāsūnarī chegūneh sāzemānī ast? Cheh nowʿ irtibāṭi bā Bahā’iyat dārad?” http://www.siasi.porsemani.ir/node/1112.

“Farāmāsūnarī farzand-i khwāndeh nā-mashrūʿ-i Yahūd,” http://masoner.persianblog.ir/post/7/.

“Farhang va-tahājum-i farhangī dar āyīne-i rahbar-i inqilāb,” March 29, 2012, http://www.farsnews.com/newstext.php?nn=13910120000657s.

“Fārs: ajdād-i Āl Saʿūd Yahūdiyān-i khaybar hastand,” 9 Farvardīn 1394/March 29, 2015, http://www.parsine.com/fa/news/232655/.

“Fatāwā Shīʿīyya tuḥarrimu sabb al-ṣaḥābah,” November 24, 2006, http://sudaneseonline.com/msg/board/400/msg/1346494097/rn/3.html.

“Fatāwā Shīʿīyya tuḥarrimu sabb al-ṣaḥābah,” *Al-Ahrām*, November 23, 2006.

“Fatvā-i Ayatollah Kāẓim Hā’irī barāye iʿẓām beh Sūriye,” http://www.teribon.ir/archives/246396/.

“Fatvā-i jihād Muqtaḍā Ṣadr ʿalayh-i Dāʿesh,” http://www.trt.net.tr/persian/mntqh/2014/12/11/ftwy-jhd-mqtdy-sdr-lyh-d-sh-145270.

“Feminism chīst?,” 29 Tīr 1395/July 19, 2016, http://www.welayatnet.com/fa/forum/فمینیسم-چیست؟.

“Feminism-i nafsānī-i gharb yā mushārakāt hame-i jānibeh-i Islam,” *Tebyān*, 2 Mordād 1382/July 24, 2003, https://article.tebyan.net/2902.

“Feminism taʿrīf kardeh va-athār-i mukharrib in jonbesh rā bayān konīd,” – http://www.andisheqom.com/fa/Question/View/1113 (accessed November 1, 2017).

“Feminism va-bāztāb-i ān dar jahān-i Islam,” 3 Bahman 1390/January 23, 2012, http://zayeri.blogfa.com/post/97.

“Feminism va-dīdgāh-i Islam dar mowred-i ān” 11 Azar 1390/December 2, 2012, http://siasi.porsemani.ir/node/2109.

“Feminism va-ṣahyūnīsm,” 20 Tīr 1386/July 11, 2007, http://banoo.blogfa.com/post-82.aspx.

"Feminism va-tanaquz dar rāhbordhā," *Howrā'* 17 (1384/2005), http://www.hawzah.net/fa/Magazine/View/6432/6446/73692/.

"Femīnīsthā va-pīshtāzān harzahgerā'ī pīrū-i prōtokol ṣahyūnīsm hastand," 31 Farvardīn 1393/April 20 2013, https://www.isna.ir/news/93013113406.

"Firqa-i inḥirāfī-i Bahā'iyat," http://rasekhoon.net/article/show/187889/-فرقه-انحرافی-بهائیت/.

"Ganjīnah-i Ma'ārif: Āzādī-i 'aqīda" 9 Azar 1389/November 30, 2010, http://www.hawzah.net/fa/Article/View/91773.

"Gharb va-ākhar al-zamān," pt. 2, http://www.mahdaviat.porsemani.ir/content/ -غرب-و-آخرالزمان۲.

"Ghulāt al-Wahhābiyya yad'ūna ilā man' al-Muslimīn min irtiyād al-mawāqi' al-Islāmiyya al-mashhur wa-tahdīmihā wa-tasayyujīhā," January 5, 2009, http://burathanews.com/arabic/news/57083.

"Goftār-i pīshīn: cherā bāyad gharb rā shenākht," July 11, 2006, http://www.tebyan.net/index.aspx?pid=24112.

"Goftegū-i 'Alī Khalīl Ismā'īl bā dustān-i javān dar masjid Imām-i Sajjād 'alayhi al-salām," – http://atm.parsiblog.com/Posts/119/.

"Gozāresh-i Fārs az neshest-i 'naqsh-i Yahūd dar vāqi'a-i khūnīn-i Karbalā' (2)," 27 Abān 1391/November 17, 2012 – http://www.farsnews.com/newstext.php?nn=1391082600113.

"Gozāresh-i kitāb-i juẕūr-i Dā'esh qirā'a fī turāth al-Wahhābiyya wa-'ulamā' al-sa'ūdiyya," http://takfir.ir/modules/smartsection/item.php?itemid=1494.

"Gozāreshī az kitāb-i mabānī-i naẓarī-i gharb-i modern," 5 Abān 1388/October 27, 2009, https://hawzah.net/fa/Article/View/82468/.

"Hame chīz dar bārah-i nohom-i Rabī' al-awwal va-bid'at 'Īd al-Zahrā' (s)," 29 Azar 1394/December 20, 2015, http://javanenghelabi.ir/news/24241.html.

"Ḥamla-i Dā'esh neshāneh-i ẓuhūr ast?," 22 Khordād 1393/June 12, 2014, https://article.tebyan.net/279563/-حمله-داعش-نشانه-ظهور-است.

"Ḥaqīqat nohom-i Rabī' al-awwal chīst?" http://ahlulbaytclub.com/HtmlFiles/Art0002286_Content.htm.

"Ḥaqīqat qabr qātil 'Umar b. al-Khaṭṭāb fī Iran," http://alburhan.com/Article/index/7688.

"Ḥażrat-I Shujā' al-Dīn Fayrūz Abū Lū'lū' raḥmat Allah 'alayhi," https://yazahrajan.blogsky.com/1391/11/07/post-177/.

"Ḥimāyat bī qayd va-sharṭ az Yahūdiyān tahdīdī 'alayh-i javāmi'-i basharī," 23 Farvardīn 1389/April 12, 2010, http://www.farsnews.net/newstext.php?nn=8901211582.

"Hoshdār-i rahbar-i mu'aẓẓam-i inqilāb-i Islāmī nisbat beh Khaṭar-i buzurg-i jarayānhā-i takfīrī," 29 Dey 1392/January 19, 2014, https://www.isna.ir/news/92102916491.

"Ḥujjat al-Islam Ṭā'ib: naḥwa be qudrat rasīdan-i Abū Bakr ba'd piyāmbar akram (s)" – 26 Bahman 1389/January 15, 2011, http://tabiin.blog.ir/1389/11/26.

"ʿĪd al-Zahrāʾ: bidʿat yā sunat?" 14 Bahman 1393/February 3, 2015, http://antifetan.blog.ir/post/7.

"Idīʾūlūzhī-i Bahāʾiyat – Bahāʾiyat va-siyāsat," 14 Abān 1390/November 5, 2011 – https://www.porseman.com/article/145286/ايدئولوژي-بهائيت-بهائيت-و-سياست.

"ʿIllal va-ʿavāmil-i dushmanī-i Yahūd bar Islam," 24 Bahman 1391/February 12, 2013, http://www.mouood.org/component/k2/item/7960--علل-و-عوامل-دشمني-يهود-با-اسلام.html.

"ʿIllat-i dushmanī-i Yahūdī bā Islām: nezhād parastī," 30 bahman 1395/February 18, 2017, http://mastoor.ir/content/view/7996/1.

"ʿIllat-i ḥamla-i Dāʿesh be ʿIrāq dar in borhahā-i zamānī chīst?," 26 Khordād 1393/June 13, 2014, http://adyannews.com/4573 /.

"ʿIllat-i izdivāj-i Umm Kulthūm bu ʿUmar," 13 Dey 1389/January 3, 2011, http://www.hawzah.net/fa/Question/View/63562.

"Inglistān va-ẓuhūr-i Vahhābiyat va-Āl Saʿūd," 27 Azar 1392/December 18, 2013, http://alwahabiyah.com/fa/Article/View/2627.

"Imām Ḥusayn va-ifshāʾ kardan naqsh-i Yahūd dar vāqiʿa-i ʿĀshūrāʾ," 26 Abān 1391/November 16, 2012, https://www.farsnews.com/news/13910826000113/.

"Imām jumʿa-i Rafsanjān khastār-i ikhrāj-i Bahāʾīyān az in shahr shod," December 4, 2014, http://www.bbc.com/persian/iran/2014/12/141202_u04_iran_bahais.

"Imām-i Jumʿa-i Tabrīz: tafrīqa-i hadaf-i aṣlī-i tashayyuʿ-i Inglīsi va-tasannon-i Amrīkāʾī," 3 Dey 1395/December 23, 2016, https://www.mehrnews.com/news/3857704/.

"Al-Imām al-Khamenei: Amrīkā wal-ṣahāyīna yuʿādūna Irān li-anna al-Islām huna akthar burūzan," 25 April 2017, https://www.tasnimnews.com/ar/news/2017/04/25/1389363/الإمام-الخامنئي-امريكا-والصهاينة-يعادون-ايران-لأن-الإسلام-هنا-أكثر-بروزاً.

"Imām Khomeini (rh) va-Bahāʾiyat," http://siasi.porsemani.ir/node/1109.

"Imām-i Zamān (ʿajala Allah taʿālā farajahu al-sharīf) va-saranjām-i Yahūd," 29 Ordībehesht 1390/May 19, 2011, http://article.tebyan.net/165478.

"Imām-i Zamān va-sar anjām-i Yahūd," 18 Azar 1396/December 9, 2017, http://pajoohe.ir/امام-زمان-ع-و-سرانجام-يهود_a-35957.aspx.

"Imkān nadārad Islam vāqiʿī zebālahā-i mithl-i Dāʿesh twolīd konad," 16 Azar 1394/December 7, 2015, https://www.tasnimnews.com/fa/news/1394/09/16/936971.

"Inḥirāf-i ʿAbd al-Raḥman Dimashqiyya (w) ʿAlī al-Rubayʿī ʿan al-Islam," August 5, 2012, https://www.facebook.com/alsadreeon/posts/401495023231756.

"Inqilāb-i Islāmī va-muqābala bā nufūẕ-i Bahāʾiyat dar Irān," 30 Azar 1396/December 21, 2017, http://basijnews.ir/fa/news/8964916.

"Inqilāb-i Islāmī va-risvāʾī-i firqa-i Bahāʾiyat," http://kanoonhend.ir/fa/news/2459/انقلاب-اسلامی-و-رسوائی-فرقه-بهائیت.

"Inqilābīm, sarbaz rahbarīm," July 26, 2016, http://www.pictaram.org/post/BIYE7yuDAdR.

"Intiṣāb-i ra'īs va-a'żā' shūrā-i 'ālī-i markaz algū-i Islāmī-Irani pīshraft," 3 Khordād 1390/ May 24, 2014, http://www.icana.ir/Fa/News/165265.
"Iqdāmāt va-barnāmahhā-i ṣahyūnīsm dar taqābul āmūzeh-i mahdaviyat dar ḥawza-i farhang," http://www.mahdi313.com/index.php?pg=articles&id=1634.
"Iran tughliqu mazār Abū Lū'lū' al-majūsī qātil 'Umar b. al-Khaṭṭāb," June 13, 2007, http://www.26sep.net/news_details.php?lng=arabic&sid=28845.
"Irtibāṭ-i farāmāsōnarī bā ṣahyūnīsm va-shayṭān *parastī*," 16 Esfand 1393/March 7, 2015, http://www.adyannet.com/fa/news/14930.
"Irtidād (2) āzādī (8)," *Ḥawza* 42 (1369/1991), http://www.hawzah.net/fa/Magazine/View/4518/4555/32889.
"Irtidād 'Abd al-Karīm Sorūsh i'lām shod," 23 Mehr 1392/October 15, 2013 http://adyan news.com/fa/news/5914/.
"Ishtirākāt-i 'aqīdatī Vahhābiyat va-Yahūdiyat," 20 Esfand 1393/March 11, 2015, http://www.jahannews.com/sound/411939.
"Islām dar bārah-i feminism cheh mīgūyad? Barābirī-i zan va-mard dar Islām," *Javān*, 4 Shahrīvar 1392/August 26, 2013, http://www.yjc.ir/fa/news/4523625/اسلام.
"Islām va-shubhāt-i Bahā'iyat chīst?," http://adyan.porsemani.ir/content/-اسلام-و-شبهات-بهائيت.
"Istidlāl beh 'ghayrat-i 'arab' barāye inkār shahādat Zahrā' salām Allah 'alayhā," 5 Farvardīn 1392/March 25, 2013, http://www.valiasr-aj.com/fa/page.php?bank=mag halat&id=146.
"Istiqbāl shaykh al-Azhar az fatvā-i maqām-i mu'aẓẓam-i rahbarī," 2 Khordād 1391/ May 22, 2012, https://fa.alalamtv.net/news/328564.
"I'tirāf-i Abū Bakr al-Baghdādī," http://www.atabatkh.com/646/-اعتراف-أبوبكر-البغدادي-به-شكست-داعش.
"Iṭṭilā'-i Yahūd az terōr-i 'Umar," http://jscenter.ir/judaism-and-islam/jewish-intrigue/5549.
"Iẓhārātī ṣarīḥ dar bārah-i marāsim 'Umarkoshūn," 23 Dey 1392/January 13, 2014, http://alef.ir/vdccmsqim2bqsm8.ala2.html?211777.
"Izdivāj-i Umm Kulthūm," 18 Ordībehesht 1388/May 18, 2009, http://porseman.org/showarticle.aspx?id=633.
"Jahānī shodan inqilāb-i Islāmī va-pāyān-i ta'rīkh." 22 Farvardīn 1394/April 11, 2015 https://www.farsnews.com/news/13940119001061.
"Jang bā Yahūd dar ākhar al-zamān dar muḥākamāt-i Qur'ānī ast," 12 Khordād 1394/ June 2, 2015, https://urlzs.com/8qqzX.
"Janghā-i khulafā' va-manfa'at-i Yahūd az ān," http://jscenter.ir/judaism-and-islam/jewish-intrigue/5507.
"Jarayān shināsī-i salafigarī-i mu'āṣir + taṣāvīr," 17 Dey 1391/January 6, 2013, https://www.mashreghnews.ir/news/176522.

"Jarayān shināsī-i ta'rīkhī-i nufūẕ bā tamarkuz bar Yahūd," 14 Bahman 1395/February 2, 2017, http://www.mehrnews.com/news/3895081.

"Jināyat-i shibh-i sufyānī: ṣaḥnehā-i ke in zan nemītavānad farāmūsh konad," 2 Dey 1393/December 23, 2014, https://www.porseman.com/article/-جنایات-شبه-سفیانی-صحنه-هایی-که-این-زن-نمی-تواند-فراموش-کند/160194.

"Jināyat-i sufyānī besiyār mushābih 'aqā'id Vahhābiyat ast," 11 Dey 1392/January 1, 2014, https://www.mehrnews.com/news/2205919/.

"Jonbesh-i feminism, ma'nāyī-i feminism," http://www.porseman.org/q/vservice.aspx?id=98942.

"Jumūd fikrī dar tafakkur-i vahhābīyyat, ānhā rā dar gamrāhī va-żalālāt qarār dādeh ast," 15 Abān 1392/November 6, 2013, http://www.farsnews.com/printable.php?nn=13920813000982.

"Ka'b al-Aḥbār va-khalīfa-i dovom," Majma' jahānī Shī'a shināsī, 18 Mordād 1395/August 8, 2016, http://shiastudies.com/fa/12608/.

"Ka'b al-Aḥbār, shakhṣī ke dar musalmānān nufūẕ kard va-talāsh kard ta'līmāt-i Yahūd rā vārid-i Islam konad," http://tvshia.com/fa/content/50285.

"Karshinās-i masā'il-i dushman shināsī: Vahhābiyat farzand-i qawm-i nāmashrū'-i Yahūd ast," 16 Ordībehesht 1393/May 6, 2014, http://www.snn.ir/detail/News/312753/164.

"Khamenei: lā ḥarb bayna al-Sunna wal-Shī'a," June 29, 2014 – http://www.elaph.com/Web/News/2014/6/918323.html#sthash.ZnyYpPNh.dpuf.

"Khamenei: al-isā'a li-zawjāt al-nabī ta'nī al-isā'a lil-rasūl nafsihi," June 12, 2106 – http://www.alraimedia.com/ar/article/foreigns/2016/06/12/686602/nr/iran.

"khashm-i serrān-i Bahā'iyat az bī tavvajuhī-i jahānīyān be ānān," 25 Khordad 1388/June 15, 2007, http://rasekhoon.net/article/show/135799.

"Khaṭṭ-i kullī-i niẓām-i Islāmī chīst?," http://www.hoviatema.ir/export/print/445?module=news.

"Khāṭira-i tekān-dehande Ayatollah Mar'ashī dar mowred-i 'Umarkoshūn," http://balatarazbalatarin.blogfa.com/post/237/-خاطره-تکان-دهنده-آیت-الله-مرعشی-در-مورد-عمر-کشون.

"Khiyānat-i Āl Sa'ūd li-felestīn wal-muslimīn," https://www.youtube.com/watch?v=WlluzFtH1NI.

"Khiyānat beh Islām dar libās maḥabbat beh ahl-i bayt ('alayhim al-salām)," 3 Dey 1393/December 24, 2014, http://sahebnews.ir/164612.

"Khiyānathā-i 'Umar beh Islam (2)," http://sedayeshia.blogsky.com/1391/11/04/post-161/.

"Khorāfāt-i 9 Rabī' dastmāyeh barāye ḥamla beh aberūyī-i tashayyu'," 20 Bahman 1391/February 8, 2013, http://www.tasnimnews.com/fa/news/1391/11/02/14537.

"Khoshūnat-i Dā'esh va-rīshehhā-i ān dar kitāb-i muqaddas-i Yahūd," http://erfaneha.parsiblog.com/Posts/389/خشونت+داعش+و+ریشه+هاي+آن+در+کتاب+مقدس+یهود.

"Khurūjī neshest-i mushtarak-i dawlat va-majlis bāyad ḥall mushkilāt-i mardom bāshad," Mehr 19, 1393/October 11, 2014, http://www.hawzah.net/fa/News/View/98018.

"Kitāb Āl Saʿyūn bā hadaf-i tabyīn jināyat-i Āl Saʿūd rivāneh bāzār shod," 24 Shahrīvar 1395/September 14, 2016, http://www.rasanews.ir/detail/News/449582/52.

"Kitāb ʿĀl Saʿyūn muntashir shod," 17 Mordād 1395/ August 7, 2016, https://www.mehr news.com/news/3734153.

"Kitāb laʿnhā-i nāmuqaddas muntashir shod" 29 Mordād 1393/August 20, 2014 – http://www.fetan.ir/home/2196.

"Kodām pādishāh Saʿūdī felestīn rā beh Yahūdiyān bakhshīd + sanad taʾrīkhī," 24 Farvardīn 1390/April 13, 2011, http://www.shia-news.com/fa/news/20538.

"Konkāshī dar kalām-i Imām (rh) bar irtijāʾ-i feminism," *Shūrā-i farhangī va-ijtimāʿī-i zanān*, 5 (Fall 1378/1999), http://www.hawzah.net/fa/Article/View/88684.

"Koshte shodan ʿUmar b. Khaṭṭāb beh dast-i Fīrūz Abū Lūʾlūʾ Irānī – sal 23 hijri qamari/27 Ẕū al-Ḥijjah," http://abulolo.persianblog.ir/tag/قتل_عمر.

"Kuffār aʿam az ahl-i kitāb va-ghayr-i ān ṭibq-i fatāwā-i Ayat Allah Bahjat nejes hastand," 3 Esfand 1389/February 22, 2011, http://www.porseshkadeh.com/Question/25560.

"Laʿnhā-i nāmuqaddas dar tabyīn 'tabarrā' muntashir shod," 31 Mordād 1393/August 22, 2014, http://www.teribon.ir/archives/270668/.

"Mabāḥīth-i mahdavyat 22: pīmān-i mushtarak beyne sufyānī va-gharbīhā," April 14, 2014, http://www.farhangnews.ir/content/208533#_edn10.

"Mafhūm āzādī az dīdgāh-i Islam," 21 Dey 1385/January 11, 2007, http://hawzah.net/Hawzah/Questions/QuestionView.aspx?LanguageID=1&QuestionID=11700&Search Text.

"Mafhūm-i āzādī dar falsafa-i gharb?" www.siasi.porsemani.ir/content/مفهوم-آزادی-در-فلسفه‌ی-غرب؟.

"Maʿlūmāt muhimma ʿan al-rāfiḍa aʿdāʾ Allāh," http://www.dd-sunnah.net/forum/showthread.php?t=13767.

"Manshūr-i sokhnān-i maqām-i muʿaẓẓam-i rahbarī dar mowred-i tahājum-i farhangī," May 25, 2012, http://bidaricyberi.blogfa.com/post-54.aspx.

"Maʿrakat al-Imām al-mahdī ʿalayhi al-salām maʿa al-Yahūd," https://www.ansarh.com/maaref_details_1165_معركة_الإمام_المهدي_عليه_السلام__مع_اليهود.html.

"Marāsim-i ʿUmarkoshūn va-ḥukm-i in marāsim az dīdgāh-i Imām-i Khamenei," http://rezazamani1375.blogfa.com/post/19.

"Matā tarānī wa-narāka: silsila-i maqālatī pīrāmūn-i mahdaviyat (pt. 1)," 7 Khordad 1394/May 28, 2015, http://www.ebnolreza.ir/cultural/tahlilvizhe/250-selseleh-maghalat-1.html.

"Mīkveh va-fasād-i akhlāqī-i ḥākhāmhā-i Yahūdī," 18 Esfand 1395/March 8, 2017, http://khabarfarsi.com/u/34721670.

"Al-Mīthāq al-ʿilmī: al-muʾtamar al-ʿālamī lil-tiyārāt al-mutashaddida wal-takfīriyya min wujhat naẓar-i ʿulamāʾ al-Islam," 1 Azar 1391/November 21, 2012, http://dinpa joohan.com/ararticle13102.html.

"Mowżūʿ-i pazhūhesh (2) dushman shināsī," *Maʿārif-i Islāmī* 68 (1386/2007), https://hawzah.net/fa/Magazine/View/5387/5606/54392.

"Mu'alafahā-i shenākht-i dushman chīst?" 7 Mehr 1392/September 29, 2013 – http://www.ghatreh.com/news/nn15863623.

"Mūʿāvin-i dabīr-i kull ḥizballah Lubnān: terōrism takfīrī ghīdeh-i sarṭānī ast keh bāyad rīsheh kon shavad," 7 Farvardīn 1395/March 26, 2016, http://www.jamnews.com/detail/News/648891.

"Muḥammad bin ʿAbd al-Wahhāb va-Yahūdiyat," 30 Bahman 1393/February 19, 2015, http://daesh93.rasekhoonblog.com/show/369903.

"*Mukhtaṣar ta'rīkh al-rāfiḍa saraṭān al-umma,*" http://www.masr4host.org/~amhzn/vb/showthread.php?t=4496.

"Muqtaḍā Ṣadr khāṭaba beh Shīrāzīhā: taklīf-i khōd rā mushakhaṣ konīd," 8 Esfand 1393/February 27, 2015, http://www.fetan.ir/home/4767.

"Al-Murshid al-aʿlā lil-thawra al-Islāmiyya ʿAlī al-Khamenei yaqūlu: yuḥarram al-nayl min rumūz ikhwāninā al-Sunna," September 30, 2010, http://www.mehrnews.com/mehr_media/image/2010/09/576469_orig.jpg/.

"Murūrī bar athār va-andīshehā-i Reżā Dāvarī Ardakānī," 22 Khordād 1394/June 12, 2015, http://www.irna.ir/fa/News/81643158/.

"Murūrī bar kitāb ʿdushman shināsī az manẓar-i rahbarī," 12 Abān 1395/November 2, 2016, http://teeh.ir/fa/news-details/2329/مروری-بر-کتاب-«دشمن-شناسی-از-منظر-رهبری».

"Musābaqa-i ṣad su'āl az Vahhābiyat dar Zāhidān," 14 Tīr 1391/July 4, 2012, http://www.farsnews.com/printable.php?nn=13910616000173.

"Muṣāḥaba-i majala-i nigāh bā dabir-i hamāyesh Ḥujjat al-Islam wal-Muslimīn Muḥammad Āsif Muḥsinī (Ḥikmat)," 29 Mīzān 1496/October 21, 2017, http://www.bsharat.com/id/9/6.html.

"Mushāvir-i aʿẓam-i khalīfa-i dovom yek Yahūdī tāzeh-musalmān būdeh," http://www.vahabiat.porsemani.ir/content/مشاور-اعظم-خلیفه-ی-دوم-یک-یهودی-تازه-مسلمان-بوده.

"Muta'asefāne dīrūz ham rokh dād/bargozārī marāsim gheyr-i akhlāqī; noh-i Rabīʿ al-awwal khorāfa-i tashayyuʿ-i londonī," December 22, 2015, https://www.parsnews.com/بخش-فرهنگی-6/330187-متاسقانه-دیروز-هم-رخ-داد-برگزاری-مراسم-غیر-اخلاقی-نه-ربیع-الاول-خرافه-تشییع-لندنی.

"Nābūdī-i qawm-i Yahūd dar dowran-i ākhar al-zamān," 24 Dey 1387/January 13, 2009, http://www.shia-news.com/fa/news/11981.

"Nābūdī-i Shīʿa beṣūrat-i narm az dīdgāh-i Fransīs Fūkūyāmā," *Islam Times*, 18 Esfand 1395/March 8, 2017, https://www.islamtimes.org/fa/article/616178.

"Naqd-i Bahā'iyat, be kam-i Bahā'iyat," 20, Dey 1389/January 10, 2011, https://www.mashreghnews.ir/news/23703.

“Naqd-i kitāb-i ‘laʿnhā-i namoaddas’ barresī-i kitāb-i ‘laʿnhā-i namoaddas’ athr-i aqā-i Mahdī Masāʾilī,” http://naghdobarresi2.blogfa.com.

“Naqd va-barresī-i sokhnān-i shaykh al-azhar, bar żede mabānī-i iʿtiqādi-i tashayyuʿ,” 24 Shahrīvar 1394/September 15, 2015, http://www.valiasr-aj.com/persian/shownews.php?idnews=8040.

“Naqd va-barresī-i uṣūl-i iʿtiqādi-i Bahāʾiyat,” http://www.hazrate-ghaem.blogfa.com/post/41/نقد-و-بررسي-اصول-اعتقادي-بهائيت.

“Naqdī: idīʾūlūzhīhā-i gharb beh ban bast rasīdeh ast,” 18 Ordībhesht 1394/May 8, 2015, http://www.isna.ir/fa/news/94021810069.

“Naqdī bar pāsokh-i aqā-i Rafsanjānī beh yek iddiʿā’,” 28 Bahman 1392/February 17, 2014 http://ravanbakhsh.blogfa.com/post-42.aspx.

“Naqsh-i Abū Bakr va-ʿUmar dar terōr-i rasūl akram ṣalā Allah ʿalayhi va-Ālihi,” https://amīremomenin.persianblog.ir/QL366j4a0Wibxqb11wrQ-نقش-ابوبکر-و-عمر-در-ترور-رسول-اکرم-صلی-الله-علیه-و-آله-.

“Naqsh-i feminism va-ṣahyūnīsm dar żāyiʿ kardan jins-i zan,” 6 Mordād 1396/July 28, 2018, https://www.yjc.ir/fa/news/6613218/.

“Naqsh-i Inglīshā dar tashkīl-i Vahhābiyat,” 15 Mordād 1393/August 6, 2014, https://www.mashreghnews.ir/news/333231.

“Naqsh-i inqilāb-i Islāmī dar ufūl-i Amrīkā va-gharb,” http://www.ghatreh.com/news/nn17859353.

“Naqsh-i Irāniān dar terōr-i ʿUmar,” 15 Abān 1386/November 6, 2007, http://oskarimbns.blogfa.com/post-1.aspx.

“Naqsh-i ṣahyūnīsm dar Yahūd setīzī,” 7 Mordād 1387/July 28, 2008, http://www.aftabir.com/articles/view/politics/world/c1c1217232350_zionism_p1.php.

“Naqsh-i Yahūd dar intikhāb ʿunwān barāye ʿUmar bin Khaṭṭāb,” 4 Esfand 1391/February 22, 2013, http://armanemahdaviyat.ir/?p=158.

“Naqsh-i Yahūd dar shahādat-i ahl-i bayt,” http://dar-al-quran.ir/اخبار/مناسبت-ها/1508-نقش-يهود-در-شهادت-اهل-بيت-ع.

“Naqsh-i Yahūd dar shahādat-i ḥażrat-i Fāṭima (s),” http://fa.alkawthartv.com/news/119907.

“Naqsh-i Yahūd dar shahādat-i Imāmān,” http://www.ahbab14.blogfa.com/post/26.

“Naqsh-i Yahūd dar taḥrīf-i ḥādithat-i Ghadīr Khumm,” – 22 Dey 1388/January 12, 2010, http://www.askdin.com/showthread.php?t=2437.

“Naqsh-i Yahūd dar vaqāyiʿ-i taʾrīkh-i Islam,” 7 Bahman 1386/January 27, 2008, http://www.farsnews.com/printable.php?nn=8609240312.

“Naqsh-i Yahūd dar vāqiʿa-i ʿĀshūrāʾ va-shahādat-i Seyyed al-Shuhadāʾ ʿalayhi al-salām,” http://intiqam.blogfa.com/post-27.aspx.

“Naqsh-i Yahūd dar vāqiʿa-i khūnīn Karbalāʾ,” https://www.mouood.org/component/k2/item/6417.

"Naqsh-i Yahūd (ṣahyūnīsm) dar vāqiʿa-i Karbalāʾ," http://21122012.blogfa.com/post-38.aspx.

"Naqsh-i Yahūdiyān dar tarvīj-i Islam setīzī," http://qods.persianblog.ir/post/153.

"Naqsh-i Yahūdiyān-i ṣahyūnīst dar ghasb-i khilāfat-i amīr al-muʾminīn ṣalvāt-i Allah ʿalayhi wa-salām" http://intiqam.blogfa.com/post-23.aspx.

"Naẓar-i Ayatollah Bahjat dar bārah-i nohom Rabīʿ al-awwl," 21 Dey 1392/January 11, 2014, http://aghigh.ir/fa/news/19525.

"Naẓar-i Ayatollah Khamenei dar mowred-i khorāfāt nohom Rabīʿ," 1 Bahman 1391/January 20, 2013, http://www.farsnews.com/newstext.php?nn=13911101000500.

"Naẓar-i Ayatollah Makārem Shīrāzī dar mowred-i marāsim-i ʿīd al-Zahrāʾ," http://www.hawzah.net/fa/News/View/96429.

"Naẓar-i Ayatollah Vaḥīd dar bārah-i bī iḥtirāmī beh khulafāʾ-i ahl-i Sunnat," 4 Ordībehesht 1390/April 24, 2011, http://www.shia-online.ir/article.asp?id=17770.

"Naẓar-i Islam dar bārah-i āzādī chīst? Va-ayā taqvā mukhālif-i āzādī ast?," http://library.tebyan.net/fa/Viewer/Text/145417/1.

"Naẓar-i Rahbarī dar bārah-i khorāfāt-i 9 Rabīʿ al-awwal," 1 Bahman 1391/January 20, 2013, https://www.mashreghnews.ir/news/187473/-نظر-رهبری-درباره-خرافات-9-ربیع-الاول.

"Naẓar-i ṣarīḥ-i rahbar-i inqilāb dar khuṣūṣ-i ʿUmarkoshūn," 1 Bahman 1391/January 20, 2013, http://www.harfeno.com/vdcf.cdmiw6doygiaw.html.

"Naẓar-i shahīd-i Beheshtī dar bārah-i āzādī," 24 Ordībehesht 1393/May 14, 2014, http://www.jahannews.com/analysis/360232.

"Naẓar-i ʿulamāʾ va-marājiʿ-i ʿuẓām bar vaḥdat miyān Shīʿa va-Sunnī," 14 Dey 1393/January 4, 2015, http://dana.ir/News/206483.html.

"Naẓariyat-i bīdārī-i Islāmī va-pāyān-i makātib-i umanīstī," 24 Ordībehesht 1391/1395/May 13, 2012, http://farsi.khamenei.ir/print-content?id=25076 (last accessed July 19, 2015).

"Naẓariyat-i pāyān-i taʾrīkh – naẓarīyat-i pāyān-i taʾrīkh-i Fūkūyāmā," http://siasi.porsemani.ir/node/2505.

"Nemādhā-i muhim Yahūdī va-māsōnī," 23 Tīr 1392/July 14, 2013, https://www.porseman.com/article/134966/نمادهای-مهم-یهودی-و-ماسونی.

"Nemāyandeh-i valī-i faqīh dar Khuzistān: Dāʿesh az neshānehhā-i khurūj-i sufyānī ast," 24 Khordād 1393/June 14, 2014, https://www.mashreghnews.ir/news/317921.

"Nemūneh-i az taḥrīf-i taʾrīkhī-i nohom Rabīʿ al-awwal/ Sīrat amīr al-muʾminīn (a) dar ittiḥād-i Islāmī," 29 Azar 1394/December 20, 2015, https://www.farsnews.ir/news/13940925001299/-از-تحریف-تاریخی-نهم‌ربیع‌الاول-سیره‌امیرالمؤمنین-ع-در.

"Neshest-i hamandīshī 'ṣahyūnīsm, feminism, umānīsm,' dar Bojnūrd bargozār shod," 8 Khordad 1391/May 28, 2012, https://iqna.ir/fa/news/1018945/-نشست-هم‌اندیشی-صهیونیسم-فمینیسم-و-اومانیسم-در-بجنورد-برگزار-شد.

"Nigāhī beh abʿād-i mukhtalif-i kongreh-i jahānī-i jarayānhā-i ifrāṭī va-takfīrī az dīdgāh-i ʿulamā'-i Islām," 2 Azar 1393/November 23, 2014, http://www.farsnews.com/newstext.php?nn=13930901000989.

"Nigāhī beh fatvā-i ta'rīkhī-i valī-i amr al-Muslimīn dar bārah-i ahl-i Sunnat," 20 Mehr 1389/October 12, 2010, https://www.farsnews.com/news/8907191487.

"Nigāhī beh feminism-i Islāmī: radd-i feminism-i Islāmī, nafy-i ḥuqūq-i zan dar Islām nīst," 30 Bahman 1390/February 19, 2012, http://snn.ir/fa/news/172554.

"Nigāhī beh kitāb ʿaz afsāneh-i Yahūd setīzī tā vāqiʿiyat-i Islām setīzī,'" 19 Ordībehesht 1394/May 9, 2015, http://www.rasanews.ir/print/259737.

"Nigāhī beh kitāb Āl Saʿyūn," 19 Shahrīvar 1395/September 9, 2016, http://www.farsnews.com/newstext.php?nn=13950618000671.

"Nigāhī beh taḥaqquq-i ʿajīb 14 pīsh-bīnī-i buzurg-i Imām Khamene'i," February 4, 2012, http://iran313.blogfa.com/post-114.aspx.

"Nigāhī beh zindigī-i Muḥammad bin ʿAbd al-Wahhāb," 4 Esfand 1394/February 23, 2016, http://www.adyannet.com/fa/news/18016.

"Niẓām-i jumhūrī-i Islāmī, muhimtarīn-i hadaf-i tahājum-i farhangī-i istikbār ast," *Akhbār-i Shīʿīyān*, 68 (1390/2011), 1–3.

"Nohom Rabīʿ al-awwal, jashn-i aghāz-i Imāmat-i Imām-i zamān ast yā jashn-i ʿīd al-Zahrā'?" 11 Bahman 1391/January 30, 2013, https://urlzs.com/beL7P.

"Nohom Rabīʿ al-awwal rūz bayʿatī dōbāreh bā Imām-i zamān ast," 11 Dey 1393/December 22, 2015, http://www.farsnews.com/newstext.php?nn=13931010001385.

"Nohom Rabīʿ; rūzī ke dushman khōshḥāl ast," 2 Dey 1394/December 23, 2015, http://www.tabnakesfahan.ir/fa/news/150317/.

"Nohom Rabīʿ al-awwal, sālrūz-i aghāz-i imāmat-i imām-i zamān (aj), zamānī barāye shādī muntaẓirān," Dāneshgāh-i Āzād Islāmī Vāḥid Hamedan, 1 Bahman 1391/January 20, 2013 http://www.iauh.ac.ir/about-university/news-archive/45-farhangi/846-9rabiolaval.html.

"Nohom-i Rabīʿ-i avval va-jashn-i mamnūʿ ʿUmarkoshān," http://www.socio-shia.com/index.php/sociology-of-shia-fields/shia-rituals/187-9rabi-note.

"Nufūẕ-i Yahūdiyān dar Islam barāye taghyīr-i dādan masīr-i dīn," 10 Esfand 1395/February 28, 2017, http://ferghenews.com/fa/news/15317.

"Ustād-i Rā'ifīpūr: Shimr Yahūdī būd," http://www.aparat.com/v/zZ39R; https://www.instagram.com/p/7GP5uBGRLD/.

"Pāsokh beh chend shubha-i muhim-i ta'rīkhī dar bārah-i anjuman-i Ḥojjatiya/bakhsh-i dovom," 11 Mehr 1396/October 3, 2017, http://ferghenews.com/fa/news/15985/.

"Pāyān-i ṣafar va-tikrār khorāfa-i 'daq albāb masājid' aʿmāl muṣṭaḥab nakhostīn rūz Rabīʿ al-awwal," 21 Azar 1394/December 12, 2015, https://www.mashreghnews.ir/news/660793/پایان-صفر-و-تکرار-خرافه-دق-الباب-مساجد-اعمال-مستحبی-نخستین.

"Pīsh-bīnī suqūṭ gharb," *Siyāsat-i rūz*, November 8, 2005.

"Pīsh-bīnī suqūṭ gharb tavassoṭ-i maqām muʿaẓẓam rahbarī," 15 Abān 1390/November 6, 2011, http://siasi.porsemani.ir/node/1806.

"Pīsh qarāvolān-i sufyānī yā ʿamālahā-i ṣalīb va-ṣahyūn," 18 Tīr 1393/July 9, 2014, https://article.tebyan.net/281196.

"Pīsh raft yā pas raft? Naqd-i algū-i gharbī az manẓar-i Rahbar-i muʿaẓẓam-i Inqilāb-i Islāmī," April 14, 2015, http://www.farsnews.com/newstext.php?nn=13930802000542.

"Pīshīneh va-kārnāmah-i Vahhābiyat (pt. 1) – Vahhābiyat va-tafrīqa," 7 Mehr 1386/September 29, 2007, http://www.farsnews.com/newstext.php?nn=8607010023.

"Pīshīneh va-kārnāmah-i Vahhābiyat (pt. 3) – ʿaqāyed va-ʿamalkard," 8 Mehr 1386/September 30, 2007, https://basirat.ir/fa/news/13511/-پیشینه-و-کارنامه-وهابیت-عقاید-و-عملکرد.

"Piyāmakhā-i tabrīk-i sālrūz-i aghāz Imāmat va-vilāyat-i imām-i zamān (AJ)," 10 Dey 1393/December 31, 2014, http://www.yjc.ir/fa/news/5087415.

"Poshtībānī-i Yahūd az saqīfa gerāyān," https://forum.hammihan.com/thread101903.html.

"Poshtībānī-i Yahūd az bānd-i Shīrāzīhā," 11 Dey 1394/January 1, 2016, http://aghigh.ir/fa/news/68925/پشتیبانی-یهود-از-باند-شیرازی‌ها.

"Qawm-i Yahūd rā behtar beshenāsīm," 26 Khordād 1392/June 16, 2013, http://article.tebyan.net/248084.

"Qawm-i Yahūd va-taskhīr-i jahān," 12 Abān 1395/November 2, 2016, http://www.rasanews.ir/print/458897.

"Qirāʾatī: muftīhā-i vahhābī tavān-i munaẓara bā ʿulamāʾ-i Shīʿa rā nadārand," 29 Dey 1392/January 19, 2014, http://shiayan.ir/3818/.

"Rābiṭa-i Islām va-feminism," http://www.andisheqom.com/public/application/index/viewData?c=11344&t=articlel – accessed November 2, 2017.

"Rābiṭa beyne shūresh-i sufyānī va-ḥavādith-i Sūrīya," 20 Mehr 1393/October 12, 2014, https://www.mashreghnews.ir/news/353477/-شباهت‌-ها-و-تفاوت‌-های-داعش-و-سفیانی.

"Rābiṭa-i Dāʿesh bā rivāyat-i sufyānī, dajjāl va-parchamhā-i siyāh," 29 Mordād 1396/August 20, 2017, http://www.hawzah.net/fa/Discussion/View/44809/-رابطه-داعش-با-روایات-سفیانی-دجال-و-پرچم-های-سیاه.

"Radd fatāwā al-Imām al-sayyid ʿAlī al-Khamenei bi-tahḥrīm sabb al-ṣaḥāba," 5 Shahrīvar 1389/August 27, 2010, http://www.alshirazi.com.

"Al-Radd al-ṣārim ʿalā aʿdāʾ al-Imām al-qāʾim," May 4, 2016, https://www.facebook.com/123825401328114/photos/a.227440030966650.1073741828.123825401328114/229390314104955/?type=3.

"Radd va-ibṭāl-i firqa-i Bahāʾiyat;" 10 Tīr 1385/July 1, 2006, https://hawzah.net/fa/Question/View/2644/.

"Rafsanjānī: digār mowżūʿiyatī nadārad keh bibīnīm cheh kesī khalīfa avval būdeh ast," 19 Farvardīn 1386/April 8, 2007, http://www.asriran.com/fa/news/14741.

"Rafsanjānī ilā matā nataqātalu ḥawla man huwa al-khalīfa al-awwal?," *al-Maṣrī al-Yawm*, December 18, 2014.

"Rafsanjānī: la'n al-ṣaḥāba wal-iḥtifāl bi-maqtal al-khalīfa 'Umar awṣalanā ilā Dā'esh," *al-Quds* (London), November 10, 2014.

"Rahbar-i mu'aẓẓam-i Inqilāb: Khaṭṭ-i kullī-i niẓām-i Islāmī chīst?," April 28, 2013, http://www.hoviatema.ir/export/print/445?module=news.

"Rāhpīmāyi 'alayh-i seh khalīfa va-ijrā-i marāsim-i 'Umarkoshān' dar Qom," 20 Dey 1393/January 10, 2015, https://urlzs.com/JPwR6.

"Rāhyābī 100 hamjins bāz beh kongreh-i Amrīkā suqūṭ-i siyāsī gharb ast," June 14, 2013, http://www.tasnimnews.com/fa/news/1394/06/28/69893.

"Ra'īs-i dāneshgāh-i adyān va-maẕāhib: Khaṭar tashayyu'-i Inglīsī jedāsāzī Shī'a az ṣufūf jahān Islām ast," 16 Ordībehesht 1394/May 6, 2015, https://khabarfarsi.com/u/2865991.

"Ra'īs-i sāzemān-i basīj-i masājid-i sepāh: tamaddun mottakī bar sarmāyeh-dārī gharb rū beh ufūl ast," June 8, 2013, http://www.farsnews.com/newstext.php?nn=13920218001340.

"Rajabī Davānī barresī kard: 'āmil-i aṣlī-i ghasb-i khilāfat Abū Bakr būd noh 'Umar," 16 Farvardīn 1391/April 4, 2012, http://www.snn.ir/detail/News/179019/1070.

"Raqṣ-i shamshīr-i jāhiliyat-i modern dar konār jāhiliyat-i qabīlagī rā hajū konīd," Khordād 21, 1396/June 11, 2017, https://www.tasnimnews.com/fa/news/1396/03/21/1432910/رقص-شمشیر-جاهلیت-مدرن-در-کنار-جاهلیت-قبیلگی-را-هجو-کنید.

"Rivāyat-i Ḥujjat al-Islam Ṭā'ib az naqsh-i Yahūd dar dastgāh-i khilāfat-i Mu'āwiya," 22 Dey 1391/January 11, 2013, http://www.farsnews.com/newstext.php?nn=13911021000692.

"Review on Yūsuf Rashād," *Naqsh-i āfarīnī-i Yahūdiyān-i makhfī dar Masīḥiyat* tr. 'Abbās Kosnakī (Tehrān: Mow'ūd, 1390), http://www.hawzah.net/fa/News/View/94273 and http://teeh.ir/fa/news-details/2733.

"Rīsheh-i Vahhābiyat va-Yahūd be gofteh-i khōd Vahhābiyat + pazhūhesh," http://fadaeyane-velayat.persianblog.ir/post/1505/.

"Rīshehhā-i Yahūdī-i Āl Sa'ūd," 8 Abān 1391/October 29, 2012, http://salafi-vahabi.blogfa.com/post/88.

"Rūḥānī: rezhīm-i ṣahyūnīstī va-khūnrīzān-i minṭaqa beh zūdī gereftār ya's khwāhand shod," 25 Azar 1395/December 15, 2016, https://www.tasnimnews.com/fa/news/1395/09/25/1268404/روحانی-رژیم-صهیونیستی-و-خونریزان-منطقه-به-زودی-گرفتار-یأس-خواهند-شد.

"Rūyikard-i femīnīstī beh dīn; bā ta'kid bar Yahūdiyat va-Masīḥiyat," 19 Ordībehesht 1395/April 30, 2016, https://urd.ac.ir/fa/cont/5966/-رویکرد-فمینیستی-به-دین؛-با-تاکید-بر-یهودیت-و-مسیحیت».

"Sabb al-ṣaḥāba jarīma wal-qatl bi-'ism al-ṣaḥāba jihād," October 10, 2013, http://burathanews.com/arabic/articles/214324.

“Ṣahyūnī setīzī,” http://antisemitism.blogfa.com/post-1.aspx.

“Ṣahyūnīsm va-andīsheh-i farāmāsūnarī-i ḥuqūq-i doghūrīn-i zanān,” 14 Mehr 1392/ October 16, 2013, http://mouood.org/component/k2/item/14159.

“Salafī kīst va-cheh mīgūyad?/cherā salafīgarī buzurgtarīn-i khaṭar pīshrū-i jahān-i Islām ast?” 16 Dey 1391/January 5, 2013, https://www.mashreghnews.ir/news/176518.

“Salafiyya cheh kesānī hastand? Aṣlītarīn-i ʿalāyim-i salafiyya chīst?” 4 Mordād 1392/ July 26, 2014, http://shiayan.ir/2901/.

“Sālrūz-i aghāz-i imāmat-i valī-i ʿaṣr (ʿaj) taʿṭīl-i rasmī mīshavad,” 13 Ordībehesht 1395/ May 2, 2016 http://www.mehrnews.com/news/3614339.

“Saqīfat banī Isrāʾīl,” http://intiqam.blogfa.com/post-23.aspx.

“Sarneveshet-i aqaliyathā-i maẕhabī dar ḥukūmat-i mahdavī,” 28 Mordād 1394/ – https://www.mashreghnews.ir/news/455524/ سرنوشت-اقلیت-های-مذهبی-در-حکومت-مهدوی.

“Sayyid Ḥasan Naṣrallah: dīn-i takfīrīha Islām nīst,” 15 Dey 1391/January 4, 2013, https://shafaqna.com/persian/services/other-news/item/31824.

“Sirdār Naqdī: nezhād-i urupaʾī dar ḥāl-i inqirāż ast,” 3 Bahman 1394/January 23, 2016, https://www.tasnimnews.com/fa/news/1396/11/03/1636397.

“Shabāhat va-tafāvothā-i Dāʿesh va-sufyānī bar asās-i rivāyat-i ākhar al-zamānī,” 14 Mehr 1393/October 6, 2014, https://www.tasnimnews.com/fa/news/1393/07/14/520096/ شباهت-ها-و-تفاوت-های-داعش-و-سفیانی-بر-اساس-روایات-آخرالزمانی.

“Shabāhathā va-tafāvothā-i tafakkur-i Dāʿesh bā Vahhābiyat chīst?,” 28 Tīr 1393/July 19, 2014, https://www.mashreghnews.ir/news/325090.

“Shādī-i ahl-i Sunnat az fatvā-i rahbarī dar bārah-i ʿAisha,” 10 Mehr 1389/October 2, 2010, https://www.mashreghnews.ir/news/8338.

“Shīʿa Inglīsī dar pay mutawaqqif sākhtan Islām siyāsī ast,” 9 Esfand 1393/ February 28, 2015, https://www.tasnimnews.com/fa/news/1393/12/09/668383/شیعه-انگلیسی-در-پی-متوقف-ساختن-اسلام-سیاسی-است.

“Shīʿa va-Sunnī, pāsokh beh shubhāt-i barādarān-i Sunnī,” http://shiaanswering.blogfa.com/.

“Shīʿīyāni keh faqaṭ chend rūz-i sāl Shīʿa-and!,” 21 Dey 1392/January 11, 2014, http://www.dana.ir/News/47164.html.

“Sukūt dar berābir firqa-i Shīrāzīhā jāyiz nīst,” 8 Esfand 1393/February 27, 2015, https://rasanews.ir/fa/news/249273/سکوت-در-برابر-فرقه-شیرازی-ها-جایز-نیست.

“Siyāsathā-i sāzimān-i nifāq barāye nābūdī-i Islām pas az piyāmbar (s),” pt. 2 – n.d., http://www.fa.tarikh.org/index.php/تاریخ-انبیا-و-معصومین-ع/پیامبر-اعظم/item/1302--سازمان-نفاق-برای-نابودی-اسلام-پس-از-پیامبر-ص-بخش-سوم?tmpl=component&print=1.

“Sokhanrānī-i ustād-i Qarahī dar ayām-i ʿĀshūrāʾ,” 21 Azar 1390/December 12, 2011, http://www.shabestan.ir/detail/News/90013.

"Sufyānī, avvalīn-i neshāneh-i ḥatmī-i ẓuhūr-w Imām-i Mahdī," 12 Khordād 1394/June 2, 2015, http://www.rajanews.com/news/213604.

"Ta'ammolī bar Bayānāt-i rahbar-i inqilāb dar dīdār khobregān rahbarī," pt. 2, March 14, 2014, http://www.bultannews.com/fa/news/195528.

"Ta'ammolī dar mushtarakāt-i 'tashayyuʿ-i Inglīsī va-tasannon-i Amrīkā'ī'," Mordād 14, 1395/August 4, 2016, https://www.fardanews.com/fa/news/552052.

"Ṭā'ib: Mashā'ī Abū Bakr-i zamān va-nufūẕī-i Yahūd ast," 14 Tīr 1395/July 4, 2016, http://www.entekhab.ir/fa/news/30644.

"Tafāvot-i ʿaqā'id Bahā'iyat bā ʿaqā'id-i adyān-i asmānī dar chīst?," http://rwgn.net/index.aspx?siteid=1&pageid=319.

"Tafāvot-i āzādī-i Islāmī va-āzādī-i gharbī," 1 Mehr 1391/22 September 2012 – http://article.tebyan.net/221126.

"Tafāvot-i jawharī-i iḥyā'-i ḥuqūq-i zanān dar Islām va-jonbesh-i feminism," 18 Bahman 1390/February 7, 2012, http://www.hawzah.net/fa/News/View/91073.

"Taḥqīqāti-i kāmil dar bārah-i nohom Rabīʿ al-awwal," http://sraj.ir/fa/index.php/2015-12-12-16-28-27/416-2015-12-20-14-44-10.

"Takfīrīhā nemād-i ʿaynī-i inḥirāf-i sufyānī hastand," 23 Khordād 1393/June 13, 2014, http://www.farsnews.com/printable.php?nn=13930323000380.

"Taktīkhā-i Shīʿa setīzī-i Vahhābiyat," http://mouood.org/index.php?option=com_k2&view=item&id=8542:%D8%B3%D8%B3.

"Talāsh barāye nābūdī-i Islām dar shahr-i Qom + taṣāvīr," 20 Dey 1393/ January 10, 2015, https://urlzs.com/hM90V.

"Tamaddun-i gharb dar maʿraż suqūṭ va-sar nīgūnī ast," IRIB News Agency, April 17, 2013, http://www.iribnews.ir/fa/news/28332.

"Tamām āncheh keh bāyad dar mowred-i gurūh-i terōristi-i Dāʿesh bedānīm," 1 Mordād 1393/July 23, 2014, http://hawzahnews.com/TextVersionDetail/335334.

"Tanaqużāt dar ā'īn-i Bahā'iyat," https://www.tebyan.net/newindex.aspx?pid=934&articleID=843884.

"Tanaqużhā-i Hāshimī pedar va-Hāshimī dokhtar," 26 Ordībehesht 1395/May 15, 2016 – http://sobheqazvin.ir/news/183717-newscontent.

"Ta'rīkh-i daqīq-i marg-i ʿUmar bin Khaṭṭāb," http://belagh1.blogfa.com/post-1130.aspx.

"Al-ta'rīkh yuthbitu yahūdiyat Āl Saʿūd," May 30, 2013, http://burathanews.com/news/196926.html.

"Tasāhul va-tasāmuḥ dar Bahā'iyat," http://www.adyan.porsemani.ir/content/-تساهل-و-تسامح-در-بهاییت.

"Tashābuh-i pīrūwān-i Vahhābiyat bā Yahūd va-Naṣārā," 4 Khordād 1393/May 25, 2014, http://www.adyannet.com/fa/news/11407.

"Tashābuh-i tashayyuʿ-i Inglīsī bā tasannon-i Amrīkā'ī/ agar marjaʿiyat rā az shīʿa begīrand, cheh chīzī bāqī mīmānad?" 16 Ordībehesht 1393/May 6, 2015, https://snn

.ir/fa/news/405406/-تشابه-تشیع-انگلیسی-با-تسنن-آمریکایی-اگر-مرجعیت-را-از-شیعه
بگیرند-چه-چیزی-باقی-می-ماند.

"Tashayyuʿ-i Inglīsī beh jāy-i faḥāshī bā manṭiq az shīʿa difāʿ conand," http://shabestan.ir/detail/News/442258.

"Tashayyuʿ-i Inglīsī va-Islam Amrīkāʾī hadaf vāhidī dārand," 6 Bahman 1393/ January 26, 2015, http://www.mehrnews.com/news/2472433.

"Tashayyuʿ-i Inglīsī va-tasannon-i Amrīkāʾī, dō tīghe yek qīchī," 8 Ordībehesht 1395/ April 27, 2016, http://qademon.ir/2196-2/.

"Tashayyuʿ-i Inglīsī intiqām-i Yahūd az ahl-i bayt (ʿlayhim al-salām) ast," Mehr 28, 1394/ October 20, 2015, http://qademon.ir/تشیع-انگلیسی-انتقام-یهود-از-اهل-بیت-علی (accessed April 25, 2016).

"Tashkīl-i Dāʿesh zayr sāyeh ḥimāyat ʿibrī, ʿarabī va-gharbī," http://www.empireoflies.ir/تشکیل-داعش-حمایت-عبری-عربی/.

"Tavalā va-tabarrā chīst?" 6 Khordād 1392/May 27, 2013, http://www.soalcity.ir/node/2075.

"Teknīkhā-i dushman shināsī az manẓar-i Imām ʿAlī," 27 Abān 1388/November 18, 2009, https://article.tebyan.net/107858/.

"Tahājum-i farhangī, marg-i tadrījī-i yek millat" http://sbmu.ac.ir/?siteid=426&pageid=22839.

"Towṭiʿah-i family yā tablīghāt-i feminism," 13 Tīr 1390/July 4, 2011, http://www.ghatreh.com/news/nn7813132.

"Towtīʾah-i Yahūd barāye javānān-i Irānī," http://javanetakı.blogfa.com/category/5/توطئه-یهود-برای-جوانان-ایرانی.

"Towżīḥ-i Hāhimī barāye sokhnānesh dar bārah-i khalīfa avval," 7 Bahman 1392/ January 27, 2014, http://www.tabnak.ir/fa/news/374212.

"Tuhmat-i Yahūdsetīzī be mathābat-i yek silāḥ-i siyāsī manfaʿat ṭalabāneh," 27 Farvradīn 1389/April 16, 2010, http://www.farsnews.net/newstext.php?nn=8901141028.

"ʿUlamāʾ bā ṭard takfīrīhā, abrūyī Islam rā ḥafẓ konand/ ṣulḥ va-arāmesh rā beh Muslimīn bargardanīm," 28 Mehr 1395/October 19, 2016, http://hawzahnews.com/detail/News/396493.

"ʿUmar bin khaṭṭāb, khalīfa-i dovom keh būd va-cheh khuṣūṣiyat-i raftārī dasht?" http://www.islamquest.net/fa/archive/question/fa34625.

"ʿUmar bin al-Khaṭṭāb al-khalīfa al-thānī/Muʾāmarat al-Muslimīn ʿalā al-nabī Muḥammad," http://marwan1433.blogspot.co.il/2013/07/5.html.

"ʿUmar bin Khaṭṭāb sutūn-i panjom-i Yahūdiyān-i Medina," 25 Dey 1393/January 15, 2015, http://amīremomenin.persianblog.ir/post/942.

"ʿUmar wal-Yahūd: dirāsa nafsiyya fī khalfiyat ʿUmar al-dīnīyya," (pt. 2), https://groups.yahoo.com/neo/groups/al-sadeq/conversations/messages/60377.

"'Umar wal-Yahūd, yahūdiyat 'Umar bin al-Khaṭṭāb wa-ta'āmurihi ma'a al-Yahūd," October 5, 2014, http://marwan1433143.blogspot.co.il/2014/10/blog-post.html.

"'Umarkoshūn!! Yek rasm khorāfī va-aḥmaqāne az sūye barkhī jahhāl-i Shī'a!" 11 Azar 1393/December 2, 2014, http://313muslims.blog.ir/post.

"Al-Uṣūl al-Yahūdiyya li-Āl Sa'ūd wa-tadmīrihim li-athār al-nabī wal-ṣaḥāba bi-Makka wal-muḥāfaẓa 'alā athār al-Yahūd bi-Khaybar (pt. 2)," June 9, 2014, https://ar-ar.facebook.com/notes/673051039417372/.

"'Użvū ḥayāt-i ra'īsa bonyād-i ḥafẓ va-nashr athār va-arzeshhā-i difā' muqaddas," http://www.nedayeurmia.ir/index.aspx?fkeyid=&siteid=8&pageid=214&newsview=264860.

"Va'da-i ilāhī nisbat be nābūdī-i Yahūdiyān," 2 Azar 1391/November 22, 2012 http://www.tebyan.net/newindex.aspx/index.aspx?pid=934&articleid=751771.

"Va'da-i ilāhī bar nābūdī-i Yahūd," http://imammahdi.ir/1396/07/15/-وعده-الهی-بر-نابودی-یهود-2/.

"Vaḥdat az manẓar-i rahbar-i mu'aẓẓam-i inqilāb," 24 Dey 1392/January 14, 2014, http://www.irna.ir/fa/News/80993797.

"Vahhābiyat-i Āl Sa'ūd va-Yahūd," 7 Farvardīn 1392/March 27, 2013, https://rasekhoon.net/forum/thread/731244.

"Vahhābiyat beh Sunnat nazdīktar ast yā modernīte?" 19 Esfand 1395/March 9, 2017, http://ferghenews.com/fa/news/15359/وهابیت-به-سنت-نزدیک-تر-است-یا-مدرنیته.

"Vahhābiyat dar khidmat-i dushmanān-i Islām," http://almazhab.org/?p=282.

"Vahhābiyat dast-i parvardah Yahūdiyat ast," 16 Mordād 1393/August 7, 2014, http://www.rasanews.ir/detail/news/215610/23.

"Vahhābiyat va-'aql setīzī," https://farsi.al-shia.org/وهابیت-و-عقل-ستیزي.

"Vahhābiyat va-naqsh-i 'aql dar shenākht-i ma'ārif-i dīnī," 10 Bahman 1394/January 30, 2016, http://www.adyannet.com/fa/news/17615.

"Vahhābiyat va-Yahūd niyākān-i Āl Sa'ūd va-Muḥammad bin 'Abd al-Wahhāb" 25 Mordād 1394/August 16, 2015, http://313-nafar.rozblog.com/61.

"Vakonesh beh ihānat-i rūḥānī-i vahhābī beh Shī'īyān," *Akhbār-i Shī'īyān* 43 (Khordād 1388/May–June 2009) sic, http://www.hawzah.net/fa/Magazine/View/5658/6891/82959/.

"VākoneshhābehdīdārīiFā'izaHāshimībāmudīr-ijāmi'a-iBahā'īyān,"May14,2016,http://www.bbc.com/persian/iran/2016/05/160514_l57_fariba_kamalabadi_meetup_reax.

"Vāqi'īyat taḥrīf-shodeh dar ta'rīkh-i Islām: goft va-gūyī ikhtiṣāṣīi bā 'alāma muḥaqqiq sayyid Ja'far Murtażā 'Āmilī," *Mow'ūd*, 76 (Khordād 1386/June 2007), http://www.hawzah.net/fa/Magazine/View/4227/5729/570578C.

"Vaqtī Bahā'iyat pāygāh-i isti'mār dar Iran mīshavad," 29 Ordībehesht 1393/May 19, 2014, https://www.mashreghnews.ir/news/310619.

"Veterans Today: Rahbar-i Dāʿesh Yahūdī va-jāsūs mossad ast," 16 Mordād 1393/ August 7, 2014, https://www.mashreghnews.ir/news/333465/-رهبر-داعش-یهودی-و-جاسوس-موساد-است.

"Vīrāyishī jadīd az nohom Rabīʿ, jahālathā, khiṣārathā muntashir mīshavad," 11 Dey 1393/January 1, 2015, http://aghigh.ir/fa/news/44604.

"Vīzhegīhā-i mushābih beyn Vahhābiyat va-Yahūd," 4 Ordībehesht 1387/April 23, 2008 – http://valiasr-aj.com/fa/page.php?bank=shobheh&id=34.

"Weblāg takhaṣṣuṣī ḥażrat-i Abū Lūʾlūʾ ʿalayhi al-salām," http://abalolo.blogfa.com/.

"Yā Āl Saʿūd yā āl Yahūd," http://www.vahabiat.porsemani.ir/content/-«سعود-یا-»آل-یهود«.

"Yā Āl Saʿūd yā āl Yahūd al-waʿd al-waʿd," April 21, 2015, https://www.youtube.com/watch?v=f-KQbyQITeg.

"Yā Āl Saʿūd yā āl Yahūd sawfa nantaqimu minkum sharr intiqām_sayyid Amīr Ḥusaynī," https://www.youtube.com/watch?v=eaI_mf4r4Qo.

"Yahūd va-ākhar al-zamān 1," http://alhadid.blogfa.com/post-55.aspx.

"Yahūd dushman-i aṣlī-i Imām-i Zamān (ʿajala Allah taʿālā farajahu)," 27 Abān 1391/ November 17, 2017, http://www.shia-news.com/fa/news/46588.

"Yahūd shināsī az nigāhī-i ustād-I Qarahī," 23 Azar 1390/December 14, 2011, http://boyekhoshebandegi.blogfa.com/post/31.

"Yahūdī makhfī yā ānūsī," 12 Dey 1391/January 1, 2013, http://afshin1939.persianblog.ir/post/633.

"Yahūdīhā va-ṣahyūnīsthā az yek qimāsh hastand," n.d. http://mahdaviun.blogfa.com/post-36.aspx.

"Yahūdiyān beh ʿUmar bin Khaṭṭāb laqab Fārūq dādand," http://www.lamia.blogsky.com/1392/10/25/post-183.

"Yahūdiyān-i makhfī," 23 Shahrīvar 1390/September 14, 2011, http://www.mouood.org/component/k2/item/2022-یهودیان-مخفی.html.

"Yahūdiyān rāz sarmāyeh dārī modern," http://www.bashgah.net/fa/content/print_version/23593.

"Yahūdiyān, sarsakhtarīn-i dushmanān," 23 Khordād 1393/June 13, 2014, http://mouood.org/component/k2/item/20369.

"Yahūdiyānī keh iddiʿāʾ-i musalmānī mīkonand," 23 Khordād 1393/June 13, 2014, https://www.mouood.org/component/k2/item/20370.

"Yahūdiyat va-Vahhābiyat naqsha-i koshtan-i Shīʿīyān rā dar sar dārand," 26 Dey 1392/ January 16, 2014, http://www.diyarebaran.ir/50026.

"Yahūdī zadegan musalmān nemā (bakhsh-i pāyānī)," http://khoroosh.parsiblog.com/category/یهود/.

"Yūḥanā muʿallīm-i Yazīd beshenāsīd," 19 Abān 1392/November 10, 2013, http://www.mouood.org/component/k2/item/15236-یوحنا-معلم-یزید-را-بشناسید.html.

"Zavāl va-ufūl-i tamaddun-i gharb dar kalām rahbarī," May 1, 2013, http://zang110.mihanblog.com/.

"Ẓuhūr-i 'Dāʿesh' neshāneh-i nazdīk shodan-i ẓuhūr-i ḥażrat-i Mahdī ast," n.d., http://www.alvadossadegh.com/fa/article/mahdaviat/mahdavi-6/82559.

"Żuʿufhā-i inqilāb manshā ʾījād tashayyuʿ-i Inglīsī shod," 18 Bahman 1393/February 7, 2015, http://www.jahannews.com/interview/405574/ضعفهای-انقلاب-منشاء-ایجاد-تشیع-انگلیسی-سیاستهای-دوران-سازندگی-تکفیری-ها-تقویت.

"5 hizār sayt Vahhābiyat barāye munḥarif kardan javānān-i Irānī faʿāliyat dārand," 3 Tīr 1391/June 12, 2012, http://www.farsnews.com/newstext.php?nn=13910603000400.

Sources in Other Languages

Abisaab, Rula Jurdi. *Converting Persia: Religion and Power in the Safavid Empire* (London: I.B. Tauris, 2004).

Abu-ʿUksa, Wael. *Freedom in the Arab World: Concepts and Ideologies in Arabic Thought in the Nineteenth Century*. Cambridge: Cambridge University Press, 2016.

Adang, Kamila. "Medieval Muslim Polemics against the Jewish Scriptures," in *Muslim Perceptions of Other Religions: A Historical Survey*, edited by Jacques Waardenburg, 143–159. Oxford: Oxford University Press, 1999.

Adang, Kamila. *Muslim writers on Judaism and the Hebrew Bible: from Ibn Rabban to Ibn Hazm* (New York: E.J. Brill, 1996).

Adib-Moghaddam, Arshin. *A Meta-History of the Clash of Civilizations: Us and Them Beyond Orientalism* (London: Hurst, 2011).

ADL Global100: An Index of Anti-Semitism 2015 – http://global100.adl.org/#country/iran.

Afary, Janet. "The War Against Feminism in the Name of the Almighty: Making Sense of Gender and Muslim Fundamentalism," *New Left Review* 224 (1997): 89–110.

Afshar, Haleh. "Khomeini's Teachings and Their Implications for Women," *Feminist Review* 12 (1982): 59–72.

Afshari, ʿAli. "Khamenei preaches Shiʿite-Sunni unity against Islamic State, US," *Al-Monitor*, October 24, 2014 – http://www.al-monitor.com/pulse/originals/2014/10/iran-khamenei-sunni-Shiʿite-ghadeer.html#ixzz4CPWxUuQF.

Afshari, Reza. "The discourse and practice of human rights violations of Iranian *Bahaʾis* in the Islamic Republic of Iran," in *The Bahaʾis of Iran: Socio-Historical Studies*, edited by Dominic Parviz Brookshaw and Seena B. Fazel, 232–277. London: Routledge, 2012.

Aghaie, Kamran Scot. *The Martyrs of Karbala: Shiʿi Symbols and Rituals in Modern Iran* (Seattle: University of Washington Press, 2004).

Aghaie, Kamran Scot. "The Origins of the Sunnite-Shi'ite Divide and the Emergence of the Taziyeh Tradition." *TDR/The Drama Review* 49, no. 4 (2005): 42–47.

Ahmadi, Fereshteh. "Islamic feminism in Iran: Feminism in a New Islamic Context," *Journal of Feminist Studies in Religion* 22, no. 2 (Fall 2006): 33–53.

Ahmed, Leila. *Women and Gender in Islam: Roots of a Modern Debate*. New Haven: Yale University Press, 1992.

Ahouie, Mahdi. "Iranian Anti-Zionism and the Holocaust: A Long Discourse Dismissed," *Radical History Review* 105 (2009): 58–78.

Akhavi, Shahrough. *Religion and Politics in Contemporary Iran: Clergy-state Relations in the Pahlavi Period.* Albany: State University of New York Press, 1980.

Algar, Hamid. "An Introduction to the History of Freemasonry in Iran," *Middle Eastern Studies* 6, no. 3 (October 1970): 276–296.

Algar, Hamid. *Wahhabism: A critical essay*. Oneonta NY: Islamic Publications of America, 2002.

Aman, Fatemeh. "Iran's Uneasy Relationship with its Sunni Minority," March 21, 2016 – http://www.mei.edu/content/article/iran%E2%80%99s-uneasy-relationship-its-sunni-minorities.

Amanat, Abbas. *Apocalyptic Islam and Iranian Shi'ism*. London: I.B. Tauris, 2009.

Amanat, Abbas. "The Historical Roots of the Persecution of Babis and *Baha'is* in Iran," *The Baha'is of Iran: socio-historical studies*, edited by Dominic Parviz Brookshaw and Seena B. Fazel, 184–197. London: Routledge, 2012.

Amanat, Abbas. *Iran Facing Others.* New York: Palgrave Macmillan, 2012.

Amanat, Abbas. "Mujtahids and missionaries: Shīʿī responses to Christian polemics in the early Qajar period," in *Religion and Society in Qajar Iran*, ed., Robert Gleave, 247–269. London: Routledge, 2004.

Amanat, Mehrdad. *Jewish Identities in Iran: Resistance and Conversion to Islam and the Baha'i Faith*. London: I.B. Tauris, 2011.

Amnesty International. "Iran: Women's rights activists treated as 'enemies of the state' in renewed crackdown," August 10, 2016, https://www.amnesty.org/en/latest/news/2016/08/iran-womens-rights-activists-treated-as-enemies-of-the-state-in-renewed-crackdown/.

Ansari, Ali. *Iran under Ahmadinejad: The politics of confrontation.* Abingdon: Routledge, 2017.

Arjomand, Said A. *After Khomeini: Iran under his Successors*. Oxford: Oxford University Press, 2009.

Ashcraft, Richard. "Locke's Political Philosophy," in *The Cambridge Companion to Locke*, ed. Vere Chappell, 226–252. Cambridge: Cambridge University Press, 1994.

Ashraf, Ahmad. "Conspiracy Theories," *Encyclopaedia Iranica*, http://www.iranicaonline.org/articles/conspiracy-theories.

Asyraf Hj. A.B. Rahman and Nooraihan 'Ali. "The Influence of Al-Mawdudi and The Jama'at Al Islami Movement On Sayyid Qutb Writings," *World Journal of Islamic History and Civilization* 2, no. 4 (2012): 232–236.

Al-Azm, Sadik Jalal. "Orientalism, Occidentalism, and Islamism: Keynote Address to 'Orientalism and Fundamentalism in Islamic and Judaic Critique: A Conference Honoring Sadik Al-Azm'," *Comparative Studies of South Asia, Africa and the Middle East* 30:1 (2010): 6–13.

Azizi, Arash. "Iran targets 'MI6 Shi'ites'," May 4, 2015 – https://www.al-monitor.com/pulse/originals/2015/04/iran-shia-shirazi-movement-secterian.html.

Al-'Azmah, 'Aziz. *Ibn Khaldun*. London: Routledge, 1990.

Badran, Margot. *Feminism in Islam: Secular and Religious Convergence*. Oxford: Oneworld, 2001.

Baer, Marc David. "An Enemy Old and New: The Do¨nme, Anti-Semitism, and Conspiracy Theories in the Ottoman Empire and Turkish Republic," *The Jewish Quarterly Review* 103, no. 4 (Fall 2013): 523–555.

Bakhshandeh, Ehsan. *Occidentalism in Iran: Representations of the West in the Iranian Media*. London: I.B. Tauris, 2015.

Bali, Rıfat N. *A Scapegoat for All Seasons: The Dönmes or Crypto-Jews of Turkey*. Istanbul: Isis Press, 2008.

Bar-Tal, Daniel. "Societal Beliefs in Times of Intractable Conflict: The Israeli Case," *International Journal of Conflict Management*, 9 (1998): 22–50.

Bar-Tal, Daniel. "From Intractable Conflict Through Conflict Resolution to Reconciliation: Psychological Analysis," *Political Psychology* 21, no. 2 (June 2000): 351–365.

Barasher, Meir. "Les fils d'Israël, prototypes de la Chi'a: notes sur quelques traditions exégétiques du chi'isme duodécimain," *Perspectives* (*Revue de l'Université Hébraïque de Jérusalem*) 9 (2002), 125–137.

Baron, Beth. *The orphan scandal: Christian missionaries and the rise of the Muslim brotherhood*. Palo Alto: Stanford University Press, 2014.

Barzegar, Abbas. "The Persistence of Heresy: Paul of Tarsus, Ibn Saba', and Historical Narrative in Sunni Identity Formation," *Numen* 58 (2011): 207–231.

Baumann Gerd and Andre Gingrich (eds.). *Grammars of Identity/Alterity: A Structural Approach*. Oxford/New York: Berghahn, 2004.

Bayat, Mangol. "The Iranian Revolution of 1978–79: Fundamentalist or Modern?" *Middle East Journal* 37, no. 1 (Winter 1983): 30–42.

Beeman, William O. "Images of the Great Satan: Representations of the United States in the Iranian revolution," in *Religion and Politics in Iran: Shi'ism from Quietism to Revolution*, edited by Nikki Keddie, 191–217. New Haven: Yale University Press, 1983.

Behrooz, Maziar. "Factionalism in Iran under Khomeini," *Middle Eastern Studies* 27, no. 4 (Oct., 1991): 597–614.

Bengio, Ofra and Meir Litvak, eds. *The Sunna and Shi'a in History: Division and Ecumenism in the Muslim Middle East*. New York: Palgrave Macmillan, 2011.

Berlin, Isaiah. *Four Essays on Liberty*. Oxford: Clarendon Press, 1969.

Blanks, David R., and Michael Frassetto. "Introduction" in *Western Views of Islam in Medieval and Early Modern Europe: Perception of Other*, edited by Blanks and Frassetto, 1–8. New York: St. Martin, 1999.

Boroujerdi, Mehrzad. *Iranian Intellectuals and the West: The Tormented Triumph of Nativism*. Syracuse: Syracuse University Press, 1996.

Boroujerdi, Mehrzad. "The Ambivalent Modernity of Iranian Intellectuals," in *Intellectual Trends in Twentieth-Century Iran: a critical survey*, edited by Negin Nabavi. 11–23. University of Florida Press, 2003.

Boroujerdi, Mehrzad. "Iranian Islam and the Faustian Bargain of Western Modernity," *Journal of Peace Research* 34, no. 1 (February 1997): 1–5.

Breakwell, Glynis M. *Coping with Threatened Identities*. London: Methuen, 1986.

Brinner, William M. "The Image of the Jew as 'Other' in Medieval Arabic Texts," *Israel Oriental Studies* XIV.

Brunner, Rainer. *Islamic Ecumenism in the 20th Century: The Azhar and Shiism between Rapprochement and Restraint*. Leiden-Boston: Brill, 2004.

Brunner, Rainer and Werner Ende, eds. *Religious, Culture and Political History*. Leiden: Brill, 2001.

Buchta, Wilfrid. "Teheran Ecumenical Society (Majmaʿ al-taqrib): a veritable ecumenical revival or a Trojan horse of Iran?" in *The Twelver Shi'a in Modern Times, Religious, Culture and Political History*, edited by R. Brunner and W. Ende, 333–353. Leiden: Brill, 2001.

Buruma, Ian and Avishai Margalit. *Occidentalism: The West in the eyes of its enemies*. New York: Penguin, 2005.

Carrier James, G. (ed.). *Occidentalism: images of the West*. Oxford: Clarendon Press, 1995.

Chehabi, Houchang E. "Anatomy of Prejudice: Reflections on secular anti-*Baha'i*sm in Iran", in *The Baha'is of Iran: socio-historical studies*, edited by Dominic Parviz Brookshaw and Seena B. Fazel, 184–199. London: Routledge, 2012.

Chehabi, Houchang E. *Iranian Politics and Religious Modernism: the Liberation Movement of Iran under the Shah and Khomeini*. London: I.B. Tauris, 1990.

Chehabi, Houchang E. "The Paranoid Style in Iranian Historiography," in *Iran in the 20th Century: Historiography and Political Culture*, edited by Touraj Atabaki, 155–176. London: I.B. Tauris, 2009.

Clawson, Patrick. "The Paradox of Anti-Americanism in Iran," *MERIA Journal* 8, no. 1 March 2004 (Electronic edition).

Cohen, Lynn E. "Bakhtin's Carnival and Pretend Role Play: A Comparison of Social Contexts." *American Journal of Play* 4 (2011): 176–203.

Cole, Juan RI. "Shaikh al-Ra'is and Sultan Abdülhamid II: The Iranian Dimension of Pan-Islam," *Histories of the Modern Middle East: New Directions*, edited by Israel Gershoni, Hakan Erdem, Ursula Wokock, 167–185. Bolder: Lynn Rienner, 2002.

Cook, David. "Messianism in the Shi'ite Crescent," *Current Trends in Islamist Ideology* 11 (April 2011): 91–103.

Cook, Michael. "Al-Nahy 'an al-Munkar," *Encyclopaedia of Islam* – http://referenceworks.brillonline.com/entries/encyclopaedia-of-islam-2/al-nahy-an-al-munkar-COM_1437.

Cragg, Kenneth. *Muhammad and the Christian: a question of response*. Darton, Longman and Todd, Limited, 1984.

Dabashi, Hamid. *Theology of Discontent: the Ideological Foundations of the Islamic Revolution in Iran*. New York: New York University Press, 1993.

Dakake, Maria Massi. *The Charismatic Community: Shi'ite Identity in Early Islam*. Albany: SUNY Press, 2007.

Davari, Reza. "Is Philosophy Global or Regional?" http://rezadavari.ir/index.php?option=com_content&view=article&id=324:is-philosophy-global-or-regional&catid=32:archive&Itemid=76.

Day, Patrick. "Is the Concept of Freedom Essentially Contestable?" *Philosophy* 61, no. 235 (January 1986): 116–123.

Donohue, John J. *The Buwayhid dynasty in Iraq 334 H./945 to 403 H./1012: Shaping Institutions for the Future*. Leiden: Brill, 2003.

Dostoyevsky, Fyodor. *The Brothers Karamazov*. Aegitas, 2016.

Elad-Altman, Israel. "The Sunni-Shia Conversion Controversy," *Current Trends in Islamist Ideology* 5 (April 2007): 1–10.

Enayat, Hamid. "Iran: Khumayni's Concept of the 'Guardianship of the Jurisconsult," in *Islam in the Political Process*, edited by James P. Piscatori, 160–180. Cambridge: Cambridge University Press, 1982.

Enayat, Hamid. *Modern Islamic Political Thought*. London: I.B. Tauris, 2005.

Esfandiari, Golnaz. "Iranian Women's Monthly Under Pressure From Hard-Liners," September 1, 2014 – https://www.rferl.org/a/iran-womens-monthly-under-pressure/26561137.html.

Faghihi, Rohollah. "Can Rouhani's Citizens' Rights Charter be enforced?" http://www.al-monitor.com/pulse/originals/2016/12/iran-rouhani-citizens-rights-charter-conservative-criticism.html.

Farhi, Farideh. "Iran's 2008 Majlis Elections: The Game of Elite Competition," *Middle East Brief* 29 (2008).

Fischer, Klaus P. *History and prophecy: Oswald Spengler and The decline of the West* (New York: P. Lang, 1989).

Fischer, Michael. *Iran: From Religious Dispute to Revolution*. Cambridge, Mass.: Harvard University Press, 1980.

Fludernik, Monika. "Identity/alterity," in *The Cambridge Companion to Narrative*, edited by David Herman, 260–273. Cambridge: Cambridge University Press, 2007.

Friedmann, Yohanan. *Tolerance and Coercion in Islam: Interfaith Relations in the Muslim Tradition*. Cambridge: Cambridge University Press, 2003.

Fukuyama, Francis. "The End of History," *National Interest*, (Summer 1989): 3–18.

Fukuyama, Francis. *The End of History and the Last Man*. London, Penguin 1992.

Funk, Nathan C. and Abdul Aziz Said. "Islam and the West: Narratives of conflict and conflict transformation," *International Journal of Peace Studies* (2004): 1–28.

Furman, Uriah. "The Future of Islam, the Future of the West in Fundamentalist Islamic Theology," *HaMizrah Hahadash*, 51 (2012, Hebrew).

Gellately, Robert. *Stalin's Curse: Battling for Communism in War and Cold War*. Oxford: Oxford University Press, 2013.

Ghanea-Hercock, Nazila. *Human Rights, the UN and the Baha'is in Iran*. Leiden: Martinus Nijhoff Publishers, 2002.

Gheissari, Ali. "Constitutional Rights and the Development of Civil Law in Iran, 1907–1941," in *The Iranian Constitutional Revolution*, edited by Vanessa Martin and Houchang Chehabi, 69–80. London: I.B. Tauris, 2010.

Gheissari, Ali. *Iranian Intellectuals in the 20th Century*. Austin: University of Texas Press, 1998.

Ghobadzadeh, Naser. "Religious secularity: A vision for revisionist political Islam," *Philosophy and Social Criticism* 39, no. 10 (2013): 1005–1027.

Ghobadzdeh, Naser and Shahram Akbarzadeh. "Sectarianism and the prevalence of 'othering' in Islamic thought," *Third World Quarterly* 36, no. 4 (2015): 691–704.

Gieling, Saskia. *Religion and War in Revolutionary Iran*. London: I.B. Tauris, 1999.

Gleave, Robert. "The Status of the Battlefield Martyr in Classical Shi'i Law," in *Concepts of Martyrdom in Modern Islam: Political and Social Perspectives of Sacrifice and Death*, edited by in Meir Hatina and Meir Litvak, 52–75. London: I.B. Tauris, 2016.

Golkar, Saeid. *Captive Society: The Basij Militia and Social Control in Iran*. Washington DC: Woodrow Wilson Center Press, 2015.

Golnar, Mehran. "Socialization of Schoolchildren in the Islamic Republic of Iran," *Iranian Studies*, 22, no. 1 (1989): 35–50.

Graham, David A. "Iran's Beleaguered Sunnis," *The Atlantic Magazine*, January 6, 2016.

Haddad, Fanar. *Sectarianism in Iraq: Antagonistic Visions of Unity.* New York: Oxford University Press, 2011.

Haghighatnejad, Reza. "What Good is Rouhani's Citizens' Rights Charter?," https://iranwire.com/en/features/4271.

Harle, Vilho. "On the Concepts of the 'Other' and the 'Enemy,'" *History of European Ideas* 19, nos. 1–3 (1994): 27–34.

Harle, Vilho. "Otherness, identity, and politics: Towards a framework of analysis," *The European Legacy* 1, no. 2 (1996): 409–414.

Hasson, Isaac. "Contemporary Polemics between neo-Wahhabis and post-Khomeinist Shiʿites." *Hudson Institute: Research Monographs on the Muslim World*, 2009.

Hasson, Isaac. "Les Šiʿites vus par les neo-wahhabites," *Arabica* 53 (2006): 299–330.

Hatina, Meir. "Debating the 'Awakening Shi'a': Sunni Perceptions of the Iranian Revolution," in *The Sunna and Shi'a in History: Division and Ecumenism in the Muslim Middle East*, edited by Ofra Bengio and Meir Litvak, 203–221. New York: Palgrave Macmillan, 2011.

Hatina Meir and Meir Litvak, eds. *Concepts of Martyrdom in Modern Islam: Political and Social Perspectives of Sacrifice and Death*. London: I.B. Tauris, 2016.

Herman, Arthur. *The idea of decline in western history*. New York: Simon and Schuster, 1997.

Heschel, Susannah. "Historiography of Antisemitism versus Anti-Judaism: A Response to Robert Morgan," *Journal for the Study of the New Testament* 33, no. (2011), 257–279.

Heern, Zack. *The Emergence of Modern Shiʿism: Islamic Reform in Iraq and Iran*. London: Oneworld, 2015.

Hunt, Emily. "Zarqawi's 'Total War' on Iraqi Shiites Exposes a Divide among Sunni Jihadists," Washington Institute Policy Watch #1049, November 15, 2005.

Huntington, Samuel P. "The clash of civilizations?" *Foreign affairs* (1993): 22–49.

Huntington, Samuel P. *The clash of Civilizations and the Remaking of World Order*. New York: Simon and Shuster, 1996.

Hussein, Jassim M. *The Occultation of the Twelfth Imam*. London: Muhammadi Trust, 1982.

Intelligence and Terrorism Information Center. January 25, 2010 – http://www.terrorism-info.org.il/malam_multimedia/English/eng_n/html/iran_e048.htm.

Iran (Islamic Republic of)'s Constitution of 1979 with Amendments through 1989 – https://www.constituteproject.org/constitution/Iran_1989.pdf?lang=en.

Iran Human Rights Documentation Center. *A Faith Denied: The Persecution of the Baha'is of Iran*. New Haven, December 2006.

Iran Human Rights Monitor – https://iran-hrm.com/index.php/2017/06/22/mohareb-punishment.

Jahanbakhsh, Farough. *Islam, Democracy and Religious Modernism in Iran (1953–2000): From Bazargan to Soroush*. Leiden: Brill, 2001.

Jaspal, Rusi. "Anti-Semitism and anti-Zionism in Iran: the role of identity processes," *Israel Affairs* 19, no. (2013): 267–84.

Jaspal, Rusi. *Antisemitism and anti-Zionism: Representation, Cognition, and Everyday Talk*. London: Routledge, 2014.

Jaspal, Rusi and Marco Cinnirella. "Coping with potentially incompatible identities: accounts of religious, ethnic and sexual identities from British Pakistani men who identify as Muslim and gay," *British Journal of Social Psychology* 49, no. 4 (2010): 849–70.

Jaspal, Rusi and Marco Cinnirella. "The construction of ethnic identity: Insights from identity process theory," *Ethnicities* 12, no. 5 (2012): 503–530.

Jaspal, Rusi and Glynis M. Breakwell (eds.). *Identity Process Theory: Identity, Social Action and Social Change*. Cambridge: Cambridge University Press, 2014.

Jensen, Sune Qvotrup. "Othering, identity formation and agency," *Qualitative studies* 2, no. 2 (2011): 63–78.

Juergensmeyer, Mark. *The New Cold War? Religious Nationalism Confronts the Secular State*. Berkeley: University of California Press, 1993.

Kabir, Mafizullah. *The Buwayhid Dynasty of Baghdad (334/946–447/1055)*. Calcutta: Iran Society, 1964.

Kadivar, Mohsen. *Apostasy, Blasphemy, and Religious Freedom in Islam: A Critique Based on Demonstrative Jurisprudence*, web-Book: July 2014, – http://en.kadivar.com/2014/07/23/an-introduction-to-apostasy-blasphemy-religious-freedom-in-islam/.

Kadivar, Muhsen. "The Freedom of Religion and Belief in Islam," in *The New Voices of Islam: Reforming Politics and Modernity – A Reader*, edited by Mehran Kamrava, 119–142. London: I.B. Tauris, 2006.

Kadivar, Mohsen. "The Freedom of Thought and Religion in Islam," https://en.kadivar.com/2006/09/29/the-freedom-of-thought-and-religion-in-islam-2/.

Kamrava, Mehran. *Iran's Intellectual Revolution* (Cambridge: Cambridge University Press, 2008).

Kamrava, Mehran. "Khomeini and the West," in *A Critical Introduction to Khomeini*, edited by Arshin, Adib-Moghaddam, 149–169. Cambridge: Cambridge University Press, 2014.

Karateke, Hakan T.H. Erdem Çıpa and Helga Anetshofer (eds.). *Disliking Others: Loathing, Hostility, and Distrust in Premodern Ottoman Lands*. Boston: Academic Studies Press, 2018.

Kazemi Mousavi, Ahmad. "Sunni-Shi'i Rapprochement (Taqrib)," in *Shi'ite Heritage: Essays on Classical and Modern Traditions*, Editor and Translator L. Clarke, 301–315. Binghamton: Binghamton University Press, 2001.

Kazimi, Nibras. "Zarqawi's Anti-Shi'a Legacy: Original or Borrowed?" *Current Trends in Islamist Ideology* 4 (November 2006): 53–72.

Kazemzadeh, Firuz. "The *Baha'is* in Iran: Twenty years of repression," *Social Research* 67:2 (2000), 537–558.

Kennedy, Hugh. "al-Mutawakkil ʿAlā ʾllāh," EI2 – https://referenceworks.brillonline.com/entries/encyclopaedia-of-islam-2/al-mutawakkil-ala-llah-SIM_5658?s.num=1&s.f.s2_parent=s.f.book.encyclopaedia-of-islam-2&s.q=Mutawakkil.

Kenney, Jeffrey T. *Muslim Rebels: Kharijites and the Politics of Extremism in Egypt*. Oxford and New York: Oxford University Press, 2006.

Kermani, Navid. "The Fear of the Guardians: 24 Army Officers Write a Letter to President Khatami," in *The Twelver Shia in Modern Times: Religion, Culture and Political History*, edited by R. Brunner and W. Ende, 354–364. Leiden: Brill 2001.

Khalaji, Mahdi. *Apocalyptic Politics: On the Rationality of Iranian Policy*. Washington Institute for Near East Policy: Policy Focus #79, January 2008.

Khalaji, Mahdi. "The Dilemmas of Pan-Islamic Unity," *Current Trends in Islamist Ideology* vol. 9 (2009): 64–79.

Khamenei, Sayyid 'Ali. "Bringing U.S. to Its Knees, in the Region, is a Miracle of the Islamic Revolution," November 22, 2017, http://english.khamenei.ir/news/5289/Bringing-U-S-to-its-knees-in-the-region-is-a-miracle-of-the Revolution.

Khamenei, Sayyid 'Ali. "Freedom of Media in the U.S. means freedom of speech for the mogul-capitalists," May 3, 2019 – http://english.khamenei.ir/news/6675/Freedom-of-Media-in-the-U-S-means-freedom-of-speech-for-the.

Khamenei, Sayyid 'Ali. "Leader: Shias allied with MI6, Sunnis tied with CIA all enemies of Islam," – 9 January 2015 – http://www7.irna.ir/en/News/81457345/.

Khamenei, Sayyid 'Ali. "The Leader's remarks in a meeting with a group of officials, ambassadors of Muslim countries," 18 July 2015 – http://www.leader.ir/langs/en/index.php?p=bayanat&id=13451.

Khamenei, Sayyid 'Ali. "The Leader: We will not allow the US to make economic, political or cultural inroads into Iran," 15 August 2015 – http://www.leader.ir/langs/en/index.php?p=contentShow&id=13484.

Khamenei, Sayyid 'Ali. "Oppression of women can be prevented via laws and edification of men" April 16, 2017 – http://english.khamenei.ir/news/4763/Oppression-of-women-can-be-prevented-via-laws-and-edification.

Khamenei, Sayyid 'Ali. "Provoking the Feelings of Sunnis is a Plot Funded by the English Treasury'," 20 September 2016 – http://english.khamenei.ir/news/4167/Provoking-the-Feelings-of-Sunnis-is-a-Plot-Funded-by-the-inglish.

Khamenei, Sayyid 'Ali. "Supreme Leader's Full Speech in International Congress;" 26 November 2014 – http://www.miu-lb.org/details.php?id=591&cid=484.

Khamenei, Sayyid 'Ali. "9320–3: Physical contact with non-Muslims," http://www.khamenei.de/fatwas/12quesions.htm.

Khamenei – https://mobile.twitter.com/khamenei_ir/status/843423686963183620.

Khamenei – http://english.khamenei.ir/news/4731/Feminism-Women-are-not-commodities-says-Ayatollah-Khamenei, 23 March 2017.

Khomeini, Ruhollah. *Islam and Revolution: Writings and Declarations of Imam Khomeini* Translated and annotated by Hamid Algar. Berkeley: Mizan Press, 1981.

Khomeini, Ruhollah. *The political will of Imam Khomeini – The Political Will of Imam Khomeini* – http://www.alseraj.net/maktaba/kotob/english/Miscellaneousbooks/LastwillofImamKhomeini/occasion/ertehal/english/will/.

Khosrokhavar, Farhad. "Neo-conservative intellectuals in Iran," *Middle East Critique* 10, no. 9 (Fall 2001): 5–30.

Kia, Mehrdad. "Pan-Islamism in Late Nineteenth-Century Iran," *Middle Eastern Studies*, 32, no. 1 (January 1996): 30–52.

Kian, Azadeh. "Islamic Feminism in Iran: A New Form of Subjugation or the Emergence of Agency," Tr. Ethan Rundell, *Critique internationale*, 46 (2010/1): 45–66.

Kister, Meir J. "On 'Concessions' and Conduct: A Study in *Ḥadīth*," *Studies on the First Century of Islamic Society*, edited by G.H.A. Juynboll, 89–107. Carbondale: Southern Illinois University Press, 1982.

Kiyan, Azadeh. "Gendered Khomeini," in *A Critical Introduction to Khomeini*, ed. Arshin Adib-Moghaddam, 170–192. Cambridge: Cambridge University Press, 2014.

Kohlberg, Etan. "Barā'a in Shi'i Doctrine," *Jerusalem Studies in Arabic And Islam*, 7 (1986): 139–75.

Kohlberg, Etan. "The Term *Rāfida* in Imāmī Shīʿī use," *Journal of the American Oriental Society* 99, no. 4 (October–December 1977).

Kohlberg, Etan. "Some Imāmī Shīʿī Views on the Ṣaḥāba." *Jerusalem Studies in Arabic and Islam* 5 (1984): 143–75.

Koron, Eugene. "Tradition Meets Modernity: On the Conflict of Halakha and Political Liberty," *Tradition* 25, no. 4 (Summer 1991): 30–35.

Kramer, Joel L. *Humanism in the Renaissance of Islam: the Cultural Revival during the Buyid Age*. Leiden: Brill, 1992.

Kramer, Martin. "Khomeini's Messengers in Mecca," in his *Arab Awakening and Islamic Revival*. New Brunswick: Transaction, 1996, 161–87.

Küntzel, Matthias. *Unholy Hatreds: Holocaust Denial and Antisemitism in Iran*. No. 8. Vidal Sasson International Center for the Study of Antisemitism, 2007.

Landau, Jacob M. *Pan-Islam: History and Politics*. Abingdon: Routledge, 2015.

Langermann, Y. Tzvi. "Medical Israiliyyat? Ancient Islamic Medical Traditions Transcribed into the Hebrew Alphabet." *Aleph: Historical Studies in Science and Judaism* 6, no. 1 (2006): 373–398.

Langmuir, Gavin. *Toward a Definition of Antisemitism*. Berkeley: University of California Press, 1990.

Laoust, Henri. "Lapensée et l'action politiques d' al-Mawardi." *Revue des Etude Islamiques* 36 (1968).

Lassner, Jacob. *The Middle East Remembered: Forged Identities, Competing Narratives, Contested Spaces*. Ann Arbor: University of Michigan Press, 2000.

Lazarus-Yafeh, Hava. "Some neglected aspects of medieval Muslim polemics against Christianity," *Harvard Theological Review* 89, no. 1 (1996): 61–84.

Lecomte, G. "al-Saḳīfa," *EI2* http://dx.doi.org/10.1163/1573-3912_ei2glos_SIM_gi_04068.

Lewis, Bernard. *The Jews of Islam*. Princeton: Princeton UP, 1984.

Lewis, Bernard. *The Muslim Discovery of Europe*. New York: Norton and Co, 1982.

Lewis, Bernard. "Ottoman observers of Ottoman decline," *Studia Islamica* (1962), 71–87.

Litvak, Meir. "The Finances of the 'Ulamā' Communities of Najaf and Karbalā', 1796–1904," *Die Welt des Islams*, New Ser., 40, no. 1 (March, 2000): 41–66.

Litvak, Meir. "Iran," in *Middle East Contemporary Survey 2000*, edited by Bruce Maddy-Weitzman, 206–245. Tel Aviv: Moshe Dayan Center for Middle Eastern and African Studies, 2002.

Litvak, Meir. "Iranian Anti-Semitism and the Holocaust," in *Antisemitism Before and Since the Holocaust: Altered Contexts and Recent Perspectives*, edited by Anthony McElligott and Jeffrey Herf, 205–229. New York: Palgrave-McMillan, 2017.

Litvak, Meir. "The Islamic Republic of Iran and the Holocaust: Anti-Semitism and Anti-Zionism," *The Journal of Israeli History*, 25, no. 1 (March 2006): 267–284.

Litvak, Meir. "'More harmful than the Jews': anti-Shi'i polemics in modern radical Sunni discourse," in *Le shi'isme imamite quarante ans après: Hommage à Etan Kohlberg*, edited by Mohammad Ali Amir-Moezzi, Meir M. Bar-Asher, Simon Hopkins, 285–306. Paris: Brepols Publishers, 2008.

Litvak, Meir. *Shi'i Scholars of nineteenth-century Iraq: the 'ulama' of Najaf and Karbala'*. Cambridge: Cambridge University Press, 2002.

Litvak Meir and Ofra Bengio. "Introduction," in *Division and Ecumenism in Islam: The Sunna and Shi'a in History*, edited by Ofra Bengio and Meir Litvak, 1–16. New York: Palgrave-McMillan, 2011.

Louër, Laurence. *Transnational Shia politics: religious and political networks in the Gulf*. New York: Columbia University Press, 2008.

MacEoin, Denis. "The *Baha'is* of Iran: the Roots of Controversy," in *BRISMES Proceedings of the 1986 International Conference on Middle Eastern Studies*, Oxford, 1986: 207–15.

MacEoin, Denis. "Bahā'īsm," Encylopaedia Iranica *Encyclopædia Iranica*, http://www.iranicaonline.org/articles/bahaism-index.

MacEoin, Denis. "From Babism to Baha'ism: Problems of militancy, quietism, and conflation in the construction of a religion," *Religion* 13, no. 3 (1983): 219–255.

MacEoin, Denis. "Orthodoxy and Heterodoxy in Nineteenth-Century Shi'ism: The Cases of Shaykhism and Babism," *Journal of the American Oriental Society* 110, no. 2 (Apr.–Jun., 1990): 323–329.

Machlis, Elisheva. *Shi'i Sectarianism in the Middle East: Modernisation and the Quest for Islamic Universalism*. London: I.B. Tauris, 2014.

Madelung, Wilfred. *The succession to Muhammad: a Study of the Early Caliphate*. Cambridge: Cambridge University Press, 1997.

Maghen, Zeev. "Occultation in Perpetuum: Shi'ite Messianism and the policies of the Islamic Republic," *The Middle East Journal* 62, no. 2 (2008): 232–257.

Maghen, Zeev. "Unity or Hegemony? Iranian Attitudes to the Sunni-Shi'i Divide," in *The Sunna and Shi'a in History: Division and Ecumenism in the Muslim Middle East*, edited by Ofra Bengio and Meir Litvak, 183–202. New York: Palgrave Macmillan, 2011.

Mamuri, 'Ali. "Shiite leaders forbid insults against Sunnis," *al-Monitor* 13 January 2015.

Marschall, Christin. *Iran's Persian Gulf Policy: From Khomeini to Khatami*. London: Routledge, 2003.

Martin, Vanessa. *Creating an Islamic state: Khomeini and the making of a new Iran*. London: I.B. Tauris, 2003.

Marcotte, Roxanne D. "Religion and Freedom: Typology of an Iranian Discussion," *Australian Religion Studies Review* 18, no. 1 (2005): 49–67.

Matsunaga, Yasuyuki. "Mohsen Kadivar, an Advocate of Postrevivalist Islam in Iran." *British Journal of Middle Eastern Studies* 34, no. 3 (2007): 317–329.

Memri, Inquiry and Analysis – no. 521, 8 June 2003 – https://www.memri.org/reports/ahmadinejad-iran-nuclear-power-ready-participate-running-world.

Memri, Inquiry and Analysis Series Report no. 517, 29 May 2009 – http://www.memri.org/report/en/print3334.htm.

Memri, Inquiry and Analysis Series no. 1068, February 12, 2014 – https://www.memri.org/reports/iran-calls-violent-shiite-reaction-against-saudi-arabia.

Memri Inquiry and Analysis Series no. 1062, February 1, 2014 – https://www.memri.org/reports/tunisian-daily-al-shurouqs-campaign-against-sexual-jihad.

Memri Special Dispatch Series, no. 98, 7 June 2000 – https://www.memri.org/reports/protocols-Elders-zion-iranian-perspective.

Memri Special Dispatch Series, no. 705, 30 April 2004 – https://www.memri.org/reports/iranian-tv-series-based-protocols-elders-zion-and-jewish-control-hollywood.

Memri Special Dispatch Series no. 855, January 28, 2005 – https://www.memri.org/reports/antisemitism-and-holocaust-denial-iranian-media.

Memri Special Dispatch Series, no. 897, 22 April 2005 – https://www.memri.org/reports/ayatollah-nouri-hamedani-%E2%80%98fight-jews-and-vanquish-them-so-hasten-coming-hidden-imam%E2%80%99.

Memri Special Dispatch no. 6759, January 27, 2017 – https://www.memri.org/reports/khamenei-associate-mehdi-taeb-jews-are-only-ones-who-need-weapons-mass-destruction-order.

Memri Special Dispatch no. 7758, November 12, 2018 – https://www.memri.org/reports/antisemitic-conference-tehran-iranian-presidency-official-denies-holocaust-fact-we-do-show.

Memritv.org clip. No 1575, 5 October 2007.

Memri clip no. 1298 – "Hizbullah Deputy Secretary-General Sheik Naim Qassem on the Difference between Jews and Zionists," 17 October 2006 – https://www.memri.org/tv/hizbullah-deputy-secretary-general-sheik-naim-qassem-difference-between-jews-and-zionists/transcript.

Memri Clip no. 4042, February 1, 2013 – https://www.memri.org/tv/head-iranian-think-tank-advising-khamenei-jews-want-nuclear-bomb-kill-muslims-and-achieve-world/transcript.

Menashri, David. *Iran: A Decade of War and Revolution* New York: Holmes and Meier, 1990.

Menashri, David. "The Jews of Iran: Between the Shah and Khomeini," in *Anti-Semitism in Times of Crisis*, edited by Sander Gilman and Steven Katz, 353–371. New York: New York University Press, 1991.

Menashri, David. *Post-Revolutionary Politics in Iran: Religion, Society, and Power.* Portland, OR: F. Cass, 2001.

Mernissi, Fatima Mernissi. *Islam and Democracy: Fear of the Modern World.* Wokingham: Basic Books, 1992.

Mirbagheri, Farid. "Narrowing the Gap or Camouflaging the Divide: An Analysis of Mohammad Khatami's 'Dialogue of Civilizations'," *British Journal of Middle Eastern Studies* 34, no. 3 (December 2007): 305–316.

Mir-Hosseini, Ziba. "Beyond 'Islam' vs 'Feminism,'" IDS Bulletin 42, no. 1 (January 2011): 67–77.

Mir-Hosseini, Ziba. "The Conservative–Reformist Conflict Over Women's Rights in Iran," *International Journal of Politics, Culture and Society* 16, no. 1 (Fall 2002): 37–53.

Mir-Hosseini, Ziba. "Debating Women: Gender and the Public Sphere in Post-Revolutionary Iran," in *Civil Society in the Muslim World Contemporary Perspectives*, edited by Amyn B. Sajoo, 95–122. London: I.B. Tauris, 2002.

Mir-Hosseini, Ziba. *Islam and Gender: The religious debate in contemporary Iran* Princeton: Princeton University Press, 1999.

Mir-Hosseini, Ziba. "Religious Modernists and the 'Woman Question': Challenges and Complicities," in *Twenty Years of Islamic Revolution: Political and Social Transition in Iran since 1979*, edited by Eric Hooglund, 74–95. Syracuse University Press, 2002.

Mirsepassi, Ali. *Intellectual Discourse and the Politics of Modernization Negotiating Modernity in Iran*. Cambridge: Cambridge University Press, 2004.

Mirsepassi, Ali. "Religious Intellectuals and Western Critiques of Secular Modernity," *Comparative Studies of South Asia, Africa and the Middle East* 26, no. 3 (2006): 416–433.

Misbah Yazdī, Muhammad Taqī. *Freedom: The Unstated Facts and Points* Tr., Mansoor Limba, n.p. Ahl al-Bayt World Assembly, 2005.

Moaddel, Mansoor. *Islamic Modernism, Nationalism and Fundamentalism: Episode and Discourse*. Chicago: University of Chicago Press, 2005.

Moghadam, Valentine M. "Islamic Feminism and Its Discontents: Toward a Resolution of the Debate," *Signs* 27, no. 4 (Summer 2002): 1135–1171.

Moghissi, Haideh. *Populism and Feminism in Iran: Women's Struggle in a Male-Defined Revolutionary Movement*. New York: St. Martin, 1994.

Mojtahed Shabestari. "Interview with Mohammad Mojtahed Shabestari (Part 1): 'Islam Is a Religion, Not a Political Agenda'" (n.d.) – https://en.qantara.de/content/interview-with-mohammad-mojtahed-shabestari-part-1-islam-is-a-religion-not-a-political-0.

Momen, Moojan. *An Introduction to Shi'i Islam*. New Haven: Yale University Press, 1985.

Moreen, Vera. "The Problems of Conversion among Iranian Jews in the Seventeenth and Eighteenth Centuries," *Iranian Studies* 19, nos. 3–4 (Summer 1986): 215–228.

Mosse, George. *Nationalism and sexuality: respectability and abnormal sexuality in modern Europe*. New York: H. Fertig, 1985.

Najmabadi, Afsaneh. "Feminism in an Islamic Republic: years of hardship, years of growth," edited by Y. Yazbeck Haddad and J. Esposito, *Islam, Gender, and Social Change*, 59–84. Oxford: Oxford University Press, 1999.

Nakash, Yitzhak. "The Visitation of the Shrines of the Imams and the Shi'i Mujtahids in the Early Twentieth Century," *Studia Islamica* 81 (1995): 153–164.

Nakash, Yitzhak. "An Attempt to Trace the Origin of the Rituals of 'Āshūrā'," *Die Welt des Islams* 33, no. 2 (Nov., 1993): 161–181.

Netzer, Amnon. "Antisemitism in Iran, 1925–1950," *Peamim* 29 (1987): 5–31 (Hebrew).

Nikou, Semira N. "Iranians split on Egypt's turmoil," *The Iran Primer*, February 3, 2011 – http://iranprimer.usip.org/blog/2011/feb/03/iranians-split-egypt%E2%80%99s-turmoil.

Nirenberg, David. *Anti-Judaism: the Western Tradition*. New York: W.W. Norton, 2013.

Okolie, Andrew C. "Introduction to the Special Issue-Identity: Now You Don't See It; Now You Do," *Identity: An International Journal of Theory and Research* 3, no. 1 (2003): 1–7.

Paivandi, Saeed. *Discrimination and Intolerance in Iran's Textbooks*. A Freedom House Publication, 2008.

Parchami, 'Ali. "The 'Arab Spring': the view from Tehran," *Contemporary Politics* 18, no. 1 (2012): 35–52.

Pew Research Center, *The Pew Global Project Attitude, February 2010*, http://pewglobal.org/reports/pdf/268.pdf.

Pardo, Eldad J. *Imperial Dreams: The Paradox of Iranian Education* (The Institute for Monitoring Peace and Tolerance in School Education [IMPACT-SE], May 2015).

Parsa, Misagh. *Democracy in Iran: Why it Failed and How it might Succeed*. Cambridge: Harvard University Press, 2016.

Parvizi Amineh, Mehdi and Shmuel N. Eisenstadt. "The Iranian revolution: The multiple contexts of the Iranian revolution." *Perspectives on Global Development and Technology* 6, no. 1 (2007): 129–157.

Perlman, Moshe. "The Medieval Polemics between Islam and Judaism," in *Religion in a Religious Age*, edited by S.D. Goitein, 103–138. Cambridge, MA: Association for Jewish Studies, 1974.

Pourjavady, Reza and Sabine Schmidtke. "Muslim Polemics against Judaism and Christianity in 18th Century Iran. The Literary Sources of Āqā Muḥammad 'Alī Bihbahānī's (1144/1732–1216/1801) Rādd-i shubahāt al-kuffār," *Studia Iranica* 35:1 (2006): 69–96.

Pratt, Douglas. "Muslim–Jewish relations: some Islamic paradigms," *Islam and Christian–Muslim Relations* 21, no. 1 (2010): 11–21.

Quandt, William B. *Saudi Arabia in the 1980s: Foreign Policy, Security, and Oil.* Washington DC: The Brookings Institution, 1981.

Rahimi, Babak. "How Iran Views the Egyptian Crisis," Jamestown Foundation – February 3, 2011 – https://jamestown.org/program/special-commentary-how-iran-views-the-egyptian-crisis/.

Rahimiyan, Orly. "'The Jew has a lot of money, too': Representations of Jews in twentieth-century Iranian culture," *Constructing Nationalism in Iran: From the Qajars to the Islamic Republic*, edited by Meir Litvak, 173–189. Abingdon: Routledge, 2017.

Rahimiyan, Orly. "The Protocols of the Elders of Zion in Iranian political and cultural discourse," in *The Global Impact of the Protocols of the Elders of Zion: A Century-Old Myth*, edited by Esther Webman, 196–219. London: Routledge, 2012.

Rajaee, Farhang. *Islamism and Modernism: The Changing Discourse in Iran.* Austin: University of Texas Press, 2007.

Ravitsky, Aviezer. "The Question of Tolerance: Between Pluralism and Paternalism," in *Freedom on the Billboards: Other Voices of Religious Thought* (Tel Aviv: Am Oved, 1999, Hebrew).

Razavi, Shahra. "Islamic politics, human rights and women's claims for equality in Iran," *Third World Quarterly* 27, no. 7 (2006): 1223–1237.

Richey, Russell E. "Denominations and denominationalism: An American morphology." *Reimagining Denominationalism: Interpretive Essays* (1994): 74–98.

Rosenthal, Frantz. *The Muslim Concept of Freedom.* Leiden: Brill, 1960.

Rosenzweig, Franz. *Ninety-Two Poems and Hymns of Yehuda Halevi* Translated by Thomas Kovach et al. (Albany: SUNY Press, 2000).

Rosiny, Stephan. "The tragedy of Fatima al-Zahra in the debate of two Shi'ite theologians in Lebanon." *The Twelver Shia in Modern Times: Religious Culture and Political History*, edited by Werner Ende and Rainer Brunner, 207–219. Leiden: Brill 2001.

Rousseau, Jean-Jacques. *The Social Contract and Other Later Political Writings* Tr. Victor Gourevitch. Cambridge: Cambridge University Press, 1997.

Sadjadpour, Karim. *Reading Khamenei: The World View of Iran's Most Powerful Leader.* Carnegie Endowment for International Peace, 2008.

Sadri, Mahmoud. "Hojjatiya," *Encyclopædia Iranica*, http://www.iranicaonline.org/articles/hojjatiya.

Sadri, Mahmoud. "Sacral Defense of Secularism: The Political Theologies of Soroush, Shabestari, and Kadivar," *International Journal of Politics, Culture and Society* 15, no. 2 (Winter 2001): 257–270.

Samaha, Nour. "Hezbollah chief urges Middle East to unite against ISIL," 16 Feb 2015 – http://www.aljazeera.com/news/2015/02/hezbollah-hassan-nasrallah-isil-150216214845193.html.

Samii, A. William. "The Nation and Its Minorities: Ethnicity, Unity, and State Policy in Iran." *Comparative Studies of South Asia, Africa and the Middle East* 20, no. 1 (2000): 128–137.

Sanasarian, Eliz. *Religious minorities in Iran*. Cambridge: Cambridge University Press, 2000.

Sande, G.N., George R. Goethals and Lisa Ferarri, Leila T. Worth. "Value Guided Attributions: maintaining the Moral Self Image and the Diabolical Enemy-Image," *Journal of Social Issues*, 45 (1989): 91–118.

Savory, Roger M. "Relations between the Safavid State and its Non-Muslim Minorities," *Islam and Christian-Muslim Relations* 14, no. 4 (October 2003): 435–458.

Scherberger, Max. "The Confrontation between Sunni and Shi'i Empires: Ottoman-Safavid Relations between the Fourteenth and the Seventeenth Century," in *The Sunna and Shi'a in History: Division and Ecumenism in Islam*, edited Ofra Bengio and Meir Litvak, 51–67. New York: Palgrave-McMillan, 2011.

Schirazi, Asghar. *The Constitution of Iran: Politics and the State in the Islamic Republic* London: I.B. Tauris, 1998.

Schimitz, M. "Kaʿb al-Aḥbār," *Encyclopaedia of Islam (EI2)*. Leiden: Brill, 1978 4:316–17.

Schmitt, Carl. *The Concept of the Political*. Expanded Edition (1932), trans. by G. Schwab. Chicago: University of Chicago Press, 2007.

Seidel, Roman. "Portrait Mohammad Shabestari: Faith, Freedom, and Reason," (n.d.) – http://en.qantara.de/content/portrait-mohammad-shabestari-faith-freedom-and-reason.

Shahbaz, Syed 'Ali. "The heretical cult of Wahhabi Takfiri Salafis," http://www.imamreza.net/eng/imamreza.php?id=11318.

Shakdem, Catherine. "Feminism – Women are not commodities says Ayatollah Khamenei," 23 March 2017 – http://english.khamenei.ir/news/4731/Feminism-Women-are-not-commodities-says-Ayatollah-Khamenei.

Sharon, Moshe. *The Baha'i Faith and its Holy Writ: The Most Holy Book (al-Kitab al-Aqdas)*. Jerusalem: Carmel Publishing, 2005 (Hebrew).

A Shi'ite Encyclopedia (Ahlul Bayt Digital Islamic Library Project, 2017, electronic edition).

Shahvar, Soli. "The Islamic Regime in Iran and Its Attitude towards the Jews: The Religious and Political Dimensions," *Immigrants and Minorities*, 27:1, pp. 94–98.

Shavit, Uriya (ed.). *The Decline of the West: the Rise of Islam? Studies in Civilizational Discourse*. Tel Aviv: Ha-Kibbutz ha-Meuchad, 2010, in Hebrew.

Silberstein, Laurence J. "Others within and others without: Rethinking Jewish identity and culture," in *The other in Jewish Thought and History: Constructions of Jewish Culture and Identity*, edited by Silberstein, Laurence J., and Robert L. Cohn, 1–34. New York: NYU Press, 1994.

Siavoshi, Sussan. "Ayatollah Khomeini and the contemporary debate on freedom." *Journal of Islamic Studies* 18:1 (2007), 14–42.

Siavoshi, Sussan. "Ayatullah Mesbah Yazdi: Politics, Knowledge, and the Good Life," *The Muslim World*, 100 (January 2010): 124–144.

Siavoshi, Sussan. "Human Rights and the Dissident Grand Ayatullah Hussain 'Ali Montazeri," *The Muslim World* 106, no. 3 (2016): 605–625.

Sivan, Emmanuel. *Islamic Fundamentalism and anti-Semitism*. Jerusalem: Israeli Academy of Sciences, 1985 (Hebrew).

Sivan, Emmanuel. *Radical Islam: Medieval Theology and Modern Politics*. New Haven: Yale University Press, 1990.

Slomp, Gabriella. *Carl Schmitt and the Politics of Hostility, Violence and Terror* New York: Palgrave-McMillan, 2009.

Smith, Peter. *The Babi and Baha'i Religions*. Cambridge: Cambridge University Press, 1987.

Smith, Peter. "A note on Babi and Baha'i numbers in Iran," *Iranian Studies* 17:2–3 (1984), 295–301.

Soage, Ana Belén. "Islamism and Modernity: The Political Thought of Sayyid Qutb," *Totalitarian Movements and Political Religions* 10, no. 2(2009): 189–203.

Soofi, Abdol S. and Sepehr Ghazinoory, eds. *Science and Innovations in Iran: development, progress, and challenges*. New York: Palgrave Macmillan, 2013.

Soroudi, Sorour. "The concept of Jewish Impurity and its Reflection in Persian and Judeo-Persian Traditions," *Irano Judaica*, III (1993): 1–29.

Soroush, Abdkarim. "Reason and Freedom," in *Reason, Freedom, and Democracy in Islam: The Essential Writings of Abdolkarim Soroush*, translated, edited, annotated, and with a critical introduction by Mahmoud Sadri and Ahmad Sadri, 88–104. New York: Oxford University Press, 2000.

Stanfield Johnson, Rosemary. "Sunni Survival in Safavid Iran: Anti-Sunni Activities during the Reign of Tahmasp I," *Iranian Studies* 27, nos. 1–4 (1994): 123–133.

Staszak, Jean-François. "Other/Otherness," in *International Encyclopedia of Human Geography*, edited by R. Kitchin and N. Thrift. Oxford: Elsevier, 2008, vol. 8, pp. 43–47.

Stein, Howard F. "The Indispensable Enemy and American-Soviet Relations," *Ethos* 17, no. 4 (December 1989), 71–90.

Steinberg, Guido. "The Shiites in the Eastern Province of Saudi Arabia (al-Ahsa'), 1913–1953," in *The Twelver Shia in Modern Times: Religious Culture and Political History*, edited by R. Brunner and W. Ende, 236–254. Leiden: Brill, 2001.

Steinberg, Guido. "The Wahhabiyya and Shi'ism, from 1744/45 to 2008," in *The Sunna and Shi'a in History: Division and Ecumenism in the Muslim Middle East*, edited by Ofra Bengio and Meir Litvak, 163–182. New York: Palgrave-McMillan, 2011.

Stewart, Devin J. "Popular Shi'ism in Medieval Egypt: Vestiges of Islamic Sectarian Polemics in Egyptian Arabic." *Studia Islamica*, 84 (1996): 35–66.

Stillman, Norman A. "Anti-Judaism and Antisemitism in the Arab and Islamic Worlds Prior to 1948," in *Antisemitism: A History*, edited by Albert S. Lindemann and Richard Levy, 117–139. Oxford: Oxford University Press, 2010.

Stümpel-Hatami, Isabel. "Christianity as Described by Persian Muslims," in *Muslim Perceptions of Other Religions: A Historical Survey*, edited by Jacques Waardenburg, 227–239. Oxford: Oxford University Press, 1999.

Subhani, Ja'far. "Takfir is totally condemned in Islam: Grand Ayatollah Subhani," 26 November 2014, http://sachtimes.com/en/world/around-the-world/1813-takfir-is-totally-condemned-in-islam-grand-ayatollah-subhani.

Szanto, Edith. "Beyond the Karbala Paradigm: Rethinking Revolution and Redemption in Twelver Shi'a Mourning Rituals," *Journal of Shi'a Islamic Studies*, VI, no. 1 (Winter 2013): 75–91.

Tabaar, Mohammad A. "The Beloved Great Satan: The Portrayal of the U.S. in the Iranian Media since 9/11," *Crossroads* 6, no. 1 (2006): 20–45.

Takeyh, Ray. "A Profile in Defiance," *The National Interest*, March 17, 2006.

Tavakoli-Targhi, Mohamad. "Anti-Baha'ism and Islamism in Iran," in *The Baha'is of Iran: socio-historical studies*, edited by Dominic Parviz Brookshaw and Seena B. Fazel, 200–231. London: Routledge, 2012.

Teitelbaum, Joshua. "The Shiites of Saudi Arabia." *Current Trends in Islamist Ideology* 10 (2010): 72–86.

Tholib, Udjang. *The Reign of the caliph al-Qadir billāh (381/991–422/1031)* (PhD Dissertation, McGill University, 2002).

Tibi, Bassam. *Islam Between Politics and Culture*. New York: Palgrave, 2001.

Tibi, Bassam. *The Challenge of Fundamentalism: Political Islam* and the New *World Disorder*. Berkeley: University of California Press, 1999.

Triandafyllidou Anna and Ruth Wodak. "Conceptual and methodological questions in the study of collective identities: An introduction," *Journal of Language and Politics* 2, no. 2 (2003): 205–223.

Tsadik, Daniel. *Between foreigners and Shi'is: Nineteenth-century Iran and its Jewish Minority*. Stanford, Calif.: Stanford University Press, 2007.

Tsadki, Daniel. "Judeo-Persian Communities of Iran, v. Qajar Period (1786–1925)," *Encyclopedia Iranica*, http://www.iranicaonline.org/articles/judeo-persian-communities-v-qajar-period.

Toynbee, Arnold J. *A Study of History*, 12 Vols. Oxford: Oxford University Press, 1961.

United State, Department of State. "Iran 2017 International Religious Freedom Report," https://www.state.gov/documents/organization/281226.pdf.

Vaglieri, L. Veccia. "Ghadir Khumm," *Encyclopaedia of Islam*. New Edition, vol. 2, 993–94.

Vahdat, Farzin. "Post-Revolutionary Islamic Discourses on Modernity in Iran: Expansion and Contraction of Human Subjectivity," *International Journal of Middle East Studies* 35, no. 4 (November 2003) 599–631.

Vahdat, Farzin. "Post-revolutionary discourses of Mohammad Mojtahed Shabestari and Mohsen Kadivar: Reconciling the terms of mediated subjectivity," *Critique: Critical Middle Eastern Studies*, 16 (Spring 2000), 31–54.

Vahdat, Farzin. "Post-revolutionary Islamic modernity in Iran: the intersubjective hermeneutics of Mohamad Mojtahed Shabestari." *Modern Muslim Intellectuals and the Qur'an* (2004): 193–224.

Vajda, George. "Isrāʾīliyyāt," *Encyclopaedia of Islam*, Second Edition http://dx.doi.org/10.1163/1573-3912_ei2glos_SIM_gi_01840.

Vakili, Valla. "Debating Religion and Politics in Iran: The Political Thought of Abdolkarim Soroush," Council on Foreign Relations, January 1996 – http://www.drsoroush.com/PDF/E-CMO-19960100-Debating_Religion_and_Politics_in_Iran-Valla_Vakili.pdf.

Van Gelder, Geert Jan and Ed de Moor (eds.). *The Middle East and Europe: Encounters and Exchanges*. Amsterdam: Rodopi, 1992.

Vatanka, Alex. "Pulling the Strings – How Khamenei Will Prevent Reform in Iran," *Foreign Affairs*, November 2015 – https://www.foreignaffairs.com/articles/iran/2015-11-25/pulling-strings.

Vinx, Lars. "Carl Schmitt", *The Stanford Encyclopedia of Philosophy* (Spring 2016 Edition) – https://plato.stanford.edu/archives/spr2016/entries/schmitt/.

Waardenburg, Jacques. "The Early Period, 610–650," in *Muslim Perceptions of Other Religions: A Historical Survey*, edited by Jacques Waardenburg, 3–17. Oxford: Oxford University Press, 1999.

Waardenburg, Jacques. "The Modern Period: 1500–1950," in *Muslim Perceptions of Other Religions: A Historical Survey*, edited by Jacques Waardenburg, 70–84. Oxford: Oxford University Pres, 1999.

Walcher, Heidi. *In the shadow of the King: Zill al-Sultan and Isfahan under the Qajars*. London: I.B. Tauris, 2008.

Warburg, Margit Warburg. "Baha'is of Iran: Power, Prejudice and Persecutions," in *Religious minorities in the Middle East domination, self-empowerment, accommodation*, edited by Anh Nga Longva, Anne Sofie Roald, 195–218, Leiden: Brill, 2011.

Ward, Seth. "Muḥammad Said: 'You Are Only a Jew from the Jews of Sepphoris': Allegations of the Jewish Ancestry of Some Umayyads," *Journal of Near Eastern Studies* 60, no. 1 (January 2001): 31–42.

Wasserstrom, Steven. *Between Muslim and Jew: The Problem of Symbiosis under Early Islam* Princeton: Princeton University Press, 2014.

Webman, Esther. "Arab Perceptions of Globalization," in *Middle Eastern Societies and the West: Accommodation or Clash of Civilization*, edited by Meir Litvak, 177–198. Tel Aviv: Dayan Center, 2006.

Webman, Esther. "The 'Jew' as a Metaphor for Evil in Arab Public Discourse," *The Journal of the Middle East and Africa* 6, nos. 3–4 (2015): 275–292.

Wehrey, Frederic et al. *Saudi-Iranian Relations Since the Fall of Saddam: Rivalry, Cooperation, and Implications for U.S. Policy*. Santa Monica: Rand Corporation, 2009.

Wiktorowicz, Quintan. "Anatomy of the Salafi Movement," *Studies in Conflict and Terrorism* 29, no. 3 (2006): 207–239.

Winter, Stephen. *The Shiites of Lebanon under Ottoman Rule, 1516–1788*. Cambridge: Cambridge University Press, 2010.

Yazdani, Mina. "*The Confessions of Dolgoruki*: The Crisis of Identity and the Creation of a Master Narrative," in *Iran Facing Others*, edited by Abbas Amanat, 245–266. New York: Palgrave Macmillan, 2012.

Yazdani, Mina. "The Islamic Revolution's Internal Other: The Case of Ayatollah Khomeini and the Baha'is of Iran," *Journal of Religious History* 36, no. 4 (December 2012): 593–604.

Yeroushalmi, David. *The Jews of Iran in the Nineteenth Century: Aspects of History, Community, and Culture*. Leiden: Brill, 2009.

Zeidan, David. "The Islamic fundamentalist view of life as a perennial battle." *Middle East Review of International Affairs* 5, no. 4 (2001) – Electronic edition.

Zimmt, Raz. "The Return of the Eulogists," *Spotlight on Iran*, 24 October 2013 – http://www.terrorism-info.org.il/en/articleprint.aspx?id=20587.

Anonymous

"Ayatollah Mesbah Yazdi Accuses the Jews," http://www.terrorism-info.org.il/en/article/18156.

"The Baba Shuja-i-din aka Abu lulu, Mausoleum," http://www.allempires.com/forum/printer_friendly_posts.asp?TID=10804.

"Egypt's Al-Azhar Stops Short of Declaring ISIS Apostates," December 13, 2014, https://eng-archive.aawsat.com/theaawsat/news-middle-east/egypts-al-azhar-stops-short-of-declaring-isis-apostates.

"Freemasonry," Holocaust Encyclopedia – https://www.ushmm.org/wlc/en/article.php?ModuleId=10007186.

"Imam Khamenei Blasts West's View of Women," 12 August 2015 – http://sayyidali.com/getting-to-know/imam-khamenei-blasts-wests-view-of-women.html; Khamenei speech at Khorasan, http://farsi.khamenei.ir/speech-content?id=21293.

"Iran women's magazine forced to close," *Al-Monitor*, May 18, 2015 – http://www.al-monitor.com/pulse/originals/2015/05/iran-womens-magazine-zanan-emrooz-suspended.html#ixzz5YVv9lQw7.

"Iranian Judiciary Chief: West Seeking to Promote Shi'itophobia to Stir Differences among Muslims," November 27, 2014, http://www.14masoomeen.org/News-Detail-mod-Iranian-Judiciary-Chief-West-Seeking-to-Promote-Shi'itophobia-to-Stir-Differences-among-Muslims-id.html.

"Mesbah Yazdi Comments on Islamic Human Rights," IRNA, 21 Apr 2000 – IAP20000421000013.

"Positive and Negative Liberty," *Stanford Encyclopedia of Philosophy*, http://plato.stanford.edu/entries/liberty-positive-negative/.

"The Paradox of Positive Liberty," *Stanford Encyclopedia of Philosophy*, http://plato.stanford.edu/entries/liberty-positive-negative/.

"Rouhani Chastise Trump in UN Speech," September 20, 2017 – http://iranprimer.usip.org/blog/2017/sep/20/rouhani-chastises-trump-un-speech.

"Rohani Officially Launches Iranian Citizens' Rights Charter," 19 December 2016 – http://www.rferl.org/a/iran-rohani-launches-citizens-rights-charter/28184867.html.

"Sistani Issues Fatwa Against Sectarian Violence in Iraq," October 11, 2013 – monitor.com/pulse/en/contents/articles/originals/2013/10/iraqi-moderates-manage-sectarianism.html##ixzz3OomGSvl2.

"Takfiris are trying to promote Islamophobia: Ayatollah Hussaini Boshehri," 26 November 2014, http://en.shabestan.ir/search/Hussaini%20Boshehri.

"Takfiris Handiwork of US, UK, Israel," November 27, 2014, http://www.islamicinvitationturkey.com/2014/11/27/takfiris-handiwork-of-us-uk-israel/.

"Takfiris misrepresent Islam as violent religion: Ayatollah Sobhani" 25 November 2014 – http://theiranproject.com/blog/2014/11/25/takfiris-misrepresent-islam-as-violent-religion-ayatollah-sobhani/.

"Why Does Egypt's Largest Muslim Beacon, Al-Azhar, Refuse to Declare IS 'Apostate'?" April 14, 2017, http://www.egyptindependent.com/why-does-egypt-s-largest-muslim-beacon-al-azhar-refuse-declare-apostate/.

Newspapers

Aftāb-i Yazd
al-Ahram Weekly
al-Akhbār (Lebanon)
Bahār
Christian Science Monitor
Frankfurter Allgemeine Zeitung
Hamshahri
Intikhāb
Irān
Iran Daily
Iran News
IRIB Television
Islam Times
Iʿtimād-i Millī
Javān
Jerusalem Post
Kayhān
Mardom Sālārī
Al-Maṣrī al-Yawm
MidEast Mirror
Middle East Insight
New York Times
Qods
Al-Ra'y (Iraq)
Risālat
Al-Sharq al-Awsaṭ
Ṣubḥ-i Ṣādiq
Star of the West
Time
Washington Post
Washington Times
Ya Lesārat al-Ḥusayn
Voice and Vision of the Islamic Republic of Iran Network
AFP
IRNA
Radio Free Europe/Radio Liberty Iran Report
Iran Observed – Middle East Institute

Index

ʿAbbāsid family 15, 97
ʿAbbāsiyān, Ḥusayn 286
ʿAbd Allah ibn Saba' 89
ʿAbd al-ʿAzīz b. Saʿūd, Amīr 17n, 153
ʿAbd al-ʿAzīz b. Saʿūd, King 153
  and Jews 172, 173
ʿAbd al-Bahā' 247, 251, 252, 256n, 269
ʿAbd al-Ḥamīd, Ṣā'ib 174
ʿAbduh, Muḥammad 176
ʿAbdülhamīd II, Sulṭān 116, 169
abrogation 75, 234
Abū Bakr, Caliph 13, 94, 95, 97, 98, 100, 114, 115, 118, 129n, 141n
Abū Ḥanīfa, al-Nuʿmān b. Thābit 158
Abū Lū'lū' Nahāvandī 128, 129, 131–134, 143
Abu-ʿUksa, Wael 195
Abūl-Qāsimī, Javād 178
Adib-Moghaddam, Arshin 11, 21
Afary, Janet 267
Afghanistan 22, 56, 155, 161, 270
Afsā, Muḥammad Jaʿfar 63
Afshar, Haleh 268
Aghājarī, Hāshim 218
Ahl al-ḥadīth 176
Aḥmadī, Nāṣir 129
Ahmadinezhad, Maḥmūd 29, 48, 275
  and the West 61, 69
Ahmed, Leila 267
Aḥsā' province 124, 153
ʿAisha, the Prophet's wife 98, 124, 128, 142, 158
Akhbārī school 114
ʿAkkā 245, 256
Āl-i Aḥmad, Jalāl 39, 41
ʿAlāmī Hashtrūdī, Muḥammad 201
ʿAlavī, Seyyed Ḥusayn 58
Alawites 119
Algeria 56
ʿAlī b. Abī Ṭālib, Imām 13, 14, 15, 26, 46, 153, 157, 164, 175, 215
  and Aisha 124, 128, 142, 158
  and Jews 96, 97, 99, 100, 101, 102, 110, 169
  and knowing the enemy 26
  Martyrdom of 26, 103
  and Muḥammad's succession 81, 88n, 89, 92, 94, 95, 100, 102, 113, 128, 144, 278, 296
  and ʿUmar 133, 141, 142, 143
ʿAlī al-Hādī, Imām 128
Allah (See also God) 143, 144
Amanat, Abbas 18, 40, 235, 237
Ammār think tank 85
America (See also the US) 20, 22, 37, 38, 39, 48, 60, 62, 165, 180
  American Islam 122, 147, 186, 296
  Arrogance 60
  Crimes 56, 86, 122, 173, 174
  Culture of 40, 44, 64, 85
  Intervention in Iran 48, 95, 117, 187, 192, 215, 238, 253, 257, 258, 260, 261
  Invasion of Iraq 51
  and Israel, Zionism 53, 54, 79, 130, 161, 168, 184, 186
  and Takfīrīs 177, 185, 186, 286, 296
Al-Amīn, Muḥsin 154
Amīnī, Ibrāhīm 109, 211, 269
Amnesty International 290
ʿAnaza 169
Anṣār al-Mahdī 81
Anti-Judaism vii, 74–79
Anti-Semitism vii, 73, 77
  and anti-Zionism 240
  Definition of 21, 78
  In Iran 23, 74, 78, 79–84
  Western 109, 266, 293, 295
Apostasy, Apostate(s) viii, 31, 127, 156, 157, 196
  and Bahā'īs 225, 226, 234, 235, 238, 239, 240, 264, 297
  and Companions 95
  Challenge to Islam 220, 221, 222, 296
  Charge against Shīʿīs 120, 130, 151, 153, 189, 191
  Charge against reformists 218
  Definition of 218, 219, 220, 221, 222, 228, 233, 235n
  Jihādī-Salafīs charging others 120, 156, 178, 179, 191

Apostasy, Apostate(s) (cont.)
of jihādī-Salafīs as apostates 189, 190, 192, 218, 294, 297
and Liberty 31, 194, 195, 213, 217, 219, 220, 223, 226, 228
Persecution of 218, 221, 231, 240, 241
Reformists and 225, 226, 228, 229
Sunnī views on 156, 176, 189, 218
Wahhābi use of 152, 153, 157, 159, 160, 161, 173, 175, 177
Arabian Peninsula 99, 172
Arabs 21, 22, 69, 74, 98, 99, 107, 111, 117–120, 125, 155, 156, 171, 174, 195, 256, 267, 280, 296
Jāhilī 103, 189, 192
upheaval 130, 155, 169, 297
Arab-Israeli conflict 6
Ardabīlī, ʿAbd al-Karīm Mūsavī 216
Arendt, Hanna 58
arrogance, global (See also America and US) 22, 23, 35, 39, 60, 177, 183, 184, 185, 212, 294
Aryanism 77
Asadabādī (Afghani), Jamal al-Dīn 176
ʿĀshūrāʾ event 103
commemoration of 16, 104, 105, 113, 127, 147, 148, 165
culture of 253
Asia 43
Assembly of Experts 55, 69, 211
Al-ʿAwā, Muḥammad Salīm 124
Axis of Resistance 119
Ayatollah Mujtahidī Seminary 52
ʿAyn al-Molk, Ḥabībollah 257
Azarī-Qommī, Aḥmad 269
Al-Azhar 125, 128, 189

Bāb, Seyyed ʿAlī Muḥammad Shīrāzī 243, 244, 256, 296
Bābī movement, Bābīsm 172, 234, 236, 243, 247, 253
Azālī Bābīs 249, 252, 254
Badran, Margot 285
Baghdad 114, 127, 155, 192, 243
Al-Baghdādī, Abū Bakr 182, 184
Bahāʾī, Bahāʾīsm ix 1, 3, 4, 5, 14, 16, 31, 32, 116, 225, 226, **234–266**, 293, 296, 298, 300, 301
Appeal of 249, 250
Apostasy of 235, 239, 240, 264
As traitors 236, 237, 250, 251, 253–254, 258, 260, 261, 265, 293
and British 172, 253, 254, 258, 296
Critique of Doctrines 234, 242–249
Deviance of 234, 239, 241–242, 250, 261, 297
and feminism 269, 275
and Jews 93, 254, 255, 262, 266
and Pahlavis 235, 257, 258, 259
Persecution of 235, 236, 237, 238, 240, 266, 297
Ritual impurity 239, 240, 263
and Qajars 252
and Russia 236, 253, 254
and US 19
and West 248, 251, 254, 259, 265
and Zionism, Israel 19, 237, 238, 252, 254, 256, 257, 258, 259, 262, 265, 275
Bahāʾī World Congress 237
Bahāʾullah, Ḥusayn ʿAlī Nūrī 234, 241–246, 248, 249, 253, 256, 262
Bahjat, Muḥammad Taqī 79n, 130, 131
Bakhtin, Mikhail 138
Baluchistan 150n, 155
Banū Qaynuqaʿ 169
Banū Qurayẓa 96, 108
Bāqir al-ʿUlūm Research Center 283
Barāʾa 113
Bar-Tal Daniel 6
Basīj militia 37, 43n, 59, 71, 82
Baṣra 168
Baʿth party (Iraq) 22, 212
Bāṭin 52, 130, 216, 246
Beheshtī, Aḥmad 55, 56
Beheshtī, Muḥammad 199, 204
Ben ʿAlī, Zein al-ʿAbidin 69
Berlin, Isaiah 198, 207, 208, 295
Bible, Hebrew 18, 75, 256n
Bidʿat 141, 164, 165, 166, 178
Bihbihānī Kirmānshāhī, Aqā Muḥammad ʿAlī 17
Bihbihānī, Muḥammad Bāqir 166
Bishārat Cultural Institute 270
Boroujerdī, Muḥammad Ḥusayn 117, 259
Britain British viii, 43, 44, 95, 161, 168, 173

and Bahā'īs 238, 253, 254, 257, 258, 260, 296
and Jihādī-Salafsts 192, 296
and Shīrāzī faction 147
and Wahhabism 167–168, 172, 173, 174
and Zionism 79, 172, 173
Būshehr 255
Būshehrī, Seyyed Hāshim Ḥusaynī 181
Būyīd family 15, 76, 114
Byzantines (see Rūm)

Cairo 117
Caliphs 13, 15, 31, 97, 101, 114, 115, 123, 125, 126, 133, 134
Caliphate 100, 118, 142n, 155
Usurpation of 81, 95, 133
capitalism 56, 59, 66, 110
decline of 60, 61, 67, 268
and feminism 274, 275
and imperialism 52
and Jews 36n, 80
Caucasus 173
China, Chinese 2, 48
Christians 7n
in Quran 8, 9, 11, 17, 18, 75, 84, 100, 108, 218, 238, 262
and Jews 20, 77, 78, 79, 87, 88, 91n, 93, 105, 152, 165, 187, 232, 263, 266
Christianity 8–12, 15, 16, 40, 75, 77, 184, 250, 256n, 264, 266
and Bahā'īs 248
denominations 123
doctrines 18, 93, 94
Jewish corruption of 91, 93, 94
Scriptures 17
Christian-messianic Zionism 99
The Church 75, 91n, 207
Catholic 266
Citizens' Rights Charter 194
clash of civilizations 12, 30, 62–64, 66
Clergy (Shīʿī) 21, 22, 29, 32, 39, 73, 80n, 105, 110–112, 114, 117, 118, 129, 138, 140–143, 145, 146, 149, 164, 197, 214, 232, 270, 272, 289, 292, 300
Religious role of 25, 121, 163, 182, 183, 193, 211, 216, 231, 234, 246, 247, 251, 257, 259, 280, 283, 286–288, 290, 291, 294, 297, 298
Political activity of 32, 158, 173, 235, 237, 238, 242, 249, 251, 253, 262, 265, 266, 293, 298
Sunni 296
Wahhābī 154
Cold War 12, 63, 208
Colonialism 43, 282n
Commanding right and forbidding wrong 208
Communism 41, 53, 65, 66, 208
Companions of the Prophet 94, 114, 158
and ʿAlī 95, 99, 113, 175
and Jews 96
New Shīʿī respect of 122, 124, 149
Sunni veneration of 112, 171
Tolerance of 161
Vilification of 113, 123, 126, 127, 131, 136, 141–143, 146
congresses, Islamic 119
Constitution of Medina 8
constitution 190, 195
Constitution, Islamic Republic 79, 194, 207, 210, 211, 216, 218, 223, 238, 251n, 262, 269
Convention on the Elimination of All of Discrimination against Women 281
converts (Jewish) 17, 92–96, 99, 110
to Christianity 218
coup (1953) 236
courts 261
for clergy 213
press 289
revolutionary 218
Cox, Percy 172
Crescent, Shīʿī 119
Crusades, Crusaders 10, 11, 36, 180
Crusader-Zionist 102
cursing (see also sabb) the enemies of the Shīʿa 31, 104, 113, 115, 123, 125–127, 131, 136, 142, 143, 146

Dabashi, Hamid 34
Al-Daghamseh, Saber 167
Damascus 13, 61
Dār al-taqrīb 117
Dashtī, Muḥammad 96
Dāvarī, Reża
on liberty 199
on the West 35, 48, 53, 56, 57, 62

Day of Judgment 65
democracy 29, 38, 50, 194, 224, 225, 229
  liberal 51, 60, 65–67, 231
Descartes, René 58
Devil worshiping 250
Dhimmīs 261
dialogue of civilizations 38, 63
Dolgorukov, Dimitry Ivanovich 236
Dönmeh 168, 169
Dostoyevsky, Fyodor 207
downtrodden 39, 67
Durkheim, Émile 241

The East 11, 35, 67, 68, 71, 196, 198, 244, 247
  Islamic 42
Egypt 120, 188, 189
Encyclopaedia Iranica 260
End of History vii, 30, 62, 65–67, 299
  Mahdavi end of 30, 51, 68, 72, 299
Enlightenment 37, 39, 49, 54, 57, 66, 80n, 163, 197, 247
  Counter- 37, 51
Eshkivarī, Ḥasan Yūsufī 30, 218
Europe 10, 11, 12, 38, 48, 49, 51, 54, 59, 138, 150, 185, 225, 240, 247, 252, 254

Faḍlallah, ʿAlī 124
Faḍlallah, Muḥammad Ḥusayn 124, 210
Family and Women News Analysis Center 286
Family Protection Law 268, 276
Fanon, Franz 41
Farhangistān-i ʿUlūm-i Islāmī 60
fascism 53
Fāṭima 96, 98, 100n, 128, 141, 278
  and Nine Rabi 129, 130, 137, 138, 143, 144
  Death of 97, 113
Fāṭimī, Amīn 275
Fāṭimīnezhād, Majīd 159
Fayāż, Ibrāhīm 247
Fayżiyya seminary 269
Fāżil Lankarānī, Muḥammad 131, 140, 174
Fāżil Maybudī, Muḥammad Taqī 216
Fedai'yan-i Islam 117
feminism ix, 32, 266, **267–291**
  and Bahā'ism 269
  and capitalism 274, 290
  and clerical monopoly 280, 287, 290, 291
  and enemies 1, 4, 5, 16
  Islamic 32, 248, 285–290
  and Islamic law 271, 276–281, 286–288
  threat to morality 281–285
  and Western cultural offensive 267–268, 271–275, 286–287, 290
  and Zionism 274–275, 290
Feuerbach, Ludwig 227
Ficicchia, Francesco 242
Fiqh-i pūyā 269
fourteen pure ones 100
France 56
freedom (see also liberty) viii, 34, 56, 65, 138, 195, 197–199, 201–203, 206, 208, 213, 230, 232, 283, 291
  and apostates 217–221
  of expression 194, 214–217, 242
  political 211, 212
  reformists' view on 222–230
  spiritual 203–207, 209, 210, 211, 228, 230, 231
  of thought 207, 213, 214, 227
  Western concepts of 196, 198, 200, 202, 203, 281, 282, 294
Freemasons 80, 110, 254, 275
Foucault, Michel 11
Fukuyama, Francis 30, 65, 66, 67, 74, 295, 299
fundamentalism 19, 267
  Islamic 12, 19

Gaza 122
gender 197, 267–270, 290
  differences 277
  equality 28, 29, 268, 269, 270, 276, 277, 279, 283, 285, 291
General Will 208
Germany
  Nazi 26, 53n
Ghadīr Khumm 95
  Day of 130
Ghazna 270
Gharbzedegī (see also Westoxication) 39, 46
Ghulāt 164
Giddens, Anthony 58
Globalization 44, 45n, 61, 64
Gobineau, Joseph Arthur 54

God 5, 7, 40, 49, 156, 197, 200, 203, 212, 213. 216, 223, 229, 251n, 273
  and Bahā'īs 234, 241, 242, 243, 244, 261, 263
  and Christians 8, 94
  duties towards 25, 26, 121, 152, 158, 195, 204, 206, 207, 219, 220, 224, 227, 228
  enemies of 20, 125, 126, 220, 221, 226
  and Jews 8–10, 78, 85, 86, 91, 94, 96, 105, 143, 170
  and Shī'īs 3, 20, 65, 67, 113, 128, 138, 144, 152, 153, 157
  submission to 31, 187, 205, 209, 230, 231
  Wahhabi concepts of 156, 162–165, 170, 187
  and Western perceptions of 55, 57, 58, 61, 67, 198, 200
  and women 276, 279
Golpāygānī, Muḥammad Reżā 239
Greece, Greek 2, 8, 35
Gulf
  Arab states of 124, 125, 154
  Persian 172, 173

Habermas, Jurgen 58, 227
Ḥabīb, Yāsir 124, 146
Habsburg Empire 173
Ḥadīth 25, 71, 87, 118, 132, 135
  fabricated 92, 96, 99, 101
  "raf' al-qalam" 138
  Shī'ī 18, 97, 98, 100n, 108
  Sunnī 8, 92
Hā'irī, Kāẓim 190
Al-Ḥallāj Ḥusayn b. Manṣūr 243
Ḥamās 119
Hamdāniyān, Fāṭima 283
Ḥamīdī, Muḥammad Mahdī 103
Ḥanbalī school 167
hardliner, trend 28, 76, 109, 111, 170, 194, 198, 213, 218, 223, 225, 226, 228, 283, 300
Ḥasan al-'Askarī, Imām 98, 139
Ḥasan b. 'Alī, Imām 103
Hāshimī, Fā'iza 264
Ḥażrat-i Valī-i 'Aṣr Institute 141
Heidegger, Martin 37, 51n, 53, 58n
Hegel, Georg Wilhelm Friedrich 57, 65
Hempher 173
Herder, Johann Gottfried 37
Hidden Imām 16, 105, 126, 182, 244
ḥijāb 212, 267, 284
Ḥijāz 153
Hitler, Adolf 56
Hobbes, Thomas 57, 201, 206n
Ḥojjatiya 236, 259, 260
Hollywood 99
homosexuality, homosexuals 59, 199, 240
Hoveida, Amīr 'Abbās 257, 258
ḥudūd 244
human rights 29, 200, 217, 222, 229, 262, 263, 270, 287
humanism vii, 35, 52, 55–60, 247, 254, 274, 275, 287, 290
Huntington, Samuel 12, 30, 62, 295
Hurmuz, Straits of 173
Ḥurūfiyya sect 242
Ḥusayn, 'Abd al-Ṣamad 115
Ḥusayn b. 'Alī Imam 26, 103, 135, 153
  Martyrdom of 14, 103, 113, 298
  Shrine of 152
Ḥusayn, Mīr Seyyed 128
Ḥusayniyān, Rūḥollah 213, 257
Ḥusaynzādeh Abūl-Ḥasan 286
hypocrites (*munāfiqīn*) 23, 26, 84, 88, 96, 105, 132, 140

Ibn al-'Alqami 192
Ibn Idrīs al-Ḥillī 132
Ibn Muljam 97
Ibn Taymiyya, Taqī al-Dīn Aḥmad 20, 128n, 155, 162
Ibrāhīm-niyā, Muḥammad 81 95, 97, 103, 104
'Īd al-Zahrā' 128, 132
Identity Process Theory (IPT) 4, 5, 298
ijtihād 18, 158, 162, 179, 191, 196, 243, 279, 280, 285–288, 300
imāmat 92, 139, 242, 243
imāms, the twelve 100n, 113, 129, 130, 143, 152, 153, 171, 176, 182, 201, 216, 283, 288
  and cursing 126, 127
  and Jews 97
  and 'Umar's death 130, 135, 138
imperialism 10, 32, 35, 40, 52, 56, 79, 86, 117, 125, 205, 212, 235, 252, 253, 255, 257, 265, 267, 271, 292, 293, 294

imperialism (cont.)
and Bahā'īs 249, 251, 252, 254, 255, 257, 258, 259 265
British 172–174, 254
clergy opposition to 253, 259
cultural 32, 39, 267, 271
Russian 236, 253
and Wahhābism 172, 177
and Zionism 78, 235, 258
India 44, 161, 173, 188
Indonesia 130
Inquisition 199
Inquisitor, Grand 207
Institute of Applied History 90
intellectuals 12, 24, 34, 46, 48, 50, 85, 116
anti-West 38
religious 29, 77, 213, 218
Western 54
West-leaning 21, 23, 39–41, 44, 268, 272
International Covenant on Civil and Political Rights 220
International House of Justice 249, 260
International Union for Muslim Scholars 124
International Conference on Radical and Takfīrī Movements 176, 178, 180, 187, 188
Iraq 14, 15, 76, 114, 127, 128, 152, 182, 259
Baʿth regime in 22, 106n
Iranian involvement in 191
ISIS in Iraq 122, 184, 185, 192, 193, 295
Al-Qāʿida organization in 20, 120, 122, 155, 174
sectarian violence in 120, 122, 129, 130, 131, 132, 155, 161, 180
Shīʿī community in 22, 112, 119, 120
Shīʿī militias in 150
Shīʿī missionary activity in 16
Sunni minority in 22
US invasion of 48, 51, 56, 155
war with Iran 21, 46, 48, 118, 154, 189, 260, 265
Ishāqī, Seyyed Ḥusayn 201, 287
Ishāqīyya sect 242
Ishārat, Bushrā 286
ISIS (Islamic State of Iraq and Shā'm, *Daʿesh*) viii, 131, 132, 150, 155, 174, 177, 179, 188, 190
and Jews, Zionism 122, 184–186, 298
and the Mahdi 181–184, 193, 298, 299
and Wahhābism 177, 186
and the West 122, 184–186
Islamic-Iranian Blueprint for Progress 70, 71
Islamic Propagation Office of the Qom Seminary 269
Islamic Revolution Guards Corps, IRGC (See also Revolution Guards) 26, 36n, 201
Islamic Unity conferences 122
Islamism 1, 109, 292
and othering 19
Islamophobia 63, 85, 181
Israel (See also Zionism) 34, 75, 79, 80, 99, 104, 105, 107, 267, 295
and Bahā'īs 19, 236, 256, 257, 260, 262, 264
children of 75
and Ḥizballah 22, 120
and Muḥammad Reża Shāh 78
and Sunnīs 91
and Takfīrīs 180, 181, 184, 190
and US 54, 118, 121, 167, 185
Israel-Lebanon War 54, 120, 172, 174, 175
Isrā'īliyyāt 93, 162
istinbāṭ 158, 280

Jaʿfar al-Ṣādiq, Imām 26, 100n, 103, 113, 117
Jaʿfarī school 119
Jāhiliyya 188, 275
Neo-jāhiliyya 188
Jamāʿat al-tablīgh 159
Jamāʿat al-taqrīb 117
Jāmiʿa-i rūḥāniyat mubāriz 28
Jamshīdī, Muḥammad Ḥusayn 45
Jannatī, Aḥmad 60, 215
Japan 34, 36, 165
Jaspal, Rusi 4, 74
Javādī Āmolī, ʿAbdollah
on gender 269, 277
on liberty 200
Javānī, Yadollah 24, 25
Jazāyīrī, Muḥammad ʿAlī Musāvī 182
Jerusalem 106, 116, 117, 143
Jesus
as a prophet 18, 93, 94
Jews and 9, 10, 96

Jews, Jewish (See also Judaism, Zionism) vii, viii, 1, 2, 3, 5, 8, 14, 15, 17, 18, 26, 31, 73–111, 143, 148, 152, 193, 204, 232, 262, 263, 266, 292, 295, 296, 300
and ʿAlī 96–98, 110
and **Bahāʾīs** 14, 235, 237, 254, 255, 256, 262, 265
and capitalism 73, 80, 254
and Christians 8, 10, 12, 78, 79, 88, 93–94
conflation with Zionism 80, 81, 95, 102
conspiracies of 79, 82–85, 87, 88, 90–96, 99, 101, 134, 173, 222, 251, 255, 256, 296
converts to Islam 84, 92–96, 99, 110
corruption of 81, 85, 86, 107, 256
distinction from Zionism 79
enmity towards Islām and Shīʿīsm 31, 73, 78, 80, 84–93, 97, 100, 101, 110, 134, 148, 186, 293, 295, 297, 298, 299and Feminism 274, 275
and Freemasons 80, 85
harm to Shīʿīsm 74, 75, 89–97, 100, 293
and imperialism 79, 111, 173, 174, 235
and Iran 76, 77, 80, 110, 232, 238, 240, 255, 262
Islamic doctrines on 10, 77, 78
and Jihādī-Salafīsts 80, 184–187, 192
and Karbalāʾ tragedy 103, 104
and Mahdi 104–109, 111, 297
metaphore of evil 74, 100, 168, 171, 186
other enemies as 85, 89, 96, 97, 100, 101, 102, 142, 148, 164, 168–172, 174, 296, 297
and the Prophet 8, 9, 10, 88, 96, 97, 100
The Qurʾān and 9, 23, 85, 88, 95, 165, 293, 295
and ritual impurity 75, 79, 110, 293, 294
and Sufyānī 106, 107
and Sunnis 76, 90, 96, 297
and ʿUmar b. Khattab 98, 99, 100, 102, 133
and Umayyads 101, 102, 103, 104, 110, 133
and Wahhābism 168–172, 80, 111, 152, 165, 167, 168–174, 192
and West 20, 36, 40, 78, 80, 103, 110, 111, 165, 168, 174, 192, 293, 294, 295
Jewish
Law 8, 9, 76, 93, 198, 204
pre-modern Shīʿī attitudes on 75, 76
racism 84, 86, 87
Scriptures 17, 18, 75, 102, 184
Shīʿī Polemics on 17
tribes 8, 88, 91
Jewish Studies Center 102
Jihādī-Salafīsts (see also Takfīrīs) 1, 3, 4, 5, 22, 31, 69, 117, 146, 151, 154, 159, 190, 193, 292, 295, 296
as apostates 127, 189, 190, 218, 297
doctrine 72, 120, 155, 156, 158, 175, 176, 177, 178, 179, 186, 187, 188, 190, 191
and Jews, Zionism 80, 148, 184, 186, 192, 297
and Khawārij 156, 178
and mainstream Sunnis 155, 156, 158, 174, 175, 176, 178, 189
and Umayyads 183
violent conduct of 151, 155, 178, 179, 180, 187, 188, 189, 190, 233, 294
and Wahhābism 151, 156, 158, 174–175, 177, 187, 301
and West 184, 186, 187, 192, 296
jizya 108, 109
Joint Comprehensive Plan of Action 70
Judaism 73, 74, 99, 109, 111, 232, 294
as a heavenly religion 10, 83, 294
and Christianity 8, 11, 15, 93, 94, 266
in Iran 78
polemics against 10, 16, 75, 76, 77, 83, 295, 300
and racism 84, 87n
relations to Shīʿīm 76, 91, 293, 296
and Sunnīsm 90
and Zionism 79, 80, 81, 82n, 294
Jurdi Abisaab, Rula 115

Kaʿb al-Aḥbār 92, 96
and Muʿāwiya 101
and ʿUmar 99, 101, 102, 133
Kachuyān, Ḥusayn 146
Kadīvar, Muḥsin 30
and Bahāʾīs 262–264
and gender equality 270, 291
and liberty 225, 226, 232
and Vilāyat-i faqīh 216, 224
Kalām 176, 178
Kalām Institute 244
Kamālabādī, Farībā 264
Kant, Immanuel 58, 196, 198, 206, 279

Al-Karakī, ʿAlī 115
Karbalāʾ 145, 152, 155, 161, 246, 300
massacre102, 103, 104, 113, 298
paradigm 14,
Karrūbī, Mahdī 217
Kāshān 18, 128, 129, 131, 143, 145
Kāshif al-Ghitāʾ, Jaʿfar 153, 157
Kāshif al-Ghitāʾ, Muḥammad Ḥusayn 116
Kasravī, Aḥmad 85
Kāẓimyan-pūr, Ghulām Reżā 171
Khalaji, Mehdi 117
Khamenei, ʿAlī 32, 85, 96, 300
and Bahāʾīs 239, 240, 250, 266
and Blueprint for Progress 70, 71
and feminism 279, 284
and global arrogance 23, 294
and Jews 79, 134, 240
and liberty 197, 202, 204n, 205, 217, 221
and Palestine 79, 180
and perception of the "enemies" 1, 22, 23, 24, 26, 70, 127, 250
and pluralism 158
and politcs 28
and rapprochement with Sunnis 119, 121, 123–125, 128, 130, 131, 134, 140, 142, 146, 147, 149, 158
and Salafis, Takfīrīs 117, 122, 127, 179–180, 184–188, 190
and Wahhābīs 186, 187
and West 35, 38, 42–45, 47, 51, 52, 54, 59, 60n, 69, 122, 123–124, 185, 187, 284
and US 22, 70, 134, 294
and Zionism 22, 79, 134, 184, 240, 294
Khanjī, Muḥammad ʿAlī 246, 251
Khātamī, Seyyed Muḥammad 21n, 29, 270
and liberty 195, 197, 222–224
on West 38, 63
Khawārij 156
and ʿAlī 157, 215
and Jihādī-Salafīs 178, 192
and Wahhābīs 160, 161
Khaybar 96, 98, 169, 171
Al-Khoʾīnī, Abū al-Ḥusayn 131, 133n
Khomeini, Rūḥollah 32, 119, 195, 261, 300
and Arab States 154
and Bahāʾīs 237, 238, 239, 248, 255, 257, 259, 265, 266
and enemies 1, 22, 172, 290
and feminism 248, 268, 269, 277, 280
and Iraq War 46
and Islamic Rule 46
and Islamic Unity 117
and Jews 40, 78, 79, 102, 107, 108, 255
and liberty 196, 197, 199, 200, 202–207, 210, 211, 212, 214, 217, 224
and mysticism 204
and politics 21, 216, 250, 251n
and the 1979 Revolution 146, 224
and Sunnis 118, 122
and the US 41
and Vilāyat-i faqīh 118, 145n, 206, 290
and West 39, 40, 117, 172
and Zionism 79, 237, 257, 294
Khorāsānī, Vaḥīd 125, 131, 144
Khorāsānis 107
Khosrō-panāh, ʿAbd al-Ḥusayn 246
Kramer, Joel 75
Kūfa 161
Kurānī, ʿAlī 182
Kurdistan 121, 150n, 155, 180

Lakzāʾī, Mahdī 271
Lankarānī, Muḥammad Fāżil 131, 140, 174
Lārījānī, Ṣādiq Āmolī 177
lesbianism 283
Lewis, Bernard 8
liberalism 18, 49, 53, 56, 60, 65, 67, 69, 198, 201, 202, 203, 215, 220, 232, 248, 275, 293, 294, 301
liberty viii, 31, 67, 138, **194–233**, 301
and feminism 292, 300
liberal concept of 196
negative 197–203, 210, 231, 232
positive 31, 197, 207–210, 232
reformist views on 222–230
spiritual 203–205
liberties, civil 194
Libya 180
Locke, John 196, 206, 279
Loew, Judah 232
Luṭfī, Luṭfallah 244

Maʿāf, Islām Mālikī 133, 135
Madāḥān 145
Madrasat Ahl al-Bayt 159
Mahdaviyat 67, 68

Mahdaviyat Center 181
Mahdi, (See also Twelfth Imam) vii, viii, 67, 68, 69, 72, 139, 193, 253, 265, 297
  Governance of 67, 299
  and ISIS 181–184
  and Jews 104–111
Mahdī seminary in Qom 81
de Maistre, Joseph 37
Majīdī, Keyvān 82
Majlis 264
  2000 elections 29
Majlisī, Muḥammad Bāqir 128, 135
Majmaʿ-i jahānī-i ahl-i bayt 119
Majmaʿ-i Ruḥāniyūn Mubāriz 29
Makārem Shīrāzī, Nāṣir
  and apostasy 158, 239
  and Bahā'īs 239, 261
  and companions 136
  and Jews 109, 111
  and moral deviations 209
  and Sunnīs 188
  and Takfīrīs 178, 180, 181, 186, 187
  and Wahhābīsm 158, 161, 165, 167, 187, 188
Manṣūrī Damghānī, Muḥammad ʿAlī 92, 95
Marājiʿ taqlīd 127, 130, 138, 142, 143, 145, 149, 216, 249
Marʿashī Najafī, Shihāb al-Dīn 143
Martyn, Henry 172
Marx, Karl 227
Marxism 18
Marwān b. al-Ḥakm 101
Masā'ilī, Mahdī 125, 126
Mashhad 181, 278, 300
  Cultural Foundation of 139
Al-Masʿūdī, ʿAlī ibn al-Ḥusayn 132
Maʿṣūmī Tehrānī, ʿAbd al-Ḥamīd 263
Mawdūdī, Abū-l-Aʿlā 117, 159, 188
Mecca 8, 95, 161, 166, 171, 183
Medina 94, 146
  Constitution of 8
  Iranian residents of 134
  Jews of 8, 81, 88, 91, 99, 100, 110, 169
  Muslims of 93
  and Prophet 8, 95, 160, 169
  Shīʿī sanctities in 161
  and Wahhābīs 161, 171
Mediterranean 119
Meyhandūst, Muḥammad Hādī 137
Middle East 51, 62, 111, 112, 119, 154, 155
  New Islamic 69, 180, 253
Ministry of Culture and Islamic Guidance 42n
Ministry of Foreign Affairs 123
Ministry of Intelligence and Security (VIVAK) 132
Mīr-Aḥmadī, Manṣūr 207
Mīr-Bāqirī, Muḥammad Mahdī 60
Mir-Hosseini, Ziba 269
Miṣbāḥ Yazdī, ʿAlī 218n
Miṣbāḥ Yazdī, Muḥammad Taqī 29, 144
  on Jews 85, 107
  on liberty 200, 201, 202, 205, 212, 213, 215, 228
  on Vilāyat-i faqīh 212
missionaries, (Christian) 17, 18, 44, 75, 271
modernity 32, 35, 53–56, 61, 192, 199, 221, 247, 248, 269, 275, 295
  Western 49, 55, 57, 72, 77, 246, 265, 271, 292
Mojtahed-Shabestari, Muḥammad 30, 229, 230
  and liberty 226, 227, 228, 232
Mongols 178, 192
Montaẓeri, Ḥusayn ʿAlī 216
  on apostasy 220, 226
  on Bahā'īsm 261, 262
Montesquieu, Charles-Louis 54
Mosaddeq, Muḥammad 38, 48
Mosul 155, 182
Mouood Cultural Institute 32, 92, 101, 103, 104, 284, 289
Muʿāwiya
  and ʿAlī 13, 157
  and Jews 101, 102, 133
Mubarak, Husni 69
Al-Mufīd Shaykh 114
Al-Mughīra b. Shuʿba 134
Muḥārib 234, 261
Muḥammad, (see also the Prophet) 12, 13, 19, 88, 234, 242, 243, 244, 263, 264
  and ʿAlī 95
  and Imām Ḥusayn 152
  and Jews 8–10, 75, 87, 89n, 96, 100, 169
  and ʿUmar
Muḥammad ʿAlī Shāh 252

Muḥammad ibn ʿAbd al-Wahhāb 20, 154, 156
and British 173
crude scholarship of 157, 162, 166
intolerance of 160, 168
Jewish descent 159–160, 168–169, 296
and Shīʿīsm 152, 173
Muḥammad Reża Shāh 21, 26, 34, 78, 237, 269, 272
and Bahāʾīs 237, 257, 258, 259
and Jews 77, 78, 215
Muḥammadī, ʿAbdollah 283
Muḥammadī, ʿAlī Reżā 241, 260
Muḥammadī, Muḥsin 90, 92
Muḥammadī-Golpāygānī, Muḥammad 187
Muḥammadpūr, ʿAlī 65, 66
Muḥsinī, Muḥammad Āsef 270
Muʿizz al-Dawla 114
Al-Mukhtār, Ibn Abī ʿUbayd Al-Thaqāfī 133
Mūsā, Prophet 45
Musaylima 157
Muslim Brothers 117, 120, 159
Musliḥī, Ḥaydar 101–103
Muslim world 4, 5, 10, 36–38, 42, 44, 64, 74, 75, 106, 112, 116, 118, 120, 147, 149, 154, 166, 173, 174, 179, 187, 254, 258, 293
Muslims 11, 25, 40, 45, 79, 86, 89, 112, 151, 163, 208, 219, 220, 229, 234, 251, 254, 257, 261, 281
and Christians 12, 263
divisions among 114, 118–121, 123, 126, 131, 147, 156–158, 160, 161, 164, 165, 168, 171, 174, 175, 177–179, 181, 184, 187–189, 191, 253
and Iran 107, 154, 211
and Jews 77, 78, 84, 85, 90–92, 96, 100, 103, 107–109, 134, 170, 171, 179–180, 185, 255, 263
non-Muslims viii, 31, 79, 109, 181, 187, 219, 228, 257, 263
and ʻOthers' 2, 8, 148, 161
Shīʿīs among 14, 31, 113, 118, 152, 153
unity among 122, 125–127, 157, 158, 249
and West 127, 185
Al-Mutawakkil, Caliph 15
Muʿtazila, Muʿtazilī theology 18, 162, 164, 195

Muṭṭaharī, Murtażā
and feminism 269, 276
and liberty 203, 205, 213, 215, 216
and West 39

Nahj al-Balāgha 101
Naʾīnī, Muḥammad Ḥusayn 195
Najaf 153, 155, 182, 300
Najafī, ʿAbbās 163
Najafī Fīrūzjāyī, ʿAbbās 163, 166
Najafī, Muḥammad Bāqir 254
Najd 156, 157, 162
Najmabadi, Afsaneh 286
Naqdī, Muḥammad Reża 59
Narāqī, Mulla Aḥmad 18
Nasab, Jaʿfar Musāvī 139
Naskh, (see abrogation)
Naṣrallah, Ḥasan 120
nationalism 60, 65
Iranian 32, 236, 266, 298
Nazi(sm) 53, 266
Nietzsche, Friedrich 37, 54, 58
Nine Rabīʿ Celebrations **132–136**, 139, 140
Nirenberg, David 74, 89
"No compulsion in religion" 213, 219, 225, 228, 243
Nūrī, ʿAbdollah 224, 270
Nūrī-Hamadānī, Ḥusayn 81, 91, 104, 130, 239
Nūrizād, Muḥammad 263
Al-Nuṣra Front 175

Occidentalism 36
Occupy Wall Street 60
Onslaught, Cultural 24, 39, 41–48, 71, 92, 93, 192, 237, 254, 267, 268, 271, 290, 294, 295, 301
Orientalism 3, 63
Book 11
Ottoman Empire 11, 12, 50, 169, 256
and the British 173
and Iran 115
and Sunnī Islam 115
and Shīʿīs 115, 116, 153

pagan(s) religions, paganism 7, 8, 41, 84
Pahlavī dynasty 43n
and Bahāʾīs 235, 252, 257, 258, 259, 265

and feminism 277
reforms 235
and West 40
Pakistan 180
killing of Shīʿīs 120, 130, 131, 155, 161
Palestine, Palestinians 56, 79, 83, 101, 106, 107, 111, 172, 180, 256, 259, 262
Parsa, Misagh 250
Pārsāniyā, Ḥamīd 284, 285
Paul, apostle 93, 94
Payām-i Zan 269
Pharaoh 45, 226
Political Culture 168, 296
Popper, Karl 58
post-modernism 57, 58n
Prague 232
Prophet (Muḥammad) 98, 99, 112, 113, 132, 156, 158, 161, 164, 178, 188, 216, 217, 221, 241, 288, 298
and ʿAlī 13, 46, 95
and apostasy 221n
birthday 119, 165
and Christians 8, 9, 263
death of 31, 68, 82, 92, 94, 94, 97, 100, 118, 128, 141, 157, 165
and Jews 8, 9, 81, 87, 88, 91, 98, 108, 142, 222, 263
Seal of the Prophets 243
succession of 16, 112, 144, 163, 292
Prophet's family 13, 96, 97, 98, 105, 113, 122, 127, 131, 137, 138, 140, 145, 160
The Protocols of the Elders of Zion 82, 110, 252, 256, 275
Pure Muḥammadan Islam 4, 122, 186, 260

Al-Qādir, Caliph 15
Qādiriyya Treatise 15
Al-Qāʿida 20, 120, 122, 131, 155, 174, 181
Qājār dynasty 76, 110, 116, 135
Qaradāwī, Yūsuf 50
Qarahī, Rūḥollah 80n, 81, 87, 90n, 102
Qarmaṭi sect 157
Qatar 129
Qazvīnī, Seyyed Muḥammad Ḥusaynī 165
Qirāʾatī, Muḥsin 166, 172
Qom 60, 81, 90, 101, 114, 119, 136n, 160, 216, 250
Qom seminary 80, 124, 135, 144, 145, 165, 177, 189, 197n, 198, 201, 246, 254, 269, 272, 278, 280, 289, 296n
Qommī, ʿAbbās 97
Qommī, Muḥammad Taqī 117
Qoṭbī, Hādī 137
Qurʾān 18, 87, 126, 153, 157, 165, 176, 179, 189, 199, 212, 213, 217, 224, 226–229, 234, 241–244, 262
on apostasy 221, 225
and Bible 75
and cursing 138, 143
on Christians 8, 9, 93, 165
fabrication of 92
on gender 277, 278
on Jews 8, 9, 23, 25, 40, 84, 85, 88, 95, 104, 107, 110, 165, 293, 295
literal reading of 162, 163
misreading of 162, 178, 285, 287, 288
Satan in 40, 140
and West 40
Quraysh 133
Quṭb, Sayyid 117, 159, 188

racism 77, 86, 284
Al-rāfiḍa, rawāfiḍ 15, 20, 76, 114
Rafsanjān (town) 239–240
Rafsanjānī, Akbar Hāshimī 28, 264
and liberty 199, 215
and sectarian rift 122, 123, 131, 140n, 144, 149
Rahbar, Muḥammad Taqī 60, 61
Rahdār, Aḥmad 64, 103
Raḥīm-pūr Azghadī, Ḥasan 81n, 274
Rāʾifī-Pūr, ʿAlī Akbar 87
Rajabī Davānī, Muḥammad Ḥusayn 135, 141n
Rajāyī Borūjnī, Muḥammad ʿAlī 166
Ramażānī Bīrjandī, ʿAlī 155n
Ramażānī-Pūr, ʿAbbās 239
Rashād, ʿAlī Akbar 281
Ravānbakhsh, Qāsim 144
Rawls, John 295
Ray 114
Rāzī, Fakhr al-Dīn 144
reformist, trend 28, 29, 47, 63, 194, 197, 202, 213, 300
and liberty 222–224

Renaissance 53, 55
Revolution, Constitutional 195, 252, 254, 272
Revolution, French 49, 199
Revolution, Young Turks 169
Revolution 1979, Islamic 1, 20, 26, 29, 34, 48, 117, 129, 130, 146, 147, 199, 269
achievements of 27, 47, 61–62, 91, 154, 174, 299
and Bahā'īs 235, 238, 258, 260
"Enemies" of 21, 22, 23, 24, 27, 28, 249, 292, 298
and feminism 268, 271, 280
and Jews 91
and Liberty 195, 196, 197, 210, **212–217**, 224
and Sunnīs 118, 154
and Wahhābism 174
and West 34, 40, 41, 45, 46, 51, 61–62, 70, 272
Revolutionary Guards 24, 35, 59, 184, 290
Reżā Shāh 77, 257, 258n
Riḍḍā, Muḥammad 50, 116
Rouhani, Ḥasan 29, 72, 131, 289, 290
On liberty 194, 225n
On sectarian rift 122
Rousseau, Jean-Jacques 54, 57, 197
Rūḥānī, Ḥusayn 61
Rūm 106, 298
Rushdie, Salman 85, 217
Russia 34, 36, 173, 253, 254
Russian imperialism 236, 253
Rūzbehānī, ʿAlī Reżā 244, 254, 258

Saʿādatī, ʿAbd al-Qādir 92, 98
Sabb (see cursing the enemies of the Shīʿa) 15, 123
Ṣābirī Maʿṣūma 281
Ṣādiqī Fasā'ī, Suheilā 283
Ṣadr, Muqtaḍā 190
Ṣafavī, Navāb 117
Ṣafavīd dynasty 164
and clergy 17, 110, 114, 128
Islam 146
and Jews 76
and Ottomans 16
and Sunnīs 114, 115, 116
and ʿUmar's death 128, 135, 149
Ṣāfī Golpāygānī, Luṭfallah 131, 140, 141n, 161
Said, Edward 3, 11
Saʿīdzādeh, Seyyed Muḥsin 269
Saʿīdī, ʿAlī 59
Al-Salaf al-ṣāliḥ 156, 163, 166, 175, 176, 178
Salafists (See also Jihadi Salafists) 20, 69, 76, 89n, 112, 163, 164, 176, 178, 181, 189, 192, 196
Sālārī, Muḥammad ʿAlī 181
Sāmarrā' 155
Al-Samāwī, Muḥammad Niʿma 181
Ṣāneʿī, Yūsuf 216, 269
saqīfa of the Banū Sāʿidah (meeting) 94, 95, 98
Sartre, Jean Paul 198
Satan 47, 84, 103, 165,
Great vii, 37, 40–41, 295
party of 101
rule of 87
Saʿūdi dynasty 160, 162, 171, 296
As Jews 169–170
Saudi Arabia 119, 124, 147, 153, 154, 156, 166, 169, 170, 175, 177, 185, 192
National Day 166
Schmitt, Carl 26, 27, 37
sectarian Sunnī-Shīʿī rift 14, 15, 16, 22, 31, 110, 114–116, 118–120, 121–123, 132, 134, 150, 159, 172
rapprochement 145–148
violence 112, 120, 129, 180
Seville 207
Shādmān, Fakhr al-Dīn 34
al-Shāfiʿī, Muḥammad ibn Idrīs 157
Shāhrūdī, Seyyed Muḥammad Ḥusaynī 144, 180, 183
Shafāʿa 152, 153, 158, 178
Sharaf al-Dīn ʿAbd al-Ḥusayn 116
Sharīfī, Saʿīd 246, 258
Shafīʿī Sarvestānī, Ismāʿīl 103, 272
Sharīʿa, 32, 118, 123, 189, 198, 206, 210, 213, 218, 221n, 234, 268, 276
Sharīʿatī, ʿAlī 39, 146
Shaykh al-Ra 'īs, Abū al-Ḥasan Mīrza 116
Shaykhism 234
Shimr b. Dhī al-Jawshan 103
Shīrāzī faction 145, 149, 293, 296
as English Shīʿīsm 146, 147
and ʿĀshūrā'commemorations 148

and Jews 148
and Takfīrīs 147
and ʿUmarkoshān ceremonies 146
and Wahhābīs 147
Shīrāzī, Ṣādiq 148
Shīrāzī, Seyyed ʿAlī Muḥammad (see Bāb)
Shirkat, Shahlā 286, 289
Shoghi Effendi 244, 249
Siavoshi, Sussan 262
Sistānī, ʿAlī 79n, 127, 182, 190
Society of Seminary Teachers 230
soft war 44, 48, 271
Soroush, AbdolKarim 30, 229, 230, 232
Soviet Union 41, 48, 54, 59, 60, 266
invasion of Afghanistan 155
Spengler, Oswald 49–51, 54
Stalin, Joseph 48, 56, 266
Subḥānī, Jaʿfar 176
and Bahāʾīsm 248, 250
and apostacy 219, 222
and companions 175
and Jews 74, 222
and Jihādī-Salafī 176, 177, 178, 179, 180
and liberty 200
and reason 162
and Wahhābism 162, 164, 173
and Zionism 222
Ṣubḥ-i Azāl, Yaḥyā ʿAlī Nūrī 249
Sufyānī 181, 193
and ISIS 182–184
and Jews, Zionism 106, 298
Ṣūfīs 18, 20, 159, 173
Suhrawardī, Shihāb al-Dīn Yaḥyā 35
Sulaymān Ibn ʿAbd al-Wahhāb 160
Sunnis vii, 1, 14, 16, 17, 22, 68, 73, 112, 117, 126, 140, 150, 155, 218
and ʿAlī 89, 90, 95, 127
and apostasy 156, 176, 189
and Christians 10, 17, 93, 105
doctrines 15, 112, 113, 121, 153, 157, 163, 165, 176, 233
in Iran 155,
and Jews 36, 75, 76, 88, 89n, 90, 91, 93, 94, 97, 100, 103, 105, 164, 296
legal schools 153, 158, 167, 176
mainstream 4, 31, 74, 90, 110, 112, 116, 118–120, 148, 149, 151, 156, 158–160, 169, 175, 176, 188, 189, 191, 192, 206, 233, 292, 294, 299, 300
reconciliation with Shīʿīs 16, 31, 90, 116–120, 122, 123–125, 127, 140, 144, 149, 150, 158, 293, 299
rift with Shīʿīs 22, 31, 61, 74, 112–116, 120, 121, 123, 126, 130–132, 134, 143, 146, 147, 154–156, 169, 174, 175, 179, 189, 192, 218, 292and Takfiris 156, 175, 188, 191
views on Shīʿīs 15, 20, 76, 89, 102, 114
and Wahhābīs 159, 160, 161, 165, 188, 191
and West 36, 41, 51, 80, 103, 127
and Zionism 81, 91
Sunnīsm, American 147, 186, 296
Supreme Council of the Cultural Revolution 146, 274
Supreme Leader (see also Khamenei) 143, 145, 154, 182, 207, 211, 212, 239, 251n, 261, 292

Tabarrā 113, 123, 125, 126, 127, 144, 149
Ṭabībzādeh Nūrī, Zahrāʾ 275
Tablīghāt-i Islāmī Organization 60
Tabrīz 92
Tabrīzī, Javād 79n, 131
Tafsīr 144, 285
Ṭāʾib, Mahdī 85, 91, 100
Ṭāʾif 161
Takāmul 203
Takfīrīs (see also Jihādī-Salafists) viii, 146, 175, 176, 190
as neo-jāhiliyya 188–189
as Non-Muslims 187–190
and apostasy 156, 179
and distortion of Islam 178–179, 188
and harm to Islam 180–181, 185, 187, 188
and Islamic Unity 179–181, 187
and Jews 187
and Khawārij 156, 178
and Mahdī 181–183
and terrorism 181
and US 177, 184–187
and violent nature 186, 188
and Wahhābism 177, 187
and Zionism 184–187
Ṭalḥa 26, 100n
Ṭālibān 22, 131

Taklīf pl. Takālīf 25, 204, 213
Tālibov Tabrīzī, ʿAbd al-Raḥman 116
Talmud 275
Taqiyya 126, 131, 149, 244
Taskhīrī, Muḥammad ʿAlī 129
Tavānā, Muḥammad ʿAlī 66
Tawassul 152, 158, 173
Al-Ṭayyib, Aḥmad. 125, 128
Tehrān 80n, 102, 237, 290
Tehrānī, Seyyed Muḥammad Ḥusayn Ḥusaynī 278
Towḥīd 178, 241
  Ahl-i towḥīd 263
Toynbee, Arnold 50, 51
Twelfth Imām (See Mahdī)

ʿUmar b. al-Khaṭṭāb 134, 140
  and ʿAlī 13, 94, 95, 96, 113, 128, 141, 143
  and Fāṭima 98, 128–130, 138, 141, 143, 144
  immoral conduct 141
  and Jews 92, 96–102, 128, 142
  cursing against 114, 115, 141, 143, 144
  Khomeini on 118
  murder of 128–139, 144
ʿUmar b. Saʿad 133
ʿUmarkoshān celebrations viii, 128–132, 134–139, 142, 145, 146, 149
Umayyad family 97, 105, 106, 134, 183
  and ʿAlī' 13
  and Jews 101–103, 110, 133, 296
  and Jihādī-Salafīs 182, 183
Umm Kulthūm 141
United States 28, 34, 36, 39, 40, 41, 42, 68, 118, 120, 150
  as enemy 70, 120, 121, 167, 175, 212, 266, 267, 294
  and Jews 102
  as Great Satan 37, 41, 47
  decline of 54, 59, 60, 61, 62, 69
  and Israel 121, 134, 167, 175, 294
  and sectarian rift 121, 134, 175
  and Takfīrīs 177, 185, 186
Unity Week 119, 127, 146
Universal Declaration of Human Rights 196, 200, 226, 262
Universities
  Adyān 271
  ʿAlāma Ṭabātabāʾī 64, 171
  Bāqir al-ʿUlūm 64
  Iṣfahān 61
  Kāshān 281
  Loristan 275
  Modarres 45
  Mufīd 216
  Muṣṭafā 58
  Shahīd-i Beheshtī 207
  Shīrāz 66
  Tehrān 283
ʿUrf 288
Uṣūlī School 167
ʿUthmān b. ʿAffān 13, 89, 102, 134

Vāʿizī, Ḥasan 54
Vakīlī, Hādī 199
Vilāyat-i faqīh 25, 67, 69, 87, 91, 118, 135, 144, 154, 176, 194, 206, 216, 218, 224, 231, 233, 290, 299
  Absolute 28, 29, 145n, 207, 212
Vilāyat-i Faqīh: Ḥukūmat-i Islāmī (book) 78
Voltaire 54

Wahhābism viii, 31, 151–177
  anti-Shīʿī nature 116, 151, 152–154, 159–161
  and the British 167, 168, 172–174, 296
  brutal conduct 156, 160, 177
  deviations from normative Islam 157, 160, 161, 164, 191
  and imperialism 147
  intolerance 157, 158, 161, 166, 177, 191
  and Jews, Zionism 80, 167–172, 192, 297
  and Jihādī-Salafīsm 119, 147, 151, 156, 174–179, 190, 301
  and mainstream Sunnīs 159
  obscurantism 156, 160, 162–167, 191
  undermining Islamic unity 161, 191
  and the US 167, 177, 296
Walāya 113
Wasserstrom, Steven 89
Webman, Esther 74
West vii, 3, 5, 23, 29, 30, 34–72, 123, 167, 247
  agression of 53, 54
  and Bahāʾīs 235, 244, 247, 248, 260
  corruption and decadence 53, 58, 59, 60, 67, 202, 203, 282
  culture 37, 38, 46, 52, 192, 196, 198, 199, 201, 247, 265, 268, 272, 274, 281, 283, 286, 288, 290, 294
  decline 41, 47–51, 54–61, 69–72, 187, 299

dichotomous to Islam 6, 11, 12, 15, 20, 34, 35, 36, 39, 40, 61–64, 66, 72, 77, 78, 105, 106, 127, 139, 168, 193, 196, 198, 209, 210, 212, 220, 266, 268, 278, 280, 284, 295–298
and feminism ix, 267, 268, 271–276, 279, 284, 286–290
and humanism 52, 55–59, 254, 274, 287, 290
and imperialism 10, 32, 35, 40, 52, 78, 79, 86, 117, 195, 235, 252, 253, 255, 257, 265, 267, 271, 292–294
and Jews 40, 78, 79, 80, 84, 103, 111, 168, 235
and Jihādī-Salafists 184–185, 187, 192, 292
as Satan 40, 41
science, technology 52
threat of 38, 39, 40, 42, 52, 70, 71, 76, 84, 103, 110, 116, 148, 173, 192, 195, 200, 222, 252, 266, 276, 290, 293, 295
and Wahhābīs 152, 167, 174, 186, 187, 192, 292
and Zionism 4, 31, 43, 167, 174, 185, 186, 235, 275, 290
Westoxication vii, 34, 62
women 137, 141, 281, 287, 301
activism 269, 271, 272, 273, 280, 290
and Bahā'īs 237, 244, 248
Islamists on 267, 268, 269, 270, 277, 278, 286, 291
legal status under Islam 206, 269, 271–273, 277–281, 283, 284, 287, 288, 291
liberal views on 273
moral conduct 281, 282, 283, 284
social roles 267, 268, 273, 276, 277, 282–285, 291
Wahhābī and Takfīrī attitudes towards 167, 178, 179
and West 272, 274, 279, 281, 282, 284, 285, 286
and Zionism 275, 276
World Forum for the [Prophet's] Family 119
World Forum for the Proximity of Islamic Schools of Thought 119 129, 133
World Islamic Congress 116
World War I 172
World War II 36, 77, 240, 294

Al-Ya'qūbī, Aḥmad ibn Abī Ya'qūb 132
Yarshater, Ehsan 261
Yazdani, Mina 266
Yazīd, Caliph
evil nature 103, 104, 110
Jewish descent 102
Yazdī, Muḥammad on liberty 205, 212, 215, 216
young Turks 169
Yūnesī, 'Alī 131
Yūsuf Khān Mustashār al-Dawla 116
Yūsufī Gharavī, Muḥammad Hādī 135

Zāhidī, Muḥammad Taqī 26
Ẓāhir 52, 162, 216, 246
Zanān 269, 270
Zanān-i Emrūz 289
Al-Zarqāwī, Abū Muṣ'ab 20, 155
Zībāyī-nezhād, Muḥammad Reżā 272
Zionism 3, 5, 31, 65, 78, 82, 102, 161
anachronistic use of the term 73, 81, 102, 103, 110
and Bahā'īs 237, 238, 239, 252, 254, 256–259, 261, 262, 265, 275, 296
conspiracies against Islam 92, 281, 293, 222
and feminism 274, 275, 290, 293, 296
and freemasons 275
and Holocaust 82
global, international 22, 43, 294
and Jihadi-Salafis 180, 181, 184–186, 192
and Judaism 73, 79–81, 95, 110
lobby 81
and Palestinians 56, 83, 172
and Sufyani 298
and Sunnī-Shī'ī rift 130, 134
threat to Islam 101, 122, 134, 148, 184, 293, 295, 296, 297
and Wahhābīsm 161, 171, 174, 181
and West 31, 134, 139, 161, 184, 186, 192, 235, 275, 293
and US 215
Zionist Islam and Muslims 148, 171
Zoroastrianism 75, 235, 238, 262, 264
Ẓū al-Qadr, Muḥammad Bāqir 35, 42, 62
Zubayr 26
Ẓuhūr 104, 243

Printed in the United States
by Baker & Taylor Publisher Services